GREEN

CONSTR

GREEN

CONSTRUCTING LANDSCAPE

MATERIALS, TECHNIQUES, STRUCTURAL COMPONENTS

ASTRID ZIMMERMANN (ED.)

Birkhäuser
Basel

CONSTRUCTING LANDSCAPE

INTRODUCTION		7
CONSTRUCTING LANDSCAPE, Essay by Cordula Loidl-Reisch		9

1	**MATERIALS**	
1.1	SOIL	15
	Components, properties, classification	15
	Bulk material	20
	Soil protection	24
	Testing and assessing foundation soil	24
1.2	PLANTS	29
	Plant propagation	29
	Woody plants	30
	Herbaceous plants (including grasses and ferns)	35
	Bulbs and tubers (geophytes)	37
	Bedding and tub plants	37
1.3	LAWNS AND OTHER SEEDED AREAS	43
	Lawns	43
	Crushed stone lawn/checker brick lawn	46
	Meadows	47
	Intermediate planting	48
1.4	WOOD	53
	Composition, properties and timber preservation	53
	Products	60
	Surface qualities	61
	Joints	62
1.5	CUT STONE	67
	Properties and products	68
	Surface properties and treatment	72
	Jointing and shaping	75
1.6	BRICK AND CLINKER	79
	Composition, properties, products	79
	Surface qualities and surface treatment	86
	Laying and shaping	90
1.7	CONCRETE	95
	Composition, properties, products	95
	Surface qualities and surface treatment	99
	Joining and molding	100
1.8	METALS	105
	Iron and steel	106
	Aluminum	117
	Copper	118
	Zinc/titanium zinc	118
1.9	OTHER BUILDING MATERIALS	123
	Plastics	123
	Bitumen and asphalt	128
	Glass	131

2 THE PRINCIPLES OF LOADBEARING STRUCTURES

2.1	LOADBEARING STRUCTURES AND THEIR DIMENSIONS	137
	Fundamentals of structural component dimensioning	137
	Assumed loads	143
	Choice of system	144
	Choice of materials	147
	Choice of cross-section	151
	Stiffening	154
2.2	FOUNDATIONS	159
	The principles of soil mechanics	159
	Principal foundation types	167
2.3	CONNECTIONS	173
	Timber connections	173
	Steel connections	180
	Concrete connections	184
	Connections between different materials	191

3 STRUCTURAL ELEMENTS AND BUILDING METHODS

3.1	GROUND MODELING AND EARTHWORKS 199	
	Terrain modeling	199
	Securing earthworks	202
	Specimen projects	208
3.2	PATHS AND SQUARES	215
	Hard surfaces—terminology	215
	Building ground	215
	Pavement	216
	Construction methods for surface courses	219
	Borders	231
	Specimen projects	233
3.3	STEPS	243
	Outdoor steps	243
	Construction methods	245
	Ramps	257
	Specimen projects	258
3.4	RAILINGS AND FENCES	267
	General requirements	267
	Construction methods	269
	Specimen projects	281
3.5	WALLS	295
	Principles	295
	Freestanding walls	295
	Retaining walls	296
	Nonstable construction methods	300
	Stable construction methods	302
	Specimen projects	314
3.6	SMALL STRUCTURES AND PERGOLAS	327
	Construction and use of materials for small structures	327
	Construction and use of materials for pergolas	334
	Specimen projects	336
3.7	SMALL BRIDGES	347
	General structure of a bridge	347
	Bridge support structures	347
	Specimen projects	350
3.8	WALKWAYS AND DECKS	357
	General essentials	357
	Foundation	358
	Substructure/support construction	359
	Covering	359
	Specimen projects	361

3.9	PLANTING TECHNIQUE AND CARE OF VEGETATION SURFACES	369
	Basics of plant growth	369
	Planting woody plants	372
	Planting and maintenance of herbaceous plants	378
	Planting and maintenance of geophytes	379
	Seasonal ornamental plants	379
	Specimen projects	380
3.10	LAWNS AND MEADOWS: LAYING OUT AND CARE	389
	Lawns	389
	Meadows	392
	Seeding ornamental annuals	393
	Specimen projects	494
3.11	SURFACE DRAINAGE	399
	Creating slopes	399
	Construction methods for drainage systems	404
	Basic calculations and parameters	411
	Specimen projects	414
3.12	WATER INSTALLATIONS	421
	General building methods and choice of location	421
	Construction methods	422
	Planting pools and ponds	428
	Specimen projects	432
3.13	VERTICAL PLANTING	445
	Creative aims	447
	Structures and attachment modes for trellis climbers	451
	Construction requirements	451
	Loads	452
	Problems with climbing plants	452
	Maintenance and checking	452
	Specimen project	453
3.14	GREEN ROOFS	457
	Forms of green roof	457
	Construction requirements and constructive elements	459
	Designs and layers in green roofs	464
	Greening methods	466
	Implementing a green roof	468
	Specimen projects	471
3.15	SPECIAL ELEMENTS	479
	Lighting elements	479
	Play and sports elements	482
	Specimen projects	485
	Seating elements	490
	Specimen projects	491

APPENDIX

LITERATURE, STANDARDS AND DIRECTIVES, ADDITIONAL INFORMATION	503
PICTURE CREDITS	519
INDEX	525

INTRODUCTION

Between the design idea and its conversion into constructed reality lie the technical details—in landscape architecture as in every design-related occupation. Only meticulous handling of these details can ensure that the quality of the design is preserved in the completed object. The basis for the—enduring—success of a construction scheme is therefore a respect for the properties of the materials used, as well as a construction method suitable for the materials and function. Given the particular conditions of "the outdoors" as a site, aspects of weather impact and the durability of facilities for public use must be paid particular attention.

This publication is aimed at anyone who is concerned with creating outdoor facilities and is looking for an introduction to technical and constructive planning. This handbook gives a basic overview of materials, construction methods, and vegetation techniques used in urban-context planning.

It is divided into three parts: "Materials", "The principles of loadbearing stuctures", and "Structural elements and building methods". The individual sections can be combined in a modular fashion.
The first part outlines materials used out of doors, presenting their basic properties as well as their surface qualities, application possibilities and products.
The second part is concerned with fundamental questions of structural engineering. This should support both the reader's own construction designs and informed discussion with structural engineers. The first chapter discusses the rules governing structural engineering. The following chapters are concerned with joints in loadbearing construction elements, soil mechanics and the different types of foundation.
The third part describes how and with what elements outdoor complexes are built. Besides small structures such as walls, fences, steps or pools, this includes paved and non-paved surfaces. In addition, drainage and various aspects of vegetation techniques are important. As well as the basics of the subject and in-depth rules, various types of construction are presented—with the aid of specimen projects with construction methods that go beyond the standard details and expand the field of application.

Plants as a construction material are a central theme in landscape architecture. Characteristics, possibilities for use and quality requirements for different plant groups are considered in the materials chapters "Plants" and "Lawns and other seeded areas". Further information can be found in the chapters on vegetation techniques (Chapters 3.9 and 3.10) and in chapters that stand in close relation to plants as a construction material (e.g. the "Green roofs" chapter). It is impossible to do justice to the complexity of this field, particularly that of growth forms and areas of use for plants, within this publication. Given the background of very different site factors created by the climatic and soil-specific peculiarities of each region, readers are referred to the appropriate subject literature. Where an overview of the most important plant species is possible and appears justified, constructive chapters are supplemented with plant tables. > **Chapters 3.12 Water installations, 3.13 Vertical planting and 3.14 Green roofs**

A region's climatic conditions determine both the use of individual plant species and the construction methods for outdoor complexes. In order to make general statements, the scope of information contained in this publication is restricted to the Central European area. However, many of the construction methods can be used in other regions or adapted with only minor changes.

The European standards handbook already provides international regulations for many areas of construction. These are the basis for the technical codes of practice quoted in this publication. In areas with non-uniform regulation, national standards or guidelines are listed instead. A country-specific inspection must take place in each individual case. The literature and reference lists at the end of each chapter may help the reader with this research. The national editions of the EU standards, which partly consist of the supplementary regulations, are also recommended.

The FLL regulatory publications, established as the standard set of rules in Germany, are listed in some chapters, even if applying them is not compulsory outside Germany. The information they contain reflects the current state of science and practical experience. Outside Germany, they can therefore be considered as guidelines or recommendations.

Constructing Landscape is conceived as a reference work on the subject of construction in landscape architecture, intended to accompany the design process from the draft stage to the best possible structural and technical solution, and provide helpful information to support this development. As well as the necessary basic technical knowledge, it is therefore also intended to provide inspiration and encouragement for constructive planning.

As guidance for further research, the appendix of this publication contains lists of literature, standards and guidelines plus further information on each theme divided according to the relevant chapter. There is also a summary of literature for all chapters.

Astrid Zimmermann
Berlin, summer 2008

CONSTRUCTING LANDSCAPE

Essay by Cordula Loidl-Reisch

This publication focuses on the fascinating interaction between landscape, seen as dynamic detailing of the earth's surface, and construction. Here landscape can be both a "substrate" for design work and also a place-related "basis". In each case, interest is focused on a mutual process: landscape and its qualities dictate the general conditions while construction, itself determined by the characteristic properties of building components, offers a response.

"Putting together"—building, erecting or manufacturing a material or immaterial structure—is the literal meaning of construction. *Construere*, the Latin verb, includes all the ideas, considerations, principles, calculations, strategies and processes that contribute to a technical product's intended functions, whether it is a machine or a building. The word's meaning also implies ordering material and endowing it with form.

The Latin word *talea* in its narrowest sense means a "severed twig", but the beautiful French verb derived from it, *détailler* (= cutting to pieces) describes what happens in the detailing process: dividing off or dividing up into smaller sections. But detail can refer in particular to single feature, or a more precise excerpt from a greater whole, often an enlarged image. So "detailed" also means something that is presented precisely and thoroughly in every aspect.

Anyone getting involved in construction should be in love with detail. This propensity—often wrongly confused with pettiness—is greatly needed because it acts as a motor for new and further developments. Arts pages make a clear distinction between people who solve puzzles and thinkers—allowing only the latter to be carefree—but developing detail needs passionate solvers of brainteasers in the best sense of the word, people whose obsessive attitude enables them to work innovatively.

A consistent approach to working through from a first draft to the detail is helpful and desirable. But if you find yourself behaving with remorseless rigor and getting mercilessly entrapped in detail at the planning stage, the best response is to season the game with a pinch of humor and juggle your own ideas around a bit.

"Construct, don't calculate!" demands Karlheinz Wagner in his "Fragil Bauen" ("Fragile Building") article (2005, p. 8), pointing out that optimizing a statical system depends to a great extent on materials, and that it is important to do justice to materials when constructing, from the first step in designing the loadbearing structure via developing detail for execution, right through to the finishing touches.

Comfort has always been a motor for structural development, and it is becoming even more important. If we believe Eva Gesine Baur's predictions in her 1999 book *Was kommt, was bleibt* (p. 60), comfort will be the strongest argument when choosing clothing in future. Is it likely to be very different for open space as a consumer product?

"The fact is that people like comfortable things." Peter Eisenman

It is understandable that interior design elements increasingly provide the ideas for objects in the open air. They insist that demands are made in terms of both aesthetics and comfort on structures that are "transferred" into the open air, where they have to be adapted to withstand considerably harder conditions in terms of weathering and drainage requirements. What can be observed is a regular transfer of elements and materials: indoors, outdoors and back.

But the choice of materials and construction is also affected by the zeitgeist and the fashion trends it generates. Here is an "angled" example: in the 1970s an angle of 45° was held in high esteem and used simply everywhere—from the ground plan of a building to the detail of an object, but we still cannot distance ourselves enough to have a completely relaxed relationship with this angle. It was followed by ruthlessly precise 90° corners, of the kind Donald Judd loved.

Even slight beveling of corners with a chamfer was taboo. Now in principle objects intended to have right angles are supposed to be prettily rounded at the corners—interior or exterior—even if this does not immediately put the whole object out of kilter.

Urban densification processes are often subject to complicated sites and sometimes general conditions that seem almost paradoxical. But stress-creating users also generate a need for special constructions: for example, cage-like structures that are built to make it possible for plants to grow without being vandalized, to protect them from damage or thoughtless use. Using climbing plants, with the idea of "deliberately conquering the airspace", can be the constructive solution in artificial sites or in tricky, cramped situations.

In contrast with this, "one size" promises pragmatically simplified planning by the use of elements that function universally, focusing on rapid building. Using "one-size products" does not necessarily mean less durability, but they do reinforce the trend towards globalized appearance. Paul Virilio expresses it very clearly in his *The Aesthetics of Disappearance*: "If a technology disappears, in reality it is being replaced by another one that is considered more efficient."

So-called "Universal Design" developed in the late 1980s, with commitment, and aware of the different qualities of users and a number of special needs: elements are constructed to guarantee a broad span of usefulness and flexibility, to admit simple and intuitive use, and requiring little physical effort to use. Alongside the ecological dimensions of creative construction, it is above all these aspects of "Universal Design" that should be seen as the greatest artistic-constructive challenge for the near future.

Furthermore, anti-aging strategies are affecting all areas of life at the present moment. Why should they leave out landscape architecture?

A desirable patina as a sign of aging makes an attractive contrast to this. Where patina exudes a sense of modernity, as when using weatherproof steel for example, with all its rusty power to convince, the effect of age is appreciated and thus makes clear on the structural level as well what designing open space, above because of its durable woodwork, is not and cannot be: short-lived.

Durability is considered desirable for open spaces in most cases, but let us look at something very different: a planned, intentional short-lived quality, as seen in "temporary gardens"—a recent, artistic and yet social form of open space design: its devotees are not depriving others of the chance to design something new and interesting in the same place and in the foreseeable future (cf. Pierre Bertaux, *La Mutation humaine*).

There are also general conditions that offer relief: temporary gardens often do not have to last for even a single summer; light, varied and also transitory materials can be used very casually—anything, as long as no one is put at risk.

Of course, people are constantly looking for new and interesting solutions, for constructions that follow fashionable trends or, even better, trends that indicate innovation. But novelty is certainly associated with:

· new materials that inevitably lead to innovative constructions; or
· to unusual combinations of materials, chosen innovatively;
· to proportions and forms that had not been usual up to this time;
· to new uses or
· new freedoms that can arise from the sensational stability of a brilliant new material; or of course
· to a generally new "view" of things.

Sensational designs will always create their own suction effect. They are models, they create desires and they make demands in terms of materials and construction. But even the most innovative constructions are ultimately part of a development process, and do not stay new for long. What can be said about them is this, by an attractive analogy with Paul Virilio's statements, based on locomotive machines, in his book *The Aesthetics of Disappearance* (1991): as soon as a type of landscape construction is new in the world, it is no longer part of what used to be missing. It is no longer what is to come, it is there, and is thus about to become outmoded.

Being aware of more or less limited durability should discourage design engineers as little as the fact that open space users can put enormous pressure on facilities. Research into vandalism and also the development of positive strategies are needed. And in the detailing process it is above all the appropriate choice of materials that can make a compensatory effect.

When the twelfth volume in the *Gartenschönheit* ("Garden Beauty") series, called *Hausgartentechnik* ("Domestic Garden Technology") appeared in 1929, landscape architecture's main sphere of operation was the gardens of houses and villas. So that publication aimed to present the current state of technology against this background (Poethig, Schneider 1929, p. 7).

Constructing Landscape—the very title makes it clear how much the discipline has gained in "space" and content in the last 80 years, and has emancipated itself from merely working on house and villa gardens (although these remain very attractive propositions): landscape architecture has become part of the landscape.

And "if one wanted to set up a rank order among the arts, even though this seems somewhat absurd, they could be arranged according to the extent to which they depend on materials, which would produce the sequence: architecture, sculpture, painting, poetry, music". We may smile at the intellectual games that the paradoxical thinker Egon Friedell plays in his *A Cultural History of the Modern Age* (first published 1927 in German), but still wonder where landscape architecture would fit into this hierarchy: somewhere between architecture and sculpture.

Constructing Landscape is intended materially here in a thoroughly rooted sense. "Constructing" as the development of an architectural structure from the landscape "substrate" itself, or from buildings that are "only" connected with the landscape.

Poethig and Schneider made it very clear at the time in the introduction to *Hausgartentechnik* that "any examination of garden art is completely avoided" (p. 7). A great deal has changed since 1929 in this respect as well.

As a publication, *Constructing Landscape* pursues more ambitious creative intentions: it would like to offer inspiration for detailed design by increasing awareness of possibilities, limitations and interdependencies.

But even at that time, Poethig and Schneider dismissed as "out-of-date" the point of view of some garden experts who put forward the view that they were not allowed to give away "technical" secrets (p. 7). This also fits in with this book's intention, which is to give insights into basic material behavior, and to demonstrate structural component properties and principles of loading and design for ease of production applying appropriate specific connection techniques.

Other important subject matter includes technical properties like the durability of materials and their connections and the environmental balance sheet, and last but not least, that objects and materials provide suitable comfort.

And so the book addresses creative people full of curiosity, critical imagination and stamina, who want to meet the challenges that can be placed by the new, and thus definitely be the source of displeasure of all kinds (freely after Sigmund Freud).

When all is said and done, it is about the ambitious aim of "breaking down" design ideas. About moving the basics of creative conception away from the higher idea, the complete whole and shifting them on to the plane of convincing details, suitable material combinations, appropriate surfaces, harmonious coloring and more.

About becoming part of the iterative process from what is devised to what is constructed and finally built, something that is intended to fulfil a particular purpose in the chosen place, and thus speak a specific "language" that is as expressive as it can possibly be.

1 MATERIALS

1.1 SOIL

COMPONENTS, PROPERTIES, CLASSIFICATION
- Soil components
- Classification by particle size (soil type)
- Soils for building purposes—workability (soil class) and suitability for building (soil group)
- Soil for growing vegetation
- Contaminated soil

BULK MATERIAL
- Naturally occuring stone aggregates
- Artificial aggregates
- Bulk material for use when growing vegetation

SOIL PROTECTION

TESTING AND ASSESSING FOUNDATION SOIL
- Soil reports
- Soil investigation

Astrid Zimmermann

1.1 SOIL

Soil is not just a base on which to build, but an essential creative tool for landscape architects. It creates form, and functions as a link between the surface and the area below it that can appear as a patch of vegetation, a pathway area or a building. It is important for almost every creative measure in outdoor space.
The different use aspects indicate the different demands made on soil and show that it is necessary to assess its properties in different ways with regard to the task in hand. > **Figs. 1.1.1.** and **1.1.2**

Even though every planned project should aim to work with the soil as found, for both economic and ecological reasons, the soil conditions on site or the planning requirements can mean that additional soil or a change of soil is required. If there is not enough soil for the purposes of the building project, e.g. because it does not have sufficient loadbearing properties, then measures have to be taken to improve the soil, or additional soil has to be bought in.

COMPONENTS, PROPERTIES, CLASSIFICATION

Soil components

Soil is formed when solid rock is broken down by physical, chemical and biological processes (for original stone types > **Chapter 1.5 Cut Stone**). The mineral components separated in these ways form deposits with more or less open space within them. Soil can have organic as well as mineral components. As soon as the first layer of soil is enriched with deposits that are organic in origin, it is called topsoil. The organic components of the topsoil are called humus. Peat is a completely organic soil.
Man-made artificial fillers or deposits of stone-like materials (e.g. slag from blast furnaces) are also called soil. Soil that has been produced locally by deposits and weathering and has not yet been changed is called "natural soil".
The soil structure is determined by the size, shape and irregularity (> **Chapter 2.2 Foundations**) of the solid soil components. The gaps make up the porous volume, which is filled with water and air (or other gases). The water to air ratio changes; an increase in water content means that the proportion of air is reduced, or vice versa. Compression reduces the porous volume.
The soil structure is impaired by interventions and redistribution. Compression caused by loads in particular can considerably reduce the porous volume, and thus the permeability of the soil. Moving it around reduces its stability.
For water in soil, a distinction is made between seepage, retained and captured water. Precipitation or condensation water seeps (pore size d > 0.01 mm), and thus

Fig. 1.1.1: Soil as a foundation:
a) preparing the ground for building

b) installing and sealing a loadbearing layer

Fig. 1.1.2: Soil as a modeled building material and future area of vegetation

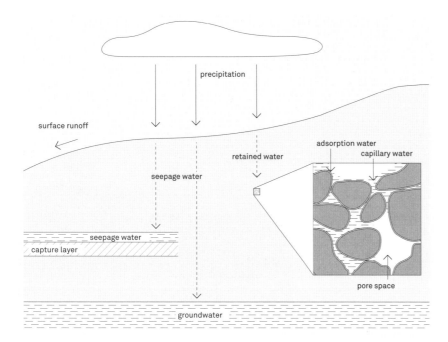

Fig. 1.1.3: Schematic representation of groundwater

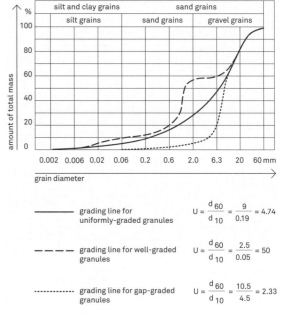

$U = \dfrac{d_{60}}{d_{10}} = \dfrac{9}{0.19} = 4.74$ — grading line for uniformly-graded granules

$U = \dfrac{d_{60}}{d_{10}} = \dfrac{2.5}{0.05} = 50$ — grading line for well-graded granules

$U = \dfrac{d_{60}}{d_{10}} = \dfrac{10.5}{4.5} = 2.33$ — grading line for gap-graded granules

Fig. 1.1.4: Sieve lines: example of uniform, well- and gap-graded soils

helps to enrich the groundwater, or stays behind as retained water (pore size d = 0.0002 to 0.01 mm) in the layers of soil above. Here it is retained as adsorption water directly on the surface of the soil particles or is retained as capillary water in the soil pores. If the pores are smaller than 0.0002 mm and the water pressure rises, then the retained water is more strongly bonded with the soil particles and it is no longer suitable for planting. > Fig. 1.1.3

Soil is categorized according to its usefulness for a particular building brief according to the properties that are relevant in this context. So there are different classifications for the different types of use.

Classification by particle size (soil type)

An initial classification, which does not provide an evaluation in terms of use, is made by identifying soil according to grain size, grain size distribution and further description of other soil characteristics according to EN ISO 14688-1 and EN ISO 14688-2. The standard identifies soil types primarily according to the size of their mineral components. This divides soils into fine-grain soil types (clay and silt), coarse-grain soil types (sand and gravel), and very coarse-grain soil types (stone and block).

Fine-grain soil types are also called cohesive and coarse-grain types noncohesive or granular. Soils of different grain fractions are defined according to their main and subsidiary component proportions. > Tab. 1.1.1

Further classifications are made for cohesive soils, for example, in terms of their plasticity and consistency, which provides information in terms of how well they can be worked and shaped. Soils with a high silt content have low plasticity, while soils with a high clay content have high plasticity. The consistency or state of a cohesive soil is defined—in association with the water content—as mushy, soft, stiff, semifirm or firm. Mushy soils are insufficiently firm, and so cannot be worked. Workability increases as the water content decreases: stiff to hard soils are considered to be adequately workable.

Noncohesive soil types can be further differentiated on the basis of grain size distribution. Grain size distribution provides information in particular a soil's compactability and shear strength. A distinction is drawn between uniformly graded, well-graded and gap-graded soils, with "uniform" indicating evenness, "well" some irregularity in the grain size and "gap-graded" a great deal of irregularity (certain grain sizes are missing). > Fig. 1.1.4 and chapter 2.2 Foundations Well-graded soils compact very well, gap-graded quite well and uniformly graded soils less well. The permeability of gap-graded gravels is greater than for well-graded ones.

Soils for building purposes—workability (soil class) and suitability for building (soil group)

Soil workability

The nature of the soil affects the amount of effort required to work, transport, store and install soil, which can differ greatly. A soil workability classification is needed in order to assess the nature and scale the soil work needed. In Germany, the relevant standard here is ATV DIN 18300. Topsoil is listed as a class in its own right, regardless of its qualities, as it always has to be worked and stored separately from the rest of the soil, so that other soil components are not worked in. > Tab. 1.1.2

Suitability for construction

Different requirements are made of soil related to its use as a basis for foundations, for soil modeling, or as drainage material.

Shear stability and compressibility are important parameters when assessing soil in terms of its suitability for foundations or for earth structures. Shear stability identifies the resistance soil presents to a load. If soil constantly yields to a load, this will cause a change of form (compressibility). All coarse-grained soils (gravels and sands and mixtures including them) and some mixed-grained soils (high fine-grained levels ≤ 0.063 mm have an adverse effect) have high to very high shear stability and good to very good compressibility. Compressibility is reduced for fine-grained soils, as the water in the pores can escape only slowly. Such soil will settle only after years or decades, while coarse-grained soils settle immediately. > **Chapter 2.2 Foundations**

The foundation base must be sufficiently capable of loadbearing to deal with loads exerted by a building and its use. Here sealing is intended to increase the soil's loadbearing capacity and anticipate possible (subsequent) settling. The degree of sealing required depends on the anticipated load. But not all soils are capable of being sealed as required. The Proctor density gives information about the required sealing levels. > **Chapter 2.2 Foundations**

Fine-grained (cohesive) soil types that also show delay in settling are difficult to compress. Noncohesive soils are more compressible. Well-graded soils have the best compressibility characteristics.

Soils with a high porous volume, so mainly gravels and sands, are more permeable than fine-grained soils, and uniformly graded soils are usual more permeable than well-graded types. The permeability of a soil is determined by the permeability characteristic k (m/s). Coarse-grained, uniformly graded soils are best for drainage. But soils with a high ratio of fine-grained material, especially light and medium-plastic soils are more

	Area	Name	Abbreviation		Grain size in mm	Description according to DIN 4022 / DIN 18196
Noncohesive soil	very coarse soil	large boulder	LBo		> 630	Y
		boulder	Bo		> 200 to 630	
		cobble	Co		> 63 to 200	X
	coarse soil	gravel	Gr		> 2 to 63	G
		coarse gravel		CGr	> 20 to 63	gG
		medium gravel		MGr	> 6.3 to 20	mG
		fine gravel		FGr	> 2 to 6.3	fG
		sand	Sa		> 0.063 to 2	S
		coarse sand		CSa	> 0.63 to 2	gS
		medium sand		MSa	> 0.2 to 0.63	mS
		fine sand		FSa	> 0.063 to 0.2	fS
Cohesive soil	fine soil	silt	Si		> 0.002 to 0.063	U
		coarse silt		CSi	> 0.02 to 0.063	gU
		medium silt		MSi	> 0.0063 to 0.02	mU
		fine silt		FSi	> 0.002 to 0.0063	fU
		clay	Cl		< 0.002	T
Other		organic soil	Or		–	H
		fillers	Mg			A

	Area	Name	Abbreviation*	Properties	
				main defining component	influencing component
	composite soil types (examples)	gravel, sand	saGR	gravel	sand
		coarse sand, fine gravel	fgrCSa	coarse sand	fine gravel
		silt, fine gravel, coarse sand	fgrcsaSi	silt	fine gravel and coarse sand
		gravel/sand	Gr/Sa	approximately equal amounts	

* Minor components are represented by lowercase letters.

Tab. 1.1.1: Subdivision and identification of soil types by grain size

Source: taken from EN ISO 14688-1 and expanded

or less impermeable to water in their compressed state and are used for sealing (e.g. for ponds). The smaller the soil particles, the higher the water will rise by capillarity. > Tab. 1.1.3

The stability of the soil increases with grain weight. This makes coarse-grained soils less prone to erosion because of their weight. But the grain size is the key factor for fine-grained soils: while high silt content reduces the stability, finer grain content produces greater cohesion, which makes the soil particles "stick" to each other. The humus content in the topsoil reduces erosion.

If water freezes it can cause a great deal of lifting and settling, and put a building's stability at risk. Sensitivity to frost is heightened by low porous volume and continuous increase in water content. If soil is frost-sensitive, frostproof foundations are needed, or a frost protection layer has to be built in; this will prevent water from rising by capillary action because of the grain characteristics. All non-cohesive soils are frostproof. Silty soils are more sensitive to frost than clayey soils. > **Chapters 2.2 Foundations** and **3.2 Paths and squares**

Soil class		Description of soil type
1	topsoil	upper layer of soil, with humus components
2	flowing soil types	flowing to pasty composition, water not easily released
3	easily workable soil types	noncohesive to weakly cohesive soils with ≥ 15% silt or clay component (dia. < 0.06 mm) and ≤ 30% stones dia. = 63–300 mm, stable organic soils (e.g. peat)
4	moderately workable soil types	mixtures of sand, gravel, silt and clay with ≥ 15% silt or clay components (dia. < 0.06 mm) and light to medium-plastic (semi)firm cohesive soil types
5	difficult-to-work soil types	similar to 3 and 4, but with > 30% stones dia. = 63–300 mm, noncohesive and cohesive soil types with ≤ 30% stones dia. = 300–600 mm and soft to semifirm plastic clays
6	easily workable rocks and comparable soil types	fractured, brittle, friable, slatey, soft or weathered rock types and comparable firm and firmed soil types with > 30% stones dia. = 300–600 mm
7	difficult-to-work rocks	rock types with a high structural firmness that are only slightly fractured or weathered. Boulders > 600 mm

Tab. 1.1.2: Soil classified by workability   Source: DIN 18300

Soil type	Permeability*	Coefficient of permeability kf (m/s)	Water content in %	Capillary rise (m)
coarse gravel	very highly permeable	over 10^{-2}		0–0.05
fine to medium gravel	highly permeable	10^{-3}–10^{-2}	1–3	0–0.05
coarse sand	highly permeable	10^{-4}–10^{-3}	1–3	0.03–0.10
medium sand	highly permeable	around 10^{-4}	2–5	0.10–0.30
fine sand	permeable	10^{-5}–10^{-4}	9–5	0.30–1.00
coarse soil, saturated			up to about 20%	
coarse silt	permeable to slightly permeable	10^{-8}–10^{-5}	10–20	1.00–3.00
medium silt	permeable to slightly permeable	10^{-8}–10^{-5}	10–20	3.00–10.00
fine silt	permeable to slightly permeable	10^{-8}–10^{-5}	10–20	10.00–30.00
medium-plastic clay	very slightly permeable	10^{-11}–10^{-8}	20–30	30.00–300.00
distinctly plastic clay	very slightly permeable	10^{-11}–10^{-8}	30–80	30.00–300.00
fine-grained soils, saturated			up to about 250	
organic silt	very slightly permeable	10^{-11}–10^{-9}	40–80	
organic clay	very slightly permeable	10^{-11}–10^{-9}	50–150	
peat, saturated			up to about 800	
* taken from DIN 18130				

Tab. 1.1.3: Permeability and capillary rise for water

	Soil group	Abbreviation	Indication of technical construction									
			Properties						Suitability			
		according to DIN 18196	shear strenght	compactibility	compressibility	permeability	sensitivity to erosion	sensitivity to frost	foundation material for construction—foundations	building material – sealing	building material – support	building material – drainage
Coarse—grained soils	uniformly graded gravel	GE	+	+o	++	--	++	++	+	--	+	++
	well-graded gravel-sand mixtures	GW	++	++	++	-o	+	++	++	--	++	+o
	gap-graded gravel-sand	GI	++	+	++	-	o	++	++	--	++	+o
	uniformly graded sand	SE	+	+o	++	-	-	++	+	--	o	+
	well-graded sand-gravel mixtures	SW	++	++	++	-o	+o	++	++	--	+	+o
	gap-graded sand-gravel mixtures	SI	+	+	++	-o	+o	++	++	--	+	+o
Mixed soils	gravel-silt mixtures	GU	++	+	++	o	+o	-o	++	-	+	-
	gravel-silt mixtures (fine-grained levels)	GU *	+	+o	+	+	-o	--	+	+o	-	--
	gravel-clay mixtures	GT	+	+	+	+o	+o	-o	++	-o	+o	-
	gravel-clay mixtures (fine-grained levels)	GT *	+o		o	+o	++	+o	-	+o	+	--
	sand-silt mixtures	SU	++	+	+	o	o	o	++	o	-o	-
	sand-silt mixtures (fine-grained levels)	SU *	+	o	+o	+	-	--	o	+o	--	--
	sand-clay mixtures	ST	+	+o	+o	+o	o	-o	+	o	-	--
	sand-clay mixtures (fine-grained levels)	ST *	+o	-o	+o	++	-o	-	o	+	--	--
Tine-grained soils	light plastic silt	UL	-o	-o	+o	+o	--	--	+o	o	--	--
	medium-plastic silt	UM	-o	-	-o	+	-	--	o	+o	--	--
	distinctly plastic silt	UA	-	-	-	++	-o	-o	-o	-o	--	--
	light plastic clay	TL	-o	-o	o	+	-	--	o	++	--	--
	medium-plastic clay	TM	-	-	-o	++	-o	-o	o	+	--	--
	distinctly plastic clay	TA	--	--	--	++	o	+o	-o	-	--	--
Others (selected)	silts with organic admixtures and organogenic silts	OU	-o	-	-o	+o	--	--	--	-	--	--
	clays with organic admixtures and organogenous clays	OT	--	--	--	++	-o	-o	--	-	--	--
	coarse to mixed grain soils with humus type admixtures (e.g. topsoil)	OH	--	--	-	++	-o	-o	--	-	--	--
	coarse to mixed grain soils with organic admixtures and and calcareous siliceous formations	OK	+	o	-o	-o	o	+o	-o	--	--	--
	undecomposed to medium-decomposed peats (humus)	HN	-	--	--	o	+o	-	--	--	--	--

-- very low	-- very poor	-- very great	-- unsuitable
- low	- poor	- great	- not very suitable
-o moderate	-o moderate	-o medium to great	-o moderately viable
o medium	o medium	o medium	o viable
+o medium to great	+o medium to great	+o small to medium	+o suitable
+ great	+ great	+ very small	+ highly suitable
++ very great	++ very great	++ negligibly small	++ very highly suitable

Tab. 1.1.4: Soil groups for building purposes

Source: DIN 18196, Table 4, extract

*Classification by suitability for building
(soil group)*

In Germany, soils are classified in groups based on DIN 18196 according to their material composition and the resultant qualities. > Tab. 1.1.4 As well as this, each soil group provides information about its suitability as a foundation material for construction, and as a building material in its own right (e.g. sealing, providing support and enabling drainage).

Soil for growing vegetation

The space that roots have to penetrate if the ground is planted, provided the plants with their basis for life, is called the vegetation support layer. Here a distinction is made between topsoil and the subsoil beneath it.

The principal criteria for the vegetation layer are water permeability and availability, root penetrability, soil reaction (pH) and nutrient supply. Apart from soil type, the organic content has a crucial effect on water and nutrient levels. Humus, along with the fine clay particles, forms the clay-humus complex, which establishes the best possible grain structure for the topsoil. The air, water and nutrient contents are improved, and the tendency to erode and silt up reduced.

Soil intended for growing vegetation must be loose and rich in cavities. For noncohesive soils the ideal pH is in the 5.5–6 (slightly acid) range and for cohesive solids in the 6.5–7.5 (neutral) range. The best possible conditions for plant growth are provided by sandy clays or clayey sands with a good grain structure, but different soil types can provide adequate growth conditions if the correct plants are chosen for the location.

To avoid structural damage, the soil in planted areas should be worked only in the places where new surfaces are to be created. In the case of cohesive soils, irreversible changes in soil structure can be brought about if the ground water content is too high because of plastic qualities. An impermeable layer of fine silt and clay elements then forms on the surface of the soil, which leads to poor air and water provision. For this reason, cohesive and highly cohesive soils should not be worked before drying out for a consistency that is at least semi-solid. This can delay the building program. This applies to soils including loamy sand and sandy loam, loamy grit and gravel, and also plastic silt and loam with or without grit and gravel content. Work on low-cohesive soils should be undertaken only after surface drying for a consistency that is at least stiff. Low-cohesive soils include slightly loamy sand, sandy loess and loamy loess and gravel. There are no restrictions for sand, or for grit and gravel.

Contaminated soil

Soils used for building or growing vegetation must contain no pollutants, or only a very limited amount. This also applies to contaminated soil in the area that is being built on. Further use or reuse is admissible according to the degree of contamination, or a full disposal process may be required. The key factors are to ensure that soil function is not impaired, and to secure the planned use by importing soil.

If the soil is to be used for areas with vegetation, protected drinking water areas or other sensitive areas (e.g. children's playgrounds), the requirements are more rigid than for technical construction and backfilling. Permitted values classifications are set by legislators or the working committees they appoint. In Germany, for example, this is the "Landesarbeitsgemeinschaft Abfall". Soils are classified (according to LAGA notification 20) on the basis of the established pollutant values. These permit unlimited or limited use (Z0 to Z2) or only dumping (Z3 to Z5).

Local environment ministries will usually supply information. In Switzerland, for example, the Federal Office of the Environment issues the appropriate compliance aids, which can be consulted online.

BULK MATERIAL

Substrates and stone aggregates are available in particular material and grain size combinations, corresponding to the grade requirements for different areas of use.

Naturally occurring stone aggregates

Naturally occurring stone aggregates are available crushed and uncrushed. The material is usually obtained from sand and gravel pits, and from quarries. The rocks are processed in a crusher to produce material in the form of crushed sand, chippings or ballast. > Fig. 1.1.5 They are used, among other things, for installing load-bearing and frost-resistant layers, drainage courses, building foundations, nonslip surfaces or as a aggregate for concrete and mortar. Crushed material is preferable if loadbearing layers are being installed, as the angular, irregular surface of the grains ensures better keying and thus greater stability. High-grade crushed sand and high-grade chippings are crushed stone aggregates that meet high grain quality requirements. They are used mainly for surface courses.

Volcanic bulk materials (e.g. pumice, tuff or lava) are uncrushed stone aggregates that may have angular grain structures. Volcanic rocks are particularly useful for roof planting and improving ventilation or drainage qualities in soil because they are light and have a very porous structure.

Cohesive soils are suitable as construction material because they can be shaped at will. Different properties, and use areas derived from them, emerge as a result of grain size composition. Loam is a soil type consisting mainly of sand, silt and clay. Loam products include light mineral mixtures, rammed clay and loam bricks for wall construction, and also loam mortar.

The grain structure of clay, especially lightly plastic clay, means that it can be compacted to produce a soil layer that is almost impermeable to water. Compacted clay is used for jobs such as pond construction. Powder products such as powdered clay or bentonite are available, as well as clay tiles.

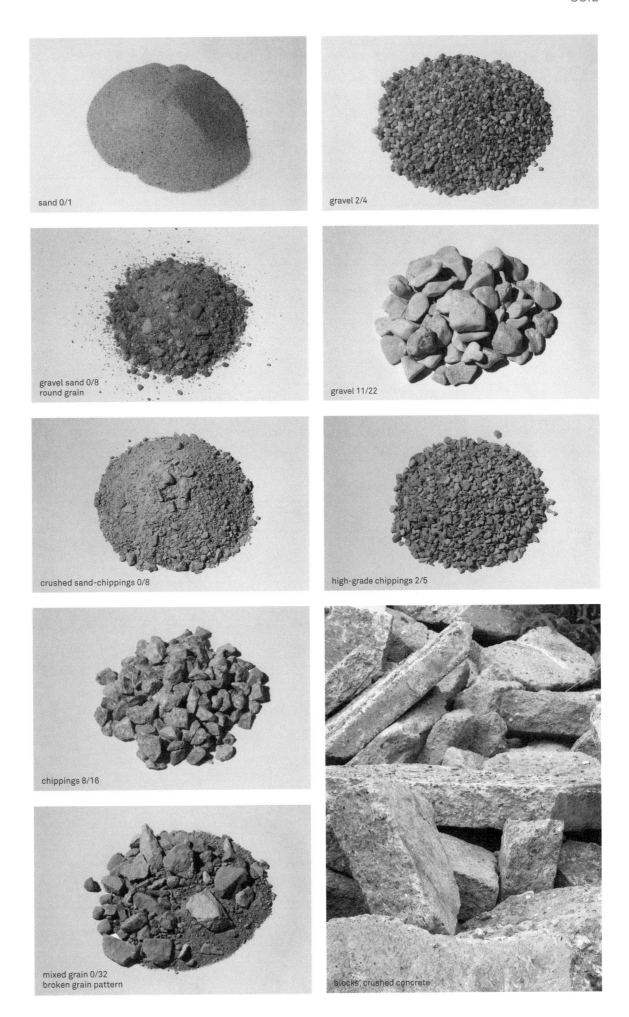

sand 0/1

gravel 2/4

gravel sand 0/8
round grain

gravel 11/22

crushed sand-chippings 0/8

high-grade chippings 2/5

chippings 8/16

mixed grain 0/32
broken grain pattern

blocks, crushed concrete

Fig. 1.1.5: Various stone
aggregates

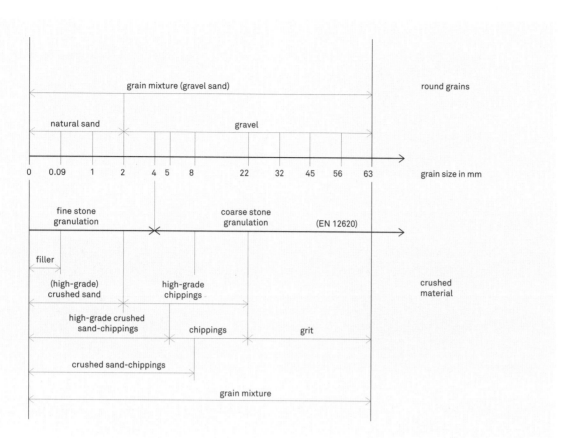

Tab. 1.1.5:
a) Stone aggregates
   by grain group and standard
   commercial description

b) Commercially available
   granulations of grit substances
   (a range of choices)

Description	Stone granulation in mm	Examples of use
Round-grained		
natural sand	0/1 (fine sand), 0/2	paving and cobble bedding and joining material, cable sand, trench reinstatement, aggregate substance (concrete, mortar) play, sport, nonslip sand: special qualities for beach volleyball, golf and riding paddocks, play areas
gravel	2/4, 4/8, 8/16, 11/22, 16/32, 32/63, 32/56, 32/63	drainage/seepage bed, aggregate substance (concrete) frost protection layers, decorative gravel
grain mixture (gravel sand)	0/3, 0/4, 0/8, 2/8, 0/16, 0/32, 0/56, 0/63	filler, nonslip (2/8), frost protection and loadbearing layers (0/32, 0/56), aggregate substance (concrete) surface layer in path construction, decorative gravel
Broken material		
filler (rock flour)	≤ 0.09	aggregate substance (concrete, asphalt)
(high-grade) crushed sand *	0/2	aggregate substance (concrete, asphalt), trench reinstatement
crushed sand-chippings	0/5, 0/8	paving and cobble bedding material, trench reinstatement
high-grade crushed sand-chippings	0/5, 0/3 1/3	paving and cobble bedding and joining material, chippings for scattering on asphalt
high-grade chippings *	2/5, 5/8, 8/11, 11/16, 16/22	surface layer in path construction, paving and cobble bedding (2/5), aggregate substance (concrete, asphalt)
chippings	5/8, 5/11, 8/11, 8/16, 11/16, 16/22, 22/32, 16/32	aggregate substance (concrete and asphalt), drainages (11/16, 11/22, 16/22, 16/32)
grit	32/45, 32/56, 45/56	absorbent strip under eaves, soil stabilization, drainage/seepage bed
mixed grain	0/32, 0/45, 0/56 also 0/16, 0/22	surfacing in path construction (smaller grain sizes) aggregate substance (concrete, asphalt), frost protection layers (0/5 to 0/56), loadbearing layers (0/32, 0/45, 0/56 **)

*   For high-grade crushed sand and high-grade chippings, higher specifications on grain size, quality and composition are set.
** also described as a grit loadbearing layer (D)

Fig. 1.1.6: Bulk materials for
covering planted areas:
a) bark mulch
b) chippings
c) dyed bark mulch
d) gravel

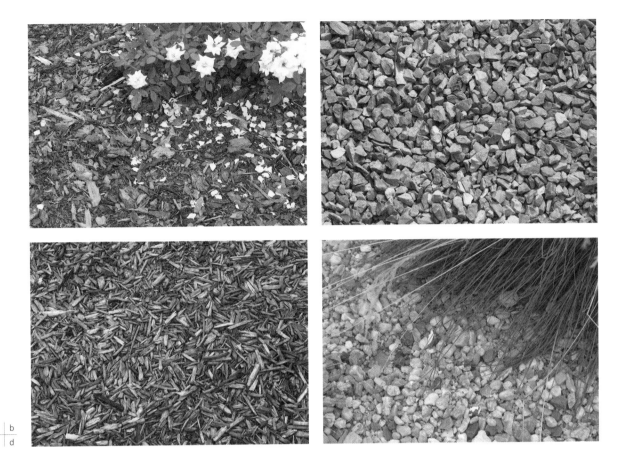

a | b
c | d

Artificial aggregates

Artificially manufactured products are available commercially, as well as naturally occurring bulk materials.
A distinction is made between recycled material made
from demolished products from the civil engineering and
building trades (concrete, asphalt or masonry), and industrial (by-)products. Lightweight expanded clay is an
industrially produced building material, produced by firing certain clay minerals, but industrial by-products are
defined as substances left over from production processes. Examples of this are blast furnace slag or refuse
incineration slag.

For reasons of sustainability and economic viability, the
use of recycled material (RC material) and industrial by-
products is to be encouraged, and is often compulsory for public construction projects. But care has to be
taken when choosing these materials, as they may be
polluted. Only material that has been tested and certified as being of the appropriate quality should be used.
Use is limited, particularly in areas that are significant
in terms of water capture and groundwater quality, and
in water protection areas. But top-quality RC material can be used without further concern in individual
cases in water protection surface areas. The groundwater level and the permeability of the particular soil
are important parameters. Bound surface layers above
the recycling material offer additional protection. A
distinction is also made in this context between water-
permeable, semipermeable and impermeable installation methods. In Germany and Switzerland, the local

water and refuse disposal authorities or the appropriate cantonal office provide information about and permission to use RC material.

Bulk material for use when growing vegetation

Topsoil must be suitable for the intended type of planting and use. It must contain no foreign matter that could
impair its function, such as building residue or refuse,
or parts of plants that rot down with difficulty or not at
all. Volcanic rock is often used as a vegetation support
layer for roof planting.

Bulk material is also used to cover planted areas to prevent weeds from growing or to improve the soil as well
as the actual soil substrate in areas where vegetation
is being cultivated.

Soil-improving bulk materials other than the various soil
types are above all compost or bark humus (shredded
and composted bark). Bark mulch (coarsely shredded
bark) or wood chippings are used as mulch, along with
the various stone aggregates such as gravel, chippings
or pumice. Quality-controlled products (in Germany
with the RAL seal of quality, for example) should be
noted when choosing bulk materials of organic origin.
> Fig 1.1.6

SOIL PROTECTION

Any work carried out in the soil will generally alter the soil structure, and so any interventions in or beside the soil should be confined to what is essential, so that the natural soil function is not impaired. Compression caused by loads exerted on the soil, or by driving over it, should be avoided, especially in (future) planting areas. Care should also be taken to ensure that no pollution occurs as a result of impurities in the form of solid materials, or liquids. Impurities in the soil are also a potential hazard for the groundwater. In areas where soil contamination cannot be avoided, the necessary measures should be taken, by sealing, for example.

Soil protection measures have a part to play during the building phase as well. This includes identifying suitable storage areas and organizing vehicular access to the building site so that the soil is protected.

Protection from erosion is required when building on soil, for intermediate storage and when redesigning modeled ground. Both temporary and permanent earthworks should be protected against atmospheric and hydrogeological influences. A distinction is made between measures involving biological manipulation and those made on a technical-structural basis. > **Chapter 3.1 Ground modeling and earthworks**

Topsoil should be appropriately protected against drying out and wind erosion. Topsoil clamps should not be piled higher than 2 m and adequate rainwater drainage should be guaranteed. If topsoil is in intermediate storage for longer than three months, then intermediate planting measures are recommended, by sowing Phacelia or mustard seed, for example. > **Chapter 1.3 Lawns and other seeded areas**

TESTING AND ASSESSING FOUNDATION SOIL

Soil reports

It is essential that an expert soil report be compiled for every construction project that entails building on existing soil. This will provide data about local soil conditions, and thus make it possible to plan appropriately. It can be omitted only in exceptional cases, for example if the project is on a very small scale, and at the same time sufficient information about local soil conditions is already available (e.g. because of previous building on the site), and if only minor technical demands have to be met in terms of the soil. Agricultural research institutions or other establishments studying soil will help to establish whether it is suitable for vegetation.

It is the client's responsibility to commission a soil report. It should be compiled to relate specifically to the project in hand, so that concrete requirements can be addressed.

The engineering practice commissioned to do the work will determine the nature and scope of the soil study on the basis of the project brief, and then draw up a geotechnical report containing information about the geological and hydrological conditions and provide instructions and recommendations for the planned building work.

The report will outline the soil profiles, and also make statements on matters including soil classifications (soil type, soil class and soil group), on sensitivity to frost and permeability, and on the groundwater levels. It will also contain precise instructions about the nature and depth of the foundations, on compacting, water retention, soil improvement and disposal of contaminated soil.

Soil investigation

Appropriate topsoil investigations require soil studies and (lab) tests carried out as preliminaries to a soil report. Planners also have other methods of investigation at their disposal. Maps and aerial photographs can be examined beforehand to acquire a first impression of the terrain. While evaluating multitemporal aerial photographs can provide information about earlier uses and the resultant changes to the soil (e.g. contamination, excavations and other digging, the various specialist maps available provide data on topography, the geological underlay, the existing soil or the water situation. Subsoil and geological maps for engineers in particular provide facts about the conditions relevant to building. Online databases are also available in many places. Environmental data catalogues can be called up via the environment ministries' Web sites and the Land or cantonal authorities in Germany and Switzerland. > **Fig. 1.1.7**

Soil conditions can be determined precisely only by carrying out investigations on the spot, as minor deviations could well occur at any time. Soil is assessed visually, e.g. by observing the terrain, observing the vegetation and addressing grain size, and manually, e.g. by kneading or shaking experiments and finger tests. > **Tab. 1.1.6**

Fig. 1.1.7: Example of engineering classification of soils; source: Umweltdatenkatalog des Landesamtes für Bergbau, Energie und Geologie (LBEG) Hanover.

Caption

Fluid soil

Easily loosened soil

Soil that can be loosened with medium difficulty

Soil that can be loosened only with difficulty

Easily loosened rock and comparable soil type

Rock that is difficult to loosen

No data

a) classification of noncohesive soil types

Grain size
(in mm)

b) classification of coherive soil types

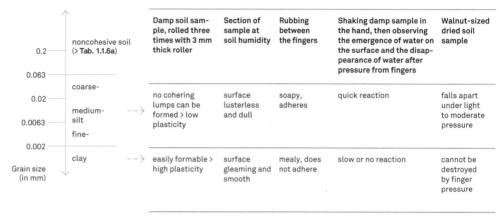

		Damp soil sample, rolled three times with 3 mm thick roller	Section of sample at soil humidity	Rubbing between the fingers	Shaking damp sample in the hand, then observing the emergence of water on the surface and the disappearance of water after pressure from fingers	Walnut-sized dried soil sample
0.2	noncohesive soil (> **Tab. 1.1.6a**)					
0.063						
0.02	coarse-	no cohering lumps can be formed > low plasticity	surface lusterless and dull	soapy, adheres	quick reaction	falls apart under light to moderate pressure
0.0063	medium-silt					
0.002	fine-					
	clay	easily formable > high plasticity	surface gleaming and smooth	mealy, does not adhere	slow or no reaction	cannot be destroyed by finger pressure

Grain size
(in mm)

Source: EN ISO 14688-1

c) indicator plants for determining soil characteristics

Soil characteristics		Indicator plants
soil reaction	highly to moderately acidic	*Calluna vulgaris*, heather *Nardus stricta*, mat grass *Rumex acetosella*, red sorrel *Scleranthus annuus*, annual knawel *Spergula arvensis*, corn spurrey *Trifolium arvense*, hare's-foot clover
	moderately acidic	*Anthemis arvensis*, corn chamomile *Chrysanthemum segetum*, corn marigold *Digitalis purpurea*, purple foxglove *Potentilla argentea*, silver cinquefoil *Scleranthus perennis*, perennial knawel *Spergularia rubra*, sand spurrey
	weakly acidic to neutral	*Alopecurus myosuroides*, slender meadow foxtail *Apera spica-venti*, common windgrass *Fumaria officinalis*, common fumitory *Matricaria chamomilla*, German chamomile *Veronica persica*, Persian speedwell
	neutral to alkaline	*Campanula persicifolia*, peach-leaved bellflower *Cenataurea scabiosa*, greater knapweed *Euonymus europaeus*, European spindle *Geranium pratense*, meadow geranium *Ligustrum vulgare*, common privet *Ranunculus arvensis*, corn buttercup *Salvia pratensis*, meadow clary *Sinapis arvensis*, wild mustard
	alkaline	*Adonis flammea*, large pheasant's-eye *Galium glaucum*, waxy bedstraw
loamy soil		*Cornus sanguinea*, common dogwood *Euonymus europaeus*, European spindle *Ranunculus arvensis*, corn buttercup *Rosa arvensis*, field rose *Rosa rubiginosa*, sweet briar *Veronica persica*, Persian speedwell
nutrient content	nitrogen-poor	*Calluna vulgaris*, heather *Erophila verna*, whitlow grass *Potentilla argentea*, silver cinquefoil *Rumex acetosella*, red sorrel *Scleranthus annuus*, annual knawel *Spergula arvensis*, corn spurrey *Sedum album*, small houseleek *Trifolium arvense*, hare's-foot clover
		Atriplex nitens, garden orache/saltbush *Atriplex patula*, common orache/saltbush *Chenopodium bonus-henricus*, Guter Heinrich *Chenopodium polyspermum*, many-seeded goosefoot *Galium aparine*, goosegrass *Lamium album*, white deadnettle *Sambucus nigra*, black elder *Stellaria media*, common chickweed *Urtica dioica*, stinging nettle *Urtica urens*, dwarf nettle

Tab. 1.1.6: Visual and manual methods for establishing soil compositions and soil properties

Source: DIN 18915 et al.; Ellenberg, H. 1979

1.2 PLANTS

PLANT PROPAGATION

WOODY PLANTS
· Grade and quality criteria
· Summer and evergreen broad-leaved woody plants
· Conifers
· Checking and accepting woody plants

HERBACEOUS PLANTS (INCLUDING GRASSES AND FERNS)
· Habitants and variety of shapes
· Groups by use
· Plant qualities

BULBS AND TUBERS (GEOPHYTES)
· Hardy geophytes

BEDDING AND TUB PLANTS

Ute Rieper

1.2 PLANTS

Plants, as living materials, are landscape architecture's typical design material. All other materials start to age once the project is complete, but plants achieve their full effect only in the course of time. Vegetation has an inherent dynamic. For one thing, plants reflect the cycle of the seasons, as they shoot, blossom and take on their fall colors, and for another, they go through life phases from youth to age. This can mean a vegetation period of up to several centuries, according to growth form. Integrating this dynamism effectively and working creatively with it is a sign of successful planning.

This chapter discusses the plant groups available to landscape architecture as material: woody plants, herbaceous plants, bulbs and corms, and seasonal plants. They are categorized according to growth forms and botanical criteria. A short introduction lists the requirements and possible uses for each group, and also the characteristic qualities that each plant displays. As the qualities of plants, being living material, are strongly influenced by the soil and climate of their situation, recommendations and empirical values are transferable to other countries only to a limited extent. There are considerable differences between the horticultural traditions of the individual European countries, defined by different climatic and socio-cultural conditions. This shows very clearly in the range of species used. Different sets of rules have to be applied against this background.

This chapter introduces the most important topics, focusing principally on the use of woody plants in urban public parks and green areas. It has not been possible to give tips about using the various plant species and kinds in this publication, with the exception of the street tree list > **Tab. 1.2.1** and the summary of lasting potential for hardy geophytes. > **Tab. 1.2.3** References are made to the relevant literature on plant use. The chapters on water features, greening buildings and planting roofs also give tips on plant use for these specific situations.

PLANT PROPAGATION

Plants propagate themselves in nature generatively, via seeds. The parent plants are heterozygous so their progeny can be very diverse. Cultivated herbaceous and woody varieties are thus bred vegetatively in horticulture, in order to preserve the qualities and genetic characteristics of the mother plant. Vegetative breeding methods include grafting and cuttings, separation and root cuttings. In grafting, a shoot or bud of the desired cultivar is attached to another type, the stock, which will also ensure varietal consistency. In addition to this, positive qualities of the stock, for example stronger stem or root formation, will also be transferred.

In present-day tree nursery practice, seed, young plants, seedlings and fully grown plants are traded throughout Europe. But as the origins of the seed, the soil and climate in the place where it is produced affect the later use of a plant, care should be taken that those conditions coincide with the new location as far as possible. Plants whose seeds or seedlings are produced in milder regions survive less well than those adapted to the situation. These problems become all the more acute the harsher the climate is in the new location. The consequence is a greater failure rate than for new planting, reduced vitality and increased susceptibility to pests. The principal limiting factors are severe frost, long periods of frost and summer drought.

Plants are offered with different root qualities. > **Tab. 1.2.4** Seedlings of summer-green woody plants and varieties of roses in particular are sold as bare-root goods. They are comparatively reasonable in price. They take root without difficulty, grow rapidly in the first year and adapt well to conditions in their new location. The only disadvantage is that young woody plants often need three to five years to give any sense of spread. The planting period is also limited to the very short dormant season. Rooted plants cannot be dug up and offered for sale until the leaves start to drop in fall.

Root ball goods are bred by regular replanting. This makes the plant form a compact, dense root ball, the only form in which relatively large woody plants can be replanted. The older the plant, the more slowly it will bed in and form new shoots. One problem is that the soil in root balls can differ considerably from the new location (e.g. clay root ball in sandy soil), as a capillary break will make the water supply more difficult. Smaller root balls are cloth-wrapped, and larger ones contained in wire mesh. Compared with bare-root goods, the planting time for root ball goods is about 2 to 4 weeks longer, in spring and autumn.

Plants can also be grown exclusively in pots and containers, which means that they can be planted almost all year round. For woody plants, the volume of the container in liters is given as well as the size. The pot is the standard form for herbaceous plants. Normally a peat-based substrate is used. As humus-rich peat balls are usually very different from the mineral soil at the new location, this can impede the water supply and rooting. Peat extraction is also problematic for nature conservation reasons. Substrates made of other raw materials have been introduced, but are not very widely used.

The best time to plant most woody and herbaceous varieties is the early fall. Roots continue to grow as long as the soil temperature is about 5 °C. Thus, freshly set plants form a well-established root system in order to be able to survive the dryer summer months in the following year. Spring planting makes sense for particularly heavy soils or for varieties that are not reliably frost-resistant. > Chapter 3.9 Planting technique and care of vegetation surfaces

WOODY PLANTS

Woody plants are perennial varieties with woody shoots above the ground. Trees are characterized by apical growth, i.e. they grow from the shoot tip and usually develop a continuous leader, or one that does not divide very much. Shrubs grow from the rhizome and usually develop large numbers of shoots. Because of their size, both groups are suitable for creating three-dimensional structures. These can be point structures (solitaire tree), cover and area (grove, group of woody plants) or linear (avenue, hedge), and grow freely or be trimmed with varying degrees of severity. There are three basic types of root system that develop in deep soil: tap root systems grow deep into the soil, vertically, and have a markedly thicker main root; heart root systems have several roots that grow more or less vertically down into the soil; and horizontal root systems with roots that run mainly diagonally to horizontally. Root systems are species-specific, and important for the plant's use criteria.

Grade and quality criteria

Woody plants are offered in various sizes, called grades. Quality standards define the grades, and the appropriate minimum sizes.

Criteria are number of shoots, height and/or width, trunk circumference for trees (at a height of 1 m), number of transplants and root formation or pot volume for shrubs and woody container plants. > Fig. 1.2.1 Over and above this, authenticity of variety, flawless health and good general vitality are required, so that the plants are in a position to establish themselves without problems. > Fig. 1.2.1

If woody plants are to be accepted as flawless when supplied, in other words if they are for sale, they have to meet other criteria. Trees and shrubs should have a shape that is typical for their species and age. For example, a young tree will naturally have a somewhat narrower crown, while a solitaire tree of the same species that has been cultivated for longer in the tree nursery and planted well away from its neighbors should have a somewhat more extensive crown. Relative age shows above all in the position of the shoots. Young trees grow vigorously and their shoots are positioned at a very steep angle. Somewhat older trees, usually larger grades that have been transplanted several times, have branches that grow at a much lower angle.

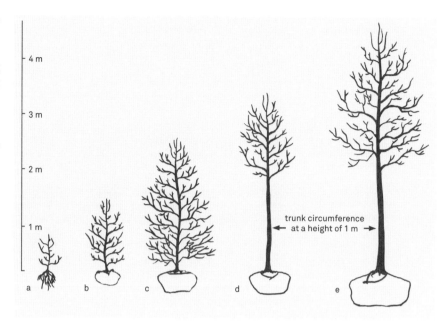

Shrubs and crowns should have a regular structure and plenty of branches. Very asymmetrical crowns and bald leading shoots, in other words trunk prolongations, are cause for complaint. The same applies to unduly curly branches and forking trunks. They reduce the long-term stability of the crown, as the branches damage each other when they start to thicken out. Cut points caused by cultivation pruning in the nursery should be at least partially healed over, i.e. new bark should have grown over them. It is also important that there are no weeds in the root balls and containers. Any sign of couch grass (Elymus repens) or ground elder (Aegopodium podagraria) should also be objected to. If herbaceous plants or low bushes are being used for underplanting, these weeds will create a maintenance problem in future and a considerable amount of extra effort. Seed-propagated weeds can essentially be tolerated. > Tab. 1.2.2

Summer and evergreen broad-leaved woody plants

Broad-leaved woody plants are dicotyledonous (with two cotyledons in the seed) angiosperms with reticulated leaves. The texture of the foliage is fine to coarse, depending on species. Decorative effect derives primarily from habit (growth form, e.g. strictly upright, weeping, wide-canopied), but also from blossom, fruit and winter color. Deciduous woody plants that are green in summer come from moderate climates with distinctive seasons. They grow new foliage annually during the growing season. Evergreens come from Mediterranean (arid) regions, or areas with mild winters, and most of them have limited frost-hardiness.

Street trees have to meet two demands. One is to tolerate the adverse conditions of their city location: urban climate with heat and summer dryness, and frequently radiation back from the facades of buildings, cramped space for their roots and poor, C-character soil, surface and underground sealing, emissions, road salt and dogs' urine.

Fig. 1.2.1: Selection of Carpinus betulus (hornbeam) grades, schematic diagram:
a) small young tree, replanted 1 x, h 60–80 cm
b) young tree, replanted 2 x, with root ball, h 125–150 cm
c) young solitaire tree, replanted 3 x, with wired root ball, w 100 –150 cm, h 250–300 cm
d) standard, replanted 3 x, with wired root ball, trunk circumference 14–16 cm
e) solitaire standard, replanted 4 x, with wired root ball w 100–150 cm, h 250–300 cm

Seq. no.	Botanical and English name	Height achieved in m	Width in m	Light penetration	Sun or shade	Suitability for urban spaces	Remarks
4	*Acer platanoides,* Plane	20–30	15–22	negligible	sun to semishade	suitable within limits	Large, fast-growing tree, with a dense, rounded crown; blossoms before the leaves shoot; sensitive to ground sealing
7	*Acer platanoides* 'Cleveland' Norway maple	10–15	7–9	negligible	sun to semishade	suitable	As no. 4, but medium-sized tree with oval, compact and regular crown, horizontal oval shape when mature, young leaves marbled in light red; resistant to urban climate
32	*Alnus spaethii,* Alder	12–15	8–10	moderate	sunny	well suited	Passed as a suitable street tree since 1995, very fast-growing, with a broad pyramidal crown, branches loosely upright; spreads more horizontally when mature, consistently straight trunk, late-falling, dark green, slightly shiny foliage (can break under snow)
35	*Betula pendula,* Silver birch	18–25 (30)	10–15 (18)	considerable	sunny	suitable within limits	Large, fast-growing tree with loosely rising crown; not resistant to urban climate and therefore not suitable for paved areas, short-lived; needs a lot of light, shallow rooted, pioneer woody plant
44	*Corylus colurna,* Turkish filbert	15–18 (23)	8–12 (16)	negligible	sun to semishade	well suited	Medium to large tree with regular, broad-based conical crown, consistently straight trunk, beware of falling fruit, edible fruit
59	*Fraxinus ornus,* Manna ash	8–12 (15)	6–8 (10)	moderate	sunny	suitable	Fast-growing small tree with weal wood with a round or broad pyramidal crown, branches rarely grow straight, pay attention to side clearance, flowering tree; do not use in paved areas; resistant to urban climate
62	*Ginkgo biloba,* Ginkgo biloba	15–30 (35)	10–15 (20)	considerable	sun to semishade	well suited	Large tree, grows in various ways, fan-shaped leaves, dioecious, disease-resistant, needs a lot of light, beware of falling fruit, fall color; resistant to urban climate
85	*Platanus acerifolia,* London plane	20–30 (40)	15–25	negligible	sunny	suitable	Large, fast-growing tree with wide crown, increasingly prone to attack by pests such as leaf-blight, wilt, lace-bug in recent years; resistant to urban climate
86	*Populus berolinensis,* Berlin poplar	18–25	8–10	moderate	sunny	suitable within limits	Large tree with broad, column-like trunk, fast-growing, forms root suckers
91	*Prunus avium,* Wild cherry	15–20 (25)	10–15	negligible	sunny	not suitable	Medium-sized tree, risk of gummosis, flowering tree, fruit falls
109	*Quercus robur,* Pedunculate or English oak	25–35 (40)	15–20 (25)	considerable	sunny	suitable	Large tree with broad conical crown, spreads widely; susceptible to pests, do not plant before December
113	*Robinia pseudoacacia,* False acacia	20–25	12–18 (22)	considerable	sunny	suitable	Large tree with open, irregular crown, fast-growing when young, flowering tree; low maintenance but susceptible to wind damage in nutrient-rich soil, dead wood forms in later years, forms root suckers; resistant to urban climate
133	*Tilia cordata,* Small-leaved lime	18–20 (30)	12–15 (20)	negligible	sun to semishade	suitable within limits	Large tree with broad, conical, dense crown, spreads vigorously when older; habit can be very variable, likes fresh, open soil; secretes honeydew
135	*Tilia cordata* 'Greenspire', 'Greenspire' small-leaved lime	18–20	10–12	negligible	sun to semishade	well suited	Like no. 133, but crown narrower, more regular and denser, broader when older; branches ascending; bark necrosis in some regions

Tab. 1.2.1: Extract from the 2006 GALK street tree list. Of a total of 145 species and varieties listed, 7 were rated as well suited, about 40 as suitable and 50 as suitable within limits. It may be better to check the suitability of individual species rather than the suitability of the species as a whole.

If trees are not to create traffic safety problems around them, the also have to meet functional requirements. Relatively high stability and safety against fracture should minimize danger from trees falling over or branches breaking off. Upright growth with a closed crown should secure the street's light profile and avoid damage from low branches. Fruit formation is undesirable as fruit falling on the pavement can be a hazard and increase the danger of people skidding. They should also not exude honeydew (aphid secretion) as this soils parked cars. Growth typical to the species should not include roots that come very near the surface, as these frequently damage roads and footpaths.

The best species for the urban climate come from sub-Mediterranean or subtropical regions, as they can tolerate heat and dryness. But most central European tree species come from woods or meadows and are thus ruled out. Some pioneer trees such as *Populus* (poplar) are unsuitable because of their aggressive roots near the surface (horizontal root system); they also grow suckers and have brittle wood. Varieties of *Acer platanoides* (plane), also a pioneer tree, are at least suitable, however.

List of recommended or unsuitable trees are often compiled to make it easier to choose suitable street tree species. In Germany, the Arbeitskreis der Grünflächenamtsleiterkonferenz (Green open space department directorial conference working party, GALK) has published a street tree list based on the experiences of local green open space departments. > Tab. 1.2.1 This working party is also in touch with experts from neighboring European countries.

Points to check	Criteria	Procedure, remarks
size	minimum height and/or number of shoots	measure or count random samples
width	minimum width given, fully developed crown for solitaires	remove transport protection from crown, requires good species knowledge as there are great differences between species
trunk circumference	minimum circumference at a height of 1 m as specified in tender	measure random samples, all items for large woody plants
species or variety	must comply with species or variety specified	difficult if no foliage, varieties can often be checked only by blossom or species, open transport protection for individual plants for easier identification
root ball quality	roots firm and dense throughout the ball, root end not too thick at the end of the ball	plants loose in the ball package? Then complain about "droopy" ball. Very thick root ends at the edge of the ball indicate overripe goods
state of health	last year's shoots, bud or foliage and bark immaculate, lichen growth	look carefully for discoloration and distortion, and for traces of pest damage, lichen indicates stagnating growth
transport and storage damage	roots, ball, trunk and shoots free from mechanical damage and without damage from heat or cold	look carefully for dried-out roots, bent shoots, fresh (painted) damage to bark and loose root balls, complain about damaged leaders if applicable (always in the case of conifers and street trees), always transport covered in case of frost or temperatures above 25 °C
freedom from weeds	ball and container goods free of root weed (couch grass!)	in case of suspicion, open root ball or check during planting

Tab. 1.2.2: Checking criteria for accepting woody plants

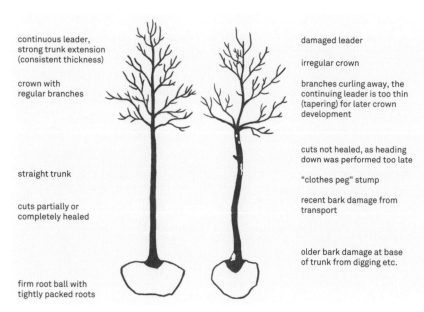

continuous leader, strong trunk extension (consistent thickness)

crown with regular branches

straight trunk

cuts partially or completely healed

firm root ball with tightly packed roots

damaged leader

irregular crown

branches curling away, the continuing leader is too thin (tapering) for later crown development

cuts not healed, as heading down was performed too late

"clothes peg" stump

recent bark damage from transport

older bark damage at base of trunk from digging etc.

Fig. 1.2.2: Avenue trees: positive and negative examples, schematic diagrams

Fig. 1.2.3: Preproduced clipped hedge elements: *Prunus laurocerasus* 'Herbergii' (cherry laurel), solitaire, 4 x replanted with wired root ball, 110 x 60 x 200, 8–10 years old

Fig. 1.2.4:
a) Spheres made of *Ligustrum vulgare* 'Atrovirens' (privet), 160–180 cm diameter, transplanted 5 x, with wired root ball, approx. 15–18 years old, trimmed annually
b) *Tilia cordata* 'Greenspire' (small-leaved lime), foot trellis, transplanted 5 x with wired root ball, trunk circumference 40–45 cm, width: 250 cm, overall height 570 cm, roughly 12–15 years old
c) *Tilia europaea* 'Pallida' (Kaiserlinden), box-shaped, transplanted 4 x with wired root ball, 45–50 cm trunk circumference, overall height approx. 400 cm, crown springs at approx. 250 cm, 1 trim annually 1, approx. 17–22 years old
d) *Buxus sempervirens* (box) as sofa, approx. 2 m wide and 1 m high. Commissioned. Made up of solitaire plants, transplanted 3–4 x, approx. 7–10 years old, structurally trimming for about 4 more years, trimmed 2 x annually

a	b
c	d

Street trees are supplied with wrapped root ball at a trunk height of 220 cm to 250 cm. The continuous leader should have even branches of medium thickness, so that the tree can be headed back in the next few years. A trunk height or a side clearance of 4.5 m is usually needed on main roads, less on minor roads. Leaders with forking or damage to the leader are definite cause for complaint. > **Fig. 1.2.2**

Hedging plants are bred from deciduous and evergreen hardwoods that tolerate clipping well and can grow like shrubs or trees. Hedging should carry twigs from the bottom upwards and grow densely, which is achieved by repeated clipping at the tree nursery. Light shrubs are supplied with bare roots, thicker shrubs with wrapped root balls or in containers. > **Tab. 1.2.4** Preproduced hedges have been available for some time now. They make newly planted areas look mature immediately upon completion. > **Fig. 1.2.3**

Topiary plants are bred from deciduous and evergreen hardwoods and more rarely from conifers, above all *Taxus baccata* (yew). Trees and shrubs that tolerate clipping, e.g. *Carpinus betulus* (hornbeam), *Fagus sylvatica* (beech), *Prunus laurocerasus* "Herbergii" (cherry laurel) and *Buxus sempervirens* (box) are suitable. There are no standard quality guidelines for topiary plants. Large tree nurseries offer a whole variety of shapes designs. Trees are bred in the shape of spheres, columns of fans; and shrubs primarily in geometrical shapes like spheres, cubes or cones. Unusual designs not included in the standard range can be bred to order by specialist tree nurseries, but at least four years or more must be allowed for them to be ready. Typically, topiary plants are used for formal outdoor areas. > **Fig. 1.2.4**

Fully grown trees are not usually brought on in a tree nursery, but are taken from their long-established location and replanted as more or less fully mature specimens. They change and make a striking effect on the space immediately after planting because of their mature or irregular, expressive habit. Transplanting costs vary from low to relatively high according to species and size, the previous location and the distance traveled. The failure rate is considerably higher than for nursery goods, as most of the roots of a large, fully grown tree are lost in transplantation. They have to be carefully, elaborately and expensively tended. Frequently trees of this kind need a permanent anchorage, as their root systems have not redeveloped sufficiently strongly. As large trees are no longer very adaptable because of their age, use that is suitable to their species or their location is all the more important. If trees' fundamental needs in terms of light and soil are not considered, the growth of transplanted large trees will stagnate, or they gradually die off.

Fruit trees are unsuitable for use in public spaces. As they are comparatively demanding in terms of soil and climate, they do not flourish in typical urban locations. They also need to be pruned regularly, annually at first, and usually neither the personnel nor the resources are available for this. In addition, dropping fruit cause problems on carriageways and grassy areas. Wild or decorative fruit trees can be a sensible alternative outside densely populated areas, as they are more robust and considerably easier to tend.

Climbing plants and creepers are leafy woody plants that cannot stand alone, but need supports from walls or props if they are to grow upwards. Many of them often come from wooded locations where they grow between trees, and prefer cool locations and fresh, humus-rich soil. They grow from heights ranging from 2 to 30 m. Climbers are supplied in containers and should show at least two strong shoots. Breakage-prone species must be staked. > **Chapter 3.13 Vertical planting**

Roses have been bred for several centuries, and an enormous range of varieties is now available. They are divided into different classes according to the way they grow or their species. Typical bedding roses include floribunda, polyanthus roses, polyanthus hybrids and species roses, which remain relatively low (0.5 to 1.5 m high) and produce a large number of blooms, usually large. These roses are very decorative and need a relatively high degree of maintenance.

Climbing roses grow to a height of 2 to 5 m according to species, and are relatively easy to maintain. Bush and park roses are wilder in character (1 to 3 m high) and are relatively undemanding. Bloom size and unusual colors used to be the aim when breeding, but for some years now roses have been bred for their resistance to disease. > **Fig. 1.2.5.**

All rose types are propagated vegetatively by budding (grafting a scion with buds attached to a briar stock). Grafted roses are supplied as year-old, bare-root plants. > **Tab. 1.2.4** Class A goods are recommended. Roses of

Fig. 1.2.5: Bush roses

this kind characteristically have three well-developed, mature, i.e. slightly lignified shoots.

Ground cover roses grow similarly to climbing roses, and their blooms are like wild roses. This group includes a particularly large number of disease-resistant varieties. They are usually planted in public green spaces. As they are normally propagated on their own roots using cuttings or live stakes, there is no risk of undesirable growth from the stock, as in the case of grafted roses. The same quality requirements as for woody plants apply to wild roses, i.e. seedlings propagated generatively.

Conifers

Conifers are gymnospermous plants. The leaves usually have parallel veins, and are needle-shaped. Their habit is mainly regular, austere, with continuous branching on the leader. Their evergreen leaves make them suitable for creating long-lasting structures. Very few conifers respond well to clipping. As they often have to rely on symbiotic mycorrhiza (fungus roots), they are supplied as rootball or container goods. > **Tab. 1.2.4** They grow from a height of about 10 cm for some dwarf varieties and up to 20 m and more, as in *Pinus sylvestris* (Scots pine), for example. Origins and locational requirements also differ considerably. Species from mountainous

Fig. 1.2.6: Gaps between tufty species are quickly colonized by runners.

Fig. 1.2.7: Mixed planting in September

a | b
c |

Fig. 1.2.8: Hardy geophytes:
a) *Tulipa* hybrids (garden tulips): new tulip bulbs are usually
   planted each year for a lavish display of flowers;
b) *Scilla siberica* (spring beauty): they flourish in the long grass and
   also survive surface wear and tear and trampling in the summer;
c) *Narcissus* hybrids (large cupped narcissi): they need cool situations
   in the summer.

positions or coastal forests are adapted to large quantities of precipitation and high humidity. Species of this kind cannot tolerate the urban climate and respond to heat, dryness and exhaust emissions by shedding their needles. This reduces their photosynthesis levels, their growth stagnates and they become more susceptible to disease.

Conifers should have dense needles and species-typical foliage color. The trunk should have a dense pattern of branches from the base upwards. In most species that grow like trees, a continuous trunk without forking should be sought. Bent shoots and damaged terminal buds are definite cause for complaint.

Checking and accepting woody plants

When a plant order is delivered to the building site, the qualities stipulated in the tender bid must be checked. Any mistakes must be queried with the tree nursery immediately. As soon as the contractors have accepted delivery of plants without objections, they guarantee to the client that the plant quality is unexceptionable. To avoid later deficiencies a specialist representative of the planning office should also be present at the time of delivery to check the correctness and quality of the plants supplied immediately. Hence **Table 1.2.2** shows the most important checking criteria.

HERBACEOUS PLANTS
(INCLUDING GRASSES AND FERNS)

Herbaceous plants are perennials whose parts growing above the earth usually die off as winter approaches. New growth comes from buds close to or below the surface of the soil. Growth can be tufty to runner-spread. > **Fig. 1.2.7**

Habitats and variety of shapes

Locations for herbaceous plants range from sunny, dry areas to damp, shady positions. The length of time each species lives ranges from a few years to several centuries, according to origin and location; and the height to which they grow from a few centimeters to two meters and more. Large numbers of hybrids and garden versions are bred, and these are easier to cultivate than their wild ancestors. An enormous range of herbaceous plant varieties has been created over the last hundred years.

Groups by use

The scope offered by the various herbaceous plant grades is enormous, and is dealt with in detail in a large number of textbooks. The possible uses for some groups can be summed up a little more simply, however.

Early flowering herbaceous plants start to shoot in spring and flower until early summer. They grow to heights of between 10 and 60 cm. After they have flowered, most species have somewhat unattractive foliage, which even dies back in some cases. The vast majority of this group comes from Europe.

Late-flowering species do not start to shoot until about May. Blossom begins in summer or fall, and can continue until the first frosts. There are many species that grow to considerable heights in this group, easily reaching 1.2 to 2 m. These species often come from North America.

Plants with decorative foliage are used primarily for shady locations where flowering plants that need a lot of sun will not flourish. They make their effect mainly through the texture of their leaves and are often offered as varieties with variegated leaves. As they often originate from forests or woodland peripheries, most of them are demanding in terms of humidity, soil quality and water supply. The latter applies to varieties with very large leaves in particular.

Most of the species share the characteristics of wild shrubs, creating their aesthetic effect through the shape in which they grow, and their foliage. The flowers are usually single, and make an overall effect, rather than as individual blooms.

The group of bedding and decorative plants can be distinguished from the wild species. Most species are tall, growing to heights of 1.2 to 2 m. Many varieties have large, individual flowers in glowing colors. They need to be planted in a sunny location on moist, nutrient-rich soil. They need a lot of care and attention, and cannot usually be attorded for public green spaces.

Grasses are a group in their own right from a botanical point of view. They are monocotyledonous herbaceous plants. Most varieties are deciduous, a limited number are evergreen. The range of situations they thrive in is very wide. Species for shady locations usually go not grow so high, and are less conspicuous. Species for sunny, damp locations can grow up to 2 m and are decorative because of their imposing height. They originate from Europe, America and Asia.

Ferns are not seed plants, but reproduce through spores, thus forming a group in their own right. Their fronds are usually singly or multiply leaved, and rarely entire. Most of them come from forest locations, and need moist, humus-rich soil and high humidity. They grow to heights from about 20 cm to 1.2 m. Deciduous species are somewhat less demanding than the evergreen varieties.

Plant qualities

Herbaceous plants should be genuine varieties, healthy and vigorous, so that they take root reliably. As the parts of the plant above ground level die off in winter in the case of deciduous herbaceous plants, grasses and ferns, the size of the root ball and thus of its nutrient reserves are a more suitable criterion for defining the state of development and the strength of growth. Herbaceous plants are usually supplied in containers. > **Tab. 1.2.4** 9 cm pots (500 cm³) are the most usual for herbaceous plants of the usual height. Tall grasses or large herbaceous plants with vigorous roots should have a container of at least 11 cm (1000 cm³). Herbaceous plants that are acceptable for purchase must be well developed, healthy and hardened off, and have dense root balls without alien growth. Complaints should be made about immature young plants with loose root balls, plants that are obviously sickly or tired, old goods. Plants for use on roofs have special characteristics. > **Chapter 3.14 Green roofs**

Special sizes: Herbaceous plants, particularly those propagated as seedlings, can also be bought as young plants. As this is an unusual size in the trade, they should be ordered from specialist growers, allowing a vegetation

Fig. 1.2.9: Summer bedding plants

Fig. 1.2.10: Spring bedding plants

Fig. 1.2.11: Tub plants

Tab. 1.2.3: Lifespan of the commonest hardy geophytes (for mass planting)

Names (botanical, English)	Natural location	Persistence/lifespan
Allium spp., wild leek	full sun, dry in summer	usually ages well, perennial
Crocus spp. crocus	full sun (semishaded), dry in summer	usually ages well
Eranthis hyemalis, winter aconite	forest edge, humus-rich soil	perennial, usually ages well
Galanthus nivalis, snowdrop	forest edge/forest, humus-rich soil	ages well, plants bulbs as soon as possible without long storage
Narcissus spp., botanical forms	usually moist, partly from fields, sun to semishade; small number of species of Alpine origin	many species and varieties age well, relatively persistent
Narcissus hybrids, large flowers	good soil, sun to semishade	usually ages well, relatively persistent
Scilla siberica, spring beauty	edge of wooded areas, humus-rich soil	ages very well, largely trample-resistant, very persistent
Tulipa spp., botanical wild tulip forms	full sun, dry in summer	ages well in favorable locations, relatively persistent
Tulipa hybrids, tulips as cultivated varieties	full sun, dry in summer	approx. 2–3 years according to species and variety, on rare occasions up to 8 years

period. The fact that they are not very decorative immediately after planting is more than made up for by very rapid development in the following year. They are better value for money, markedly more adaptable and build up a strong root system more rapidly than would be the case if they were cultivated in pots for longer. Older herbaceous plants within particularly large pot balls can be used to achieve an immediate decorative effect.

BULBS AND TUBERS (GEOPHYTES)

Geophytes are perennial herbaceous plants whose growth above ground level recedes after flowering. Their bulbous or tuberous organs enable them to survive unfavorable seasonal phenomena such as summer droughts or underground frost. Good combinations of bulbs and tubers can produce flowers almost all the year round. There are hardy and frost-sensitive varieties.

Hardy geophytes

In the wild state, geophytes come from three typical locations: forests with humus-rich soil and good moisture supply; sunny fresh to damp meadows or pasture; and sunny steppes that are dry in summer. If they are used correctly for their needs they can permanently enliven large areas planted in a natural style and parkland meadows, and enrich prestigious bedding plants in groups or as patterns.

BEDDING AND TUB PLANTS

Decorative planting of this kind is usually used for prestigious areas or at horticultural shows. Normally summer flowering plants are used, and then replaced with the first frosts. For summer blossom, annual flowering and decorative foliage plants, frost-sensitive geophytes such as dahlias, semishrubs such as pelargonium hybrids, and decorative vegetable varieties. These can be combined with tub plants. > Fig. 1.2.9

Frost-resistant biennials such as *Cheiranthus* (also called *Erysimum*) (wallflower) or *Myositis sylvatica* (forget-me-not) are used for spring blossom, usually combined with hardy geophytes such as garden tulips or narcissi. > Fig. 1.2.10

Apart from a few species, these decorative plants need sunny locations with good soil and water supply. Bedding plants involve a great deal of material and maintenance, but the decorative effect when they are in full bloom is incomparable.

Tub plants are frost-sensitive semishrubs or decorative woody plants such as *Citrus* plants, and these are kept in the greenhouse for protection in the cold season. They are used in historical gardens or prestigious areas. Tub plants need intensive, expert care both in the summer season and in their winter quarters. There are no general definitions of quality.

Plant group	Normal supply	Growing patterns	Decorative effect immediately after planting	Time to plant	Cost of planting material	Maintenance levels to full effect	Risks, remarks
Deciduous foliage plants							
bare-rooted	particularly for young and hedging plants	adapts well, strong growth	little	outside growing season, fall (spring)	little	little to average, according to planting scheme	can dry out when stored in cold store, dry out rapidly if tamped down inappropriately
root ball plants	standard, sturdier goods, particularly street trees	relatively good, slows down with age and size	average to high	fall and spring	average to high	average, high in warm spring	stagnation if in wrong soil type or if planted too late in spring
container plants	possible	generally slow to develop	average to very high	all year round if frost-free	high to very high	high to very high	difficult rooting because of peat ball, matted, uncut roots grow badly into deeper soil
Evergreen woody plants							
bare-rooted	unusual	-	-	-	-	-	
root ball plants	standard	relatively good development	average to high	early fall (spring)	average to high	average to high	dry out through frost if planted in late fall, dry out if planted too late in spring
container plants	possible	slow growth, especially when in flower	average to very high	all year round if frost-free	high to very high	average to very high	goods age quickly in summer quarters, inclined to dry out after planting
Climbers and creepers							
bare-rooted	unusual	-	-	-	-	-	-
root ball plants	unusual	-	-	-	-	-	-
container plants	standard, younger plants	relatively good development	little to average	fall (spring)	little to average	average	if transport safety packaging left in place the growing shoots can be caught up
Roses							
bare-rooted	usual	quick to establish itself, robust growth	little	fall (spring)	little	little to average	goods dry out in storage (cold store) after spring planting
root ball plants	unusual	-	-	-	-	-	-
container plants	possible	slow to start growing	average to very high	may be planted all year round, even when in flower	high to very high	average to high	some problems caused by peat balls and matted roots
Conifers							
bare-rooted	unusual	-	-	-	-	-	-
root ball plants	standard	establishes itself relatively well	average to high	early fall, spring	average to high	average to high	dry out through frost if planted in late fall, dry out if planted too late in spring
container plants	possible	slow to take root	average to high	all year round if frost-free	high to very high	high to very high	drying out when planted in summer
Herbaceous plants (including grasses and ferns)							
bare-rooted	(only for amateur gardeners)						
pot plants	standard	establishes itself relatively well	little to average	fall, spring to early summer	little to average	little to average	more watering effort needed if planted after early summer
wedge root ball plants, young plants	by order	very good	little	fall, spring	little	average	
container plants	by order	slow to take root	average to high	spring, summer, fall	high	average to high	drying out when planted in summer

Plant group	Normal supply	Growing patterns	Decorative effect immediately after planting	Time to plant	Cost of planting material	Maintenance levels to full effect	Risks, remarks
Hardy geophytes							
clean tubers and resting bulbs	standard	takes root well (easy to plant)	none	early fall	little	little	too little root formation for late fall planting, hardly any flowers for tulips in second established year
pot and container plants	unusual, possibly for planting on in spring	slow growth, mainly blossom	average to high	spring	high	average	forced hothouse goods usually not weatherproof
Frost-sensitive geophytes							
clean tubers	traditionally possible	develops well, strong plants	none	after night frosts, about mid-May	average	average to high	poor tubers so not shoot and cause gaps slugs eat shoots
rooted cuttings in pot	usual	develops well, plants tend to be small	average	after night frosts, about mid-May	little to average	average to high	wrong varieties sometimes recognized
forced tubers in pot or container	usual within limitations, e.g. for replacement purposes	tends to develop slowly in some cases	average to high	after night frosts, about mid-May to summer	high to very high	average	sun scorching on hothouse goods
Ornamental annuals							
potted, in bud	usual	takes root and grows on well	little to average	after night frosts, about mid-May	little	little to average	can become overgrown with weeds until plants are larger
potted, in flower	usual	little further development	average to high	after night frosts, about mid-May	little to average	little to average	more prone to dry out because of scant root system
Ornamental biennials							
young plant, potted	usual	takes root and grows on well	little	fall	little	average	necessary in combination with hardy geophytes
mature plant, in bud	within limits	little further development	average	spring	average	little to average	unhardened goods threatened by frost and rain
Tub plants							
bare-rooted	unusual	-	-	-	-	-	-
root ball plants	unusual	-	-	-	-	-	-
container plants	usual	relatively good development	average to high	after night frosts, about mid-May	average to high	little to average	unhardened goods suffer from sun scorching, wintering is customary

Tab. 1.2.4: Normal trade sizes—advantages and disadvantages

1.3 LAWNS AND OTHER SEEDED AREAS

LAWNS
- Origins of lawn grasses
- The most important grass species and their properties
- Suitable locations for successful lawn establishment
- Choosing the grass
- Lawn seed mixtures
- Turf rolls
- Organic seed

CRUSHED STONE LAWN/CHECKER BRICK LAWN

MEADOWS
- Suitable locations and meadow seed mixtures
- Transforming existing meadows or lawns

INTERMEDIATE PLANTING

Alexander von Birgelen

1.3 LAWNS AND OTHER SEEDED AREAS

LAWNS

A lawn is a dynamic group made up of several thousand individual plants. The range of uses extends from carpet-like show lawns, via intensively used areas for sport and games, areas for sunbathing, to extensively used meadow-like areas. As well as being a flexible design tool, lawns are becoming increasingly important because of their ecological features. Grass, like other areas of vegetation, contributes to improving the urban climate, as it captures carbon dioxide and dust, produces oxygen, which raised the humidity of the air, and reduces temperature fluctuation. On a suitable base, lawns help rainwater to seep away, and form an important source of nutrition and a habitat for various birds, small animals and creatures that live in the soil.

A group of plants is defined as a lawn if it is made up preponderantly of thick-growing grasses, and their roots and runners have grown into and become attached to the layer of vegetation or the soil below. A visually appealing lawn, which is cut regularly to keep it even and attractive to walk on usually has no agricultural purpose and can also contain other plants according to its intended use. > Fig. 1.3.2

Origins of lawn grasses

All lawn grasses are part of the large grass family. Known species suitable for lawns come from the so-called sub-grasses of the pasture and meadow groups. These come to predominate over taller grasses if land is increasingly grazed or mown, as they react to cutting by tillering. That is to say, they grow thickly close to the ground as long as they have sufficient light, water and nutrients.

The most important grass species and their properties

Grasses with special properties are needed to produce an evenly short, dense lawn that is more or less hard-wearing and visually appealing. Suitable types stay green for a long time, tolerate cutting and have densely packed, upright blades that are as short and narrow as possible. The chosen grasses should be durable, frost-hardy, drought tolerant and resistant to disease. They should grow well while young, and also rejuvenate well, so that they can stand up to constant wear.

Summing up these requirements when looking for suitable lawn grasses, the choice is reduced from several thousand species of grass to very few chosen types. Most of these belong to the four groups of bent grass (*Agrostis*), fescue (*Festuca*), meadow grass (*Poa*) and rye grass (*Lolium*). > Tab. 1.3.2

Suitable locations for successful lawn establishment

Lawn or turf is made up of various grasses whose growth, like all plants, depends on certain factors relating to location. Temperature and light as growth factors cannot usually be altered, so for a healthy lawn it is essential to choose a suitable sunny to semishady location and a mixture of lawn grasses that is appropriate to the prevailing temperatures. The greater the

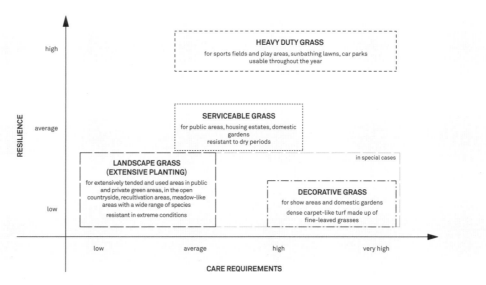

Fig. 1.3.1: Resilience and care requirements for various lawn types as per DIN 18917

Fig. 1.3.2: Various lawn types
> Fig. 1.3.1 in appropriate
contexts:
a) hard-wearing turf for sport,
   Allianz Arena in Munich
b) ornamental lawn as a decorative element for the Het
   Loo baroque park (Holland)
c) moderately hard-wearing
   utility lawn in a public park in
   Zurich
d) extensive maintenance
   landscape lawn after demolition work in a rapidly shrinking residential area in Wolfen
   Nord (Saxony-Anhalt,
   Germany)

a	b
c	d

amount of shade, or the shade-tolerance of the grass, the more its growth, density, durability and thus also its viability as a lawn will decrease. Other important factors such as the availability of water, soil aeration and nutrient supply can be positively influenced by preparatory soil improvement and later by appropriate maintenance measures.

Choosing the grass

The choice of grass should be addressed in terms of the particular growth factors, potential uses and possible maintenance program. If one or more of these factors change it usually affects the combination of species directly. The range is constantly on the move, individual species can disappear completely or new ones introduce themselves from elsewhere. The consequence of this is usually that the lawn can no longer meet the demands placed on it. For this reason, before trying to establish a lawn, appropriate thought should be given to what the lawn is for and how much maintenance can be provided. > Fig. 1.3.1 The combination of species or varieties for the grass mixture, the soil structure, work on preparing the ground and the scale of maintenance available all depend on these requirements. The key point is: the greater the demands to be made on the lawn, the more work will have to be put into it in the long term.

Lawn seed mixtures

Lawns based on monocultures are very seldom found and not to be recommended because of their susceptibility and the demands they make in terms of location and maintenance. In order to create a firm sward, grasses with different growth forms are combined. Slow-growing clump grasses, that can rarely form a complete sward on their own, create a solid framework for a lawn. The faster-growing grasses with their surface (creeping) or underground runners (stolons) spread into the gaps between the clumps and fill them in. > Fig. 1.3.3

As a rule, a lawn is made up of two to five types of grass. Several varieties of the same species are included, to improve adaptation to the location. Here the choice of variety is very important, as a variety that is suitable for a particular purpose can influence the sward quality of the lawn considerably, even if it is present only as a very small proportion of the overall weight. A greater number of species makes sense only "for safety" if a large area of lawn is to be planted with very great variations in the nature of the location in small areas.

Expert knowledge is needed to create the correct mixture, so consumers have to rely on the mixtures that are available commercially. High-quality seed should always be chosen, as only this can guarantee continuing

	Bent grasses (Agrostis species)		Meadow grasses (Poa species)		Fescue (Festuca species)					rye grasses (Lolium species)
	Agrostis capillaris common bent	*Agrostis stolonifera* creeping bent	*Poa pratensis* Smooth meadowgrass	*Poa supina* supine bluegrass	*Festuca arundinacea* tall fescue	*Festuca brevipila* (*F. ovina ssp duriuscula*) hard fescue	*Festuca nigrescens* (*F. rubra commutata*) chewings fescue	*Festuca rubra rubra* red fescue	*Festuca trichophylla* (*F. rubra trichophylla*) sheep fescue	*Lolium perenne* prennial rye grass
Growth form	runners	runners	runners	runners	clumps	clumps	clumps	runners	short runners	clumps
Growth vigor	ag	ag	sg, sd	sg, sd	ag	ag, sd	ag	ag	ag	sg, sd
Texture [1]	medium	medium	medium-coarse	fine	coarse	fine	fine	fine	fine	medium
Color	light green	blue cast	dark to gray-green	light green	green	gray to blue-gray	deep gray-green	deep gray-green	dark green	dark green
Nutrient requirements	low to medium	medium	high	high	medium	low	low	low	low	medium to high
Drought resistance	low to medium	low to medium	medium	low	high	high	high	high	high	medium
Resilience	low to medium	low to medium	high	high, for sites in semishade	medium	low	low	low	low	high
Use in various lawns with regular seed mixtures [2]	2, 4, 6, 7, 8	4; in 7 for moist sites	2, 3, 4, 5, 6, 7	2, 4, 7 for sites in semishade	2	2, 6, 7, 8	1, 2, 4, 5, 6, 7, 8	1, 2, 4, 7, 8	1, 2, 4, 5, 6, 7	1, 2, 3, 4, 5, 7

[1] texture derives from blade width (narrow blade = fine structure), [2] see table 1.3.2
sg = slow germination, ag = average germination, sd = slow development

Tab. 1.3.1: Important Central European lawn grasses and their properties

Sources: Taschenbuch der Gräser, Exkursionsflora von Deutschland, vol. 4, www.rasengesellschaft.de

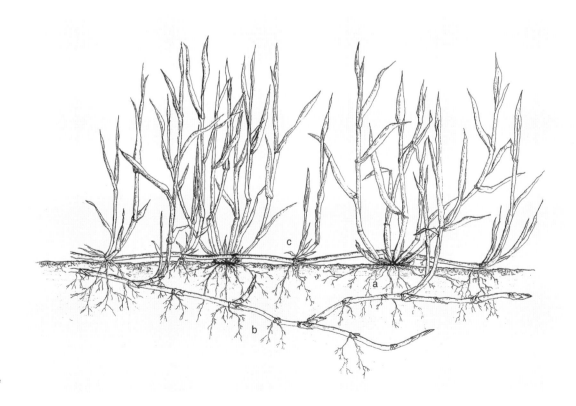

Fig. 1.3.3: (Drawing by Ivette Grafe) A lawn sward generally consists of grasses that grow in clumps (a) which form the basic framework, and grasses that spread very rapidly vegetatively with their runners above (c) or below (b) ground level, which are able to close gaps very quickly.

successful lawn growth, though it must be used appropriately, and care taken with creating and maintaining the lawn. The German research organization Landschaftsentwicklung Landschaftsbau e.V. (FLL) publishes suitable regular seed mixtures (RSM) annually for different areas of use and location conditions. The combination of species and mixture proportions for the grasses for particular purposes are defined here. RSM is seen as the quality standard in Germany, but also sets a good standard for seed quality in neighboring countries such as Switzerland and Austria. These mixtures can be bought ready-mixed or prepared by seed merchants to meet particular requirements. > Tab. 1.3.2 Lawn-seed mixtures that are often sold at lower prices but without certification usually produce a green effect quickly, but it does not last for very long. In cheap mixtures of this kind, neither the individual varieties nor their proportion in terms of weight is fixed. They contain a high proportion of species that can be grown cheaply, and also some varieties from crop growing. The price difference between the individual seed mixtures is thus based on the grass species or varieties included. High-quality lawn seed is subject to years of testing for suitability. As a rule they produce fewer seedpods and thus less seed, which is desirable if a lawn is to look even. The cost difference will be made up for at the latest by the better sward quality and less growth that needs cutting, as the cultivated lawn varieties are lower and denser in their growth.

Turf rolls

Prefabricated items from stocks of specially cultivated turf are available ready for planting as turf pieces or turf rolls. Using turf rather than sowing seed is more expensive in terms of purchase, transport and installation. Unlike sowing seed, it offers the advantage that a sward can be established in a much shorter time. Hence an area of green grass is available more quickly, and it can be used sooner for sports or games, for example. Additionally, there is less risk of erosion, it is harder for alien species to invade and the site can usually be completed earlier. As turf can be delivered and installed practically all the year round (except in case of rain, frost and snow), using turf means that a wider range of times is available for acquiring a new lawn. Turf rolls are now generally available in most commercial seed mixes. If sufficient notice is given, the seed mixture and the soil substrate can be adapted to the special conditions on site, in order to make sure that the turf will establish itself better once installed. > Fig. 1.3.4

Organic seed

Organic seed comes from a precisely defined source, and is not crossed or mixed with plants from other sources. The seed should come from suitable and natural sites as near as possible to the place where it is to be marketed. This means that it is better adapted to local conditions than normal seed, and thus has a lower failure rate. This quality is particularly marked in extreme locations, and is often used for planting as part of a biological engineering

scheme, for example. Site suitability derives from the ecotypes summed up under species, which in fact differ in terms of place and inherited characteristics; they are also called subspecies, varieties and forms.

The reason for all the fuss and argument about this method is the problem, familiar for some time now, of the increasing loss of genetic and thus biological diversity. Ecotypes are particularly badly affected by this. The principal cause for concern is the wide-ranging use of standardized landscape grass seed mixes using seed alien to the area in open countryside, often in the course of compensation and replacement work.

On the basis of this research, the European Council issued a decision on maintaining biodiversity in 1993 (93/626/EC), which serves as a model for national legislation in the European countries. Germany incorporated it into the Federal Nature Conservation Act in 1998. There are still some difficulties in implementing these requirements, but it is hoped that they can be cleared up soon. For example, the Nature Conservation Act's requirements in terms of producing and selling seed contradict the EU directives on seed traffic and the German act governing seed that evolved from this.

Various processes are available in landscape construction for producing seed for ecotypes defined by a particular natural area and suitable for location, site and function: the hay mulch or Heudrusch methods, seed from mown hay, planting seed from collected or increased ecotype seed stock, and grassland soil transfer.

CRUSHED STONE LAWN/CHECKER BRICK LAWN

Crushed stone and checker brick lawns are suitable for areas where there is occasional traffic. The lawn seed mixture should contain grasses or leafed plants that root strongly and have a high level of resistance to dry conditions.

The composition of the seed mixture depends on the site conditions and the degree of use anticipated, which can range from low to high. Suitable standard seed mixtures here are the RSM for car park areas or the utility lawn mixture for warm, dry sites. > Tab. 1.3.2

But the seed mixtures cannot cope with unduly high traffic levels, either as crushed stone or checker brick lawns. The gaps that often appear in grassy areas of this type in practice show that sufficient attention is not paid to this at the planning stage.

Fig. 1.3.4: Turf is usually supplied in rolled strips and spread out like a carpet on site, then worked on.

Lawn seed mixtures	Climate/location	Wear/use	Maintenance	Designation iaw. RSM
Ornamental lawns				
ornamental lawns	no restrictions	low / prestige green space, domestic gardens	high	1.1
Utility lawns				
dry sites (variants 1 and 2)	dry areas / dry sites	v 1 low to medium, v 2 medium to high / public grass that can be used, housing estates, domestic gardens	low to high, according to intensity of use	2.2
grassed play area	up to 1000 m above sea level / no restriction	medium to high / grass intended for heavy use (e.g. grass for games or sunbathing, domestic gardens)	medium	2.3
herb lawns	no restrictions / for all sites except very moist, nutrient rich soils	public grass that can be used, housing estates, domestic gardens	low to to very low	2.4
Sports fields				
new	no restrictions	high, all year round / sports fields	medium to high	3.1
regeneration	no restrictions	high/ regeneration of games and sports fields	medium to high	3.2
Golf courses				
green (variants 1–3)	no restrictions	v 1 and v 2 for high to top quality; v 3 for high quality, especially on high sites	very high	4.1
tee	no restrictions	hard-wearing and good ability to regenerate, especially when resown	high to very high	4.3
fairway (variants 1–3)	no restrictions	v 1 for all sites, especially if soil is under threat of erosion, silting or weed growth; v 2 and v 3 for soil under threat of erosion, silting or weed growth in dry and moist conditions	medium to high	4.4
Grass for car parks				
grass for car parks (variants 1–3)	no restrictions / v 1 no restrictions, v 2 warm and dry sites, v 3 areas subject to medium to heavy wear	low to high / crushed stone lawn, checker bricks	low to medium	5.1
Roof planting				
extensive roof planting	no restrictions	high degree of drought tolerance and good ability to regenerate / roof areas with vegetation support layers approx. 10–15 cm thick	low	6.1
Landscape lawn				
site with or without leaf growth	no restrictions / for all situations except extremely dry, alkaline, wet or shady	open landscape, recultivation areas, extensively used and/or maintained areas of public or private grass	low to to very low	7.1
dry sites with or without leaf growth	inland area / extremely dry sites on alkaline soil	open landscape, recultivation areas, extensively used and/or maintained areas of public or private grass	low to very low	7.2
wet sites	no restrictions / sites threatened by accumulated moisture	open landscape, recultivation areas, extensively used and/or maintained areas of public or private grass	low to very low	7.3
semi-shade	no restrictions / light semi-shade	open landscape, recultivation areas, extensively used and/or maintained areas of public or private grass	low to very low	7.4
Habitat development areas				
habitats (variants 1–4)	no restrictions (except for extreme situations) / for sties low to moderately well provided with nutrients, moderately dry to occasionally wet sites	for recultivation, compensation and habitat development areas, by roads or railways and busy and/or well-tended areas of public or private grass	low to very low	8.1

Tab. 1.3.2: Commercially available lawn seed mixtures for the most important areas of use and the resultant maintenance needs, in accordance with the German regular seed mixtures (RSM). Individual seed mixes vary according to the range of species and varieties, local legislation and site conditions (e.g. special mixtures for sites above 1000 m).

Source: FLL: *RSM 2006. Regel-Saatgut-Mischungen Rasen*

> Chapter 3.2 Paths and squares The required maintenance also depends on the intensity of use, and lie in the low to medium range in comparison with other lawn types.

MEADOWS

A meadow is a complex plant community made up of grasses and a more or less high proportion of colorfully flowering, light-loving plant types. Unlike the lawn, which is kept short on a permanent basis, the species-rich meadow is mown only once or twice per year, and the less species-rich meadow is multiply mowed up to six times per year. As well as local factors such as soil and climate, recurrent mowing helps to determine the way the species are composed. It establishes the rhythm of growth, flowering, fruit formation and seed ripeness. Meadows normally need very little maintenance, but they are not very hard-wearing either.

Suitable locations and meadow seed mixtures

Today's meadows, which are mainly artificial, grow in potential woodland where they have to be cleared of woody plant growth on a regular basis. Several hundred meadow types are now known to plant sociology. These can be divided into several basic types and their associated sub-types according to nutrient supply, moisture and soil reaction. > Figs. 1.3.5–1.3.6

The spectrum ranges from natural dry and semi-dry grassy areas on poor soil, often with gaps but very rich in

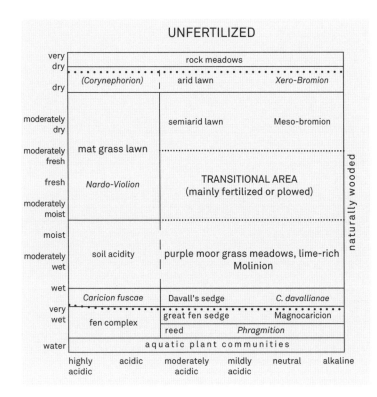

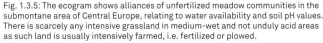

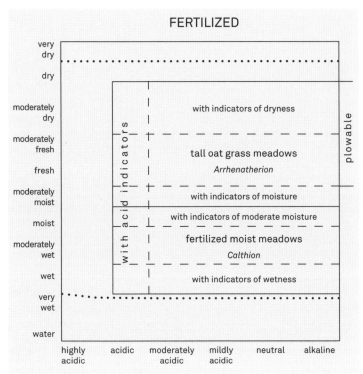

Fig. 1.3.5: The ecogram shows alliances of unfertilized meadow communities in the submontane area of Central Europe, relating to water availability and soil pH values. There is scarcely any intensive grassland in medium-wet and not unduly acid areas as such land is usually intensively farmed, i.e. fertilized or plowed.

Fig. 1.3.6: The ecogram shows different meadow types in nutrient-rich locations that are replacing the meadow types shown in Fig. 1.3.4 as a result of fertilization or nutrients introduced by flooding. There are no fertilized meadows in very dry locations, as additional nutrients make too little difference here. Such meadow communities are also absent in very acid locations, as fertilizing also means introducing bases.

species, via the increasingly rare tall oat-grass meadow, to the intensively used nutrient-rich commercial or manured grassland, which is low on blossom but rich in grass. > Figs. 1.3.7–1.3.9

To establish a new meadow, seed mixes can be made up to order, or meadow mixes from specialist meadow seed merchants based on patterns of plant sociology can be used. If appropriate source areas are available, natural planting methods can be used and these can then be upgraded by adding other species. > Chapter 1.3 Lawns and other seeded areas, Lawns, Organic seed

Many commercial meadow mixtures contain large numbers of short-lived species that are unsuitable for establishing a long-lasting meadow. The great number of field plant species that bloom strikingly in the first year is reduced dramatically even in the second year, as these species cannot establish themselves permanently on meadow sites.

Transforming existing meadows or lawns

One possibility for creating meadows in abundant bloom is to transform existing lawns that need multiple mowing, or fertilized pasture. Depending on the starting conditions, this can take some years. Cutting back on mowing, reducing nutrients in the soil by removing mown material, and deliberately introducing species by planting or sowing are required here.

INTERMEDIATE PLANTING

Intermediate planting is brought into play mainly to improve or protect the soil, or for aesthetic reasons.

If suitable plants are chosen, an intensively rooted stock can be introduced quickly as effective protection against erosion and as ground cover to suppress weed growth. If additional measures are carried out to improve the soil, for example to improve structure and enrich humus, then the recommended plants have a large mass of organic substance that is slow to degrade and bulky where necessary. Such material is simply plowed into the areas concerned at an appropriate time. Leguminous plants are suitable for additional nitrogen enrichment in the soil, and so are various species of clover and lupins that are able to integrate nitrogen from the air with the aid of nodule bacteria. The root systems of plants such as narrowleaf lupin (Lupinus angustifolius) are also able to loosen the soil up to a depth of 2 m.

Information about germination periods, sowing times, speed of development, soil requirements and life span should also be taken into account if the right choice of plants is to be made. > Tab. 1.3.3

The creative aspect comes to the fore when sowing decorative annuals as intermediate planting. Here mainly short-lived flowering varieties tend to be used. The aim is to create attractive images that can be produced rapidly at a reasonable price, for empty areas that are temporarily available. The disadvantage here is the long, usually unattractive development phase from sowing to full development of the planted area. Good soil preparation is also needed, and a selection of plants suitable for the location. > Fig. 1.3.10

Plant species	Weed suppression/ ground cover	Root depth	Soil	Remarks
Helianthus annus, annual sunflower	poor	deep (150–200 cm)	for all soils, acidic to high lime requirement	annual, grows rapidly
Lathyrus sativus, grass pea	good	average (80–150 cm)	for all soils, acidic to limy	annual, durable, enriched by atmospheric nitrogen by nodule bacteria, clear fertilization effect from 6 weeks of cultivation
Lupinus albus, white lupin	very good	deep (150–200 cm)	light to average soils, acidic to low lime content	annual, very grows rapidly, enriched by atmospheric nitrogen by nodule bacteria, clear fertilization effect from 6 weeks of cultivation
Lupinus angustifolius, narrow-leaf lupin	very good	deep (150–200 cm)	very light to average soils, acidic to low lime content	annual, grows rapidly, enriched by atmospheric nitrogen by nodule bacteria, clear fertilization effect from 6 weeks of cultivation
Lupinus luteus, yellow lupin	very good	deep (150–200 cm)	very light to average soils, acidic to low lime content	annual, slow growing, enriched by atmospheric nitrogen by nodule bacteria, clear fertilization effect from 6 weeks of cultivation
Medicago, Melilotus, Trifolium, various clover species	poor–average, varies by species	average to deep, varies according to species (from 80 cm to 200 cm)	light to heavy soils, acidic to limy, according to clover variety	slow development, annual and perennial clover species, enriched by atmospheric nitrogen by nodule bacteria, clear fertilization effect from 6 weeks of cultivation
Phacelia tanacetfolia, phacelia tansy	very good	shallow, according to soil type accumulates very quickly	light to medium-heavy soils, strongly acidic to high lime content	annual, accumulates very quickly, neutral to crop rotation, bee pasture
Pisum sativum, garden pea	good	average (80–150 cm)	average to heavy soils, acidic to high lime content	annual, slow development, enriched by atmospheric nitrogen by nodule bacteria, clear fertilization effect from 6 weeks of cultivation
Raphanus sativus, cultivated radish	good	average (80–150 cm)	for all soils, acidic to moderately limy	annual, grows rapidly
Sinapis alba, white mustard	very good	average (80–150 cm)	light to heavy soils, acidi to high lime content	annual, rapid-growing green manure, fine root mass improves the soil structure as live planting

Source: Handbuch Gartenpraxis, RSM 2006

Tab. 1.3.3: Important plant species for soil improvement measures and soil protection for prior or intermediate planting.

Fig. 1.3.7: Silicate neglected grassland on a nutrient-poor sandy substrate in Stein/Pfreimd (Bavaria). The principal flowers are white-flowering common yarrow (*Achillea millefolium*), yellow-flowering lady's bedstraw (*Galium verum*) and the red flower of maiden pink (*Dianthus deltoides*). The dominant grass is common bentgrass (*Agrostis capillaris*).

Fig. 1.3.8: Valley meadow with false oat-grass in Heppenheim (Hessen). The main floral aspects are the yellow-flowering wild parsnip (*Pastinaca sativa*), the crimson blooms of brown knapweed (*Centaurea jacea*), the white umbels of the greater burnet saxifrage (*Pimpinella major*) and the white-flowering annual known as eastern daily fleabane (*Erigeron annuus*).

Fig. 1.3.9: A heavily fertilized meadow in Thuringia, with a relatively small number of species. In late May the grasses dominate this meadow community, e.g. soft brome (*Bromus hordeaceus*).

Fig. 1.3.10: Mainly short-lived plant species sown in a public green area in Ladenburg. The principal impression is given by red corn poppies (*Papaver rhoeas*), the white umbels of Queen Anne's lace (*Ammi majus*) and the yellow-brown flowers of golden tickseed (*Coreopsis tinctoria*).

1.4 WOOD

COMPOSITION, PROPERTIES AND TIMBER PRESERVATION
- Anatomical structure and chemical composition
- Physical properties
- Mechanical and technological properties
- Natural resistance and weathering
- Timber preservation measures

PRODUCTS
- Solid timber products
- Engineered wood materials
- Solid wood product grades
- Cutting, drying and surface treatment
- Grading

SURFACE QUALITIES
- Surface treatment and coloring
- Wood treatment

JOINTS

Gero Heck

1.4 WOOD

Fig 1.4.1: Stack of mechanically debarked round timber

There are 25,000 to 30,000 existing tree species, of which about 600 are regularly traded internationally, while in Europe about 30 well-known tree species are worked. Forests cover about 30% of the land world-wide. About 50% of them are in the developing and newly industrialized countries in the tropics and subtropics. Despite a wide range of protection activities, the countries of the southern hemisphere lose 12–15 million hectares of forest annually, so the use of tropical timbers in Europe should be weighed up carefully and critically. Regionally available tree species can usually be selected as an alternative, thus avoiding transporting timber halfway round the globe, with all the associated irreversible damage to the ecosystem and habitats.

Sustainable forestry can be supported worldwide by using timber products with forest approval seals certified by one of two international bodies, the FSC (Forestry Stewardship Council) or the PFEC (Programme for the Endorsement of Forest Certification schemes). > Fig. 1.4.2

COMPOSITION, PROPERTIES AND TIMBER PRESERVATION

In general, the term wood or timber applies to the solid or hard substance that grows from the shoot axes (trunk, branches and twigs) of trees and shrubs. Wood from tree trunks is most commonly used for building.

Anatomical structure and chemical composition

Wood substance is created in divisible plant cells. The cambium takes care of secondary thickness growth. As the cambium cells divide and differentiate, the bark, consisting of phloem and crusta, develops outwards and timber cells are formed inside.

In regions with distinct seasons, growth slows down periodically, producing alternating wide-bore, water-carrying early timber cells and thick-walled late timber cells, largely performing a strengthening function.

This cyclical growth behavior produces annual rings, discernible more or less distinctly in the trunk cross-section according to the tree species. Evergreen trees from the tropics do not show annual rings, because they grow uninterruptedly; occasionally the growth areas show signs of the rainy and dry seasons. > Fig. 1.4.3 As the tree gets older, medullation can occur as a result of interrupted water flow and cell death. Heartwood materials then form and are stored in the cell walls. If the heartwood area is clearly separated from the surrounding sapwood by being darker in color, the trees are known as heartwood trees (e.g. oak, pine, larch, Robinia). If there is no discernible difference in color, but the reduced moisture content suggests medullation in the inner area, then the trees are known as even-textured trees (e.g. spruce, fir, beech). In even-textured heartwood trees the heartwood is a different color, followed by an even-textured area (e.g. ash, elm). Sapwood trees are uniform in their coloring. There is no medullation. Water and nutrients are conveyed over the whole cross-section of the trunk (e.g. birch, alder, poplar). > Fig 1.4.4

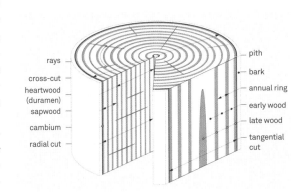

Fig. 1.4.3: Schematic diagram of a trunk section

Fig. 1.4.2: Certification seals from the two international organizations

Fig. 1.4.4: Cross-section of a larch trunk. It is already possible to make a macroscopic distinction between heartwood and sapwood and the individual annual rings.

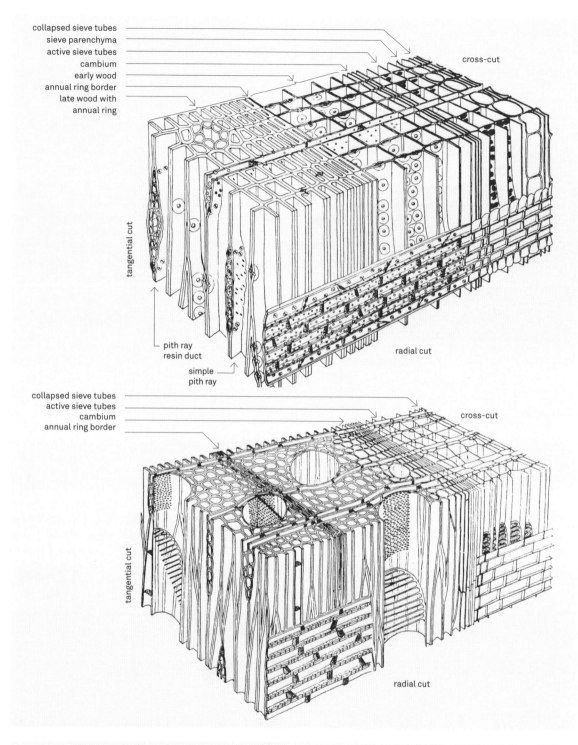

collapsed sieve tubes
sieve parenchyma
active sieve tubes
cambium
early wood
annual ring border
late wood with
annual ring

cross-cut

tangential cut

pith ray
resin duct

simple
pith ray

radial cut

collapsed sieve tubes
active sieve tubes
cambium
annual ring border

cross-cut

tangential cut

radial cut

Fig. 1.4.5: Microstructure, wood and inner bark of a coniferous tree (above) and a deciduous tree (below)

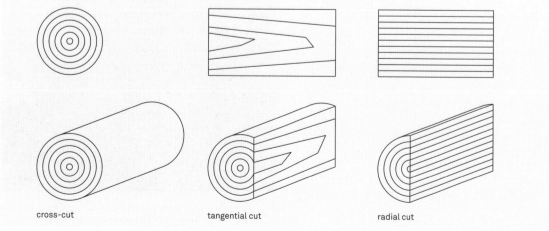

cross-cut

tangential cut

radial cut

Fig. 1.4.6: Directional cuts in wood

The molecular components of wood are 40–50% cellulose, 20–30% hemicellulose and 20–39% lignin. Other wood components (dyes, oils, tanning agents, resins) are generally present in quantities well below 5% of the timber substance. They are usually specific to a particular type of wood, and determine color, odor and resistance in terms of timber preservation.

Cells are the basic building blocks in wood. Numerous cell types are distinguished on the basis of their functions in the living tree, for example strengthening, conducting substances and storing material. > Fig. 1.4.5 Most cells are elongated, and are therefore also known as fibers. The position and direction of the cells, together with the annual rings, create the grain patterns typical of each tree species.

Plant cells' ability to adopt various growth directions is known as anisotropy. Put in simple terms, the woody tissue can be described as a bundle of tubes offset to each other in a longitudinal direction. Anisotropy explains why various cuts in wood look completely different (crosscut, radial and tangential cut) and the equally different behavior of wood longitudinally to and across the fiber. > Fig 1.4.6

Physical properties

As timber cells in all wood varieties have walls of a uniform 1500 kg/m³ density, the major difference in the bulk density of timbers lies in the different proportions of cell wall material and pore space in any given woody tissue. The bulk density is an important characteristic value for tree species and timber materials. Generally speaking, elastic qualities and rigidity, hardness and abrasion resistance, the degrees of swelling and shrinkage and difficulties in working and drying out all increase with rising bulk density. > Tab. 1.4.1

Wood moisture always relates to wood weight and can be determined as a quotient of water mass in the wood and the mass of the oven-dry wood (pure wood mass). Wood is hygroscopic, i.e. it takes water up and releases it according to the ambient moisture conditions. If wood is used for building, so-called equilibrium moisture content becomes the mean value. In constructions exposed to the weather on all sides this lies at 18 ± 6%. The term fiber saturation is used when only the cell walls are saturated with water and the cavities are free of water. > Fig. 1.4.7 The moisture content at fiber saturation lies between 22 and 35%. Below fiber saturation, if the bound moisture is withdrawn from the cell walls, the wood starts to shrink. Conversely, the wood swells from oven-dry (wood moisture 0%) to fiber saturation. Swelling and shrinkage are much more marked in the direction of the fiber than across it. The changes in dimension that inevitably occur in all wooden components subject to moisture fluctuation must be taken into account. As cells and cell walls occur with differing degrees of frequency in the various spatial directions within wood, the dimensions change irregularly as well, and so the wood warps. > Fig. 1.4.8

Mechanical and technological properties

Below a certain limiting stress, the limit of elasticity, wood and timber-derived products behave approximately elastically. Changes of form in wooden components can be defined using the moduli of rigidity and elasticity as characteristic values. The more rigid the material, the higher the values.

The direction of load is a key factor for wood and timber-derived products, as wood is anisotropic. Wood is much more rigid in the grain direction than transversely to it. Wood increases in hardness and abrasion resistance with increasing bulk density and decreasing moisture content. Wood is 1.5 to 2.5% harder on the end-grain face than on the side faces.

Natural resistance and weathering

Natural resistance is wood's inherent ability to resist attack from organisms that can destroy it. A five-class system, ranging from "very resistant" to "not resistant" is used to classify natural resistance to fungi that can damage wood severely. The system ranks the wood's durability at a predominantly or constant wood moisture level of over 20% (EN 350-2). The stated degree of resistance applies only to the heartwood. Sapwood is classed as not resistant regardless of tree species. Weathering occurs in wood if it is exposed to sunlight, precipitation and atmospheric oxygen for a long time without protection. The first stage is that the lignin starts to break down on the surface of the wood by photo-oxidation. In the case of light-colored wood, the chemical changes mainly produce yellowing, sometimes deepening towards a shade of brown over time. But in areas exposed to long periods of rain, the dark lignin breakdown products are continually rinsed out, and the wood surface finally takes on the whitish color of cellulose. This bleaching out looks like a graying process. > Fig. 1.4.9 Black to bluish discoloration is usually caused by mildew growing on the surface or blue stain fungi that grow in the wood cells without attacking the wood substance.

Timber preservation measures

Wood is subject to numerous stresses that can combine in damaging and destroying the wood substance, e.g. fungi, insects, sunlight, temperature fluctuation, wind, rain, ground moisture, humidity, splashing, reactions with metals and chemicals. It is possible to preserve the properties and lifespan of wood and timber derived products by taking preventive structural and chemical timber protection measures. Structural timber protection and the use of tree species with high natural resistance are definitely to be preferred to chemical measures.

EN 335 defines the use classes for particular contexts and geographical locations. The current conditions for use can be consulted in order to establish, on the basis of its natural resistance, whether the selected timber (EN 350) needs additional protection or not (EN 460). > Tab. 1.4.2 At the time of writing, national standards still exist alongside the European standards. The national standards take precedence in matters of practical timber protection, i.e. for construction methods

Scientific name / Trade name	Origin	Average bulk density at 12% moisture (kg/m³)	Elasticity module (N/mm²)	Degree of shrinkage and swelling per 1% wood moisture variation below the fiber saturation point, average value for tangential and radial shrinkage (%)	Dimensional stability	Natural resistance of the heartwood to fungus/ resistance class [1]	Sapwood width
Conifers							
Abies alba Fir (silver fir)	Europe, North America	460	11,000	0.24	good	4	indistinct
Larix decidua Larch (European)	Europe	600	13,800	0.24	good	3–4	narrow
Picea abies Spruce	Europe	460	11,000	0.24	good	4	indistinct
Pinus sylvestris Scots pine	Europe	520	11,000	0.24	average to good	3–4	narrow to average
Pinus elliottii, P. taeda, P. palustris Pitch Pine	North America	660	13,000	0.24	average to good	3	average
Pseudotsuga menziesii Douglas fir	North America, cultivated in Great Britain	520	13,000	0.24	good	3–4	narrow
Thuja plicata Western Red Cedar	North America, cultivated in Great Britain	370	8 000	0.15	very good	2–3	narrow to average
Deciduous timbers							
Acer pseudoplatanus, A. platanoides Sycamore maple, Norway maple	Europe	640	10,500	0.20	average to good	5	indistinct
Afzelia bipindensis Afzelia	West Africa	800	13,500	0.24	very good	1	narrow
Castanea sativa Spanish chestnut	Europe	590	9 000	0.19	good	2	narrow
Eucalyptus diversicolor Eucalyptus	Australia	880				2	narrow
Fagus sylvatica Beech	Europe	710	14,000	0.30	slight	5	indistinct
Lophira alata Azobe	West Africa	1060	17,000	0.36	slight to average	2	narrow
Quercus robur, Quercus petraea Oak	Europe	710	13,000	0.24	average	2	narrow
Robinia pseudoacacia Robinia	North America, Europe	740	13,600	0.29	average	1–2	very narrow
Shorea laevis, S. atrinervosa, S. glauca, S .sp.pl. (section Shorea) Balau	South-east Asia	930	18,700	0.29	slight	2	narrow
Shorea curtisii, S. pauciflora, S.sp.pl. (section Rubroshorea) Dark Red Meranti	South-east Asia	680	14,500	0.24	good	2–4	narrow
Tectona grandis Teak	Asia, cultivated in Asia etc.	680	13,000	0.20	very good	1–3	narrow

[1] Natural resistance fungus/resistance class

1 very resistant
2 resistant
3 moderately resistant
4 slightly resistant
5 not resistant

Tab. 1.4.1: Important tree species and their properties

Fig. 1.4.7: Free and bound water:
1: free water in the cell cavities
2: bound water in the cell walls

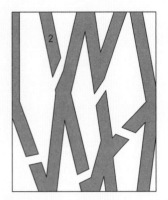

wood moisture > 30%   wood moisture approx 30%   wood moisture < 30%

Fig. 1.4.8: Qualitative changes
of form in wood cross-sections
when absorbing and releasing
water

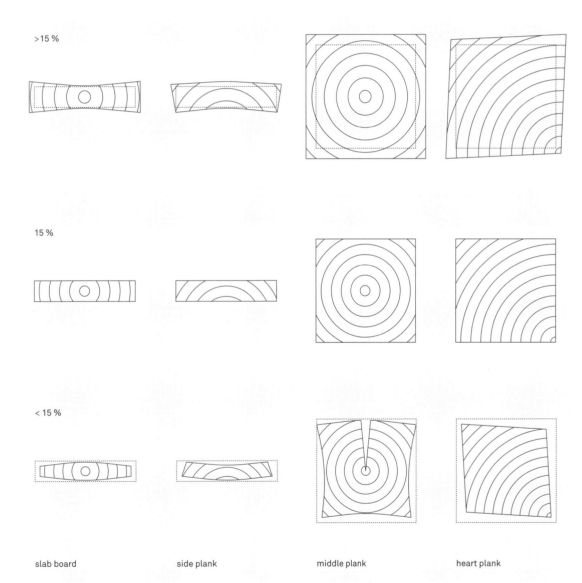

>15 %

15 %

< 15 %

slab board   side plank   middle plank   heart plank

Fig. 1.4.9: Color changes in wood
caused by weathering

Use class	General conditions for use	Exposure to moisture	Wood discoloration and wood rot fungus	Soft rot fungus	Beetles	Termites	Marine organisms	Precautions
1	indoors, covered	dry, 20% max.	-	-	x	(x)	-	use wood types of durability classes 1 to 5; where construction elements are inadequate and cannot be checked, treat with insect-resistant wood preservers
2	indoors or covered	occasionally > 20%	x	-	x	(x)	-	use wood types of durability classes 1 to 5; for durability classes 4 to 5, treat with insect and fungus-resistant wood preservers where necessary
3.1	outdoors, not in contact with the ground, protected	occasionally > 20%	x	-	x	(x)	-	use wood types of durability classes 1 to 2; for durability classes 4 to 5 and possibly durability class 3, treat with insect, fungus and weathering-resistant wood preservers
3.2	outdoors, not in contact with the ground, unprotected	frequently > 20%	x	-	x	(x)	-	same as use class 3.1
4.1	outdoors, in contact with the ground and/ or fresh water	predominantly or constantly > 20%	x	x	x	(x)	-	use wood types of durability class 1; for durability classes 3 to 5 and possibly durability class 2, treat with insect, fungus, weathering and soft rot-resistant wood preservers
4.2	outdoors, in contact with the ground (high stress) and/or fresh water	constantly > 20%	x	x	x	(x)	-	same as use class 4.1
5	in seawater	constantly > 20%	x	x	x	(x)	x	use wood types of durability class 1; for durability classes 2 to 5, treat with insect, fungus, weathering and soft rot-resistant wood preservers

x   occurs throughout Europe
(x)   localized occurrence in Europe

Tab. 1.4.2: Connections
between the use class (EN 335),
the required resistance classes
(EN 350) and the use of timber
preservatives

involving loadbearing timber components or the use of timber preservatives.

Preventive structural timber protection

To prevent harmful changes in the moisture content of wood and timber derived products and thus to guarantee the best possible timber protection, the following preliminary considerations should be taken into account, along with measures relating to structure and building physics:

· select the tree species appropriate to planned outdoor use
· install at the moisture content anticipated as the average during use
· construct protruding roof structures and coverings from weather-resistant materials > Fig. 1.4.10
· provide adequate gaps between wooden components and adjacent surfaces, to protect them against snow and splashing; 30 cm high splash protection zone in the base, 15 cm when a gravel strip is being used; keep column bottoms as open to diffusion as possible and protect them from splashing > Fig. 1.4.11
· protect against rising damp by installing barrier layers
· ensure water is carried off quickly by creating inclines, ideally in the direction of the grain. Also create drip edges on the underside of structural components > Fig. 1.4.12

· protect end-grain wood by covering, beveling edges or chamfering > Fig. 1.4.13
· prevent water from accumulating in corners, grooves and joints; keep contact area for wood joints under 5 cm wide, e.g. by using 3 mm stainless steel spacers > Fig. 1.4.14
· avoid dust or earth accumulating in cracks, as this can lead to wood rot in persistently moist conditions
· avoid encasing in concrete (for palisades, for example)
· structural components should be dried rapidly using the most effective ventilation possible
· use the smallest possible material cross-section in order to prevent damage from swelling and shrinking and to encourage rapid drying after wet conditions
· sink relief grooves for larger timber cross-sections to avoid unmonitored cracks through which insects and water could penetrate the wood > Fig. 1.4.15
· arrange horizontal timbers with the right-hand side, pointing towards the heart, on top, so that water runs out of cracks running towards the heart and the top side curves upwards
· avoid wedge finger joints or do not expose them to direct weathering
· use corrosion-resistant connecting devices
· install heat-treated timber; the heat treatment produces higher resistance (not suitable for loadbearing building components)

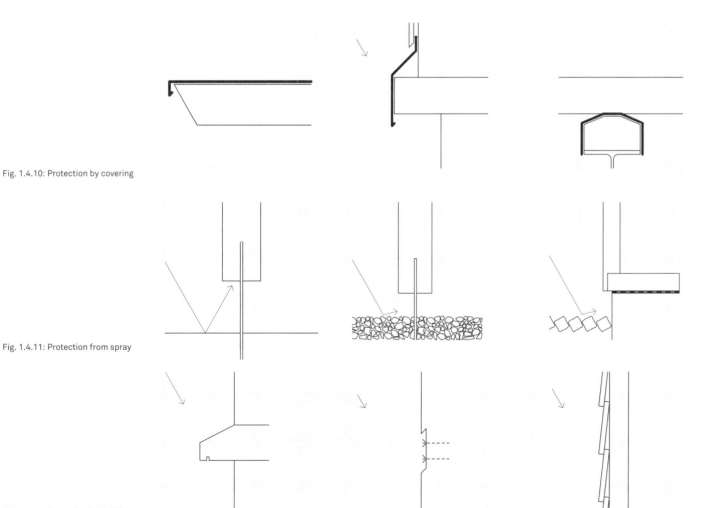

Fig. 1.4.10: Protection by covering

Fig. 1.4.11: Protection from spray

Fig. 1.4.12: Protection by draining off water

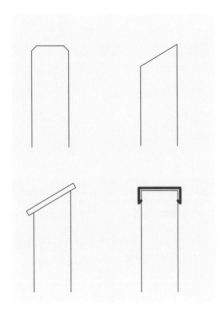

Fig. 1.4.13: End-grain wood protection

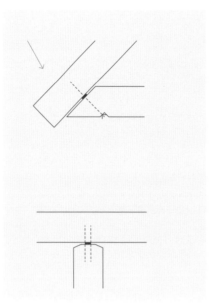

Fig. 1.4.14: Protection by preventing water from accumulating

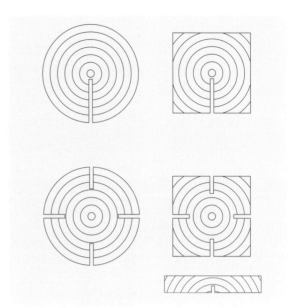

Fig. 1.4.15: Avoiding crack formation with relief grooves

Preventive chemical timber protection

The timber protection methods prescribed for loadbearing timber sections act as recommendations in protecting nonloadbearing components. These can be specified according to the individual case. Preventive chemical timber protection is achieved with biocidal agents. The possible uses for timber protection methods are defined precisely by the construction authorities in their regulations. Any work on the timber should be concluded before the protective treatment. If wooden structural components are sawed, drilled, planed or shaped subsequently, further treatment should be carried out. Timbers exposed to weathering on all sides should ideally have protection applied by a pressure boiler process.

PRODUCTS

Solid timber products

Timber products used outdoors include round and sawn timbers in solid wood and laminated timber, which is improved by gluing. > Fig. 1.4.16

Round timber means trunks or parts of trunks that have had their bark removed. There are three possible methods here: manual bark removal retaining the original shape of the trunk, mechanical bark removal with slight surface smoothing, or calibration, resulting in an even diameter and completely smooth surface.

Sawn or engineering timber is a timber product at least 6 mm thick, produced by sawing round timber parallel to the axis of the trunk, using frame saws or log band saws. Sawn timbers are classified as laths, boards, planks or square timber according to thickness.
> Tab. 1.4.3 and fig. 1.4.17

Laminated wood is an improved solid timber product, consisting of flat planks or strips glued together with their grain running parallel in two, three or more plies. As these plies can be shaped very easily, it is possible to produce curved structural components. Only

Fig. 1.4.16: Solid timber products: round timber, sawn timber and laminated timber

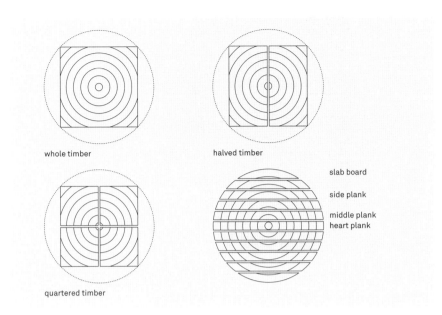

whole timber

halved timber

slab board

side plank

middle plank
heart plank

quartered timber

Fig. 1.4.17: Trunk divisions for sawn wood

	Thickness t height h	Width b
Lath	d ≤ 40 mm	b > 80 mm
Board	d ≤ 40 mm	b ≥ 80 mm
Plank	d < 40 mm	b > 3 d
Square timber	b ≤ h ≤ 3 b	b > 40 mm

Tab. 1.4.3: Sawn wood categories

synthetic resin adhesives tested for durability in all climatic conditions may be used for components that will be exposed to weathering (e.g. resorcinol resin adhesive). Laminated timber is recommended for large cross-sections. Its structure makes it very rigid and very little prone to cracks, with a high loadbearing capacity. It meets high standards visually.

Engineered wood materials

Sheets or rods pressed from small timber pieces are known as timber-derived products. The wood is reduced by sawing (planks), peeling or cutting (veneers), chip removal (wood wool, chips) or shredding, and then compacted, usually with the addition of resins or mineral bonding agents.

Most engineered wood products such as OSB board, synthetic resin bonded chipboard or fiberboard are not suitable for open-air structures subject to weathering. But exterior grade plywood (EN 13986) may be used for constructions exposed to weathering. Plywood is made up of crosswise adhesive-bonded plies. A distinction is made between veneer plywood and rod and slat plywood.

Solid wood product grades

The purpose of use determines the choice of a suitable wood species, but selecting the correct quality of timber, in other words the timber grade, is also important. Solid timber product grades can by affected by the various production phases.

Cutting, drying and surface treatment

Any tendency to crack, twist or wind can be markedly reduced by splitting the trunk in line with the pith (split-heart cut) or by separating out a heart plank containing the pith (split with heart removed). So if appearance is an important factor, a split-heart cut or a split with the heart removed should be chosen.

Unfortunate consequences such as warping, crack formation or attack from fungi and insects that damage wood can be minimized if the wood can be built into the structure at the moisture level that is anticipated in that location in the long term. Wood has to be dried to achieve the correct moisture content for working and for the location where it is to be used subsequently. In the case of solid wood, the required moisture content should be specified in the invitation to tender. Engineering timber can be worked rough-sawn. If a greater level of surface quality and precision of fit is required, planed surfaces and chamfered edges are used. If a rough edge is undesirable, a square-edged cut must be specified separately.

Grading

A distinction is made in grading between the grade prescribed by building regulations for loadbearing timbers and grading by aesthetic impression. Qualities that are also aesthetically relevant are taken into account when grading visually: branch distribution, grain direction, pith, width of annual rings, cracks, rough edges, crookedness, discoloration, and insect damage. So when grading by aesthetic impression it is possible to work by the grading characteristics of visual grading and fix other standards.

SURFACE QUALITIES

Wood can perform a variety of functions, and the way it looks is correspondingly varied. Timber structure also varies considerably. No one place is like another, and the living quality of the cell structure remains visible. Each timber species has its own unmistakable grain and coloring. In the case of unprotected wood, the weathering process can create signs of characterful aging if it is consciously included in the design. Wood is perceived as warm because of its good thermal insulation properties: it is pleasant to sit on a wooden bench or to walk on wooden decking in bare feet.

Surface treatment and coloring

It is possible to apply color to wood for outdoor use. The wood substrate must be appropriate, and correctly prepared: the moisture content must be below 20%, weathered timber has to be removed, along with resin that has oozed out, mildew must be cleaned off and a protective antimildew undercoat applied. The wood is then ready to be painted or varnished. Paint and varnish have to be renewed at regular intervals, so it does not make sense to treat the surface of many outdoor structures, because it is impossible or too expensive to repaint or revarnish. Colorless coatings, oils and waxes are not suitable for use in the open air.

One other possible way of coloring wood is fuming. Wood containing tanning agents (e.g. oak) takes on a brown to black aging hue if exposed to ammonia vapors for several hours in an airtight fuming chamber, though this effect will last for only a limited period in the open air. > Fig. 1.4.18

Wood treatment

Wood is easy and uncomplicated to work as a building material. Customary methods include sawing, drilling, planing and smoothing, chiseling, slitting and chamfering. Round timbers with the bark removed, rough-sawn or planed cut timber can be used for building according to design intentions and the intended use of the wooden structure. Wood is available rough-edged, square-edged or chamfered. Timber sections with special, nonrectangular cross-sections can be prepared by planing and chamfering. Freer forms and irregular surfaces can be created by using a chainsaw. > Fig. 1.4.19 Sandblasting or brushing the surface of the wood can bring out the early and late timber structure in relief.

JOINTS

Until the last century, carpentry joints were the only way of jointing wood durably by a forced-closed method. But the wide range of joints developed by traditional craft carpenters are very rarely used today. Timber has to be very carefully worked and finished to make them, and the process is wage-intensive and thus relatively expensive. As well as this, it is very difficult to calculate the load bearing capacity of these wood joints adequately, and large cross-sections are required. However, these are joints that correspond with the technical characteristics of the material. The way the force is transferred is immediately intelligible, and they can be deployed with considerable creativity because of the uniform use of material. > Fig. 1.4.20 Connections using mechanical devices have become accepted for modern engineering timber construction. The commonest connecting methods include nails, screws, dowel, bolts, lay-in and bolted connectors and a number of timber connections made up of shaped sheet metal parts. > Fig. 1.4.21 At least one zinc coating is required to protect such steel connectors against corrosion for outdoor use. Noncorroding lightweight metal or stainless steel products are more suitable. Care should be taken that connecting devices, wood and wood protection products are compatible when using any wood jointing technique.

Fig. 1.4.18: Coloring wood containing tanning agents by fuming

Fig. 1.4.19: Working wood with a chainsaw: nature playground at the National Garden Show (BUGA) in Potsdam

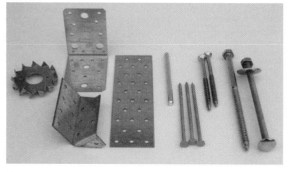

Fig. 1.4.21: Connections used in engineering timber construction

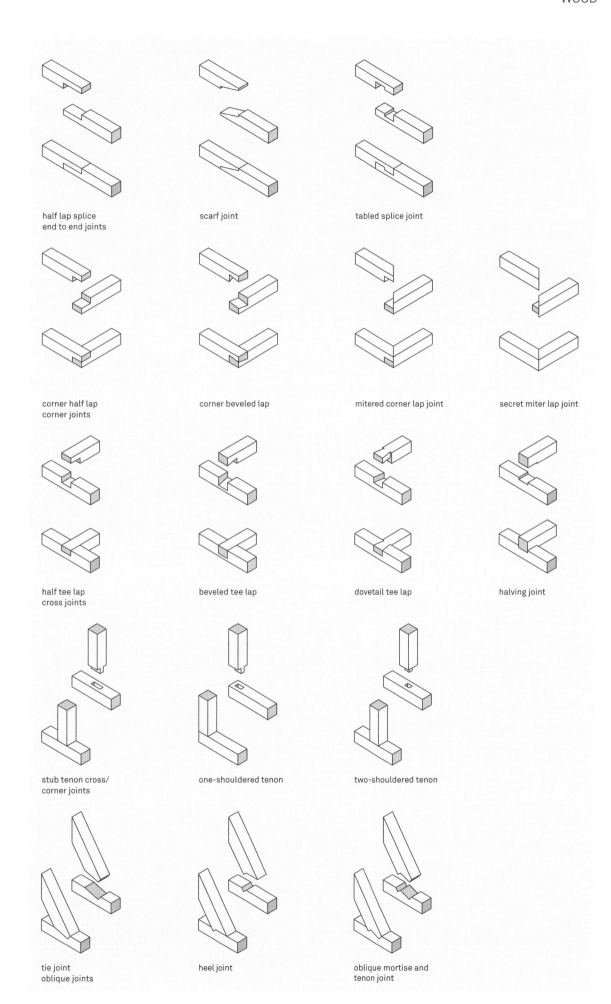

half lap splice
end to end joints

scarf joint

tabled splice joint

corner half lap
corner joints

corner beveled lap

mitered corner lap joint

secret miter lap joint

half tee lap
cross joints

beveled tee lap

dovetail tee lap

halving joint

stub tenon cross/
corner joints

one-shouldered tenon

two-shouldered tenon

tie joint
oblique joints

heel joint

oblique mortise and
tenon joint

Fig. 1.4.20: Carpenters'
wood joints

1.5   CUT STONE

PROPERTIES AND PRODUCTS
- Stone families and groups according to their mode of origin
- Qualities and properties
- Extraction and products

SURFACE PROPERTIES AND TREATMENT
- Possible treatments
- Care and Protection

JOINTING AND SHAPING

Hanna Bornholdt

1.5 CUT STONE

Buildings in natural stone are unique. There is scarcely a material with so many structures, colors and markings as stone. This variety can be further enhanced by different surface treatments, giving planners a range of materials and enabling them to make paving, walls, steps and water features in the open air look exactly as they wish.

Naming and classifying stone is a broad subject. When allocating stone to categories, science has to wrestle with each stone's particular qualities, and it is often impossible to decide with the naked eye which group it belongs to. Unlike plant and animals, many stone types are not easy to distinguish from each other. Some researchers identify > **Fig. 1.5.1** 1000 existing stone types, while others manage 100.

One old rule in stone lore states: stones that look the same may well belong to quite different types. This fact suggests how difficult it is for planners and individuals working with stone to make appropriate choices for a building project.

Scientific nomenclature often runs counter to commercial categories. Trade names are commonly fixed by quarry owners, importers or merchants looking for the most impressive names they can find. They do not always take account of the type of stone they have in front of them, and omit to use scientific terms, thus causing confusion. Standard EN 12670 thus lays down

Fig. 1.5.1: A number of different stone types were used for the collected stone paving in the Botanical Garden of the Villa Carlotta in Cadenabbia, Italy. It was impossible to name them precisely before carrying out petrochemical tests.

a terminological basis for geological and petrological definitions of stone types, and their classification. To avoid misunderstandings, each stone type is listed with its trade name, its petrochemical name, its quarry location, and descriptive attributes (color, granularity).

The way in which stone is formed, along with its chemical composition, is one of the main stone classification criteria. Classification takes place according to the genetic principle outlined below. > **Tab. 1.5.1**

Natural stone														
Magmatites **(igneous rocks)**						**Sediments** **(sedimentary rocks)**						**Metamorphites** **(metamorphic rocks)**		
plutonic rocks (deep-seated rocks)						biogenic, chem. sediments (chem. sedimentary rocks)						orthogenic (from igneous rocks)		
granite	sye-nite	diorite	gabbro	peridotite	foyaite	limestone	dolomite	slabby limestone	traver-tine	muschelkalk	calcare-ous tuff	orthogneiss	chlorite slate	serpentine
microplutonites (dike rocks)						clastic sediments (fragmented rocks)						other sediments (transformed sedimentary rocks)		
pegma-tite	aplite	lamprophyry				breccia	sandstone (psammite)	clay rock (pelite)	pyroclastic rock			quartzite	paragneiss	micaceous slate
vulcanites (eruptive rocks)												marble	clayey shale	phyllite
						breccia	sandstone	shale clay	volcanic tuffs					
rhyolite (porphyry)	basalt	lava	diabas	tuff		conglomerate	rocks silica sandstone							
							calcareous sandstone							
							greywacke schist							

Tab. 1.5.1: Stone type systematics

PROPERTIES AND PRODUCTS

Stone families and groups according to their mode of origin

Magmatites (igneous rocks)

Igneous rocks are formed from viscous, molten magma. They are distinguished according to where they solidified between plutonic or intrusive, volcanic or extrusive and microplutonic rocks. > Fig. 1.5.2

Plutonic rocks (named after Pluto, the Roman god of the underworld) are created when the magma cools within the earth's crust. The minerals can crystallize out well because of the slow cooling and the pressure of the layers above them. The best-known types are granite, syenite, diorite and gabbro. Plutonic rocks become increasingly darker within this sequence. Their particular characteristics are large crystals, visible to the naked eye, minerals that are mixed higgledy-piggeldy, nondirectional and compact in appearance, without cavities. Their properties mean that they are very strong (high proportion of quartz) and in most cases highly resistant to a whole variety of aggressors. Plutonic rocks are very easy to split, their surfaces take work and polish in particular very well. Their frost resistance and resistance to pressure and wear makes them usable almost without restriction for garden and landscape construction, and they are the most commonly used stone types. > Figs. 1.5.3–1.5.5

Volcanic rocks are created when volcanic pressure forces molten magma to the surface, where it cools. The most important stone groups are rhyolite (porphyry), basalt, diabas/dolerite, lava tufa, pumice stone and scoria. Basalt is the most common and best-known volcanic rock, and is a uniform, dark, dense stone. It is used as a paving stone, and is one of the strongest and most weather-resistant natural stones. Its dense pores make it excellent for polishing. Basalt paving that is heavily walked on and driven over can become very smooth. (Basalt) lava is created on eruption from the crater and in its basic form contains a large number of small cavities. Basalt and basalt lava are important for providing rough stone, crushed stone and chippings. The dark chippings make a good covering layer for roadmaking. It is also used in small sizes (mosaic, small stone). > Figs. 1.5.6–1.5.8

Microplutonic rocks are formed inside the earth's crust when low-viscosity magma penetrates cracks in rocks. They are similar in structure to other plutonic rocks, but as they cool more rapidly they crystallize less regularly and can contain insets of different rock type. The most important groups are the pegmatites, aplites and lamprophyres.

Sedimentary rocks

Sandstone is formed when weathered rocks are compacted (diagenesis) and particles, above all isolated quartz grains, are cemented in by clay, calcium carbonate or silica. Silica-bound sandstone is characterized by being reasonably strong and frost-resistant in outdoor use. One typical characteristic of sandstone is its

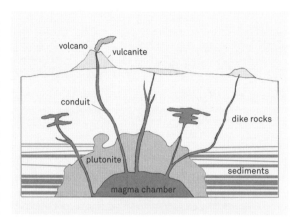

Fig. 1.5.2: Schematic diagram of the origin of rocks and the resultant classification

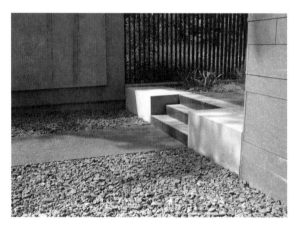

Fig. 1.5.3: Steps and facade in gabbro ("Nero Assoluto", South Africa), stair stringers or yellow sandstone ("Sunrise", South Africa), and red sandstone rubble ("Thambach sandstone", Germany), South African Embassy, Berlin

Fig. 1.5.4: Large red granite slabs, sculpture garden, Neue Nationalgalerie Berlin

Fig. 1.5.5: Framing walls and inflow gutters in dark grey, finely structured granite, mosaic paving in Polish "Strigau granite" and large paving stone in Ukrainian basalt in a Berlin roof garden

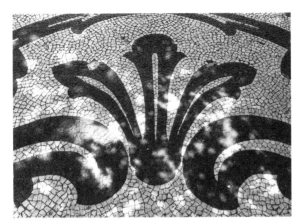

Fig. 1.5.6: Mosaic paving in basalt
and limestone, Praça de São
Mamede, Lisbon

Fig. 1.5.7: Rhyolite (porphyry)
walls and facades, Santa Maria
degli Angeli Chapel, Monte Ta-
maro, Switzerland

1.5.8: Slab cladding in porous basalt lava ("Plaidt basalt-lava"),
private garden, Zurich

stratification, creating many warm color shades and soft structures in red, yellow, brown, green and grey. Sandstone features in many historical buildings, and is considered easy to work. Sandstone acquires a patina and goes green in particularly shady places and if there is sufficient moisture. This property is much prized for sculpture, but the slipperiness that this can also cause makes it less suitable for roadmaking. > **Fig. 1.5.9**
Limestone and carbonate rocks are formed as a result of chemical conditions. Materials such as lime, dolomite and gypsum dissolve in water, break down and form deposits. Typical features of limestone are the remains of fossils such as shells, snails or sea lilies they often contain. A large number of limestone types exist, as a result of origins in various geological ages, and the types of

fossils in them, as well as numerous variations in color and marking. Categories include muschelkalk, travertine, calcareous tuff, dolomite, limestone and laminated limestone. Many dense, strong limestone types are wrongly called marble, which can lead to structural miscalculations. The constructional properties in relation to durability and appearance of sedimentary rocks differ on the basis of the minerals included and the different ways they are formed. The freshwater limestones travertine and calcareous tuff have clearly defined pores, a very varied structure, clear stratification and colors ranging from yellow to ocher. Muschelkalk is the commonest limestone, and can be used universally because of its almost unlimited durability and ease of working. > **Figs. 1.5.10–1.5.12**

Metamorphic rocks
Igneous and sedimentary rocks can be shifted into deeper strata by movements in the earth's crust and changed there by pressure and high temperature in such a way that new rock types are formed. This process is called metamorphosis, and it often causes stratification (fine lines) or cleaving (layered texture) in the rock, but this should not be confused with the stratification in a sedimentary rock. Metamorphic rocks are almost entirely free of cavities, are strongly textured and often have a silky, glimmering sheen. Chemical composition, appearance and thus the possibilities for use in construction vary considerably in metamorphic rocks. The most important types are quartzite, gneiss, marble and slate.

Fig. 1.5.9: Coursed masonry in red
Main sandstone, flood defenses
in Miltenberg, Germany

Gneiss rocks are light-colored, feldspar-rich metamorphic rocks and with granites the commonest continental surface-crust rock. If the original material is igneous, such rock is called orthogneiss. > Fig. 1.5.13 If it is formed from a sedimentary material, it is called paragneiss. Both are similar to granite, and are also often traded as granites, even though the stratification marks a clear distinction. Confusion with granite can lead to technical miscalculations in terms of strength and frost resistance.

Quartzites are very hard metamorphic rocks with a quartz content of over 85%. Their stratified structure makes them easy to split. The stone is highly abrasion resistant, which makes it useful for paving slabs and steps in areas with heavy traffic, particularly in its natural split form. Clayey shales are thin-plated, splittable anthracite black rocks with a very dense, fine-grained appearance. Clayey shale is increasingly used outdoors in the form of solid stone, slabs or walling units. > Figs. 1.5.14 and 1.5.15

Qualities and properties

Each rock type has special properties and characteristics, so the places in which different types are used vary correspondingly. At the beginning of a planning process,

Fig. 1.5.10: Mosaic pavement in black and white limestone, Avenida da Liberdade, Lisbon

Fig. 1.5.11: Free-standing wall in Thuringian travertine (Langensalza) in a private garden in Berlin

Fig. 1.5.12: Gabion wall filled with Harz limestone (Devonian massive limestone), Wernigerode regional horticultural show, Germany

Fig. 1.5.13: Natural split coursed masonry in Stainz hard gneiss, Riem cemetery, Munich, Germany

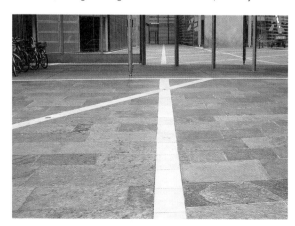

Fig. 1.5.14: Slate ("Otta phyllite" Norway) and marble paving, Scandinavian Embassies, Berlin

Fig. 1.5.15: Slate water table, Bundesgartenschau Park, Potsdam, Germany

	Technical qualities						Durability	Comfort
	bulk density (kg/m³)	compressive strength (N/m²)	frost resistance	water absorption (mass %)	tensile bending strength (MPa) with the support	abrasion resistance (cm³/50 cm²)	thermal conductivity (W/mK)	
Magmatites								
granite	2600–2800	130–270	●	0.1–0.9	5–18	5–8	2.8 (1.6–3.4)	
syenite	2600–2800	160–240	●	0.2–0.9	5–18	5–8	3.5	
diorite	2800–3000	170–300	●	0.2–0.4	6–22	5–8	3.5	
gabbro	2800–3000	170–300	●	0.2–0.4	6–22	5–8	3.5	
rhyolite (porphyry)	2500–2800	180–300	●	0.2–0.7	10–22	5–8	3.5	
basalt	2900–3000	240–400	●	0.1–0.3	13–25	5–8	3.5 (1.2–2.0)	
diabas	2800–2900	180–250	●	0.1–0.4	15–25	5–8	3.5	
Sedimentary rocks								
breccia	2600–2750	50–160	○	0.5–1.0	--		2.3	
conglomerate	2200–2500	20–160	●	0.8–10	2–15	14–80	2.3 (1.2–3.4)	
sandstone	2000–2700	30–150	● (○)	0.2–10	--	9–35	2.3 (1.2–3.4)	
quartz sandstone	2600–2700	120–200	○	0.2–0.5	--	7–8	2.3 (2.1)	
greywacke	2600–2650	150–300	●	0.2–0.5	11–25	7–8	2.3	
volcanic tuffs	1800–2000	20–30	○	6–15	0–5	10–35	2.3 (0.4–1.7)	
limestone	2600–2900	75–240	●–○	0.1–3	3–19	15–40	2.3 (2.0–3.4)	
shell limestone	2600–2900	80–180	●–○	0.2–0.6	3–16	15–40	2.3 (2.0–3.4)	
dolomite	2600–2900	75–240	○	0.1–3	3–19	15–40	2.3	
travertine	2400–2500	20–60	● (○)	2–5	2–13	20–45	2.3	
calcareous tuff	1700–2200	30–50	○	1–10	--	n.b.	0.85–1.7	
aragonitic limestone	2600–3000	100–200	●	0.3–0.4	--	4–10	3.5 (1.6–2.1)	
Metamorphic rocks								
paragneiss	2600–3000	100–200	●	0.3–0.4	4–12	4–10	3.5 (1.6–2.1)	
quartzite	2600–2700	150–300	●	0.2–0.5	13–25	7–8	3.5	
micaceous slate	2600–2800	140–200	○	0.2–0.4	--	15–25	2.2	
clayey shale	2700–2800	50–80	●	0.5–0.6	1–8	n.b.	2.2 (1.2–2.1)	
marble	2600–2900	75–240	○	0.1–3	3–19	15–40	3.5 (2.0–2.6)	

● highly suitable
○ less highly suitable

Tab. 1.5.2: Technical properties
of stone

a natural stone is usually chosen first of all for visual reasons such as color, structure, grain patterns or texture. After this come checks on whether the stone can meet the technical requirements and stand up to loads and the effect of chemicals, in order to avoid subsequent structural damage and legal claims. According to the way it is to be used, the stone must meet requirements relating to frost resistance, abrasion resistance, pressure resistance, thermal expansion, tensile bending strength and absorbency. General data giving a general idea of how stone behaves can be obtained from stone type tables. > Tab. 1.5.2 For natural stone whose properties in the open air cannot be established from experience, a recognized material testing service should provide a test certificate in conformity with European standards. Frost resistance in particular should be established for graded natural stone that will be in direct contact with soil or will always be wet (for example in shady areas or in water features). Paving and stairs in busy areas should be tested for abrasion resistance, loadbearing components like plinths or columns for pressure resistance, and cantilevered or protruding steps for tensile bending strength. Experience shows that general test certificates can be meaningless, for example because the test material is taken from the best parts of a quarry and the material supplied can differ considerably from this. Adjacent seams or similar looking stone is not tested specially and individually. It makes sense to have proof of suitability for the stone that is actually going to be used, to avoid problems later. It is also recommended that stone already tried out in the same location be used. > Fig. 1.5.16

Fig. 1.5.16: Frost damage to Portuguese limestone on the Pamukkale fountain in Berlin. The stone was not sufficiently tested for frost resistance before being used.

Extraction and products

Stone is usually mined open-cast on sites with good transport access (foothills and plains). Quarries mine rough blocks and provide rubble, ballast and chippings. The requirement is to extract more or less regularly formed cut stone blocks and minimize damage during the splitting process. The rough blocks are extracted by drilling and blasting, splitting (e.g. granite, sandstone) with hydraulic equipment, drill-split fragmentation (limestone), hole-to-hole cutting, slitting (limestone, sandstone, travertine) or using the oxy-acetylene process (1600°C), high pressure waterjet cutting or laser technology.

The rough blocks extracted from the quarry can be used for large, homogeneous pieces of work such as steps, large-format slabs, steles, columns or fountain basins. Stonemasons break the rough blocks down using splitting or slitting processes, and make them into usable smaller units. The splitting process is uses to produce naturally split natural stone construction elements without a high quality of finish, such as rubble stone, paving stones, kerbstones or split-face stones. The environment-friendly qualities of natural stone can be considerably enhanced by using materials from the immediate region and short transport routed. At the same time, choosing materials that occur locally or regionally has the advantage that planners and clients can examine the material for suitability at the quarry or on the stonemasons' premises. > Fig. 1.5.17

The following criteria are also important when choosing and building with natural stone:

· the availability of the material
· the sizes that can be delivered
· delivery at the correct time
· the continuing availability of the same material and
· additional workability at the building site

Cut stone can often be reworked and reused once a building is demolished. Granite paving stones in particular can be used to an almost unlimited extent, and thus have a good eco-balance.

SURFACE PROPERTIES AND TREATMENT

Possible treatments

Natural stone makes its impact through its structure and its color. Both these emerge only as a result of surface treatment. > Fig. 1.5.3 The effect can be increased or eliminated. So polishing or fine grinding help the stone's structure and color to make a greater impact, while flamed stone can change color. Trials should therefore be conducted with the chosen stone, rather than relying on general samples.

For surface treatment, the cut stones are processed in different ways, manually or mechanically on conveyor belts. Figures 1.5.18 a–i show some possible surface treatments.

	quarry rough	rough cut	pointed	bush-hammered	carved	chiseled	sand-blasted	diamond-sawed	polished	buffed	flamed
Magmatites											
granite	+	+	+	+				+	+	+	+
syenite	+	+	+	+				+	+	+	
diorite	+	+	+	+				+	+	+	
gabbro	+	+	+	+				+	+	+	
rhyolith (porphyry)	+	+	+	+				+	+	+	
basalt	+	+	+	+				+	+	+	
diabase	+	+	+	+	+			+	+		
lava tuff	+	+	+	+	+	+	+	+	+		
Sediments											
conglomerate	+	+	+	+		+		+	+		
breccia	+	+	+	+	+	+	+	+	+		
quartz sandstone	+	+	+	+	+	+	+	+	+	+	
sandstone	+	+	+		+	+	+	+	+		
greywack	+	+	+		+	+	+	+	+		
volcanic tuff	+	+	+		+	+	+	+	+		
limestone	+	+	+	+	+	+	+	+	+	+	
muschelkalk	+	+	+	+	+	+	+	+	+	+	
travertine	+	+	+	+	+	+	+	+	+	+	
limestone tuff	+	+	+					+			
dolomite	+	+	+	+	+	+	+	+			
Metamorphites											
ortho-/paragneiss	+	+	+	+	+			+	+	+	+
quartzite	+							+	+	+	
mica slate	+							+			
chlorite slate	+							+	+	+	
serpentenite					+			+	+	+	
marble	+	+	+	+	+	+	+	+	+	+	
phyllite	+							+			
clay slate	+								+	+	
granulite	+	+	+	+				+	+	+	

Tab. 1.5.3: Manual and mechanical surface treatments for natural stone

Magmatites
1 Balmoral granite
2 Baltic Brown granite
3 Bianco Cristal granite
4 Bohus Red granite
5 Claire du Tarn granite
6 Grigio Sardo granite
7 Epprechtstein granite
8 Flossenburg granite
9 Furstenstein Diorit
10 Kaltrum granite
11 Knaupsholz granite
12 Kösseine granite
13 Kuru Grey granite
14 Lausitz granite
15 Meissen granite
16 Metter granite
17 Mittweida granite
18 Neuhauser granite
19 Pedrogoa Gabbro
20 Rosa Porrino granite
21 Silesian granite
22 Schrems granite
23 Silvestre granite
24 Tittling granite

Volcanic rocks
25 Basaltina volcanic
26 Beucha rhyolite (granite-
    porphyry)
27 Gondomar
28 Greifenstein basalt
29 Labrador Antique syenite
30 Londorf basalt-lava
31 Oberscheld diabas
32 Plaidt basalt-lava
33 Rhenish basalt-lava
34 Trentino rhyolite
35 Weidenhahr Trachyte

Microplutonic
36 Snowflake lamprophyre

Sedimentary rocks
Limostone and carbonite rocks
37 Aachener blue stone
38 Adnet limestone
39 Belgian granite
40 Cannstatt travertine
41 Comblanchien stone
42 Crailsheim muschelkalk
43 Gönningen calcareous tuff
44 Harz limestone (Devonian
    massive limestone)
45 Huglfing (Pollingen) tuff
    limestone
46 Kirchheime muschelkalk
    (Kernstein)
47 Kirchheim muschelkalk
    (Blaubank)
48 Krensheim muschelkalk
49 Langensalza travertine
50 Oberdorla muschelkalk
51 Portuguese limestone
52 Roman travertine
53 Wachenzell dolomite

Sandstone
54 Bateig sandstone
55 Bentheim sandstone
56 Bollingen sandstone
57 Cotta sandstone
58 Neksö sandstone
59 Pfaffenhofen sandstone
60 Red Main sandstone

61 Seeberg sandstone
62 Sirkwitz-Rachwitz
    sandstone
63 Warthau sandstone
64 Weser sandstone
65 Worzeldorf sandstone

Slate
66 Fredeburg slate
67 Harz slate
68 Mayen slate

Metamorphic rocks
69 Alta quartzite
70 Andean orthogneiss
71 Calanca paragneiss
72 Graubündnen orthogneiss
73 Iragna paragneiss
74 Maggia paragneiss
75 Odenwald orthogneiss
76 Otta phyllite
77 Tauerngrün serpentinite
78 Theuma Frucht slate
79 Verde Alpi serpentinite
80 Welsh slate
81 Walser quartzite

Volcanic tuff
82 Ettringen tuff
83 Rochlitz rhyolite tuff
84 Roman tuff

Fig. 1.5.17: Selection of natural
stones in Europe

a	b	c
d	e	f
g	h	i

Fig. 1.5.18: Manual and mechanical surface
treatments for cut stone:
a) bush-hammered Metten granite
b) rough cut Metten granite
c) flamed Metten granite
d) sand-blasted Metten granite
e) polished Metten granite
f) coarsely pointed Jura limestone
g) bush-hammered Jura limestone
h) chiseled Jura limestone
i) diamond-sawed Jura limestone

Care and protection

Natural stone acquires a natural patina in the course of time. Igneous and most metamorphic rocks are very durable, and weather very little. Sandstones acquire a patina more rapidly when subjected to direct weathering. Algae, in particular, rapidly gain a purchase in the micropores, so the surface of the stone can very quickly turn green if there is a lot of moisture. Porous rocks, in other words travertines, calcareous tufa and coarse-pored lava provide good conditions for germination and growth. Algae and lichens flourish above all in moist areas, places near the ground, in constant shade, under trees, in badly ventilated corners, or where there is often dripping water. This is usually merely aesthetically unappealing, but can also cause slippery conditions. If undesirable stains appear, these can often be cleaned off with ordinary soft soap and warm water. Thorough soaking in soapsuds makes cleaning with a brush easier and leaves behind a light film of grease that inhibits new soiling. The roughness of the stone surface determines how firmly the dirt sticks. For example, chewing gum can be removed from a polished or laser-treated floor with a sharp scraper, but dry ice systems or chemicals have to be used on flamed or bush-hammered surfaces. Other cleaning methods for removing stains are compressed steam equipment, laser-beam processes, cement streaking removers or special surface cleaning products for natural stone. If acids are used, great care is needed for many stone surfaces.

Natural stone is very durable. But under the present environmental conditions, many kinds of stone like for example sandstone and stone containing lime need a more weatherproof or water-repellent surface treatment. The stone surfaces are regularly painted, impregnated or sealed with fluosilicic acid, hydrofluoric acid, silicic acid esters or silicone resins. Care needs to be taken with water-repellent impregnations, to avoid damaging the crust that is to be applied and prevent water penetration. Stone can be impregnated with wax to protect it against graffiti.

Some discolorations and stains are determined by the composition of the stones themselves. Hence many stones, if they are exposed to moisture after building, are inclined to "rust" because of embedded minerals containing iron. Stains are often caused during the building work. Calcium hydroxide in the cement, unbound aggregates or formwork lubricant stains can be washed in by the water and cause surface discoloration. Salt deposits, such as efflorescence, leaching or sintering out can be removed in some cases by dry brushing or washing with a great deal of water, or in stubborn cases with special cleaning materials. Salt deposits can be avoided by using trass cement as a bonding agent.

Fig. 1.5.19: Travertine slab covering, joints filled with drain gravel, roof garden in Berlin

JOINTING AND SHAPING

Cut stone is mainly used as for paving and as slabs. Broken, frost-resistant minerals should be used as a substructure and as bedding for path coverings. Natural stone is sensitive to accumulated moisture in the covering structure, so as well as planning the height, it is necessary to plan drainage to ensure that the base layer and the foundation course are drained correctly. > Chapter 3.2 Paths and squares. The joints between the slabs and in the paved areas have to be fully and solidly jointed with high-quality material to at least 2/3 of the height of the stone. > Fig. 1.5.19 Often the water drainage capacity on the sealed level of roof or terrace areas is inadequate, especially when surface and facade water is intended to flow over them. Products to be laid in terrace areas promise protection from damage by frost and moisture. Natural stone slabs are laid on single-sized aggregate concrete, and mesh laths and plastic channels under the mortar ensure that precipitation water will run off rapidly horizontally, and also provide ventilation. Natural stone masonry is used in garden and landscape construction either as solid masonry or as facing masonry without an air space. > Chapter 3.5 Walls Coursed stone is coursed to correspond with its natural stratification in solid walls; the stone courses must not the stone height more than four to five times.

Nonloadbearing frostproof leaves are either suspended or built up in front of the loadbearing wall or internal leaf (usually a concrete core) and secured with clamps, plugs or forked ties. Lime efflorescence in walls can be avoided if the concrete is made as thick as possible without too high a water content, and both the natural stone and the concrete core are at the same temperature when setting. Generally speaking, an appropriate way to prevent efflorescence in natural stone walls is to use trass cement, iron Portland cement or blast furnace cement. Cement mortar is usually unsuitable.

1.6 BRICK AND CLINKER

COMPOSITION, PROPERTIES, PRODUCTS
· Shaping
· Formats and dimensions
· Molded bricks
· Care and protection
· Reusability

SURFACE QUALITIES AND SURFACE TREATMENT
· Surface treatment
· Coloring
· Firing bricks

LAYING AND SHAPING
· Brick masonry
· Paved areas

Petra Zadel-Sodtke

1.6 BRICK AND CLINKER

The term "brick" includes all fired earthenware materials. Clinker is the term for special bricks made of high-quality, dense clays fired to sintering point. As a term, brick includes the historical handmade wall brick, and new bricks with historical quality (monument brick). Only weather- and frost-resistant bricks are used for durable outdoor structures. The categories used include facing bricks and glazed bricks, facing tiles and engineering clinker, floor tiles and paving clinker, and also roof tiles and terracotta slabs. Back-up bricks are not suitable, as they are not frost-resistant. Other ceramic building materials are also used, such as frost-resistant stoneware, outdoor tiles and heavy ceramic slabs.

Bricks differ not just in format, but also, above all, in their surface quality. In this respect we are dealing with a building material that offers a wide range of design possibilities in the interplay of bond and joint patterns. The brick manufacturing process breaks down into extracting and preparing raw materials, shaping and finally drying and firing. Coloring during preparation or decorating before firing are additional means of finishing the surface.

COMPOSITION, PROPERTIES, PRODUCTS

Bricks consist mainly of the raw material clay, and aggregates can include sand, ash or oxides (pigments). Raw materials containing clay can be found in mountainous regions, in valleys, on riverbanks, on the bottom of lakes or the sea, and are categorized as common clay, brick clay, clay stone, shale clay and clayey shale. Not all clays are suitable for brick manufacture. Raw materials containing clay have very different properties, and have to be handled appropriately.

Shaping

The oldest shaping method involves "striking" bricks by hand. Here the clay mass is pressed into wooden or iron molds, with or without bottoms. The molds have to be moistened or coated beforehand with water, oil or sand, so that the clay will come out afterwards; hence these bricks are also known as water-struck bricks, hand-struck bricks or sand-struck bricks. Individual brickworks specialize in these processes for use in monument conservation, and also copy bricks if required. Hand manufacture was generally superseded with the introduction of the extruder (1861) and the screw-extruder (1863).

In machine manufacture, a distinction is made between struck bricks (machine-struck bricks) and pressed bricks, although a machine-struck brick looks very little different from a handmade brick. > Tab. 1.6.1, lines 1–3 Pressed bricks are made in molds in brick presses as semi-dry pressed bricks and dry pressed bricks, or with the aid of nozzles (fitted to the extruder) as extruder bricks. Bricks with holes can be made only by extrusion. > Fig. 1.6.1

Not all coring or perforation types are suitable for outdoor use because some of them are not frost- and

Brick category by shaping process	Appearance	
	handmade	machine made
Water-struck bricks	fine, smoothed, dense surface with clay or water streaks	similar to handmade water-struck bricks, but with piston print on one side
Hand-struck bricks and Formbak bricks (Dutch term)	rough, uneven surface structure, sand-surfaced on all sides, with an irregular pattern of indentations and pressing creases, irregular edges	rough-pored, sand-covered surface on all sides, with piston print on one side
Hand-struck bricks	sharp-edged, with smooth surfaces on all sides and narrow pressing creases, usually without sand-covered surface, finely sieved sand occasionally applied	irregular, sand-covered surfaces, pressing creases with trapped sand, cylinder print on one side
	machine made	
Extruded bricks	even, smooth pressing skin, cut surfaces without pressing skin, some with cutting marks and grooves, sharp-edged, sometimes burred, irregular shallow indentations on the surface caused by brunt out materials (e.g. sawdust, polystyrene), vacuum-pressed green bricks with especially smooth pressing skin and high density	
Semidry pressed bricks	surface usually smooth, somewhat structured according to the way the raw material is prepared	
Dry-pressed bricks	smooth surface on all sides, sharp edges, dense, structured brick body, very accurate to prescribed dimensions	

Tab. 1.6.1: Effect of the shaping process on visual properties

Fig. 1.6.1: Properties of the brick surface created by molding processes:
a) water-struck
b) sand-struck
c) handmade
d) extruder without vacuum
e) extruder with vacuum
f) dry press

a	b
c	d
e	f

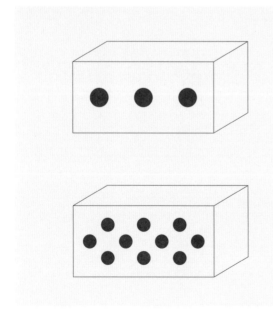
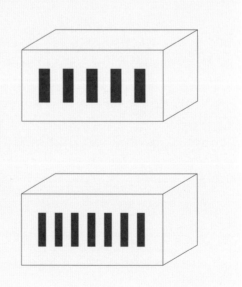

Fig. 1.6.2: Solid bricks with a coring

Tab. 1.6.2: Standard formats for some European countries

Country	Length (cm)	Width (cm)	Height (cm)
Germany	24	11.5	7.1 (NF)
		11.5	5.2 (DF)
Belgium	19	9	5
Denmark	22.8	10.8	5.4
Finland	27	13	7.5
France	22	11	6
United Kingdom	21.5	10.25	6.5
Italy	25	12	5.5
Holland	21	10	5
Norway	23	11	6.5
Austria	25	12	6.5
Sweden	25	12	6.2
Switzerland	25	12	6
Spain	25	12	5

weather-resistant. Only facing bricks and clinker with a maximum of 50% coring are suitable as exposed brick, and the cross section of individual perforations must not exceed ≤ 2.5 cm². > **Fig. 1.6.2** Thus only absolutely solid bricks without coring, solid bricks with some coring and bricks with vertical or horizontal coring with A coring in accordance with DIN 105-1 are permitted. Only solid bricks without coring are structurally admissible in areas where there is drilling, in order to prevent water from penetrating the masonry.

Formats and dimensions

Brick formats and brick proportions

As well as the German normal format NF, thin format DF and multiple thin formats (e.g. 2DF, 3DF, 20DF etc.) DIN formats, other standard formats are used in Europe. > **Tab. 1.6.2**

There are also further standard commercial brick formats. > **Fig. 1.6.3a, b** Here the brick formats differ not simply in their nominal dimensions, but also in their proportions. This also produces different horizontal effects in the bond pattern. > **Tab. 1.6.3** As the list of brick proportions shows—scaled to a unit height—several length variations are available for shaping the overall appearance of a building.

a | b

Fig. 1.6.3: Various standard commercial formats

Proportion group l / h	Proportion l / h	Name	Short mark	Dimensions l / w / h (in cm)	Proportions l / w / h
24		Flat tile (straight cut)		36 x 15 x 1.5	24 / 10 / 1
12		Floor clinker slab, thin		30 x 30 x 2.5	12 / 12 / 1
9.5		Bar format (since c. 2003)		49 x 11 x 5.2	9.4 / 2.2 / 1
7.5		Floor clinker slab, thick		30 x 30 x 4	7.5 / 7.5 / 1
7		Belgian thin format		21 x 10 x 3	7 / 3.3 / 1
6		German Römer		24 x 11.5 x 4	6 / 2 / 1
5.5		Bavarian format, large	BFG	36 x 18 x 6.5	5.5 / 2.8 / 1
		Special format	SF	34 x 16.5 x 6.5	5.2 / 2.5 / 1
		Dutch Vecht format	VF	21 x 10 x 4	5.3 / 2.5 / 1
5		Dutch standard format		20 x 10 x 4	5 / 2.5 / 1
4.5		Bavarian format, small	BFK	29 x 14 x 6.5	4.5 / 2.2 / 1
		Thin format	DF	24 x 11.5 x 5.2	4.6 / 2.2 / 1
		Dutch Lilliput format		16 x 7.5 x 3.5	4.6 / 2.1 / 1
4		Kiel format, thin	KF	23 x 11 x 5.5	4.2 / 2.0 / 1
		Oldenburg format	OF	22 x 10.5 x 5.2	4.2 / 2 / 1
		Dutch Waal format, thin	WF	21 x 10 x 5	4.2 / 2 / 1
3.5		Normal format	NF	24 x 11.5 x 7.1	3.4 / 1.6 / 1
		New Reich format	NRF	24 x 11.5 x 6.5	3.7 / 1.8 / 1
		Kiel format, thick	KDF	23 x 11 x 6.5	3.5 / 1.7 / 1
3		Frankenstein (since c. 2003)		36.5 x 24 x 11.5	3.1 / 2.1 / 1
		Euro module	EM	29 x 9 x 9	3.2 / 1 / 1
		Dutch Waal format, thick	WDF	21 x 10 x 6.5	3.2 / 1.5 / 1
2.5		Prussian smallest format		14.8 x 11.8 x 5.6	2.6 / 2.1 / 1
2		3 x thin format	3DF	24 x 17.5 x 11.3	2.1 / 1.5 / 1
		2 x thin format	2DF	24 x 11.5 x 11.3	2.1 / 1 / 1
1.5		Euro module	EM	29 x 9 x 19	1.5 / 0.5 / 1
		Euro module	EM	19 x 9 x 14	1.4 / 0.6 / 1
1		Terracotta		24 x 7.1 x 24.0	1 / 0.3 / 1

Tab. 1.6.3: Some brick formats compared: length/height proportions relating to a unit height h = 1

Cut bricks and nominal dimensions

Cut bricks have to be used to ensure the right interlock in different masonry bonds. These cut bricks can be prepared on site or delivered preformed. Cuboid cut bricks are called full bricks, ¾ bricks, ½ bricks and ¼ bricks according to their size. They can be halved across their length, width and height. Vertically halved bricks are difficult to manufacture in craft terms and are often structurally suspect as well. But it makes a particular aesthetic effect in paving made up of historical bricks (with the polished cut surface facing upwards).

It is recommended to use the precise nominal dimensions of bricks—these differ from the nominal dimensions stated in DIN 1023—to achieve identical values when using a computer program to establish the built dimensions for brick courses laid one above the other. Given a uniform joint thickness of 1 cm for vertical and horizontal joints, the precise nominal dimensions for the German national format will be 24 x 11.5 x 7.33 cm. > **Fig. 1.6.4** Dimensions for the German thin format will be 24 x 11.5 x 5.25 cm, with the following dimensions for cut bricks: three-quarters NF 17.75 x 11.5 x 7.33 cm; quarter NF 5.25 x 11.5 x 7.33 cm; halved across width NF 11.5 x 11.5 x 7.33 cm; halved across length NF 24 x 5.25 x 7.33 cm and halved across height NF 24 x 11.5 x 3.16 cm. > **Fig. 1.6.5**

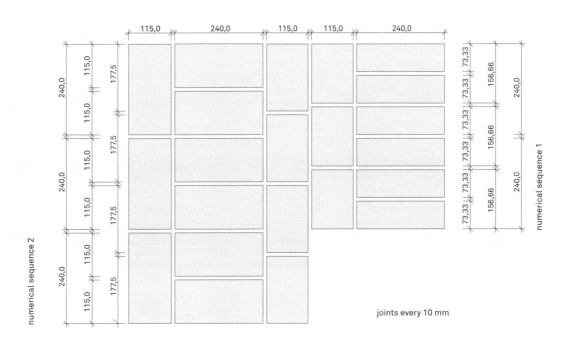

Fig. 1.6.4: Derivation of the precise nominal dimensions for the German normal format (NF)

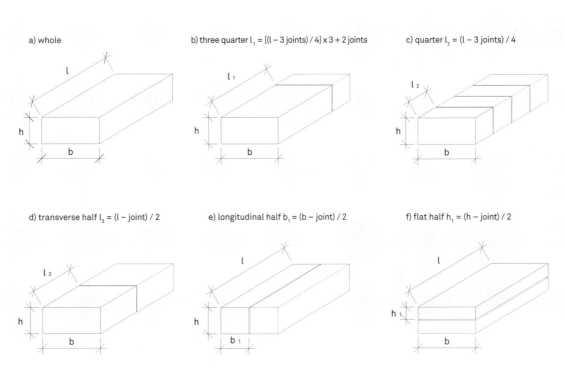

a) whole

b) three quarter $l_1 = [(l - 3 \text{ joints}) / 4] \times 3 + 2 \text{ joints}$

c) quarter $l_2 = (l - 3 \text{ joints}) / 4$

d) transverse half $l_3 = (l - \text{joint}) / 2$

e) longitudinal half $b_1 = (b - \text{joint}) / 2$

f) flat half $h_1 = (h - \text{joint}) / 2$

Fig. 1.6.5: Cuboid brick and related cut bricks

Molded bricks

Further complementary molded bricks are available in addition to the cuboid brick, the normal brick and the cut brick, so that elaborate geometrical patterns can be created. > Figs. 1.6.6–1.6.8

Molded bricks are also available to provide additional horizontal reinforcement for wall coping. > Fig. 1.6.9

Molded bricks can be used in a number of ways. For example, a beveled brick can be used in a corner, for a well, or as a door jamb. > Fig. 1.6.10

Rhomboidal, triangular, hexagonal and square molded bricks are also available as paving stones. The general molded brick program for house bricks and paving stones is complemented by special forms like handrail bricks or perforated lawn clinker, drainage clinker and flexible shapes with chamber systems for drainage. > Fig. 1.6.11

Care and protection

Brick walls or paved areas are easy to care for and usually need no protection. Generally speaking, the cleansing effects of rain, sun and regular use are sufficient. Roofed areas should be cleaned from time to time with water without chemical cleaning agents or washed down with a high-pressure cleaner if very badly soiled.

Cleaning by sandblasting or a dry blasting process are recommended for wall clinker. Here it should be noted that this can cause loss of surface brick, which could also be interpreted as premature aging.

So far no transparent antigraffiti coating can be recommended for brick—as opposed to concrete—as unattractive gray deposits usually build up underneath it.

Reusability

Historic bricks, preserved as recycled bricks by controlled demolition, are the principal material used for restoration purposes. But their patina and attractive looks also commend them for new building.

Clinker and hard-fired bricks are also used in crushed form. As crushed recycled materials they are used as brick gravel, concrete aggregate and ballast substrate for terraces, as an aggregate for frost protection and ballast layers, as fillers and embankment building materials and as a substrate for planted joints and openings in paving or slab coverings, or also as a substrate for trees.

To produce brick gravel with particle sizes of 8/16, 16/32 and 32/64, demolition material is crushed and processed in drum mills. This product, which does not contain fragments of rendering or mortar, is suitable not only for drainage beds, but because it is so attractive

a) beveled corner
b) beveled end
c) fully beveled
d) rounded off
e) rounded off concave
f) rounded
g) semicircular
h) straight wedge
i) curved wedge
j) top curved
k) profiled
l) bent
m) angled
n) pierced
o) sloped slab

Fig. 1.6.6: Molded bricks for masonry

Fig. 1.6.8: Molded paving slabs

Fig. 1.6.7: Selected molded bricks

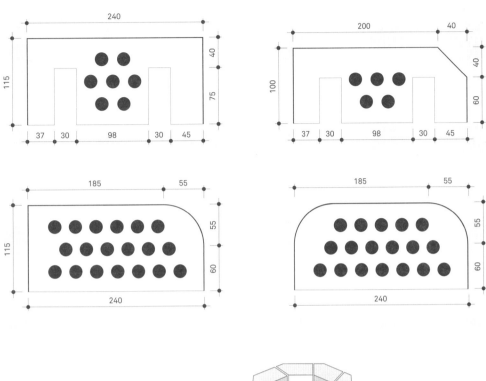

Fig. 1.6.9: Molded bricks for wall coping

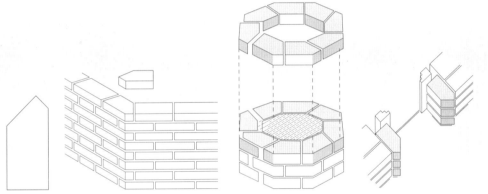

Fig. 1.6.10: A multi-purpose molded brick

Fig. 1.6.11: Perforated lawn bricks

Fig. 1.6.12: Brick gravel made from demolished bricks, belTerra

a | b

as a design feature, for covering paths or as decorative gravel in garden design. > Fig. 1.6.12

SURFACE QUALITIES AND SURFACE TREATMENT

Every brick is both uniform and individual: uniform, because all bricks in a series are of similar size and the same shape; individual, because no brick is like any other in detail and so is unique. So bricks can make an impact through their modular quality (cuboid shape), variety of outline (uneven outline), variety of surface structure (uneven structure) and variety of coloring.

The visual characteristics of bricks arise from the plastic consistency of the original material, the manufacturing phases and the specific firing method. The firing and shaping process produces specific characteristics such as water streaks (water-struck bricks), natural pressure folds with trapped sand (sand-struck bricks), smooth surfaces with narrow pressure folds (oil-struck bricks) and traces or grooves from cutting caused by a cutting wire. Mechanical shaping and even firing in gas-fired tunnel kilns produced accurately dimensioned but monotonous looking bricks that were often used in the 1970s and 1980s. Visual irregularities are not a fault in bricks, but a quality that is appreciated.

It is possible to manufacture hand-struck bricks mechanically using industrial processes like water-struck brick presses, striking presses and hand molding presses to produce the same natural impression given by hand-struck bricks. It is also possible to make industrially produced extruded bricks look natural deliberately by taking them off the conveyor belt by hand and by firing with charcoal or vitrifying material in a circular kiln. > Fig. 1.6.13 a, b

Fig. 1.6.13:
a) Solid facing brick, Waal thick format, extruded brick removed by hand, coal-fired in circular kiln (from France, manufacturer unknown)
b) Solid clinker, Reich format, melted, circular kiln firing with coal, vitrified architecture grading (Klinker- und Ziegelwerk Wansleben, Germany)
c) Solid clinker, Waal thick format, machine sand-struck (from England, manufacturer unknown)
d) Solid facing brick, machine hand-struck, Waal thick format (Neerbosch Baksteen, Holland)
e) Facing brick, Waal thick format, machine hand-struck in tunnel kiln, sprayed (KDB Holland)
f) Solid clinker, Reich format, extruder press, original coal firing in circular kiln (AKA Klinkergruppe, Germany)

a	b
c	d
e	f

In addition to this, transport and storage of green bricks while they are still damp will often add marks made by hands, in the storage place (animal prints) and by conveyor belts, supporting boards or palettes. The bricks carry irregular, shallow indentations as a result of cauterized materials or the typical pressing skin. > **Fig. 1.6.14**
Surface designs with intricate repetitions, added subsequently, make the bricks look artificial and lifeless, as this destroys the balance between natural and artificial aspects. > **Fig. 1.6.15** The grooves differ in direction, curvature, number, width and depth, and in the frequency of interruptions and the intensity of shadow.

Surface treatment

Additional structuring processes make a variety of surface designs possible. These can be applied either to the freshly pressed extruded clay, the damp green or blank brick, the dried green brick or the fired brick. > **Tab. 1.6.4 and fig. 1.6.16**
Floor tiles and paving clinker should not be laid with the unduly smooth firing skin face upwards for outdoor use to avoid slipping and make them easy to walk on. Cut, pared or tumbled surfaces are suitable for nonslip surfaces.

Coloring

Brick color derives from the firing process. The desired color is achieved by choosing particular clays to which materials that will provide color (aggregates) can be added. The bricks are colored throughout or receive a coat of surface color. Coloring is also affected by the firing atmosphere (oxygen content, moisture content etc.) and the addition of certain firing additives (e.g. wood chips).
The color range of unglazed bricks includes the classic brick colors red, orange and yellow, and also numerous color tones, for example white or yellow nuances, bright yellow, reddish yellow, pink, pink with color tinge, bright orange, bright red, reddish brown, light reddish brown, light reddish blue, brown, blackish brown and anthracite. We distinguish between ten types of brick by their color. > **Tab. 1.6.5**

Fig. 1.6.14: Visible foot with surface structure caused by transport on conveyor belt

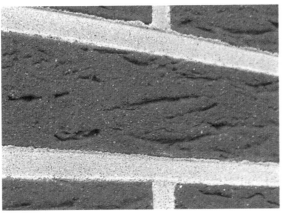

Fig. 1.6.15: Comparison of natural and artificial look in surface structure:
a) hand-struck bricks with pressing creases
b) extruded bricks with pitting rolled in

a/b

Structuring process	Effect
a) on the moist extruded clay or blank	
untreated, natural pressing skin	smooth
compressed air	sanded (fine, course)
blade	pared
sponges	with water streaks
brushes	brushed
blade or wire brush	roughened
Roller (profiled brick)	pitted
	undulating
	etc.
b) on the dry green brick	
sandpaper	rubbed
compressed air	sprayed
comb-like tool	chiseled
c) on the fired brick	
sand-blaster	sand-blasted
knife	bossed
drum mill	tumbled

Tab. 1.6.4: Brick surface structuring processess

Brick category	Coloring process	
natural bricks	raw material firing color	
through-colored bricks	aggregates	
reduced bricks	firing atmosphere	
steamed bricks		
flamed bricks		
coated bricks	surface coating	applied color
engobe bricks	engobe	
glazed bricks	glaze	
color sprayed bricks	applied pigment	
color sand-surfaced bricks		

Tab. 1.6.5: Coloring processes for bricks

a	b
c	d
e	f

Fig. 1.6.16: Additional surface structures:
a) cut
b) brushed
c) pitted and heavily sanded
d) brushed and coarsely sanded
e) bossed
f) tumbled

To preserve the coloring despite abrasion or chipping, only through-colored bricks should be used, or bricks that are extremely similar in terms of color. So in areas at risk of vandalism or where there will be very heavy use, bricks with applied colors should be avoided.

Firing bricks

The fine particles of the raw material are irreversibly combined to form a solid body by firing, effectively becoming stone. The clay is matured according to its composition at temperatures between 800 and 1200°C. Above the maturation point, each clay has its individual sintering and melting point. A distinction is made according to firing temperature between mature bricks (facing bricks), clinker and vitrified bricks. Bricks fired to the sintering temperature are called clinker. Bricks fired to their melting point, so that the clay melts and the whole mass becomes glazed, are called vitrified or burr bricks. Vitrified bricks are classified as mis-fired, but they are sometimes made deliberately for their expressive distortions and coloring. > Fig. 1.6.17

The bricks are placed in the kiln on top of each other, so that the whole stack can be heated as evenly as possible. The brick at the bottom is partially protected from the firing atmosphere by the bricks above it, which produces setting stripes. > Fig. 1.6.18 In the case of vitrified

Fig. 1.6.17: Vitrified bricks

bricks, the bricks placed one on top of the other fuse together partially and have to be separated, which produced particularly marked surface protrusions.

Very few brickworks still use coal or peat as fuel, both of which leave traces on the surface. Such bricks are coal-fired bricks or peat-fired bricks. Field-fired bricks, which are fired with wood in scove kilns, are a rarity, and are now made only in Belgian brickworks. Generally speaking, genuine coal-, peat- and field-fired bricks are seen as the most visually expressive products—because of their irregular surfaces and lively, nuanced firing colors. > Fig. 1.6.19

Fig. 1.6.18: Setting stripes on bricks:
a) matured bricks

b) clinker

c) vitrified brick

Fig. 1.6.19: Brick category by fuel
a) coal-fired brick

b) peat-fired brick

c) field-fired brick

LAYING AND SHAPING

The choice of material and the arrangement of the joints produces a wide range of appearances for masonry and paving bonds, and these can be reinforced or weakened by the quality of the materials. > Fig. 1.6.20

Brick masonry

Brick walls are always jointed with mortar. Here the showing faces can be pointed either during building as a trowel finish or after building as subsequent pointing. In subsequent pointing, a distinction is made between pointing after 4–5 courses have been completed and pointing after all the masonry has been finished and has set fully.

The following joint types can be used for a trowel finish: dry joint, flush joint, center-scratched flush joint, smoothed joint, raked-out joint, dummy joint, hollow joint, center-scratched hollow joint, V-shaped joint and bulging joint. > Chapter 3.5 Walls

Standard joint thicknesses for vertical and horizontal joints can be worked out by considering the length/width and length/height proportions of the brick dimensions. > Tab. 1.6.2

Paved areas

In the case of paved areas open to road traffic, great care must be taken from brick to brick that the joints are filled with sand, gravel sand, crushed sand, chippings or a crushed sand and chipping mixture of the appropriate particle size and are 3–5 mm wide, to enable the necessary transfer of forces (e.g. compression and shear forces). No dry joints should be used, and mortar only in exceptional cases, to avoid faults in the paving. > Chapter 3.2 Paths and spares

The most common sizes for brick paving stones in Germany are 20 x 10 cm, 22 x 10.5 cm and 24 x 11.8 cm, and the most usual heights are 4.5, 5.2, 6.2 and 7.1 cm. Brick paving stones can be beveled or sharp-edged.

Fig. 1.6.20: Design diversity for variety in appearance: masonary (a-p) and paving bonds (q-z)

a–p

1.7 CONCRETE

COMPOSITION, PROPERTIES, PRODUCTS
· Cement
· Additives and admixtures
· Exposure classes
· Reinforced concrete
· Watertight concrete
· Self-compacting concrete
· Fiber and otherwise reinforced concrete
· Vacuum concrete
· Precast concrete units

SURFACE QUALITIES AND SURFACE TREATMENT
· Exposed concrete
· Color and surface creation
· Photoconcrete
· Ground and polished concrete

JOINING AND MOLDING
· Concrete as a construction aid and as a foundation
  construction material
· Concrete as a free-form moldable construction material

Thomas Brunsch

1.7 CONCRETE

Concretes are self-hardening mixtures based on cement as a bonding agent. After the plastic fresh concrete has fully stabilized, a construction material is created which resembles natural stone in appearance and technical construction properties. Concrete is therefore often referred to as artificial stone.

The basic concrete formula comprises granular mineral aggregate, cement and water. > Fig. 1.7.1

This process is also called hydration, as water triggers cement hardening. From cement paste, a mixture of cement and water, interlocking needle-like crystal structures form over a period of months. These microscopic structures are able to bond mineral and metallic substances stably over a long period of time. In order to alter the properties of concrete in a targeted way, additives and admixtures are added to it during industrial manufacture. This is described as the five-component system of concrete. The controllable variation of its properties makes concrete, like glass or steel, a thoroughly modern material. The almost inexhaustible range of current developments, such as self-compacting or translucent concrete, show how much future potential still remains in this construction material.

COMPOSITION, PROPERTIES, PRODUCTS

Concrete manufacture involves formulas or mixing instructions that determine the composition of the end product and ensure its quality. The main bulk of a formula consists of aggregates. In the main, round-grained (sand and gravel) or broken (grit and crushed stone) mineral substances are used in concrete manufacture. Cement acts as glue, permeating the mixture and giving it strength. > Fig. 1.7.2

The hardening of this cement, also called setting, is a process clearly visible after a few hours. It takes years to fully conclude. Cement sets hydraulically; that is, where air is excluded as well as under water. Cemented stone created in this way cannot be dissolved by water. Depending on the amount of water added, fresh concrete is a friable, slightly pasty or flowing gray mass, which is freely moldable. The ratio of cement content to water content is described as the water/cement value (W/C). A high frost and de-icing salt resistance, achieved through a low water/cement value of 0.5 (equivalent to a mixing ratio of 1 liter of water to 2 kg of cement), is important in the outside use of concrete.

The shape of the solid concrete is usually defined using molds. In the industrial manufacture of nonreinforced finished concrete parts, precise steel molds are used, into which concrete at soil humidity is pressed at high pressure and shaken. > Fig. 1.7.3

Concrete processed on the construction site is called cast in-situ concrete. The molds in which it hardens are called formwork. Modern formwork consists of industrially manufactured system modules. However, they may also be manually produced from wood. Cast in-situ

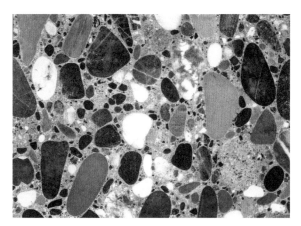

Fig. 1.7.1: Cut concrete—the coarser granular mineral aggregates are embedded in the finer components.

Fig. 1.7.2: The surface of this wall was created by planned variation of aggregate, cement types and moisture in the concrete. The metal elements were poured in.

Fig. 1.7.3: Steps and surface made from anthracite-colored pressed concrete finished parts

concrete used for visible surfaces is described as exposed concrete. The manufacture of exposed concrete requires concrete with a sluggishly flowing to fluid consistency and a grading curve set accordingly. It is compacted using an internal vibrator. > Fig. 1.7.4

Like natural stone, concrete has great compressive stability. Compressive strength is listed according to the strength class required, meaning that C 20/25 concrete reaches a compressive strength of 20 to 25 N per mm². Concrete that reaches a compressive strength of 55 to 67 N per mm² is described as high-strength concrete. Depending on aggregate, nonreinforced concrete weighs between 2.0 and over 2.6 kg per dm³. > Tab. 1.7.1

Cement

Cement consists of a mixture of ⅔ lime and ¼ clay, fired to the sinter limit. At a temperature of about 1400°C, what is known as Portland cement clinker is created. This is ground down to a fine dust to create Portland cement.

The cement standard EN 197-1 distinguishes 27 cements commonly used in Europe, divided into 5 classes. CEM I describes plain Portland cement. CEM II to V encompass various mixtures of Portland cement with other hydraulic substances, e.g. granulated sand (CEM II / Portland-slag cement).

The setting of cement is an exothermic process that releases warmth. Quick-drying cements with high hydration heats are distinguished from slow-hardening cements with low hydration heats. Slow-hardening cements are used in structural elements with a large mass, as even slight expansion due to heat could lead to cracks. > Fig. 1.7.5 and chapter 2.1 Loadbearing structures and their dimensions

In the autumn and winter months, quick-drying cements are usually preferable, as low ambient temperatures retard the setting process.

Additives and admixtures

Additives are added to concrete in large amounts to alter certain properties such as color or density. They are taken into account in the formula; that is, according to the amount of them in the concrete, more cement must be added. Examples of additives are industrial ashes and dusts or rock flour. These materials serve as (pore) fillers > Fig. 1.7.6

Self-compacting concrete, for instance, contains high levels of rock flour. Other additives are color pigments and trass. These substances often have a hydraulic or latent hydraulic effect, like the cement. This means that they react with the lime in the cement and form cemented stone.

Admixtures are added in small amounts to alter the chemical or physical properties of the concrete. The commonest are retarders (VZ), which extend the processing time. Further admixtures are: plasticizers (BV), superplasticizers (FM), air entrainers (LP), sealants (DM), accelerants (BE), grouting aids (EH) and stabilizers (ST). > Fig. 1.7.7

Strength class	Cement content in kg/m³		Suitable for:
C 12/15	270	standard concrete, X0	nonreinforced concrete
C 20/25	280	concrete by properties	reinforced concrete
C 25/30	300		
C 30/37	≥ 300		

Tab. 1.7.1: Strength classes of concrete

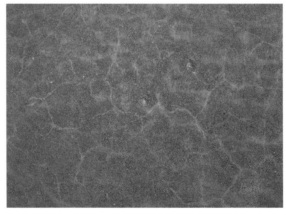

Fig. 1.7.5: Typical shrinkage cracks in colored concrete

Fig. 1.7.4: Cast in-situ garden terrace with embedded found natural stone

Fig. 1.7.6: Reinforced exposed concrete elements: Fillers help to optimize the surface.

Exposure classes

Different stresses on the concrete, e.g. humidity, frost or chemical attack (acids, salt etc.) mean that the composition must be adapted to the site and its conditions. Exposure classes define a particular purpose or site where a concrete can be used. The minimum quality of cement required can be calculated from this. In particular, the cement content, the water/cement value and the concrete needed to cover the reinforcement must be paid close attention to in outside concrete under high stress. > Tab. 1.7.2

The following exposure classes are recognized: XC— reinforcement corrosion due to carbonation, XD—reinforcement corrosion due to chloride, XS—reinforcement corrosion due to seawater, XF—frost attack with or without de-icing agents XA—reinforcement corrosion due to chemical attack, XM—wear and tear, XO—concrete with no risk of attack. An additional number quantifies the intensity of stress: For instance, XS1 means "salt in the air" and XS2 means "submerged in seawater".

Reinforced concrete

The installation of reinforcement significantly improves the static properties of concrete, especially its relatively low tensile strength. As a rule, construction steel is used for this. Reinforced concrete is also described as reinforced concrete. However, in special cases, high-grade steel or various fibers may be used. In theory, any material with good tensile strength and appropriate durability may be used.

For conventional steel reinforcement, concrete steel mats, concrete steel rods and other specially manufactured elements such as baskets are used. The steel is arranged throughout the cross-section of the concrete element so that it reinforces the concrete where high tensile forces exist. The load bearing capacity the structural element is required to have determines the steel areas' dimensions. For structural elements under high stress or relevant to safety these are to be ascertained by a statistician. > Chapter 2.1 Loadbearing structures and their dimensions

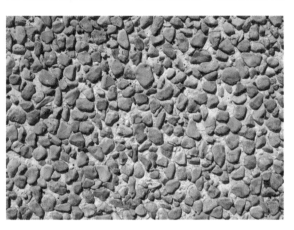

Fig. 1.7.7: No-fines concrete: treated with retarders, the concrete surface sets later than the core concrete. If the fine components are washed out, no-fines concrete is created.

Exposure class	Form of attack	Example / assigned to	Minimum compressive strength class	Minimum cement content kg/m³	Max. water/ cement value
	Environmental conditions				
X0	**no corrosion or attack risk**				
X0	structural elements where environment is nonhostile to concrete	filling concrete, granular sub-base	C 8/10		
XC	**reinforcement corrosion due to carbonation**				
XC1	dry or constantly wet	non-reinforced foundations and no frost; structural elements that are constantly submerged in water	C 12/15	240	0.75
XC2	wet, rarely dry	foundations	C 16/20	240	0.75
XC3	moderate humidity	roofed-in structural elements in contact with outside air, e.g. open halls	C 20/25	260	0.65
XC4	alternating wet and dry	exterior construction with direct exposure to precipitation	C 25/30	280	0.60
XD	**reinforcement corrosion due to chloride, excluding seawater**				
XD1	moderate humidity	e.g. individual garage	C 30/37	300	0.55
XD2	wet, rarely dry	saltwater swimming baths	C 35/47	320	0.50
XD3	Alternating wet, rarely dry	road surfacing	C 35/45	320	0.45
XS	reinforcement corrosion due to chloride from seawater				
XS1	salt in air	outdoor structural elements near the coast	C 30/37	300	0.55
XS2	under water	structural elements in harbors that are continually underwater	C 35/45	320	0.50
XS3	tidal zones, splash zones	quay walls	C 35/45	320	0.45
XF	**frost attack with or without de-icing agents**				
XF1	moderate water saturation without de-icing agents	outdoor structural elements	C 25/30	280	0.60
XF2	moderate water saturation with de-icing agents	routes treated with de-icing salt	C 25/30 (LP) C 35/45	320 300	0.50 0.55
XF3	high water saturation without de-icing agents	horizontal concrete surfaces exposed to precipitation and frost, pools	C 25/30 with air-entraining agent C 35/45	300 320	0.55 0.5
XF4	high water saturation with de-icing agents	Road surfaces exposed to de-icing agents	C 30/37 with air-entraining agent	320	0.5

Tab. 1.7.2: Exposure classes and concrete qualities according to EN 206 and Zement-Merkblatt Betontechnik B9

One disadvantage of steel reinforcement is that relatively high coverage of the steel reinforcements is necessary to protect the steel from corrosion. Rusting steel expands to many times original size. This causes an explosive effect that may cause spalling of the concrete's surface. The minimum of concrete covering the reinforcement should be 2.5 cm, in the case of outdoor weathering and where the reinforced structural elements have a thickness of at least 6–8 cm. With increased chemical attack, or close to the sea, 5.5 cm concrete cover is appropriate. To maintain precise intervals between steel reinforcers and formwork facing and prevent displacement by vibrations, a sufficient number of suitable spacers must be used.

Watertight concrete

WU describes watertight concrete, or concrete with a high resistance to water permeation. This property is due to a granular mixture low in cavities and a low water/cement value. To minimize the intrusion of water through cracks, reinforcement to limit the breadth of cracks is required > Chapter 2.1 Loadbearing structures and their dimensions

Watertight expansion and construction joints are achieved using an appropriate joint tape.

Self-compacting concrete

Self-compacting concrete is concrete with exceptional flow and de-aeration properties, made possible by the development of a new generation of high-performance concrete plasticizers (HBV).

Consistency and viscosity of self-compacting fresh concrete is approximately that of honey. This concrete therefore flows around obstacles and fills cavities properly without further compaction. Exposed concrete surfaces of self-compacting concrete appear extremely homogenous. > Fig. 1.7.9 As this concrete shows a significantly higher flour and fine grain in the grading curve, it can be assumed that the surface will remain homogenous as the

Fig. 1.7.9: Steles made from self-compacting concrete, Memorial to the Murdered Jews of Europe, Berlin

concrete ages and little gravel will be released. As this process is still new, conclusive statements on its ageing process and durability when exposed to the elements are not yet possible.

Fiber and otherwise reinforced concrete

The low tensile strength and ductility (ability to expand and deform) of concrete means that it tends to crack, with the edges tending to spall or break off. In the manufacture of large cast in-situ concrete paving slabs, double-chamfered pieces of steel wire are added to minimize these phenomena. Concrete reinforced in this way is described as steel fiber concrete. Unlike reinforced concrete, where the reinforcing steel is arranged according to where the tensions will be, the steel in steel fiber concrete is distributed evenly throughout the whole cross-section.

Alternative reinforcements such as fibers or high-grade steel are not prone to destructive corrosion and are higher-performance than construction steel, but are also dearer. Due to the reduced need for concrete cover, filigree structures can be created. High-quality surfaces can also be produced. > Fig. 1.7.10

In translucent concrete, optical glass fibers act as reinforcement. As light is carried by the fibers with virtually no loss, differences in brightness and even colors can be distinguished through meter-thick walls. > Fig. 1.7.11

Vacuum concrete

The vacuum process is mainly used for paving slabs. It allows the concrete to be installed with a high water content, making compaction easier. Afterwards, the excess water can be sucked out of the concrete using vacuum mats and vacuum pumps. This process can be used to create an optimal water/cement value. Finally, the fresh concrete is smoothed with a power trowel. By optimizing the concrete's water/cement value, the vacuum process improves proneness to shrinkage cracks, frost resistance and the concrete's final strength.

Fig. 1.7.8: Reinforcement corrosion

Fig. 1.7.10: Fiber concrete:
a) facade panel
b) seating
c) seating elements made from
   glass fiber concrete

Precast concrete units

Industrially produced concrete elements are known as precast concrete or precast concrete units. The basic distinction is between nonreinforced elements, mainly manufactured from pressed concrete, and reinforced exposed concrete elements.

Pressed concrete has a rough surface, allowing purchase (useful for pedestrian surfaces and paving), on which the grains of aggregate are clearly visible. Concretes for paving stones are made using special formulas, attaining extremely high strengths. This means that paving stones do not have to be beveled—that is, the upper visible edge of the stone is not tapered off, but left as a right angle. Non-beveled paving stones are used for road surfaces and car parks, as they reduce the noise made by vehicle tires. In the case of more cost-intensive elements, the visible layer often consists of facing concrete. This is concrete optimized as a visual material, for instance by the addition of color pigments or ornamental crushed stone, and can be reworked mechanically. > Fig. 1.7.12 Other products made from pressed concrete include curbstones, wall elements, corner brackets, steps, palisades and ducts.

Finished concrete parts made from exposed concrete have a distinctive smooth surface, with no visible aggregate grains. To avoid damage to edges caused during processing, transport or use, exposed concrete elements are produced as standard with beveling—nonbeveled and colored exposed concrete parts are a specialized manufacture and can only be obtained from specialized producers.

SURFACE QUALITIES AND SURFACE TREATMENT

The basic color of new "natural" concrete is a warm and dull light-to-middle gray, varying according to the fresh concrete's humidity and cement type and content. The concrete color can be varied considerably by a careful choice of cement and by using appropriate colorants and aggregates. In addition, numerous surface treatment techniques that also affect color are used in industrial manufacture. Blasting, usually using water, quartz sand or steel shot, is the most significant treatment. Fundamentally, this amounts to a premature ageing by deliberately wearing down the cement's surface. > Fig. 1.7.13 Basically, all forms of surface treatment used on natural stone can be used. > Chapter 1.5 Cut stone, Surface properties and treatment

Exposed concrete

Today, exposed concrete is usually produced using non-absorbent formwork. This formwork consists of specially coated wood or artificial panels with many-layered glue laminating, producing absolutely even surfaces with no warp, although this also means that they do not absorb excess water from the concrete. Under certain circumstances, non-absorbent formwork may promote "blushing effect" in the concrete surface.

Fig. 1.7.12: Surface of a terrace paving slab: blasted facing concrete with a diagonal structure

Fig. 1.7.11: Translucent concrete

Fig. 1.7.13: Sandblasted square in the middle of a concrete surface with a natural patina caused by aging

Formwork made from natural wood, on the other hand, has an absorptive effect and takes up water from the fresh concrete. Together with the natural wood structure, concrete formed in this way gives a more living, but also more uniformly colored impression. Fewer pores and "blushes" in the concrete surface are created. > **Fig. 1.7.15**

When using a nonabsorbent formwork, highly standardized concrete processing is necessary, as moisture differences, compaction differences or releasing agent excesses will be visible in the concrete's surface. Even changes in the weather can create differences in surface color.

Exposed concrete surface evaluation criteria are: surface texture and porosity, formwork element transition precision, evenness of color tone, evenness of surface, outer edges and anchor holes. Where the requirements on an exposed concrete surface are high, formwork and formwork systems, releasing agents and concrete formulas must agree precisely. This may involve a trial is being carried out. As the production process is protected from weathering, the surface of exposed precast concrete units can be manufactured with greater precision and perfection than cast in-situ concrete.

Color and surface creation

In construction, concrete color can be changed with the choice of aggregate and cement. White cement in combination with light aggregates such as quartz sand and quartz gravel produces an entirely white concrete. A brown color can be created by using oil-shale cement as a bonding agent.

A broad palette of colors can be achieved by using specialized powdered or liquid concrete paints. However, as with many construction materials exposed to the elements, the color fades over the years, sometimes significantly, especially red and blue tones. A green color is achieved using chrome oxide. Adding cobalt blue results in a blue tone. Iron oxide pigments produce a yellow, red, brown or black color. > **Fig. 1.7.16**

The amount of color added is usually between 1 and 10%. If a greater amount is added, the achievable color effect remains the same. A more intensive impression of color is created if white cement rather than gray is used. In the past, iron powder was sometimes mixed with the concrete to create a rusted patina. A new procedure from Finland makes use of the same principle; the concrete is mixed with copper powder. Depending on the catalyst used, the concrete is colored a lasting blue or green. The color of concrete treated in this way gives a more natural and living impression than conventional colored concrete. Blasting gives concrete parts a coloration and structure similar to that of natural stone, as the amount of aggregate in the visible surface is increased.

The installation of structured stencils made from artificial materials in the formwork (cast in-situ concrete and precast concrete units) allows the concrete surface to be formed without subsequent working. These stencils can be used multiple times, and can also be used to create complex surface structures. > **Fig. 1.7.17** As well as crushed stone aggregate, colored or mirrored mineral glass can be mixed with the concrete as aggregate,

as long as it is alkali-proof. The colored glass effect is only visible after the concrete surface has been ground. > **Fig. 1.7.18**

Photoconcrete

Photoconcrete describes a concrete surface inscribed with visual information. The information—picture or text—cannot be changed once it has been written into the concrete. This process involves a sheet printed with a design in retarders preventing the concrete surface from hardening. This sheet can be installed in the formwork. When in due course the concrete surface is stripped of formwork and washed down, the printed visual information can be seen in the concrete skin's differences in surface composition. The raw, washed-out areas appear darker than the formwork smooth expanses. > **Fig. 1.7.19**

A process for use on already set concrete surfaces involves a partially perforated sheet. The sheet is glued to the concrete surface and acid-washed using a special gel. The effect is largely similar to that of the process mentioned above.

Ground and polished concrete

Ground concrete is known as terrazzo. Ground concrete surfaces can be polished to a high shine if the concrete is of a high quality. It requires high density and strength, achieved through a low water/cement value and painstaking compaction. Any coarse pores are filled with fine mortar and ground or polished again. Several working processes involve successively finer abrasive granules, finishing with special polishing compounds to create a homogenous, highly polished surface. > **Fig. 1.7.20**

JOINING AND MOLDING

Concrete as a construction aid and as a foundation construction material

A significant portion of the concrete used in landscaping, the foundation concrete, is invisible to users. Foundation concrete is processed at natural soil humidity (consistency band C1—as specified for stiff concrete by EN 1045) within the strength class C12/15 (or, in the case of higher requirements, C20/25). Tamping or pressing compacts the concrete at soil humidity sufficiently to hold the inbuilt elements in place.

In processing foundation concrete, a number of basic rules must be observed to avoid constructional faults. These apply to all concrete processing:

1. Foundation concrete is often transported to the construction site as finished concrete and processed on the same day. To ensure that it can be processed over several hours, retarders must be added to the concrete, especially where the ambient temperature is high. Non-processed concrete in which the setting process has already begun can no longer be used.
2. In order to prevent impurities in the concrete caused by substances in the soil, a base course of a neutral material (e.g. gravelly sand) should be provided at footing level, particularly where the soil is highly cohesive.

Fig. 1.7.14: Concrete surfaces:
a) the smoothed concrete surface is uniformly ground in the same direction by strokes with a fine broom
b) ground surface with crushed granite aggregate
c) ground surface with crushed diabase aggregate
d) polished and blasted concrete surface

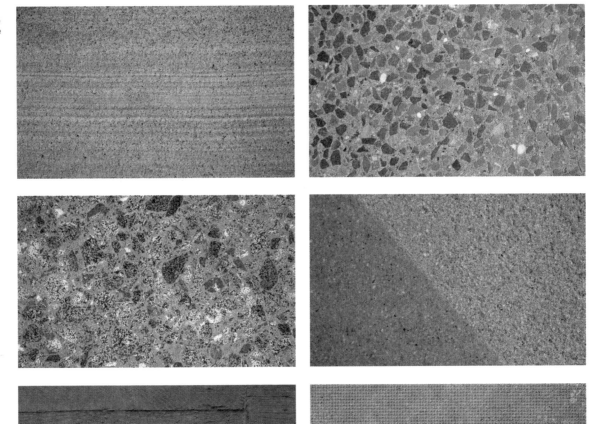

a	b
c	d

Fig. 1.7.15: Exposed concrete surface: natural wood formwork, colored yellow

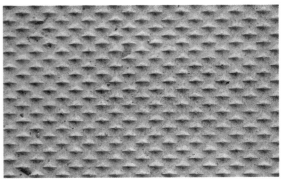

Fig. 1.7.16: Surface of red-colored concrete, where white cement has been used

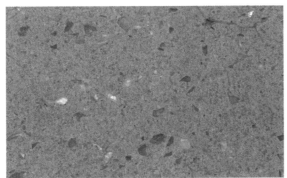

Fig. 1.7.18: Cast in-situ concrete with glass aggregate

a
b
c

Fig. 1.7.17: Surface structures created by a variety of formwork installations: a) screen-print plate, b+c) textured plate

Fig. 1.7.19: Photoconcrete

3. Concrete at soil humidity with a low water content must be protected from drying out. And its position, once installed, should not be changed by agitation or load.
4. Concrete should not be processed at temperatures lower than +5°C, as extensive freezing has a significant effect on strength development. > Fig. 1.7.21

Concrete as a free-form moldable construction material

Cast in-situ concrete can be shaped in any way permitted by formwork, i.e. any form from which the formwork can be detached after hardening. Undercut forms (widening out inside the structural element) can only be produced using "lost formwork". Styrodur or other materials can be used for this, and removed along with the rest of the formwork. Free plastic forms are almost impossible for conventional formwork, as the formwork boards and plates are flat. An alternative to creating free-form objects is milled Styrodur formwork; however, this permits only limited surface quality. > Fig. 1.7.22

Concrete can only really be freely formed using application technology, e.g. sprayed concrete. The reinforcement is bent into the required shape and sprayed with concrete, using special nozzles. The surface created in this way is relatively raw, but can be further processed and structured, or trowelled manually. > Fig. 1.7.23

A further option in free-forming concrete involves stencils. Reusable individual stencils are taken directly from a model using polyurethane elastomeres, detached and provided with a supporting formwork, e.g. one made from concrete. The surface quality achieved is generally higher than with conventional formwork. > Chapter 2.3 Connections

Building with precast concrete units

Finished part construction differs from cast in-situ concrete and its monolithic character. The structure is not cast "in one piece", but made from layers of joined individual elements. These can be connected in different ways. To prevent damage due to heat expansion, it is important to leave sufficient expansion joints between the components. Their arrangement depends on the size of the structure and its design.

Fig. 1.7.21: Corner bracket elements set into a concrete foundation

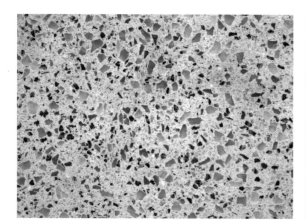

Fig. 1.7.20: Polished white concrete with crushed quartz aggregate

Fig. 1.7.22: Free-formed abutment to a pedestrian bridge in Lyon

Fig. 1.7.23: Application technology— imitation tree trunk in concrete

1.8 METALS

IRON AND STEEL
· Properties, products and surface properties
· Shaping and jointing

ALUMINUM
· Properties and products
· Surface properties
· Shaping and jointing

COPPER
· Properties and products
· Surface properties
· Jointing and shaping

ZINC/TITANIUM ZINC
· Properties and products
· Surface properties
· Jointing and shaping

Astrid Zimmermann

1.8 METALS

Most of the metals commonly used in the building industry do not occur naturally, so extracting and producing them usually involve energy-intensive processes such as smelting.

The different properties of metals concentrate their use in particular fields. Steel is used as a building material because of its specific properties (great strength, great rigidity, low thermal expansion), but other metals are often preferred for their unusual surface properties (e.g. green patina for copper), better formability or greater resistance to corrosion (aluminum, copper). Modern surface treatment processes, improved technical properties and also technological developments like the CNC manufacturing process mean that the possible uses of metallic materials are constantly being expanded. > Fig. 1.8.1

Nonferrous metals can often be shaped more easily than ferrous materials. However, their thermal expansion is greater, and they change shape more after installation, which can be important for construction.
Of the precious metals, only copper is regularly used in building; gold or silver, for example, appear very rarely. Gold leaf in particular is suitable for decoration, and is used to make particular points more attractive.
> Fig. 1.8.2
Almost all metallic materials are not used in pure form, but have their properties optimized by the introduction of alloys. Only a few alloys, the properties of which differ very considerably, can be discussed here.

Fig. 1.8.1: Silhouette-style processing of weatherproof steel using CNC-controlled laser beams: shelter in Landshut by Hild und K Architekten

Fig. 1.8.2: Cavities in an exposed concrete wall decorated with gold leaf

IRON AND STEEL

Iron is the fourth most common element in the earth's crust, with a share of 5% by mass. It is usually present in the form of iron oxide, in iron ores such as hematite or magnetite. Pig iron is extracted by reducing the iron oxides in blast furnaces. Slag is produced as a by-product. The subsequent processes turn pig iron into either cast iron or steel. Steel is made by reducing the carbon content to 2% and less, in a refining or converting process. > Fig. 1.8.3 Steel is highly malleable, while a high carbon content in iron gives it good casting properties.

Iron- and steel-making is a very energy-intensive process. But cast iron and steel are almost 100% recyclable. A large proportion of current production comes from scrap iron or steel, but because of the high demand for steel products the recycling rate is well below 50%.

Properties, products and surface properties

Cast iron

A distinction is drawn between white and black malleable cast iron, cast iron with flake graphite (gray cast iron), and cast iron with nodular graphite (also called spheroidal or ductile cast iron). Cast iron is so brittle that generally it cannot be worked any further, and only chip generating processes, like milling, are possible. White malleable cast iron is an exception here: it can be welded. Cast iron with flake graphite is distinguished from cast iron with nodular graphite by the carbon, which is present as different forms of graphite. The spherical shape of the graphite in spheroidal cast iron gives greater tensile strength, greater failing strain and elastic deformation. Together with high abrasion resistance, this means that spheroidal cast iron is particularly suitable for road-making, where high loads have to be borne. Generally speaking, cast iron is adequately corrosion-resistant in the presence of (drainage) water and de-icing substances.

Cast iron needs to be coated only when the increased presence of specific corrosive agents (in the soil, for example), demand it.

Surface coatings for sewerage covers are usually applied simply to improve the visual effect. It is possible to apply color using a powder coating or dip painting.

Typical molded parts in spheroidal and gray cast iron are shaft covers, covers for street and yard drains, pipe conduits, tree discs, as well as street furniture such as benches or bollards. > Fig. 1.8.4

Steel

Steel contains alloy elements other than carbon. Steel types acquire their different properties from the combination of these alloys and their relative percentages. The general construction steels, which include nonalloy steels and fine grain construction steels, are the steel types most used in steel construction. Here the material properties of nonalloy steels usually provide good value for money. As well as the general construction steels, weatherproof and stainless steels

Fig. 1.8.3: Hot broad strip mill in a steel works

Fig. 1.8.4: Cast-iron drainage gutter

are important in construction, and particularly in use for design purposes. As they are more corrosion-resistant, they offer an important complement to the general construction steels. > Tab. 1.8.1

Another material, concrete steel, is used as the reinforcing elements in the compound material reinforced concrete, in the form or concrete bar steel, or as concrete steel fabric. > Chapter 1.7 Concrete Prestressed concrete uses an appropriate prestressed steel. Cast steel occupies a special place; it is used for the manufacture of special molded parts (e.g. as connecting nodes).

Because of its material properties, steel is suitable for comparatively slender structures. Sectional steel, bar steel, and steel cables can be used for substructures, as well as for visible constructions that contribute a formal element. Sheet steel and steel fabric also make it possible to design areas or cladding. Connecting elements and molded parts are used when fitting together building components made of different materials.

		Name	Standard	Abbreviation acc. to EN 1560	Material number acc. to EN 1560	National/former abbreviations, product names	
Cast iron > 2% carbon	malleable cast	white malleable cast	EN 1562	EN-GJMW-350-4	0.8035	GTW-35 (D)	
		black malleable cast		EN-GJMB-350-10	0.8135	GTS-35-10	
		gray cast iron (cast iron with flake graphite)	EN 1561	EN-GJL-250	EN-JL 1040	GG-25 (D)	
		nodular cast iron (cast iron with nodular graphite)	EN 1563	EN-GJS-400-15	EN-JS 1030	GGG-40 (D)	
				abbreviation acc. to EN 10027-1	material number acc. to EN 10027-2		
Steel max. 2% carbon		cast steel	EN 10340	G200	1.0420	GS 38 (D)	
		concrete steel	EN 10080	B500		BSt 500 (D)	
		unalloyed construction steel	EN 10025-2	S235JR	1.0038	St 37-2 (D), E 24-2 (F), Fe 360 B (I), AE 235 B (E)	
				S355J0	1.0553	St 52-3 U (D), E 36-3 (F), 50 C (GB) Fe 510 C (I), AE 355 C (E)	
		fine grained construction steel max. 0.2% carbon	EN 10025-4	S460M	1.8827	StE 460 TM (D), Fe E 460 KGTM (I)	
		weatherproof construction steel 0.25–0.55% copper, 0.3–1.25% chromium	EN 10025-5	S235J2W P max. 0.04%	1.8961	WTSt 37-3 (D), E 24 W 4 (F), COR-TEN B, Allwesta 360 F, DIWETEN 235	
				S355J2WP P 0.06–0.15%	1.8946	E 36 WA 4 (F), COR-TEN A, Allwesta 510 FP (not approved in D)	
				abbreviation acc. to EN 10088-1			
		stainless steel min. 10.5% chromium, max. 1.2% carbon	EN 10088-1	X5CrNi18-10	1.4301	V2A	2332(S), 304 S 15 (GB), Z 6 CN 18.09 (F), NIROSTA 4301
				X6CrNiTi18-10	1.4541		2337 (S), 321 S 31 (GB), Z 6 CNT 18.10 (F), NIROSTA 4541
				X5CrNiMo17-12-2	1.4401	V4A	2347 (S), 316 S 31 (GB), Z 7 CND 17.02.02 (F), NIROSTA 4401
				X6CrNiMoTi17-12-2	1.4571		2350 (S), 320 S 31 (GB), Z 6 CNDT 17.12 (F), NIROSTA 4571

Tab. 1.8.1: Survey of selected iron and steel materials and their designations

	Sheets and strips	Cored panels, profile end corrugated sheets	Profiles (I, T, U, Z, L and others)	Cavity profiles	Bars	Cables	Wires and wire mesh	Joint elements	Cast parts
Cast iron									x
General construction steel	x	x	x	x	x	x	x	x	x
Weatherproof steel	x	x	x	x	x			not fully available	
Stainless steel	x	x	x	x	x	x	x	x	x
Aluminum	x	x	x	x	x			only rivet	x
Copper or copper alloys	x	x	x	x	x		x	x	x
Zinc / titanium zinc	x	x		tubes					x (fittings)

Tab. 1.8.2: Metal products

Name	Profile shape	Large and small dimensions h x b (x t)	Weight	Notes
Broad-flanged profiles				
broad I-girders (broad-flanged girders)				
HEA (IPBl) light finish		HEA 100 (96 x 100 mm) HEA 1000 (990 x 300 mm)	16.7 kg/m 272.0 kg/m	especially as columns and supports for large loads
HEB (IPB) standard finish		HEB 100 (100 x 100 mm) HEB 1000 (990 x 300 mm)	20.4 kg/m 314.0 kg/m	
HEM (IPBv) reinforced finish		HEM 100 (120 x 106 mm) HEM 1000 (990 x 300 mm)	41.8 kg/m 349.0 kg/m	
semibroad I-girders				
IPE		IPE 80 (80 x 46 mm) IPE 600 (600 x 220 mm)	6.0 kg/m 122.0 kg/m	light, slender profiles for small loads, above all as flexural girders
halved I-girders				
IPET		IPET 80 (40 x 46 mm) IPET 600 (300 x 220 mm)	3.0 kg/m 61.2 kg/m	
U-steel				
UAP		UAP 80 (80 x 45 mm) UAP 300 x 100 (300 x 100 mm)	8.38 kg/m 46.0 kg/m	good for combination in pairs, thus raising loadbearing capacity
UPE		UPE 80 (80 x 50 mm) UPE 400 (400 x 115 mm)	7.9 kg/m 72.2 kg/m	
steel angle				
equilateral		20 x 3 (20 x 20 x 3 mm) 250 x 35 (250 x 250 x 35 mm)	0.88 kg/m 128 kg/m	
nonequilateral		30 x 20 x 3 (30 x 20 x 3 mm) 200 x 150 x 15 (200 x 150 x 15 mm)	1.12 kg/m 39.6 kg/m	
sharp-edged		LS 20 x 3 (20 x 20 x 3 mm) LS 50 x 5 (50 x 50 x 5 mm)	0.87 kg/m 3.73 kg/m	only in small dimensions
T-steel				
sharp-edged		TPS 20 (20 x 20 x 3 mm) TPS 40 (40 x 40 x 5 mm)	0.87 kg/m 2.94 kg/m	only in small dimensions
Z-steel				
round edged		Z 30 (30 x 38 mm) Z 160 (160 x 70 mm)	3.39 kg/m 21.6 kg/m	
Profiles with angled internal surfaces				
narrow I-girders				
I (INP) with parallel flanges		I 80 (80 x 42 mm) I 550 (550 x 200 mm)	5.9 kg/m 166.0 kg/m	
U-steel				
U		U 30 x 15 (30 x 15 mm) U 65 (65 x 42 mm)	1.74 kg/m 7.09 kg/m	less suitable for screw connection because of the angled flange area, more reasonably priced than profiles
UNP		UNP 80 (80 x 45 mm) UNP 400 (400 x 110 mm)	8.64 kg/m 71.8 kg/m	
T-steel				
T		T 30 (30 x 30 mm) T 140 (140 x 140 mm)	1.77 kg/m 31.3 kg/m	
Bar steel				
round steel		6 (Ø 6 mm) 250 (Ø 250 mm)	0.22 kg/m 385 kg/m	for stiffening in skeleton structures, as suspensions and tension bars
square steel		6 (6 x 6 mm) 150 (150 x 150 mm)	0.28 kg/m 177.0 kg/m	
flat steel		5 x 10 (5 x 10 mm) / 5 x 100 (5 x 100 mm) 6 x 150 (6 x 150 mm) / 60 x 150 (60 x 150 mm)	0.39 / 3.93 kg/m 7.06 / 70.7 kg/m	
broad flat steel		5 x 160 (5 x 160 mm) / 80 x 160 (80 x 160 mm) 5 x 1200 (5 x 1200 mm) / 80 x 1200 (80 x 1200 mm)	6.28 / 100 kg/m 47.1 / 754 kg/m	
Cavity profiles				
square cavity profiles		40 (40 x 40 x 3/5 mm) 400 (400 x 400 x 10/16 mm)	3.41 / 5.28 kg/m 122 / 191 kg/m	for post-and-rail structures
rectangular cavity profiles		50 x 30 (50 x 30 x 3/4 mm) 500 x 300 (500 x 300 x 10/20 mm)	3.41 / 4.39 kg/m 122 / 235 kg/m	
circular cavity profiles		33.7 (Ø 33.7 mm x 2.6/4 mm) 1219 (Ø 1219 mm x 10/25 mm)	1.99 / 2.93 kg/m 298 / 736 kg/m	

Tab. 1.8.3: Selection of common steel sections

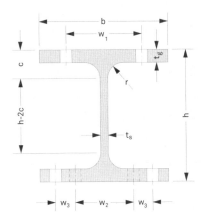

Abbreviation	h	b	t_s	t_g	r	h-2c	A cm²	G kg/m	d¹ (max.)	w¹ w²	w³
HE-B 100	100	100	6	10	12	56	26.0	20.4	13	56	-
HE-B 240	240	240	10	17	21	164	106.0	83.2	25	96	35

Fig.1.8.5: Example extract from a section table: measurements and properties of two wide I-girders: HE-B 100 and 240

Rolled and hollow sections, strip steel, simple and sectional sheets as well as perforated sheets, bars, wire and wire fabrics make up the essential steel product range, along with the jointing and fastening elements. > Tab. 1.8.2 Special products can be made to order, but these are restricted to specialized building jobs on the grounds of cost. Various standards govern the products and their dimensions. Specialist associations and manufacturers offer information about the usual formats, as well as handbooks on sectional steel. Alongside the general dimensions, information about cross-section values, and the size and number of possible drilling formats are also of interest to planners. > Tab. 1.8.3 and fig. 1.8.5

Steel as a ground covering can be extremely slippery. In the open air, especially in areas to which the public has access, care must be taken that the appropriate materials are used, e.g. expanded metals or nonslip coatings. Steels for use in the open air are usually exposed to weathering, so their durability depends considerably on active and passive anticorrosion measures.

General construction steels

General construction steels are steels with only a small proportion of alloy elements (> EN 10020). The properties of nonalloy steels meet most of the demands made by landscape architecture. As far as welding properties are concerned, the JR, J0, J2 and K2 grades are generally adequate (abbreviation at the end of the short type description). Alternative fine-grain construction steels are used only for high-stressed welded structures, e.g. for large buildings and bridge construction.
General construction steels usually have to be protected against corrosion by covering or coating. They tend to rust, which would produce surface changes and destroy the material in the long run. This is caused by an (electro-)chemical reaction on the surface of the steel, which

Fig. 1.8.6: Galvanized component with aperture for ventilation or run-off

intensifies with rising (atmospheric) humidity and as a reaction to impurities in the air and hygroscopic salts (e.g. de-icing salt). > Tab. 1.8.4 It only makes sense to omit protection measures against corrosion for general construction steels if the components are not being installed for the duration, have no loadbearing function, or if materials of the appropriate thickness are provided. The chosen surface treatment will make an essential difference to the appearance of the steel.

Protection against corrosion: A distinction is drawn between active and passive protection against corrosion. Active protection against corrosion includes all the structural measures that can reduce the possibility of exposure to corrosive materials by appropriate surface design. This includes construction methods that prevent water from accumulating (avoiding pockets and other cavities) and make it possible for water to run off quickly, inside the structure and at ground level. Any irregularities on the surface of a component, such as overlapping, sharp edges or corners should be avoided. Measures should be taken against contact corrosion by using different metals and steel types. > Fig. 1.8.7 Active corrosion protection also includes using materials that resistant corrosion because of their alloy components, such as weatherproof and stainless steels.

Passive corrosion protection means applying coverings and coatings to keep corrosive materials away from the surface of the steel. Coverings usually consist of metallic materials, mainly zinc, applied by hot-dip or thermal spray processes. Coatings are created by applying (colored) liquid or powder coatings. A combination of the two processes is called a duplex system. > Tab. 1.8.5 Pure coatings are the least economical corrosion protection process, and should be used only if the structure is to be used for only a few years, or if galvanization is impossible for technical production reasons.

Metallic coverings: the commonest process for applying metallic coverings is hot-dip galvanizing: a distinction is drawn between discontinuous (piece and tube galvanization) and continuous (strip and wire galvanization) processes. In piece galvanization (> EN ISO 1461), individual items are coated with zinc by dipping in a zinc bath. To ensure even coating, and to avoid including air, a sufficient number of holes should be provided for flow or ventilation, and closed cavities or large overlapping areas avoided. > Fig. 1.8.6 In addition, the size of the items is restricted by the size of the bath. The usual dimensions for such baths are lengths of 7 to 17.5 m, widths of 1.3 to 2 m and depths of 1.8 to 3.2 m. Flat components with the same thickness throughout are preferred. Excessively long items can be treated by double dipping up to a certain size. Careful checks should always be carried out to establish whether a hot galvanizing plant with the appropriate facilities is available, to avoid supply bottlenecks and high transport costs.

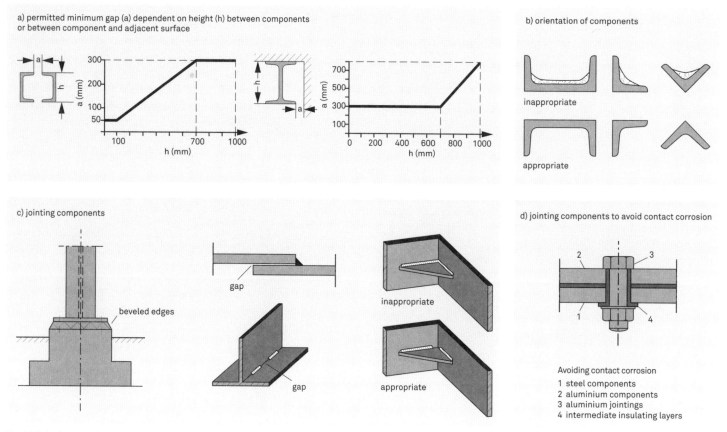

Fig. 1.8.7: Active corrosion protection measures

Corrosion category and corrosion load	Environmental conditions relevant or unalloyed construction steels	Environmental conditions (moisture readings) relevant to weatherproof construction steels	Average corrosion in µm/a			Notes
			zinc	unalloyed construction steel	weatherproof steel * after 10 years	
C1 insignificant	not relevant outdoors		≤ 0.1	≤ 1.3		
C2 slight (low)	atmospheres with low pollution. Mainly rural areas	alternately wet-dry with only brief condensation (indirect wetting with good ventilation)	> 0.1–0.7	1.3–25	0.1–2 0.1–1 *	95% of German territory falls into these categories. Unalloyed steels can be adequately protection by galvanization.
C2/C3		alternately wet-dry with only brief condensation (indirect exposure to moisture with good ventilation) and high sulfur dioxide loads				
C3 moderate (average)	urban and industrial atmosphere, moderate pollution with sulfur dioxide. Coastal areas with low salt load	alternately wet-dry determined by atmosphere only (well ventilated, smooth structures)	> 0.7–2.1	25–50	2–8 1–5 *	
C3/C4		alternately wet-dry with only brief condensation (indirect wetting with good ventilation) and high salt loads				
C4 strong (severe)	industrial and coastal areas with moderate salt loading	alternately wet-dry determined by atmosphere only (well ventilated, smooth structures) and high sulfur dioxide load or high salt load oralternately wet-dry with longer wet periods than those caused by the climate alone (e.g. structure with dirty nests)	> 2.1–4.2	50–80	8–15 5–10 *	unalloyed steels should be protected by duplex system.
C4 / C5		alternately wet-dry with very long wet periods: effectively permanently wet				
C5-I very strong (industry)	industrial areas with high wetness levels and aggressive atmosphere	alternately wet-dry with longer to very long wet periods, high sulfur dioxide load or high salt load	> 4.2–8.4	80–200		unalloyed steels should be protected by duplex system. The use of weatherproof steels is not recommended.
C5-M very strong (sea)	coasts and offshore areas with high salt loading		> 4.2–8.4	80–200		

Tab. 1.8.4: Corrosion categories and corrosion rates for alloy and weatherproof steels

Source: EN ISO 12944-2, Table 1 and Stahl-Informations-Zentrum: Merkblatt 434: Wetterfester Baustahl, Table 3, changed and with additions

Heating up in the zinc bath can cause diminished internal stress and consequent warping of the steel components. To avoid this, care should be taken that components that are to be welded are manufactured to low stress levels. For example, components that are symmetrically welded run a lower risk of warping. In the case of sheet metal constructions, care should be taken about expansion of the metal, and possible warping and denting should be avoided. This can be done in terms of construction by creating shallow surface channels or folds. If components warp, correspondingly morc time will be needed for subsequent fitting on the building site.

As a layer of iron and zinc forms on the surface of the steel in the dipping process, this approach produces relatively robust coatings that can also cope with mechanical loading to a certain extent. However, this protective coating is destroyed by chip generating processes, e.g. drilling, so these should be carried out before the galvanization process whenever possible. Galvanized components can be welded. Any damage to the zinc coating can be corrected on site, but the original level of durability will not be achieved. Steel materials that are suitable for hot-dip galvanizing should be used. Care must be taken in all cases that design is carried out appropriately for hot-dip galvanizing in accordance with EN ISO 14713.

Coating processes: The commonest coating processes are powder coating and painting. Powder painting, in which the colored powder is sprayed on electrostatically and then baked is the more environmentally friendly process, as it is always carried out without solvents. It also produces a more robust coating. But unlike painting, powder coating cannot be repaired on site, and is more inclined to form uneven patches. The surface structures and degrees of gloss in both processes are different, so that they cannot be used in direct juxtaposition to each other. > Fig. 1.8.8 Color shades are chosen on the basis of standardized color systems. The commonest systems are RAL, DB-Eisenglimmer, NCS (Natural Color System) or MCS (Metallic Color System). One fundamental problem with color coatings is the risk of damage through mechanical loading, which can cause cracks, or force the color off. For this reason, restoring and renewing the coating system should by considered at the planning stage, and factored in as a maintenance measure.

Contact corrosion: Contact corrosion is electrochemical corrosion caused when a precious and a nonprecious metal come into contact. The addition of an electrolyte (usually moisture) brings about an anodic reaction in the less precious metal when two metals have a different electronic potential (e.g. weatherproof steel or

Nature of protection	Galvanizing (batch galvanizing acc. to EN ISO 1461)	Preparing the galvanized surface	Coating systems with reference to EN ISO 12944-5			Corrosion category and protection duration acc. EN ISO 12944-1 (short = 2–5 years, average = 5–15 years, long > 15 years)
			basic coating	cover coating including intermediate coating	specified layer thickness	
single coating	without	-	80 µm 2K-EP-liquid coating *	2 x 60 µm 2K-EP- or 2K-PUR-liquid coating *	200 µm	to C3 (long protection) or C4 (short protection)
coating by galvanization	the minimum thickness of the coating according to the thickness of the component is: < 1.5 mm = 45 µm ≥ 1.5 to < 3 mm = 55 µm ≥ 3 to < 6 mm = 70 µm > 6 mm = 85 µm (50–150 µm are usual in practice, greater thicknesses require the selection of suitable steel)	-	-	-	-	C2 or C3 (several decades)
duplex system with powder coating		dusting		80 µm SP- or EP/SP-powder coating	80 µm	to C3 (long protection) or C4 (short protection)
		chromating process for yellow coating				to C4 (long protection)
duplex system with multiple powder coating		dusting	60 µm EP-powder coating	70 µm SP- or EP/SP-powder coating	130 µm	to C3 (long protection) or C4 (average protection)
		chromating process for yellow coating n				to C5-I (average protection) or C5-M (long protection)
duplex system with multiple liquid paint coating		dusting	40 µm 2K-EP-liquid coating *	80 µm 2K-EP- or 2K-PUR-liquid coating*	120 µm	to C4 (average protection) or C5-I (short protection)
		cleaning	40 µm 2K-EP-Komb- or 1K-AY-hydro-liquid coating *	80 µm 2K-EP- or 2K-PUR-liquid coating *	120 µm	to C4 (average protection) or C5-I (short protection)
		cleaning	80 µm 2K-EP- or 1K-AY-hydro-liquid coating *	80 µm 2K-EP- or 2K-PUR-liquid coating *	160 µm	to C4 (long protection) or C5-I (short protection) or C5-M (short protection)
		dusting	80 µm 2K-EP-liquid coating *	2 x 80 µm 2K-EP- or 2K-PUR-liquid coating *	240 µm	to C5-I (average protection) or C5-M (long protection)

Abbreviations for the basic binder materials:
EP   = epoxy resin
EP-Komb = epoxy resin/combinations
SP   = polyester resin
EP/SP   = epoxy polyester resin
PUR   = polyurethane hardening polyester resin

AY   = acrylic resin
AY-Hydro = acrylic resins, water soluble (to reduce solvent emissions in liquid paint processes)
PVC   = vinyl chloride co-polymers

* dual-component (2K) coating materials are more stable than single-component (1K) coating materials

Tab. 1.8.5: Specimen illustration of some coverings and coatings

Fig. 1.8.8 Color coating on steel sheets

Weatherproof construction steel

Weatherproof construction steel is high-grade steel with a minimal addition of alloys. It differs from nonalloy construction steels because chromium and copper have been added as alloy elements. Working with phosphorus, these will form a barrier layer on the surface of the material that will adhere relatively firmly and provide a good seal. It prevents corrosive materials from penetrating to the surface of the metal, thus inhibiting the corrosion process (by about half in comparison with nonalloy steel).

This coating contributes to the characteristic appearance of the metal—its rust-red coloring. It is only after about ten years that the color can be considered relatively stable. Furthermore, the layer builds up in different ways according to the weather conditions and the extent to which the component is exposed. In normal cases, the color of weatherproof steel changes from light orange at the beginning via dark orange and reddish brown, until it finally takes on a dark brown to violet tinge. > Fig. 1.8.9

stainless steel in contact with galvanized steel). If it is not possible to avoid combining precious and nonprecious metals, then a nonconductive divider, such as plastic washers, should be used. > Fig. 1.8.7 and tab. 1.8.6

The following points should be considered in general construction steels are to be used appropriately:

· ensure that there are sufficient protective layers to meet the required life of the treated metal and to suit (C2–C5) the environmental conditions > Tab. 1.8.4
· apply structural protection against corrosion
· avoid contact corrosion
· make provision for maintaining or renewing a painted coating
· provide inadequate steel components with durable protection against corrosion or use thicker material

One essential requirement for the formation of the protective layer is an air humidity of at least 65% and a regular shift from moist to dry. If these conditions are not fulfilled, it is impossible for an even protective coating to form. If the conditions are permanently moist, the steel will rust like a nonalloy steel. But in areas with little rain and low humidity there is little material damage, as very little or no rust is formed. In such cases, the typical surface quality does not appear, or appears only in some parts of the structure.

Weatherproof steels differ little in their mechanical properties from nonalloy construction steels.

		Material with small area / jointing elements					contact with other materials
		weatherproof steel	stainless steel	zinc / galvanized steel	aluminum	copper	
Large areas of material	weatherproof steel	+ (limited availability of jointing materials)	o tolerable	o only with coating if directly exposed to wetting	o limited use with indirect wetting	– limited use with indirect wetting	coat with bitumen if in contact with ground
	stainless steel	–	+	–	o / –	+	use special qualities for ground contact
	zinc / galvanized steel	–	+	+	+	o	
	aluminum	–	+	o	+	o / –	avoid contact with wet concrete, cement mortar and lime mortar or use insulating paint
	copper	–	+	–	–	+	
key: + good o uncertain - bad							

Tab. 1.8.6: Compatibility between different metals on exposure to atmosphere

Source: Informationsstelle Edelstahl Rostfrei: Merkblatt 829, Tab. 7; changed and with additions

a-b

c-d

e-f

g

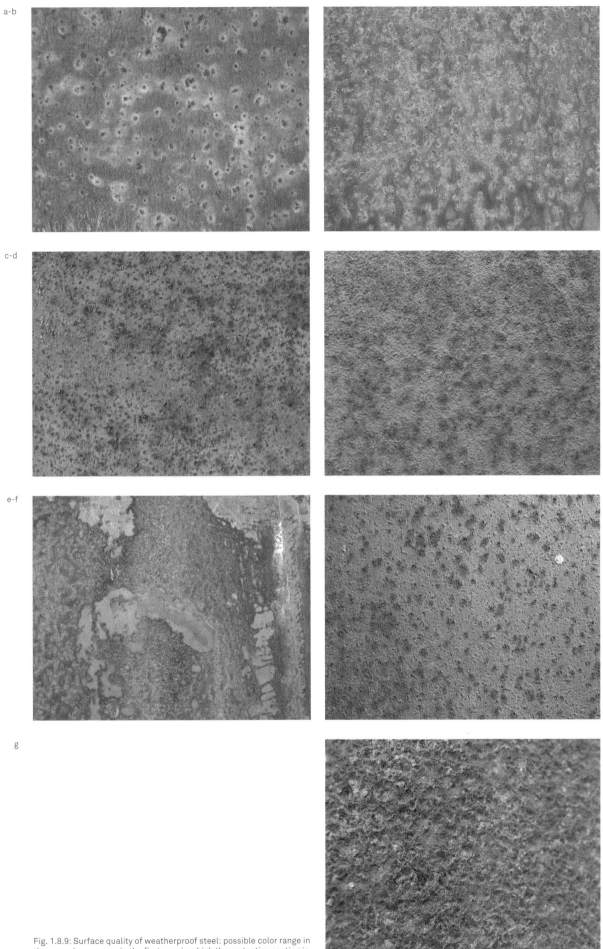

Fig. 1.8.9: Surface quality of weatherproof steel: possible color range in
the corrosion process in the first year in which the protective coating is
forming (a) to the final appearance of the structure (g)

EN 10025-5 divides them into two main groups, characterized by a variation in phosphorus content. The increased phosphorus content creates a stronger protective layer, and ensures that the orange color will last for longer. (In Germany this is not permitted under DASt-Richtlinie 007 or Bauregelliste A.)

It is possible to apply color coatings to weatherproof steels. This can increase the durability of the material. Using weatherproof steel in a manner appropriate to the material means:

· avoiding structural details that cause moisture to accumulate
· ensuring rapid water drainage at ground level > **Fig. 1.8.10** or avoid contact with the ground completely
· not permitting capillary formation through overlapping joints; welded seams are to be preferred
· installing to a maximum of corrosion category C4 > **Tab. 1.8.4**
· keeping vegetation away from the structure
· avoiding the build-up of dirt in adjacent areas or on adjacent components caused when rusty water drains off
· avoiding contact corrosion
· adapting the thickness of the material to local conditions
· it is possible to paint the components with bitumen on invisible sides or when the structure is in contact with the ground

If an even surface color is particularly desirable, care should also be taken that:

· wetting is even and there is no contact with the ground

Fig. 1.8.10: Water drainage channel at the foot of a wall clad with weatherproof steel

Fig. 1.8.11: Rolling residue, as here on a heavy plate, can be prevented by blasting the surface.

· steel with a blasted surface is used (appropriate material can be ordered from the factory) or remove marks left by assembly by subsequent blasting > **Fig. 1.8.11**
· precorroded material is used that is already light orange in color as a result of treatment with a solution containing hydrochloric acid (watch delivery times!)

If it is not possible to use such steels appropriately, the use of nonalloy construction steels should be considered as an alternative on grounds of cost. This applies particularly if the building components do not have an essential loadbearing function or if materials of an appropriate thickness can be used.

Stainless steels

The salient characteristic of stainless steels is their excellent corrosion resistance. Because of the alloys present in it, the steel forms a chromium-rich oxide layer on the surface that reforms even after damage, so no further protection against corrosion is needed. The austenitic chromium-nickel steels, with a chromium content of at least 16% and at least 8% nickel can be used outdoors. The further addition of molybdenum as an alloy increases corrosion resistance even more for some steel types, so that they will function adequately in an industrial atmosphere or near the coast (including materials 1.4401 and 1.4571).

Stainless steels are easy to reshape, but a greater degree of force is required than for nonalloy steels.

Stainless steel products leave the factory with a surface that can be complemented with other surface finishes (according to EN 10088-2 or 10088-4). A whole variety of finishes can be delivered, according to requirements and the desired visual effect for the surface. Smooth surfaces are less susceptible to corrosion. Electrolytic coloring is also an option. Here a transparent film is applied to the surface by the electrochemical treatment, and according to the thickness of the layer this creates color effects in blue, purple, red, green, gold or black. > **Fig. 1.8.12** Surface damage should be avoided. It is also possible to introduce color by using a powder coating rather than electrolytic coloring, but this procedure is rarely used.

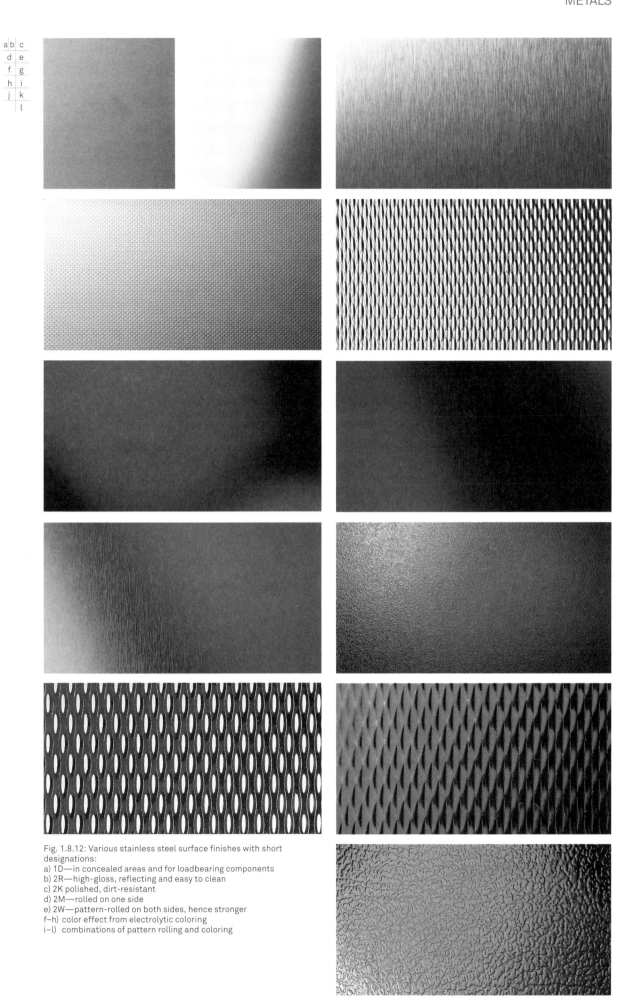

Fig. 1.8.12: Various stainless steel surface finishes with short designations:
a) 1D—in concealed areas and for loadbearing components
b) 2R—high-gloss, reflecting and easy to clean
c) 2K polished, dirt-resistant
d) 2M—rolled on one side
e) 2W—pattern-rolled on both sides, hence stronger
f–h) color effect from electrolytic coloring
i–l) combinations of pattern rolling and coloring

Steel typematerial no.	Situation											
	country			town			industry			near sea		
	N	M	H	N	M	H	N	M	H	N	M	H
1.4301 1.4541	+	+	+	+	+	(+)	(+)	(+)	−	+	(+)	−
1.4401 1.4571	X	X	X	X	+	+	+	+	(+)	+	+	(+)

N = lowest corrosion load in the given situation (e.g. low temperature and low air humidity)

M = average corrosion load in the given situation

H = high corrosion load in the given situation (e.g. persistently high air humidity, high ambient temperatures, especially aggressive air pollution)

X = fundamentally meets requirements, but cheaper steel could be adequate

+ = probably the best choice of material in terms of corrosion resistance and cost

(+) = adequate behavior as long as certain precautions are taken; smooth surfaces and regular cleaning and particularly

− = severe corrosion anticipated

Tab. 1.8.7: Stainless steels for different locations

Source: Informationsstelle Edelstahl Rostfrei: Merkblatt 828, extract from Table 2

Using stainless steel in a manner appropriate to the material means:

· choosing the steel type appropriate to the job and the surroundings > Tab. 1.8.7
· avoiding structural details that cause moisture to accumulate
· avoiding contact corrosion
· avoiding (clean where necessary) film rust deposits (other ferrous particles caused by cutting, grinding and welding), as these reduce corrosion resistance
· carrying out maintenance surface cleaning, especially for structural components exposed to rain

Shaping and jointing

Shaping

Most steel products have to be further processed for use for a particular purpose, by reshaping, separating or drilling. So steel tubes for handrails of steel strips for curved paths or flowerbed edging can be bent into shape. Curved large forms can be prefabricated at the factory using special machines. > Fig. 1.8.13 Bent or beveled edges and folds are other shaping possibilities. If steels are to be reshaped cold this must be pointed out when ordering/tendering, as appropriate grades have to be used.

Chip generating procedures include milling, drilling and sawing. This means that the steel products will acquire their final dimensions and where appropriate be prepared for the chosen jointing technique. Manufacturers offer a particular grade of steel for laser cutting.

Forging steel is a special (craft) process in which the material acquires a different shape from hammering or pressing tools, when the material is hot or cold, according to requirements. The starting materials are usually round, squared or flat steels. > Fig. 1.8.14

Cast iron, unlike steel, is very suitable for pouring, and is thus used particularly for making folded parts. Thus further working is possible only to a limited extent. Only chip generating processes, such as milling, are possible.

Jointing

For jointing a distinction is drawn between permanent and nonpermanent joints. Nonpermanent joints make rapid assembly on site possible, and are thus also good for maintenance and repair work.

Screwing is a nonpermanent, point connection between two or more structural components. It usually involves a screw, a washer and a nut. Swinging or moving parts are additionally secured (check nut, lock washer, cotter pin) on the nut side.

Pegging means that two components are fitted precisely one inside the other. Pegged joints make sense if smaller components than originally desired have

Fig. 1.8.14: Forged railing

Fig. 1.8.13: Large shapes created mechanically in the factory: Allerpark in Wolfsburg

Fig. 1.8.15: Steel joints:
a) pegged
b) screw joint
c) welded seam

a | b | c

Fig. 1.8.16: Aluminum rooftop:
a) extruded part on a bicycle
shelter
b) edging system for lawn and
path borders

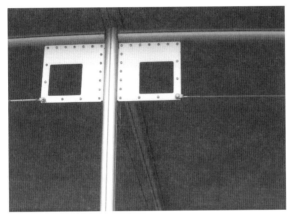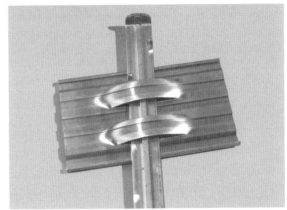

a | b

to be devised for reasons of transport or production.
> Fig. 1.8.15

Permanent connections offer more protection in public spaces against undesirable demolition. But they can make repairs and maintenance more difficult.

Welding is one of the most important processes. Most of the normal fusion and resistance welding processes can be carried out on nonalloy, weatherproof and stainless steels. The particular features of the individual steel grades should be noted. Coatings should ideally be applied after welding. > Fig. 1.8.15

Permanent connections can also be created by riveting. The classical process using a full rivet is now used almost exclusively for repairs, as it is relatively expensive, time-consuming and noisy. The less elaborate process using a blind rivet, where the work is done from one side only, is used to joint thin metal sheets, for example.

Gluing steel is becoming increasingly important. This avoids the negative side-effects of screwing or welding, including weakening the basic material or visual impairment. The result is a flat, flush joint, though its thermal resistance is low. Gluing systems are constantly being improved, so they will be better suited even to outdoor use in future.

ALUMINUM

Properties and products

Aluminum has a share of about 8% of the earth's crust, so appears even more copiously than iron. But a great deal more energy is needed to extract and process it, which makes it more expensive. Some of these higher costs are compensated for by the material's long life and the fact that it needs no maintenance. Aluminum is also highly recyclable: the process requires only 5% of the energy originally used. It can be shaped almost at will, has a high degree of resistance to corrosion, and weighs very little. These reasons are very often cited when arguing in its favor against other metals. Aluminum is highly suitable for structural design, and is frequently used in combination with glass for canopies, small structures and greenhouses.

After the manufacturing process, a distinction is drawn between extruded profiles such as bars and rods, solid and hollow sections, and also precision sections and rolled products such as strips and sheets, including wall cladding panels, rooftop sheets and cladding. A large number of prefabricated elements are also supplied for open-air use, including lighting masts, bollards handrails, plant tubs, tree grilles and enclosure systems and frames for climbing plants. Other products include molded parts in cast aluminum such as door and window fittings or parts. > Fig. 1.8.16

Surface properties

Aluminum builds up almost no form of durable protective layer on its surface that would protect the material from corrosion. This can be produced artificially by electrolytic oxidation, which makes greater layer thicknesses possible, and increases resistance to corrosion. Grinding, brushing or polishing can produce various decorative surface effects.

Electrolytic coloring or color anodization can produce shades from silver gray via bronze color to dark gray and black. As an alternative, the porous anodized layer can be colored adsorptively.

Painting and powder coating are other common processes for coloring aluminum. The preferred approach for aluminum strips is to use a coil-coating process in special plants.

Shaping and jointing

As the material can be shaped so easily, it is possible to use chip-generating techniques, and also to reshape sheets in particular by bending, and folding edges. All the usual jointing techniques such as screwing, riveting, welding, gluing and pegging can be used. Special processes are needed for welding. As the material is so easy to shape, folded joints can also be used for aluminum.

COPPER

Properties and products

Copper as a material manufactured from copper ore resists corrosion well and is easy to shape. It has a characteristic green patina. The most common copper alloys are the copper-tin alloys (bronze) and wrought copper alloys, better known as brass. > **Fig. 1.8.17** Brass and bronze are stronger and harder than copper. They resist corrosion very well, and bronze resists even seawater. Brass is very easy to shape, while bronze is not so malleable, and is used above all as a casting material.

Copper is used mainly for roof coverings and gutters, as wall cladding, and for furnishings and jointing elements. Like brass, copper has a bactericidal effect. Sections, sheets, strips, rods, tubes, wires and jointing elements are produced for the building industry.
Germany covers about 50% of its copper requirements from recycling.

Surface properties

Oxidation will produce a dark-brown shade even after a year in untreated copper. After about eight or more years (dependent on the degree of air pollution), this changes into a light green patina made up of basic copper salts. Patina may not form or may form more slowly on steep to vertical sides, sides that do not face the prevailing wind and in rural atmospheres.
Copper sheets and strips in particular can be supplied with treated surfaces. In addition to this, special alloys can produce a material that retains its golden-brown

coloring permanently. Tin coatings create a permanent matt gray shade. > **Fig. 1.8.18**
Brass, according to the particular alloy, takes on a golden-red to light yellow coloring, bronze a salmon pink to greenish yellow hue.
The surface of all the materials can be processed for decorative purposes by grinding, blasting and polishing.

Jointing and shaping

Chipless processes (e.g. rolling, pressing, stamping or bending) can all be used for copper, in the case of bronze they have to be cold processes. Chip-generating processes, are less useful, with brass having better properties here.
Joints are produced by screwing, folding, riveting or soldering. Brass and copper can be welded to a limited extent. All the common welding methods can be used for the de-oxidized, oxygen-free copper that is usually deployed in the building industry.

ZINC/TITANIUM ZINC

Properties and products

Zinc's high levels of weather resistance are exploited when galvanizing steel structural elements, but they also make it interesting to contemplate using the material directly, especially for cladding and drainage facilities. But as zinc is so brittle, it is used mainly as a zinc alloy, usually as titanium zinc. Titanium zinc is sufficiently corrosion-resistant, but if it is exposed to moisture over a long period without adequate ventilation it can be subject to corrosion. Strips, sheets and tubes are manufactured in zinc alloy form. These are used in the field of roof covering, and as a covering sheet for upstands or posts. Construction zinc has a recycling rate of up to 95%.

Surface properties

The commercially available zinc alloys form a matt, grayish blue patina if exposed to the atmosphere. Special surface treatment processes can also create shades of gray to anthracite.

Jointing and shaping

Zinc alloys can be turned up at the edges, bent, rounded and folded. Structural components can be jointed by soft soldering. Titanium zinc is also suitable for welding.

Fig. 1.8.17: Brass fountain on the KPM site, Berlin (Topotek 1 practice)

Fig. 1.8.19: Zinc coping

Fig. 1.8.18:
a) Copper sheet with special alloy, making a permanent golden shade possible: temporary pavilion of the Münster 2007 sculpture projects (modulorbeat practice)
b) Copper panels with typical coloring (prepatinated copper sheet)

 a b

1.9 OTHER BUILDING MATERIALS

PLASTICS
- Composition, properties and products
- Surface qualities
- Shaping and jointing

BITUMEN AND ASPHALT
- Composition, properties and products
- Surface qualities
- Forming and jointing

GLASS
- Composition, properties, products
- Surface qualities and treatment
- Forming and jointing

Astrid Zimmermann

1.9 OTHER BUILDING MATERIALS

PLASTICS

Composition, properties and products

The special properties of plastics are the almost limitless ways in which they can be shaped, their resistance to weathering and chemicals, their low ability to absorb water, their low density and the possibility of adding color and creating transparent building materials. Most plastics are based on carbonaceous, reactive monomers bonded by chemical synthesis to form macronuclear compounds: polymers. The source materials for synthetic plastic production are derived mainly from crude oil. Natural polymers, such as natural rubber (latex) or cellulose form the basis for semisynthetic plastics.

Plastics with widely differing properties, particularly in terms of their elasticity and plasticity, can be produced by using different methods of synthesis and by adding other chemical elements. Generally speaking, the mechanical properties of plastics are governed by the temperature and duration of the stress applied. Many tend to form tension cracks if subjected to long periods of tensile load (e.g. polystyrene, polyethylene or polycarbonate), and at low temperatures they tend to become brittle. This is even more likely as a result of persistent exposure to weathering. So plastics intended for outdoor use must have the appropriate properties.

It is technically possible to reuse plastics. Homogenous waste is a prerequisite for material recycling, in which new products are produced by treating the plastics. Material recycling is not usually possible for compound plastics and plastics that cannot be melted (elastomers, duroplast).

The alternative is the possibility of raw material recycling, where the plastics are reduced to gases and oils by breaking down and reconstructing the molecular compounds, and can then be used for various industrial production processes. They can also be incinerated to produce energy.

A distinction is made between thermoplastics, duroplastics and elastomers, according to the degree of molecular cross-linking and the resulting properties.

Thermoplastics (also known as plastomers) are based on unlinked polymers. Their molecular chains are held in position by intermolecular forces. These become mobile when warmed, meaning that these substances melt easily. Within a certain temperature range, they can be easily shaped or welded. The substance can be cooled or reheated any number of times as long as it is not overheated, which would cause the material to disintegrate. The material can also be made more workable using chemical substances (e.g. organic solvents). Depending on their composition, thermoplastics may be soft or hard at the point of use. They are predominantly used in landscape architecture as prefabricated parts, tiles, cables and as geoplastics. > **Tab. 1.9.1**
Geoplastics is a term meaning films, fleeces or woven matting used for sealing and root barrier sheets, filtration and drainage layers and building protection and erosion control mats. Woven plastic and plastic canopies are also used as solar arrays and protection from rain. These plastics are easily moldable, allowing the creation of very different prefabricated parts. Very thin walls are also possible, allowing thin-walled tubes, tiles or seats for chairs to be produced. Due to the low risk of breakage, plastic tiles can also be used as an

a | b

Fig. 1.9.1:
a) Epoxy resin-sand mixture forming larger than life animal tracks at the BUGA Munich in 2005
b) An experiment with colored epoxy resin as a jointing material

Name / abbreviation		Properties, notes	Selected products and areas of use
thermoplastics			
polycarbonate	PC	completely transparent, impact resistant, flameproof, outdoors only with addition UV protection, can be glued, machining possible	stay bridges and corrugated sheets
polyethylene	PE	milky to opaque, good resistance, impact resistant even when cold, inclined to form tension cracks, resistant to oil, bitumen and chemicals, can be welded, machining possible within limits	
· soft	PE-LD	very flexible very adaptable in sheet form	sealing foil and other geoplastics, (fabric) tarpaulins, light piping
· hard	PE-HD	more robust than PE-LD, particularly durable: type "PE 100"	drainage, seepage, pressure and sewage pipes, sealing foils at tips, molded parts
polypropylene	PP	weakly transparent to opaque, particularly heat-resistant, can be welded, well suited to machining	pressure and outlet pipes, high temperature pipes (HT), panels, cables, molded parts, geoplastics
polymethyl methacrylate	PMMA	very translucent, transparent or dense, resistant to light and weathering, can be polished, welded and glued, machining possible, splinter-proof	sheets ("acrylic glass," familiar trade name > PLEXIGLAS®), wall and floor coatings
polystyrene foam · expanded · extruded	EPS XPS	not UV-resistant, insulating effect	insulating panels (frost protection for road building) and drainage panels, recycled and pulverized for soil improvement
polyvinylchloride	PVC	can be supplied glass-clear, transparent or with dense color, resistant to chemicals, largely not compatible with bitumen or polystyrene, can be welded, glued, and machined	
· soft PVC	PVC-P	soft/rubbery	geoplastics (esp. sealing foils), tarpaulins, joint tapes, molded part (e.g. play equipment)
· hard PVC	PVC-U	hard, more weather resistant than PVC-P, tension cracks can form	drainage and seepage pipes, pressure and sewage pipes (to max. 60/40°C), panels, molded parts
ethylene-tetrafluorethylene	ETFE	light-fast, noncombustible, almost self-cleaning	(translucent) foils
flexible polyolefines	FPO (TPO)	dimensionally stable, resistant to weathering and aging, highly workable, tear-proof, mechanically robust, compatible with bitumen and polystyrene	sealing foils
thermosets			
epoxy resins	EP	hardened: glassy and hard, pressure- and friction-proof, resistant to chemicals and moisture, excellent adhesion with almost all materials, good workability when hardened	adhesives, binding agents, reaction resins for coating, casting resin
unsaturated polyester resins	UP	hardened: glassy and hard, well-balanced mechanical and chemical properties, easy to work, stable in shape	binding agents, paints, UP fiber geoplastics
polyurethane resins	PUR	hardened: glassy and hard, slight yellowing with time, very tough and good UV resistance, good workability when hardened	binding agents, sealants, coatings, paints, to bond loose stones / granulate
elastomers			
natural rubber	NR	little UV and weathering resistance	tires, balloons, sealing
ethyl-propylene-diene rubber	EPDM	highly resistant to UV and weathering, temperature stable to −45°C and 120°C, adaptable and highly flexible even when cold, resistant to chemicals, not resistant to mineral oil, bitumen compatible to a limited extent, can be glued	sealing foils, granulate (also recycling granulate) for floor coverings
styrene-butadiene rubber	SBR	black, high abrasion resistance, adequately weatherproof, low elasticity, reasonably priced	ties, conveyor belts, sealing, rubber mats
polyurethane rubber	PUR	mechanically strong, resistant to oil and ozone	sealants
chloro-butadiene rubber	CR	resistant to chemicals, oil and ozone	adhesive, cable cladding, conveyor belts
silicone / silicone rubber	SI/SIR	transparent, water repellent, very temperature resistant, (approx. to -60°C and 200°C or higher)	coatings, sealants
PUR-bound rubber granulates		elastic, weather resistant	elastic layers for floor coverings/artificial grass
glass-fiber—reinforced rubber (GFK)—"fiberglass"			
fiberglass—reinforced polyester resin	UP-GF	holds shape, resistant to weathering, temperature and chemicals, can be machined with special tools	pools, pipes, corrugated, flat and formwork panels, pipes (for special requirements), drainage gutters and inlet boxes, molded parts, freely designed shapes
fiberglass—reinforced epoxy resin	EP-GF		

Tab. 1.9.1: Range of plastics, their properties and use

	a	
b	c	d
	e	f
g		h

Fig. 1.9.2: Thermoplastics:
a) PVC covers
b) cable conduits made from PE-HD
c) seepage pipe made from PVC-U
d) Geoplastic: fleece combined with geogrid to improve the soil's loadbearing capacity
e) acrylic glass wall
f) molded chairs
g) crates made from PEHD stacked to form a wall
h) ETFE sheet, Allianz Arena Munich

alternative to glass, e.g. in dividing walls or in canopies. > **Fig. 1.9.4**

Thermoplastics can be easily recycled as functional material. Through the production of recycled plastic granules or the direct melting down of plastic waste, secondary raw materials can be derived for use in new products such as lawn grids (PE-HD recycled plastics), drainage channels (mixed plastics) and seat moldings for benches. Duroplastics (also known as duromers or artificial resins) have molecules with close-meshed cross-links. These are created during the manufacture process by a chemical reaction in the still moldable, i.e. freely flowing primary products (mainly consisting of resins and hardeners). After this the plastic substance hardens and cannot be altered—only surface working is possible. At the point of use, duromers are hard. Only a few types show soft elastic behavior due to somewhat widely meshed cross-linking. Duroplastics' resistance to high temperatures offsets a certain brittleness. They are mainly used as bonding agents and glues and in coating materials and resin varnishes. In landscape architecture, duroplasts are used as bonding agents in elastic floor surfacing and composite fiber materials, or to stabilize stone aggregates. In fixing technology, they are one of the components of reaction resin mortar (compound dowel). > **Chapter 2.3 Connections** They are also used to produce watertight joint seals. > **Fig. 1.9.1b** Duromers in common use include epoxy resins, polyester resins and polyurethane resins. > **Tab. 1.9.1**

Epoxy resins' adjustable drying time, adaptable to different temperatures and humidities, their low shrinkage during hardening and their good mechanical properties after hardening are ideal for usage outdoors. On the other hand, polyurethane resins have better weathering and UV resistance.

Unhardened artificial resins are usually irritant or caustic, and their fumes or grinding dust may be allergenic. Possibilities for recycling duromer plastics are limited, especially where it is part of a composite with other substances and separation is difficult. As well as energy produced through incineration, regranulate derived from particle recycling can be added to new products in small amounts.

Natural and synthetic latex are elastomers. These include ethyl propylene diene latex, styrene butadiene latex and polyurethane latex. Their distinguishing feature is the wide-meshed chemical cross-linking of their macromolecules. These cross-links permit the material to expand at use temperature. It returns to its original state once the force causing this effect is removed. This is also described as rubber-elastic behavior. Elastomers are almost or entirely impossible to melt. Most synthetic elastomers have a higher resistance to abrasion and a better resistance to heat, ozone and UV than natural latex. In landscape architecture, because of their elastic composition, elastomers are largely used to surface sport and play areas, as fall protection and building protection mats, as elements of play apparatus and as a sealing and jointing material. EDPM is also used to make sealing sheets. These are more durable, more elastic and workable at lower temperatures than thermoplastic sheets. > **Fig. 1.9.3 and tab. 1.9.1**

Elastomers have limited recycling possibilities. They can only be reused when ground down into granulates. Recycled rubber granulates, usually bonded with

a | b
c | d

Fig. 1.9.3: Elastomers:
a) nonbonded EPDM granulate
b) PUR bonded EPDM granulate
c) play area made from rubber mats
d) nonslip rubber surface on wood boards

Fig. 1.9.4: Composite plastics:
a) PUR-bonded EPDM surface
b) wall cladding, flat tiles of
   UP-GF
c) wall cladding, corrugated tiles
   of UP-GF
d) canopy, flat tiles of UP-GF
e) roof construction of UP-GF-
   moldings, Expo 02 in Yverdon-
   les-Bains, Switzerland

a	b
c	e
d	

a	b

Fig. 1.9.5: Color deviation between
core molding and surface layer:
bench seat before and after
mechanical damage

polyurethane resin, are processed into building protection mats, elastic layers for beneath sports surfaces or, mixed with primary grade EDPM granulate, as installed surface layers.

Silicones have the same properties as elastomeres. However, unlike carbon-based plastics, they are made from inorganic (semiorganic) silicon-oxygen bonding. Silicones are extremely water-repellant and weather-resistant. They are used in joint sealing substances and as an element in coatings.

Fiber and particle composite plastics: When a matrix, usually a duroplast, and a fibrous material or material consisting of small granules are mixed, a composite plastic is created. For instance, EDPM granulates are mixed with polyurethane resin (PUR) as a bonding agent to produce elastic sport and play area surfaces. Mixing and installation usually take place onsite, but prefabricated tiles are also available. > **Fig. 1.9.4**

Fiber-reinforced plastics are utilized when high specifications for rigidity, strength and maintaining of shape are involved. This makes plastic loadbearing construction elements possible. Artificial, glass or other fibers are the basis for fiber-reinforced plastics. Glass-fiber-reinforced plastics are often used in construction. While mechanical properties are determined by the fibers and their positions in relation to each other (directional or nondirectional), other properties are dictated by the matrix used. For materials used in construction, duroplastics are normally used, due to their high heat resistance, durability, good adhesive properties and very good surface qualities. Molded elements such as containers for ponds, tiles, moldings or pipes as well as individually shaped forms are produced from glass-fiber-reinforced plastics. > **Fig. 1.9.4**

Surface qualities

Generally speaking, plastics are easy to color. Depending on pigmentation, colors are likely to change over the course of time. White and black pigmentations ensure the most durable coloration. In transparent plastics, such as polycarbonate and polyvinyl chloride, yellowing may take place over the course of time.

Many plastics have a surface that is smooth before polishing. Others can be polished.

Secondary plastics are often given a coating of new acrylic plastic, which is particularly UV-resistant and colorfast, to create better surface quality. If the moldings are cut or damaged, there may be color deviations between the core substance and the coating. > **Fig. 1.9.5**

Many plastic surfaces become electrostatically charged easily, which can mean they readily become dirty. They may be antistatically equipped to combat this.

Shaping and jointing

Thermoplastic finished parts, fiber-reinforced plastics and elastomers are produced in factories. Films or fleeces can be positioned or molded onsite. For freeform construction elements made from fiber-reinforced plastic, negative molds are created. The reactive resin and the fiber substances are then applied in layers.

Most thermoplastic substances can be welded. Only thermoplastics of the same type can be bonded with each other. Where possible, plastic sheets are prefabricated in the factory. This increases the quality and thereby the durability of the seams, and speeds up the construction process. The alternative to welding is adhesion using seam tapes. Pipes are joined by means of flanges or plug-in sleeves. Alternatively, adhesive sleeve connections may be used. Tiles can be joined linearly or at points using bolt and snap-in connections. > **Fig. 1.9.6**

In some cases there may be incompatibility between plastics or where a plastic is in contact with another substance, for instance between soft PVC and bitumens or polystyrene. In these cases, neutralizing fleeces or dividing agents should be used.

BITUMEN AND ASPHALT

Composition, properties and products

Bitumen is derived from distilled suitable (heavy) crude oils. In the further stages of the process, it is optimized for the intended area of use. It is almost insoluble in water, and is therefore a good waterproofing substance. Due to its good adhesive and thermoplastic properties it can also be used as a bonding agent in the production of asphalt. Bitumen also occurs as a natural raw material, usually mixed with minerals as "natural asphalt". Large deposits exist on the island of Trinidad. Smaller deposits exist in Europe; it is mined today in Eschershausen in the Weserbergland (Germany). Adding natural asphalt can improve the properties of synthetic bitumen—particularly where specifications are high, as in road and bridge construction.

In landscape architecture, it is mainly road construction asphalt that is used. Oxidation bitumen is also used

Fig. 1.9.6: Jointing of an acrylic glass tile using linear snap-in connection

Fig. 1.9.7: Asphalt drill core made of rolled asphalt

Depending on the form of installation, bonding agent and aggregate, this may be described as concrete asphalt, stone matrix asphalt, water-permeable asphalt (drainage asphalt), or poured asphalt. Asphalt is mainly used in path and road construction and as a sealing layer (ponds, landfills). In path and road constructions it is used with different compositions as a base course, bond course or surface course. > Fig. 1.9.7 and chapter 3.2 Paths and squares

Reclaimed asphalt can be added to hot-mix asphalt in the form of asphalt granulate. Today the amount is usually about 20%. In asphalt base courses it may be up to 100%.

for building protection (sealing sheets, adhesive masses and coatings) and polymer bitumen for intensively used traffic surfaces and high-grade, UV-resistant sealing sheets.

In sealing structures, bitumen can be used in the form of a coating, adhesive or putty mass, or as sealing sheets. For this purpose, bitumen is applied to a supporting material, which gives the material its strength. Support materials include dry roofing felt, polyester fleece, woven glass and metal band inserts. Bitumen-soaked sheets are gritted in order to avoid sticking during transport and to increase heat resistance.

For use as asphalt, hot bitumen is mixed with stone aggregate. This bonding results in a low-cavity mixture with high tolerance of load and weather factors.

Surface qualities

Bitumen is black. Its color and its surface qualities can be changed using additional aggregates or additional coatings.

Use of certain chippings and pigments (e.g. red iron oxide) in the surface layer, a rolled-in scattering of chippings or exposing the mineral components through bead blasting or polishing make various design effects on the asphalt's surface possible. Special colorings can be achieved if the bitumen is replaced with colorless bonding agents. They bring out the colors of the stone aggregates and can be colored using pigments. This process involves more effort and expenditure. Apparatus and mixing facilities must be cleaned first. > Fig. 1.9.8 Stencils can also be used to structure the asphalt surface. > Figs. 1.9.9 and 1.9.11

Fig. 1.9.8:
a) Stone matrix asphalt surface layer 0/8: colorful effect created using synthetic bonding agents with an admixture of red and green pigments, e.g. liparite stone aggregate (red) and diabase (green) with 10% broken glass in each 2/8
b) Gray stone matrix asphalt 0/8 with an admixture of green glass

a | b

Marking substance	Thickness of layer (average value)	Resistance to stress	Remarks
1-component colorants (e.g. High-Solid paint)	0.3–0.6 mm	low	best process
cold spray plastic	0.3–1.2 mm	low to medium	seasonal markings, in combination with 2c cold plastic, or for remarking
2-component (2c)-cold plastic	1.5–3 (5) mm	medium to high	applied by machine or manually (except for structural road markings), surface finish, smooth coating, profiled and structural markings, greater layer thicknesses of up to 5 mm (only for tactile-visual markings and structural markings)
inlay		high	yellow and white stripes (standardized traffic symbols) are available. Easier to remove than the other marking substances
hot spray plastic	1.5 mm	high	installed by burning on at about 200°C using an installation machine. For prefabricated marking symbols, a blowtorch is used
hot plastic	3–5 mm		

Tab. 1.9.2: Range of common marking substances for asphalt surfaces

Additional effects can be created on asphalt surfaces by coatings applied to areas or (road surface) markings. Various processes such as 1-component colorants, cold plastic, hot plastic (thermoplastic used for marking) or thermoplastic inlay can be used > Tab. 1.9.2. Linear structures are usually applied using marking machines, or "stripers". Traffic symbols and individual shapes are applied using templates/masking. Prefabricated pictograms in hot plastic are also available. White and yellow are common in traffic management, whereas other colors such as red, green and blue are available on demand. > Figs. 1.9.10 and 1.9.11 Abrasive materials such as quartz sand also improve purchase on the road surface. Reflective beads (glass beads) increase visibility at night. Most marking substances can also be used on other surface coatings.

Forming and jointing

Sealing sheets are installed with covers on the jointing. Depending on the materials, they are glued or welded. Rolled asphalt (asphalt concrete, stone matrix asphalt) is installed hot, using finishers. Finally, it is rolled. Its working temperature is about 180°C. Rolled asphalt can also be installed and compacted manually, creating a surface that is visibly more irregular.

In poured asphalt, the bonding agent components create a cavityless substance that can be poured and does not need to be compacted. Poured asphalt is installed using special installation planks, or manually. The working temperature for poured asphalt is about 250°C. It is particularly suitable for difficult surface sectors. > Fig. 1.9.12 Prefabricated parts can also be created from poured asphalt using formwork.

To reduce health risks from fumes and aerosols during asphalt processing, low-temperature asphalts are increasingly used. By adding certain substances, the temperature required can be reduced to about 130°C (for rolled asphalt) or 210°C (for poured asphalt).

When working asphalt, it is not always possible to avoid seams. In road construction, this usually means crosswise seams marking the end of one day's work and the start of another. Dependent on the breadth of finishers, lengthwise seams are necessary in installations involving large surface areas. The use of two finishers optimizes "hot on hot" execution of the two adjacent installation strips. If the products used will only allow a "hot on cold" installation, the contact surfaces should be executed at a 70–80° angle. The seams will subsequently be visible. Where asphalt connects with structural elements, such as kerbstones, channels, walls, parts of buildings or concrete surfaces, joints must be provided for. These can be created using joint grouting

Fig. 1.9.9: Stamped asphalt: creating a paved pattern

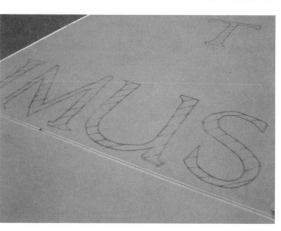

a | b

Fig. 1.9.10: 2-component cold plastic color application, 1.6. to 1.8 mm thick, with scattered beads (reflection), Sulzer site in Winterthur, Switzerland

a | b

Fig. 1.9.11a+b): Combination of stamped asphalt and applied color (hot plastic) in a design for an urban square

Fig. 1.9.12: Black poured asphalt on a light rolled asphalt covering

a
b

or joint tape. Joint tape is either applied to the edges before joining (advance joint filling), or subsequently laid over the joint. The connection is created by using primer and partially melting the joint sealant. The joint grouting substance is molded into the joint, which has also been treated with primer.

GLASS

Composition, properties, products

Glass is a noncrystalline (amorphous) material. Its significant property is its transparency. Visible light can penetrate it, while UV light cannot. Glass also has good chemical resistance and a low coefficient of thermal expansion. It is resistant to acid and alkaline damage, with the exception of fluorine compounds such as fluoric acid. Glass tends to be brittle, easily causing breakage. Faults or small cracks in its surface can also lead to breakage, without any external influences coming to bear. In safety glass, this characteristic is reduced as far as possible by means of various processes.

The main component of glass is quartz sand (silicon dioxide SiO_2)—about 70–80%. Soda-lime glass, usually involved in the manufacture of flat glass, contains the additional ingredients calcium oxide (CaO) and sodium oxide (Na_2O).
The main ingredients of boron silicate glass, apart from silicon dioxide, are boron oxide and aluminum oxide. It is very fire-resistant. In landscape architecture, it is mainly used as glass fibers in glass fiber-reinforced plastics.

Flat glass is usually produced as float glass. This involves pouring glass at 1100°C into a bath of tin. The lighter glass "floats" on the surface. It hardens through a slow cooling process. These plates of glass may reach thicknesses of 2 to 25 mm and dimensions of 3210 x 6000 mm.

Cast glass (rolled glass) is shaped using forming rollers. Structured surfaces can be created by means of rolling. Cast glass has limited transparency. During the rolling process, wire mesh can be worked in, creating safety glass or fireproof glass.

Fig. 1.9.13: Glass blocks:
a) in the form of concrete glass, which can be walked on, over an underground garage
b) in a nonloadbearing wall

Channel-shaped glass types, with or without wire inserts, are also manufactured using a rolling process. They are U-shaped in cross-section, making them statically loadbearing elements. They are often used in walls in sports areas, for instance, as they cannot be broken by flying balls. Lengths of 4000 to 7000 mm and standard widths of 232 to 498 mm are available.

Glass blocks are created in a pressing process. For hollow glass blocks, two halves are welded together while still viscous. Glass blocks are produced in formats ranging from 11.5 x 11.5 x 8 cm to 30 x 30 x 10 cm, and fixed one atop the other using cement mortar, with or without reinforcement. For loadbearing, structural

Fig. 1.9.14: Glass parapet, open staircase at Marie-Elisabeth-Lüders-Haus, Berlin

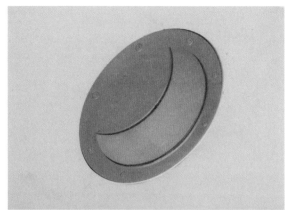

Fig. 1.9.15: Partially tempered glass (TVG) in a wall element

Fig. 1.9.16: Broken glass as a surface layer

elements called concrete glass types, are set into load-bearing reinforced concrete elements. > **Fig. 1.9.13**
Safety glass types have a higher stability than normal glass types, and break without splintering. Since in most outdoor use of glass it is desirable or even essential to minimize the risk of injury through broken glass, safety glass should be used preferentially. In landscape architecture, it is used for overhead glass canopies, wall segments (pavilions, noise protection walls, circular walls) and parapets. > **Fig. 1.9.14**
In various manufacturing processes, a base glass (e.g. float glass) is processed to become one-pane safety glass (ESG), partially tempered glass (TVG), laminated safety glass (VSG) or wire mesh glass. The glass surface is tempered by thermal treatment and associated rapid cooling. Tensile stress is created within the glass, and compressive stress is created in its surface. This prevents brittleness and crack formation. The glass is able to bear a load.
When one-pane safety glass (ESG) breaks, it forms very small, nonsharp pieces, thus also losing its loadbearing capacity, whereas partially tempered glass (TVG) is cooled more slowly during the manufacturing process, thereby acquiring lower internal stresses. The glass breaks into larger pieces. In combination, however, a certain degree of loadbearing capacity is retained. By sticking two or more layers together using polyvinyl butyral sheets, laminated safety glass (VSG) is created. In case of breakage, the sheet binds the glass

splinters. Depending on the glass's thickness, load-bearing glass types or bulletproof glass types can be created. > **Fig. 1.9.15**
In high-rise construction in particular, uses for other glass types with specialized protective functions exist, e.g. insulating glass (warmth retention) or laminated fire-proof glass.
Glass production is energy-intensive and costly for the environment. Production allows elements of used material to be melted down and reused. Broken glass is also used as aggregate in concrete and asphalt, and as a decorative drop-on material. > **Fig. 1.9.16**

Surface qualities and treatment

Glass can be given a matt finish using sand or powder blasting. In order to create a pattern, the areas that are to be left as they are can be covered with templates (varnish, wax or resin layers). Alternatively, an etching process using fluoric acid or hydrochloric acid can be used.

Polishing creates a raw, light matt or smooth glass surface. Application may be computerized (CNC) or manual. Engraving enables decorations and writing in relief. > **Figs. 1.9.17 and 1.9.18**

Glass can be colored durin g the manufacturing process by adding metal oxides. Iron oxides, for instance, give a green tone. This also appears in normal sand, indicating small amounts of iron oxide in the sand. Low-iron white

Fig. 1.9.17: Frosted glass:
a) floor slabs
b) facade of the Kunsthaus in
Bregenz (etched glass)

a | b

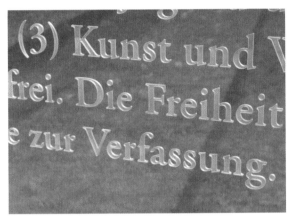

Fig. 1.9.18: Lines of script carved
using a laser, glass tiles
bordering the grounds at
Jakob-Kaiser-Haus, Berlin

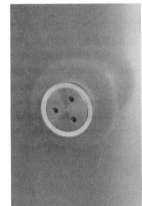

a | b | c | d

Fig. 1.9.19:
a) Linear snap joint
b) Point snap joint
c) Screw joint
d) Point fastener with four snap
joints

glass does not have these components, and is permeable to UV light. Blue, brown to violet, yellow, bronze and pink are other possible metal oxide colorings.

Patterns of color can be applied to surfaces using enamel paints or screen printing. Mirrored, nonreflective and self-cleaning glass can also be manufactured using microstructuring or coating systems.

Standing water in contact with glass should be avoided, as it can cause leaching and a consequent opacity in the glass.

Forming and jointing
Pieces of flat glass of up to 10 mm thick can be molded using sagging or pressing techniques. The pane of glass is heated, and the pliable material is sagged or pressed into a prepared mold.

Machining processes are possible for glass working materials. The material is cooled to allow drilling to be undertaken.

The glass is cut using a steel wheel or diamond, and broken at the cut. Cutting can also be performed with a jet of water or a laser beam. The edges can be tooled afterwards, to reduce their sharpness or to remove optical or technical production problems.

Flat glass can be linearly mounted or point mounted. Linear support is the mounting technique with the lower degree of stress. Today, this is usually done by clamping the glass between aluminum and steel—or more rarely wood or plastic—moldings (glazing brackets). Point mountings are created using screw or snap-in connections. Plastic inserts (sealants) cushion stress forces and make the mounting tight. > Figs. 1.9.19 and 1.9.6

2   THE PRINCIPLES OF LOADBEARING STRUCTURES

2.1   LOADBEARING STRUCTURES AND THEIR DIMENSIONS

FUNDAMENTALS OF STRUCTURAL COMPONENT DIMENSIONING
·   Force—the key value in statics
·   Balance of forces
·   Theory of material strength
·   Summary of working steps in component dimensioning

ASSUMED LOADS
·   Load differentiation
·   Load values

CHOICE OF SYSTEM
·   Bending-active loadbearing systems
·   Plate-active loadbearing systems
·   Bar-active loadbearing systems
·   Form-active loadbearing systems

CHOICE OF MATERIALS
·   Material properties
·   Choosing materials

CHOICE OF CROSS-SECTION
·   Tension
·   Pressure
·   Bending

STIFFENING
·   Nature and arrangement of stiffening elements

Bernd Funke

2.1 LOADBEARING STRUCTURES AND THEIR DIMENSIONS

FUNDAMENTALS OF STRUCTURAL COMPONENT DIMENSIONING

Force—the key value in statics

Definition and unit
Isaac Newton (1643–1727) was the first person to formulate the relationship between bodies and the forces that affect them.

Newton's First Law:
A body will remain at rest or continue to move at constant velocity as long as no force is acting upon it or the forces affecting it are in equilibrium.

For example, if you hold a ball in your hand, the muscle power you can feel being used and the force that the weight of the ball exerts are in equilibrium (i.e. they cancel each other out). The ball is at rest.

Newton's Second Law:
The net force acting on a body will cause the body to change its velocity, i.e. accelerate, in the direction of the force.

If the ball is thrown, the muscle power used must be greater than the force exerted by the weight of the ball. That is to say that the acceleration of a body requires a resultant force that is not in a state of equilibrium with any other force. The connection between the resultant force F, the mass m and the acceleration can be formulated mathematically in the equation "force = mass · acceleration". The unit of force is the newton (units are written in square brackets in the following formulae):

$$F = m \cdot a\,[N] \qquad \left(\left[kg \cdot \frac{m}{s^2}\right] = [N] = \text{Newton}\right)$$

If this formula is used to calculate the force exerted by the weight of a body, then its weight is determined a the product of its mass and the gravitational acceleration acting upon it $g = 9.81\frac{m}{s^2}$.

Consequently, the weight G of a person with a mass of 100 kg works out as

$$G = m \cdot g = 100\,kg \cdot 9.81\frac{m}{s^2} = 981\,kg \cdot \frac{m}{s^2} \approx 1{,}000\,N = 1\,kN$$
(1 Kilonewton).

This force exerted by weight is also known as a "man load". > Fig. 2.1.1

$$1\,\text{Man} \triangleq 1\,kN$$

Representing forces
Forces can be represented very vividly as vectors (arrows). The force has a line of action (position of the arrow in space), a direction (indicated by the tip of the arrow) and a value (length of the arrow). A co-ordinate system is needed for this vector representation of forces. > Fig. 2.1.2

Deconstructing and combining forces
The principles of deconstructing and combining forces are shown in figure 2.1.3. Forces in a single plane (here the x-y plane) are shown, for greater clarity.

Fig 2.1.1: Man load

Orienting the coordinate axes in relation to each other using the "right hand rule"

"arrow axis" = line along which force acts
"arrow point" = direction in which force acts
"arrow length" = magnitude of force

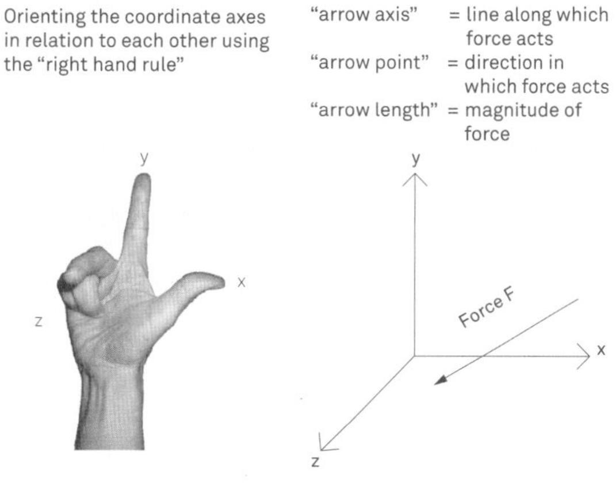

a) determining the coordinate system

b) force vector in three-dimensional space

Fig. 2.1.2: Representing forces

Moments (torsional forces)

Two forces F of the same magnitude, working in parallel but in opposition, represent a torsional force and are called a pair of forces or a "moment". > Fig. 2.1.4 Given the fact that the two forces F cancel each other out because of their magnitude and direction of action (they are in equilibrium), the body they are acting on does not move. But as they are at a distance from each other, they turn the body around their common center ("propeller effect"). The magnitude of the moment is calculated as the product of force F and eccentricity e (moment arm of the forces in relation to each other). Or in brief: "moment = force · moment arm"

$$M = F \cdot e \ [Nm] \qquad ([N \cdot m] = [Nm] = \text{Newtonmeter})$$

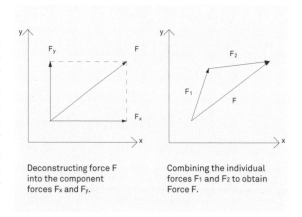

Deconstructing force F into the component forces F_x and F_y.

Combining the individual forces F_1 and F_2 to obtain Force F.

Fig. 2.1.3: Deconstructing and combining forces

Balance of forces

Seen scientifically, statics is the "theory of the balance of forces and of the rest of bodies". In this context, it is possible to derive the following statement from Newton's First Law:

A body is at rest if all the forces acting on that body are balanced, i.e. they cancel each other out. > Fig. 2.1.5

Condition of equilibrium

As buildings should be at rest, the loading and reacting forces must be in equilibrium.

loading forces = reacting forces (action = reaction)

The loading forces are the forces acting on the support member (external acting forces), also called action. They are established in the context of assumed load on the basis of the intended use and the acting forces to be expected as a result.

The reacting forces are the internal reaction forces (internal and bearing forces) created in the support member and other supports as a consequence of force transfer, also called reaction. It is these forces that hold the component in position despite the loads acting on it. As a rule, the internal reaction forces vary along the length of the support member ("internal force path"), which means that their maximum values can be determined by statics. But in special cases, for example optimized loadbearing systems in the form of "fishbelly girders" (popular in landscape architecture as the main girders for small bridges), the internal forces has to be following along the full length of the supporting member.

Applying the condition of equilibrium

If a loadbearing system is drawn up and the chosen loads (external action forces) noted on it, the resultant cutting and bearing forces (internal reaction forces) are unknown at first. To be able to calculate them they must first be rendered "visible" by using the "method of sections," in which the internal reaction forces are "isolated" (hence the name internal forces). This process is examined in figure 2.1.6, taking the simple case of a "beams on two supports."

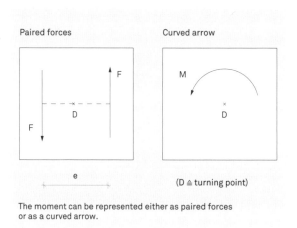

Paired forces

Curved arrow

The moment can be represented either as paired forces or as a curved arrow.

(D ≙ turning point)

Fig. 2.1.4: Representing torsional forces (moments)

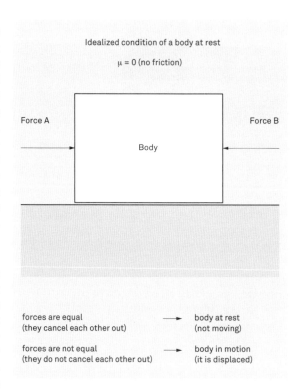

Idealized condition of a body at rest

$\mu = 0$ (no friction)

Force A

Body

Force B

forces are equal
(they cancel each other out)
→ body at rest
(not moving)

forces are not equal
(they do not cancel each other out)
→ body in motion
(it is displaced)

Fig. 2.1.5: Balance of forces

Load situation	Requirements on components	Isolating internal reaction force	Description of this cutting force	Illustration of the cutting force on the cut-out element of the loadbearing member according to cutting force convention (> Fig. 2.1.7)
 e.g. tension cable	tension	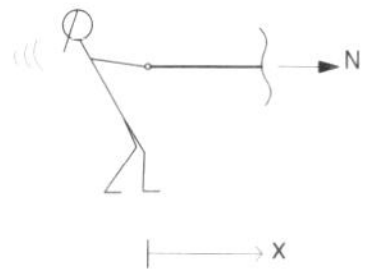 N	positive normal force (tensile force)	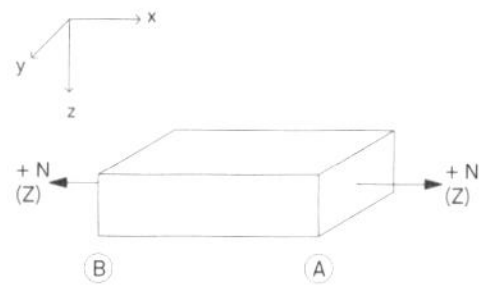 +N (Z) / +N (Z)
 e.g. compression rod	compression	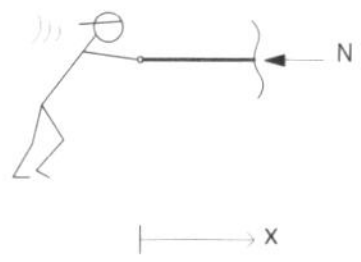 N	negative normal force (compressive force)	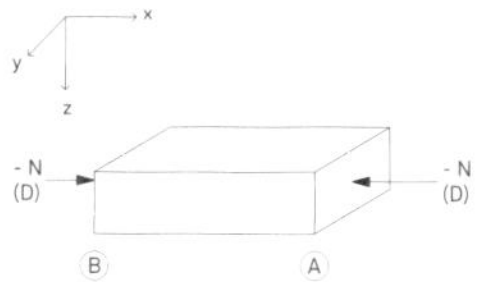 −N (D) / −N (D)
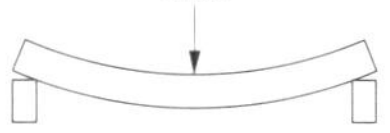 force F / e.g. shear bolts	thrust or shear	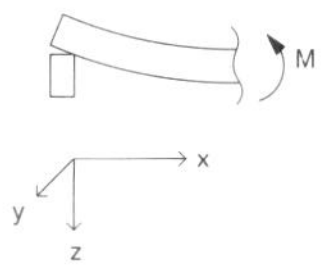 M	cross force ** (shear)	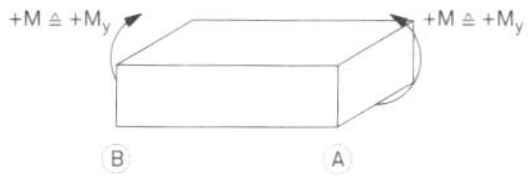 +M ≙ +M_y / +M ≙ +M_y
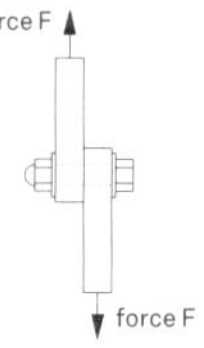 force F / force F / e.g. flexural beams	bending	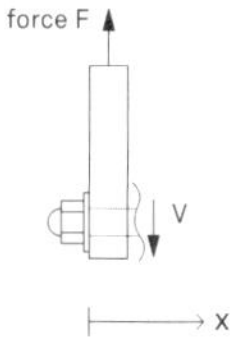 force F / V / bolts, longitudinal direction	bending moment or simple moment	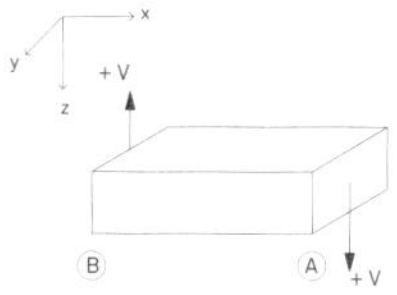 +V / +V
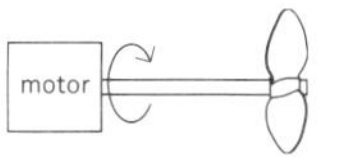 motor / e.g. propeller shaft	torsion	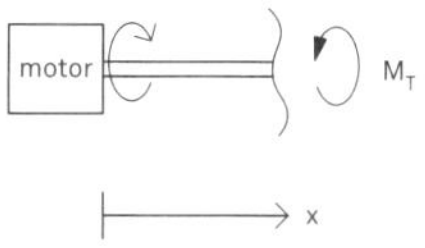 motor / M_T	torsion moment	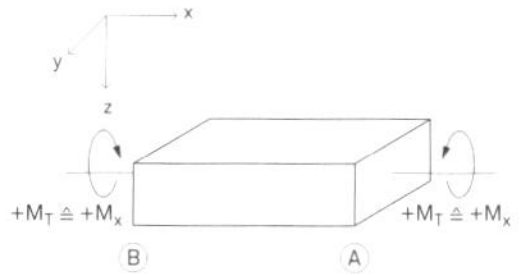 +M_T ≙ +M_x / +M_T ≙ +M_x

*   Normal force acts longitudinally to the structural component (along the x axis). This description is used because the lengthwise direction of a loadbearing member is called the normal direction
** Cross force acts perpendicular to the length (the y and z direction).

Tab. 2.1.1: Possible internal forces (internal reaction forces)

The first step here is to isolate the bearing members ("external cut"). Consequence: if the bearing member is cut off from a supporting member, it falls down. To stop this happening, the as yet unknown bearing forces are applied at the cutting point instead. They restore the balance of forces and hold the support member in the required position. Now both the load force (G = weight of the child) and the supporting forces (AV, BV and BH —bearing forces acting vertically and horizontally) are applied to the support member. The next step is that three force equations can be drawn up to meet the requirement that all the forces and torsion forces must cancel each other out (condition of equilibrium):

· sum of all horizontal forces (x direction) equals zero
· sum of all vertical forces (y direction) equals zero and
· sum of all torsional forces (moments) equals zero.

Finally, the three equations are used to calculate the three unknown bearing forces (solving three equations with three unknowns).

Once all the supporting forces are known, the second stage involves cutting through the supporting member itself ("internal cut"), applying the internal reaction forces at the point of section, and finally calculating the three internal forces N, V and M, > Tab. 2.1.1 and fig. 2.1.7 by analogy with the condition of equilibrium. This process is called internal force determination.

Theory of material strength

After the condition of equilibrium has been used to calculate the inner reaction forces (internal forces) from the action forces (loads) acting on the support member from the outside, these can be used in turn to calculate the

Loadbearing problem to be solved

Fixing the loadbearing system and assumed load

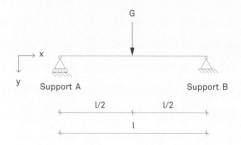

System: Beam on two supports
Load: Weight G of the child in the middle of the beam

Support A can be moved horizontally ("roller bearing") in order to deal with changes in the length of the beam without restraint, e.g. as a result of temperature or humidity fluctuations, i.e., it transfers only vertical loads.

External sections: determining the supporting loads

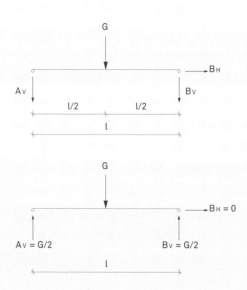

Support A can transfer only a vertical force A, and support B both a vertical force B and a horizontal force BH.

Calculation of the three reaction forces via the three equilibrium conditions: Sum of all horizontal forces, sum of all vertical forces and sum of all moments (torsional forces) around the point (B = 0).

$\sum FH = 0 = B_H$ $\rightarrow B_H = 0$ equation 1
$\sum FH = 0 = G + A_V + B_V$ $\rightarrow B_V = -G - A_V$ equation 2

$\sum M^B = 0 = G \cdot \dfrac{l}{2} + A_V \cdot l$ $\rightarrow A_V = -G / 2$ equation 3

Placing equation 3 in equation 2.

$$\rightarrow B_V = -G + \frac{G}{2} = -\frac{G}{2}$$

Result:

$$A_V = -\frac{G}{2} \qquad B_V = -\frac{G}{2} \qquad BH = 0$$

A negative force means that it works in the opposite direction, which is why it makes sense to invert the force arrows A_V and B_V in the diagram and that their signs change as well.

Internal section: determining the internal forces

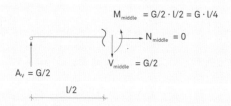

The section in the middle of the beam is discussed as an example as this is the placing with the greatest bending moment. In the case of flexible support members like this balancing beeam the bending moment is relevant in terms of measurement as a rule, and thus determines the required beam cross-section. To this end, the beam is cut through left of force G and the right-hand half of the beam removed. The internal forces transferred from the beam are shown instead of this.

Calculating the three internal forces via the three equilibrium conditions:

$\sum F_H = 0 = N_{middle}$ $\rightarrow N_{middle} = 0$ equation 1
$\sum F_V = 0 = V_{middle} - A_V$ $\rightarrow V_{middle} = A_V$ equation 2

$\sum M^{middle} = 0 = M_{middle} - A_V \cdot \dfrac{l}{2}$ $\rightarrow M_{middle} = A_V \dfrac{l}{2}$ equation 3

$\sum M_{middle} \triangleq$ sum of all moments acting around the beam's central point

Placing reaction force $A_V = \dfrac{G}{2}$ in equations 2 and 3.

Result:
$N_{middle} = 0 \qquad V_{middle} = \dfrac{G}{2} \qquad M_{middle} = G \cdot \dfrac{l}{4}$

Fig. 2.1.6: Reaction and internal forces on the beam on two supports

a) Coordinate orientation,
   taking a beam as an example

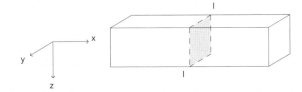

The lengthwise direction of a supportive component is described as the x direction. The two
cross directions (vertical and horizontal to the lengthwise direction) are described as the
y and z directions. In construction statics, their orientation in relation to the x direction is
obtained by means of the "right hand rule". (> Fig. 2.1.2)

b) Orienting the forces
   on the borders of the cut

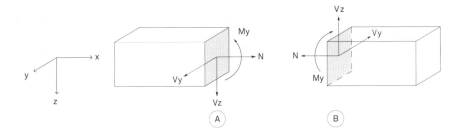

A Positive cut border (first cut border in positive x direction):
   At the positive cut border, all positive cutting forces point in the positive coordinate
   directions x, y and z.

B Negative cut border (second cut border in positive x direction):
   At the negative cut border, all positive cutting forces point in the negative coordinate
   directions x, y and z, and are therefore shown as inverse.

c) Right fist rule

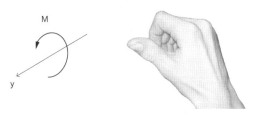

Showing a positive moment using the "right hand rule":
The thumb points in the coordinate direction and the fingers show the direction of the
positive moment around this coordinate axis.

Fig. 2.1.7: Internal force convention

required component resistance. This should be chosen
so that its strength can be used to support the calculated
internal forces without fracture (loadbearing capacity).

Tension

The reference value for the force to be supported F (internal force) and the available component cross-section
is tension σ (sigma):

$$\sigma = \frac{F}{A}\left[\frac{N}{m^2}\right].$$

Each force acting on a body creates tension within it. The
tension thus represents the actual load on the material.
If force F acts on a small area A_{small}, then the tension is
great. If the same force F acts on a large area A_{large}, then
the tension is small as the force can be distributed over
a large area.

After determining the internal forces and choosing a
component cross-section it is then possible to use
to two of them to calculate the material load that
will occur in the form of the actual tension actual σ.
> Tab. 2.1.2

Load situation	Cutting force	Required strength	Description of tension	Magnitude of tension	Associated tension figures
	+N = tension	tensile strength	tensile tension	$\sigma = N/A$ (+)	$\sigma_z = Z/A$
	-N = compression	compressive strength	compression tension	$\sigma = N/A$ (-)	$\sigma_D = D/A$
force F	±M = bending moment	thrust strength or shear strength	thrust tension (shear tension)	$\sigma = M/W$ (+ or -)	$s_D = M/W$ compressive zone / tension zone 1/6h, e = 2/3h, 1/6h $s_z = M/W$
force F	±Q = cross force	bending strength	bending tension	$\tau \cong Q/A$ (+ or -)	$\tau = Q/A$
motor	±M$_T$ = torsion moment	torsion strength	torsion tension	$\tau_T = M_T/W_T$ (+ or -)	$\tau_T = M_T/W_T$

A = cross-sectional area [cm²]
W = moment of resistance [cm³]. This value depends on the cross-section.
WT = moment of resistance for torsion [cm³]. This value depends on the cross-section.

Tab. 2.1.2: Possible tensions (material loads)

Material strength

Strength is the measure for a body's resistance. The higher its strength, the greater the force (or load) it can withstand, where its cross-section remains the same. Strength can be defined as permissible strain (a quotient calculated from the permissible force together with the cross-section surface). It is determined by the choice of materials, and therefore represents the material-specific loadbearing capacity.

Tension comparison

Finally the actual tensions actual σ can be compared with the admissible tensions adm. σ (material strengths). The admissible tensions for the various materials (strength of wood, steel, concrete, etc.) are established with loading experiments in the lab (loading to breaking point) and can be taken from the appropriate standard ratings and the current construction tables.

If the actual tension is smaller or equal to the admissible tension, then the component cross-section is sufficiently capable of bearing the load. That is to say that the required component cross-section can be established from the equation

$$\text{actual.}\sigma = \frac{F}{A} \le \text{adm.}\sigma,$$

If this procedure suggest cross-sections that are too large for financial or design reasons, then either the material strength (adm. σ) and/or the static system (actual F) must be changed.

$$\text{reqd.}A \ge \frac{\text{actual.}F}{\text{adm.}\sigma}.$$

As loads, material strengths and cross-sectional dimensions are subject to a certain range of variation, appropriate safety reserves must be allowed for when making the tension comparison. This can be done by increasing the actions by certain safety coefficients and reducing the resistance by other safety coefficients.

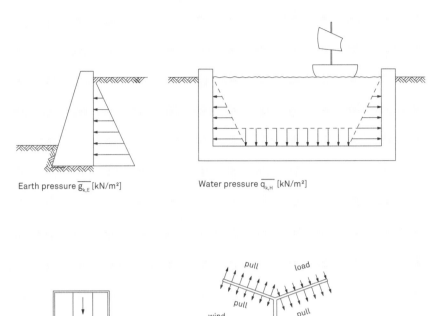

Earth pressure $\overline{g_{k,E}}$ [kN/m²]

Water pressure $\overline{q_{k,H}}$ [kN/m²]

Functional load $Q_{k,N}$ [kN]

Wind load $q_{k,W}$ [kN/m²]
Wind load and pull

(k stands for the characteristic, largest possible value of an effect)

Fig. 2.1.8: Some selected action (loads)

Summary of the working steps for component dimensioning.

1. Assumed loads
The loads to be expected (actions) must be fixed first when calculating a loadbearing system –> action.
2. Establishing internal force
The internal reaction forces (bearing and internal forces) generated in the loadbearing structure can be calculated by using the condition of equilibrium –> reaction.
3. Dimensioning / choice of material and cross-section
The cross-sectional dimensions needed to absorb the calculated internal forces can be established on the basis of "strength theory" (component load ≤ component resistance).

ASSUMED LOADS
All the force and deformation values acting on a loadbearing structure are called actions. Deformation values (not discussed further below) can include changes of length as a result of varying temperatures in the structure (change from summer to winter) or subsidence affecting the foundations, for example.
> Fig. 2.1.8

Load differentiation
Loads are essentially categorized in terms of the following criteria:

Duration of the effect
· constant loads G (e.g. own dead weight, permanent pressure from soil or water)
· varying loads Q (e.g. permitted load, wind load and snow load)
· exceptional loads A: usually of short duration, highly unlikely to occur, but with a high potential for creating damage (e.g. explosions, collision with vehicle or ship)

Effect of acceleration on the loadbearing structure
· static loads: these cause no significant acceleration in the loadbearing structure (e.g. dead weight and permitted loads)
· dynamic loads and seismic actions (earthquakes): these cause considerable acceleration or considerable changes in stress (e.g. traffic loads on bridges or the aerodynamic effect of wind loads)

Direction
· vertical loads (e.g. dead weight)
· horizontal loads (e.g. wind)

Nature of the load
· individual loads (point loads)
· area loads
> Fig. 2.1.9

Load values
The names, units and values for the actions on which a statical calculation is based can be taken from the appropriate standards for actions on loadbearing structures (DIN 1055, DIN special report 101 and DIN EN 1991) or the current construction tables. These give the weightings (unit weight forces) for all current construction and storage materials for establishing dead weight, the usual permitted loads, wind loads, snow loads, ice loads etc. The most important loads for buildings can be found in table 2.1.3.

For assessing the order of magnitude, it should be mentioned once again that a mass of 100 kg exerts a weight

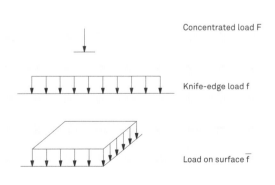

Concentrated load F

Knife-edge load f

Load on surface $\overline{f}$

Fig. 2.1.9: Possible load types

Duration of effect	Load type	Concentrated load [kN]	Knife-edge load [kN/m]	Load on surface [kN/m²]
continuous	dead weight earth pressure * water pressure *	G_k G_k,E G_k,H	g_k g_k,E g_k,H	$\overline{g_k}$ $\overline{g_k,E}$ $\overline{g_k,H}$
variable	functional load wind load snow load	Q_k,N Q_k,W Q_k,S	q_k,N q_k,W q_k,S	$\overline{q_k,N}$ $\overline{q_k,W}$ $\overline{q_k,S}$
* when under sustained stress				

Tab. 2.1.3: The commonest types of load for buildings

force of 1 kN (man load). Consequently a mass of 1 t (e.g. 1 m³ of water) exerts a weight force of 10 kN.

CHOICE OF SYSTEM

Loadbearing systems are structured according to a wide variety of criteria. Categorization by the nature of the loadbearing system has remained one of the most lucid and generally comprehensible structures. Here four groups can be distinguished: bending-active, surface-active, bar-active and form-active loadbearing systems.

Bending-active loadbearing systems

Bending-active loadbearing systems are linear or flat loadbearing elements, with sufficiently large cross-sectional dimensions, that transfer their load mainly via "bending stress." > Figs. 2.1.10 and 2.1.11

This system is used mainly to produce loadbearing structures with flat surfaces, e.g. beams with a flat top or ceilings with an upper space intended for use. The loadbearing method involves a beam- or slab-shaped element loaded at right angles to its longitudinal axis and thus bent downwards. This creates bending stress and thus a bending element as the internal reaction force. To absorb this element (pair of forces made up of a tensile and a compressive force, > Fig. 2.1.33) a certain cross-sectional height is required. This ensures that an adequate moment arm (e) is created between the tensile force (Z) and the compression force (D), so that these do not become too great ($Z = D = \frac{M}{e}$).

So the following applies to flexurally stressed components: a large cross-sectional height available creates small internal forces and thus small tensions; but then a small height leads to large internal forces and large tensions, and thus to a need for very strong materials (e.g. steel).

Care should be taken that the tensile forces acting on the stretched loadbearing elements can be absorbed (pressure builds up on the compressed side). So for example steel and wood are strong enough to be used under stress, but concrete is not. This is why bending loadbearing members in concrete must be reinforced with steel on the tension side.

Plate-active loadbearing systems

Plate-active loadbearing systems are rigid flat loadbearing elements ("plates") formed in such a way that they transfer their loads mainly through compression or tensile stress (normal forces on a flat plane, where possible avoiding high bending stresses). > Figs. 2.1.12 and 2.1.13

In simple terms, it is possible to imagine a plate loadbearing system in such a way that internal tensile and compression struts are formed within a flat plane (almost an "internal truss"). This means that bending stresses are low and no components need to be particularly thick. Plate-active loadbearing structures make it possible to create relatively filigree loadbearing structures (e.g. slender roof support systems), although as horizontal loadbearing elements they still need to be developed in three dimensions (topographical surface).

Bar-active loadbearing systems

Bar-active loadbearing systems are loadbearing elements made up of rigid bars and shaped so that their loads are mainly transferred into the bars by pressure or tension. > Figs. 2.1.14 and 2.1.15

This means that flat and three-dimensional loadbearing structures can be built with minimal use of materials. It could also be said that the plate-active loadbearing systems described above are reduced to the tensile and compression struts created. As slender bars are sensitive to bending stress, the loads can generally be applied only to the nodes in the bar system, i.e. a flat secondary support system is required for a load over a flat surface ("collects the loads" and is supported by the primary construction nodes).

Fig. 2.1.10: Bending-active loadbearing system

Fig. 2.1.12: Plate-active loadbearing system

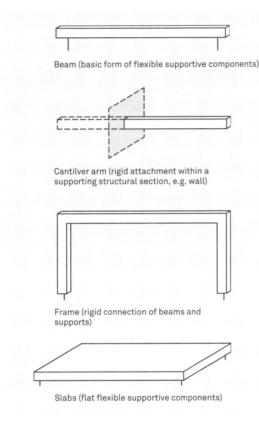

Fig. 2.1.11: The major bending-active loadbearing systems

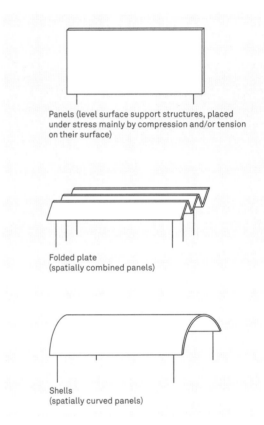

Fig. 2.1.13: The major plate-active loadbearing systems

Form-active loadbearing systems

Form-active loadbearing systems are loadbearing elements that transfer their loads either through tensile forces alone (cables and membranes) or through compression forces alone (arches and arch shells), because their loads are appropriately formed. > Figs. 2.1.16 and 2.1.17

Here, particular geometrical forms are selected that are used in a physical or mathematical experiment as "balanced form", without bending or shear stress ("funicular or pressure line"). A funicular line is the name for the geometry adopted by a freely suspended cable hanging under a certain load (for example its dead weight as line load) between two support points. As a cable can take only tensile stress, the form must be one involving only tensile forces and no other static forces. If the funicular line is turned upside down as an intellectual exercise, this produces a pressure line, in which only tensile forces occur with the same load, but applied in the opposite direction. So very efficient loadbearing structures (maximum span with minimum use of materials) can be created that are interesting in their formal language, but that fall into a relatively load-specific category. Care should be taken in this connection that tensioned structures (cables and tents) can adapt their shape appropriately to changing loads (stabilize themselves), whereas pressured structures (arches or arch shells) are inclined to shift sideways if subjected to varying loads (buckling or bulging).

Fig. 2.1.14: Bar-active loadbearing system

Fig. 2.1.16: Form-active loadbearing system

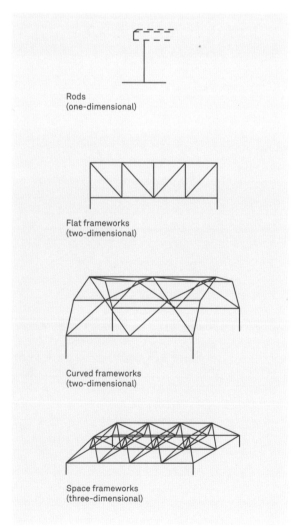

Rods
(one-dimensional)

Flat frameworks
(two-dimensional)

Curved frameworks
(two-dimensional)

Space frameworks
(three-dimensional)

Fig. 2.1.15: The major bar-active loadbearing systems

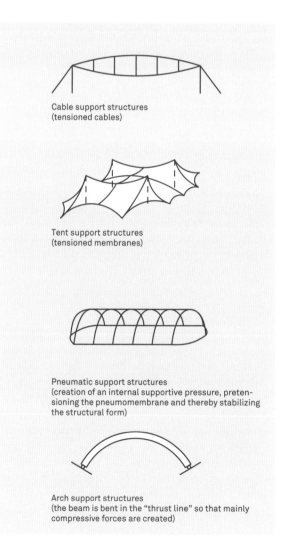

Cable support structures
(tensioned cables)

Tent support structures
(tensioned membranes)

Pneumatic support structures
(creation of an internal supportive pressure, preten-
sioning the pneumomembrane and thereby stabilizing
the structural form)

Arch support structures
(the beam is bent in the "thrust line" so that mainly
compressive forces are created)

Fig. 2.1.17: The major form-active loadbearing systems

Construction material	Material behavior	Properties	Strength	E-module [MN/m²]
steel e.g. S 235 (St 37–2)	isotropic	tensile strength compressive strength	$f_{u,k}$ = 360 N/mm² (tensile and compressive strength)	210,000
glass e.g. silicate glass	isotropic	tensile strength compressive strength	max. ^{Z} = 30–90 N/mm² (tensile strength) max. ^{D} = 700–900 N/mm² (compressive strength)	~ 70,000
wood e.g. S 10/C24M (NH, Gk II)	anisotropic	tensile strength compressive strength	$f_{t,0,k}$ = 14 N/mm² (tensile strength parallel to fibers) $f_{t,90,k}$ = 0.4 N/mm² (tensile strength parallel to fibers) $f_{c,0,k}$ = 21 N/mm² (compressive strength parallel to fibers) $f_{c,90,k}$ = 2.5 N/mm² (compressive strength perpendicular to fibers)	10,000 (Europ. conifers) 12,500 (Europ. deciduous trees)
concrete e.g. C 20/25 (B25)	limitedly isotropic	compressive strength	$f_{ck,cyl}$ = 20 N/mm² (cylinder compressive strength) $f_{ck,cube}$ = 25 N/mm² (cube compressive strength)	26,000 (C 12/15) 29,000 (C 20/25) 35,000 (C 40/50)
brickwork e.g. MZ 20/III	anisotropic	compressive strength	$_R$ = 6 N/mm² (compressive strength computational value)	1500–10,000
ground e.g. sand	very limitedly isotropic	compressive strength	adm. ^{D} ≈ 0.3 N/mm² = 300 kN/m² (permitted bearing pressure)	20–250 *
1 N/mm² = 1 MN/m² = 1000 kN/m²				* stiffness modulus E_s
The E-moduli listed for woods apply parallel to fibers. Values perpendicular to fibers are significantly lower. E -conifers ~ 300 MN/m².				

Tab. 2.1.4: Selected characteristic material values

CHOICE OF MATERIALS

Material properties

The loadbearing properties of any given material (load-bearing capacity and deformation behavior) are determined primarily by two material parameters, material strength and the elasticity module (e-module for short).

Material strength

As described above, material strength represents the specific loadbearing capacity of a material and is specified in terms of the maximum tension that can be absorbed adm. σ or the characteristic strength f_k. This makes it the key parameter for the loadbearing strength (failure strength) of a structural component. > Tab. 2.1.4

Elasticity module

If a body is placed under tension by the application of a load, it will inevitably be deformed. > **Fig. 2.1.18** The degree of deformation depends on the elasticity of the material. The characteristic value for the elasticity of materials is the e-module. > **Tab. 2.1.4**

The product of e-module and cross-sectional area A (E · A) is called elastic strength. For tension- and pressure-loaded components, the greater the elastic strength, the smaller the change of length will be. This means that if distortion is to be kept low, either E or A or both must be high (strong material and/or large cross-section). Similar observations can also me made for components subjected to bending. Here the product of e-module and moment of plane area I (E · I) is called bending strength (I [m⁴] is a cross-sectional parameter that is given in current construction tables for all the usual cross-sections). > **Fig. 2.1.19**

Fig. 2.1.18: Elasticity of materials

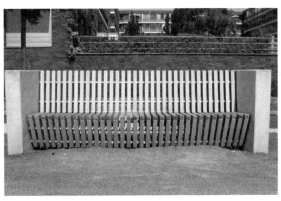

Fig. 2.1.19: Limiting deformation (the stainless steel loadbearing bars for the timber strip bench were dimensioned separately to avoid undue bending)

Material-specific e-modules are determined by loading tests in which the deformations produced are then measures. > **Tab. 2.1.4**

Choosing materials

Materials should be chosen to maintain both loadbearing capacity (actual $\sigma \leq$ adm. σ) and fitness for purpose (no undue deformations). So the choice of material depends to no small extent on the size of the actual load (actual σ). For tension and compression loads, the actual tension can be calculated using the familiar formula $\sigma = F/A$. To establish the actual tension in the case of bending loads, another cross-sectional parameter, the moment of resistance W [m³], is needed. W is also listed in current construction tables for all the usual cross-sections. Bending stress then comes out as

$$\sigma = \frac{M}{W}\left[\frac{N}{m^2}\right] \quad \left(\left[\frac{N\cdot m}{m^3}\right]=\left[\frac{N}{m^2}\right]\right).$$

Hence in cases of greater bending tension (capital M), the cross-section will also need a greater moment of resistance W to limit the bending tension generated. Open cross-sections (I-girders, cavity girders etc.) are suitable for creating large moments of resistance. > **Tab. 2.1.5** That is to say, it must be possible to create the shape required with the material without undue effort (e.g. steel or concrete).

Here, the ratio of the moment of resistance to the area has become accepted as an indicator for bending efficiency. The larger W/A is, the more efficiently a material cross-section can be deployed for bending and buckling loads.

Some essential features and the preferred fields for using individual building materials will be discussed below.

Wood

Wood is an anisotropic and inhomogeneous material that grows organically. > **Fig. 2.1.20** As it is possible to imagine the grain structure of wood as a bundle of tubes, its properties in terms of strength differ considerably longitudinally ‖ and transversely ⊥ to the grain.

Anisotropy: The influence of the angle φ between the grain direction and the stress direction can be seen in the diagram in figure 2.1.21.

Inhomogeneity: Wood's naturally inhomogeneous properties, e.g. in the form of branches, also has a negative effect on loadbearing capacity. Essentially this has already been considered in the admissible tensions for dimensioning standards, but care should be taken if there are particularly significant deficiencies in the grain structure, as they could pose a threat to tensile strength.

This forms the basis of the following rule for carpenters: lay beams so that the branches are in the compression zone. > **Fig. 2.1.22**

Fig. 2.1.20: Wood as a material

Cross section (all measurements in cm)	H = 10, B = 8	b = 16, h = 24, s = 1, H = 26, B = 18	b/2 = 13,3/2 (b = 13,3), h = 11,6, s = 1,3, H = 16, t = 2,2, B = 14,6	D = 10	d = 39,38, t = 0,63, D = 40,64
Surface A [cm²]	B H	B H - b h	2 B t + s h	$\frac{\pi\ D^2}{4}$	$\frac{\pi\ (D^2 - d^2)}{4}$
	8 10 = 80 cm²	18 26 - 16 24 = 84 cm²	2 14.6 2.2 + 1.3 11.6 = 79.3 cm²	π 10²/4 = 78.5 cm²	π (40.64² - 39.38²)/4 = 79.2 cm²
Moment of resistance W [cm³]	$\frac{B \cdot H^2}{6}$	$\frac{(B\ H^3 - b\ h^3)}{6\ H}$	$\frac{(B\ H^3 - b\ h^3)}{6\ H}$	$\frac{\pi\ D^3}{32}$	$\frac{\pi\ (D^4 - d^4)}{32\ D}$
	8 10²/6 = 133.3 cm³	(18 26³ - 16 24³)/6 26 = 610.2 cm³ (≈ 4.6 times this size)	(14.6 16³ - 13.3 11.6³)/6 16 = 406.7 cm³ (≈ 3.1 times this size)	π 10³/32 = 98.17 cm³ (≈ 0.7 times this size)	π (40.64⁴ - 39.38⁴)/32 40.64 = 780 cm³ (≈ 5.9 times this size)

Although all five cross-sections have a similar surface area, their resistance moments vary relatively highly depending on the geometry of the cross section. The fact that the cross-sectional values of the box and I-sections do not precisely agree with the corresponding section values for a hollow steel molding 260 x 180 x 10 or HEM 140 is due to their being based on an idealized cross-section form without corner arcs.

Tab. 2.1.5: Cross-sectional values for different shapes

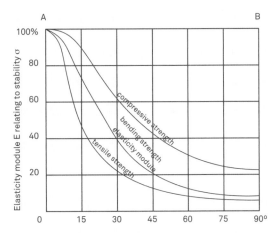

Fig. 2.1.21: Dependence of mechanical timber properties on the angle of stress to the grain direction

A Stress parallel to fibers
B Stress perpendicular to fibers

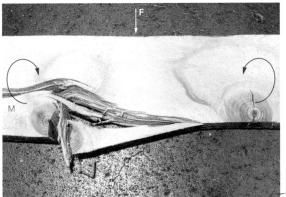

Fig. 2.1.22: Bending fracture in timber with many branches

Fig. 2.1.23: Steel as a material

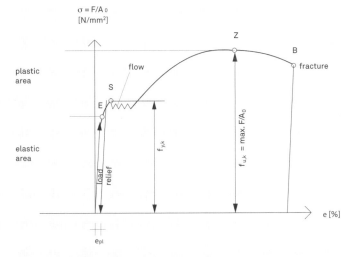

In order to represent the process clearly, the initial phase of the tension-expansion relationship (up to limit of stretch S) is shown flatter than it would actually be.

E = limit of elasticity   (permanent expansion ε_{pl} = 0.01%)
S = limit of stretch $f_{y,k}$ (permanent expansion of ε_{pl} = 0.2%)
Z = tensile strength $f_{u,k}$ (max. tension that can be tolerated, exceeding this limit causes failure)
B = breaking tension (< $f_{u,k}$)   (tension immediately before breaking)
A_0 = initial cross section   (cross section with no load [mm²])

Fig. 2.1.24: Tension-elongation diagram for structural steel S 235

Steel

Unlike wood, steel > Fig. 2.1.23 is a homogeneous isotropic building material and shows the same material behavior in all directions.

The particular feature of steel in terms of loadbearing behavior is the switch from elastic to plastic deformation under a certain level of stress (limit of elasticity). > Fig. 2.1.24 On exceeding the strain limit, the point of so-called "fluidity" is reached, at which elongation increases without the load having to be increased. After the load is removed, a steel body subject to elastic load returns to its original geometry. But if the load is applied in the plastic field this will cause a plastic (permanent) deformation.

Concrete

Concrete > Fig. 2.1.25 is an artificial stone made by mixing aggregates, cement (limestone fired to sinter point and then finely ground) and water as result of hardening of the cement paste (cement plus water). It has good loadbearing behavior under compression load. But it can transfer tensile forces only to a limited extent (no tensile strength can be listed to prove stability). Steel is therefore generally inserted (reinforcement) to absorb tensile forces. Concrete can be shaped in a variety of ways, and so relatively high building heights and moments of resistance can be created. The material is thus highly suitable for bending-active loadbearing systems. Special attention should however be paid to protecting the reinforcement adequately against corrosion (see also exposition classes according to standard > Fig. 1.7.2). The following two chemical reactions involving cement are especially important in this context.

Hydratation: Cement's reaction with water (hardening) is called hydratation, as various calcium hydrate compounds are formed. The set cement derives its strength from these. Calcium hydroxide ($Ca(OH)_2$) is also produced, which makes the concrete matrix alkaline (pH ~ 12).

Carbonatization: The reinforcement's natural protection against corrosion from the calcium hydroxide is lost as a result of carbonatization over the course of time. Calcium hydroxide reacts with the carbon dioxide in the atmosphere to produce calcium carbonate ($CaCO_3$). This process is very rapid in urban and industrial air.

Carbonatization gradually reduces the pH of the concrete. If the pH is < 9, there is no basic protection against corrosion and the reinforcing steel starts to rust because of the presence of both oxygen and water.
The progress of carbonatization and the associated lost of protection against corrosion in the reinforcing steel depend on a range of environmental and manufacturing conditions. > Tab. 2.1.6

Protection against corrosion can also be impaired by unduly large and wide cracks. It is therefore important to restrict the width of cracks when dimensioning

	Condition	Degree of carbonization/mode of action
Environmental factors	underwater or at low air humidity (e.g. interior components)	practically zero
	outdoors, unprotected	slow (concrete pores filled with water act as a CO_2 retardant)
	outdoors, roofed over	2 to 3 times as fast as outdoor unprotected material (no water-filled concrete pores)
	industrial air (high CO_2-content)	significantly accelerated
Production factors	low water-cement value ω	acts as a carbonization retardant $$w = \frac{\text{water content}}{\text{cement content}}[-] \text{ preferably} \leq 0.6 \left(\frac{\left[\frac{kg}{m^3}\right]}{\left[\frac{kg}{m^3}\right]} = [-] \right)$$ The following building site rule applies: *Do not try to improve the workability of concrete by adding excessive water!*
	sufficient concrete cover	carbonization front reaches the reinforcement as late as possible

Tab. 2.1.6: Progress of carbonatization dependent on environmental and manufacturing conditions

Fig. 2.1.25: Concrete as a material

Abb. 2.1.26: Masonry as a material

reinforced concrete building components. Cracks can be created by stress from both loads and indirect action. Indirect action cracks are often caused by shrinkage and settlement differences, for example.

As it is fundamentally impossible to prevent cracks from forming in concrete, they must be distributed as finely as possible to avoid the formation of a small number of large ones. For this reason, a certain minimum reinforcement is incorporated (structural reinforcement, even for smaller loads), and also the mesh in the reinforcement net is kept as small as possible (many small-diameter bars as far apart as possible). If this process leads to unduly large degrees of reinforcement, indirect action that might cause cracks can be reduced by the planned arrangement of expansion joints or contraction joints approx. 6 to 10 m apart. Contraction joints create nominal cracks, as it were. These are arranged structurally so that the differences in length that occur can be absorbed without damage. > **Chapter 2.3. Connections**

Masonry

Masonry is constructed from stone and mortar. > **Fig. 2.1.26** It is an inhomogeneous and anisotropic hybrid building

material with a loadbearing capacity that depends on the strength of the stone used and the quality of the selected mortar (mortar group). > **Tab. 2.1.7** Special cases include dry masonry (no mortar—limited loadbearing capacity) and reinforced masonry (has steel inserts in its joints to absorb bending and tensile stress—increased loadbearing capacity, see DIN 1053-3 and EC 6).

Assignment of erf. stone strength to mortar groups according to DIN/mortar classes according to EN 998-2			Brickwork strength classes	Computational values of compressive strength R [MN/m²]
IIa	III	IIIa	M	
2	-	-	1,5	1,3
4	-	-	2,5	2,1
6	-	-	3,5	3,0
12	-	-	5	4,3
20	12	-	6	5,1
28	20	-	7	6,0
-	28	20	9	7,7
-	36	28	11	9,0
-	48	36	13	10,5
-	60	48	16	12,5
-	-	60	20	15,0

Tab. 2.1.7: Strength classes of brickwork

Working material	Cross-section	W/A (resistance moment / cross-sectional area)	Strength	Application	Regulation references
solid wood	quadratic, rectangular, round	low	low to medium compressive strength, tensile strength lower than compressive strength (negligible longitudinal to fibers, significant across fibers)	bending- and bar-active support systems under low stress	measurement according to DIN 1052 and EN 1995 (EC 5)
laminated wood (BSH)	high rectangular and special cross-sections	medium		bending-active support systems under medium to high stress (but sensitive to changes in moisture and relatively cost-intensive)	
solid steel	round, square box and flat steel	low	high tensile and compressive strength (due to the slender cross-sections resulting from high strength. compressive stress creates a danger of folding)	tensile bars and compressive components under pressure (e.g. short compression stamps and bearings) and reinforcement steel for concrete	measurement according to DIN 18800 and EN 1993 (EC 3)
molding steel	large variety of moldings	medium to high		bending- and bar-active support systems and compression rods under high stress	
concrete	individual	variable	medium compressive strength, tensile strength only when combined with steel inserts (reinforcement)	bending- and plate-active support systems (only as supports in bending-active support systems and only where compressive stress is involved in formative support systems. e.g. arches)	measurement according to DIN 1045 (new) and EN 1992 (EC 2)
brickwork	variable (generally cubic)	low	low to medium compressive strength, tensile strength only when combined with steel inserts (reinforced brickwork)	compressive components under low stress or with correspondingly large cross-sections, tensile and bending stress only in exceptional cases	measurement according to DIN 1053 and EN 1996 (EC 6)

Tab. 2.1.8: Key materials and their possible uses

CHOICE OF CROSS-SECTION

The choice of cross-section depends essentially on cross-sectional loading, i.e. on the internal forces acting in the cross-section. > Tabs. 2.1.1 and 2.1.2 As a rule, tensile, compression and bending forces are relevant to dimensioning. Load from transverse forces is crucial only in the case of large loads close to the point of support or in the case of jointing devices (e.g. screws and welded joints). Torsion (special case) is not considered further here.

Tension

Accompanying internal force is the positive normal force +N. Under tension all that has to be done is to choose an adequately large cross-section area A (which is thus capable of loadbearing). Here the geometry of the cross-section is irrelevant, so that a common solution is a full cross-section in very strong material (e.g. steel or carbon fiber). Because these materials are so strong, large forces can be transferred with small cross-sections. > Fig. 2.1.27

$$actual.\sigma_z = \frac{F_z}{A} = \frac{+\,N}{A} = \frac{\text{tensile force}}{\text{area}} \le adm.\,\sigma_z$$

This means that any desired form can be chosen for the cross-section, as only the area of the cross-section is relevant to loadbearing capacity.

Pressure

Accompanying internal force is the negative normal force "-N". A distinction is made between two kind of compression members > Figs. 2.1.28 and 2.1.29:

· Compact compression members
  The remarks on tension above apply equally to compact compression members. The cross-sectional

Fig. 2.1.27: Loadbearing cable for a suspension bridge (tension element)

Fig. 2.1.28: Roofing uprights (compression elements)

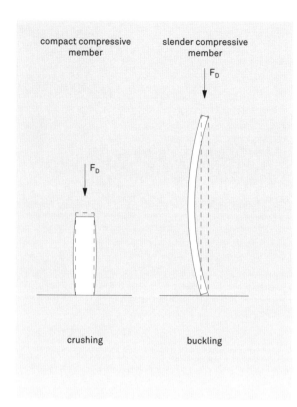

Fig. 2.1.29: Compression member types

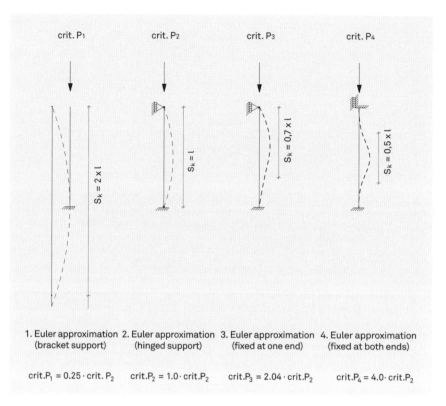

Fig. 2.1.30: Influence of support on buckling strength

geometry is unimportant, as it simply has to be large enough (stacked sheets, pressure pistons, short uprights with a large cross-section etc.)

$$actual.\sigma_D = \frac{F_D}{A} = \frac{-N}{A} = \frac{compressive\ force}{area} \leq adm.\sigma_D.$$

This means that any desired form can be chosen for the cross-section, as only the area of the cross-section is relevant to loadbearing capacity.

· Slender compression members
But the cross-sectional geometry is crucial for slender compression members (e.g. slender uprights) as these are in danger of buckling. "Buckling" is best explained by the "ruler effect". If you press on a vertically placed ruler, it moves in the direction of the weak axis. This sideways movement under pressure is called "buckling" and is relevant to the dimensioning of slender compression members. > Fig. 2.1.29
According to Leonhard Euler (1707–1783) the critical buckling load is calculated as follows:

$$P_{cr} = \frac{\pi^2 \cdot E \cdot I}{s_k^2} \quad \text{(Euler formula)}.$$

It depends on π (mathematical constant), the e-module, the cross-section (moment of plane area I) and the bedding mode (buckling length s_k). Four Euler cases are distinguished with respect to the buckling length s_k. > Fig. 2.1.30

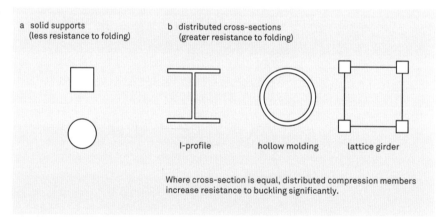

Where cross-section is equal, distributed compression members increase resistance to buckling significantly.

Fig. 2.1.31: Influence of cross-sectional shape on buckling strength

As the moment of plane area I (see construction tables, e.g. rectangular cross-section $I = b \cdot h^3/12$), increases by analogy with the moment of resistance W as the cross-section increasingly "breaks up", the following relationship is produced between the chosen cross-section and the critical buckling load:

· solid cross-sections have low buckling strength (P_{cr} is small)
· open cross-sections have high buckling strength (P_{cr} is large). > Fig. 2.1.31

$$actual.P = F_D = -N = \frac{compressive}{force} \leq P_{cr} = \frac{critical\ buckling}{load}$$

This means that a cross-section cannot be chosen at random, as cross-section geometry is one of the factors in determining loadbearing capacity. Open cross-sections (e.g. I-profiles) have much greater buckling strength than solid cross-sections with the same area!

Bending

The accompanying internal force is the bending moment M. > **Fig. 2.1.33a** This bending moment affects the cross-section as a pair of forces acting longitudinally to the supporting member consisting of a compression force D in the bending pressure zone and a tensile force Z in the bending tension zone. > **Fig. 2.1.33b** So the cross-section is not subject to even loading, but to a stress flow with *max.* σ_D on the pressured edge and *max.* σ_Z on the tensioned edge. Thus the cross-section in tension-free in the neutral fiber area (transition between compression and tension zone). > **Fig. 2.1.33c**

As discussed above, a corresponding moment of resistance W is needed to transfer a bending moment M. The moment of resistance rises with increased height and openness (I-profile, hollow profile etc.) for the cross-section, as the moment arm e between the internal forces D and Z becomes greater. Efforts are made here to arrange

Fig. 2.1.32: Girders in a bridge (bending element)

the greatest possible proportion of profile cross section as far as possible from the profile centre of gravity. The more open a cross-section is, the greater the moment of resistance W and thus its bending resistance.

$$actual.\sigma_{D,Z} = \frac{M}{W} = \frac{\text{bending moment}}{\text{moment of resistance}} \leq adm.\sigma_{D,Z}.$$

If large structural heights are possible, then the moment arm of the internal forces and thus W as well

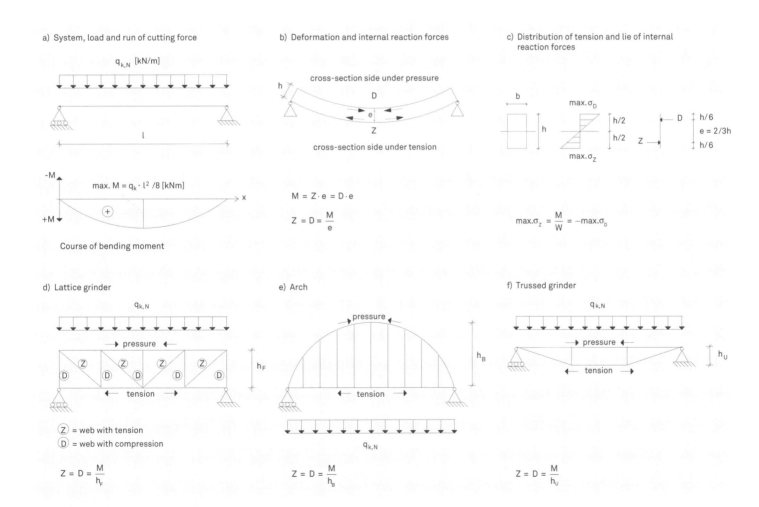

Fig. 2.1.33: Bending loadbearing structures

can be maximized effectively by splaying the cross-section (loadbearing arches, lattices and trussing). > Figs. 2.1.33d–f This generally produces considerable savings in terms of material.

This means that a cross-section cannot be chosen at random, as cross-section geometry is one of the factors in determining loadbearing capacity. From this it follows that open cross-sections with a large moment of resistance W (e.g. the top and bottom chords in a trussed beam) have much greater resistance to bending than solid cross-sections with the same area!

STIFFENING

Buildings must be adequately stiffened, i.e. they must be in a position to transfer all forces acting horizontally (wind, plumb line deviation, former soil pressure, collision with vehicle etc.). A sufficient number of vertical and horizontal loadbearing stiffening elements should be deployed to this end.

Nature and arrangement of stiffening elements

At least three vertical sheets (e.g. walls) and one horizontal sheet (e.g. roof) are required to stiffen a single-storey building. The axes of the vertical sheets should not intersect within the ground plan. > Fig. 2.1.34

Various sheet- or plate-like loadbearing elements can be used to stiffen a building component. > Fig. 2.1.35

The wind load represented in figure 2.1.36 on a roof stiffened by the rear wall and two side walls illustrates the flow of forces in this structure. The wind acts on the rear wall horizontally. The upper edge of this is supported by the roof and the lower edge by the foundations. The roof functions as a sheet and transfers the wind force from the rear wall to the two side walls. As these also act as sheets, they disperse the forces downwards in the form of diagonal compression struts and transfer them to the foundations there. Finally, the foundations have to safely transfer all the force of the wind acting horizontally to the subsoil (base friction on the underside of the foundations). As the figure shows, two things are important for overall stability. For one thing, the sheets and the connections between them have to have sufficient loadbearing capacity to be able to transfer the forces that build up. Then the structure as a whole must be heavy enough not be toppled over by the wind. This danger of tipping is best illustrated by the "chair model". If horizontal pressure is exerted on the back of a chair, the chair legs lift off the floor on the side facing the pressure. If there is sufficient imposed load on the chair (e.g. if someone is sitting on it), they do not lift. That is to say that the vertical tension forces created on the wind pressure side have to be out-pressured either by sufficient dead weight, or alternatively by anchoring in the round.

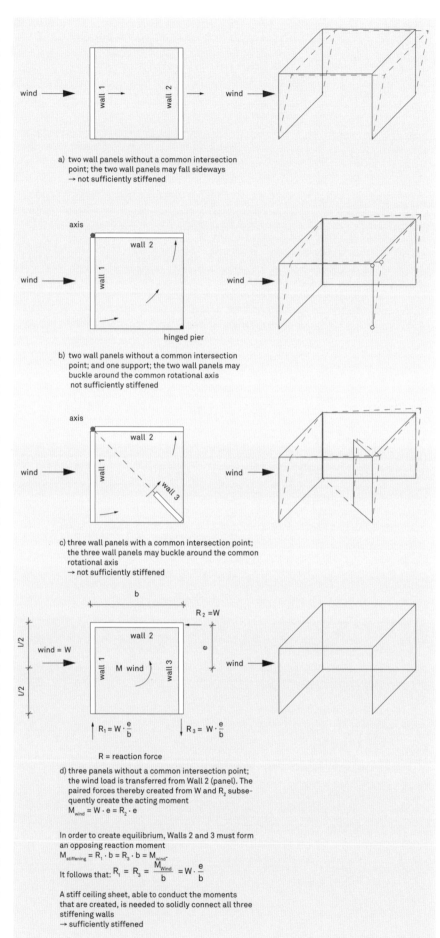

Fig. 2.1.34: Arranging stiffening elements

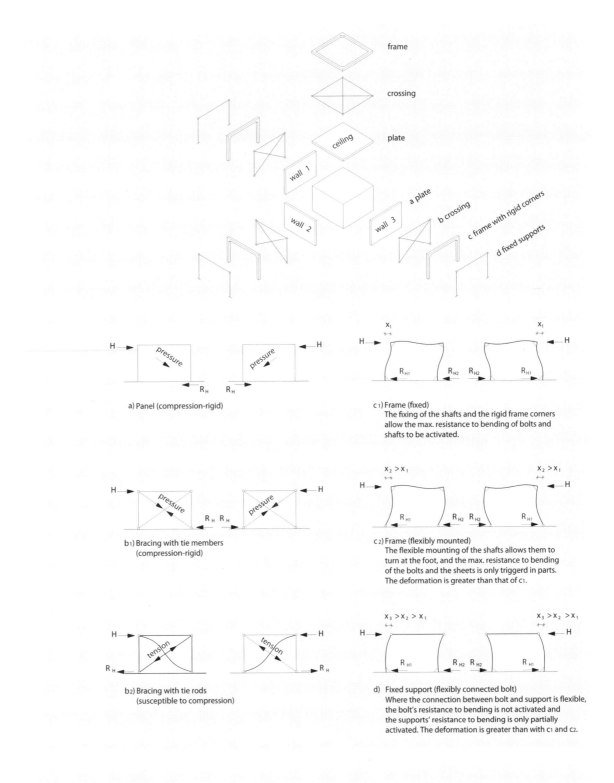

frame

crossing

plate

ceiling

wall 1

wall 2

wall 3

a plate

b crossing

c frame with rigid corners

d fixed supports

a) Panel (compression-rigid)

b1) Bracing with tie members
(compression-rigid)

b2) Bracing with tie rods
(susceptible to compression)

c1) Frame (fixed)
The fixing of the shafts and the rigid frame corners
allow the max. resistance to bending of bolts and
shafts to be activated.

c2) Frame (flexibly mounted)
The flexible mounting of the shafts allows them to
turn at the foot, and the max. resistance to bending
of the bolts and the sheets is only triggerd in parts.
The deformation is greater than that of c1.

d) Fixed support (flexibly connected bolt)
Where the connection between bolt and support is flexible,
the bolt's resistance to bending is not activated and
the supports' resistance to bending is only partially
activated. The deformation is greater than with c1 and c2.

Fig. 2.1.35: Possible types
of stiffening element

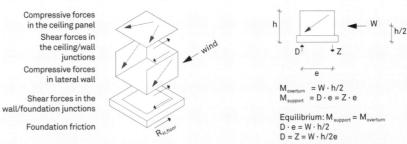

Compressive forces
in the ceiling panel
Shear forces in
the ceiling/wall
junctions
Compressive forces
in lateral wall

Shear forces in the
wall/foundation junctions

Foundation friction

wind

$M_{overturn} = W \cdot h/2$
$M_{support} = D \cdot e = Z \cdot e$

Equilibrium: $M_{support} = M_{overturn}$
$D \cdot e = W \cdot h/2$
$D = Z = W \cdot h/2e$

(D increases the existing base compression due to
vertical load and Z must either be overpressed by
the roofing's own weight or anchored in the ground.)

Fig. 2.1.36: Flow of force in roof
stiffening against wind load and
the tilt load created

2.2 FOUNDATIONS

THE PRINCIPLES OF SOIL MECHANICS
· Important parameters for the loadbearing behavior of soils
· Foundation design aspects
· Allowable load on the subsoil
· Frost in the soil

PRINCIPAL FOUNDATION TYPES
· Shallow foundations
· Deep foundations

Bernd Funke

2.2 FOUNDATIONS

THE PRINCIPLES OF SOIL MECHANICS

Soil mechanics is the study of forces and their effects in the ground. In principle, all construction works cause changes in the forces in the ground due to the increase or decrease in the loads associated with such works (e.g. as a result of excavations). We distinguish here between foundations (structures in the soil) and earthworks (structures built with soil). In the end it is the soil-structure interaction that determines the design of a foundation.

Important parameters for the loadbearing behavior of soils

To complement the principles of soil classification (soil types, particle sizes, etc.) introduced in section 1.1, a number of further features and parameters important for the loadbearing behavior of soils are described below.

Particle-size distribution

This is the distribution of the different particle sizes throughout the soil and is a primary classification factor for inorganic soils. The uniformity coefficient U is one variable used to describe the particle-size distribution. It is the quotient of particle diameter d_{60} and particle diameter d_{10}.

Explanation: To determine the particle size, in a laboratory test a soil sample is passed through a standardized stack of sieves with ever finer mesh sizes. The mesh size of the sieve through which 60% by mass of the soil passes is called d_{60}. The sieve with the mesh size d_{10}, on the other hand, allows only 10% by mass of the soil to pass through.

$$U = \frac{d_{60}}{d_{10}} [-]$$

$$U = \frac{(60\% \text{ by mass of the particles have a diameter } d \leq d_{60\,[mm]})}{(10\% \text{ by mass of the particles have a diameter } d \leq d_{10\,[mm]})}$$

Soils with U < 5 are uniform (closely graded), those with 5 ≤ U ≤ 15 nonuniform (well-graded), and those with U > 15 extremely nonuniform (gap-graded). Nonuniform soils are easier to compact than uniform ones, because in nonuniform soils the smaller particles can fill the voids between the larger grains. Such soils are therefore also more susceptible to settlement. So in order to carry the same applied load, nonuniform soils must generally be compacted more than uniform soils.

Density

One of the most important parameters for the bearing capacity of a soil is its density.
In-situ density D: This specifies the ratio of the density of the soil in its natural state to the loosest possible state (trickling from the hand) and to its densest possible state (firmly compacted with considerable energy).

The greater the proportion of voids in a soil, the lower its in-situ density. The in-situ density D is calculated from the following ratio of possible dry densities (the d suffix here stands for "dry"):

$$D = \frac{\rho_d - \min.\rho_d}{\max.\rho_d - \min.\rho_d} [-] \text{ rather } D = \frac{\text{exist } \Delta\rho_d}{\max.\Delta\rho_d} \quad \text{> Fig. 2.2.1}$$

where:
ρ_d = in-situ dry density
$\min.\rho_d$ = minimum dry density after loosening
$\max.\rho_d$ = maximum dry density after compacting

The dry density is measured in mass per volume $\left[\frac{t}{m^3}\right]$.

The maximum in-situ density is max. D = 1, i.e. the in-situ soil has reached its highest possible density. The minimum in-situ density is min. D = 0, i.e. the in-situ soil has reached its lowest possible density. The soil strata are therefore described with in-situ densities between 0 and 1. > Tab. 2.2.1
A soil can be compacted in order to increase its bearing capacity; this increases its in-situ density and the variable used to measure this increase is the degree of

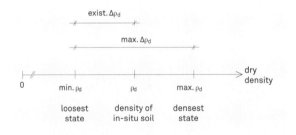

Fig. 2.2.1: Possible dry densities

State	Very loose	Loose	Med. dense	Dense
In-situ density D	< 0.15	0.15–0.30	0.30–0.50	> 0.50

Tab. 2.2.1: Guidance values for the relationship between the in-situ state and the in-situ density D as measured

compaction D_{Pr}. A sample of soil is taken to determine the degree of compaction D_{Pr} directly. Afterwards, the dry density ρ_d of the in-situ soil is determined in the laboratory. Following that, the sample is placed in a standardized container with a standardized weight and compacted with a certain number of hammer blows (Proctor test to DIN 18127). The parameters of this compaction are defined in such a way that the sample of soil is compacted by applying a standardized work of magnitude $A = 0.6$ [MNm/m³]. The dry density, also known as the Proctor density ρ_{Pr}, of this soil sample compacted in this standard way is then calculated. Finally, the degree of compaction ρ_{Pr} the quotient of the dry density ρ_d (dry density of soil to be tested prior to standardized compaction) and the Proctor density ρ_{Pr} (dry density after standardized compaction) can be worked out.

$$D_{Pr} = \frac{\rho_d}{\rho_{Pr}} \cdot 100 [\%]$$

As the compactability of a soil is heavily dependent on its water content, at least five samples with different water contents must be made from the sample of soil, then compacted, and finally examined with respect to their dry densities. Plotting the results of these individual samples on a graph produces a curve known as the Proctor curve. The peak (maximum) value on this curve is the Proctor density ρ_{Pr} and should be entered into the above equation. > **Fig. 2.2.2 and tab. 2.2.2**

In the vicinity of foundations, a degree of compaction of $D_{Pr} \geq 95\%$ is generally required in uniform soils, and D_{Pr}

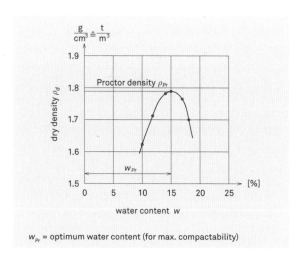

w_{Pr} = optimum water content (for max. compactability)

Fig. 2.2.2: Proctor curve as a function of the dry density ρ_d required after compaction and depending on the water content w_{Pr}

Soil type	ρ_{Pr} in $\frac{g}{cm^3}$	w_{Pr} [%]
clay, high plasticity	1.44	30
clay, low plasticity	1.62	22
sandy clay	1.70	17
sandy silt	1.75	14
medium sand	1.85	11
gravelly sand	1.98	10
gravel-sand mix	2.12	7

Tab. 2.2.2: Guidance values for the Proctor density ρ_{Pr} and associated water content w_{Pr} of various soils

$\geq 98\%$ in nonuniform soils. In practice, the degree of compaction D_{Pr} can be determined using one of the following four methods:

1. Soil sample (direct determination according to DIN 4021, 18125 and 18127, also DIN EN ISO 22475-1): Taking a sample of soil (e.g. using a sampling tube), determining ρ_d and ρ_{Pr} and subsequently calculating D_{Pr}. This is a very precise method that, however, makes it necessary to obtain samples of soil and investigate them in a laboratory.

2. Plate bearing test (indirect determination according to DIN 18134, currently not covered by a Euronorm, planned for DIN EN ISO 22476-3): Measuring the deformation of the soil when subjected to a static load applied via a standard plate and determining the degree of compaction by calculating back from the elastic moduli E_{v1} (initial loading) and E_{v2} (re-loading) determined. As the plate bearing test can only be used reliably for limited stratum thicknesses up to approx. 1 m, it is preferably used for layered fill over a large area.

3. Dynamic penetration test (indirect determination according to DIN 4094-3 and DIN EN ISO 22476-2): Recording the number of blows required to drive a cone with defined dimensions into the soil, which allows conclusions to be drawn about the degree of compaction. The number of blows required for 10 cm penetration is called the n_{10} value. For example, in loose soils $n_{10} \leq 3$ and in dense soils $n_{10} > 15$ when using a lightweight cone (investigation depths down to approx. 10 m). Owing to the relatively small amount of work involved, dynamic penetration tests are particularly suitable for obtaining a rough guide to the existing soil conditions. They can also be used to reach greater depths and hence localize the boundaries to strata and disruptions in the soil. Over larger areas, they are often used to check the consistency of the soil between the points at which soil samples have been taken.

4. Cone penetration test (indirect determination according to DIN 4094-1 and DIN EN ISO 22476-1): Measuring the resistance, skin friction and excess pore water pressure upon pressing a cone with defined dimensions into the soil at a steady rate and subsequently calculating back to find the degree of compaction. Cone penetration tests supply more accurate results than dynamic penetration tests but involve more work because appropriate heavy plant (e.g. CPT rig anchored to the ground) has to be provided.

Furthermore, road-building and landscaping projects can also make use of "drive-over tests," which simply involve driving a truck with a 5 t wheel load over the ground to be investigated. The depth of the wheel tracks in the ground allows conclusions to be drawn regarding the strength and deformation behavior of the existing soil. Even though this method is no more than an approximate, visual examination, it can be permitted as a test if agreed in the contract.

Shear strength τ_f

The shear strength τ_f of a soil ensures that it does not "flow like water", but instead can stand without support over a certain height or can be formed into a stable embankment, for example. If the shear strength of the soil is exceeded, a wedge-shaped body of soil slides down a slip (rupture/failure) plane at the slip plane angle ϑ. > **Fig. 2.2.3** consists of an adhesion component plus a friction component. The adhesion component occurs only in cohesive soils and corresponds to the cohesion c'. Due to the flake-like form of their relatively fine particles, cohesive soils, once wet, develop surface forces that cause the flakes to bond together. > **Chapter 1.1 Soil** The friction component builds up because the weight of the soil exerts a pressure on the slip plane, which in turn generates a friction force. If we relate the emerging friction force to the area of the shear plane, this results in the maximum shear stress that can be transferred $\tau_{friction} = \tan\varphi' \cdot \sigma'$ ($\varphi' =$ effective angle of friction of soil, e.g. from published tables; $\sigma' =$ effective compressive stress at slip plane).

The shear strength τ_f is therefore calculated as follows: $\tau_f = c' + \tan\varphi' \cdot \sigma'$ (adhesion component + friction component). > **Fig. 2.2.4**
The shear strength is lowest in dry, nonplastic soils and highest in nonsaturated, highly cohesive soils.

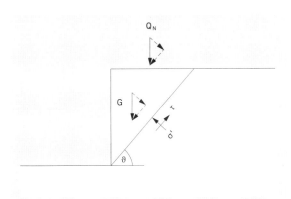

$\sigma' =$ effective normal stress (compressive stress) on slip plane, which generates friction and consequently shear resistance.
τ = shear stress in slip plane. If this is greater than the shear strength τ_f, the wedge of soil slides downwards.

Fig. 2.2.3: Wedge of soil with self-weight G and imposed load Q_N sliding down the slip plane at the slip plane angle ϑ

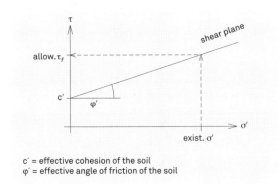

$c' =$ effective cohesion of the soil
$\varphi' =$ effective angle of friction of the soil

Fig. 2.2.4: Shear strength after Coulomb

Foundation design aspects

A number of foundation design relationships important for foundations and retaining structures are explained below.

Settlement

Settlement is a vertical, downward deformation of the subsoil and can be due to various causes:

· Compression of the subsoil by loads (e.g. as a result of the applied load of a foundation or fill, and here the rule is: the greater the load, the greater the settlement). In landscape architecture this is normally of only minor importance owing to the (usually) not very great foundation loads.
· Compression of the subsoil due to a change in the bearing capacity (e.g. as a result of lateral destabilization of the subsoil due to neighboring excavation works).
· Settlement of the subsoil due to a drop in the water table. Like all materials, soil experiences buoyancy in water. Pumping away the water and lowering the water table reduces or even eliminates this buoyancy effect. The self-weight of the soil increases, the stresses in the subsoil rise and the effect is equivalent to an additional applied load.
· Settlement of the subsoil due to the drying-out of cohesive soils (e.g. below large ground slabs or sealed ground).
· Heave and settlement of the subsoil due to the effects of frost. Changes in the volume of water in the soil due to freeze-thaw cycles can also cause changes in the volume of the subsoil.
· Settlement of the subsoil as a result of changes at greater depths (e.g. due to subterranean erosion or underground movements in mining areas).

The planner's aim must be to determine any expected settlements and, if necessary, to control their magnitude through the design of the structure. We basically distinguish between uniform and differential settlement; the latter are generally critical because these can lead to cracking, tilting and other damage to structures. > **Fig. 2.2.5**

If greater differential settlement is to be expected as a result of the subsoil's heterogeneity, this can be dealt with using the following constructional measures:

· Design the foundations in such a way that essentially uniform settlement can be expected below the entire structure (e.g. replace thin strata with lower bearing capacities or use piles to transfer foundation loads to deeper, thicker strata with better bearing characteristics).
· Design the structure to be so stiff that it does not deform and essentially "bridges over" areas of subsoil with a lower bearing capacity. However, such an approach is only viable with sagging effects because in the case of hogging and tilting, out-of-plumb columns and instability might be the result.

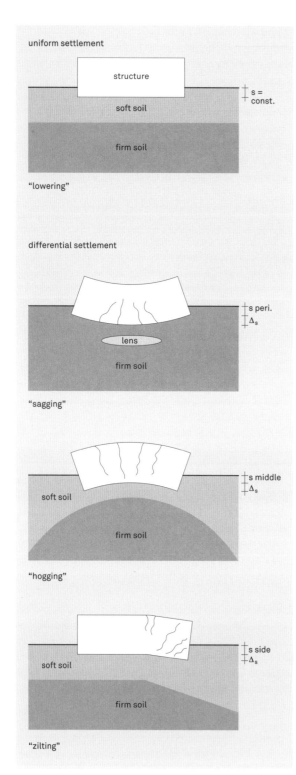

Fig. 2.2.5: Possible types of settlement

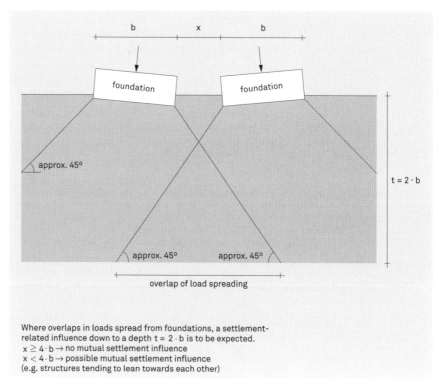

Where overlaps in loads spread from foundations, a settlement-related influence down to a depth $t = 2 \cdot b$ is to be expected.
$x \geq 4 \cdot b \rightarrow$ no mutual settlement influence
$x < 4 \cdot b \rightarrow$ possible mutual settlement influence
(e.g. structures tending to lean towards each other)

Fig. 2.2.6: Mutual settlement effects of adjacent foundations

· Design the structure to have sufficient flexibility to accommodate the expected deformations without damage. In the case of bridges, for example, differential settlement at different piers can be compensated for by providing hinges.

Furthermore, note that closely spaced foundations can be affected by the settlement effects of neighboring foundations. > Fig. 2.2.6

Heave failure

As the load on a foundation increases, so the compaction of the soil underneath it also increases. Once the maximum possible compaction has been reached and the bearing capacity of the soil exceeded, the foundation begins to displace the soil sideways. The soil is pushed sideways and upwards on a slip plane (failure plane in which the shear strength has been exceeded) and heaves up adjacent to the foundation. The load necessary for this corresponds to the ultimate bearing capacity of the soil. > Fig. 2.2.7 The failure behavior of soils is easy to demonstrate with a small experiment. Fill a dish with sugar and place a glass on the sugar. Then press down on the glass with your hand and increase the pressure slowly. Once the ultimate bearing capacity of the "no-fines" sugar is exceeded, it is forced upwards around the glass.

The failure load depends on the shear parameters of the soil plus the size, geometry and embedment depth d of the foundation. Heavily loaded, shallow foundations are especially critical with respect to the risk of heave failure. This is also the reason why excavations alongside foundations may not extend down as far as the underside of the foundation. The minimum embedment depth required is 50 cm. In addition, the risk of heave failure increases in the presence of cohesive soils with a high water content and in the presence of horizontal forces (e.g. also due to the horizontal component of a compressive force applied at an angle) because they reinforce the lateral sliding along the slip plane.

Ground failure

If a retaining structure (e.g. a gravity wall) together with part of the surrounding soil slides along a slip plane, we speak of a ground failure. > Fig. 2.2.8

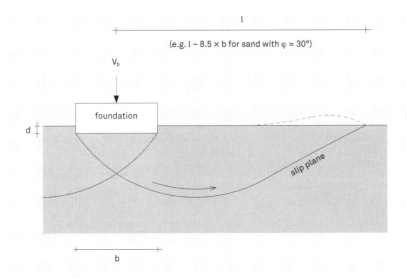

The slip (failure/rupture) plane is approximately the shape of a logarithmic spiral and its position depends on the angle of the internal friction of the soil φ'. The ultimate load depends on the pressure below the foundation, the cohesion of the soil c' (only in the case of cohesive soils), the embedment depth d, and the foundation width b.

Fig. 2.2.7: Heave failure

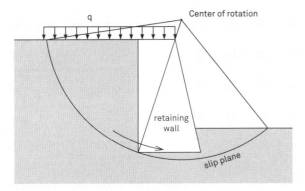

The slip plane is approximately the shape of a circular arc.

Fig. 2.2.8: Ground failure

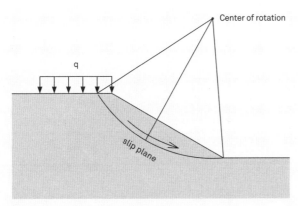

The slip plane is approximately the shape of a circular arc.

Fig. 2.2.9: Slope failure

A ground failure can be caused by an excessive surcharge q behind the structure or a structure with the wrong geometry (insufficient embedment, too narrow, inadequate anchorage, etc.). In terms of soil mechanics, the "driving forces" (tangential components of vertical loads) acting on the slip plane are greater than the retaining forces (friction forces generated by the normal components). Other reasons for ground failure can be unfavorable groundwater conditions (e.g. a build-up of water behind the retaining structure) or soil strata with inadequate shear strength.

Slope failure

If an embankment to a dam or cutting slides down a slip plane together with part of the underlying soil, we speak of a slope failure. > Fig. 2.2.9

Slope failure can be caused by an excessively steep embankment angle, an excessive surcharge q at the top of the embankment or the presence of unfavorable soil strata (e.g. clay strata that act as slip planes).

Earth pressure

The lateral pressure of the soil on a retaining structure is known as earth pressure. This, too, is easy to demonstrate with a little experiment. If a cardboard box is filled with dry sand, the sides of the box bulge outwards as a result of the ensuing horizontal pressure. This horizontal earth pressure is similar to the hydrostatic pressure of liquids ($p_{liquid} = \gamma_{liquid} \cdot h_{liquid}$), except that its magnitude is less owing to the shear strength of the soil (internal resistance). The earth pressure coefficient k is used to take account of the influence of the shear strength on the magnitude of the earth pressure: $p_{earth} = \gamma_{earth} \cdot h_{earth} \cdot k$. In the example with the cardboard box, $k < 1$ and the pressure is therefore less. Figuratively, we could also say that the sand cannot "flow apart" like water, and therefore does not exert such a high pressure. However, the entire weight of the sand (without any reduction) acts on the base of the cardboard box. Consequently, the loads on the structure due to the in-situ soil have to be calculated separately for the horizontal and vertical directions—in contrast to liquids, which exert the same pressure in all directions. The vertical pressure due to backfilling over the structure is known as an earth surcharge, the magnitude of which is $g_{earth} = \gamma_{earth} \cdot h_{earth}$.

The magnitude of the ensuing earth pressure depends on the shear parameters of the soil (internal friction ϕ and cohesion c'), and on the resulting displacement of the structure towards the soil, where the earth pressure coefficient k must not necessarily be less than 1. We distinguish between active earth pressure, at-rest earth pressure and passive earth pressure. > Figs. 2.2.10 and 2.2.11

If the structure moves away from the supporting soil (which, for example, corresponds to the deformation behavior of conventional retaining walls), active earth pressure e_a with the coefficient $k_a < 1$ becomes relevant.

a) Active earth pressure E_a

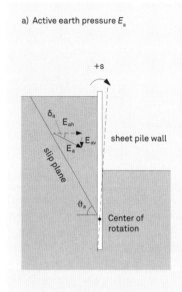

b) At-rest earth pressure E_0

c) Passive earth pressure E_p

The retaining structure (e.g. a sheet pile wall) yields slightly under the action of the earth pressure and is displaced away from the soil (+s).

ϑ_a = active slip plane angle
δ_a = active wall friction angle

The active wedge of soil slides downwards behind the wall. This movement leads to friction on the retaining structure so that the active body of soil "pushes" the wall downwards. Consequently, the vertical component of the active earth pressure E_{av} acts downwards.

The retaining structure (e.g. a gravity wall founded on rock) does not move (s = 0).

The retaining structure (e.g. the abutment to an arch bridge) is pressed towards the ground by the horizontal force H (horizontal thrust at springing) and compresses the soil (-s). This consequently mobilizes ground resistance, which is known as passive earth pressure.

ϑ_p = passive slip plane angle
δ_p = passive wall friction angle

The passive wedge of soil behind the foundation is displaced upwards. This upward movement leads to friction on the retaining structure so that the soil "pulls" this with it. Consequently, the vertical component of the passive earth pressure E_{pv} acts upwards.

Fig. 2.2.10: Types of earth pressure

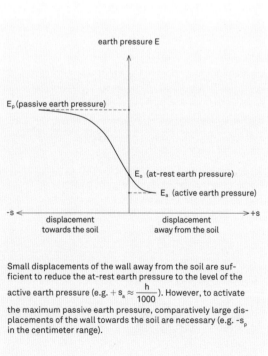

a) Wall movement in relation to the soil

+s = Displacement away from the soil
- s = Displacement towards the soil

b) Stress distribution in the soil and horizontal earth pressure forces

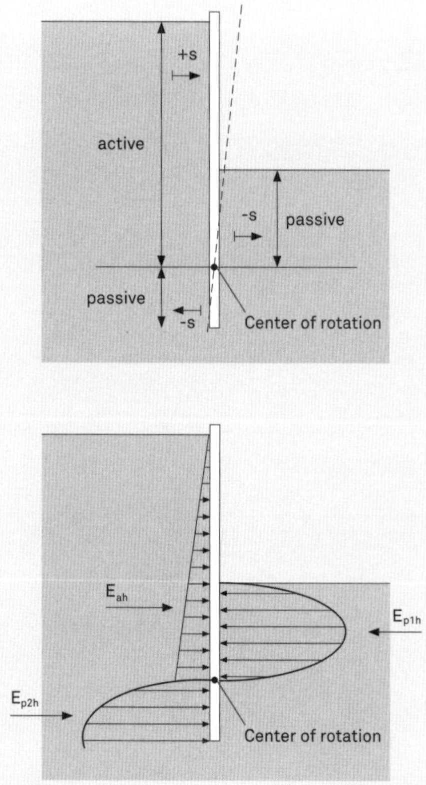

Small displacements of the wall away from the soil are sufficient to reduce the at-rest earth pressure to the level of the active earth pressure (e.g. $+s_a \approx \dfrac{h}{1000}$). However, to activate the maximum passive earth pressure, comparatively large displacements of the wall towards the soil are necessary (e.g. $-s_p$ in the centimeter range).

Fig. 2.2.11: The magnitude of the earth pressure depending on the movement of the retaining structure

Fig. 2.2.12: Active and passive earth pressures on a retaining wall whose base is fully fixed in the ground

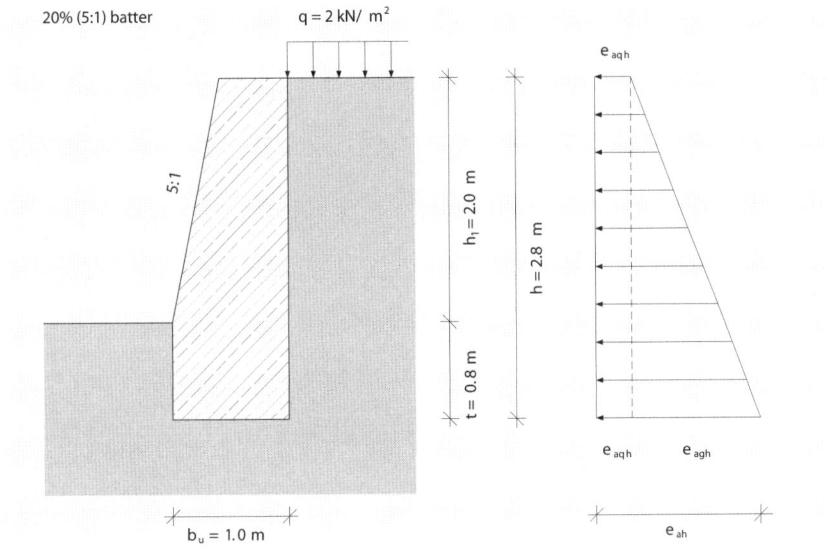

Fig. 2.2.13: Earth pressure
on a gravity wall

moves towards it. In this case the internal resistance increases the pressure because it has to be overcome as well. > **Fig. 2.2.12** In addition, the horizontal movement of a retaining structure causes a vertical movement of the ground behind it (the wedge of soil slides up or down the slip plane). This is why the wall friction angle δ (roughness of the rear face of the wall) has an influence on the magnitude of the earth pressure.

The earth pressure e due to the self-weight of the soil is the product of the unit weight of the soil γ (gamma!), the depth of the in-situ soil h (at the base of the wall the height of the retaining structure, > **Fig. 2.2.13**) and the earth pressure coefficient k. Here, the earth pressure coefficient k represents the transverse pressure component of the vertical soil stresses dependent on the wall movement and the friction parameters φ and δ > **Tab. 2.2.3**

$$e = \gamma \cdot h \cdot k \left[\frac{kN}{m^2} \right].$$

This is the smallest possible earth pressure because the soil, as a result of its shear strength (internal resistance), cannot follow the movement of the wall unhindered. If the retaining structure is so stiff and well supported that it does not move (which, for example, is the case with a structure backfilled on both sides and with adequate wall thickness), at-rest earth pressure e_0 with the coefficient $k_a < k_0 < 1$ becomes relevant. The associated earth pressure is therefore greater than in the case of active earth pressure because the soil does not have to follow the wall and hence no pressure-relieving transverse movement occurs. If the retaining structure moves towards the soil (e.g. in the region of the valley-side ground abutment to a palisade, where the embedded end of the palisade is supported by the soil), passive earth pressure ep with the coefficient $k_p > 1$ becomes relevant. This is the maximum possible earth pressure because the ground is compressed and compacted as the wall

The following units of measurement are relevant here:

$$\gamma \left[\frac{kN}{m^3} \right], \; h[m], \; k[-].$$

In the presence of a cohesive soil, the earth pressure due to cohesion is calculated separately and superimposed on the other earth pressures, but this aspect will not be dealt with any further at this point.

In the standard situation, retaining structures (sheet pile walls, palisades, cantilever retaining walls, etc.) are designed for the horizontal component of the active pressure with the earth pressure coefficient k_{ah} owing to the movement of the wall away from the soil. > **Tab. 2.2.3** If there is an additional surcharge, the associated earth pressure component is the product of the additional surcharge q and the earth pressure coefficient k_{ah}. The total

Type		δ \ φ	17.5°	20°	22.5°	25°	27.5°	30°	32.5°	35°	37.5°	40°
Active	k_a k_{ah} k_{ah}	0 $+\frac{1}{3}\varphi$ $+\frac{2}{3}\varphi$	0.54 0.50 0.47	0.49 0.46 0.43	0.45 0.41 0.38	0.41 0.37 0.35	0.37 0.34 0.31	0.33 0.30 0.28	0.30 0.27 0.25	0.27 0.25 0.22	0.24 0.22 0.20	0.22 0.20 0.18
At-rest	k_0	0	0.70	0.66	0.62	0.58	0.54	0.50	0.46	0.43	0.39	0.36
Passive	k_p k_{ph} k_{ph}	0 $-\frac{1}{3}\varphi$ $-\frac{2}{3}\varphi$	1.86 2.11 2.32	2.04 2.37 2.66	2.24 2.67 3.06	2.46 3.03 3.56	2.72 3.45 4.17	3.00 3.96 4.94	3.32 4.59 5.93	3.69 5.36 7.20	4.11 6.34 8.89	4.60 7.59 11.16

φ = angle of internal friction of the soil
δ = wall friction angle
  δ = 0° wall with smooth rear face, e.g. with waterproofing
  δ = $\frac{1}{3}\varphi$ wall with slightly rough rear face, e.g. concrete with plastic formwork or precast elements
  δ = $\frac{2}{3}\varphi$ wall with rough rear face, e.g. steel, concrete, timber
k_a = coefficient for active earth pressure without wall friction (acts horizontally because without friction there is no vertical component)
k_{ah} = coefficient for horizontal component of active earth pressure with wall friction
k_0 = coefficient for at-rest earth pressure (inevitably horizontal because without movement there is no friction)
k_p = coefficient for passive earth pressure without wall friction (acts horizontally because without friction there is no vertical component)
k_{ph} = coefficient for horizontal component of passive earth pressure with wall friction

Tab. 2.2.3: Earth pressure coefficients for retaining structures with vertical rear face and level ground

of the horizontal active earth pressure due to soil load and the additional surcharge is as follows

$$e_{ah} = e_{agh} + e_{aqh} = (\gamma \cdot h + q) \cdot k_{ah} \quad \text{> Fig. 2.2.13}$$

Allowable load on the subsoil

The allowable load on the subsoil can be determined from the bearing capacity and the anticipated deformation behavior of the soil in-situ. In doing this, it is important to verify that, on the one hand, no failure conditions occur (failure of the subsoil due to heave, ground or slope failures) and, on the other, the settlement to be expected does not assume an order of magnitude that is damaging for the structure.

In simple cases, the allowable bearing pressures σ_{allow} for pad and strip footings can be taken from the design tables in DIN 1054 (depending on the structure's susceptibility to settlement, foundation width and embedment depth). Provided these allowable bearing pressures are not exceeded, a specific heave failure and settlement analysis is not obligatory. However, certain conditions have to be fulfilled when using the tables (e.g. rigid foundation, minimum foundation width = 30 cm, no dynamic loads, uniform soil conditions). This method, valid in Germany, is not currently covered in the associated Eurocode DIN EN 1997 (EC 7). Nevertheless, its "simple structure" means it has a rule-of-thumb character and is therefore certainly adequate for an initial estimate of the bearing capacity. > Tabs. 2.2.4–2.2.7

The analysis is such that the existing bearing pressure is checked to ensure that it is less than or equal to the allowable bearing pressure. The existing bearing pressure σ_{exist} is the quotient of the vertical force at the underside of the foundation (total of all loads) and the bearing area of the foundation.

$$\sigma_{exist} = \frac{F}{A} = \frac{V_{u/s\,found}}{A_F} \leq \sigma_{allow} \left[\frac{kN}{m^2} \right].$$

The loadbearing properties of the soil in the area of the proposed foundation should always be checked ahead of the design work. It should always be remembered that even mature soil might have insufficient bearing capacity, a fact that applies to organic and soft soils in particular. Moreover, nonmature soils and uncompacted fill generally have only a low bearing capacity because the uncoordinated placement of the soil produces a relatively loose density. If the bearing capacity of the soil is inadequate, it can be compacted or replaced, or a deeper foundation can be constructed.

Minimum embedment depth of foundation [m]	Allowable bearing pressure [kN/m²] depending on width of strip footing			
	0.5 m	1 m	1.5 m	2 m
0.5	200	300	400	500
1	270	370	470	570
1.5	340	440	540	640
2	400	500	600	700
for structures with foundation depths ≥ 0.3 m and foundation widths ≥ 0.3 m	150			

Tab. 2.2.4: Allowable bearing pressures σ_{allow} for nonplastic soils under structures not sensitive to settlement (DIN 1054, Tab. A.1, not covered by a Euronorm)

Minimum embedment depth of foundation [m]	Allowable bearing pressure [kN/m²] depending on width of strip footing					
	0.5 m	1 m	1.5 m	2 m	2.5 m	3 m
0.5	200	300	330	280	250	220
1	270	370	360	310	270	240
1.5	340	440	390	340	290	260
2	400	500	420	360	310	280
for structures with foundation depths ≥ 0.3 m and foundation widths ≥ 0.3 m	150					

* A structure is sensitive to settlement when settlement can damage its constructional elements (e.g. stiff constructions continuous over several spans).

Tab. 2.2.5: Allowable bearing pressures σ_{allow} for nonplastic soils under structures sensitive to settlement * (DIN 1054, Tab. A.2, not covered by a Euronorm)

DIN 1054 states that in order to be able to use the allowable bearing pressures given in the tables for nonplastic soils, the following conditions must be fulfilled, depending on the soil group and the uniformity coefficient:

Soil group to DIN 18196	Uniformity coefficient U	In-situ density D	Degree of compaction D_{Pr}	Penetration resistance P_c [MN/m²]
SE, GE, SU GU, GT	≤ 3	≥ 0.3 (≥ 0.5)	≥ 95% (≥ 98%)	≥ 7.5 (≥ 15)
SE, SW, SI, GE GW, GT, SU, BV	> 3	≥ 0.45 (≥ 0.65)	≥ 98% (≥ 100%)	≥ 7.5 (≥ 15)

U ≤ 3 → uniform soils
U > 3 → nonuniform soils
The minimum values specified corresponded to a medium density. The values in brackets represent a higher density, and so σ_{allow} may be increased by 50%.

Tab. 2.2.6: Requirements for the application of Tab. 2.2.4 and Tab. 2.2.5

Soil type	Soil group	Consistency	Embedment depth [mm]			
			0.5	1	1.5	2
pure silt	UL	semifirm	130	180	220	250
mixed-grain soil	SU, ST, ST, GU, GT	stiff semifirm firm	150 220 330	180 280 380	220 330 440	250 370 500
clayey silty soil	UM, TL, TM	stiff semifirm firm	120 170 280	140 210 320	160 250 360	180 280 400
fatty clay	TA	stiff semifirm firm	90 140 200	110 180 240	130 210 270	150 230 300

Tab. 2.2.7: Allowable bearing pressures σ_{allow} [kN/m²] for cohesive soils (DIN 1054, Tab. A.3–A.6, not covered by a Euronorm)

Frost in the soil

If the external temperature drops below 0°C for a longer period, frost penetrates the soil parallel to the ground surface. As it does so, it freezes any water present in the soil and increases its volume by approx. 9%.

Soils not sensitive to frost

In soils without capillary action (e.g. sands and gravels), it can be assumed in the normal case that frost does not cause any significant changes to the volume of the soil. If the soil is not saturated, the volume of pores is generally sufficient to accommodate the increased volume of the pore water as it freezes. In saturated soils, the water not yet frozen is displaced by the pore water upon freezing. However, as in this displacement process certain resistances have to be overcome, in unfavorable cases frost heave is still possible where there is no or too little vertical load (which forms the resistance for the displacement).

Soils sensitive to frost

In soils with capillary action (e.g. mixed- and fine-grain silts), water in the soil is transported into the freezing zone by capillary action, which means that the water content of the frozen part of the soil increases significantly. As a result, ice lenses often form, which can cause considerable increases in volume in the centimeter range or even greater, depending on the amount of water available.

Upon thawing, the areas that had been subjected to ice lens formation are often oversaturated and pulpy. They therefore lose their bearing capacity and tend to yield under load. As a result, soils sensitive to frost are potentially at risk on two counts: first, heave as the ground freezes, and second, settlement and sliding as the ground thaws, both of which can cause damage to the construction above. For example, frost heave can crack pavements, which then, once the ice has thawed, may subside under imposed loads owing to the weakening of the base below the pavement due to oversaturation. > Chapter 1.1 Soil, Frost sensitivity

In order to prevent stability risks, loadbearing structures must be founded in such a way that they cannot be damaged by frost. The foundation must either be embedded so deep in the ground that frost does not penetrate as far as the underside of the foundation (normally approx. 80 cm in Central Europe), or it must be founded on a suitable, appropriately thick subbase (e.g. adequately compacted gravel or ballast). In some cases it may also be necessary to consider construction conditions that extend beyond the winter period. For example, the ground below foundations that are not yet backfilled could freeze and hence destabilize the existing soil structure.

In the case of nonloadbearing constructions, the potential risks and damage to a foundation that could be affected by frost must be weighed up against the cost of providing a foundation that is safe in freezing conditions. It is not only the risks to the construction itself that are relevant here, but also any safety risks associated with the effects of frost. Constructions that must comply with safety requirements, e.g. well-used paved areas and stairs in public areas, should therefore be founded on suitable subbases if the subsoil could be a problem in freezing conditions. Such constructions can be further protected by draining the subsoil.

PRINCIPAL FOUNDATION TYPES

Foundations are divided into shallow foundations (foundations with a small embedment depth) and deep foundations (foundations with a large embedment depth). > Fig. 2.2.14

Shallow foundations

Shallow foundations are used when the subsoil below the structure possesses adequate bearing capacity and the ground does not have to provide a fixed-end condition for the structure above. Essentially, we distinguish between pad foundations, strip footings and raft foundations.

Pad foundations and strip footings

When the loads of the structure are transferred to the foundation level by way of columns and piers, the most obvious solution is to support these on individual pad foundations. Where, on the other hand, concrete or masonry walls carry the loads down to foundation level, strip footings will probably be required. However, in the case of heavy loads, these solutions are only possible

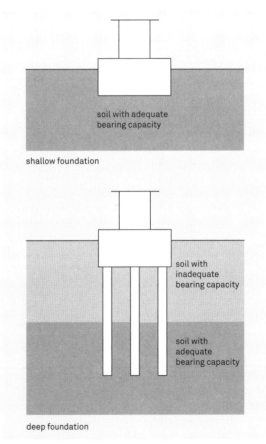

Fig. 2.2.14: Types of foundation

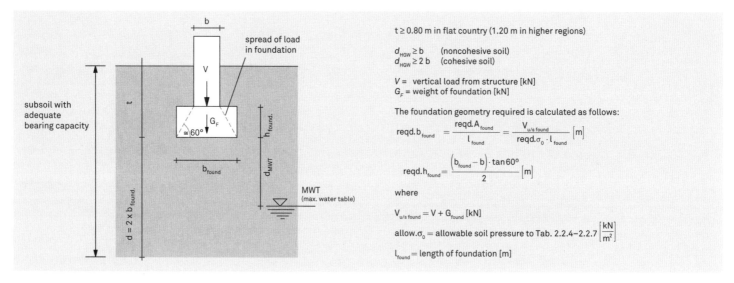

$t \geq 0.80$ m in flat country (1.20 m in higher regions)

$d_{HGW} \geq b$ (noncohesive soil)
$d_{HGW} \geq 2\,b$ (cohesive soil)

$V = $ vertical load from structure [kN]
$G_F = $ weight of foundation [kN]

The foundation geometry required is calculated as follows:

$$\text{reqd.}\,b_{found} = \frac{\text{reqd.}\,A_{found}}{l_{found}} = \frac{V_{u/s\,found}}{\text{reqd.}\,\sigma_0 \cdot l_{found}}\;[m]$$

$$\text{reqd.}\,h_{found} = \frac{\left(b_{found} - b\right) \cdot \tan 60^\circ}{2}\;[m]$$

where

$$V_{u/s\,found} = V + G_{found}\;[kN]$$

$\text{allow.}\,\sigma_0 = $ allowable soil pressure to Tab. 2.2.4–2.2.7 $\left[\frac{kN}{m^2}\right]$

$l_{found} = $ length of foundation [m]

Fig. 2.2.15: Conditions and calculations for a foundation for the "simple standard case"

when the subsoil has an adequate bearing capacity for the bearing pressure that ensues below these relatively small foundations, and when the structure can accommodate any differential settlement between the individual foundations without suffering any damage. Furthermore, it should be ensured that the horizontal forces (bracing forces, e.g. due to wind, earth pressure or unplanned eccentricities in the structure) can be transferred safely to the subsoil by way of friction at the underside of the foundation. Therefore, with respect to horizontal load-carrying ability, interconnected strip footings (a "foundation grillage" offering mutual support) are much more accommodating than pad foundations. The pressure distribution beneath a pad foundation takes on a multi-layered bulbous shape ("bulbs of pressure"), and the pressure in the ground decreases relatively quickly with the depth. For example, at a depth of twice the foundation width, it is already reduced to approx. 20% of the pressure at the underside of the foundation. The following simplified approach can be used to determine the required foundation area for standard situations:
The required foundation area reqd. A_{found} is the quotient of the vertical force at the underside of the foundation $V_{u/s\,found}$ and the allowable bearing pressure $\sigma_{allow.}$ > Tabs. 2.2.4–2.2.7 The vertical force at the underside of the foundation is determined as part of the structural calculations and for simple cases an initial estimate is obtained by simply adding together the loads of the structure (> Tab. 2.1.3 and design tables generally available).

$$\text{reqd.}\,A_{found} = \frac{V_{u/s\,found}}{\sigma_{allow.}}\,[m^2] \qquad \left(\left[\frac{kN}{\frac{kN}{m^2}}\right] = [m^2]\right).$$

The following conditions must apply in order to use this equation:
· Subsoil with consistent bearing capacity below the foundation and a stratum thickness at least twice that of the foundation width
· Frost-free at formation level
· Adequate clearance from groundwater.

For pad foundations and strip footings, this results in the relationships illustrated in **Fig. 2.2.15.**
These days, for reasons of durability, foundations are generally constructed using concrete of grades C12/15 to C20/25. If the load can spread adequately within the foundation (spreading angle $\cong 60°$), the foundation can be left unreinforced. > **Fig. 2.2.15** But in unreinforced (= mass concrete) foundations with a greater width, the depths can become quite considerable owing to the spread of the load required. To save concrete, such foundations can be stepped or splayed (which saves the upper sections of the concrete that do not carry any load). However, the cost-savings brought about by the reduction in the amount of concrete must be weighed up against the extra costs for formwork and construction joints. Where a greater number of pad foundations is involved, a study should be carried out to check whether the use of precast foundations is more economic. > **Fig. 2.2.16**
If the foundation width required leads to an uneconomic foundation depth, the foundation can be reinforced (= reinforced concrete), which means it must then be designed as an individual structural member in bending. > **Fig. 2.2.17**
The plan layout of a foundation should be simple and regular, preferably symmetrical in both directions, so that settlement is as uniform as possible (no tilting of the foundation). > **Fig. 2.2.18**

As in the end every foundation disrupts the surrounding ground and influences the properties and behavior of this area to a greater or lesser extent, foundations no longer required following the demolition of the structure above should also be removed.

Raft foundations

Where the bearing capacity of the in-situ subsoil is not adequate to carry the loads via pad foundations or strip footings, a raft foundation in the form of a reinforced concrete construction is a popular solution. Such a foundation allows the loads of the structure to

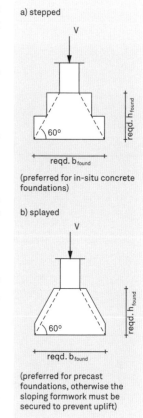

a) stepped

(preferred for in-situ concrete foundations)

b) splayed

(preferred for precast foundations, otherwise the sloping formwork must be secured to prevent uplift)

Fig. 2.2.16: Mass concrete foundations

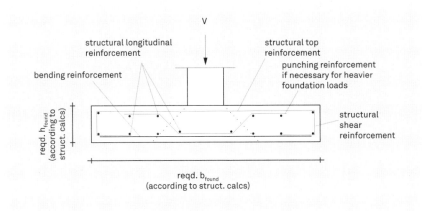

Fig. 2.2.17: Reinforced concrete strip footing

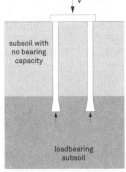

loads carried by skin friction

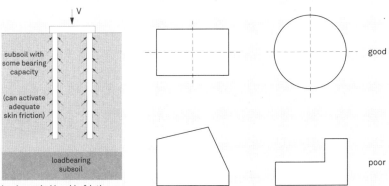

Fig. 2.2.18: Good and poor plan forms for foundations

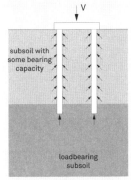

loads carried by end bearing

loads carried by skin friction
and end bearing

Fig. 2.2.19: Loadbearing behavior
of piled foundations

be distributed over the entire plan area of the structure, thus reducing the pressure beneath the foundation accordingly. Furthermore, the settlement behavior of rafts is much better than that of separate foundations (pad foundations, strip footings) because both the average settlement and any differential settlement are on average approx. 30% lower. In addition, it is easier to bridge over any heterogeneities in the subsoil. From the structural viewpoint, raft foundations are relatively complex elements because the structure and the subsoil have an influence on each other's deformation behavior. In this context we also speak of "elastically bedded plates."

Another advantage is the generally seamless, planar construction, which considerably eases the waterproofing against moisture rising from the ground. In the presence of hydrostatic pressure, a reinforced concrete ground slab and the reinforced concrete external walls built off the slab can be built watertight (waterproof concrete: selection of a sufficiently dense concrete mix, reinforcement designed to limit crack widths, watertight joints **> Fig. 2.3.31, p. 188**) without the need for any additional bituminous or synthetic waterproofing materials. If, however, hairline cracks do appear, which leave traces of moisture

on the inside of the wall, they do not necessarily have to be sealed with a suitable injected material. If the defect is acceptable temporarily, over the course of time the cracks tend to seal themselves.

With all reinforced concrete foundations, care should be taken to ensure that the concrete is not contaminated by the surrounding soil, neither while fixing the reinforcement nor while casting the concrete. For this reason, such foundations are always placed on a blinding layer (min. 5 cm thick plain concrete or other suitable material) and the sides are cast against formwork (not directly against the soil).

Additional ground improvement measures

Where the bearing capacity of the subsoil at formation level is not even adequate for a raft foundation, ground improvement measures represent another option. The following main methods are available:

· Static compaction (e.g. by preloading the soil with fill or driving closely spaced short wooden piles)
· Dynamic compaction (e.g. by vibration, rolling or dropping weights)
· Soil replacement (excavation of the soil with inadequate bearing capacity and replacing it with better material, compacting it layer by layer, e.g. gravel-sand mixtures or recycled materials)
· Soil consolidation (e.g. by grouting : injection of suspensions based on cement or clay/cement)

Where the subsoil quality reaches its limits, the measures listed above can often overcome the need to use expensive deep foundations.

Deep foundations

Where soil strata with adequate loadbearing capacity are only available at greater depths, ruling out the use of shallow foundations (possibly in conjunction with ground improvement measures) for technical or economic reasons, then deep foundations are generally the only answer. We divide deep foundations into piled foundations and caissons (for special situations only, which will not be explored further here).

Piled foundations involve driving vertical, sometimes also inclined ("raking piles" for resisting horizontal forces) elements into the subsoil. The forces are transferred into a loadbearing soil stratum by way of skin friction or end bearing, or a combination of the two. The loadbearing behavior is therefore one of the main distinguishing features of piles. **> Fig. 2.2.19**

Furthermore, we also distinguish piles according to the way they are installed:

· Driven piles: mainly steel or reinforced concrete (often timber in the past)
· Bored piles: mainly reinforced concrete (up to 3 m dia.)
· Injected piles: reinforced concrete bored piles with small diameters (0.1–0.3 m).

These piles carry loads exclusively via skin friction, which is why the concrete, or rather cement grout, must be injected into the bored hole and against the soil under pressure (approx. 5–20 bar).

2.3 CONNECTIONS

TIMBER CONNECTIONS
·   Carpentry joints
·   Mechanical connections
·   Glued joints
·   General recommendations

STEEL CONNECTIONS
·   Bolted connections
·   Welded connections

CONCRETE CONNECTIONS
·   Joints for in-situ concrete
·   Joints between precast elements

CONNECTIONS BETWEEN DIFFERENT MATERIALS
·   Steel-timber connections
·   Concrete-steel connections
·   Concrete-timber connections

Bernd Funke

2.3 CONNECTIONS

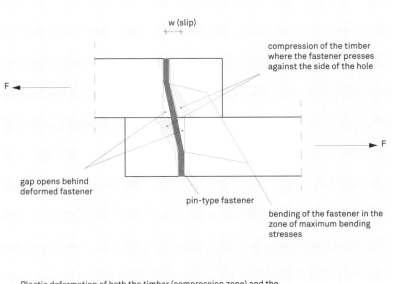

w (slip)

F ←

compression of the timber
where the fastener presses
against the side of the hole

→ F

gap opens behind
deformed fastener

pin-type fastener

bending of the fastener in the
zone of maximum bending
stresses

Plastic deformation of both the timber (compression zone) and the
steel fastener (bending zone) occurs

Fig. 2.3.1: Deformation of a
pin-type timber connection

TIMBER CONNECTIONS

In principle, we distinguish between nonrigid and rigid connections in timber construction. The nonrigid connections, which are divided into carpentry joints and mechanical connections, experience a certain amount of deformation (slip) under load. > Fig. 2.3.1 By contrast, "rigid" connections, which are produced by gluing the pieces of timber together, are very much stiffer, and the deformations that occur up to failure are comparatively small. Table 2.3.1 shows the different load-deformation behavior characteristics of a number of selected connectors. An overview of timber connections is given in figure 2.3.2.

Carpentry joints

We basically distinguish between squared section joints and timber wall joints. > Fig. 2.3.3 The former are also known as "simple wooden joints" and there are essentially eight different types, > Fig. 2.3.4 whereas the latter are divided into connections for log construction and connections for stave construction, in which the transition from carpentry to joinery is already evident. > Figs. 2.3.5 and 2.3.6 Further distinguishing features are the position of the joint (vertical or horizontal), the joint form > Fig. 2.3.7 and whether it forms a flush or non-flush connection.

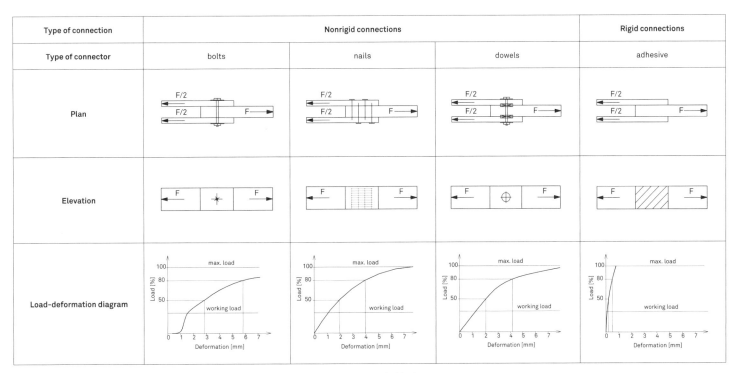

Type of connection	Nonrigid connections			Rigid connections
Type of connector	bolts	nails	dowels	adhesive
Plan	F/2 F/2 F	F/2 F/2 F	F/2 F/2 F	F/2 F/2 F
Elevation	F ← ✳ → F	F ← → F	F ← ⊕ → F	F ← → F
Load-deformation diagram				

Tab. 2.3.1: Load-deformation behavior of various connectors using the example of a lap joint in double shear

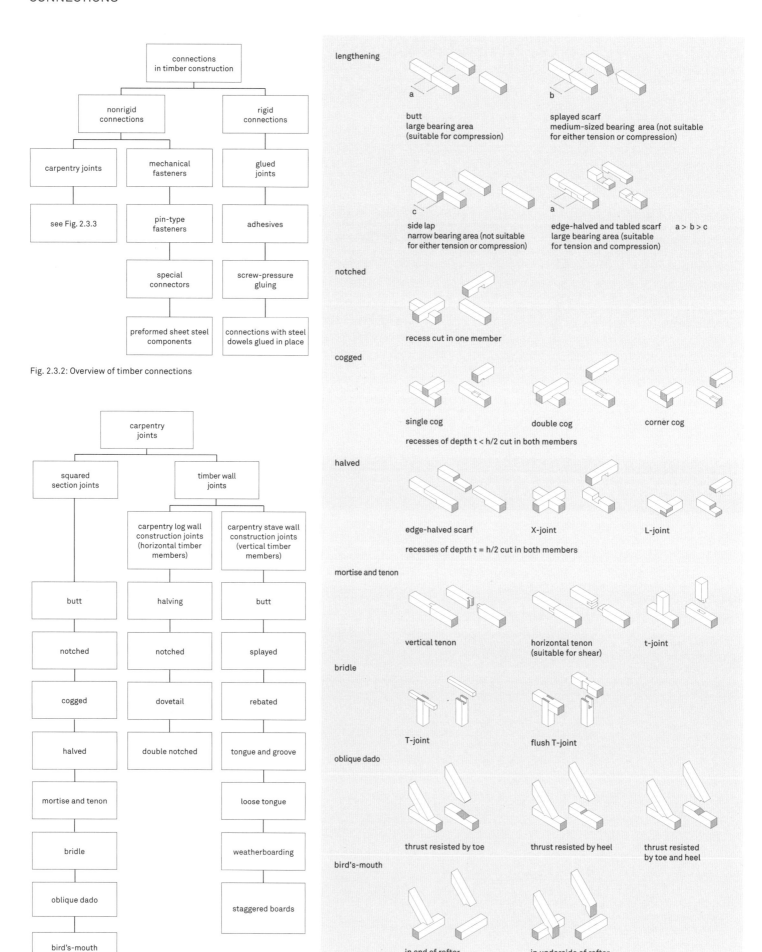

```
                    connections
                 in timber construction
                          │
          ┌───────────────┴───────────────┐
     nonrigid                          rigid
    connections                     connections
          │                             │
  ┌───────┼───────┐                     │
carpentry   mechanical             glued
 joints     fasteners              joints
  │            │                       │
see Fig. 2.3.3  pin-type            adhesives
             fasteners                 │
                │                  screw-pressure
             special                  gluing
            connectors                 │
                │                  connections with steel
         preformed sheet steel     dowels glued in place
            components
```

Fig. 2.3.2: Overview of timber connections

```
                carpentry
                  joints
                    │
        ┌───────────┴───────────┐
   squared                  timber wall
section joints                joints
     │                          │
     │              ┌───────────┴───────────┐
     │        carpentry log wall      carpentry stave wall
   butt      construction joints      construction joints
             (horizontal timber        (vertical timber
               members)                  members)
     │              │                       │
  notched        halving                  butt
     │              │                       │
  cogged         notched                 splayed
     │              │                       │
  halved         dovetail                rebated
     │              │                       │
mortise and    double notched        tongue and groove
  tenon             │                       │
     │              │                   loose tongue
  bridle            │                       │
     │              │                  weatherboarding
oblique dado        │                       │
     │              │                  staggered boards
bird's-mouth
```

Fig. 2.3.3: Overview of carpentry joints

lengthening

butt
large bearing area
(suitable for compression)

splayed scarf
medium-sized bearing area (not suitable
for either tension or compression)

side lap
narrow bearing area (not suitable
for either tension or compression)

edge-halved and tabled scarf   a > b > c
large bearing area (suitable
for tension and compression)

notched

recess cut in one member

cogged

single cog   double cog   corner cog

recesses of depth t < h/2 cut in both members

halved

edge-halved scarf   X-joint   L-joint

recesses of depth t = h/2 cut in both members

mortise and tenon

vertical tenon   horizontal tenon   t-joint
                      (suitable for shear)

bridle

T-joint   flush T-joint

oblique dado

thrust resisted by toe   thrust resisted by heel   thrust resisted
                                                             by toe and heel

bird's-mouth

in end of rafter   in underside of rafter

Fig. 2.3.4: Carpentry squared section joints

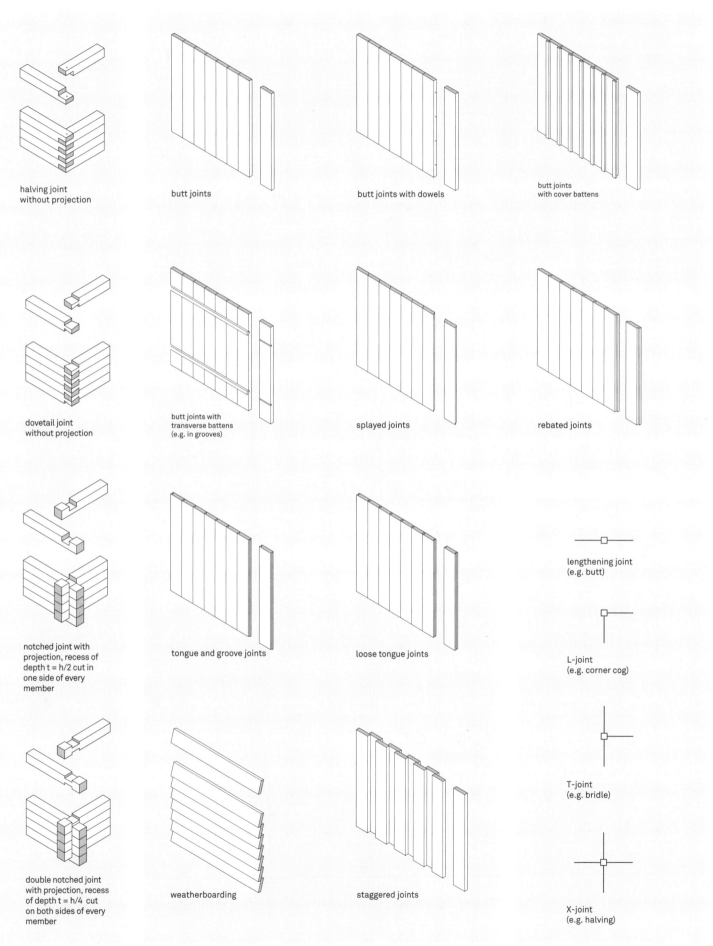

halving joint
without projection

butt joints

butt joints with dowels

butt joints
with cover battens

dovetail joint
without projection

butt joints with
transverse battens
(e.g. in grooves)

splayed joints

rebated joints

notched joint with
projection, recess of
depth t = h/2 cut in
one side of every
member

tongue and groove joints

loose tongue joints

lengthening joint
(e.g. butt)

L-joint
(e.g. corner cog)

T-joint
(e.g. bridle)

double notched joint
with projection, recess
of depth t = h/4 cut
on both sides of every
member

weatherboarding

staggered joints

X-joint
(e.g. halving)

Fig. 2.3.5: Carpentry log wall
construction joints

Fig. 2.3.6: Carpentry stave wall construction joints

Fig. 2.3.7: Joint forms

Mechanical connections

The mechanical connections are basically all metal fasteners. They are divided into pin-type fasteners, special connectors and preformed sheet steel components. Connections with pin-type connectors or dowels are divided into connections in single, double and multiple shear. > **Fig. 2.3.8** The multiple shear design principle is based on the fact that it is advantageous to distribute greater forces over more than one shear plane. As well as reducing the shear stresses in the individual fasteners, this method reduces the bearing pressure on the sides of the holes in the timber as well.

Pin-type fasteners

Pin-type fasteners include nails, staples, wood screws, dowels, standard and close-tolerance bolts, and threaded rods. > **Fig. 2.3.9** With all plain-shank fasteners (nails, staples, dowels, etc.), it is important to ensure that—owing to their pull-out characteristics—they are not permanently loaded in tension. However, a temporary tension load, e.g. wind suction, is permissible. As pin-type fasteners exert a certain cleaving effect on the timber, adequate edge distances and fastener spacings must always be ensured. > **Fig. 2.3.10**

Nails and staples

Round wire nails are primarily used when only shear forces have to be transferred. As drilling pilot holes with a diameter of $0.90d_n$ for nails considerably improve the quality of a nailed connection (25% higher loadbearing capacity and a reduced risk of splitting the wood), the extra work (and costs) involved should always be considered when high-quality connections are required. Where tensile forces in the direction of the fastener could also occur, nails with a screw-like profile are often used. Preformed sheet metal components are fixed with annular-ringed shank or helical-threaded shank nails—types of nail with a rolled profile and hence a better pull-out strength.

One particularly efficient type of fastener is the staple—because it is shot-fired into the timber by machine. To reduce the risk of splitting the wood, the back of the staple should be inserted at an angle of at least 30° to the direction of the grain. In wood-based products, staples should not be driven deeper than 2 mm into the material. Staples are used most of all in panel construction for fixing boards made from wood-based products to solid timber frames, but also in other areas of industrialized woodworking.

Wood screws

Wood screws are available in normal and self-drilling versions. The normal wood screws are covered by DIN standards (round head with slot, countersunk head with slot, hexagon head) and require pilot holes with diameter d_s equal to the length of the shank and diameter $0.7d_s$ equal to the length of the thread. Self-drilling screws require a national technical approval, have different head types to match particular screwing tools (e.g. Pozidriv, Allen key, Torx) and need no pilot holes.

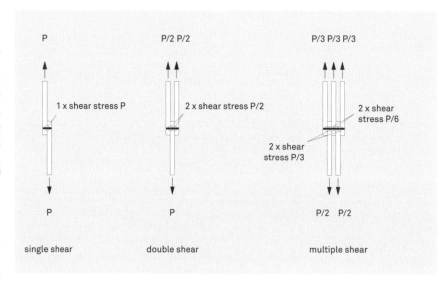

Fig. 2.3.8: Connections in single, double and multiple shear

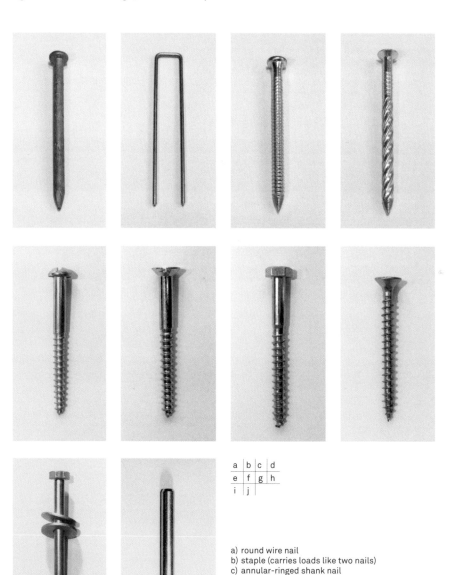

a) round wire nail
b) staple (carries loads like two nails)
c) annular-ringed shank nail
d) helical-threaded shank nail
e) round head wood screw with slot (to DIN 96)
f) countersunk head wood screw with slot (to DIN 97)
g) hexagon head wood screw (to DIN 571)
h) self-drilling wood screw (national technical approval required)
i) bolt (with nut and washers)
j) steel dowel (tight-fitting)

Fig. 2.3.9: Pin-type fasteners

a   preventing splitting by selecting sufficient edge distance and spacing between fasteners

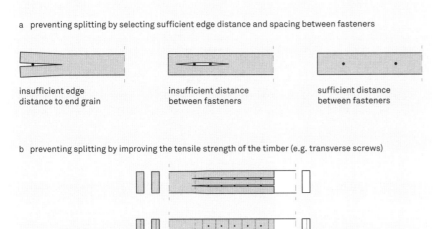

insufficient edge
distance to end grain

insufficient distance
between fasteners

sufficient distance
between fasteners

b   preventing splitting by improving the tensile strength of the timber (e.g. transverse screws)

c   When using nails, the risk of splitting the timber can be reduced by drilling pilot holes or
    staggering the arrangement of the nails by d/2.

Fig. 2.3.10: The cleaving effect of pin-type fasteners and reasonable solutions

a   collar-post connection with dowels

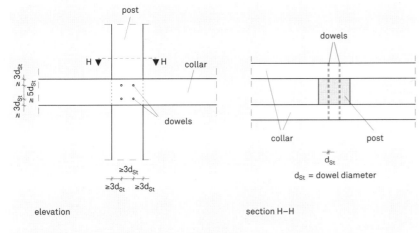

(The horizontal position of the collar [slipping off the dowels]
must be ensured by some suitable means.)

b   truss node with gusset plates and dowels

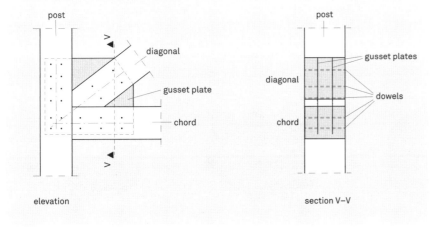

Fig. 2.3.12: Dowelled connections

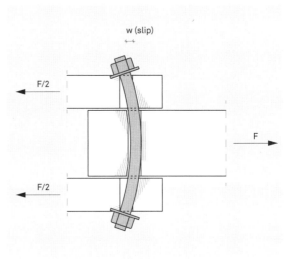

Fig. 2.3.11: Deformation behavior of a bolted connection

Screws inserted properly (turned and not hammered!)
are two to three times stronger than standard nails,
which is why they are preferred for connections involving tensile forces in the direction of the fastener.

Bolts and threaded rods

Loadbearing bolted connections must comprise at least
two bolts with a diameter of $d_B \geq 12$ mm. Owing to their relatively large slip, such connections exhibit comparatively
unfavorable deformation behavior. > Fig. 2.3.11 Nuts have
to be retightened several times because of the slow yielding of the timber. For these reasons, bolted connections
are less suitable for heavily loaded, permanent constructions. However, their simple dismantling makes them fa-
vorites for temporary structures.

Dowels

Dowels are plain cylindrical steel pins with diameters
of 8–24 mm that are driven into predrilled holes of the
same diameter. This tight fitting means that the members
meeting at the joint need no further means of connection.
In principle, dowels carry loads in the same way as nails,
although the force transfer can only take place at 90° to
the axis of the dowel. Dowelled joints are in the form of
single, double and multiple shear connections, but there
must be at least four shear planes per dowel connection. Dowels can be used for timber-timber and also tim-
ber-sheet steel connections. > Fig. 2.3.12 Owing to their
technically appealing appearance and the multitude of
sheet steel connecting components available (gusset
plates, corner angles, tension straps, hinges, etc.), dowels
are especially popular in timber engineering.

Special connectors

In order to overcome the relatively large slip associated
with the straightforward bolted connection, bolts can be
combined with special connectors, which are let into the
wood and thus transfer the shear forces. The bolt merely ensures that the connector, and thus the position of
the shear plane, remains in place. It therefore acts as
a clamping bolt, holding the pieces of timber together

and at the same time enables the transfer of a certain amount of tension in the direction of the bolt. > Fig. 2.3.13

We distinguish between shear-plate connectors (fitted into a prepared recess), toothed-plate connectors (pressed into the timber with a special tool), and combinations of these two forms. > Fig. 2.3.14 DIN 1052-2 and EN 912 define the shapes and dimensions of these special connectors. They are produced in single-sided forms (for steel-timber or detachable connections) and also double-sided forms (for timber-timber connections). > Fig. 2.3.15 The type A1 split-ring connector may also be used for end-grain connections in glued laminated timber (e.g. flush T-joints). > Fig. 2.3.16

Preformed sheet steel components

The use of perforated plates and specially shaped sheet steel framing anchors, joist hangers and other connectors has led to considerable rationalization in timber engineering. These preformed sheet steel components are fixed with annular-ringed shank nails to both the timber members to be joined together (the number of nails used depends on the structural calculations). As the material used is normally quite thin, particular attention should be paid to ensuring that the corrosion protection remains intact. > Fig. 2.3.17

Special gusset plate connections are popular for the fabrication of timber trusses, in particular the "Greim" > Fig. 2.3.18 and "Gang-Nail" systems. > Fig. 2.3.19

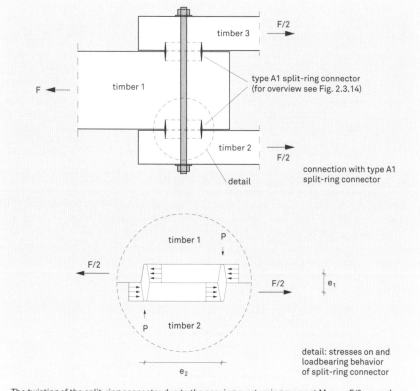

connection with type A1 split-ring connector

detail: stresses on and loadbearing behavior of split-ring connector

The twisting of the split-ring connector due to the ensuing overturning moment $M_{o/turn} = F/2 \cdot e_1$ and the fact that the timber sections are forced apart by this (connector is levered out o f position) are prevented by an opposing restraining moment $M_{restrain} = P \cdot e_2$. Prestressing the bolt holds together the timber sections and creates this restraining moment.

Fig. 2.3.13: Loadbearing behavior of special connectors (using the example of a split-ring connector)

a) special connectors (Appel system)

b) special connectors (Bulldog system)

c) special connectors (Geka system)
Circular plate let into timber, teeth pressed in.

type A1 split-ring connector (double-sided)

type C1 double-sided toothed-plate connector

type C10 double-sided toothed-plate connector

(The single-sided connectors have an opening in the middle with a defined size and a "rim" in order to create a structural connection with the through-bolt and hence to the steel plate.)

Fig. 2.3.14: Overview of special connectors

type B1 shear-plane connector (single-sided)

type C2 single-sided toothed-plate connector

type C20 single-sided toothed-plate connector

left | right

drawing of detail | symbolic drawing

a) timber-timber connection with double-sided connectors and through-bolts

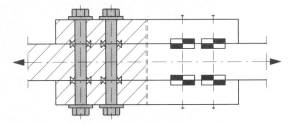

b) steel-timber connection with single-sided connectors and through-bolts

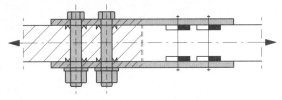

c) elevation of detail (applies to both types of connection)

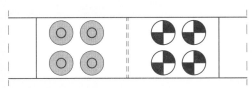

Fig. 2.3.15: Single- and double-sided special connectors

plan

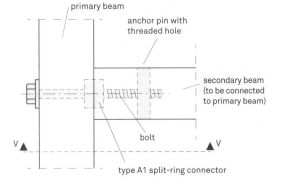

- primary beam
- anchor pin with threaded hole
- secondary beam (to be connected to primary beam)
- bolt
- type A1 split-ring connector

section V–V

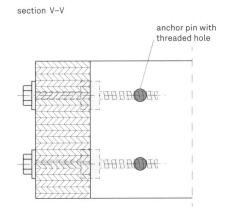

- anchor pin with threaded hole

Fig. 2.3.16: Connection between glued laminated timber members using type A1 split-ring connectors in end grain

perforated plate

rafter-purlin connector

bracket

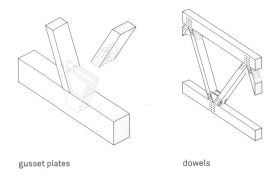

gusset plates | dowels

Fig. 2.3.18: Timber truss connection using the "Greim" system

Fig. 2.3.17: Sheet steel connectors: a) joist hanger, b) angle bracket

a | b

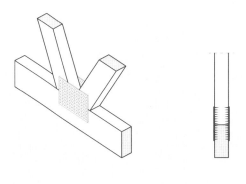

Fig. 2.3.19: Timber truss connection using the "Gang-Nail" system

Glued joints

Good stiffness and the resulting minimal displacement at the face of the joint distinguish glued joints from all other types of timber connection. Modern high-strength, waterproof and mold-resistant adhesives based on synthetic resins have generally replaced the natural glues used exclusively in the past for joints between timber members. Glued joints may be produced only by authorized companies that hold an appropriate license for such work and are inspected regularly by an approved body. Glued joints in particular are dependent on very high standards of workmanship based on considerable knowledge and experience (max. 15% wood moisture content, standard climate, constant clamping pressure, etc.) because any defects in the finished glued joint are usually not apparent.

"Bonding" is used in the production of certain wood-based products, e.g. glued laminated timber and plywood, as well as for joints in timber trusses, timber frames and sign-wave web joists. Figure 2.3.20 shows an example of a glued joint between the chords and diagonals of a timber lattice beam. Splices in longer components are often in the form of finger joints. > Fig. 2.3.21 One of the newer forms of construction is timber-concrete composite construction for suspended timber floors. Here, steel dowels are glued into predrilled holes in the timber. The concrete topping is cast around the projecting ends of the dowels, creating a shear-resistant connection between the timber and the concrete.

General recommendations

To conclude this section, here are a few general recommendations for timber connections:
Single nails ("one nail is akin to no nails") and nails driven into end grain are not permitted. If using more than one type of fastener, the stiffnesses should be as consistent as possible. Glue (rigid) should not be used together with, for example, nails, screws or dowels (nonrigid). Any tension forces at 90° to the axis of the connection should be taken into account when choosing the type of fastener. Hardwoods with a density $\sigma_k \geq 500 \frac{kg}{m^3}$ must be predrilled for pin-type fasteners (also recommended for softwoods). The ensuing bending effects must be taken into account in the case of one-sided connections between timber members subjected to tension or compression. > Fig. 2.3.22

STEEL CONNECTIONS

Steel constructions are generally built in two steps: extensive factory (pre)fabrication of elements that can be easily transported and erected, followed by assembly and erection on the building site. This approach enables the vast majority of factory connections to be welded owing to the defined, easily controlled working conditions. Welding saves material and also weight (no additional endplates, brackets or other connecting elements). The on-site connections are preferably bolted owing to the simplicity of this form of joint and the fact that the work is not dependent on the weather.

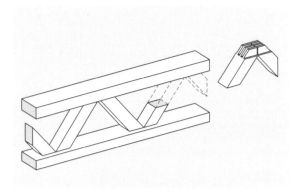

Fig. 2.3.20: Glued timber lattice beam

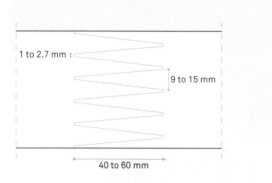

1 to 2.7 mm

9 to 15 mm

40 to 60 mm

Fig. 2.3.21: Finger joint showing the dimensions required

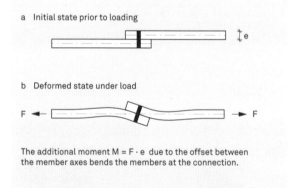

a   Initial state prior to loading

↕ e

b   Deformed state under load

F ←   → F

The additional moment M = F · e due to the offset between the member axes bends the members at the connection.

Fig. 2.3.22 Bending action on a one-sided tension/compression connection

Bolted joints

Types of bolt

Steel structures make use of hexagon head bolts with hexagonal nuts and washers. > Fig. 2.3.23 and tab. 2.3.2 These bolts have a metric thread and are distinguished according to their thread diameter (which leads to the designations M12 to M36). Four grades of steel are used for such bolts. > Tab. 2.3.3 The high-strength friction-grip bolts of strength grades 8.8 and 10.9 have larger AF sizes (AF = distance across flats) so that they can be prestressed by tightening them with a torque (larger AF size = large lever arm = large moment). The hole clearance Δd (Δd = hole diameter d_L – bolt diameter d_s) is used to distinguish between bolts with a permissible $\Delta d = 0.3 - 2$ mm and close-tolerance bolts with a permissible $\Delta d \leq 0.3$ mm. When using close-tolerance bolts, the holes for the bolts are first drilled with a smaller diameter and then bored out to the required

Bolt size	d=d$_s$ [mm]	D [mm]	min e [mm]	s [mm]	k [mm]	m [mm]
M12	12	24	19.85	18	8	10
M16	16	30	26.17	24	10	13
M20	20	37	32.95	30	13	16
M22	22	39	37.29	34	14	18
M24	24	44	39.55	36	15	19
M27	27	50	45.20	41	17	22
M30	30	56	50.85	46	19	24
M36	36	60	60.79	55	23	29

Tab. 2.3.2: Dimensions of hexagon head bolts > **Fig. 2.3.23**

Strength grade *	Tensile strength $f_{u,b,k}$ [N/mm²]	Yield strength $f_{y,b,k}$ [N/mm²]	Typical applications
4.6	400	240	bolts for steel grade S235 (formerly St 37)
5.6	500	300	bolts for steel grade S355 (formerly St 52)
8.8	800	640	high-strength bolts for steel grades S235 and S355
10.9	1000	900	

Explanation of x.y strength grade designation using the example of grade 5.6
x = 5 and y = 6
x = 1st number of strength grade
y = 2nd number of strength grade

tensile strength = x · 100 = 5 · 100 = 500 [N/mm²]
(max. permissible tensile stress prior to failure)

yield strength = tensile strength · 0.y = 500 · 0.6 = 300 [N/mm²]
(permissible tensile strength prior to the onset of larger deformations—"yielding")

Tab. 2.3.3: Bolt strength grades (to EN 20898-1)

Type of bolt	Bolt * to	Washer * to	Nut * to	Strength grades used	Permissible hole clearance	Geometry and dimensions
hexagon head bolt (black bolt)	DIN 7990	DIN 7989, A	DIN EN 24032 DIN EN 24034	4.6 and 5.6	$0.3 < \Delta d \leq 2$	> Fig. 2.3.23
hexagon head close-tolerance bolt	DIN 7968	DIN 7989, B	DIN EN 24032 DIN EN 24034	4.6 and 5.6	$\Delta d \leq 0.3$	**
hexagon head bolt with large AF size (high-strength bolt)	DIN 6914	DIN 6916 6917 6918	DIN 6915	8.8 and 10.9	$0.3 \leq \Delta d \leq 2$	**
hexagon head close-tolerance bolt with large AF size (high-strength close-tolerance bolt)	DIN 7999	DIN 6916 6917 6918	DIN 6915	8.8 and 10.9	$\Delta d \leq 0.3$	**

* Bolts and nuts of strength grades 4.6, 5.6, 8.8 and 10.9 to EN 20898 plus washers with a strength at least equal to that of the bolt
** See standard design tables and EN 20225

Tab. 2.3.4: Overview of bolt types for steel construction

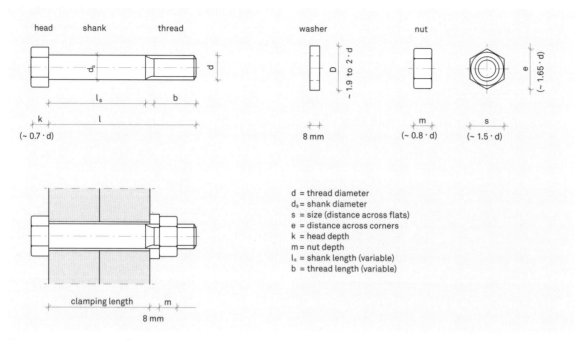

Fig. 2.3.23: Hexagon head bolt (black bolt)

d = thread diameter
d_s = shank diameter
s = size (distance across flats)
e = distance across corners
k = head depth
m = nut depth
l_s = shank length (variable)
b = thread length (variable)

dimensions (with minimal tolerance) during assembly, prior to inserting the bolts. Close-tolerance bolts are necessary if even the smallest displacement within a connection could cause problems, for example, when a combination of bolted and welded connections is employed. A greater clearance in the bolt holes would mean the neighboring nonslip, and hence stiffer, welded connection would have to carry the entire load.

Consequently, there are four types of bolt, each available in two strength grades, i.e. eight bolt types in total. Table 2.3.4 provides an overview of the bolt types used in steel construction.

Types of connection

The system for describing bolted connections is essentially divided into shear/bearing (SL) and friction-grip (GV) connections. When the load acts perpendicular to the bolt axis, the bolt is subjected to shear and the steel components being connected to bearing pressure on the side of the hole. If the bolted connection also has to transfer friction forces perpendicular to the bolt axis in addition to shear, a "friction-grip" (= nonslip) connection is required. In this type of connection, the mating faces of the components are suitably roughened and high-strength bolts used to generate a high, defined prestressing force. Figure 2.3.24 illustrates the two fundamental loadbearing methods SL and GV.

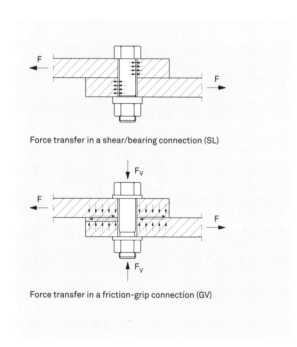

Force transfer in a shear/bearing connection (SL)

Force transfer in a friction-grip connection (GV)

Fig. 2.3.24: Loadbearing behavior of SL and GV connections

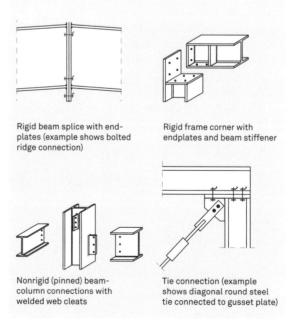

Rigid beam splice with end-plates (example shows bolted ridge connection)

Rigid frame corner with endplates and beam stiffener

Nonrigid (pinned) beam-column connections with welded web cleats

Tie connection (example shows diagonal round steel tie connected to gusset plate)

Fig. 2.3.25: Examples of bolted connections in steel construction

Type of connection	Abbreviation	Types of bolt used	Prestress	Permissible hole clearance [mm]
shear/bearing connection	SL	· black bolts 4.6/5.6 · high-strength bolts 8.8/10.9 (without larger tensile stresses)	No	$0.3 < \Delta d \leq 2$
close-tolerance shear/bearing connection	SLP	· close-tolerance bolts 4.6/5.6 · high-strength close-tolerance bolts 8.8/10.9 (without larger tensile stresses)	No	$\Delta d \leq 0.3$ (minor shear deformation)
prestressed shear/bearing connection	SLV	high-strength bolts 8.8/10.9 (with larger tensile stresses)	Yes	$0.3 < \Delta d \leq 2$
prestressed close-tolerance shear/bearing connection	SLVP	high-strength (bracket with larger tensile stresses)	Yes	$\Delta d \leq 0.3$ (minor shear deformation)
prestressed friction-grip connection	GV	high-strength bolts 8.8/10.9	Yes	$0.3 < \Delta d \leq 2$
prestressed close-tolerance friction grip connection	GVP	high-strength bolts 8.8/10.9	Yes	$\Delta d \leq 0.3$ (minor shear deformation)

Tab. 2.3.5: Overview of bolted connections in steel construction

The use of close-tolerance bolts (minimal hole clearance) enables the deformation due to shear to be minimized in both types of connection, giving connection types SLP and GVP.

When high-strength bolts are used in SL or SLP connections in order to transfer greater tensile forces in the direction of the bolt axis, these must also be tightened with a defined torque, giving connection types SLV and SLVP. Table 2.3.5 provides an overview of these different types of connection.

Owing to their simple, inexpensive assembly, SL connections are used in the majority of situations. Where greater tensile forces are involved, prestressed SLV connections are generally used. And when it is necessary to limit the deformation due to shear, SLP connections are required. SLVP, GV and GVP connections are generally reserved for special applications (e.g. bridge-building). Figure 2.3.25 shows examples of bolted connections.

Welded connections

We basically distinguish between fusion welding (mating faces are melted and joined together in the fluid state) and pressure welding (mating faces are heated up to make them malleable and then joined together under pressure through mechanical compression).

Fusion welding produces linear joints (seams). The most important methods are metal arc welding (for use on site), shielded arc welding (for factory usage, e.g. carbon dioxide welding), and submerged arc welding (for factory usage, automatic method for fabricating large welded sections).

Pressure welding produces individual discrete welds. The most important techniques are resistance welding (connecting thinner materials, e.g. spot welding of sheet metal) and metal arc pressure welding (connecting thicker materials, e.g. welding shear studs to beam flanges).

Types of welded joint

We distinguish between six basic types of joint depending on the geometrical position of the workpieces to be connected. > Tab. 2.3.6 These are either formed as butt welds (weld seam between the edges of the workpieces to be connected) or fillet welds (weld seam in the corner between the workpieces to be connected). Butt welds are further divided into those with and without full penetration (edges fully or not fully welded), and fillet welds into those with normal and those with deep penetration). Furthermore, the joint edges of butt joints can be prepared differently depending on the thickness of the material. Tables 2.3.7 and 2.3.8 provide an overview of the different types of welded joints.

Type of joint		Possible welds		
Name	Geometry	Type of weld	Example	
butt joint		butt weld	square butt joint	
lap joint*		fillet weld	2 no. fillet welds	
T-joint		butt weld or fillet weld	2 no. fillet welds	
L-joint (corner joint)		butt weld or fillet weld	bevel L-joint	
X-joint (cross-joint)		butt weld or fillet weld	2 no. double J-groove butt joints	
inclined T-joint		butt weld or fillet weld	butt joint at toe	

* Two steel plates lying on top of each other should be regarded as critical in terms of corrosion protection and should be avoided in external applications wherever possible.

Tab. 2.3.6: Overview of welded joints

The welding procedure

Larger welded joints must be built up in layers (runs).
> Fig. 2.3.26 The maximum run thickness possible in manual metal arc welding is approx. 4 mm, in shielded arc welding approx. 5 mm and submerged arc welding approx. 7 mm.

Too rapid cooling of the steel heated by the welding procedure brings with it the risk of embrittlement, and so welding should not be carried out during frosty conditions, or the workpieces must be preheated at least. Furthermore, weld seams must be appropriately reworked (transitions between weld bead and parent metal should be ground smooth to avoid stress concentrations) and the connections protected against corrosion by applying a suitable protective coating.

Besides the choice of suitable materials, equipment and joint and good planning (e.g. sequence of welds to minimize heat distortion), the quality of a welded joint is essentially dependent on the skill of the welder. Companies that carry out welding work in factories or on building sites must therefore hold an appropriate license ("minor" or "major" depending on the degree of difficulty of the welding work). In addition, only welders with a valid welding certificate to EN 287 may carry out such work. Figure 2.3.27 shows examples of welded connections.

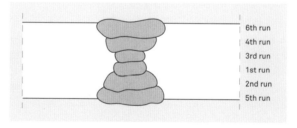

Fig. 2.3.26: Layer-by-layer build-up of welded metal in a double V-groove butt joint

6th run
4th run
3rd run
1st run
2nd run
5th run

CONCRETE CONNECTIONS

There are three basic ways of building concrete and reinforced concrete structures: in-situ construction, precast construction, and semiprecast construction.

In situ concrete construction means casting the individual components from wet concrete on the building site exactly where they are required in the finished structure. The associated operations are building formwork, fixing reinforcement, pouring concrete, striking formwork, and curing (i.e. keeping the concrete moist during hydration of the cement). As it is normally impossible to cast the entire structure in one operation, "construction joints" are necessary. This means that the final monolithic concrete structure has to be divided into

Plate thickness	Type of weld	Form
t ≤ 4 mm	square butt	~ 0.5 t to t — t
3 ≤ t ≤ 10 mm	V-groove butt	~ 60° / 0 to 4 mm — t
6 ≤ t ≤ 40 mm	Y-groove butt (= V-groove with deeper root face)	~ 60° / 2 to 4 mm / 1 to 4 mm — t
t > 10 mm	U-groove butt	~ 10° / ~ 3 mm / 1 to 4 mm — t
t > 15 mm	double bevel butt with backing bar	~ 5 to 20° / 5 to 15 mm — t

The joint forms associated with the respective plate thicknesses are valid for welding from one side. These welds can also be formed from two sides in the case of thicker workpieces. They are then known as double welds (e.g. double V-groove etc.). Sometimes only one side of the joint is prepared (e.g. J-groove, bevel).

Tab. 2.3.7: Edge preparation for butt welds

Type of weld			Symbol	Geometry
Butt welds	with root penetration	square butt	‖	
		V-groove	V	
		Y-groove	Y	
		U-groove	Y	
		double V-groove	X	
		double Y-groove	X	
		double U-groove	X	
		bevel	V	
		J-groove	U	
		double bevel	K	
		double J-groove	K	
	without root penetration	three-plate weld	⤙	
		bevel	r	
		double bevel	K	
Fillet welds	normal	fillet	◿	
		double fillet	▷	
	with deep penetration	fillet	◿	
		double fillet	▷	

Tab. 2.3.8: Overview of weld seam types

a joints in trusses made from hollow sections

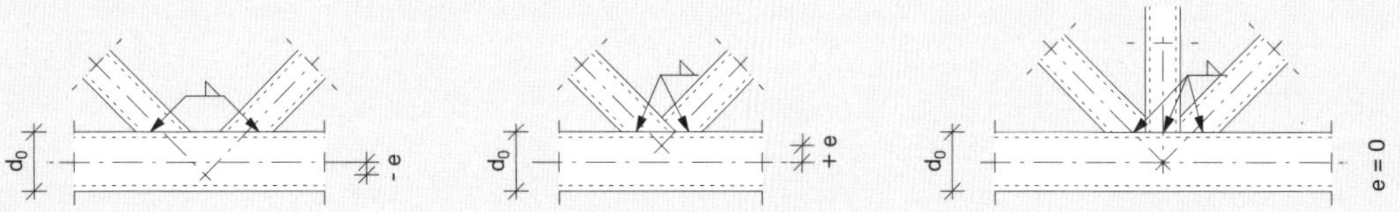

bottom chord-diagonals
joint with gap

bottom chord-diagonals
joint with overlap

bottom chord-diagonals-post joint

Joint eccentricity e should lie within the ratio $-0.55 \geq \frac{e}{d_0} \geq +0.25$.

b joints between circular hollow sections

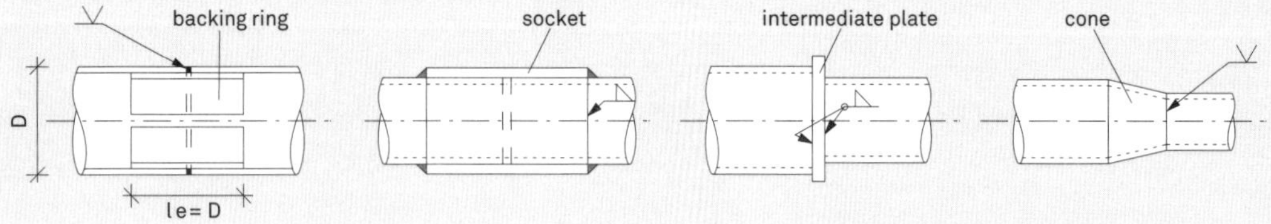

backing ring

socket

intermediate plate

cone

$le = D$

c rigid frame corner with stiffener and haunc)hed beam

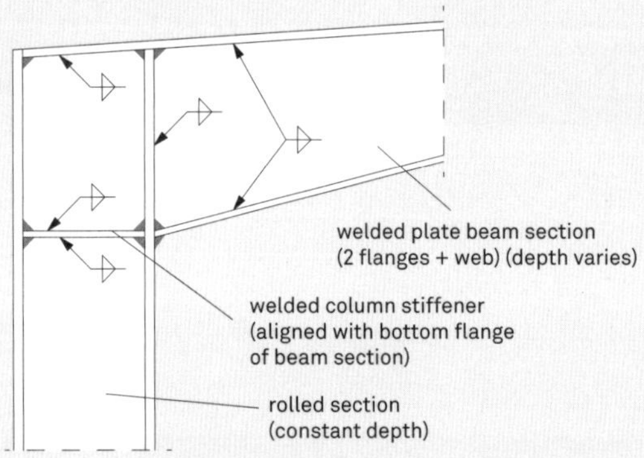

welded plate beam section
(2 flanges + web) (depth varies)

welded column stiffener
(aligned with bottom flange
of beam section)

rolled section
(constant depth)

d ridge joint with one endplate

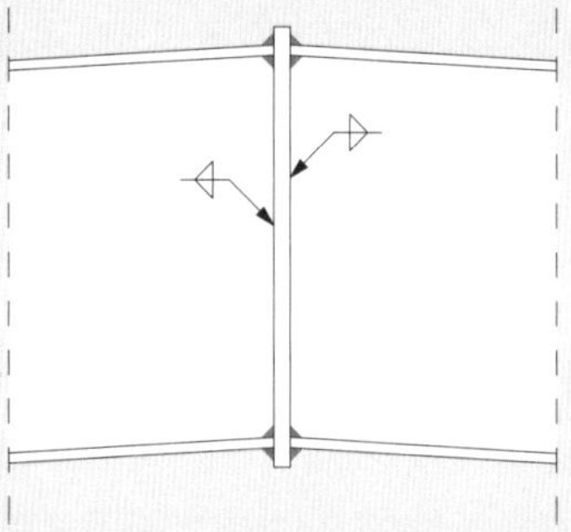

e joints in trusses made with I-sections

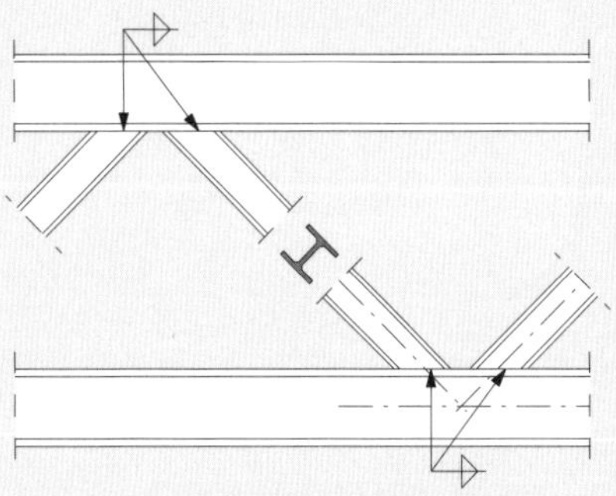

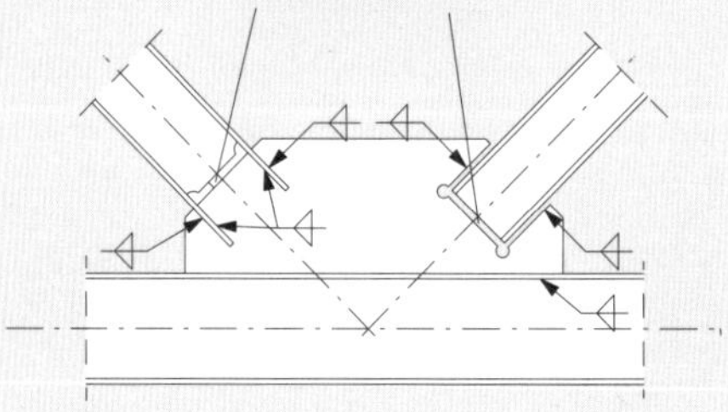

gap
(to allow for tolerances,
subsequently filled
with weld metal)

diagonals connected directly to chords

(This type of joint can carry heavy loads but
is more expensive because the diagonals
have to be cut at an angle exactly to size.)

diagonals connected via gusset plate

(This type of joint cannot carry such heavy loads
as when the diagonals are connected directly
to the chords, but is less expensive.)

symbols for welds > Tab. 2.3.8

Fig. 2.3.27: Examples of welded
connections

several segments, called pours (e.g. phase 1: ground slab; phase 2: walls and columns; phase 3: roof slab). Moreover, expansion joints and dummy joints (crack inducers) must be included where necessary.

For concrete structures that can be broken down into standardized parts, the use of precast concrete elements can represent a more economic solution (e.g. a concrete retaining wall made from L-shaped elements).

If in-situ concrete is combined with precast concrete, we arrive at a semiprecast concrete construction. In this form of building, semiprecast components with a reduced material thickness are fabricated in the factory in such a way that they can be supplemented with in situ concrete on the building site to produce the total cross section necessary for the structural requirements. > Fig. 2.3.28 Consequently, the semiprecast elements serve as permanent formwork for the in-situ concrete and also contain a significant portion of the reinforcement. When there are many identical standard components in a structure, the time-consuming and costly on-site works of constructing the formwork and fixing the reinforcement can be reduced quite considerably. At the same time, semiprecast elements are much lighter than fully precast elements, which means that the weights to be moved during transport and erection are also reduced. Special waterstops are now available to seal the construction joints where elements are exposed to moisture or water. Despite its many advantages, the semiprecast form of concrete construction is used more or less exclusively for buildings (enclosed structures with wall and roof finishes). The reason for this is that the joints between the elements remain visible, as well as the sandwich structure of the precast and in-situ concrete where the tops of walls are exposed (cladding, fascia plates, etc. if necessary).

Joints for in-situ concrete

Construction joints (monolithic connections)
A construction joint is required wherever the next section of concrete cannot be cast against the previous section before it has hardened. If a monolithic element is required at this point, both the concrete and the reinforcement of both sections must be adequately joined together. In order to guarantee the quality of the concrete, only horizontal construction joints may be allowed to cure openly. Vertical, beveled or stepped construction joints must always be cast against formwork (e.g. the concrete may not be allowed to slump uncontrolled into a sort of slope).

Horizontal construction joints are generally specified above and below suspended floors and roofs. The vertical reinforcement projects through such joints (starter bars). These starter bars must be at least as long as the lap length ls required so that the vertical reinforcement of the subsequent section of concrete

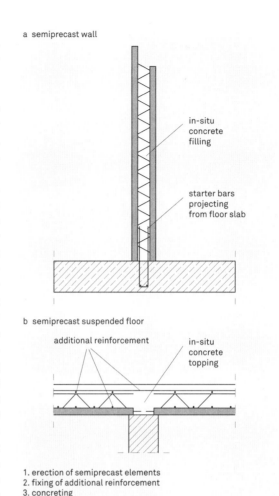

a semiprecast wall

in-situ concrete filling

starter bars projecting from floor slab

b semiprecast suspended floor

additional reinforcement

in-situ concrete topping

1. erection of semiprecast elements
2. fixing of additional reinforcement
3. concreting

Fig. 2.3.28: Semiprecast concrete form of construction sequence of operations

can be connected to the lower bars and transfer the forces. A lap joint between reinforcing bars means they are placed immediately alongside each other (and often tied together with tying wire to keep them in place) so that the forces they carry are transferred from one to the other via the bond with the surrounding concrete (from steel to concrete to steel).

Formwork made from expanded metal has proved worthwhile for vertical construction joints of low height (e.g. construction joints in ground slabs). For one thing, they produce a rough surface and hence a good bond between the two sections of concrete; and for another, the reinforcing bars for a lap joint can be easily passed above or below the expanded metal. > Fig. 2.3.29

With a greater height of formwork and hence a higher pressure due to the wet concrete (e.g. the vertical construction joint in a 3 m high wall), the construction joint must be provided with a complete formwork face. If the formwork cannot be drilled for the reinforcing bars, either bent-back starter bars or mechanical couplers can be used. Starter bars bent back into a housing in the concrete are less expensive than mechanical couplers and the shape of the housing ensures a good shear key at the construction joint. However, bending

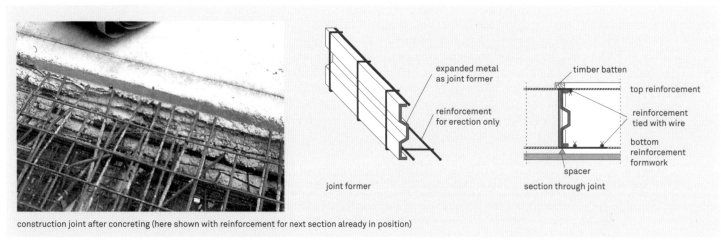

construction joint after concreting (here shown with reinforcement for next section already in position)

Fig. 2.3.29: Using expanded metal as the formwork for a vertical construction joint

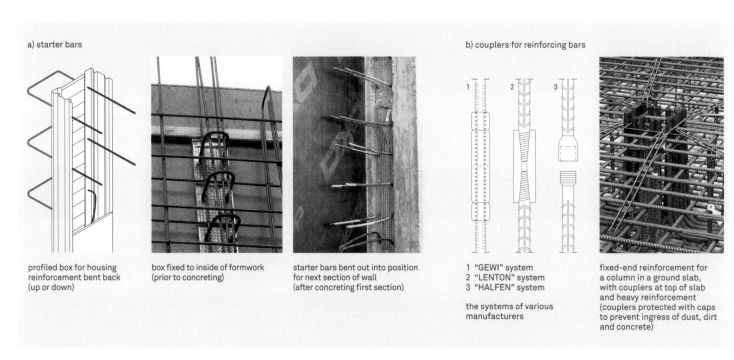

Fig. 2.3.30: Reinforcement details at construction joints with formwork and in heavily reinforced sections

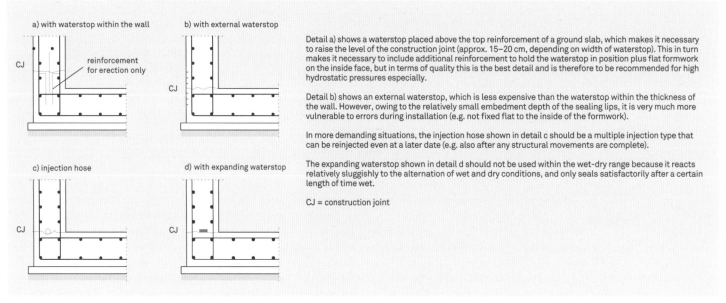

Detail a) shows a waterstop placed above the top reinforcement of a ground slab, which makes it necessary to raise the level of the construction joint (approx. 15–20 cm, depending on width of waterstop). This in turn makes it necessary to include additional reinforcement to hold the waterstop in position plus flat formwork on the inside face, but in terms of quality this is the best detail and is therefore to be recommended for high hydrostatic pressures especially.

Detail b) shows an external waterstop, which is less expensive than the waterstop within the thickness of the wall. However, owing to the relatively small embedment depth of the sealing lips, it is very much more vulnerable to errors during installation (e.g. not fixed flat to the inside of the formwork).

In more demanding situations, the injection hose shown in detail c should be a multiple injection type that can be reinjected even at a later date (e.g. also after any structural movements are complete).

The expanding waterstop shown in detail d should not be used within the wet-dry range because it reacts relatively sluggishly to the alternation of wet and dry conditions, and only seals satisfactorily after a certain length of time wet.

CJ = construction joint

Fig. 2.3.31: Sealed construction joints using the example of a ground slab-wall junction

the bars back manually on site is limited to bars with a diameter $d_s \leq 14$ mm. Couplers, on the other hand, can be used in extremely diverse formwork situations and also in heavily reinforced sections (rather the exception in landscape architecture), where there is often insufficient space for lapping the reinforcement. > Fig. 2.3.30

Where construction joints have to be sealed, e.g. water tanks or basement structures embedded in groundwater, internal and external waterstops, injection hoses, or expanding waterstops are required. > Fig. 2.3.31

Expansion joints

Where a structure is subjected to greater deformation (e.g. as a result of differential settlement or seasonal temperature fluctuations), it can be advisable to provide expansion joints in order to prevent excessive restraint stresses. Care should be taken to ensure that these joints provide a complete separation of the entire component, also passing through all fitting-out components (e.g. wall and floor finishes). Expansion joints should be dimensioned so that the anticipated deformation and differential deformations can be accommodated without restraint. They must therefore be filled with a sufficiently resilient material (e.g. mineral-fiber boards, corrugated bituminous boards where exposed to moisture) and, if necessary, made watertight by including suitable expansion-type waterstops. > Fig. 2.3.32 To protect against becoming clogged with dirt, sand and other foreign matter that could prevent movement, expansion joints must be finished with an elastic seal (e.g. preformed gasket).

Dummy joints

In order to avoid damaging crack widths due to restraint stresses (e.g. caused by shrinkage), it is necessary either to provide an adequate, closely spaced grid of crack-control reinforcement or to include suitable crack-inducing joints (dummy/contraction joints). Restraint stresses are dissipated in these joints by

inducing a crack. > Fig. 2.3.33 The basic principle of the various types of dummy joint is to weaken the cross section by approx. 30% at the joint and reduce the amount of reinforcement to such an extent that the tensile strength at the position of the joint is significantly lowered.

Joints between precast elements

Precast concrete elements normally include connectors designed to permit simple erection. The aim here is to carry the design loads via direct contact (concrete to concrete) wherever possible. A bed of grout or a plastic pad (e.g. elastomeric bearing) is used to compensate for any unevenness in the concrete mating faces. Furthermore, a simple way of securing the positions of the members must be selected (e.g. interlocking members or steel bolts and dowels). > Fig. 2.3.34

Planar precast concrete components (e.g. road pavements, retaining wall elements) are very often required to have joints that although interlocking (preventing horizontal or vertical misalignment), should not transfer forces (compensating for expansion and contraction). The edges of such planar components are provided with dowels in sleeves, which can only transfer forces

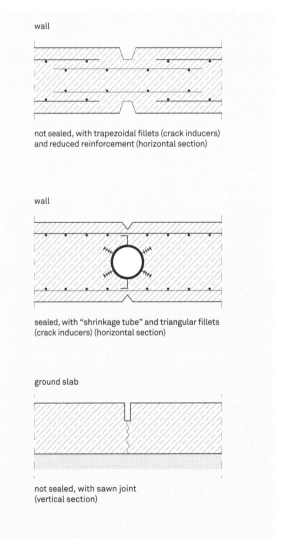

wall

not sealed, with trapezoidal fillets (crack inducers) and reduced reinforcement (horizontal section)

wall

sealed, with "shrinkage tube" and triangular fillets (crack inducers) (horizontal section)

ground slab

not sealed, with sawn joint (vertical section)

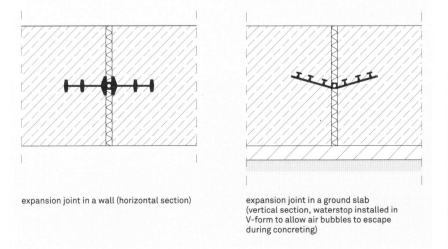

expansion joint in a wall (horizontal section)

expansion joint in a ground slab (vertical section, waterstop installed in V-form to allow air bubbles to escape during concreting)

Fig. 2.3.32: Watertight expansion joints

Fig. 2.3.33: Dummy joints for inducing cracks

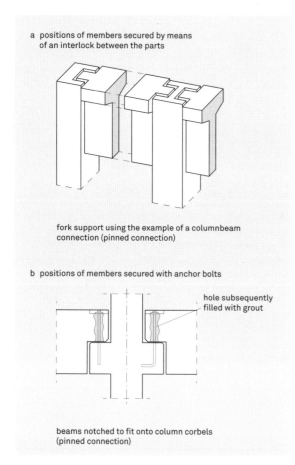

a positions of members secured by means
of an interlock between the parts

fork support using the example of a columnbeam
connection (pinned connection)

b positions of members secured with anchor bolts

hole subsequently
filled with grout

beams notched to fit onto column corbels
(pinned connection)

Fig. 2.3.34: Securing the positions of precast concrete components

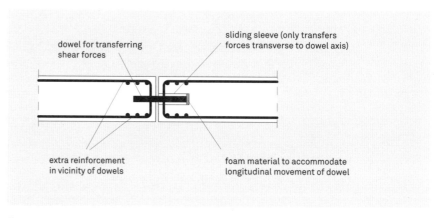

dowel for transferring
shear forces

sliding sleeve (only transfers
forces transverse to dowel axis)

extra reinforcement
in vicinity of dowels

foam material to accommodate
longitudinal movement of dowel

Fig. 2.3.35: Dowelled joint in slab

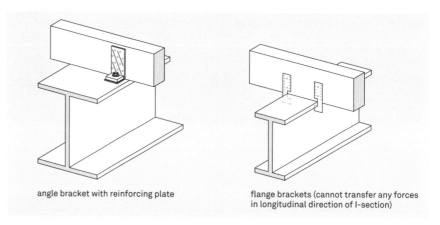

angle bracket with reinforcing plate

flange brackets (cannot transfer any forces
in longitudinal direction of I-section)

Fig. 2.3.36: Steel-timber connections with preformed sheet steel
components

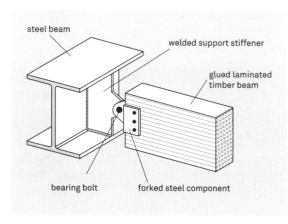

steel beam

welded support stiffener

glued laminated
timber beam

bearing bolt

forked steel component

Fig. 2.3.38: Hinged connection between steel and timber beams

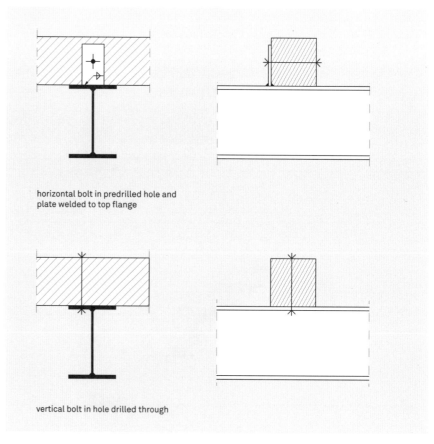

horizontal bolt in predrilled hole and
plate welded to top flange

vertical bolt in hole drilled through

Fig. 2.3.37: Steel-timber connections with threaded rods

transverse to their axis, not in the longitudinal direction (joint dowelling). Normal dowels are used for smaller loads, > Fig. 2.3.35 special dowels, with appropriate force-transfer elements to reduce the local concrete compression, for greater loads.

CONNECTIONS BETWEEN DIFFERENT MATERIALS

Steel-timber connections

Greater loads or spans often make use of primary constructions in steel (e.g. steel purlins) and secondary constructions in timber (e.g. timber rafters with timber roof decking). Preformed sheet steel components are often used for concealed steel-timber connections. These are either hooked or bolted to the steel and nailed to the timber. > Fig. 2.3.36 Where the connections are visible in the finished structure, one very common method is to weld plates or cleats to the steel and connect the timber members with horizontal bolts. Such connections can also be concealed by letting the plates into the timber members and using dowels instead of bolts. Connections in which the timber members are fixed with vertical bolts passing through holes drilled through the top flange are less common (the bolts project through the top of the timber member and cause high compressive forces perpendicular to the grain in the case of overturning forces). > Fig. 2.3.37 Fork and shoe components are suitable for hinged connections with greater angles of rotation. > Fig. 2.3.38 The information given in the sections on steel and timber connections (e.g. welding or bolting on the steel side and

dowels or nails on the timber side) are relevant for the fixing of such preformed components.

Concrete-steel connections

Connections to concrete components can be made using cast-in items, pockets or drilled anchors.

Connections with cast-in items

Suitable anchorage elements are simply cast into the structural concrete. There are two main types of cast-in items that can be used for permanent connections: Cast-in channels: These are C-shaped steel sections with anchor studs welded to the back, i.e. on the concrete side (e.g. shear studs or T-shaped anchors). > Fig. 2.3.39 To prevent the channels being filled with cement slurry, they are factory-filled with a rigid foam material that can be easily removed after striking the formwork. The steel components are fixed to the channels with special hammer-head bolts, which are inserted into the channel, turned through 90° and then tightened. When forces have to be carried in the longitudinal direction of the channel, special serrated channels and matching hammer-head bolts can be employed.

Adequate corrosion resistance for cast-in channels is achieved either by hot-dip galvanizing (internal applications) or by using stainless steel (external applications). Cast-in channels are very popular for attaching components designed to carry low and moderate loads. > Fig. 2.3.40 Cast-in plates: These are steel plates with shear studs, reinforcing bars, or "fishtail anchors" welded to the back,

a) hot-rolled section with T-shaped anchors and hammer-head bolts

Head turned lengthwise for inserting into the channel

Head transverse for tightening in the channel

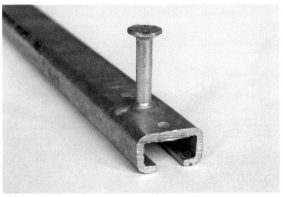

Fig. 2.3.39: Cast-in channels

b) cold-rolled section with T-shaped anchors and masonry ties for junctions between masonry and concrete

For joints with normal-weight mortar

For joints with thin-bed mortar

i.e. the concrete side, in order to transfer the forces. Once the formwork has been struck and the concrete has reached its design strength, steel components can be welded to the "outside" of the cast-in plate. This method allows, for example, posts for handrails, or cleats or brackets for supporting steel beams to be simply and securely fixed to concrete components. > Fig. 2.3.41
As the heat generated during welding can distort thin steel plates, a minimum thickness of $d \geq 8$ mm is recommended. Suitable corrosion protection must be applied after completing the welding work (factory galvanizing is ruled out because of the subsequent welding). The corrosion resistance of such cast-in items is therefore limited when they are used externally. If possible, drilled anchors should be used in such instances. Cast-in plates are useful for attaching heavier loads because they are custom items that can be designed exactly for the loads involved.

Connections with pockets

In this method, pockets, holes or recesses are formed (e.g. with polystyrene) in the structural concrete. These serve as housings for appropriate anchors that are installed later and then filled with grout. It is necessary to ensure good workmanship when forming such pockets, particularly for external applications. Pockets must be clean and all pocket formers (e.g. polystyrene) removed. They must be free from voids and a good bond between the grout and the surrounding concrete must be ensured because otherwise adequate durability of the anchorage cannot be guaranteed. Any moisture that infiltrates the joint between grout and concrete can lead to frost splitting and corrosion of the anchors. For this reason, this type of fixing is used in potentially wet areas only when greater forces have to be transferred (stainless steel anchors in drilled holes are used for smaller loads). The anchors commonly used are:

· Holding-down bolts with washers, nuts and locknuts (for securing the positions of baseplates)
· Holding-down bolts in profiled sleeves or in conjunction with anchor bars (for transferring tensile forces)
· Shear connectors (for transferring shear forces)

· Sufficiently large and thick baseplates in conjunction with tension-resistant holding-down bolts, or pocket foundations (for resisting fixed-end moments) > Figs. 2.3.42 and 2.3.43

Connections with drilled anchors

The most important advantages of drilled anchor connections are their excellent flexibility, wide range of applications, and good economy. "Heavy-duty anchors" are used for loadbearing connections. There are three anchor systems in common use:

Bonded anchors: This type of anchor comprises a threaded rod that is inserted into a drilled hole and then glued in place with a two-part reaction-resin mortar. The mortar normally consists of an organic resin (e.g. based on epoxy or polyester), an appropriate hardener, and special fine aggregate (e.g. finely ground quartz sand). To ensure that the bond remains permanent, no cracks are allowed in the concrete because otherwise the drilled hole may enlarge and cause the mortar compound to become detached from the surrounding concrete. Normal bonded anchors may therefore be used only in the compression zone of the concrete (e.g. columns, top side of single-span beams).
Special bonded expansion anchors are available when anchors are required in the tension zone (risk of cracks). > Fig. 2.3.44 Bonded anchors can also be used in masonry. Special perforated sleeves, which enable the mortar compound to be installed properly, are available for use in perforated bricks.
Metal expansion anchors: These expansion anchors have an expanding steel sleeve that is inserted into the drilled hole. Upon tightening the threaded bar or bolt, a cone is pressed against the sleeve, forcing it to spread out. This expansion generates friction forces between the expanding sleeve and the side of the drilled hole, which means that such anchors can also carry tensile forces. We distinguish between two types of expansion: torque-controlled expansion (tightening the bolt with a defined torque) and travel-controlled expansion (driving in the bolt to a defined depth). The former type of anchor can compensate for smaller inaccuracies in the drilled hole and exhibits a certain safety reserve because it expands

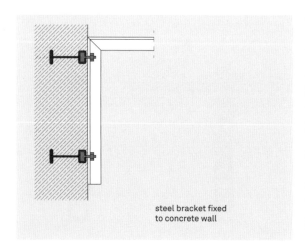

steel bracket fixed
to concrete wall

Fig. 2.3.40: Concrete-steel connection with cast-in channels

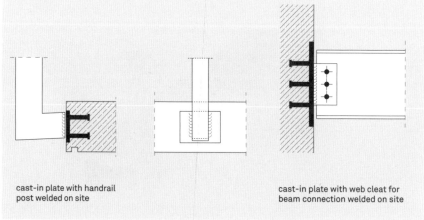

cast-in plate with handrail
post welded on site

cast-in plate with web cleat for
beam connection welded on site

Fig. 2.3.41: Concrete-steel connections with cast-in plates

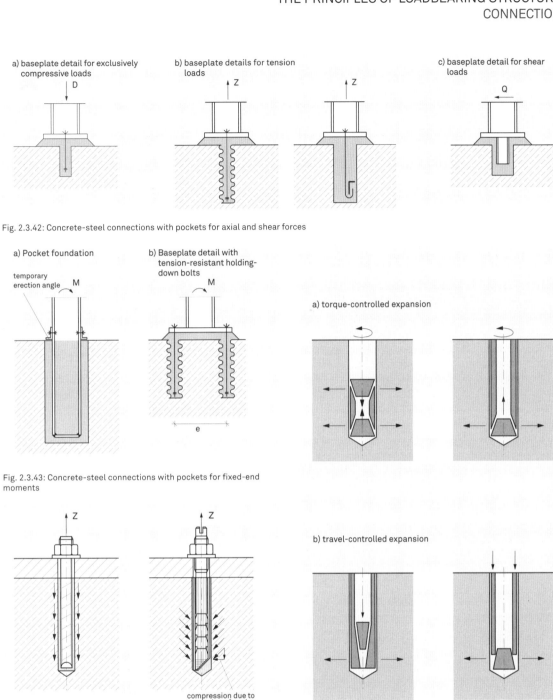

a) baseplate detail for exclusively compressive loads

b) baseplate details for tension loads

c) baseplate detail for shear loads

Fig. 2.3.42: Concrete-steel connections with pockets for axial and shear forces

a) Pocket foundation

temporary erection angle

b) Baseplate detail with tension-resistant holding-down bolts

Fig. 2.3.43: Concrete-steel connections with pockets for fixed-end moments

a) torque-controlled expansion

b) travel-controlled expansion

compression due to expansion of anchor

Bonded anchor for uncracked concrete (compression zone)

Bonded anchor for cracked concrete (tension zone)

Fig. 2.3.44: Bonded anchors

Fig. 2.3.45: Metal expansion anchors

a) undercut wider at top

b) undercut wider at bottom

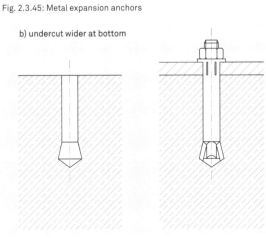

Fig. 2.3.46: Undercut anchor

further when overloaded in tension. The latter type of anchor (hammerset anchor) is quicker to install and can generate much greater expansion forces. > **Fig. 2.3.45** As the expansion forces lead to additional transverse stresses in the concrete, adequate edge distances are especially important with expansion anchors.

Cracks in the concrete may cause the drilled hole to enlarge, resulting in a decrease in the expansion force, in turn leading to a drop in the forces that can be carried. In order to overcome this problem, metal anchors have also been developed for the tension zone—undercut anchors. Undercut anchors: The installation of an undercut anchor begins with the drilling of a cylindrical hole. The second step involves cutting a conical enlargement in the base of the hole (with a special drill or a self-cutting anchor). Finally, a special expansion sleeve is inserted, the cone of which expands into the enlarged part of the hole and thus forms a mechanical interlock between the side of the hole and the anchor. > **Fig. 2.3.46** This mechanical interlock means that the expansion forces required are not as great as those of standard metal expansion anchors, which leads to an advantageous reduction in the additional stresses in the concrete caused by the anchor. The design of a drilled anchor connection with adequate loadbearing capacity (type, number, and positioning of anchors) is carried out within the scope of the structural calculations, and depends on the loads to be anchored, and the loading on and geometry of the concrete component (compression or tension zone, embedment depth possible depending on thickness of component, edge distances, and anchor spacings possible, etc.). > **Fig. 2.3.47** All drilled anchors must have a national technical approval.

To guarantee adequate corrosion protection, all customary anchor types are available in galvanized (internal applications) and stainless steel (external applications) versions.

As the concrete-steel bond is exposed to an increased risk of corrosion from potential capillary action, corresponding active and passive corrosion protection measures are necessary. > **Fig. 2.3.48** Besides ensuring that the steel has adequate corrosion protection (e.g. duplex coating or hot-dip galvanizing), ponding in the area around the connection should be prevented by sloping the sides of the grout and forming local falls in the surrounding concrete.

Concrete-timber connections

As the connections between timber sections and concrete components essentially correspond to those between steel sections and concrete, only a few special aspects of concrete-timber connections need to be mentioned here.

If several identical structural timber members (e.g. posts) have to be connected, sole plates are popular because these simplify alignment and erection. > **Fig. 2.3.49** However, care should be taken to ensure that the structural members bearing on them are not too heavily loaded because the sole plate is stressed perpendicular to the

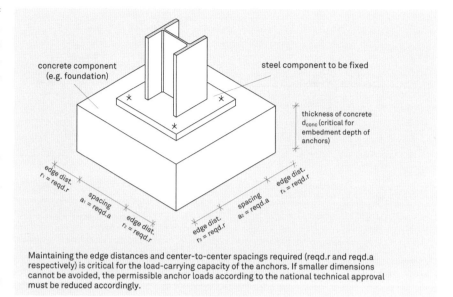

Maintaining the edge distances and center-to-center spacings required (reqd.r and reqd.a respectively) is critical for the load-carrying capacity of the anchors. If smaller dimensions cannot be avoided, the permissible anchor loads according to the national technical approval must be reduced accordingly.

Fig. 2.3.47: Edge distances and spacings required for fixings with drilled anchors

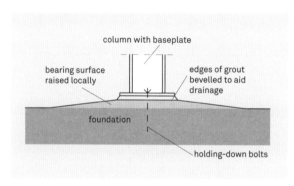

Fig. 2.3.48: Column base detail for an external application

grain. For this reason, timber columns carrying heavy loads must be supported directly (i.e. with their end grain) on the concrete or on a steel component (e.g. preformed sheet steel shoes, plates, shear connectors or other steel anchors). > **Fig. 2.3.50**

Another standard detail is the fixing of a timber beam or rafter to a concrete structure. Here again, the forms of connector described above (e.g. cast-in channels) can be used depending on the respective constructional situation. > **Fig. 2.3.51**

As condensation can form on the surface of the concrete even below covered areas (due to the cooler concrete surface compared to the ambient air), an isolating bearing pad to prevent rising moisture should always be placed between the concrete and the timber (e.g. bituminous felt for smaller loads).

External timber columns should be supported in preformed sheet steel shoes clear of the concrete to protect them against standing and splashing water. These components are available in various forms depending on the loads to be carried. > **Fig. 2.3.52** In areas exposed directly to splashing water, the clearance between the concrete and the underside of column should be as large as possible in order to improve durability ($h_A \geq 15$ cm is recommended).

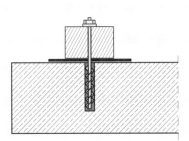

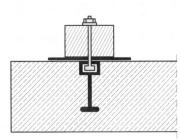

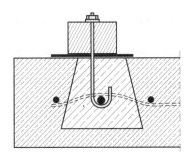

Connection using bonded anchor (positions of fixings can be varied exactly to suit, but take into account edge distances and spacings of bonded anchors; suitable for smaller tension and shear loads)

Connection using cast-in channel (positions of fixing points variable in longitudinal direction of cast-in channel, but fixed in transverse direction; suitable for smaller to moderate tension and shear loads)

Connection using holding-down bolts in pockets (positions of fixings must be defined, can also be designed for intermediate and larger tension and shear loads depending on type and arrangement of holding-down bolts detail)

Fig. 2.3.49: Connection between timber sole plate and concrete slab

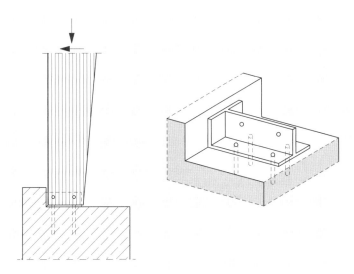

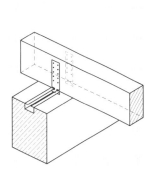

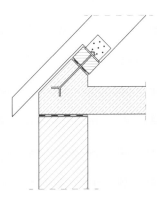

Concrete beam with cast-in channel

Rafter fixed to concrete upstand with cast-in bolts (do not position bolts directly in the load transfer zone of the rafters)

Fig. 2.3.50: Base detail for a glued laminated timber column with upstand on foundation and welded steel baseplate

Fig. 2.3.51: Connection of timber beam and rafter to concrete construction

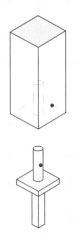

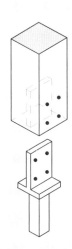

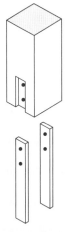

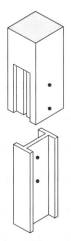

Dowel let into column, with baseplate and steel post
(for larger compression loads and smaller tensile and horizontal forces)

Plate let into column, with baseplate and steel post
(for larger compression loads and moderate tensile and horizontal forces)

Fishplates let into column sides, fixed with threaded rods
(for smaller compressive, tensile and horizontal forces)

I-section let into column, fixed with close-tolerance bolts
(for rigid connections)

Fig. 2.3.52: Base details for external timber columns

3 STRUCTURAL ELEMENTS AND BUILDING METHODS

3.1 GROUND MODELING AND EARTHWORKS

TERRAIN MODELING
·   Shaping the earth mass
·   Slope incline

SECURING EARTHWORKS
·   Soil improvement
·   Surface and deep drainage
·   Simple slope protection
·   Reinforced slopes
·   Excavation pits and service trenches

SPECIMEN PROJECTS

Astrid Zimmermann, Bernd Funke

3.1 GROUND MODELING AND EARTHWORKS

With the exception of constructions carried out in exceptional locations, such as green roofs, every open-air design involves earth to some extent. Earth provides the base for construction, > **Chapter 2.2** but it is also a material used in modeling of the new surface. Every intervention in the earth mass creates a change in the soil structure. This may make the soil less stable, and also influences its suitability as a plant habitat. During soil installation and following completion of earth sculptures, various greening or securing measures may be necessary to reinforce the earth. These depend on the type of soil involved, the incline of the sloping earth, and the type of surface reinforcement planned.

TERRAIN MODELING

Shaping the earth mass

An earth mass is shaped by removing or applying layers of soil. > **Fig. 3.1.1** The humus-enriched topsoil should always be handled separately from the soil layers beneath. It should always be removed first before any further earth modeling takes place.

The soil layers beneath are then removed, either laterally or in layers. When advantages and disadvantages have been weighed, a combination of lateral removal and layered installation will prove to be the best combination in most cases. > **Tab. 3.1.1**

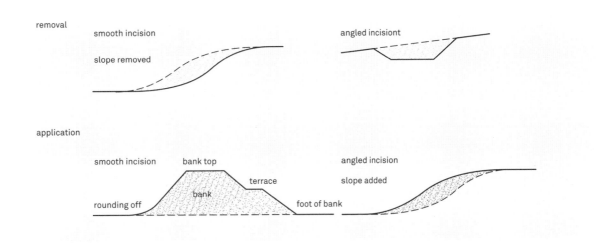

Fig. 3.1.1: Forming the earth mass, terms

	Characteristics/requirements		Advantages	Disadvantages
Layer removal	layer thicknesses 0.2–1 m	removal direction change	possible to remove changing soil types in layers	susceptible to weathering, as large areas exposed
Step removal		removal direction unchanged, slope cut slope		
Lateral removal	covers the full height of the intended removal depth	removal direction parallel to slope	less susceptible to weather as exposed area small	mixed soil types
Top removal		removal direction frontal to slope		
Layer installation	When installing on slopes with an incline of ≥ 1:5 it is necessary to key in with the base layers > **Fig. 3.1.2**	Installation by layer, usually ≤ 0.50 m, must be leveled be for adding another layer	possible to compact individual layers well, later settlement minimized	susceptible to weathering, as large areas exposed
Lateral installation		When tipped on to a slope, the loose material settling into the natural angle of the slope > **Tab. 3.1.3**	–	Compaction possible only at top tipping edge, sorting or grain sizes: larger components settle at the foot of the slope: leads to cavity formation

Tab. 3.1.1: Comparison of lateral and layer soil removal and installation

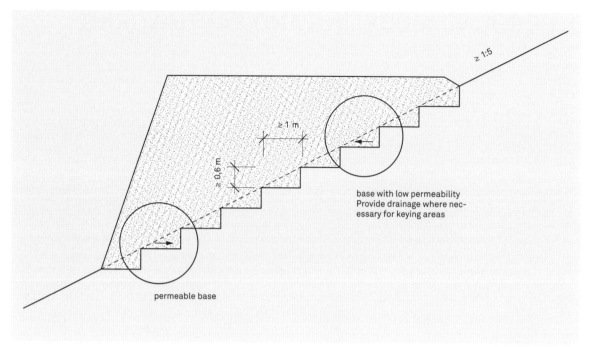

Fig. 3.1.2: Keying with base layer for inclined areas > 1:5

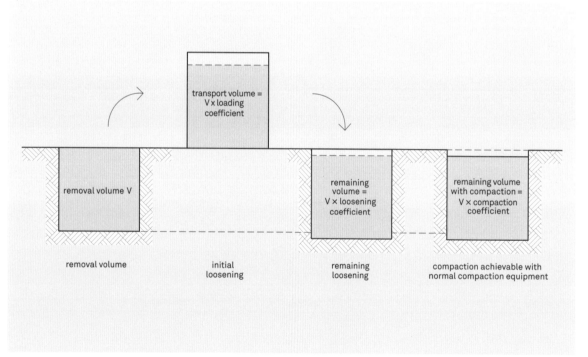

Fig. 3.1.3: Changeable soil volume

Soil type	Loading coefficient (initial loosening)	Loosening coefficient (loosening remaining once soil has settled under its own weight)	Compaction coefficient (loosening remaining after compaction)
Sand	1.15–1.25	1.01–1.02	0.95–0.85
Gravel-sand	1.20–1.25	1.01–1.02	0.95–0.85
Gravel	1.25–1.30	1.01–1.02	1.00–0.92
Coarse silt	1.05–1.20	1.03–1.05	0.95–0.75
Silt	1.15–1.25	1.04–1.06	0.95–0.85
Clay	1.20–1.30	1.05–1.08	1.02–0.90

Tab. 3.1.2: Reference values for soil loosening (after Floss)

Before new soil is added, the base material usually has to be compacted, > Chapter 2.2 with the exception of areas intended for rooting later vegetation. If the ground water levels are high, an anti-capillary layer should be laid down. When adding different kinds of soil, the cohesive soil from the lower, non-cohesive layers should be incorporated in the top layers.

Loosening and adding soil leads to volume changes. These have a part to play in both the calculation of quantities to be transported, and also in calculating the quantities to be added later. > Tab. 3.1.2 and fig. 3.1.3 Fundamentally, an effort should be made to balance the quantities brought in and taken away for every building project, as both the removal and delivery of soil generate additional expense.

Slope incline

Depending on soil type, an angle of elevation is "naturally" created during soil removal or application. > Tab. 3.1.3 The removal area can be steeper than the application area if this is taking place on soil with vegetation, as vegetated soils cohere more strongly and are therefore more stable. If the earth mass is intended to be steeper than the natural slope, additional safety measures may be needed, based on static soil calculations if necessary. For angles of elevation in construction trenches, particular limits apply. > Tab. 3.1.4

Steep slopes can be given greater stability using terraces than a single continuous slope without terraces.

The conditions for planned vegetation change the steeper the slope becomes. So lawns that need a great deal of tending (a good water supply and regular mowing, for example), should be laid with a slope incline no greater than 15% if machines have to be used. Dry lawns, meadows or robust ground cover need less care, and are thus better for steeper slopes. So only certain forms of planting should be chosen dependent on the incline, and if the incline is steeper than 1:1 additional measures are needed to secure the slope. > Figs. 3.1.4 and 3.1.5

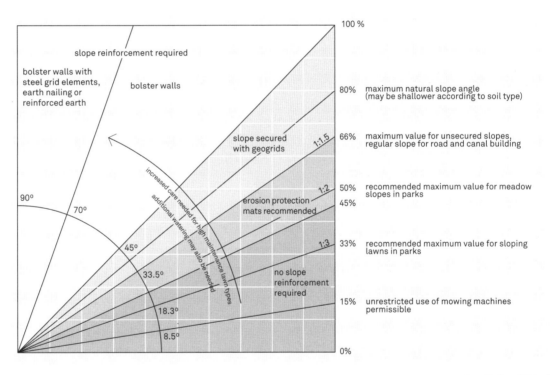

Fig. 3.1.4: Possible approaches to planting and support work dependent on slope incline (some values rounded off)

Tab. 3.1.3: Natural soil angles dependent on soil type (without stability check)

Soil type	Height of slope	Removal	Added
Gravel and gravel sand		1:1.5	1:1.5
Coarse sand		1:1.7	1:1.7
Fine sand		1:2	1:2
Cohesive soils	< 3 m	1:1.25	1:1.25 silt (I_p < 10): 1:1.6
	3–6 m	1:1.25 silt (I_p < 10): 1:1.6	1:2 silt (I_p 10–20): 1:1.6
	6–9 m	silt (I_p 10–20): 1:1.4 silt (I_p < 10): 1:1.75 clay: 1:1.25	silt (I_p 10–20): 1:1.8 silt (I_p < 10): 1:2.2 clay: 1:1.25
	9–12 m	silt (I_p 10–20): 1:1.6 silt (I_p < 10): 1:1.9 clay (I_p 20–30): 1:1.7 clay (I_p > 30): 1:1.5	silt (I_p 10–20): 1:1.9 silt (I_p < 10): 1:2.3 clay (I_p 20–30): 1:1.7 clay (I_p > 30): 1:1.5
	12–15 m	1:2 silt (I_p 10–20): 1:1.7	1:2 silt (I_p < 10): 1:2.4

Fig. 3.1.5: Lawn needing intensive care on a level surface in combination with meadow needing less intensive care on the slope

Fig. 3.1.6: Slopes reinforced with natural stones

The steeper the slope becomes, the more "angled" the transitions become from the slope to the foot of the slope, and to the top of the slope. The "edges" are then very susceptible to erosion, and mowing a lawn area will be more difficult. Countermeasures include rounding off or reinforcing the edges.

Steeply sloping lawns are highly prone to erosion if used intensively. Thus it is always worth considering whether planting of this kind makes sense in public spaces and whether additional protection against erosion or reinforcement for the edges of the steep slope should be provided. > **Fig. 3.1.6**

SECURING EARTHWORKS

Soil improvement
The most important subsoil improvement measures are described in **Chapter 2.2 Foundations and chapter 3.2 Paths and Squares**.

Two basic possibilities are available for stabilizing or improving the structure of the available loose material to be used for terrain modeling. One is mechanical soil improvement by adding (missing) mineral grains, which are worked into the existing soil. But it is scarcely possible to mix grains evenly, especially in the case of cohesive soils. Hence a second less problematical approach can be taken in such cases by improving the soil structure with binding agents. Adding lime improves the soil's manageability and compactability. Cement can also be used as a binding agent.

Surface and deep drainage
Consistent drainage is also particularly effective against erosion damage from surface and underground water, as well as reinforcing or planting the surface. Alongside creating a slope on the terrain and capturing and draining surface water off by ditches, further measures are needed, especially in relatively impermeable soils and if underground water has to be tackled (seepage, stratum and spring water). Seepage facilities, such as seepage runs and seepage layers, then have to be provided. > **Fig. 3.1.7**

Simple slope protection
The "most natural" protection against erosion for slopes is planting, i.e. using the roots to secure the soil (see also Chapters 3.9 and 3.10). A combination of extensive and intensive roots has a positive effect, as for example when using herbaceous plants and grasses, or the combination of shallow and deep roots when using woody plants, as this makes it possible to achieve even rooting throughout the soil.

Simple planting with lawn seed or lawn planting is usually not very effective in the early stages, because insufficient coverage and the roots have not yet gained sufficient hold. Here, turf offers more rapid protection against erosion. > **Chapter 3.9** But additional measures may have to be taken to secure slopes, particularly if they are very steep. Shallow slopes can also be protected with a simple covering of mineral aggregates, to avoid surface erosion problems. > **Specimen project Mobile Life Campus, Wolfsburg**

Erosion protection mats
The effectiveness of simple planting can be optimized by erosion protection mats. Geotextiles are used, usually made of coconut, jute, straw, or a combination of these materials. They provide temporary protection for the soil covering until the vegetation has developed, and rot down over the early years (jute 1–2 years, coconut 3–4 years). If longer protection is needed, the mats can be combined with an additional artificial geotextile or a steel net. The erosion protection will then last for longer, and it is also possible to stop stones from escaping.

Erosion protection mats are laid on the slope after seeding, with a side overlap of at least 10 cm. At the end of the roll the beginning of the next sheet should be laid with a 20–50 cm overlap under the end. At the top and bottom of the slope the ends should be buried or fixed at a depth of 20 cm. It might also be necessary to fix the sheets by nailing along the overlaps; possibly also in the middle of the sheet. Wooden pegs or steel craps (U- or L-shaped steel nails) are used for fastening. About 3 fixing points per meter or 5–8 per square meter should be provided along the overlaps. Installation

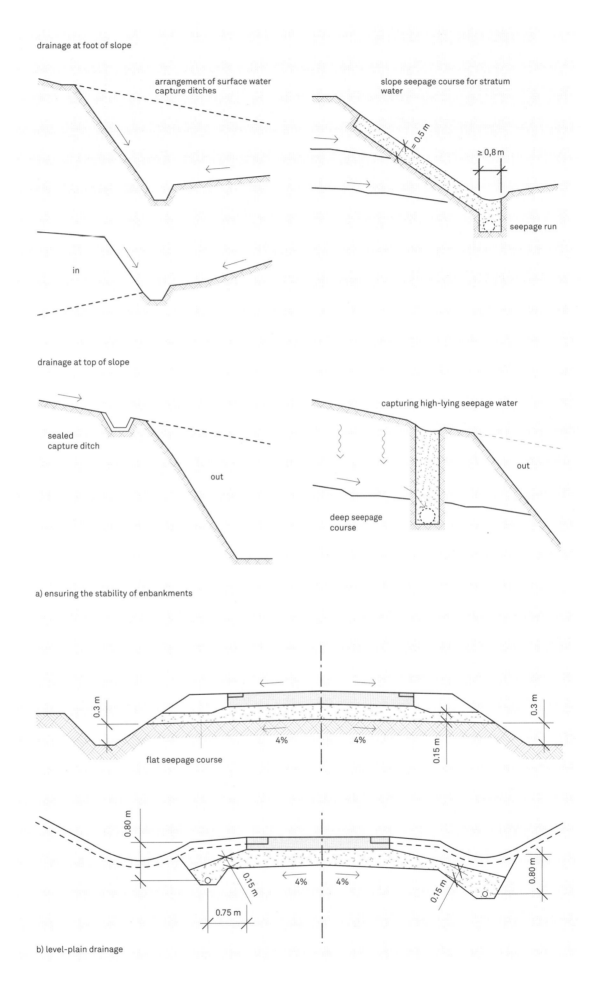

drainage at foot of slope

arrangement of surface water capture ditches

slope seepage course for stratum water

= 0.5 m

≥ 0,8 m

seepage run

in

drainage at top of slope

sealed capture ditch

out

capturing high-lying seepage water

out

deep seepage course

a) ensuring the stability of enbankments

0.3 m

0.3 m

4%

4%

0.15 m

flat seepage course

0.80 m

0.80 m

0.15 m

4%

4%

0.15 m

0.75 m

b) level-plain drainage

Fig. 3.1.7: Measures for draining earthworks

methods for these can vary according to mat type and manufacturer. > Fig. 3.1.8

Seeded mats are supplied with the appropriate seeds incorporated; in the case of vegetation mats the geo-textiles serve a support for precultivated plants (e.g. for sedum mats). > Chapter 3.14

Reinforced slopes

As sloped become steeper and are low in shear strength in the case of natural soil, earthworks have to have to be additionally stabilized. The measures range from simple reinforcement with geogrids to rein-forced steep slopes that can look like retaining walls. > Chapter 3.5

Shallow slopes

Simple reinforcement with geogrids is usually ade-quate for newly created slopes with an incline of up to 45°. The geogrids are laid between the layers of earth used to make the slope, and the depth to which they are tied in and the distances between the layers are calculated from the statical requirements. The com-pleted surface of the slope is finally covered with an erosion protection mat.

It is possible to reuse soil with low shear strength if us-ing this building method, so there is no need to substi-tute different soil. > Fig. 3.1.9

Engineering biology techniques such as slope fascines, woven fences, or hedge brush layers can be used to se-cure slopes, especially in the open countryside, utiliz-ing dead or living woody plants. > Fig. 3.1.10

Soil nailing and reinforced earth

Other reinforcement techniques are used for inclines greater than 45°. Rather like filled supporting bodies (e.g. gabions), > Chapter 3.5 this process creates a "mono-lithic" body of soil that has the loadbearing capacity of a heavyweight wall. The soil is reinforced, so that—like reinforced concrete—it is able to a withstand tensile forces as well (creating a composite body). To compact the soil, and to protect the surface mechanically, it is covered at the front (lining), and the cover is attached firmly to the reinforcement. Here, the nature of the proc-ess depends on the method used to create the difference in terrain level.

If the difference in terrain level is created by digging, then the newly created slope (natural soil) is nailed. This process is called "soil nailing". But if it is created by piling material up, then the added soil is reinforced. This process is known as "reinforced earth".

To create earth nailing, the natural soil is reinforced with tie rods, called soil nails, and covered at the top with a layer of gunned concrete. This process is used both for temporary support (e.g. around excavation pits), and also to secure rises in terrain permanently. As a rule, soil nails are made of GEWI steels (concrete steel with a coarse thread profile) or perforated steel tubes. The soil nails, with spacers, are inserted into drilled holes.

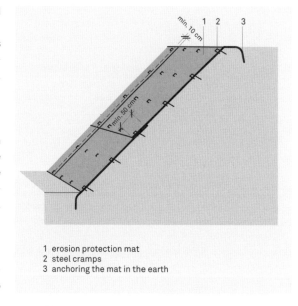

1 erosion protection mat
2 steel cramps
3 anchoring the mat in the earth

Fig. 3.1.8: Installing erosion protection/vegetation mats, example

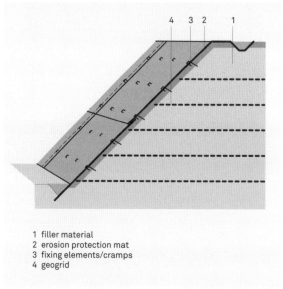

1 filler material
2 erosion protection mat
3 fixing elements/cramps
4 geogrid

Fig. 3.1.9: Planted shallow slope, example

Cement mortar is injected at the same time, filling the cavity between the bars and the earth. If the structure is intended to last, then adequate protection against corrosion should be provided (e.g. earth nails with a cement mortar coating and profiled protective tubing). The gunned concrete shell is reinforced with concrete-steel mats and is usually between 10 and 35 cm thick, according to load (tensile force of the soil nails) and the degree of durability sought.

The soil nails are arranged in a statically determined grid (1 x 1 m to 2.5 x 2.5 m) and need to be up to 0.6–0.9 times the height of the wall created.

Creating soil nailing requires stepped excavations, and proceeds in phases. In order to make the working se-quence practicable, the soil must be capable of stand-ing unsupported to a height of about 1.5 m (gravel soil and soils prone to water inrush are thus unsuitable). Areas about 1.5 m deep in each case are dug out stage by stage, working from top to bottom. The concrete steel mats are installed and reinforced with gunned

a) slope fascines

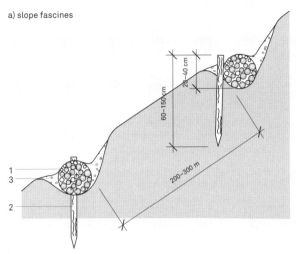

1 roll of live willow branches (can also be dead material), d = 2–4 cm, l = 200–600 cm, bound with wire
2 wooden peg, d = 5–15 cm, or steel rods, d = 1–2 cm, about 100 cm apart
3 added soil

b) bush and hedging layers with added material / in a cut slope

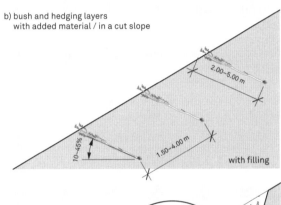

1 filled ground (loose material)
2 round timber, d = 18–25 cm
3 living branches from timber types that can shoot (mainly willows), in dense soils approx. 60 cm long, in loose, filled ground 200–400 cm long
4 rooted deciduous timber

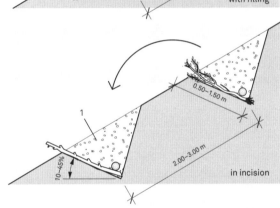

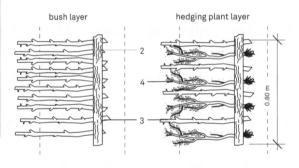

c) hurdles

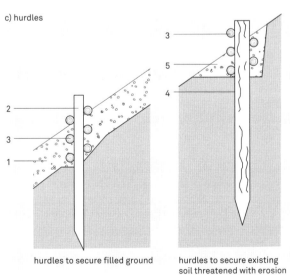

1 filled ground
2 metal bar
3 wickerwork
4 wooden pile, l = 100 cm
5 filled cut
6 spikes (wooden pegs), l = 30–80 cm
7 direction of work

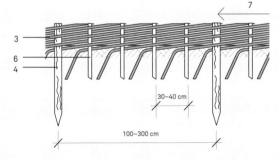

Fig. 3.1.10: Slope securing methods using engineering biology (selection)

concrete. Then the soil nails are introduced and anchored to the gunned concrete. > Fig. 3.1.11
For earth reinforcement (reinforced earth), lining elements are placed one above the other in stages, the rear tensile reinforcement is put in place, and the filling material is laid and compacted layer by layer.

Possible lining elements include both prefabricated reinforced concrete parts and profile steel sheeting, curving outwards like a shell. The reinforcement generally consists of galvanized sheet steel or plastic strips. The height of the layers corresponds to the difference in height of the reinforcement courses, and varies from system to system between approx. 30 and 75 cm.
The reinforcing wall is usually based on a prepared strip foundation. Here, the base joint of the reinforced body of earth should be tied into the native soil to a depth of 0.1–0.2 times the wall height (excavation of the foundation base). The length required for the reinforcement strips is about of the same as that required for the soil nailing (approx. 0.6–0.9 times the wall height). > Fig. 3.1.12

One variant on slope reinforcement is geogrid retention. Here, the body of soil is first stiffened with geogrids and then reinforced. The geogrids are laid out in sheets, and the soil placed on top and compacted. Finally, the geogrid is folded in towards the back from the formwork side. This working sequence means that layer after layer of "padding" is piled one on top of the other. Geogrid walls need no foundations. Because of their resilience, deformations (caused by settlement, for example) can be absorbed without damaging the construction as a whole. Geogrid walls can be planted or faced in stone.
> Fig. 3.1.13 Soil nailing can also be combined with a geogrid wall in front to produce a planted surface.

Geogrid walls can be used to create slopes up to an incline of 90°. For inclines over 70°, check whether the additional use of steel lattice elements is required to give the slope surface additional stability. > Fig. 3.1.14
If steep slopes are reinforced directly by planting, this is known as "living earth reinforcement." > Fig. 3.1.15
The geogrid wall, also reinforced with geotextiles, is combined with suspended or bush layers, which means that steeper slopes can be created using the simple layer construction method.

Excavation pits and service trenches
When creating excavation pits and service trenches, the extent of the excavation should be kept to a minimum for financial reasons, and because of constricted working space. Various stabilization measures are used, dependent on the depth of the pit and the soil type.

In stable, natural soil, the walls on a slope can be constructed vertically and without further stabilization measures to heights of up to 1.25 m (applies in Germany and Austria; for Switzerland the figure is ≥ 1.5 m). If the excavation is to be deeper, reinforcement is needed, or the soil should be slanted back. Slanted excavation pit walls must have a terrace at least 1.5 m wide from a height of 3 m. Slope angles can be created as in Table 3.1.4 without needed any further stability certification. Here, there should be a strip carrying no load at least 0.6 m wide at the top of the slope.
> Fig. 3.1.16
Soil types and the required excavation depth must be specified when putting excavation pit work out to tender. Further detail is regulated by standards in particular countries, for example DIN 4124, ÖNORM 2205, and SIA 318.

Soil type	Max. slope angle β
noncohesive and soft cohesive soil	45°
stiff to semifirm cohesive soil	60°
light rock	80°
heavy rock	90°

Tab. 3.1.4: Slope angles for an excavation pit depth > 1.25 m

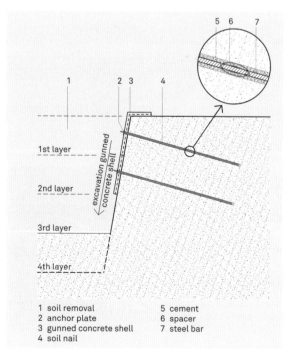

1 soil removal
2 anchor plate
3 gunned concrete shell
4 soil nail
5 cement
6 spacer
7 steel bar

Fig. 3.1.11: Soil nailing (when soil removed)

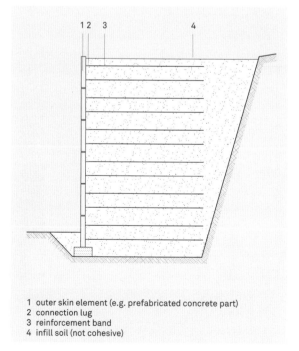

1 outer skin element (e.g. prefabricated concrete part)
2 connection lug
3 reinforcement band
4 infill soil (not cohesive)

Fig. 3.1.12: Soil reinforcement (when soil added)

1 erosion protection mat
2 geogrid
3 anchor bar
4 filler material
5 topsoil
6 drainage
7 seepage run, clad in filter fleece
8 sandbags
9 facing

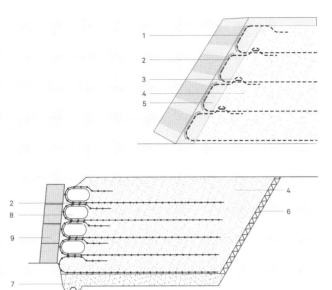

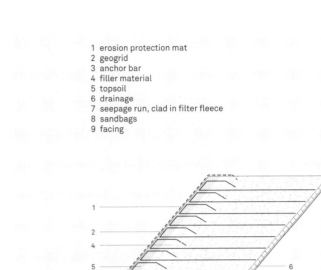

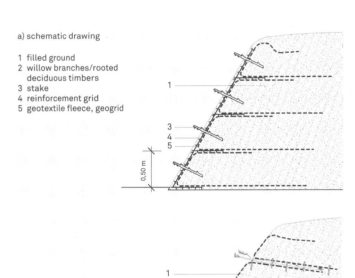

Fig. 3.1.13: Construction methods for geogrid walls, example

1 erosion protection
2 filler material
3 topsoil
4 geogrid
5 steel grid
  elements
6 spacer
7 structural
  steel mat
8 U-clamps

a) schematic drawing

1 filled ground
2 willow branches/rooted
  deciduous timbers
3 stake
4 reinforcement grid
5 geotextile fleece, geogrid

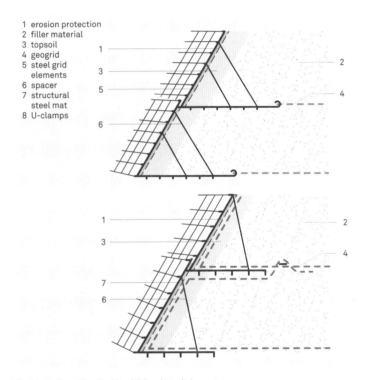

Fig. 3.1.14: Geogrid wall with additional steel elements

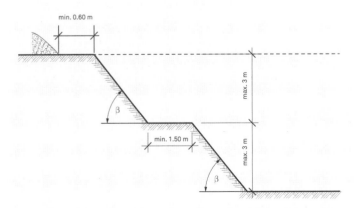

Fig. 3.1.15: Soil reinforced with living matter

Fig. 3.1.16: Slanting excavation pit sides

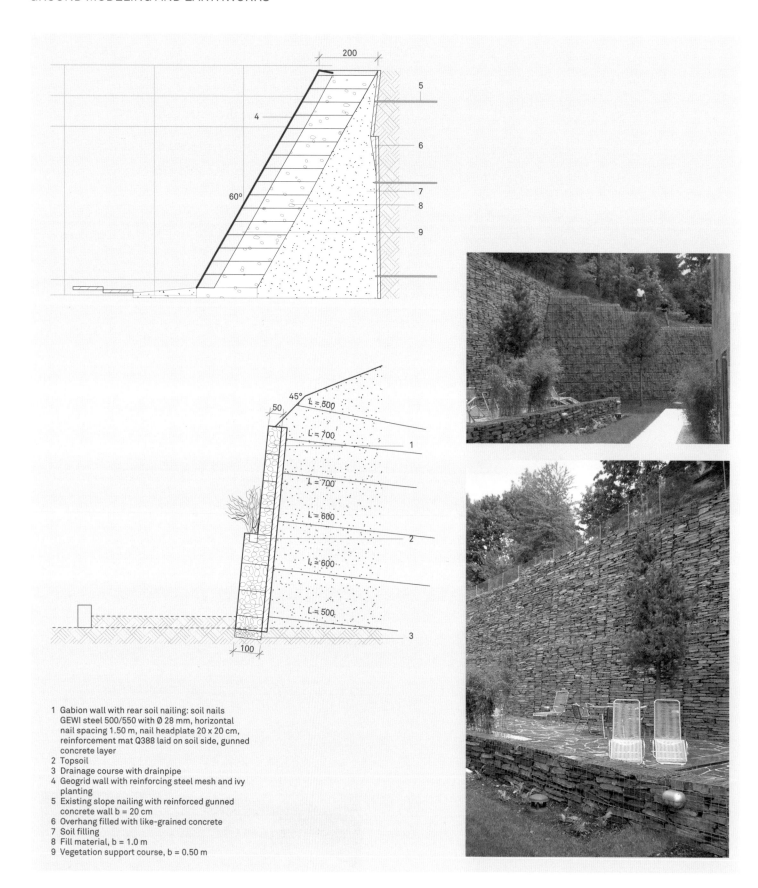

1 Gabion wall with rear soil nailing: soil nails
  GEWI steel 500/550 with Ø 28 mm, horizontal
  nail spacing 1.50 m, nail headplate 20 x 20 cm,
  reinforcement mat Q388 laid on soil side, gunned
  concrete layer
2 Topsoil
3 Drainage course with drainpipe
4 Geogrid wall with reinforcing steel mesh and ivy
  planting
5 Existing slope nailing with reinforced gunned
  concrete wall b = 20 cm
6 Overhang filled with like-grained concrete
7 Soil filling
8 Fill material, b = 1.0 m
9 Vegetation support course, b = 0.50 m

STEEP SLOPE AT THE KURMITTELHAUS, LOBENSTEIN,
GERMANY

Landscape architect: Birgit Hammer
Completion: 2003

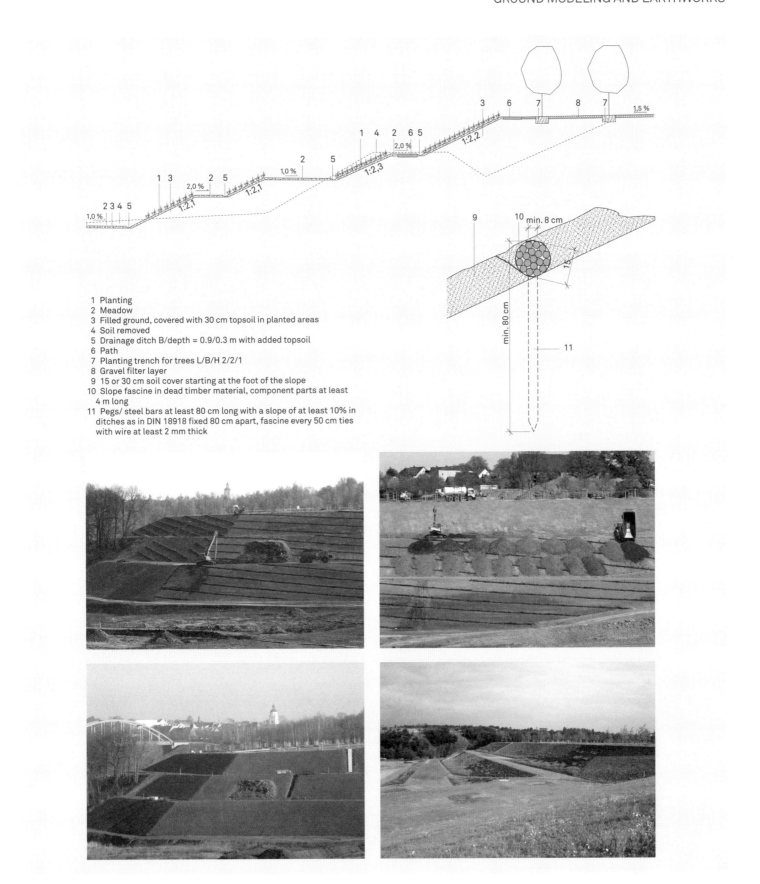

1 Planting
2 Meadow
3 Filled ground, covered with 30 cm topsoil in planted areas
4 Soil removed
5 Drainage ditch B/depth = 0.9/0.3 m with added topsoil
6 Path
7 Planting trench for trees L/B/H 2/2/1
8 Gravel filter layer
9 15 or 30 cm soil cover starting at the foot of the slope
10 Slope fascine in dead timber material, component parts at least
   4 m long
11 Pegs/ steel bars at least 80 cm long with a slope of at least 10% in
   ditches as in DIN 18918 fixed 80 cm apart, fascine every 50 cm ties
   with wire at least 2 mm thick

NEW LANDSCAPE IN RONNEBURG: SOUTH TERRACE, GERMANY

Landscape architects: Fagus GmbH, Markkleeberg
Specialized geological planning: G.U.B. Ingenieurgesellschaft
mbH, Zwickau, Jörg Friedrich
Completion: 2007

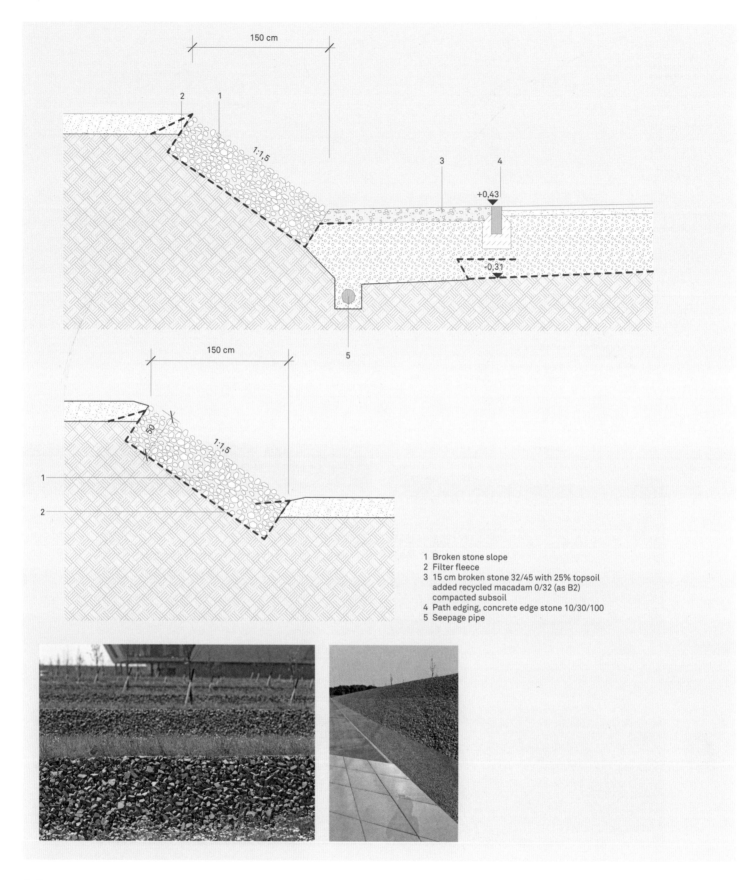

1 Broken stone slope
2 Filter fleece
3 15 cm broken stone 32/45 with 25% topsoil
  added recycled macadam 0/32 (as B2)
  compacted subsoil
4 Path edging, concrete edge stone 10/30/100
5 Seepage pipe

STONE BANKING: MOBILE LIFE CAMPUS, WOLFSBURG,
GERMANY

Landscape architects: Topotek 1
Architects: Henn Architekten
Completion: 2004

1 Precast concrete
  edging 10/15/100
2 Hard-wearing grass
  60 cm topsoil
  40 cm subsoil
  expanded glass rubble 0/56
  filter fleece 340 g/m²
3 Hard-wearing grass
  20 cm topsoil
  30 cm subsoil
  expanded glass rubble 0/56
  filter fleece 340 g/m²
4 10 cm rubble drainage 16/32
  building protection mat
  seal
  floor
5 Concrete foundation C12/15
6 Firmly compacted subsoil
7 10 cm chippings 11/22
  gravel 0/32
  filter fleece 340 g/m²
  drainage course

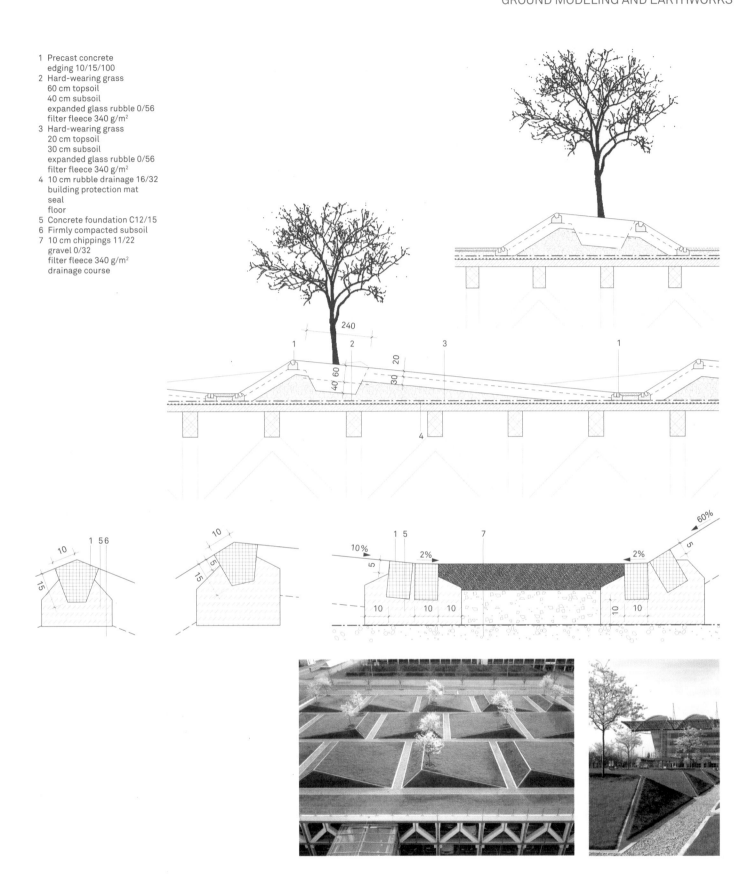

GRASSY MOUND, PARKING DECK TERMINAL 2, MUNICH
AIRPORT, GERMANY

Rainer Schmidt Landschaftsarchitekten, Munich
Architects: Koch und Partner Munich/Dresden
Completion: 2003

3.2   PATHS AND SQUARES

HARD SURFACES—TERMINOLOGY

BUILDING GROUND

PAVEMENT
- Frost protection course and base course
- Assessing structural thickness

CONSTRUCTION METHODS FOR SURFACE COURSES
- Concrete surfaces
- Asphalt surfaces
- Paved surfaces—nonbonded construction
- Tiled covering—nonbonded construction
- Paved and tiled covering—bonded construction
- Water-bound path surfaces/stamped earth covering
- Seepage-enabled surface courses
- Plastic coatings

BORDERS

SPECIMEN PROJECTS

Axel Klapka

3.2 PATHS AND SQUARES

Paths and squares are a significant part of public spaces. Their covering therefore contributes significantly to a location's appearance. As well as surface quality, the loads they must support, ranging from pedestrians to heavy goods vehicle traffic, are important parameters for construction.

HARD SURFACES—TERMINOLOGY

Hard surfaces are divided into bonded and nonbonded construction methods. > Fig. 3.2.2 Paved and tiled coverings and water-bound path surfaces constructed on compacted base courses are grouped under nonbonded construction methods. Bonded construction methods, on the other hand, involve base and surface courses that form a rigid structure due to a bonding agent such as bitumen, cement or plastic. This group primarily includes asphalt and concrete cover, along with polymer-bonded surfaces. Combinations of bonded and nonbonded materials also occur in special construction methods. It should be remembered that, while bonded constructions are significantly more rigid and can therefore support higher loads, they do not have the elasticity that allows nonbonded constructions to compensate for higher shear forces. This means that nonbonded construction is standard where, for instance, damage to paving surfaces must be avoided.

In constructing area and path surfaces, the structure's total thickness is calculated with reference to the properties of the building ground, the desired surface and load. From this, the necessary degree of ground excavation or fill can be calculated for the plot's topography. Path construction generally consists of the compacted building ground and the pavement. > Fig. 3.2.3
Indicators of construction thicknesses in this chapter are based on the traffic load caused by haulage and maintenance vehicles on frost-sensitive soils. These are condition found in park paths, entrance driveways, and service roads. > Pavement, Assessing structural thickness

BUILDING GROUND

The building ground consists of the soil onsite, which is either naturally placed (subsoil) or banked soil (substructure). Its loadbearing capacity and compactability and its drainage potential should be assessed in a soil survey before planning.
A leveled area with a gradient that corresponds to that of the covering to be laid, but no less than 2.5%, should be created on the building ground's surface. This ensures uniformly strong superstructures and planum drainage. In cohesive soil types, a geofleece or a separating course of sand should be laid to prevent the migration of fine particles of the existing soil into the frost protection course or base course immediately above it, as this adversely affects structural stability and drainage. Further, in the case of frost-sensitive soils and on groundwater-affected sites a planum drainage should be arranged with a coefficient of permeability of $k_f > 1 \times 10^{-6}$.

a) paving clinker nonbonded construction

b) asphalt-bonded construction

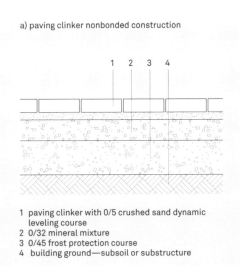

1 paving clinker with 0/5 crushed sand dynamic
   leveling course
2 0/32 mineral mixture
3 0/45 frost protection course
4 building ground—subsoil or substructure

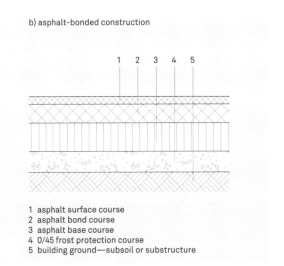

1 asphalt surface course
2 asphalt bond course
3 asphalt base course
4 0/45 frost protection course
5 building ground—subsoil or substructure

Fig. 3.2.1: Paved road in Knossos,
c. 1800 BC

Fig. 3.2.2

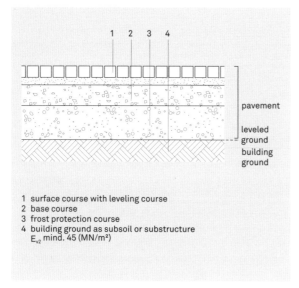

1 surface course with leveling course
2 base course
3 frost protection course
4 building ground as subsoil or substructure
  E_{v2} mind. 45 (MN/m²)

Fig. 3.2.3: Structure of area and path surfaces

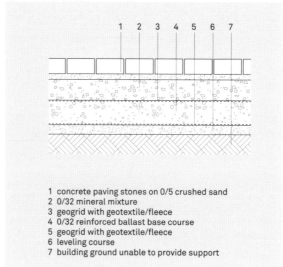

1 concrete paving stones on 0/5 crushed sand
2 0/32 mineral mixture
3 geogrid with geotextile/fleece
4 0/32 reinforced ballast base course
5 geogrid with geotextile/fleece
6 leveling course
7 building ground unable to provide support

Fig. 3.2.4: Specimen soil-conditioning measures

As a basis for the pavement, a loadbearing capacity of 45 MN/m² on the leveled building ground is required. If the value falls short of this, soil conditioning measures should be applied. Soil may be replaced with better loadbearing materials, mortared by adding cement, or improved in loadbearing capacity by drainage or the installation of a geogrid. > Fig. 3.2.4

PAVEMENT

The pavement consists of the frost protection course, the base course, and the surface course, which is the visible, functional surface. An appropriately dimensioned pavement prevents the damage that would otherwise be created by load or frost action. For base courses, broken, water-permeable and graduated mineral granulations of granulation groups 0/22 to 0/45 (bulk material base courses) are preferred, as these give greater structural stability than gravel base courses. For gravel base courses, structural heights should be 5 cm thicker than for bulk material base courses. The material must have compressive and shear strength, be frost-safe, and free of organic elements. The grain distribution of the layers lying on top of one another should be adjusted so that the grading curves lie as close together as possible. For paved or tiled surfaces, the filtration stability this creates should be maintained from the frost protection course to the joint filling.

Frost protection course and base course

In addition to protecting against wear and tear, the frost protection course also prevents deformation of the path structure during freezing and thaw periods. It is necessary where the soil is frost-sensitive (silt and clay) and the geographical location of the project area (the frost action zone) or high precipitation levels increase the frost risk. > Tab. 3.2.1

Loadbearing capacity is expressed in the combactability of the construction material mixture and is given as an E_{v2} module in meganewtons/square meter (MN/m²). Frost protection courses may be constructed from frost-safe soil, ballast, gravel or sand mixtures or recycled construction materials.

The base course is the actual stabilizing layer for the surface course. If the building ground is frost-safe and sufficiently compactable, the base course is laid without a frost protection course. The base courses consist of bulk material, gravel or sand mixtures or recycled construction materials of granulation groups 0/22 to 0/45.

The total thickness of the frost protection course and the base course should correspond to at least three times the largest grain size used, e.g. a minimum thickness of 10 cm for granulation group 0/32. If surface courses are to consist of a covering of small elements, as with mosaic paving, or will have to withstand dynamic forces, smaller grain sizes are chosen than for rigid or large-format coverings. > Tabs. 3.2.2 and 3.2.3

Class	Frost-sensitivity	Soil group according to DIN 18196
F1	not frost-sensitive	coarse-grained soils of groups: GW, GI, GE, SW, SI, SE
F2	slightly to moderately frost-sensitive	mixed-grained soils and soils with organic admixtures of groups: TA, OT, OH, OK, ST [1], GT [1], SU [1], GU [1]
F3	very frost-sensitive	fine-grained and mixed-grained soils of groups: TL, TM, UL, UM, UA, OU, ST *, GT *, SU *, GU *

[1] Note: these belong to F1 if the grain percentage is lower than 0.063 mm for a weight of 5.0% where U > 15.0 or 15.0% weight where U < 6.0.
* In the area 6.0 < U < 15.0 the grain percentage of under 0.063 required for inclusion in F1 can be linearly interpolated (see image ZTV E-StB)

Tab. 3.2.1: Frost-sensitivity by soil groups (according to RStO)

If no edging is included, the support course is extended at least 20 cm beyond the surface course at each side. So that base course or bedding mixtures can be checked, proof that compositions have been observed should be delivered along with the materials.

Assessing structural thickness

Specimen calculations of the structural thickness of individual layers can be given. This is analogous to the "Richtlinie zur Standardisierung des Oberbaues von Verkehrsflächen (RStO)" (Guidelines for standardizing the superstructure of traffic areas), which apply in Germany. Aside from the type of surface course, three factors should be assessed during planning:

· The use seen by the surface and the load caused by traffic;
· The frost-sensitivity of the subsoil;
· Local climatic conditions.

First, the construction class is determined according to **Tabs. 3.2.4–3.2.6**. Subsequently, the frost action zone should be determined according to **Fig. 3.2.5**.
Once the frost-sensitivity class has been graded, the necessary structure can be extrapolated from **Tab. 3.2.7**. The value for the thickness of the frost-safe pavement given in this table refers to the base and surface courses including any necessary frost protection course. The

Frost action zone I
Frost action zone II
Frost action zone III

Fig. 3.2.5: Frost action zones (according to RStO)

E_v2—values given on the leveled ground for	≥ 45 (MN/m²)		≥ 80 (MN/m²)	
Mixture for base course to be constructed	ballast, chippings-sand	gravel-sand	ballast, chippings-sand	gravel-sand
Desired E_v2 value on the base course to be constructed as				
Frost protection course with				
≥ 100 (MN/m²)	20 cm	25 cm	15 cm	20 cm
≥ 120 (MN/m²)	30 cm	35 cm	20 cm	25 cm
Ballast or gravel base course				
≥ 120 (MN/m²)	25 cm	30 cm	-	-
≥ 150 (MN/m²)	30 cm	40 cm	-	-

Tab. 3.2.2: Reference values for thickness of frost protection course or base course, correlated with the compacted building ground (according to RStO)

Given E_v2 value on the frost protection course for	≥ 100 (MN/m²)		≥ 120 (MN/m²)	
Mixture for base course to be constructed	ballast, chippings-sand	gravel-sand	ballast, chippings-sand	gravel-sand
Desired E_v2 value on the bulk material or gravel base course for				
≥ 120 (MN/m²)	15 cm	20 cm	-	-
≥ 150 (MN/m²)	20 cm	30 cm	15 cm	20 cm

Tab. 3.2.3: Reference values for thickness of base course correlated with the compacted frost protection course (according to RStO)

Assessment-relevant stress B Equivalent to 10-t axial transitions in a million	Construction class
over 32	SV
over 10–32	I
over 3–10	II
over 0.8–3	III
over 0.3–0.8	IV
over 0.1–0.3	V
up to 0.1	VI

Tab. 3.2.4: Assessment in terms of axial transmission (according to RStO)

Road type	Construction class
Expressway, industrial distributor road	SV / I / II
Main road, industrial road, road in industrial estate	II / III
Residential distributor road, pedestrian zone with freight traffic	III / IV
Service road, vehicle-used residential route, pedestrian zone (without bus traffic)	V / VI

Tab. 3.2.5: Assessment in terms of road type (according to RStO)

Traffic type	Construction class
Parking surface in continual use	
Heavy traffic	III / IV
Car traffic with a low percentage of heavy vehicle traffic	V
Car traffic	VI
Occasionally used parking space	
Heavy traffic	IV / V
Car traffic with a low percentage of heavy vehicle traffic	V / VI
Car traffic	as required

Tab. 3.2.6: Assessment for stationary traffic surfaces (according to RStO)

Frost-sensitivity class	Thickness in cm by construction class		
	SV / I / II	III / IV	V / VI
F2	55	50	40
F3	65	60	50

Tab. 3.2.7: Construction methods on F2 and F3 subsoil/substructure (according to RStO)

Conditions on site		A	B	C	D
Frost action	Zone I	± 0 cm			
	Zone II	+ 5 cm			
	Zone III	+15 cm			
Gradient	cutting, preliminary cut, embankment ≤ 2.0 m		+ 5 cm		
	in nonpermeable areas at about terrain height		± 0 cm		
	embankment > 2.0 m		- 5 cm		
Water situation	favorable			± 0 cm	
	unfavorable in terms of ZTV E-StB			+ 5 cm	
Construction of edge areas (e.g. shoulder, cycle paths, footpaths)	outside nonpermeable area and in nonpermeable areas with water-permeable edge areas				± 0 cm
	in nonpermeable areas with partially water-permeable edge areas as well as those with drainage installations				- 5 cm
	in nonpermeable areas with water-permeable edge areas or with drainage installations and nonpermeable lateral developments				- 10 cm

Tab. 3.2.8: Factors influencing frost-safety (according to RStO)

Surface layer	Use	Surface qualities
Concrete surfaces	ranging from roads and paths for heavy traffic to low-maintenance park paths	restricted to concrete gray and common colorations for concrete construction Surface finishes: smooth to coarse brush stroke to masonry finishes
Asphalt surfaces	roads and paths for heavy traffic to low-maintenance park paths	broad amplitude, from simple "blacktop" through treated surfaces to colored coatings
Concrete paving	paths and residential roads	from concrete gray to high-value natural stone inserts
Natural stone paving	paths and residential roads, area surfaces	as for naturally occurring stone in all its worked varieties
Clinker paving	paths and residential roads, area surfaces	color palette depends on clay used and possible metal aggregate
Concrete tiles	area and path surfaces	from concrete gray to high-value natural stone inserts
Natural stone tiles	area and path surfaces	as for naturally occurring stone in all its worked varieties
Water-bound path surface	paths and areas without vehicle traffic	many color tones from white to anthracite. Natural, soft appearance
Polymer-modified surfaces	sports and play areas	broad palette of colors, soft appearance
Special con-structions	paths and surfaces with light traffic	alternating with lawn or plants, more natural appearance

Tab. 3.2.9: Use and surface quality of various surface courses

spectrum of different specifications results from the variable factors influencing frost-safety in each case. For paved surfaces in construction class VI, the minimum thickness of frost protection course is calculated from the required total pavement thickness of 35 cm, deducting the base course and surface course's necessary structural thickness of 26 cm. For an F2 soil, the thickness of the frost protection course is 9 cm. If additional factors have an adverse effect on frost-safety, they should be taken account of in the thickness of the pavement according to Tab. 3.2.8. If the soil is not frost-sensitive, the frost protection course can be dispensed with, provided that the subsoil is sufficiently compactable. If the necessary compactability is not in place, the dimensions of the base course should be increased in thickness by 9 cm to make up for the absent frost protection course. > Figs. 3.2.2 and 3.2.3

CONSTRUCTION METHODS FOR SURFACE COURSES

For all the surface courses presented in the following pages, the structural thicknesses correspond to the loadbearing capacity of the building ground, the construction of the base courses and the expected use. All these examples involve the building classes VI as defined by RStO. > Tab. 3.2.9

Concrete surfaces

Concrete surfaces are rigid, high-strength surfaces. In creating them, many diverse possibilities for surface structure and color are available to the planner. > Fig. 3.2.8

Construction methods

A single-layer structure with a 14–18 cm thick, nonreinforced concrete surface laid on a 0/32 ballast base course is generally used for park paths. > Fig. 3.2.6 A foil or light geofleece prevents cement slurry from seeping into the base course. To successfully construct a concrete path surface, it is essential to comply with regulations for cement transport and processing, particularly those of EN 206. From the perspective of construction, concrete surfaces do not need borders.

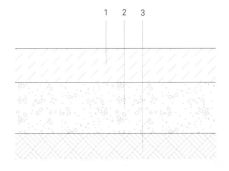

1 concrete surface, 18 cm
2 0/32 frost protection course, 27 cm
3 building ground as subsoil or substructure

Fig. 3.2.6: Standard concrete surface constructions

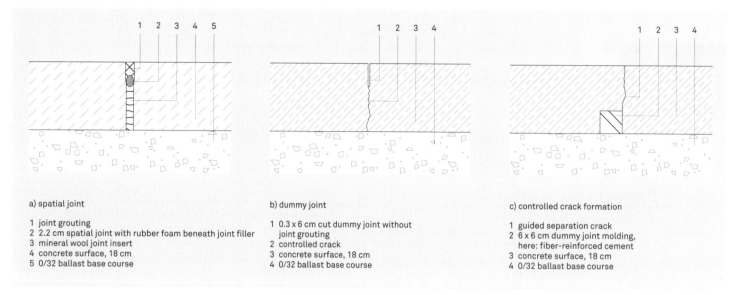

a) spatial joint

1 joint grouting
2 2.2 cm spatial joint with rubber foam beneath joint filler
3 mineral wool joint insert
4 concrete surface, 18 cm
5 0/32 ballast base course

b) dummy joint

1 0.3 x 6 cm cut dummy joint without
   joint grouting
2 controlled crack
3 concrete surface, 18 cm
4 0/32 ballast base course

c) controlled crack formation

1 guided separation crack
2 6 x 6 cm dummy joint molding,
   here: fiber-reinforced cement
3 concrete surface, 18 cm
4 0/32 ballast base course

Fig. 3.2.7: Joint forms

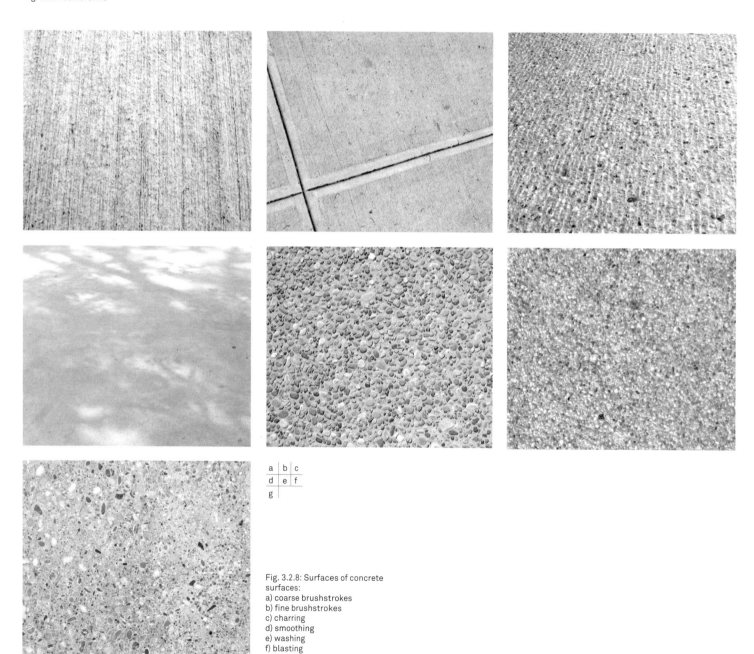

Fig. 3.2.8: Surfaces of concrete
surfaces:
a) coarse brushstrokes
b) fine brushstrokes
c) charring
d) smoothing
e) washing
f) blasting
g) grinding

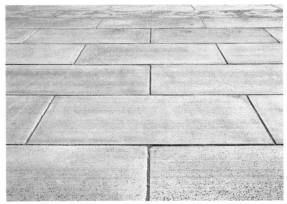

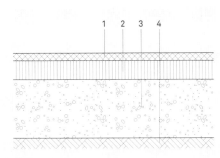

Fig. 3.2.9: Large-format ground slabs:
a) Bundesgartenschau Potsdam
b) Boat landing Plaza, Berlin

a | b

1 asphalt surface course, 4 cm
2 asphalt base course, 10 cm
3 0/45 frost protection course, 31 cm
4 building ground as subsoil or substructure

Fig. 3.2.10: Standard asphalt surface construction

They are laid between formwork molds. For a larger surface, installation with slipform pavers is possible. Concrete as delivered is distributed evenly between the formwork molds, uniformly compacted using vibrating screeds and ground down.

Concrete

When laid by hand, concrete surfaces are made using concrete mixed with superplasticizers. In a difficult installation situation or in case of heavy loading at an early stage it is made from high-early-strength concrete, otherwise it is made of soft road pavement concrete (in Germany, TL Beton-StB 2006 is referred to). Superplasticizers (FM) are added to the concrete on the construction site. It is workable within 30 minutes. The quality of the concrete should satisfy the following requirements:

Compressive strength class: C30/37
Exposure class: XF4
Consistency class: F3, flow consistency 42–48 cm (FM)
Moisture class: WF

When hardening, the concrete should be protected from evaporation, rain and frost. Depending on the temperature, the duration of this post-processing should be
· at approximately 15°C, min. 6 days
· at approximately 5°C, min. 10 days

Joints

For concrete surfaces, joints are necessary to avoid cracks and to compensate for lengthwise expansion. At solid incorporated elements and for end-of-day joints, spatial joints are arranged. Dummy joints are used for controlled crack formation in the surface. When arranging the joints, the ratio of slab size to slab thickness is decisive. > Chapter 2.3 Connections, Joints for in-situ concrete

The arrangement of the joints divides the surface into slabs. The slabs' lengths should not exceed 25 times their thickness for rectangular formats and 30 times their thickness for quadratic formats. Maximum slab sizes of 5 x 5 m and maximum path sections of 4 m in length can be given as standard values. The closer together the length and breadth of the slabs lie, the less

their tendency to form cracks. There should be no re-entrant angles within a slab. Lengthwise and crosswise joints should cross one another and not be diametrically opposed. Joints are arranged in free-form flat molds with the smallest possible cross section. > Fig. 3.2.7

Surface creation

Like other concrete surfaces, in-situ concrete path surfaces can be postprocessed to increase grip or for design purposes. After smoothing, but before hardening is completed, it is possible, using various procedures, to give the surface a structure. > Fig. 3.2.8 and chapter 1.7 Concrete

Ground slabs

Ground slabs are finished concrete parts, intermediate between in-situ concrete surfaces and standard commercially available concrete tiles. Finished parts are reinforced. They have to withstand tensile forces in order to be transported. Depending on their dimensions, ground slabs can withstand high traffic loads. Production of sharp-cornered special construction forms, for instance, is possible. > Fig. 3.2.9

Asphalt surfaces

Composition

An advantage of asphalt surfaces is their simple wide-surface installation, which makes them economical as a covering for areas and paths. Asphalt is a mixture of aggregates from broken and nonbroken natural stone minerals, sometimes with recycled granulated asphalt additions and bitumen as a bonding agent. Changing the percentages of the components changes the properties of the asphalt. The mineral substances form the support structure and are mixed according to the load expected and the desired surface structure (see EN 13108).

The functioning of asphalt construction methods is based on the thermoviscous properties of bitumen. Road paving asphalt is divided into different types for different stresses. Soft bonding agents (e.g. 160/220) are used for flexible mounting and low traffic, while harder bonding agents (e.g. 50/70) are used for higher loads.

Construction methods

A distinction is made between single-, two- and three-layered construction methods. The choice of construction is made in the light of expected traffic load. > Fig. 3.2.10

Asphalt base courses create a uniform, stable base for further construction. They are also used to stabilize paved surfaces enabled for high loads. > **Paved and tiled covering—bonded construction**

Asphalt bond courses are added in between base course and surface course where especially high thrust forces are present. This is generally only the case for intensively used roads with heavy traffic.

Asphalt surface courses, as the functional course, are under particularly high stress and are divided into asphalt concrete, stone matrix asphalt and poured asphalt owing to different types of use and surface textures > **Tab. 3.2.10**. The connecting effect between the courses is achieved by spraying the underlay (the asphalt base course) with bonding agents containing bitumen before laying the asphalt surface course.

Asphalt concrete forms a compact, smooth surface. It is laid hot using pavers and roller compaction. Asphalt concrete can also be laid and compacted manually for adaptation work.

Stone matrix asphalt consists of a high percentage of coarse-grained chippings with gap grading, with the cavities filled by asphalt mastic. It was developed for particularly high loads. Depending on grain size, its appearance can be that of a coarse-grained surface structure. Like asphalt concrete, stone matrix asphalt is laid using pavers and rollers.

For poured asphalt, the bonding agent and aggregate are adjusted to each other so that all pores are filled. By means of a surplus of bonding agent, which enables the flowing capacity of poured asphalt, a viscous mass is created that is watertight and does not need to be compacted after laying. In order to achieve a minimum surface grip, the surface course should be gritted while it is hot. Poured asphalt can be installed equally well manually or with pavers and is particularly suitable for small surfaces and those with many corners.

For asphalt base-surface courses, the base course is combined with the surface course. This construction method is primarily used in rural path construction, where requirements for surface quality and deformation stability are low. They are manufactured with a grain size of 0/16 at thicknesses of 5–10 cm. > **Tab. 3.2.11**

Water-permeable asphalt enables some of the rainwater to seep through the pavement. Grain size mixtures with a high percentage of pores and suitable bitumen used for base and surface courses ensure water drainage. This construction method should not be used in highly polluted areas, water protection zones and complexes where drainage can occur laterally into green spaces.

Processes for creating the surface

The structure and coloration of the top covering of new or existing asphalt surfaces can be influenced using

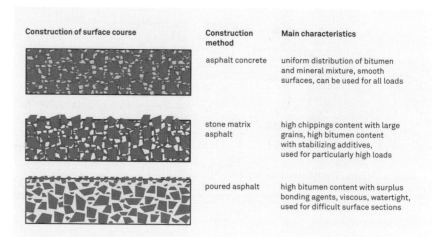

Construction of surface course	Construction method	Main characteristics
	asphalt concrete	uniform distribution of bitumen and mineral mixture, smooth surfaces, can be used for all loads
	stone matrix asphalt	high chippings content with large grains, high bitumen content with stabilizing additives, used for particularly high loads
	poured asphalt	high bitumen content with surplus bonding agents, viscous, watertight, used for difficult surface sections

Tab. 3.2.10: Asphalt surface courses

Course	Mix type/mix sort	Recommended course thickness in cm
Asphalt surface courses	asphalt concrete 0/5	2.0
	asphalt concrete 0/8	3.0
	asphalt concrete 0/11	4.0
	asphalt concrete 0/11S	4.0
	asphalt concrete 0/16S	5.0
	stone matrix asphalt 0/5	2.0
	stone matrix asphalt 0/8	3.0
	stone matrix asphalt 0/8S	3.5
	stone matrix asphalt 0/11S	4.0
	poured asphalt 0/5	2.0
	poured asphalt 0/8	2.5
	poured asphalt 0/11	3.5
	poured asphalt 0/11S	3.5
Asphalt base courses	mix type 0/16	5.0–8.0
	mix type 0/22	8.0–10.0
	mix type 0/32	8.0–14.0
Asphalt base-surface courses	mix type 0/16	8.0
	mix type 0/22	8.0–10.0
	mix type 0/32	8.0–10.0

Tab. 3.2.11: Recommended construction thicknesses for asphalt

Fig. 3.2.11: Asphalt surfaces:
a) asphalt concrete
b) stone matrix asphalt
c) poured asphalt
d) bitumen emulsion gritted
   with chippings
e) epoxy resin gritted
   with chippings
f) poured asphalt gritted
   with chippings
g) bead-blasted asphalt
   concrete
h) colored asphalt

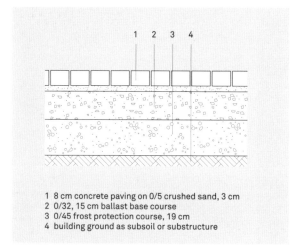

1 8 cm concrete paving on 0/5 crushed sand, 3 cm
2 0/32, 15 cm ballast base course
3 0/45 frost protection course, 19 cm
4 building ground as subsoil or substructure

Fig. 3.2.12: Standard paved surface construction

special procedures. The choice of technique depends
on function and desired appearance:

· Special bitumen emulsions on asphalt concrete gritted
  with rolled-in chippings,
· Colorable epoxy resin coating on asphalt concrete gritted with rolled-in sand or chippings,
· Poured asphalt as a surface course with chippings or
  gravel rolled in while material is hot. The gritting material is delivered dust-free and warmed,
· Bead-blasting to expose mineral components,
· Colored asphalt > Fig. 3.2.11

Paved surfaces, nonbonded construction

Paved surfaces permit a high degree of individual design. They are easy to maintain and their manufacture
is easily manageable. Only a small selection of the wide
range of possible materials and laying patterns can be
shown here. > Fig. 3.2.12

Construction methods

Paved surfaces can be created using bonded and
nonbonded construction methods. The nonbonded
construction method is standard due to its high dynamic loadbearing capacity and easy maintenance. The
paved surface consists of the paving stones, the bedding, and the joint filling. Paving stones may be natural
stone, clinker or concrete. The thickness of the stones
depends on the compressive strength of the material
and the load it will be expected to take. Moving traffic
creates dynamic forces working in several directions.
The paving stones transmit vertical loads to the bedding
and base course. Horizontal loads, created by vehicles
turning, have a thrusting and twisting effect on the paving. These forces act most strongly on the faces of the
stones and cause edge pressures which decrease with
the size of the stones (see the requirements for paving
stones in EN 1338, EN 1344, EN 1342). Paving stones are
laid in bond patterns. This gives the structure stability,
particularly when exposed to shear forces. > Figs. 3.2.13
and 3.2.14

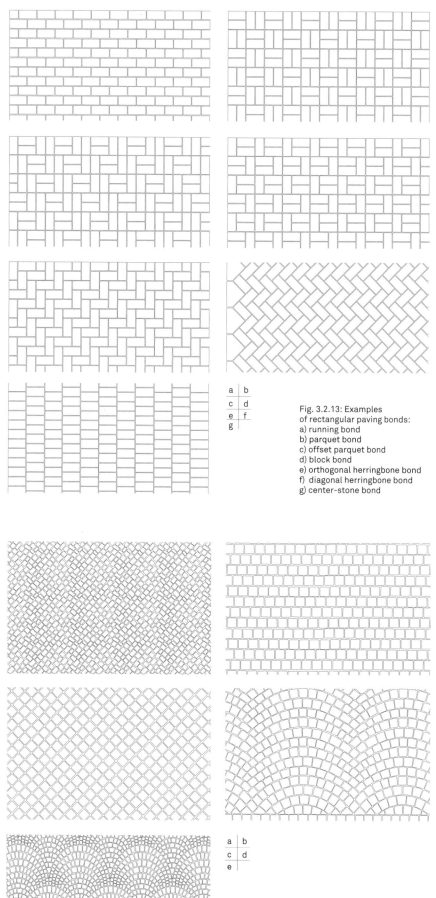

a	b
c	d
e	f
g	

Fig. 3.2.13: Examples
of rectangular paving bonds:
a) running bond
b) parquet bond
c) offset parquet bond
d) block bond
e) orthogonal herringbone bond
f) diagonal herringbone bond
g) center-stone bond

a	b
c	d
e	

Fig. 3.2.14: Examples
of ashlar paving bonds:
a) polygonal
b) rectangular bond
c) coursed paving
d) segmented arc
e) fan paving

Bedding

Paving bedding serves as a support for paving stones and should compensate for the different heights of the individual stones. It should be manufactured with a uniform thickness of at least 3 cm but not more than 5 cm in the installed state on the base course. The minimum thickness ensures correct embedding of paving stones, while keeping to the maximum thickness avoids ruts appearing in the covering. Crushed sand/chipping mixtures with grain sizes of 0/4, 0/5 or 0/8 with graded granular composition and high resistance to grain fragmentation are used as bedding material. The construction material mix must also be nonfrost-sensitive and filter stable to the base course or joint filling. When laid and compacted, the water-permeability should be guaranteed at least k_f 1 x 10^{-6}.

Joints

Joints balance out dimensional tolerances and stone expansion caused by temperature and prevent the edges from breaking. The correct joint breadth depends on the stone's size and on the surface of its sides. The jointing material is matched to the bedding material. Sands available in granulations 0/2 and 0/4 are used, with graduated crushed sand-chippings mixtures with grain sizes over 0/4 used for broader joints.

The main principle when arranging joints is that paving laid diagonally to the direction of traffic has the greatest resistance to horizontal forces, as the edge pressure is distributed between many surfaces. For perpendicularly laid paving, long joints running in the traffic direction should be avoided.

Compaction

Once the paving has been tapped into place with a rubber mallet, and the joint sand applied and swept in, the paving and the bedding are compacted using compaction plates, working from the edges to the middle. After compaction, more joint material is applied to the surface and swept in. Repeated "aftersanding" is generally necessary before the joint material has completely settled.

Concrete paving

Concrete paving is available in various constructions and formats. In addition to interlocking stones, which are often used for loadbearing traffic surfaces, special paving systems are available that take into account curbs, paving stones for radii and special forms, as well as the possibility of combining different stones. The laying of simple systems can be automated as a rational means of concrete paving surface creation. The paving stones are produced with spacers, making laying with uniform joints easier. When planning, the modular dimensions of the laying pattern resulting from the paving stones' nominal dimensions and the joint width is to be ascertained. > **Fig. 3.2.15**

It is possible to develop individual paving systems if the surface area is sufficiently big. Specialized molds are created in concrete paving factories for this purpose and can also be used for further productions. > **Fig. 3.2.16**

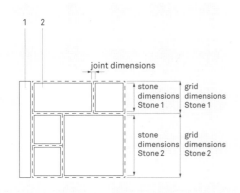

1 edge border—concrete edge stones
2 concrete tiles in a laying pattern

Fig. 3.2.15: Schema for modular dimensions and nominal dimensions

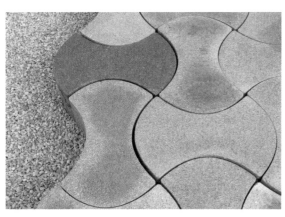

Fig. 3.2.16: "Schmetterling" paving system, design by Keller Landschaftsarchitekten

Natural stone paving

Natural stone paving is produced with split and dressed edges and surfaces. Dressed paving stones are characterized by one or more technical processings to satisfy high requirements on their form and appearance. Split side surfaces create better traction with the joint filling substance. According to EN 1342 (specifications for natural stone paving), relatively large dimensional tolerances are possible. For a regular paved surface, the higher classifications of dimensional tolerances should always be taken as a basis. Where requirements on the paving profile are particularly high, it is a good idea to personally establish and specify the tolerances in their exact dimensions.

In regulations, paving stones are described by their dimensions, e.g. 100/100/100. In Germany, natural stone paving is also classified as follows:

· Mosaic paving up to 50–60 mm
· Small paving up to 70–100 mm
· Large paving up to 110–300 mm

Mosaic paving is particularly suited to segmented-arc paving, individual patterns, or ornaments on surfaces not used by vehicles. Small stone paving is suitable for low-speed vehicle traffic, given the proper structure. It is laid as rectangular bond, polygonally, or in segmented arcs.

Large stone paving is generally made available as a sawn product and laid as a running bond or herringbone bond. Natural stone paving can be dressed using stonemasons' techniques to comply with slip safety or aesthetic requirements. > Chapter 1.5 Cut stone, Possible treatments, and tab. 1.5.2 Technical properties
The compressive strength, frost and de-icing salt resistance and weathering resistance of natural stone should be confirmed by an appropriate certificate of suitability. > Chapter 1.5 Cut stone, Qualities and properties
To verify color tone, working technique and laying pattern, the preparation of sample surfaces, kept as a reference until completion, is recommended.

Paving clinker and paving brick

In areas under vehicular use, paving clinker and paving brick with thicknesses of 60–80 mm are used, while thicknesses of 45 mm are used in areas not used by vehicles. For vehicle-used areas, the strength (ultimate flexural load) of the stones should be greater than 80 N/mm². For areas not used by vehicles, it should be greater than 30 N/mm². Clinker or bricks may be laid flat or on edge, with a joint width of 3–5 mm (narrow jointed) or 8–10 mm (wide jointed for areas with low load and for laying in mortar bedding).

Pebble paving

Paving with gravel is one of the oldest paving forms. Pebbles are pressed on edge into the sand bedding. One variant involves split river pebbles, laid horizontally. This construction method was used in Antiquity for decorative paving in gardens and courts, and later for route construction. The limited skid resistance and loadbearing capacity as well as the high manufacturing cost of this paving type mean that it is now rarely used. It may appear, for instance, in areas under historical preservation or private gardens. > Fig. 3.2.17

Tiled coverings—nonbonded construction

Tiled coverings are particularly suited to large surfaces. They are made from natural stone, clinker/brick and concrete stones. As tiles have a low stability due to the unfavorable relationship of length to thickness, these are only suitable for traffic load when produced in special thicknesses. In principle the construction methods and technical rules for tiled coverings are no different from paving construction methods. For this reason, only issues specific to tiled construction methods are addressed below. > Fig. 3.2.18

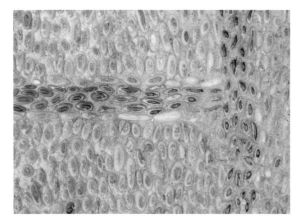

Fig. 3.2.17: Gravel paving

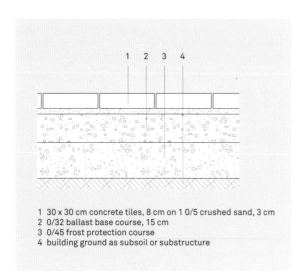

1 30 x 30 cm concrete tiles, 8 cm on 1 0/5 crushed sand, 3 cm
2 0/32 ballast base course, 15 cm
3 0/45 frost protection course
4 building ground as subsoil or substructure

Fig. 3.2.18: Standard tiled covering construction

Fig. 3.2.19: Examples of tile bonds:
a) square bond, orthogonal
b) strip bond
c) square bond, diagonal
d) random length strip pattern
e) Roman formation
f) polygonal bond

a	b
c	d
e	f

Construction methods

Dimensional stability requirements for tiles are high, as they have a high surface area and height differences can therefore only be minimally compensated for during compaction. Furthermore, there is a risk of breakage in non-uniform base courses or beddings. For vehicle-used surfaces, the target base course loadbearing capacity is therefore 180 MN/m². Bedding should be produced with a thickness of 2–4 cm. To create a regular joint profile, joint guides or spacers are used. > EN 1341 and EN 1339 Natural stone tiles are available in regular, sawn formats and free formats (polygonal tiles) with split surfaces and/or interrupted edges. > Fig. 3.2.19

Paved and tiled covering—bonded construction

Bonded paving or tiling construction methods are used where particular loads or surface properties, e.g. water impermeability, cannot be achieved with a nonbonded paving or tiling surface. Base course, bedding material and joint filling material consist of construction material mixtures with bonding agents on a cement, artificial resin or bitumen base. A rigid overall construction is created, with this property depending on the adhesive tensile strength between the covering and the bedding material as well as the physical properties of the layers. In construction, it is impossible to prevent hairline cracks from forming in the joint and bedding material, meaning that water can enter and has to be conducted away by a sufficiently water-permeable bedding and base course.

Base course

Water-permeable base courses can be constructed using drainage concrete or water-permeable asphalt. They are dimensioned according to the expected traffic load, as prescribed for this construction method. For both construction methods, a certain amount of fine granulate is omitted during manufacture (gap grading 2/4 and 4/8 mm), creating pores. The loadbearing capacity is lower than for the standard construction method. The water-permeability should have a k_f value of at least

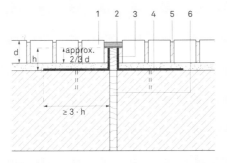

1 mosaic paving on mortar bedding
2 joint filling in accordance with ZTV Fug-StB
   (elastic, fuel-resistant), with separator layer
3 joint tape as preliminary to filling
4 L-steel angle, perforated or broken, secured to underlay
   (concrete surface)
5 joint mortar
6 existing movement joint in concrete surface

Fig. 3.2.20: Standard movement joint construction

5.4×10^{-5} m/s. To further promote water conduction, a water-permeable frost protection course or planum drainage is laid out beneath the base course. To avoid uncontrolled crack formation in the surface course, the drainage concrete course is notched, to allow controlled crack formation and correspond to the later joint grid of the surface course. For joint arrangement, the dimensions given in the section "Concrete surfaces" apply. > Chapter Construction methods for surface courses, Concrete surfaces, and fig. 3.2.20

Bedding

Defined factory-made mortars are used for the 4–6 cm thick bedding, as mixing on the construction site would be subject to significant variations. Here also, water-permeability of at least 1×10^{-6} m/s is acceptable. In addition, resistance to frost-thaw alternation, an adhesive tensile strength of 1.5 N/mm² and a compressive strength of 30 N/mm² must be established. To avoid lime blooms, which form due to the alkaline reaction that takes place as the cement hardens, particularly when sedimentary stone is used, trass cement mortar (Portland-Puzzolan cement) with 40–50% trass is available.

Joint filling

Unlike bedding, joint mortar should be largely non-water-permeable, but otherwise it should possess similar physical properties to the bedding material. It should also fill the joint space, leaving no gaps. Fundamentally, the requirements are the same as for bedding mortar. However, the compressive strength is set higher, at least 45 N/mm², and a higher fluidity is required. As mechanical compaction can change the structure, self-compacting mortars should be used.

Paving

Paving stones with a nominal thickness of at least 45 mm should be used. For vehicle-used surfaces the thickness should be 60–80 mm and for heavy traffic surfaces it should be 100–120 mm. To improve the adhesive tensile strength in relation to bedding and joint mortar, the side surfaces and undersides should be raw and clean. Sawn stones can also be given an applied adhesive bridge. Joint width should be at least 6–10 mm, 10 mm for paving bricks and up to 15 mm for nondressed natural stones.

Tiles

For tiled coverings, similar indications to those given above for paving can be applied. The standards given in the section "Tiled coverings, nonbonded construction" also apply. Tiled coverings with bonded construction should not be used in areas under vehicular use. When laying natural stone tiles, discoloration caused by reaction with the bedding mortar is unavoidable.

Movement joints

In order to avoid thermal tensions within the pavement and at solid incorporated elements or junctions with buildings, movement joints are installed. These must be allowed for

when constructing the base course, conforming to the subsequent joint profile of the surface. For vehicle-used surfaces, these require an abutment. > Fig. 3.2.20
Joint inserts, fusible joint tape or grouting compounds can be used as joint filling compounds.

Special construction methods

For paved surfaces with heavy traffic, for instance in old town centers, increased stability can be achieved by using a combination of water-permeable, bonded base courses with nonbonded surface courses. In this case, a geotextile filter should be laid beneath the bedding to preserve the base course's water-permeability. The bedding should be produced with a uniform thickness of 4 cm. Due to the forces created when the surface is driven over, hard minerals are more suitable for paving, bedding and joint filling.

Water-bound path surfaces/stamped covering

The water-bound path surface is a traditional and economical construction method for foot and cycle paths (with occasional vehicle traffic in a dry state). Its inexpensive manufacture is however offset by increased maintenance and management costs.

This construction method is a suitable single-layer design for simple, often temporary path and area surfaces, two-layer design for larger surfaces without exceptional incidence of shear forces, or three-layer design for sport surfaces and intensively used surfaces. Mineral rubble of various granulations is used for the surface layer, without added bonding agents or stabilizers. The surface course is bonded by means of a certain water content. A distinction is made between mixtures of various parent rocks, usually composed of locally available materials, and layered broken material made from a single parent rock. > Fig. 3.2.21

Construction methods

To achieve water bonding, the surface course is manufactured from mixtures with granulations of 0/5 or 0/8. An 8–21% percentage of granulations smaller than 0.063 mm ensures the necessary water storage capacity while allowing water-permeability of at least 1×10^{-6} m/s.

Fig. 3.2.21: Examples of colors for water-bound path surfaces

Broken rock mixtures with a granulation of 0/32 and water-permeability of at least 10^{-4} m/s are used for the base courses. A loadbearing capacity of 80 MN/m² must always be achieved for the base course. For foot and cycle paths without exceptional requirements, the whole structure of a water-bonded pavement should be no less than 20 cm thick. For paths with occasional automobile use on frost-sensitive soil, depending on composition, the total construction depth should be no less than 40–50 cm.

Single-layer construction methods

The single-layer construction method involves a ballast base course gritted with materials at 0% (0/4) or sand and chippings granulations of 2/5 mm to 8/16 mm. In this way, a simple loadbearing surface can be created with a 0/4 covering (recommended thickness 2 cm). Historical sites, beer gardens, rambling paths, or temporary parking areas are produced by shoveling thin sand or chipping granulations onto the base course. Due to the low thickness of the loose material on the base course, a high loadbearing capacity is achieved.

Fig. 3.2.22

a) standard single-layer construction method

1 0/4 grit
2 0/32 ballast base course, 12 cm
3 building ground as subsoil or substructure

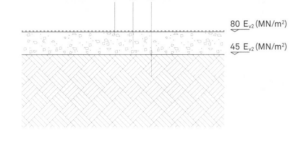

b) standard 2-layer construction method

1 surface course, 4 cm
2 0/32 ballast base course, 12 cm
3 building ground as subsoil or substructure

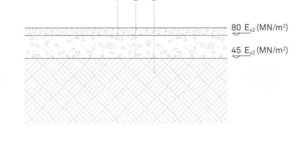

c) standard 3-layer construction method

1 surface course, 4 cm
2 dynamic course, 6–8 cm
3 0/32 ballast base course, 12 cm
4 building ground as subsoil or substructure

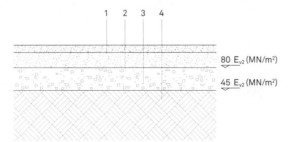

Care should be taken that, after the surface wears out, the base course does not disrupt the site's appearance. > Fig. 3.2.22a

Two-layer construction method

For the two-layer construction method, the water-bound surface course is applied to the base course. > Fig. 3.2.22b

Three-layer construction method

The three-layer construction method can incorporate an additional dynamic course, enabling it to withstand and compensate for shear forces occasioned during sports, or on intensively used surfaces in public areas. The dynamic course usually has a granulation of 0/11, 0/16 or 0/22, and should be the same color as the surface course. The structural thicknesses are 6–8 cm. While possessing a water-permeability of at least 1×10^{-5} m/s, the dynamic course should have a water storage capacity of at least 15% by volume. > Fig. 3.2.22c

Installation

Installation takes place at normal soil humidity. Dynamic and surface course compaction should be performed using statically effective compaction equipment (rollers) to avoid decomposition. When compacted, surface courses should be at least 3 cm, and preferably 4 cm, thick. Slopes of more than 5% should be avoided, as the surface course cannot withstand the erosive force of the flowing water.

Maintenance

After the winter months in particular, water-bound path surfaces should be maintained by checking for holes and eluviations and possibly performing leveling work. Renewed compaction with rollers is required after frost and thaw periods, as the material is loosened by freezing, which can cause decomposition.

Seepage-enabled surface courses

For areas with low traffic load, such as fire service installation areas or occasionally used parking areas, seepage-enabled construction methods form a vegetation-supporting, loadbearing surface course. Paved and tiled surfaces with extra-broad joints, special lawn grid systems made from concrete, clay or plastic or ballast lawn surfaces are used. Openings are filled with chippings, or, in green joints, a mixture of soil and chippings. Water-permeable asphalt, concrete and paving concrete coverings also exist. These allow water in the base courses to exit via connected pores.

Construction methods

Construction methods are divided into seepage-enabled traffic surface reinforcement, green surface reinforcement, and ballast lawns, depending on load and desired surface composition. The permeability of chipping-filled joints is higher than that of green joints. The subsoil should have a water-permeability of k_f 1×10^{-6} m/s, while that of the base course should be k_f 1×10^{-5} m/s.

Load class [1]	Total weight permitted (vehicle type)	Annual use	Alternation of vehicles	Ballast lawn	Greenable coverings
1	≤ 3.5 t (car) [2]	occasional	1–2 x weekly	+	+
2 [4]	≤ 3.5 t (car) [2]	continual	1–3 x daily	-	o
	≤ 11.5 t (truck) [3]	occasional	1–2 x weekly	-	o
3 [4]	≤ 3.5 t (car) [2]	periodic	1 x daily	+	+
	≤ 11.5 t (truck) [3]	occasional	1–3 x daily	-	+
4	vehicles ≥ 11.5 t (truck) [3]	case by case basis		+	+

+ = suitable, o = may be suitable, - = unsuitable

[1] Referring to RStO
[2] Total weight permitted
[3] Axle load
[4] Depending on load, damage to vegetation and the vegetation base layer should be expected.

Tab. 3.2.12: Load classes for ballast lawns and greenable areas

Regardless of the seepage type, additional drainage installations should be provided to conduct surface water. For seepage-enabled traffic surface reinforcement, paving and tiling systems with widened joints or seepage openings can be used. The 10–35 mm wide joints or ready-formed holes are filled with water-permeable chippings with a granulation of 1/3 or 2/5. The bedding should consist of the same material.

Open-pored paving concrete stones and tiles are also available commercially. As the pores are easily blocked, long-term functioning can be ensured only if regularly cleaned. Greenable covers made from paving or tiles, or honeycomb and grid elements, represent a compromise between the required traffic load and a "greened" appearance. Greenable surface reinforcements are divided into load classes, according to their traffic load and intensity of function. > Tab. 3.2.12

A mixture of 10–20% topsoil, 10–20% lava and 60–80% crushed sand-chippings mixture is used for bedding and joint filling. This ensures loadbearing capacity and sufficient vegetation space for greening. > Fig. 3.2.23a

Ballast lawns are used for surfaces under low strength. They approximate to a solid turf layer. They consist of a vegetation base layer. Where traffic load is high, this may contain an additional ballast base course. The vegetation base layer or ballast base course is applied to the 25 or 45 MN/m[2] compacted and roughened building ground planum. The vegetation base course consists of a mixture of 0/32 gravel (about 65%), topsoil of soil group 2 (about 20%), and lava (about 15%). Conditions for growth can be improved by adding compost. The organic substance content should however not be greater than 3% of the total mass. The vegetation base layer must possess sufficient water-permeability as well as sufficient water storage capacity. To protect the mixture, compaction is performed statically, until a loadbearing capacity of at least 45 MN/m[2] is reached. For ballast lawns, the load classes given in Fig. 3.2.23 apply.

Plastic coatings

Originally developed for sport areas, plastic coatings are also used as fall protection coating for play areas. They also offer design possibilities for varied and colored areas. Plastic coatings are standardized for light athletics, tennis and multipurpose sports facilities. Their composition is adjusted for elastic, damping or dynamic

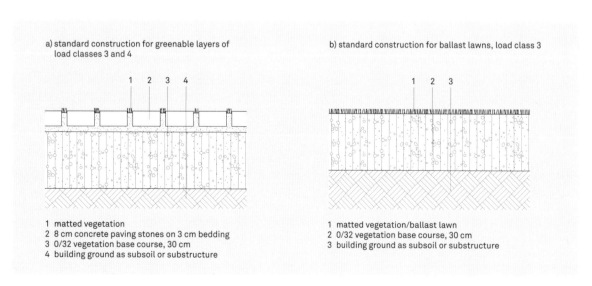

a) standard construction for greenable layers of load classes 3 and 4

b) standard construction for ballast lawns, load class 3

1 matted vegetation
2 8 cm concrete paving stones on 3 cm bedding
3 0/32 vegetation base course, 30 cm
4 building ground as subsoil or substructure

1 matted vegetation/ballast lawn
2 0/32 vegetation base course, 30 cm
3 building ground as subsoil or substructure

Fig. 3.2.23

properties, depending on their function. Coatings are divided into coating types (EN 14877) specific to sport type/function. Certified systems for each separate function are available from manufacturers.

Construction methods

Plastic coatings may be manufactured using a nonwater-permeable or water-permeable construction method, single- or two-layered. Nonpermeable systems require a stronger incline, to ensure a more rapid runoff of water. Drainage installations should be provided for both construction methods. Two-layered surface courses consist of a base layer of polyurethane-bonded granulated rubber and an upper or functional layer of polyurethane-bonded EPDM granulated rubber. Single-layer surface courses consist solely of the functional surface. The coatings are poured onto a bituminous bonded base

course. The asphalt base course and the nonbonded ballast base course beneath it ensure stability. In water-permeable construction methods, these courses conduct the precipitation water away. > Fig. 3.2.24 and tab. 3.2.13

BORDERS

Borders have both a design and a constructive function. They act as abutments for the covering during pavement laying, and protect the covering from damage. Where surface course edges are under particularly high loads, the borders prevent subsidence and crack formation in edge areas. Drainage installations may be constructed like borders, as open or closed gutters. For edge borders, drainage should be paid particular attention to, as incidental surface water generally flows toward the edges. For this reason, the enclosed covering should be laid at least 3 mm higher than the borders. > Fig. 3.2.25

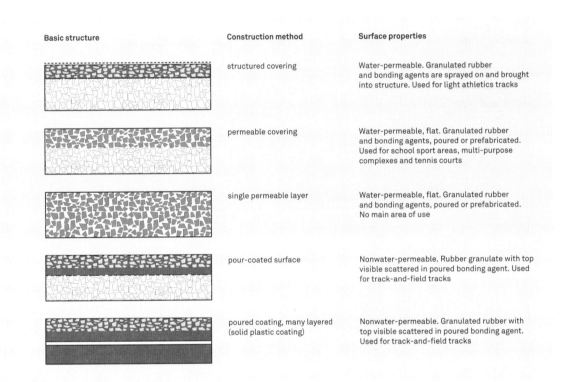

Basic structure	Construction method	Surface properties
	structured covering	Water-permeable. Granulated rubber and bonding agents are sprayed on and brought into structure. Used for light athletics tracks
	permeable covering	Water-permeable, flat. Granulated rubber and bonding agents, poured or prefabricated. Used for school sport areas, multi-purpose complexes and tennis courts
	single permeable layer	Water-permeable, flat. Granulated rubber and bonding agents, poured or prefabricated. No main area of use
	pour-coated surface	Nonwater-permeable. Rubber granulate with top visible scattered in poured bonding agent. Used for track-and-field tracks
	poured coating, many layered (solid plastic coating)	Nonwater-permeable. Granulated rubber with top visible scattered in poured bonding agent. Used for track-and-field tracks

Tab. 3.2.13: Coating types and areas of use

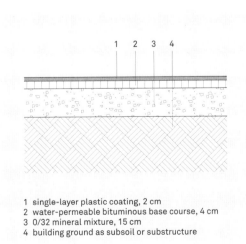

1 single-layer plastic coating, 2 cm
2 water-permeable bituminous base course, 4 cm
3 0/32 mineral mixture, 15 cm
4 building ground as subsoil or substructure

Fig. 3.2.24: Standard plastic coating construction

For asphalt paths with sufficiently broad base courses, the edges can be post-processed using properly equipped pavers, avoiding the need for bordering.

As well as the high and low curbs familiar from road construction, edge stones and steel edging are used in landscape construction. In case of vehicular traffic load, bordering is laid on a 20 cm thick concrete foundation, which absorbs vertical compressive load. Horizontal forces are absorbed by a one-sided back support, which should be 15 cm wide. For exclusively pedestrian paths, the concrete foundation and back support can be reduced to 10 cm. When in doubt, the manufacturers' indications, or, for exceptional loads, the static calculations should be taken as a basis. Concrete foundation and back support are manufactured from C12/15 and require formwork for proper installation.

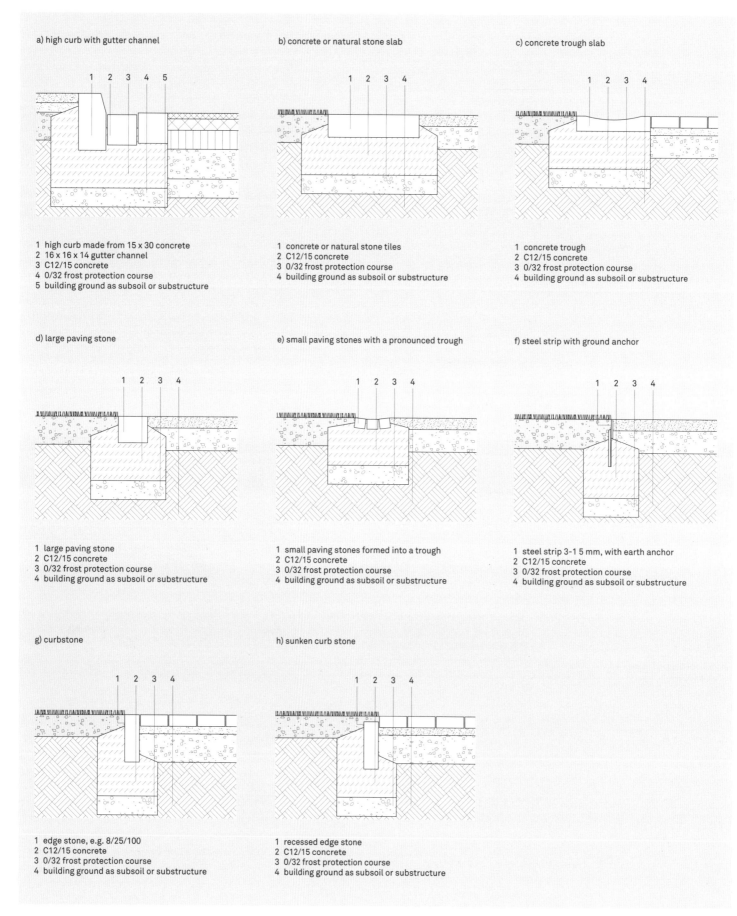

a) high curb with gutter channel

1 high curb made from 15 x 30 concrete
2 16 x 16 x 14 gutter channel
3 C12/15 concrete
4 0/32 frost protection course
5 building ground as subsoil or substructure

b) concrete or natural stone slab

1 concrete or natural stone tiles
2 C12/15 concrete
3 0/32 frost protection course
4 building ground as subsoil or substructure

c) concrete trough slab

1 concrete trough
2 C12/15 concrete
3 0/32 frost protection course
4 building ground as subsoil or substructure

d) large paving stone

1 large paving stone
2 C12/15 concrete
3 0/32 frost protection course
4 building ground as subsoil or substructure

e) small paving stones with a pronounced trough

1 small paving stones formed into a trough
2 C12/15 concrete
3 0/32 frost protection course
4 building ground as subsoil or substructure

f) steel strip with ground anchor

1 steel strip 3-1 5 mm, with earth anchor
2 C12/15 concrete
3 0/32 frost protection course
4 building ground as subsoil or substructure

g) curbstone

1 edge stone, e.g. 8/25/100
2 C12/15 concrete
3 0/32 frost protection course
4 building ground as subsoil or substructure

h) sunken curb stone

1 recessed edge stone
2 C12/15 concrete
3 0/32 frost protection course
4 building ground as subsoil or substructure

Fig. 3.2.25: Borders

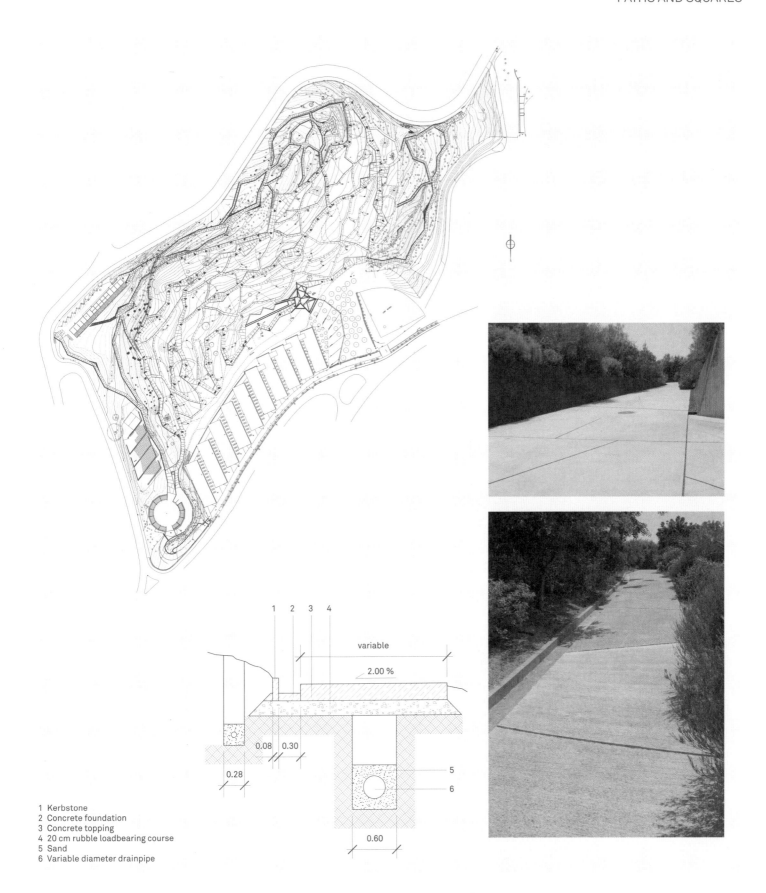

1 Kerbstone
2 Concrete foundation
3 Concrete topping
4 20 cm rubble loadbearing course
5 Sand
6 Variable diameter drainpipe

BOTANICAL GARDEN, BARCELONA, SPAIN

Architects: Carlos Ferrater, José Luis Canosa
Landscape architect: Isabel Figueras
Completion: 1999

The geometric arrangement of the in-situ concrete surfaces is based on a grid of triangles that fits into the
changes in height in the terrain. Machine-smoothed
surfaces and brushed surfaces divide the path system
into main paths and side paths.

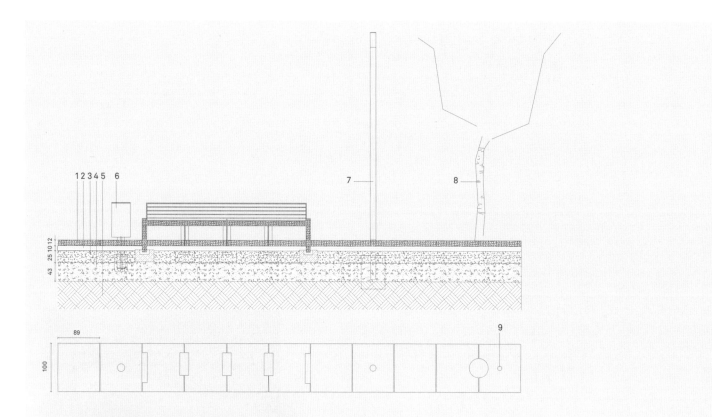

1 2 3 4 5   6   7   8

43 25 10 12

89

100

9

1 Basanite natural stone tiles, black-grey sawn +
   coarse-spalted surface, all lateral surfaces sawn
   over whole surface
2 Bedding, C8/10 shingle concrete, d = 10 cm
3 Ballast base course 0/32
   (E_{v2} min 150 MN/m^2)
4 Frost protection course 0/56
   (E_{v2} min 120 MN/m^2)
5 Leveled ground (E_{v2} min 45 MN/m^2)
6 Garbage can
7 Light pylon
8 Crataegus lavallei "Carrierei"
9 Drilled hole for tree watering system

As part of the redevelopment of the old town, all surfaces were created in construction class III. Large
granite paving with a variety of dimensions was used. It
was laid in rectangular crazy paving bond and in polygonal bond. Surfaces under especially high loads were
given an asphalt base course.

OLD TOWN SCHMALKALDEN, GERMANY

Landscape architects: terra.nova, Munich
Completion: 2005

1 "Altmarkt" edge plate (standard dimensions: L: 24–40 cm, W: 25 cm, H: 12 cm) granite, red-brown, light, medium grain underside and lateral surfaces beveled on all sides, natural-cleft surface
2 "Altmarkt" large stone paving (standard dimensions: L/W: 12–22 cm, H: 16 cm) granite, red-brown, dark, medium grain, approx. 50% of total amount;
granite, red-brown, dark, fine grain, approx. 30% of total amount; granite, red-brown, light, medium grain, approx. 20% of total amount underside and lateral surfaces beveled on all sides, sawn and flashed surface
3 Natural stone paving (d = 16 cm)
4 2/5 chipping bedding
5 Asphalt base course, WPA 0/22 (E_{v2} min. 180 MN/m²)
6 0/56 frost protection course (E_{v2} min. 120 MN/m²)
7 Leveled ground (E_{v2} min. 45 MN/m²)
8 Soil exchange with 0/56 frost protection course
9 Existing soil
10 "Kirche" eaves slab (standard dimensions: L: 60–190 cm, W: 80 cm, H: 12 cm) quartzite, red-brown, medium grain, underside and lateral surfaces beveled on all sides, surface sawn and flashed
11 "Kirchhof" paving (standard dimensions: L/W: 8–16 cm, H: 12 cm) granite, anthracite, medium grain, approx. 50% of total amount;

granite, red-brown, dark, medium-grain, approx. 30% of whole amount, basalt, black-anthracite, medium grain, approx. 20% of total amount, underside and lateral surfaces beveled on all sides, natural-cleft surface
12 Natural stone paving (d = 12 cm)
13 2/5 chipping bedding
14 WPA 0/22 asphalt base course (E_{v2} min. 180 MN/m²)
15 0/56 frost protection course (E_{v2} min. 120 MN/m²)
16 Leveled ground (E_{v2} min. 45 MN/m²)
17 Soil exchange with 0/56 frost protection course
18 Existing soil
19 "Hinter der Kirche" tiled strip (standard dimensions: L: 100 cm, W: 90 cm, H: 12 cm) basanite, black-gray, medium grain lateral surfaces sawn on all sides, underside beveled, surface sawn and coarse-spalted
20 "Kirchof" paving made from available cleared stone, granite, basalt, diabase (re-installed in "Hinter der Kirche" square)
21 Natural stone paving (d = 12–18 cm)
22 2/5 chipping bedding
23 Ballast base course 0/32 (E_{v2} min 150 MN/m²)
24 Frost protection course 0/56 (E_{v2} min. 120 MN/m²)
25 Leveled ground (E_{v2} min. 45 MN/m²)
26 Soil exchange with frost protection course 0/56
27 In-situ soil

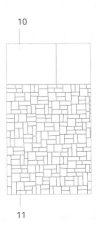
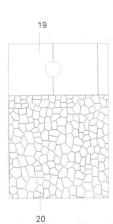
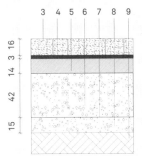
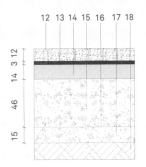
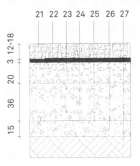

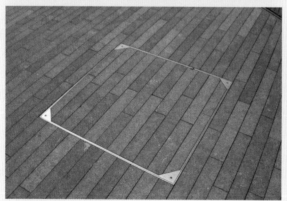

THE SCOOP, LONDON, UNITED KINGDOM

Architect & Master planner: Foster and Partners
Landscape Architect: Townshend Landscape Architects
Lighting Designer: Equation Lighting
Engineer: Ove Arup and Partners
Completion: 2007

A carpet of natural stone paving forms a uniform surface as a platform for activities and events. The paving, produced in a special format, is consistently laid in the same direction. Different surface patterns are used to mark areas of special interest.

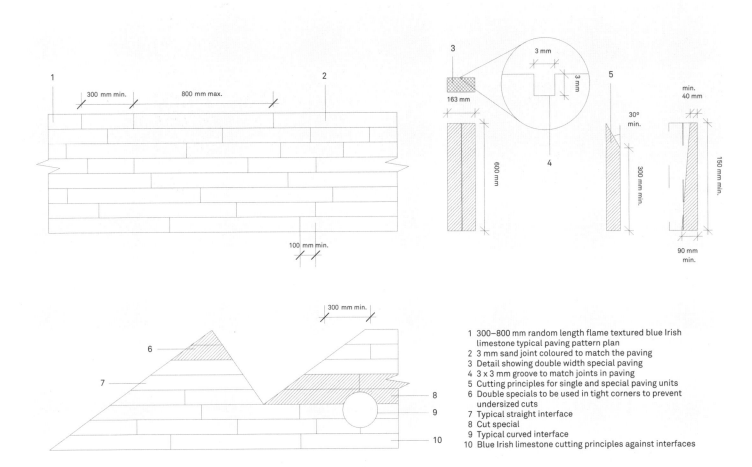

1 300–800 mm random length flame textured blue Irish limestone typical paving pattern plan
2 3 mm sand joint coloured to match the paving
3 Detail showing double width special paving
4 3 x 3 mm groove to match joints in paving
5 Cutting principles for single and special paving units
6 Double specials to be used in tight corners to prevent undersized cuts
7 Typical straight interface
8 Cut special
9 Typical curved interface
10 Blue Irish limestone cutting principles against interfaces

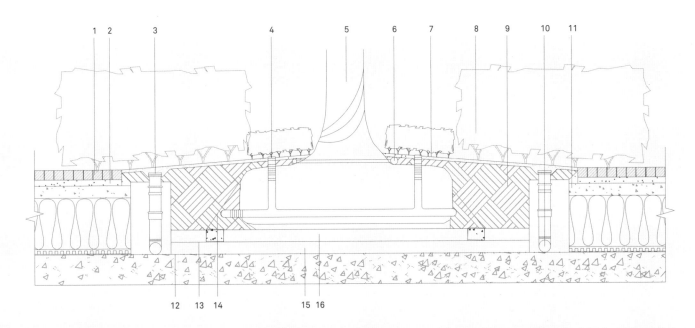

1 80 x 80 mm x random length flame textured blue limestone paving
2 50 mm class 1 semidry mortar bed
3 Dip pipe with cap
4 Aeration and watering pipe with cap
5 Tree
6 Irrigation necklace
7 25 mm blue Irish limestone chippings
8 Shrub planting
9 500 mm max., 450 mm min. topsoil
10 Land drainage
11 Concrete haunching
12 Waterproof membrane
13 Root barrier
14 Underground guying
15 100 mm layer of 10 mm river washed, rounded gravel
16 100 mm medium grade (55% minimum–60%) washed

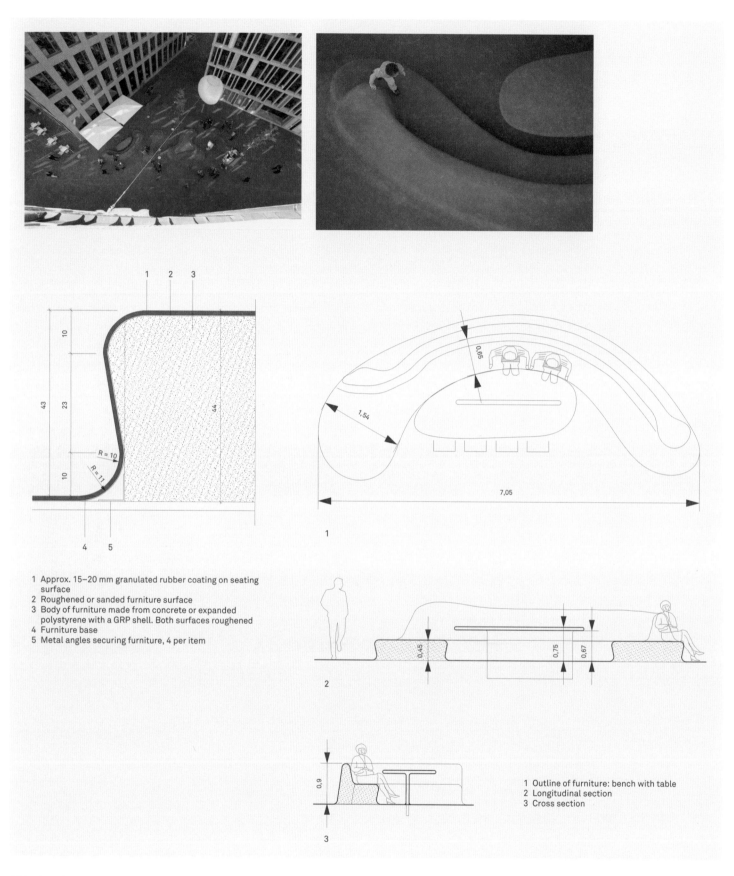

1 Approx. 15–20 mm granulated rubber coating on seating
 surface
2 Roughened or sanded furniture surface
3 Body of furniture made from concrete or expanded
 polystyrene with a GRP shell. Both surfaces roughened
4 Furniture base
5 Metal angles securing furniture, 4 per item

1 Outline of furniture: bench with table
2 Longitudinal section
3 Cross section

CITYLOUNGE ST. GALLEN, SWITZERLAND

Collaboration between Pipilotti Rist and Carlos
Martinez (Architect)
Completion: 2005

The idea of a lounge open to the public, a "town living room" provided the main theme,
which was realized using a uniform granulated rubber coating on a water-permeable
asphalt base course. The colored poured coating lies over all the furniture and other
structures "like a sheet". The coating can be driven on, is resistant to frost and deic-
ing salt, and can be machine-cleaned.

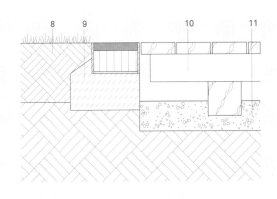

in concrete tile/grating area, can be driven on

in vegetation area, cannot be driven on

1 2,5 cm red tartan EPDM on 7.5 cm bitumen base course
2 Steel strip
3 Grating filled with sand filter and soil
4 0/22 verge ballast
5 Base course
6 Approx. 100 x 100 x 12 cm concrete tile
7 Point foundation
8 Topsoil
9 Continuous back support
10 Wood terrace
11 Rolled gravel

BEATLINE—GARDEN OF THE BARCODE HOUSE, MUNICH

Landscape architects: Keller Landschaftsarchitekten
Architects: MVRDV and Stadler Onischke
Completion: 2005

The Beat Line – a line, presented in material terms through a steel setting with a red plastic filling – lends rhythm to the outdoor area and creates a connection between the various spaces.

Application of last layer

Casting of the "course"

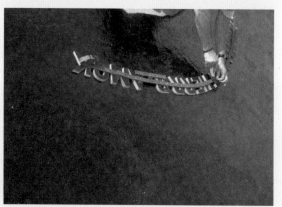

Stamping of the titles using wooden stencils

60 tons of pouring asphalt were prepared for this floor relief in memory of the work of Rainer Werner Fassbinder. It was the installed over an area of 400 m² in five layers, one on top of the other. The "ebb and flow" of the asphalt lake finishes flush with the adjacent light beige asphalt areas. Wooden stencils were used to stamp the titles of films and stage and radio plays by Fassbinder into the asphalt before it hardened off.

ASPHALT LAKE, RAINER WERNER FASSBINDER PLATZ,
MUNICH, GERMANY

Artist: Wilhelm Koch, Amberg
Technical planning: realgrün landschaftsarchitekten,
Munich
Completion: 2007

3.3 STEPS

OUTDOOR STEPS
- Rise ration and dimensions
- Handrails
- Anti-slip precautions and protection against standing water

CONSTRUCTION METHODS
- Staircase forms
- Loadbearing structures
- Foundations
- Step types
- Transverse slopes and inclined steps

RAMPS

SPECIMEN PROJECTS

Astrid Zimmermann

3.3 STEPS

OUTDOOR STEPS

Steps are a special element within a path. They make it easier to walk at places where a marked longitudinal incline would make a climb too difficult, and they create a pedestrian connection between areas of significantly different height. They structure the run of a pathway or a terrain, forming an important creative resource for contouring relief and for bordering or accentuating areas.

Rise ratio and dimensions

Paths are replaced by steps from a rise of about 18% or 10°. As it becomes difficult to walk along paths easily from a rise of even 12%, one alternative form is stepped paths, which are characterized by a continuous alternation of one step and one platform. > Figs. 3.3.1 and 3.3.4

As outdoor steps are usually constructed with an incline, a distinction has to be made between their height and their incline (height plus incline). The rise is the same as the height only when steps are built without an incline (e.g. inside buildings, or when the steps are constructed from gridded material and so no incline is needed). The rise ratio of a step is derived from the rise (r) and the tread (t), and is expressed as r/t (e.g. 15/33). The actual structural dimensions of a step can deviate from the rise ratio; for example, it is derived from the height (h) and the step width (w) for a solid rectangular step. > Fig. 3.3.2

A sequence of three or more steps is called a flight of steps. Two flights of steps are connected by a landing. > Fig. 3.3.3

The size of the step is derived from the human stride, and varies in relation to the rise. The dimensions of steps can be experienced very differently according to an individual's stride and depending on whether that person is going up or down the stairs. As early as 1683 the architect François Blondel suggested a stride rule for calculating the rise of a step; it is still used today and forms the basis for several standards. For example, DIN 18065 establishes the following formula: $2r + t = 59–65$ cm. Standard dimensions for steps in buildings, for example 17/29 (given an average stride length of 63 cm), which is seen as ideal for steps in houses, would be very

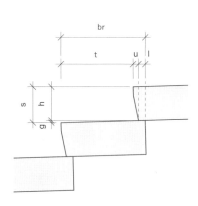

h = step height
g = step incline
s = rise
br = step run
t – tread
u = nosing
l = support

Fig. 3.3.2: Steps: terms

Fig. 3.3.1: Stepped path to the Campidoglio in Rome

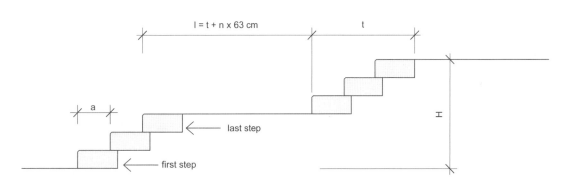

t = tread
f = flight of steps
l = length of landing
n = number of steps
h = step height

Fig. 3.3.3: Flight of steps: terms

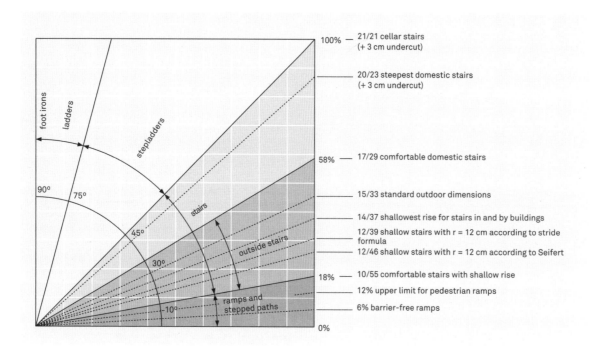

Fig. 3.3.4: Rises for stairs, ramps and ladders

	according to stride formula for stairs in buildings		according to Alwin Seifert for s < 17	
s	tread t $t = 63 - 2r$	stride length $2h + r$	tread t $r = 94 - 4s$	stride length $2h + r$
9	45	63	58	76
10	43	63	54	74
11	41	63	50	72
12	39	63	46	70
13	37	63	42	68
14	35	63	38	66
15	33	63	34	64
16	31	63	30	62

Tab. 3.3.1: Comparison of outdoor stair calculations with r < 17 according to stride formula (stride length = 63 cm) and according to Seifert (variable stride length)

steep and uncomfortable to climb in the open air. Shallower rises are more appropriate here. > Fig. 3.3.4 But the lower the rise, the greater the length of stride, so that the above-mentioned formula no longer produces satisfactory results for small rises, as studies by Mielke, Seifert or Mader have shown. Alwin Seifert arrived at step dimensions for "relaxed walking" with considerably longer stride length (Niesel 2003, p. 291). These values can be consulted when designing stairs with a rise of less than 17 cm. > Tab. 3.3.1 Stairs at the entrance to buildings should not rise less than 14 cm, however (rises under 14 cm are not permissible under DIN 18065-1 in and by buildings).

Landings are placed between the flights of steps for structuring, changes of direction, or to make walking easier. A landing should be provided after 18 steps at the latest (cf. DIN 18065). The length of the landing is derived from the tread and the multiple of the of the assumed stride length of 63 cm (l = r + n . 63 cm). > Fig. 3.3.3

Handrails

A handrail must be provided for flights with more than 3 steps. If steps are more than 3 m wide, additional handrails are required in public places. If there is a risk of falling sideways, the handrails must be appropriately braced. > Chapter 3.5 Railings and fences If there is no risk of falling, handrails can also be placed centrally if the steps are wide enough.

Anti-slip precautions and protection against standing water

Specific demands are made on outdoor stairs because of the effects of the weather. To increase safety, appropriate covering materials should be selected to prevent slipperiness. Measure should also be taken to drain off precipitation water, which is achieved primarily by inclining the step towards the front edge. The incline should be 1–3%, but at least 0.5 cm per step. This not only prevents water from standing or ice from accumulating on the step, but also stops water penetrating the foundations, thus restricting damage from freezing water.

In order to capture water running off higher areas, and in the case of longer stair structures, drainage gutters should be placed before the top step, and below each individual step in the case of stepped paths. > Chapter 3.11 Flights of steps that are constantly in the shade should be checked particularly carefully in terms of the material used because of the poor drying that can be expected. This applies in particular to steps in wood, metal and stone with polished surfaces, which should be used only in conjunction with antislip surface treatment. Exceptions here are roofed stairs or climatic conditions that admit different construction methods.

CONSTRUCTION METHODS

Staircase forms

Straight steps with one or more flights are not the only staircase form. Changes in direction in the flights produce a number of forms for staircases. Such changes are produced by a landing (angled stairs) or by arranging the steps in a spiral. > Fig. 3.3.5

Steps can also be distinguished by their position in the run of walls or on the terrain, and there are also steps with and without protected sides. > Figs. 3.3.6–3.3.9 Steps without side sections on an embankment are well suited to step shapes that clearly tie into the ground at the sides (e.g. solid rectangular steps).

Loadbearing structures

Steps in the open air are often constructed directly on the subsoil. The load is then transferred either over the whole area via stepped concrete slab foundations

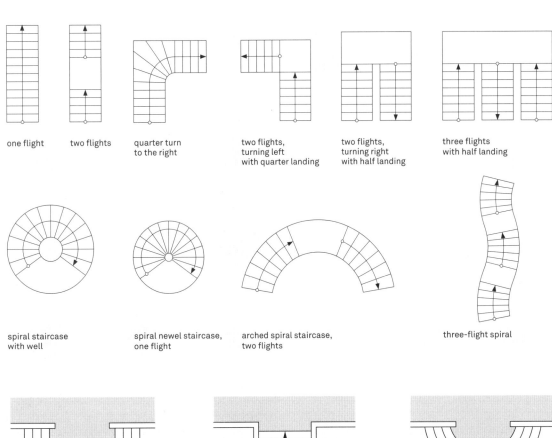

one flight   two flights   quarter turn to the right   two flights, turning left with quarter landing   two flights, turning right with half landing   three flights with half landing

spiral staircase with well   spiral newel staircase, one flight   arched spiral staircase, two flights   three-flight spiral

Fig. 3.3.5: Steps with straight and spiral flights

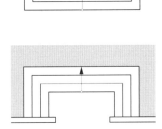
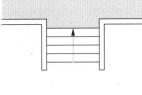
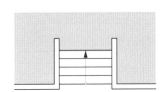
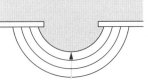

Fig. 3.3.6: Steps placed in front of a structure, and recessed steps

a | b
  | c

Fig. 3.3.7:
a) Step on embankment
b) Step in the embankment
c) Self-supporting steps

inclined side

stepped side

landing side

Fig. 3.3.8: Run of stringers

a
b

Fig. 3.3.9: Sides made of
a) concrete,
b) natural stone masonry

Fig. 3.3.10: Schematic diagram
of possible loadbearing systems

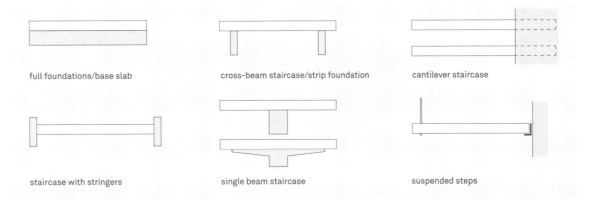

full foundations/base slab

cross-beam staircase/strip foundation

cantilever staircase

staircase with stringers

single beam staircase

suspended steps

a | b

Fig. 3.3.11: Cross-beam
staircases:
a) grid step on step-welded steel
   I-girders
b) step support placed on top

a | b
  | c

Fig. 3.3.12: Stringer staircases:
a) solid rectangular steps in natural stone, attached to the wall
   at the side
b) steel side section, with steps welded on at the side
c) inserted steps in a wooden staircase, the first step in natural
   stone protects against moisture on the floor

Fig. 3.3.13: Spiral staircase with stringers on the Killesberg viewing tower, Stuttgart: steps supported on braced net cables on one side, outer side section constructed as a steel tube works against torsion forces generated, inner side section in flat steel

Fig. 3.3.14: Cantilever steps in natural stone

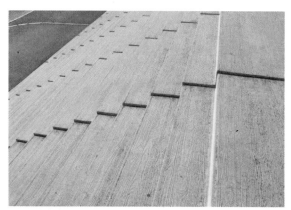

$$\frac{a}{b}$$

Fig. 3.3.15: Monolithic base slab and steps for concrete staircases: staircase segments, surface in timber formwork
a) several monolithic stair segments arranged next to each other, surface in timber shuttering;
b) with smooth shuttered surface.

Fig. 3.3.16: Monolithic steps hewn into the rock

or—in the case of narrow or short flight of steps—via full foundations. Solid rectangular steps can also be placed on strip foundations, where the load from individual steps is transferred via point supports—similarly to cross-beam steps. > Fig. 3.3.10

In self-supporting staircases, the steps are placed on a reinforced concrete base slab over their full area, or on point supports on one, two or more cross beams. Base slabs and cross beams with an appropriately stepped surface can be prefabricated in reinforced concrete. If timber or steel structures are being used, the necessary support for the steps is created by placing brackets on the cross beams or by creating stepped cross beams. > Figs. 3.3.10, 3.3.11 and 3.3.22 Alternatively the steps can also be fixed between the two supports at the sides of the stairs. > Figs. 3.3.10 and 3.3.12 Cross beams and stringers are commonly manufactured in steel. Timber structures are found less often in the open air because they do not stand up to weathering as well, and are most commonly used in sheltered areas, such as attics inside buildings. > Fig. 3.3.13
Almost all steel section types are used for side-section and cross-beam structures. They are made of flat steel (minimum thickness 10 mm), as hollow or U-sections, or for cross beams also as I-sections. > Fig. 3.3.13
For a cantilever staircase, the steps are fixed into the wall on one side only or—according to the material—screwed or welded into a wall or a side section, or fastening with dowel pins. When steps are tied into a wall, the load-bearing capacity is provided by adequate thickness in the steps and the depth to which they are tied in. Hard stone (granite, for example) can project up to 1.50 m. > Fig. 3.3.14 For a spiral staircase, the cantilever steps are carried by a central newel. The steps are connected either to the central newel or via a cylindrical mating part on the steps. Suspended steps hang on cables or rods from the ceiling or a supporting member on one side. On the other side they are anchored by a bracket to a wall or a side section of the staircase. > Fig. 3.3.10

In monolithic stairs, the steps and loadbearing structure are manufactured in a single piece. > Figs. 3.3.15 and 3.3.16

Foundations

Foundations for steps should be frost-protected, and in exceptional cases frost-resistant as well, on a horizontal foundation base on loadbearing subsoil (settled ground or compacted subsoil). The foundation type is chosen in relation to the location and the anticipated loading. Frost-protected, rigid foundations in concrete should always be provided if large loads are anticipated, a staircase is being built on a public site, or long flights of steps are planned. > Chapter 2.2, foundation base slabs or strip foundations are usually deployed for large staircases, to minimize excavation work and material costs for the foundations. Foundations are protected against frost by concrete strip foundations under the first and last steps in the case of foundation base slabs.

For self-supporting structures, the base slabs, cross beams or stringers are supported on point or strip foundations at the first step. The top of the staircase is often supported on a wall at the last step, or attached to a bracket fastened to the building. If such an approach is impossible, such as in long staircases, intermediate supports must be used. In timber staircases, the first step can be in stone, as structural protection for the timber. > Fig. 3.3.17
For full foundations, stepping the foundation base can reduce material costs, but here it is not possible to exclude different settlement rates, which may produce cracks in the foundations. Stepping should thus be used only on solid ground, and loose ground must not be allowed to slip off. > Fig. 3.3.18

Because construction loads may be distributed unevenly, staircase stringers and the steps themselves should generally be constructed separately. > Fig. 3.3.19
Nonrigid construction methods are particularly suitable for single steps and for small staircases with solid rectangular steps not intended for intensive use. If the footing is not frost-protected, the nonrigid foundation (e.g. gravel sand 0/32) must have frost-protected foundations. > Fig. 3.3.20
On settled, permeable ground, it is possible to provide foundations for the steps on reduced-depth concrete foundation only if there are few steps and low load intensity. Full foundations or strip foundations are then placed on a frost protection layer 15–20 cm thick. Alternatively, the first step alone can be supported on a frost-protected strip foundation. > Fig. 3.3.21

Wooden steps must be supported either on a stone base or a steel foot. Again, both variants must have stable, frost-protected foundations. > Fig. 3.3.22, and chapter 2.3 Connections

Step types

Various types of steps are used, depending on the load-bearing structure and the material. Almost every type of step can be executed in stone. Wood and steel are used mainly for slab steps and for variations on them. > Fig. 3.3.23 For solid rectangular steps it makes sense to use a nosing or undercut. The setback line at the front of the step forms a dummy joint, making the step look lighter, and easier to walk on. > Fig. 3.3.24

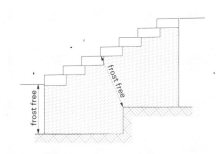

Fig. 3.3.18: Stepped foundations (only on settled ground!)

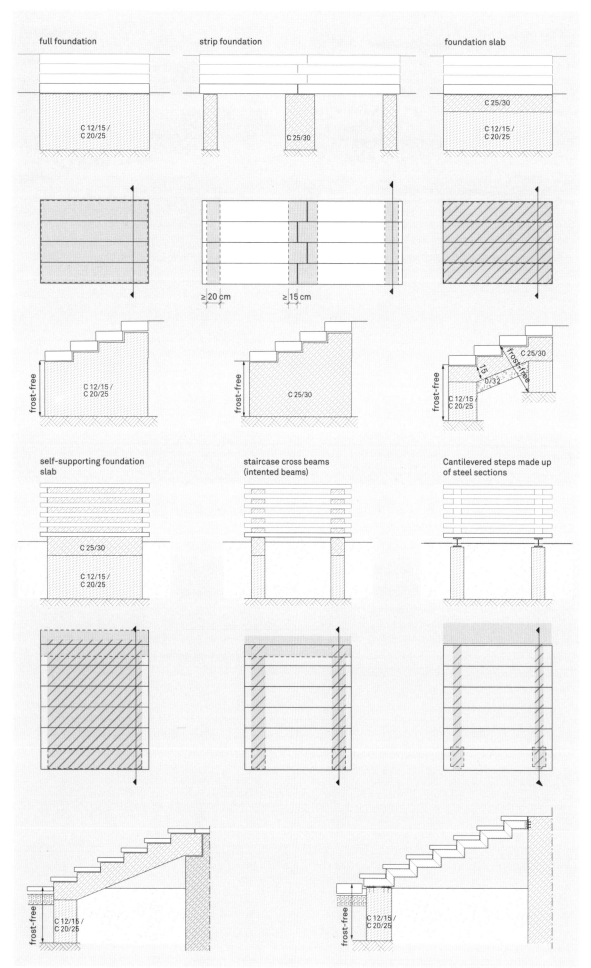

full foundation

strip foundation

foundation slab

C 25/30

C 12/15 /
C 20/25

C 25/30

C 12/15 /
C 20/25

≥ 20 cm   ≥ 15 cm

frost-free

C 12/15 /
C 20/25

frost-free

C 25/30

frost-free

C 25/30

15   0/32

frost-free

C 12/15 /
C 20/25

self-supporting foundation
slab

staircase cross beams
(intented beams)

Cantilevered steps made up
of steel sections

C 25/30

C 12/15 /
C 20/25

frost-free

C 12/15 /
C 20/25

frost-free

C 12/15 /
C 20/25

Fig. 3.3.17: Possible staircase
foundations

Fig. 3.3.22: Wooden staircase: cross beams and upright members supported on sandstone plinths

Fig. 3.3.24: Solid steps with slab and rebate

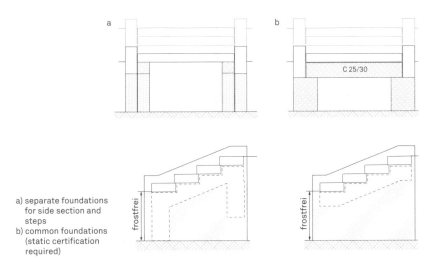

a) separate foundations for side section and steps
b) common foundations (static certification required)

Fig. 3.3.19: Staircase stringers

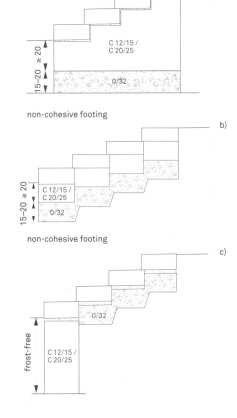

a) non-cohesive footing

b) non-cohesive footing

c)

Fig. 3.3.21: Foundations using less material

footing frost-protected!

footing not frost-protected!

Fig. 3.3.20: Non-rigid foundations for solid rectangular steps

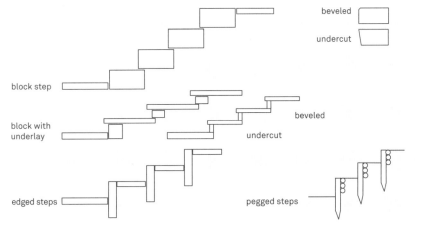

block step

block with underlay

edged steps

beveled

undercut

beveled

undercut

pegged steps

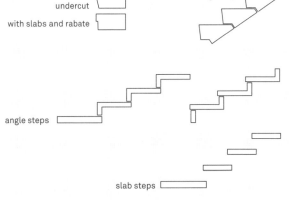

with slabs and undercut

with slabs and rabate

wedge steps

angle steps

slab steps

Fig. 3.3.23: Step types

Steps in concrete and natural stone

Because they are comparatively weather-resistant, stone steps are particularly suitable for outdoor staircases, which are often set on open ground.

They are usually placed on the support structure on a 2–3 cm thick compensation layer of mortar (e.g. M 20). If cast in-situ concrete is used, the steps can also be laid directly on the wet concrete. For single cross-beam constructions the steps have to be additionally secured, for example with dowel or a connecting reinforcement. > Chapter 2.3 Connections

Small stone formats and "bricked in" (e.g. clinker steps). Slabs and angle steps can also be glued. To create corners, stone steps should not be mitered, and acute angle should be avoided at all costs. > Fig. 3.3.25

Solid rectangular steps are characteristically highly stable even on nonrigid foundations. These steps cut in one solid block of natural or cast stone can be supplied in widths of up to 2 m in natural stone or 4 m in cast stone. Course joints are executed dry. The first step can be placed on the adjacent path covering or 3–5 cm under the top edge of the path covering. The latter approach is to be preferred, as this means a clean conclusion (especially if the path covering settles at a later stage), and at the same time provides an abutment against step slippage. This will mean different dimensions for this step, which should be taken into account. > Fig. 3.3.26 The same applies to the understep in slab steps.

Wedge-shaped steps, like solid rectangular steps, are solid elements, but they have a beveled underside and thus need a correspondingly oblique support structure.

Slab steps in natural or cast stone must always have a rigid support structure. If constructed using the open method (self-supporting structure on loadbearing cross beams), an understep of ≥ 3 cm should be built in for safety reasons, and if the stairs are set on a base slab, this is to be recommended for visual reasons. > Fig. 3.3.27 Slab steps can also be fixed to masonry by their sides, then at least a quarter, or preferably a third of their length must be tied into the wall. > Fig. 3.3.12a

Adding an understep to the tread creates a step with underlay. The slab thickness is about 5–9 cm for cast stone, and natural stone slabs are available in lesser thicknesses according to the stone type. The understep can also be broader. On nonrigid foundations in particular, the width must be ≥ 1/3 of the tread width. A rigid construction method should always be preferred for public spaces and greater numbers of steps. > Fig. 3.3.28 The tread slab should be laid dry on the understep if at all possible. If using relatively small or light naturally split materials, a compensation layer of 8–10 mm of mortar makes it possible to support the slab on the understep securely.

Angle steps are supplied in cast stone. They are laid on concrete foundations or a base slab with an appropriately stepped surface. Special dimensions are offered for constructing (seating) stands. > Fig. 3.3.23

Clinker or brick steps are constructed as masonry. Constructing the front of the tread as an edge course will help it to last longer. > Figs. 3.3.29 and 3.3.30 Small, slab-like natural stones can also be used to create steps in this way.

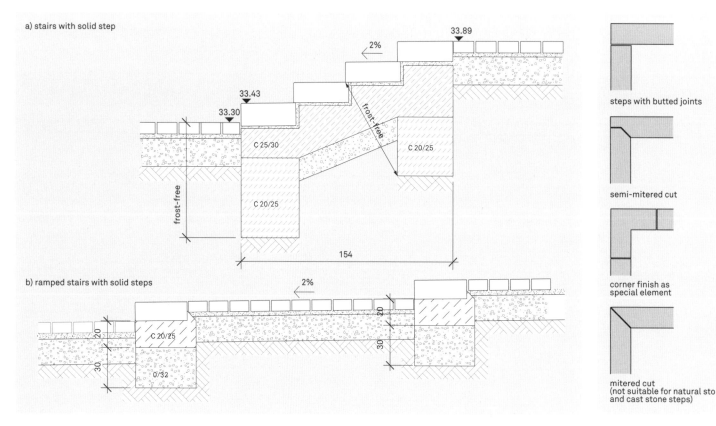

a) stairs with solid step

33.89

2%

33.43

33.30

frost-free

frost-free

C 25/30

C 20/25

C 20/25

154

b) ramped stairs with solid steps

2%

20

C 20/25

30

20

30

0/32

Fig. 3.3.26

steps with butted joints

semi-mitered cut

corner finish as special element

mitered cut
(not suitable for natural sto and cast stone steps)

Fig. 3.3.25: Corner formation

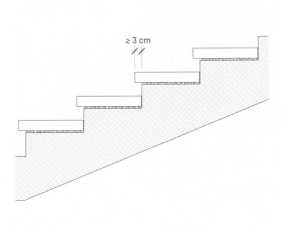

1 tread slab
2 underlay stone
3 mortar
4 frost protection layer 0/45

Fig. 3.3.27: Slab step set on base slab/cross beam

Fig. 3.3.28: Step with understep

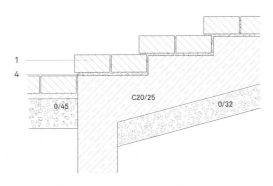

1 clinker/brick laid as edge course (edgewise)
2 clinker/brick laid flat as header course
3 clinker/brick laid flat, stretcher in front of header course
4 mortar bed
5 mortar and broken stone filler
6 underlay stone as special format

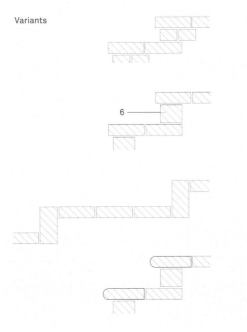

Fig. 3.3.29: Masonry steps

Variants

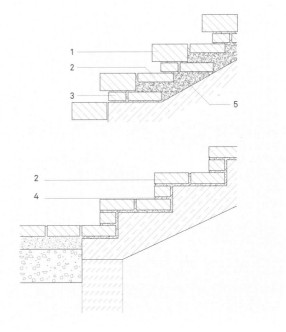

Fig. 3.3.30: Construction methods for masonry clinker steps

 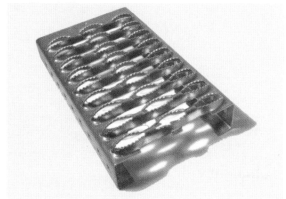

a | b

Fig. 3.3.31:
a) Grooved sheet metal as step covering
b) Safety grid with surface markings

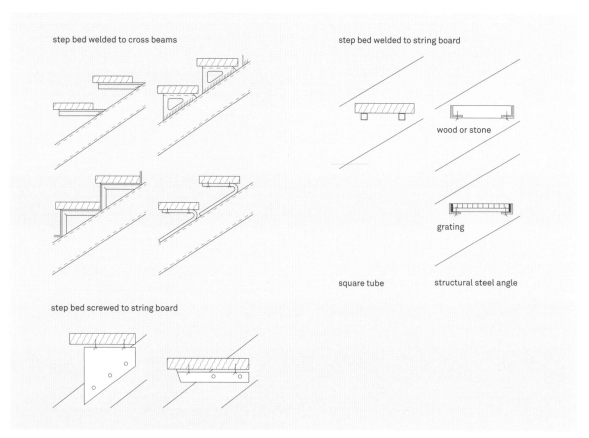

step bed welded to cross beams

step bed welded to string board

wood or stone

grating

square tube   structural steel angle

step bed screwed to string board

Fig. 3.3.32: Steel and timber steps on steel support structure

Fig. 3.3.33: Canted sheet metal (8 mm) in weatherproof steel welded to
flat steel supports as a supporting structure, handrail in stainless steel

Metal steps

Steps in steel or other metals are usually installed as slab-shaped grids or as canted sheet metal. To guarantee a nonslip surface, sheet metal with grooves or other markings, safety grids with markings or special antislip extruded grids, and if necessary safety edges are used. > Fig. 3.3.31

As a rule, the steps are manufactured on a support structure in the same material and welded or screwed to the loadbearing spar or a stringer. > Fig. 3.3.32 It is also possible to make entire flights of steps from a canted metal sheet. > Fig. 3.3.33

Fig. 3.3.34: First step made of two wooden planks

Fig. 3.3.36: Staircase in timber units

Wooden steps

Wooden steps are generally used as a kind of slab step. Here the tread of a step can consist of a board or a plank, or of several pieces of wood arranged together. > Fig. 3.3.34 The slab-like steps are pushed into the side stringers, or can be screwed on to steel or concrete support structures. If the support structure is in the form of cross beams, the steps are screwed on or attached with wooden dowelling (if the cross beams are made of wood). > Fig. 3.3.35 Slab steps ≥ 50 mm thick should be chosen.

Solid timber steps are used as wedge steps, set on a cross beam with an appropriate diagonal. Timber planks are used as solid steps in gardens or on side paths. They are laid on nonrigid foundations. They last for a limited amount of time because of the contact with the ground. > Fig. 3.3.36

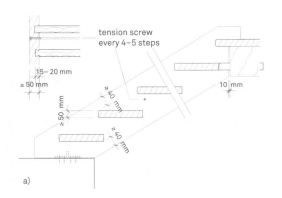

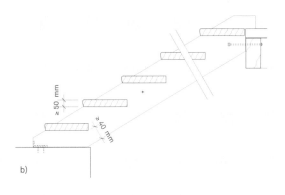

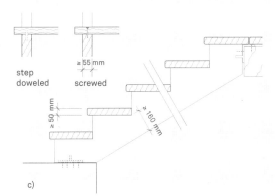

a) semi-mortised stairs
b) inserted stairs
c) bracket stairs

Fig. 3.3.35: Timber structures

a | b

Fig. 3.3.37: Edged steps: a) natural stone edge with graveled pavement tread; b) edge made of railway lines

Edged steps

The advantage offered by a flight of edged step is that it is possible to create a water-permeable layer behind the edge. It is common to find different materials used for the edge (e.g. edging stone or metal edge) and the tread area (e.g. paved area or water-bound path covering). > Fig. 3.3.37 The edge is—similarly to an edging or curb stone—set on a concrete strip foundation with a rear support. When the tread area is narrow, the strip foundation makes the seepage space between the steps very constricted, which is why edged are usually reserved for use where large treads are possible. Alternatively, a drainage tube set vertically in the foundations can guarantee that the tread area will be kept free of standing water. > Fig. 3.3.38

There can be a variation on edged steps in the form of pegs rammed into the ground (approx. 50 cm long and 6–12 cm in diameter) support horizontally placed round timbers or a wooden board, thus forming the edge, which is back-filled with loose material. This is a simply and reasonably priced construction method, though it is suitable only for temporary use or for less busy areas. > Fig. 3.3.23

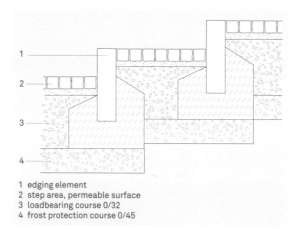

1 edging element
2 step area, permeable surface
3 loadbearing course 0/32
4 frost protection course 0/45

Fig. 3.3.38: Edged step construction methods

Fig. 3.3.39: Inclined steps at the top of the stairs

Fig. 3.3.40: Side with transverse slope at the foot of the stairs

Fig. 3.3.41: Stairs constructed in front of another structure and leaning forward

Transverse slopes and inclined steps

Steps should always be horizontal, as a transverse slope makes it difficult to walk securely. It is better to use inclined steps than to allow the steps to slope transversely if differences in level are needed. The best place to compensate for a transverse slope is at the foot of the stairs, especially if the slope on the pathway serving the steps is steady. > Figs. 3.3.39 and 3.3.40

But it is not possible to avoid a transverse slope if constructing steps in front of another structure. The transverse slope should then be placed on the less frequented sides of the staircase. > Fig. 3.3.41

RAMPS

If it is impossible to construct stairs because of use or for formal reasons, a difference in height has to be tackled with a ramp. Barrier-free access is usually required for public green spaces and for public buildings. It is in fact tolerable for a pathway to rise by 10–15%, but for people with walking difficulties, a slope of over 8% is stressful. Hence it is recommended that the requirements for "barrier-free construction" are also met for buildings that are not public. In Germany, DIN 18024 requires a maximum rise of 6% for barrier-free ramp structures. These must be broken by a landing after a maximum of 6 m. In Austria, however, landings are required every 10 m. Given that the regulations differ, the appropriate local rules should be taken into account in every case.

Ramps are to be provided with edge guards 10 cm high and handrails. > Figs. 3.3.42 and 3.3.43 They must be constructed without a transverse slope, as this would restrict wheelchair movement. Drainage must be via gutters running transversely to the direction of the path. Essentially, the rules for the construction of ramps are the same as for paths. When using paving, the last three or four rows of paving stones should be set in concrete in order to counteract any shear forces that may be generated.

Fig. 3.3.42: Opposed ramp with handrail and edge guards

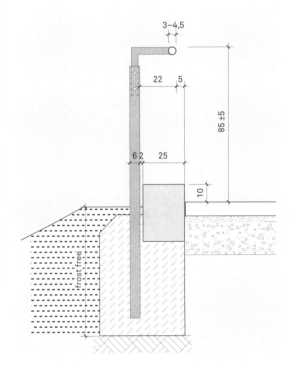

Fig. 3.3.43: Installation example of ramp stringer and handrail

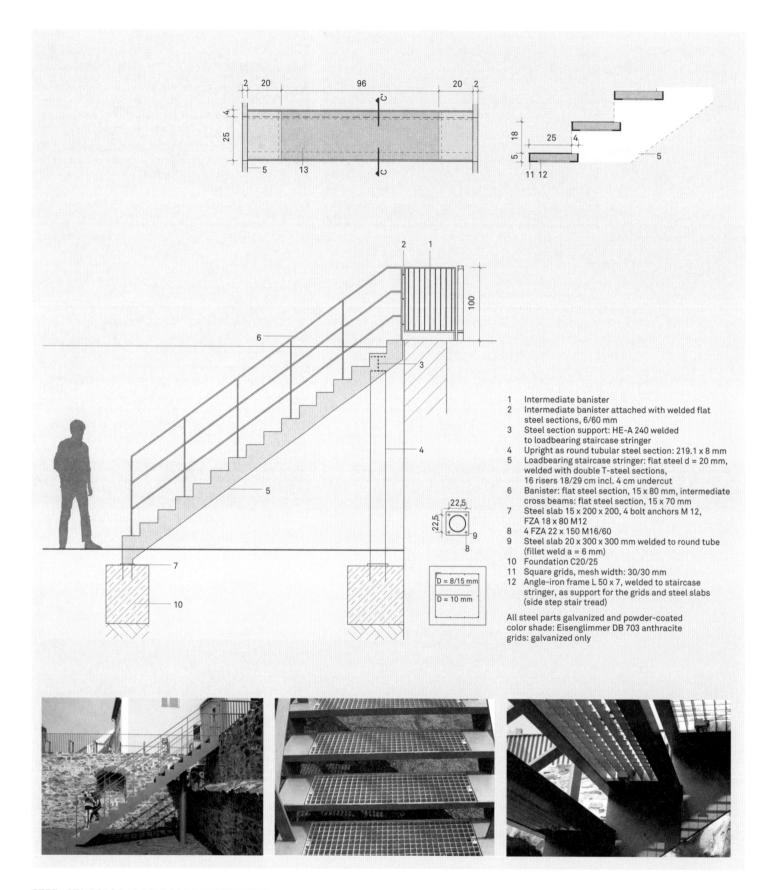

1   Intermediate banister
2   Intermediate banister attached with welded flat
    steel sections, 6/60 mm
3   Steel section support: HE-A 240 welded
    to loadbearing staircase stringer
4   Upright as round tubular steel section: 219.1 x 8 mm
5   Loadbearing staircase stringer: flat steel d = 20 mm,
    welded with double T-steel sections,
    16 risers 18/29 cm incl. 4 cm undercut
6   Banister: flat steel section, 15 x 80 mm, intermediate
    cross beams: flat steel section, 15 x 70 mm
7   Steel slab 15 x 200 x 200, 4 bolt anchors M 12,
    FZA 18 x 80 M12
8   4 FZA 22 x 150 M16/60
9   Steel slab 20 x 300 x 300 mm welded to round tube
    (fillet weld a = 6 mm)
10 Foundation C20/25
11 Square grids, mesh width: 30/30 mm
12 Angle-iron frame L 50 x 7, welded to staircase
    stringer, as support for the grids and steel slabs
    (side step stair tread)

All steel parts galvanized and powder-coated
color shade: Eisenglimmer DB 703 anthracite
grids: galvanized only

STEEL STAIRCASE AT SCHLOSS GROSSENHAIN
(SAXONY), GERMANY

Landscape architect:
Weidinger Landschaftsarchitekten, Berlin
Completion: 2002

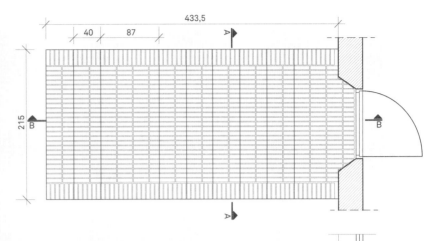

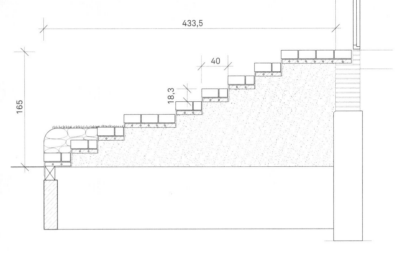

1 Bricks by Petersen Tegl: PM anthracite, 250 x 120 x 52 mm
2 Mortar
3 Coal-fired bricks by Petersen Tegl: D48 (water-struck hard-fired,
   dark color mix)/D38 (water-struck, old, alt rosé)/D32 (water-struck,
   yellow), Danish standard format (DNF): 228 x 108 x 54 mm
4 In-situ concrete, reinforced
5 Concrete rendering
6 Hollow blocks
7 Sand
8 In-situ concrete foundations
9 Cyclopean wall

CLINKER STAIRCASE, RESIDENTIAL BUILDING
IN CHARLOTTENLUND, DENMARK

Architect: Alexander Damsbo, Copenhagen
Completion: 2006

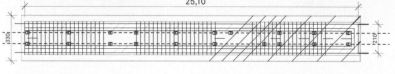

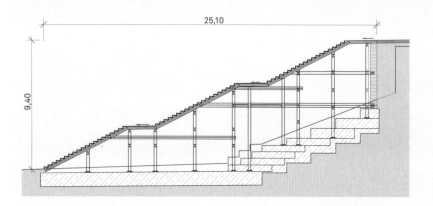

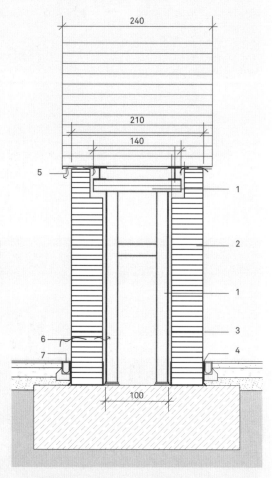

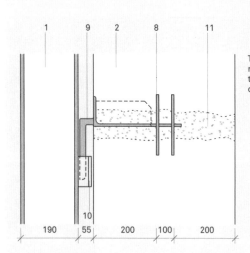

The moveable anchor laterally connecting the rammed clay walls with the steel construction permits vertical movement of the wall (settling).

1 Support structure in steel girders HEA200, galvanized
2 Rammed clay, wall thickness 50 cm
3 Cement horizon sealing
4 Bituminous wall sealing
5 Anti-insect grid
6 Ventilation pipe
7 Box gutter DN 100
8 Vertical wall anchorage
9 L-shaped steel anchorage 200 x 200 x 10 with L-shaped steel 200 x 20, cropped, l = 100, welded
10 Tuck-in flap in flat steel 35 x 10, welded with HEA 200
11 Mortar strip

Each flight of steps with 20 steps 15/31, sheet steel steps

LESSERSTIEGE IN NORDHAUSEN, GERMANY

Architects: Atelier Worschech, Erfurt
Clay construction: Jörg Zimmer, Wernigshausen
Completion: 2004

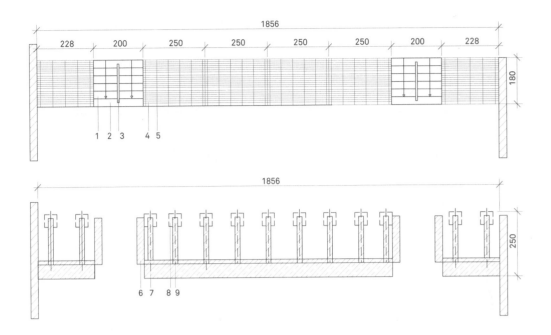

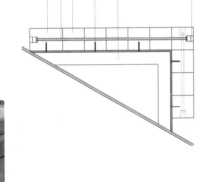

1 Concrete block steps 16/35 on 3 cm mortar bed, strip foundation, C20/25, 30 cm wide, 10 cm supporting bed 0/45
2 Concrete block step 16/30
3 Handrail
4 Squared timbers 80 x 120 or 80 x 80 mm
5 Threaded bars (axial spacing 50 cm) screwed on both sides
6 Strip foundation, C20/25
7 Support angle element, h = 105 cm, foot side length: 70 cm
8 25 cm point foundation C20/25, 50 x 50 x 85 cm
9 Steel girder IPE 200
10 Wood screw, nickel plated
11 T-steel 50 x 50 x 6 mm
12 Wooden plugs
13 Cast stone slab d = 8 cm, on 5 cm crushed sand chippings,
   27 cm macadam base
14 Slit gutter
15 Flat steel band framing (SB20)
16 Compound adhesive anchor M16
17 L-steel made up of two flat steel elements welded together,
   d = 15 mm
18 Base plate, d = 16 mm

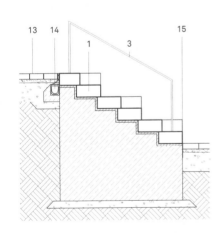

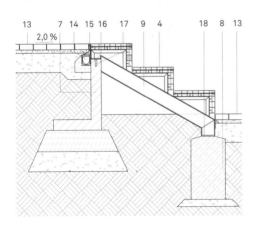

TWO TIMBER-COVERED STAIRCASES
AT MARKLEEBERGER SEE, GERMANY

Landscape architect: Till Rehwaldt, Dresden
Completion: 2006

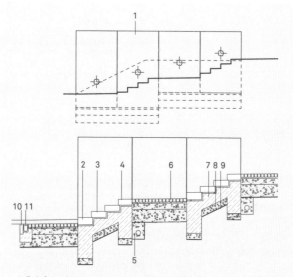

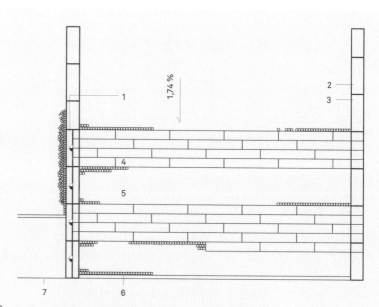

1 Reinforced concrete parts, h = 200 and 250 cm, each with one gap
   for built-in light, d = 18 cm, t = 15.5 cm, built-in light on building side
2 Solid rectangular step 211/38/18 cm natural stone on mortar bed 3 cm
3 Solid rectangular steps 211/38/14.5 cm natural stone
4 Solid rectangular step 211/34.75/14.5 cm natural stone
5 Gravel 8/16 with seepage run, full seepage pipe DN100
6 Small stone paving, in series, hard sandstone
7 Concrete C 25/30
8 Macadam base 0/45
9 Filter fleece
10 Curb below ground from existing structure
11 Drainage gutter NW100

1 Shear wall/prefabricated concrete element
2 Edging/concrete prefabricated part, l = 138.5 cm
3 Handrail north/galvanized steel, micaceous paint
4 Solid rectangular step/natural stone
5 Natural small stone paving, in series
6 Drainage gutter NW100
7 Inserted element

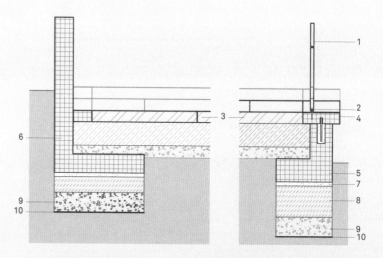

1 Handrail, steel galvanized, micaceous paint
2 Anchorage with socket cup screws, V2A injection resin dowel
3 Solid rectangular step, natural stone on prefabricated part and
   macadam base 0/45
4 North edging stone/ prefabricated concrete part with attached
   reinforcement
5 Retaining wall, l = 138.5 cm, height variable 45–115 cm with gap in the
   coping to anchor the connection reinforcement for the edging stone
6 Retaining wall/reinforced concrete part, l = 138.5 cm
7 5 cm mortar
8 Strip foundation C 12/15
9 Macadam base 0/45
10 Filter fleece

STAIRCASE, STRUDELBACHHALLE WEISSACH, GERMANY

Landscape architect: relais Landschaftsarchitekten,
Berlin
Architects: Peter W. Schmidt, Pforzheim/Berlin
Completion: 2005

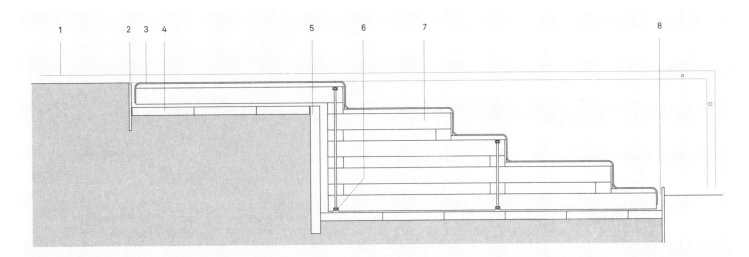

1 Asphalt
2 Steel edge 15 mm
3 Blue rubber covering (non-slip), attached to support structure
   with nails/staples
4 Concrete slabs, 40 x 40 x 5 cm, laid on incline
5 Concrete slabs 190 x 80 x 6 cm
6 Nut with washer, threaded pole
7 Support structure in waterproof glued hollow panels (boiler
   pressure impregnated pine), 28 mm and 10 mm, also concave
   and convex strip, step rise: 17 cm
8 Joint 30 mm
9 Retaining wall in concrete elements
10 Drain

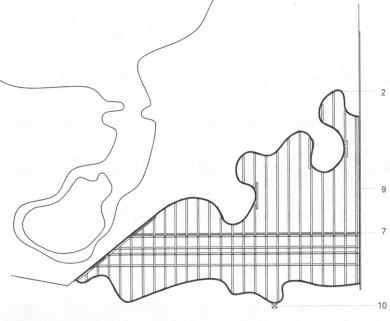

STAIRCASE WITH RUBBER COVERING, MUNICIPAL
GARDENS IN BRYGGEN, NØRRESUNDBY, DENMARK

Landscape architects:
SLA A/S, Copenhagen, Stig L. Andersson
Completion: 2005

3.4 RAILINGS AND FENCES

GENERAL REQUIREMENTS
· Minimum heights and dimensions
· Static requirements

CONSTRUCTION METHODS
· Choice of materials
· Wood-and-steel constructions
· Anchoring and foundation
· Handrails
· Gates

SPECIMEN PROJECTS

Astrid Zimmermann

3.4 RAILINGS AND FENCES

Railings in open spaces mainly serve to prevent falls where terrain height changes, or on stairs, bridges or walkway installations. Fences, on the other hand, are used to mark off a plot of ground, as visual or weather protection, or to catch balls. Most railing and fence constructions are post constructions. Secure post anchoring is therefore equally important in both cases. However, on the more specific level the different functional requirements lead to a certain amount of difference in the details. For instance, railings almost always have a handrail or some other usable element on top, e.g. a broad ledge for leaning on. Fences do not require this element. A fence may actually be required to have a top that prevents anyone climbing over.

GENERAL REQUIREMENTS

Minimum heights and dimensions

Minimum height and dimensional requirements have not been fixed internationally. When planning, the (national) building regulations and, in the case of special usages—e.g. in schools or workplaces—further regulations should therefore be referred to. The limits below should be taken as examples. They are based on what the regulations most commonly require.

Railings should generally be provided for any drop height greater than 1 m. (One exception to this is Bavaria, where the limit is 0.5 m.) If the drop is less than 12 m, the minimum height of the railing should be set at

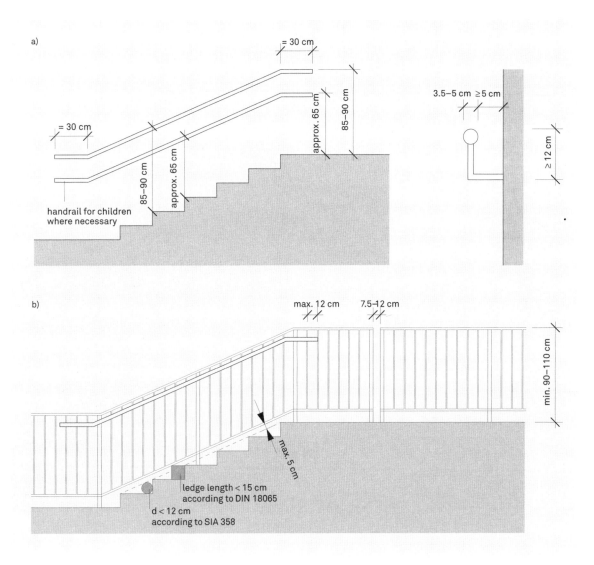

Fig. 3.4.1: Dimensional requirements:
a) handrails
b) railings

Fig. 3.4.2: Railings with angled handrail. Climbing over is additionally hindered by a grid on the lower part of the railings

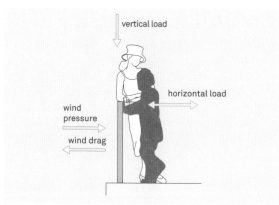

Fig. 3.4.4: Load on railings and fences

Fig. 3.4.3: Handrail for steps where no risk of falling exists

1 m. There are exceptions: for steps and in some countries, 0.90 m is allowed. For a drop of > 12 m, a railing of 1.10 m in height should be provided.

Guidelines for barrier-free construction require a handrail height of 85 cm (cf. DIN 18024) or 90 cm. For higher railings, the railings and the handrail should therefore be separated. > Fig. 3.4.1 Ideally, handrails should be round, with a diameter of 3.5–4.5 (5) cm (i.e. a circumference of 11–15 cm). This is particularly true of public stairways and ramp installations where a lack of barriers is required.

Further safety measures must be observed to protect children. The distance between longitudinal and diagonal struts should not be greater than 12 cm (in France and for play areas ≤ 11 cm). Where there is no risk of falling, larger spaces are permitted. These should however be wider than 23 cm to prevent limbs becoming trapped. Grids and mesh with a mesh size of ≤ 40 mm provide the best protection. Railings with horizontal struts can also be given an angled handrail to prevent people climbing over. > Fig. 3.4.2

Where no risk of falling exists, e.g. for steps on slopes, a simple handrail is sufficient. > Fig. 3.4.3

Static requirements

Various loads act on railings and fences, influencing the dimensions of individual components and the form of anchoring used. These are mainly horizontal loads—i.e. largely caused by persons leaning against or bumping into a railing or fence.

Wind loads play a role mainly in exposed sites and where wide-area railing or fence panels are used. Regional differences in wind load should be taken into account. Vertical loads must also be taken into account in the case of lateral railing anchoring or where the structure is secured from beneath. As well as dead load, these include loads imposed by people and possible hanging loads (loads caused by potential vegetation in planned greening, plant boxes). > Fig. 3.4.4 The fact that the greatest load is present in the lower part of a post is often reflected by a corresponding profile. > Fig. 3.4.5

The attacking loads, comparable to the leverage effect on a crowbar, must be intercepted by the post anchoring. Where railings are secured using screw anchors, both the load value of the screw anchors and the length of the counter-lever arm created by the size of the base plate and the screw anchorage point are important. If the post is anchored in a concrete foundation, the counter-lever arm is created by the embedment depth of the post in the foundation. Additionally, the foundation's strength affects loadbearing capacity. > Fig. 3.4.6

Fig. 3.4.5: Railing posts profiled in accordance with static loads. The lower part is thicker than the upper

For railings, load is normally set horizontally at handrail height at 100 kg per meter (1 kN/m). For private property, 0.5 kN/m is a sufficient assumed load. For construction assignments under normal requirements, these values can be used to measure the components and dimension the fastening devices. This should be agreed with the manufacturers or companies carrying out work. If a sophisticated assessment of the load estimates is needed, this must be undertaken by a structural engineer, who will also determine the type of anchoring used and component measurements.

Standard railings and fences (e.g. ball catch fences made from grille elements) are available from manufacturers in the appropriate material thicknesses. Additionally, manufacturers provide installation recommendations for anchoring or foundations.

CONSTRUCTION METHODS

Choice of materials

The main materials for fence and railing constructions are wood and steel. Steel permits filigree constructions. If properly protected from corrosion, it also has higher durability than wood. Steel is therefore of particular interest for use in loadbearing components. Steel fences and railings are usually assembled in sections in the factory —by welding, for instance—so that soldering onsite is minimized and the items can be assembled using screws or interlocking. > Fig. 3.4.7
With a timber fence, the laths present a relatively continuous exposed surface. The individual elements can easily be screwed or nailed together onsite. The top of the wooden elements should be made in accordance with constructive timber protection regulations. > Figs. 3.4.8 and 3.4.9, and chapter 1.4 Wood railing constructions are usually found as part of wooden bridges or walkways. > Fig. 3.4.10

Posts can also be made from masonry or concrete, often in combination with a masonry pedestal.
Other materials are possible. They must be specially tested for suitability if necessary (e.g. glass or plastic railing infills).

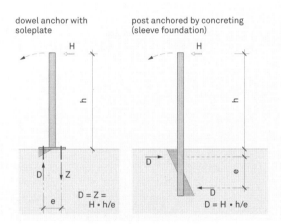

dowel anchor with soleplate

post anchored by concreting (sleeve foundation)

H = horizontal force
h = counter-lever arm for horizontal force
e = counter-lever arm for anchorage
D = compression force on anchorage (concrete load)
Z = tensile force on anchorage (dowel load))

$D = Z = H \cdot h/e$

$D = H \cdot h/e$

Fig. 3.4.6: Counter-lever arm depending on the securing method used

Fig. 3.4.7: Grille elements welded in the factory, screwed to clinker posts

Fig. 3.4.8: Lath fence: posts and laths with slanted surfaces

Fig. 3.4.9: Web members made from round timbers. The metal caps serve as protection from rainwater

Fig. 3.4.10: Wooden bridge with wooden railings

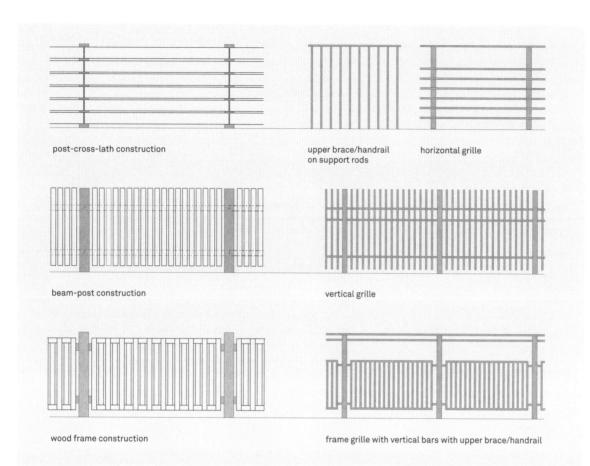

Fig. 3.4.11: Basic types of fence and railing construction (selection)

post-cross-lath construction

upper brace/handrail on support rods

horizontal grille

beam-post construction

vertical grille

wood frame construction

frame grille with vertical bars with upper brace/handrail

Fig. 3.4.12: Beam-post construction with construction timbers screwed to three crossbars

Fig. 3.4.13: Low enclosing fence with a single crossbar

Fig. 3.4.14: Post-frame construction topped by a handrail

Wood-and-steel constructions

The simplest construction method for railings and fences involves arranging horizontal filler elements between the posts. > Fig. 3.4.11 For wooden fences, these filler elements are boards, laths or (half-)round timbers. For steel constructions, narrower elements such as steel bars or steel cables are generally used. However, steel moldings of different dimensions can also be used.

If crossbars are arranged between the posts, with slats or filler elements arranged on these vertically, this is described as a post-bar construction. > Figs. 3.4.11 and 3.4.12 Narrow steel moldings and steel bars are described as upper and lower braces.
Additional bars or braces can be arranged in between for aesthetic or constructional reasons. For railings, the upper brace can double as the handrail. Sometimes there are no other horizontal struts. Lower excluding or enclosing fences can also be constructed with a single crossbar. > Fig. 3.4.13

For a post-frame construction, a frame is placed between the posts. This transfers the loads of the rods, grids or laths secured within to the posts. > Fig. 3.4.14 The profile thicknesses of the panels can be less than those of the frame construction. Construction methods where the individual frames are connected with each other and mounted directly on the subsoil are an exceptional case. The function of the posts is taken over by the vertical, external frame elements. > Fig. 3.4.15

If there are no horizontal bars, braces or panels at all and the posts stand immediately next to each other, this is a picket or palisade fence or picket fencing. Depending on material use and thickness, spacers between the vertical elements may be necessary. > Figs. 3.4.16 and 3.4.17 The posts take up the main loads of the construction and transfer them to the ground. They are dimensioned according to the desired component height, intervals between the posts and expected stresses. > Tab. 3.4.1 If thin steel moldings are to be used, lateral struts can stabilize the posts. A cross section that widens towards the base can also be chosen for the posts. Flat-rolled steel bars and box moldings are also strengthened by a spigot in the lower area. > Fig. 3.4.18
Squared, rounded or half-round timbers are used for wooden fences. For steel constructions, the moldings available range from round and quadratic hollow pipe moldings to moldings with parallel flange surfaces, e.g. T- or I-steel members. A composite post can also be formed from several elements, e.g. two or four angle irons or two flat-rolled steel bars.
The line taken by railings and fences on sloping sites involves particular considerations. Moderate slopes can usually be compensated for by angling the horizontal components. On uniform slopes (and steps) it is possible to lay the crossbars and braces parallel to the

Fig. 3.4.17: Fence made from flat-rolled steel elements. In the upper part, spacers are welded between the posts

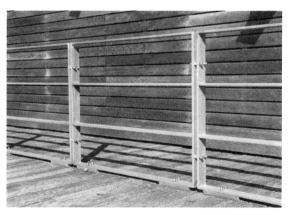

Fig. 3.4.15: Frame screwed to ground slab

Fig. 3.4.16: Picket railings made from stainless steel round pipe posts

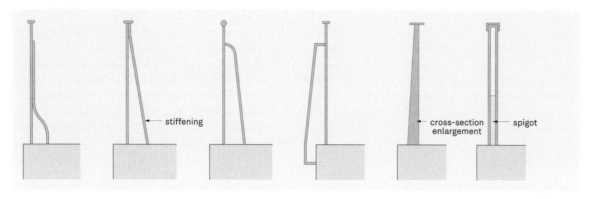

Fig. 3.4.18: Post stiffening

Component	Profile/type	Fence-/railing height	Dimensions *
Wooden posts	squared timber	800 mm	approx. 100/100 mm
		1000 mm	approx. 110/110 mm
		1000 1500 mm	approx. 120/120 mm
		1500 2000 mm	approx. 140/140 mm
	round timber		100/100–140/140 mm
	half-round timber (pickets)	800 mm	70–90 mm
		1200 mm	80–100 mm
		1200–1500 mm	90–110 mm
Steel posts	quadratic pipe	1200 mm 2000 mm	min. 40/40/3 mm min. 60/60/4 mm
	rectangular pipe	1200 mm 2000 mm	min. 20/40/2.5 mm min. 40/60/4 mm
	round pipe	1200 mm 2000 mm	min. 60/4 mm min. 76/4 mm
	round steel	1200 mm	min. d = 30 mm (less where distance between posts is less)
	square steel	1200 mm	min. 25/25 mm
	flat-rolled steel	1200 mm	min. d = 10 mm (arranged in pairs)
	I-molding	1200 mm	min. HEB 100/IPE 80
	T-molding	600 mm	min. 40/40/5 mm
		1200 mm	min. 60/60/7 mm
Masonry posts (bonded masonry)	masonry	1500 mm 2500 mm	min. 240/240 mm min. 365(240)/365 mm (with steel concrete core if necessary)
	natural stone masonry		min. 300/300 mm
Steel concrete posts	finished parts	2000 mm **	min. 100/100 mm
		2500 mm **	min. 150/150 mm
	in-situ concrete		min. 250/250 mm
Posts made from natural stone (monolith) (varies according to stone material)	example: granite	1500 mm ** 2500 mm **	min. 120/120 mm min. 100/250 mm
	example: sandstone	1500 mm ** 2500 mm **	min. 120/120 mm and 100/250 mm from about 160/160 mm

*   Does not apply to gate posts. Thickness also depends on the intervals between the posts.
** Total height. The part of the post embedded in ground should be deducted.

Tab. 3.4.1: Specimen standard values for dimensioning of posts for fences and railings

Fig. 3.4.19: Aligning fences and railings on terrain and for steps

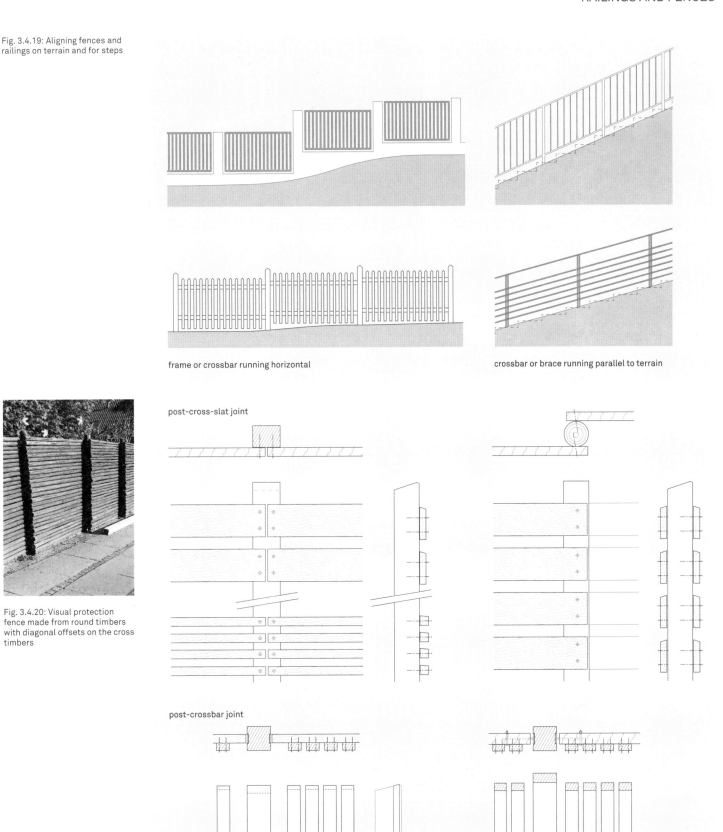

frame or crossbar running horizontal

crossbar or brace running parallel to terrain

post-cross-slat joint

Fig. 3.4.20: Visual protection fence made from round timbers with diagonal offsets on the cross timbers

post-crossbar joint

corner connectors

T-shaped timber connectors, embedded in wood

posts in cross section

posts in cross section

Fig. 3.4.21: Slats and crossbars connected to posts

Fig. 3.4.22: Wattle fence bordering a plot of land

Fig. 3.4.23: Railing made from steel pipes welded to crossbars
(flat-rolled steel) and base plate. Base plate screwed in place

terrain. On nonuniform terrain, masonry pedestals may help to even out changes in level. > Fig. 3.4.19

For timber construction methods, components are connected using nails or screws. Screws create a more stable joint. Crossbars should therefore always be secured to posts using screws, as they are subject to greater forces than the laths. If larger cross sections are to be connected or the crossbars are being installed between the laths and the post, bolted joints are used. > 2.3 Chapter Connections, Timber connections When mounting horizontal laths or two crossbars at the same height on posts, the problem of insufficient contact surfaces often arises. Relatively large or rectangular post cross sections must therefore be used. Alternatively, laths and cross sections can be installed with a lateral offset. This is particularly suitable for round timber posts, for which the contact area is seriously limited by the post cross section. Another possibility is to use timber connectors made from steel. > Figs. 3.4.20 and 3.4.21

The required dimensions of the wooden beams depend on the distances between the posts and the load to be sustained, and therefore vary widely. Minimum measurements are around—for instance—35 x 55 mm and 40 x 40 mm, average measurements 40 x 60 mm and 40 x 100 mm up to 60 x 160 mm. Steel moldings or flat-rolled steel bars can also be used as substitute crossbars. These permit comparatively small profiles, but may be aesthetically disrupting if both sides of the fence are visually important.

For wattle fences, the laths are replaced by flexible twigs made from any suitable wood. These are woven directly between the posts or crossbars and fixed at the ends with nails. > Fig. 3.4.22 The material is usually derived from year-old shoots and may be willow, hazel, birch, poplar or ash, depending on local availability.

If shoots on willow twigs are desired, the material must be installed directly after cutting and in contact with the ground (where the weaving direction is diagonal or vertical). > Fig. 3.1.9c

In steel constructions, the panels of grille railings or cage fences usually consist of grilles with vertical and/or horizontal struts. These are welded to the upper and lower braces, the crossbars or the frame. Steel bars or

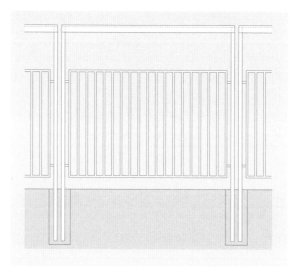

Fig. 3.4.24: Prefabricated railing segments with welded flat-rolled
steel posts

flat-rolled steel bars are generally used. For loadbearing braces, crossbars and frames in particular, L-, U- and T-moldings are also suitable, as well as rectangular pipes. > Fig. 3.4.23 Steel frames can also be filled using mesh grids, gratings, sheet metal or mesh.

The prefabricated grille elements or frames are usually then screwed to the posts onsite. Alternatively, the posts can be directly welded on. > Fig. 3.4.24 Longer sections spanning several posts are easily possible provided suitably large galvanizing apparatus is available. > Chapter 1.8 Metals, Iron and Steel

Fence segments are usually secured by fishplates welded to the posts. > Fig. 3.4.25 Bars can also be directly screwed to concrete posts. > Fig. 3.4.26 For "Hespeneisen" (specially profiled iron bars that are mainly used as crossbars), riveted joints are also used. Steel cable nets can also be used as railing panels. They are laid on the upper and lower braces and fixed in place using special fasteners. > Fig. 3.4.27

Horizontal infills made from steel cables (d = 4–6 mm) should either be anchored to every post or, if they are drawn through drilled holes or clamps, fixed at every post using stoppers. This is the only way to absorb the

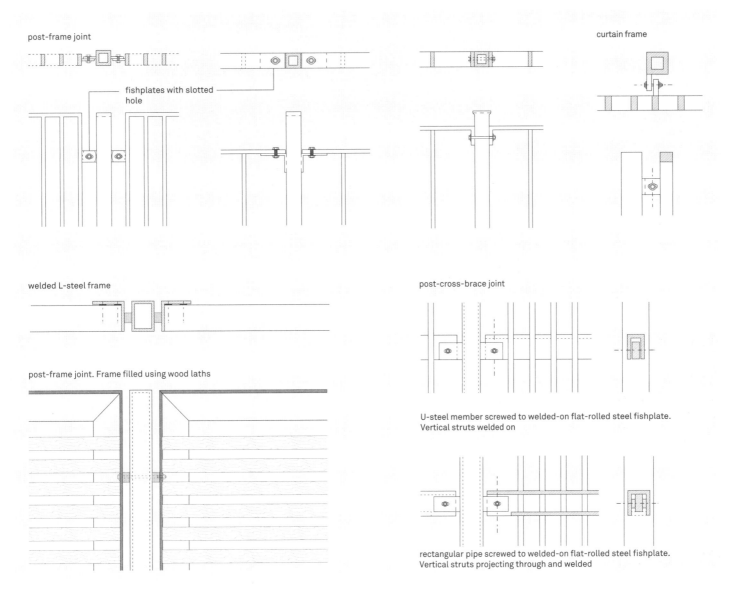

post-frame joint

fishplates with slotted hole

curtain frame

welded L-steel frame

post-frame joint. Frame filled using wood laths

post-cross-brace joint

U-steel member screwed to welded-on flat-rolled steel fishplate.
Vertical struts welded on

rectangular pipe screwed to welded-on flat-rolled steel fishplate.
Vertical struts projecting through and welded

Fig. 3.4.25: Frames and cross-braces connected to posts

Fig. 3.4.26: Quadratic pipe bar screwed to concrete posts

Fig. 3.4.27: Steel cable net suspended on steel cables

Fig. 3.4.28: Cables anchored to a railing with welded screw terminal

Fig. 3.4.29: Steel subconstruction with wood laths:
a + b) front and reverse view of a railing at a viewing point
c) reverse of a fence construction

Fig. 3.4.30: Ball catch fence—steel mat fence   Fig. 3.4.31: Steel mesh fence

load at every post. Prestressing the cables causes additional forces to act on the posts (particularly the end posts). These must be taken into account in dimensioning and anchoring. > Fig. 3.4.28

Steel constructions make a good loadbearing structure for railings and fence panels made from other materials. For instance, post-bar constructions made from steel with wood lathing are common. > Fig. 3.4.29

Steel mat fences are prefabricated fences, and are available from various manufacturers. Depending on manufacture, steel mats are made from steel bars with diameters of 5–8 m. They provide a functional enclosing fence for plots and sports areas, which can however be seen through.

Mesh with a width of 50 x 200 mm is offered as standard. For ball catch fences higher than 2000 mm, meshes of 100 x 200 mm are used. > Fig. 3.4.30 Specialized systems with special soundproofing are also available for sports facilities. The distance between the posts is generally 2.52 m.

The dimensioning of the posts is calculated according to static requirements from the height of the fence and the place of use.

For a wire mesh fence, three taut wires are stretched between the posts at different heights, taking on the function of crossbars. The plastic-coated wire mesh is secured to these. End and intermediate posts must be additionally stabilized using cross-struts. > Figs. 3.4.31 and 3.4.32

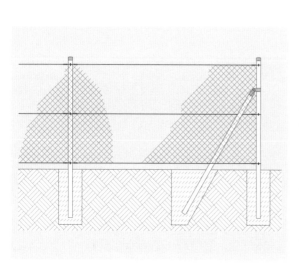

Fig. 3.4.32: Stiffening of corner or end posts using cross-struts

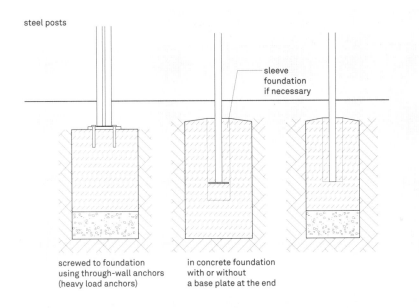

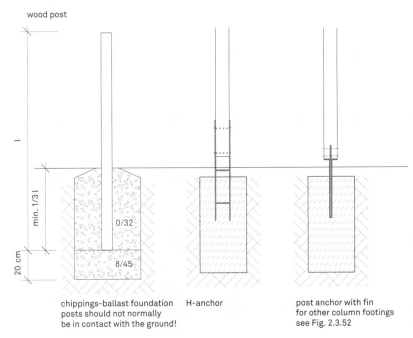

Fig. 3.4.33: Post anchoring in a concrete foundation

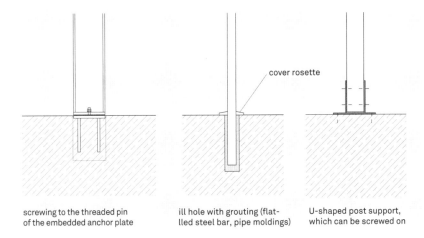

Fig. 3.4.34: Post anchoring in concrete surfaces, natural quarried stone and masonry

Anchoring and foundation

Sufficient rigidity in the fence or railing construction is achieved primarily through dimensioning and profile of the posts and their foundations or anchoring.

Anchoring in a concrete foundation

Wooden posts require a steel column footing anchored in the concrete foundation. The distance between the post and the ground can be reduced by 5–10 cm in relation to the regulation construction method, as too great an interval would impair the functional aspects of a fence. Column footings are poured directly into the concrete foundation or screwed to it. Simple construction methods and soundproofing walls—for which gaps between the fence and the ground are undesirable—are an exception. In these cases, the wooden posts can also be placed directly in the ground. In this case, only impregnated or very durable timber should be used. The posts should be installed in a drainage course in a chippings-ballast mix. > Fig. 3.4.33

Metal posts are directly cemented in. From a construction point of view, it is advisable to use sleeve foundations. Inserting a kind of sleeve creates a recess that can later accommodate the post. Finally, a stable connection is created by filling the gap with grouting mortar.

Metal posts made from flat-rolled steel and pipe moldings are given a welded-on ground slab for stability if necessary. This is concreted into the foundation. Installation takes place 5–30 cm beneath the ground's upper edge, depending on ground covering, so that the foundation is not visible and any covering can be applied around the posts. > Fig. 3.4.33 and chapter 2.3

Depending on the height of the construction, the foundation should be embedded 80–100 cm deep into the ground. A 50 cm deep foundation is sufficient for simple fences of up to a meter in height. Foundation work should be carried out on frost-free soil. Alternatively, a frost protection layer should be installed above the frost-free layer.
Concrete strength should generally be C 20/25. For lower stresses, C 12/15 is also used. Greater loads are intercepted by a reinforced foundation (C 25/30).

Surface anchoring methods

Various screw anchor joints exist for anchoring posts on existing concrete surfaces, in natural quarried stone and masonry. > Chapter 2.3 Connections For metal posts, a base plate is welded on to accommodate the through-wall anchors (heavy-duty anchors). The wall can also be drilled into following construction, so that the post can then be inserted and fixed in place by grouting. > Figs. 3.4.34 and 3.4.35 Wooden posts are placed in suitable brackets to be screwed in.
With screw anchor fastening around the edges or lateral fastening to a projecting plate, there is a risk of spalling and breaking up (concrete failure cone). The edge and axial distances required by different screw

Fig. 3.4.35: Covering the drilled hole:
a) with rosette
b) with chippings

a | b

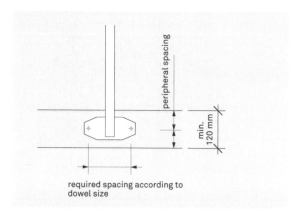

Fig. 3.4.36: Arranging screw anchor holes so as to avoid breakups and spalling during lateral anchoring

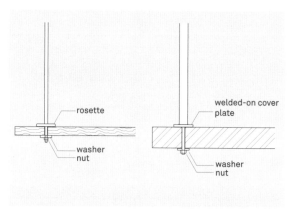

Fig. 3.4.37: Support rods secured by screwing to wooden step/ stone slab

Fig. 3.4.38 (a+b): Securing a rail for a bridge: the stainless steel railing rods (d = 16 mm) pass through the natural stone slabs and are screwed on the underside. The handrail is then welded on.

a | b

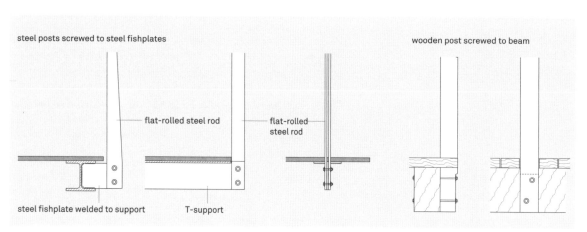

Fig. 3.4.39: Securing the posts for freestanding constructions

anchor sizes should be taken into account. In principle, the size of the screw anchor and thereby the size of the required edge and axial distances can be reduced by reducing the distances between the posts, and thus the loads acting on the individual posts. > Fig. 3.4.36 and chapter 2.3 Connections

On thin slabs or steps, posts can often be secured using screws alone. For this purpose, a threaded rod is welded to the bottom end of the post, which is stuck through a drilled hole and secured on the underside using a nut. A cover rosette or cover plate on the upper face diverts the load. > Figs. 3.4.37 and 3.4.38

For freestanding constructions, the railing post is secured by screwing it to a support or a welded-on fishplate. For wood constructions, the handrail can be screwed to the girder. > Fig. 3.4.39

Handrails

Handrails should be continuous where possible. If sections do have to be joined together, a smooth connection is important. Steel pipes can be extended using (for instance) pipe connectors. Flat-rolled steel bars can be extended by overlapping two fishplates. > Fig. 3.4.40 Handrails made from nonrusting steel can also be welded onsite without risking a negative impact on corrosion protection.

Fig. 3.4.40: Extending a flat-rolled steel handrail by means of overlapping and screwing

Fig. 3.4.42: Handrail made from non-rusting steel. Handrail, handrail strut and flat-rolled steel anchoring plate are welded together. The steel pipe is closed by an end cap.

1 handrail screwed to handgrip strut
2 handrail strut
3 rosette
4 wall anchor

1 flat-rolled steel handrail
2 handrail support, flat-rolled steel corner
3 anchor plate
4 screw/screw anchor

1 round steel bar handrail
2 handrail support
3 flat-rolled steel bar with screw joint
4 flat-rolled steel posts

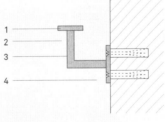

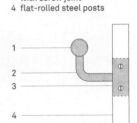

anchoring using wall anchor. The handrail is screwed on

anchoring the anchor plate using screw anchors. Handrail welded to handrail support and anchor plate

screwing to posts

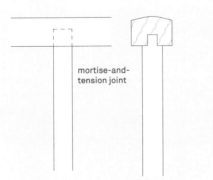

mortise-and-tension joint

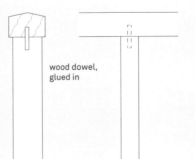

wood dowel, glued in

anchoring of wooden handrails to wooden posts

Fig. 3.4.41: Anchoring possibilities for handrails

Fig. 3.4.44: Steel gate with grille construction

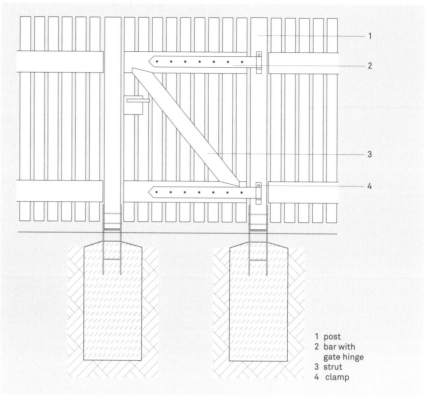

1 post
2 bar with
  gate hinge
3 strut
4 clamp

Fig. 3.4.43: Specimen design for a wooden gate

Fig. 3.4.45: Hinge on a steel gate, welded to posts

A handrail can be anchored laterally in a wall using screw anchor joints. Alternatively, the handrail strut can be welded to a concreted anchor plate. The handrail can then be secured to the handrail support using screws or plug-in joints. > **Fig. 3.4.41** The handrail is often connected to a railing via a welded-on flat-rolled steel bar screwed to the post. > **Fig. 3.4.42** Wooden handrails are screwed to the handrail support or connected to the subconstruction by mortise and tenon or dowel.

Gates

Depending on the planned height and width, wooden gates are designed either as a frame construction or—for simple wooden fences—lath gates with an additional cross-strut for stability. > **Fig. 3.4.43** Steel gates are also built as frame constructions, or as grille constructions if the material thickness is appropriate. > **Fig. 3.4.44**

Various fittings are available for securing wooden components. These are anchored to posts using clamps or hinges. > **Fig. 3.4.45** Fitted moldings, locks or catches can be used to latch the gate.

Gateposts should normally be made thicker than standard fence posts or stabilized using additional cross-struts. Gateposts should have foundations of at least ≥ 90 cm.

1 Posts, I-molding IPB 100, l =1160 mm, screwed to existing
   ground plate in cap beam using domed nut
2 Frame grille element: flat-rolled steel 50/10; web members:
   flat-rolled steel 50/5, web member intervals 30–130 mm
3 Handrail: 2 x 100/15 flat-rolled steel, expansion joint 1–2 mm
4 Flat-rolled steel spacer 50/40/10. Distance approx. 50 cm,
   welded all round to upper rail
5 Cap plate 100/100/8 with drilled holes for screws
6 Walkway IPB support, cut out
7 Plate 8 mm, flange flush on both sides, welded to walkway
8 Flat-rolled steel 40/50/10 fishplate, with slotted drilled hole,
   welded to IPB beam
9 Frame filler element with cut thread, screwed to fishplate
   using domed nut
10 Flat-rolled steel 40/50/10 fishplate, with cut thread, welded
   to IPB beam
11 Frame filler element with drilled slotted hole, screwed to
   fishplate using domed nut
12 Domed nut with washer
13 Base plate 100/100/10 welded to IPB beam, with drill holes
   to admit threaded pin, drilled slotted hole for aligning post
   with other posts
14 Bitumen/neoprene and leveling course for perpendicular
   alignment of posts
15 Ground plate in place onsite and cast in the cap beam of the
   sheet-pile wall

RAILING IN TEXTIMA GROUNDS, GROSSENHAIN
(SAXONY), GERMANY

Weidinger Landschaftsarchitekten, Berlin
Completed: 2002

Upper flat-rolled steel rail with hot-dip galvanized spacers all other metal parts with corrosion protection and top
coating; all visible domed nut joints hot-dip galvanized,
countersunk bolts hot-dip galvanized

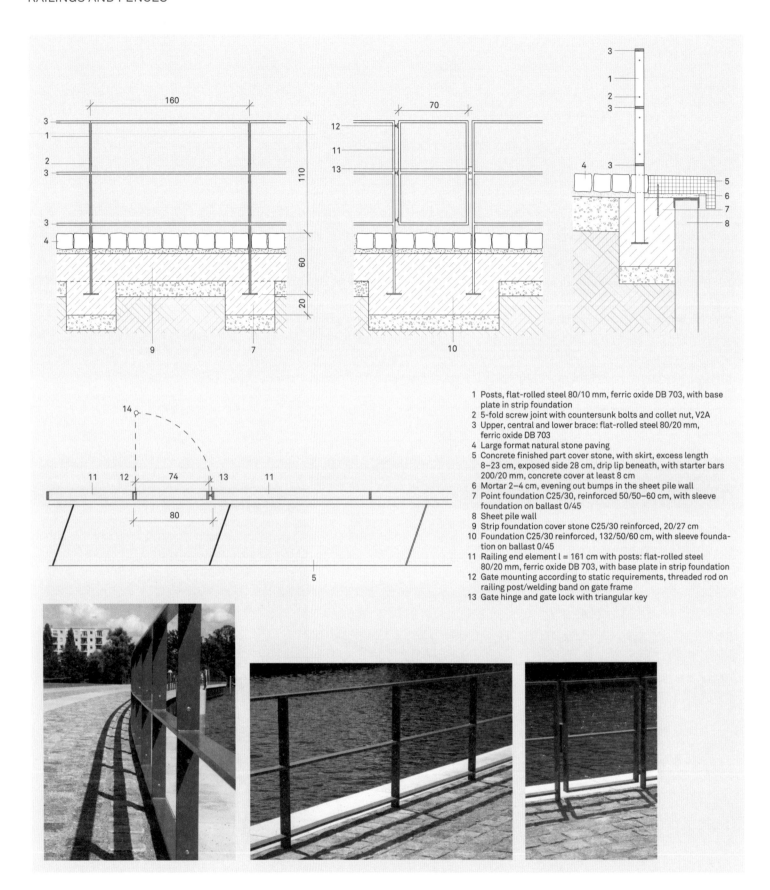

1 Posts, flat-rolled steel 80/10 mm, ferric oxide DB 703, with base plate in strip foundation
2 5-fold screw joint with countersunk bolts and collet nut, V2A
3 Upper, central and lower brace: flat-rolled steel 80/20 mm, ferric oxide DB 703
4 Large format natural stone paving
5 Concrete finished part cover stone, with skirt, excess length 8–23 cm, exposed side 28 cm, drip lip beneath, with starter bars 200/20 mm, concrete cover at least 8 cm
6 Mortar 2–4 cm, evening out bumps in the sheet pile wall
7 Point foundation C25/30, reinforced 50/50–60 cm, with sleeve foundation on ballast 0/45
8 Sheet pile wall
9 Strip foundation cover stone C25/30 reinforced, 20/27 cm
10 Foundation C25/30 reinforced, 132/50/60 cm, with sleeve foundation on ballast 0/45
11 Railing end element l = 161 cm with posts: flat-rolled steel 80/20 mm, ferric oxide DB 703, with base plate in strip foundation
12 Gate mounting according to static requirements, threaded rod on railing post/welding band on gate frame
13 Gate hinge and gate lock with triangular key

RAILING IN MASELAKEPARK, BERLIN, GERMANY

relais Landschaftsarchitekten, Berlin
Completed: 2007

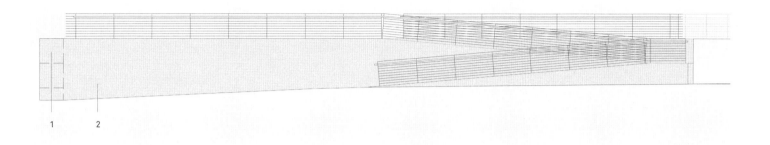

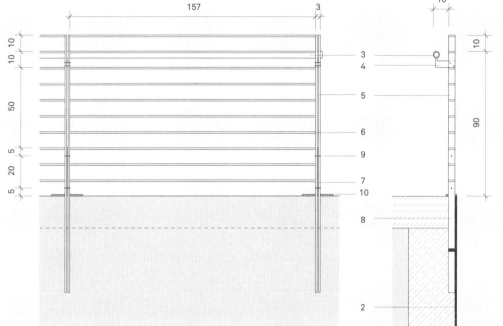

1 Gabions
2 Steel wall, nonalloyed construction steel,
   d = 10 mm, secured to corner retaining wall
   using cap bolts
3 Stainless steel handrail, d = 42 mm, welded
   to flat-rolled steel corner (4)
4 Flat-rolled steel d = 10 mm welded, screwed
   to posts
5 Flat-rolled steel posts d = 10 mm, b = 40 mm,
   nonalloyed construction steel
6 Flat-rolled steel lengthwise struts
   10/40/1570 mm welded to flat-rolled steel
   posts, nonalloyed
7 Distance piece/flat-rolled steel
   10/40/300 mm or 500 mm
8 Railing posts welded to steel wall from
   behind before concreting in
9 Screwing of distance piece/ flat-rolled steel
   bar 10/40/300
10 Cover plate made from non-alloy steel,
   200/40/20 mm, with recess, soldered to
   flat-rolled steel bars of posts

RAILING WITH HANDRAIL, WERNIGERODE, GERMANY

hutterreimann + cejka Landschaftsarchitektur,
Berlin Vienna
Completion: 2006

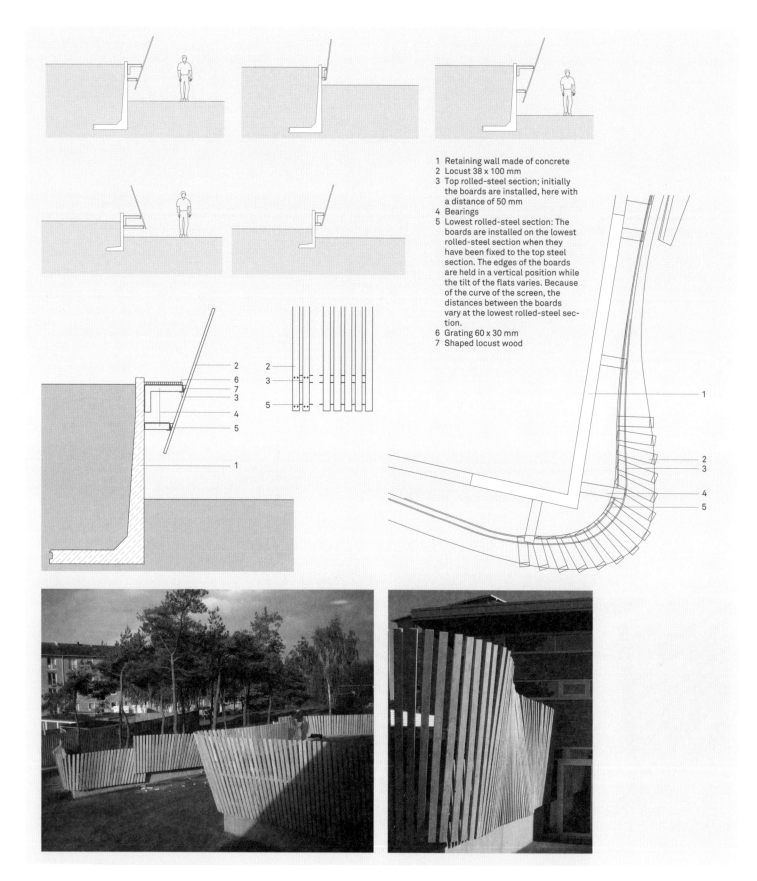

1 Retaining wall made of concrete
2 Locust 38 x 100 mm
3 Top rolled-steel section; initially
  the boards are installed, here with
  a distance of 50 mm
4 Bearings
5 Lowest rolled-steel section: The
  boards are installed on the lowest
  rolled-steel section when they
  have been fixed to the top steel
  section. The edges of the boards
  are held in a vertical position while
  the tilt of the flats varies. Because
  of the curve of the screen, the
  distances between the boards
  vary at the lowest rolled-steel section.
6 Grating 60 x 30 mm
7 Shaped locust wood

WOODEN FENCE, MOTALAVEJ (MOTALA STREET),
KORSØR, DENMARK

SLA A/S, Stig L. Andersson, Copenhagen
Completion: 2007

The billowing screens draping the asphalt ramp at the
new community building are reinterpretations of the
classic wooden fence. They are constructed of wooden
boards mounted on concrete walls using rolled steel
profiles, while steel grating covers the area between
the walls and the screens.

1 Planed larch planks, 1900 x 150 x 34 mm or 1300 x 150 x 34 mm,
   class I/II, rift/half rift cut, unmarked, beveled on top, slit below,
   hole for connecting rod, distance iL 150 mm
2 Threaded rod, galvanized
3 Spacers, spacer sleeves made from chrome steel
4 Concrete foundation
5 Flat iron metal blade, galvanized
6 Support iron molding metal truss, galvanized

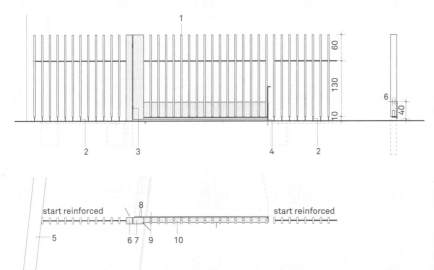

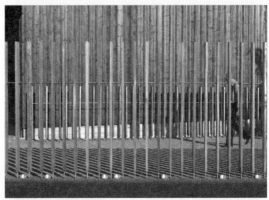

1 Lathing: 34 x 150 x 1900 mm, planed larch.
   Interval 150 mm. On metal blades
2 Metal blades welded to metal molding on point
   foundation
3 2 strong ball-bearing mounted belt closing
   devices with thrust transfer
4 Locking device
   Moveable bolt for latching, galvanized round
   steel molding, height approx. 80 cm, 2 ground
   sockets
5 Existing dry packing
6 Gateposts: rectangular hollow molding

galvanized steel 15/15 cm, wall thickness
poured at frost level or deeper, closed at top
7 Post: hollow molding 25/15 cm, galvanized
   with coating, closed at top
8 Post welded to flat iron bar
9 Wood planks secured from behind using
   countersunk bolts
10 Flat iron bar galvanized with coating.
   Mounting in prefabricated elements. Element
   length approx. 240 cm. Fence runs along the
   natural gradient. Threaded rod parallel to
   terrain gradient. Planks remain vertical.

WOODEN FENCE WITH GATE, WEIACH, SWITZERLAND

Kuhn Truninger Landschaftsarchitekten, Zurich
Completion: 2004

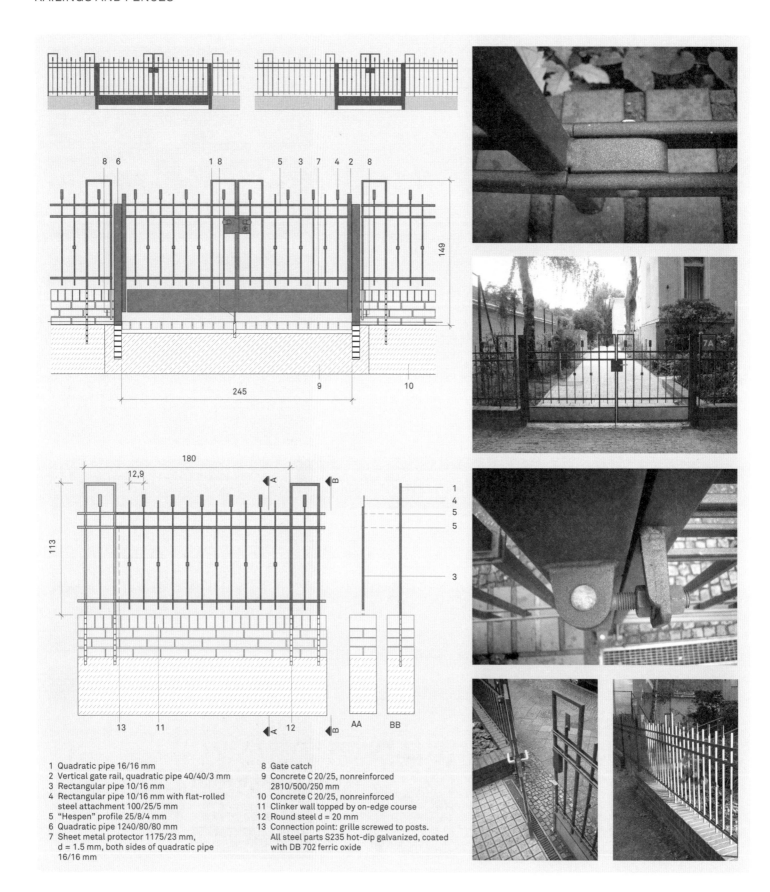

1 Quadratic pipe 16/16 mm
2 Vertical gate rail, quadratic pipe 40/40/3 mm
3 Rectangular pipe 10/16 mm
4 Rectangular pipe 10/16 mm with flat-rolled
  steel attachment 100/25/5 mm
5 "Hespen" profile 25/8/4 mm
6 Quadratic pipe 1240/80/80 mm
7 Sheet metal protector 1175/23 mm,
  d = 1.5 mm, both sides of quadratic pipe
  16/16 mm

8 Gate catch
9 Concrete C 20/25, nonreinforced
  2810/500/250 mm
10 Concrete C 20/25, nonreinforced
11 Clinker wall topped by on-edge course
12 Round steel d = 20 mm
13 Connection point: grille screwed to posts.
   All steel parts S235 hot-dip galvanized, coated
   with DB 702 ferric oxide

STEEL FENCE AND GATE, LUTHERSTIFT, BERLIN,
GERMANY

LA.BAR Landschaftsarchitekten, Berlin
Completion: 2006

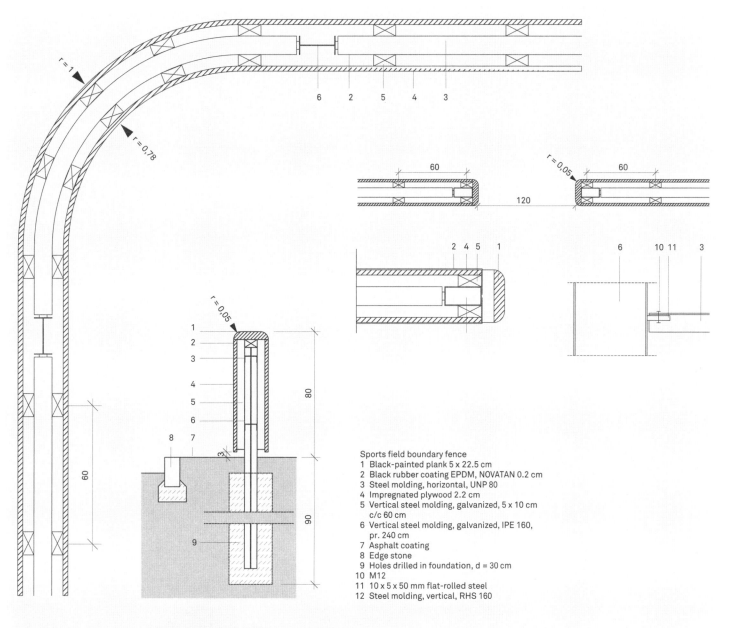

Sports field boundary fence
1 Black-painted plank 5 x 22.5 cm
2 Black rubber coating EPDM, NOVATAN 0.2 cm
3 Steel molding, horizontal, UNP 80
4 Impregnated plywood 2.2 cm
5 Vertical steel molding, galvanized, 5 x 10 cm
   c/c 60 cm
6 Vertical steel molding, galvanized, IPE 160,
   pr. 240 cm
7 Asphalt coating
8 Edge stone
9 Holes drilled in foundation, d = 30 cm
10 M12
11 10 x 5 x 50 mm flat-rolled steel
12 Steel molding, vertical, RHS 160

SPORTS FIELD BOUNDARY FENCE, PRAGS
BOULEVARD, COPENHAGEN, DENMARK

Arkitekt Kristine Jensens Tegnestue, Århus
Completion: 2005

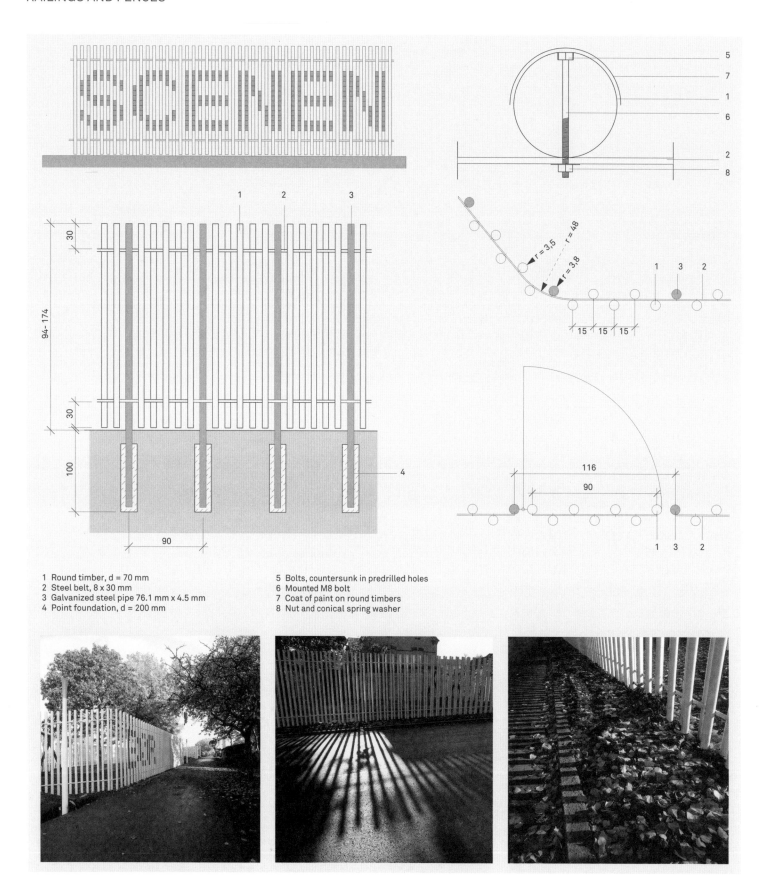

1 Round timber, d = 70 mm
2 Steel belt, 8 x 30 mm
3 Galvanized steel pipe 76.1 mm x 4.5 mm
4 Point foundation, d = 200 mm

5 Bolts, countersunk in predrilled holes
6 Mounted M8 bolt
7 Coat of paint on round timbers
8 Nut and conical spring washer

FENCE, PRAGS BOULEVARD, COPENHAGEN,
DENMARK

Arkitekt Kristine Jensens Tegnestue, Århus
Completion: 2005

298

288.5

60

section view A–A (horizontal frame)

section B–B

section C–C

5
10
6
1

1
2
3
4

B

C

1 | 14 | 5 | 4 | 8 | 4

7
3
4
8
9

1 Wood slats: Siberian larch, sort class 10, wood moisture ≤ 18%
Format: 4/14 cm, length: 280 cm, sharp-edged, planed level
2 Strut: sharp-edged L-steel, 140 x 14
3 Strut/lower intermediate frame joint: threaded pin, d = 12 mm, welded to
underplate. Above: slotted hole, secured using domed nut
4 Post/column footing joint: threaded rod, d = 14 mm, welded to underplate.
Above: slotted hole, secured using domed nut
5 Post/upper intermediate frame joint: threaded rod, d = 12 mm, welded to
underplate. Above: slotted hole, secured using domed nut

6 Upper intermediate frame: flat-rolled steel 160/20 mm. At the corners: overlapping
of steel frame
7 Lower frame: 160/20 mm flat-rolled steel. At the corners: overlapping of steel frame
8 Corner column footing: cross-shaped molding, 100/100/10 mm, above: steel plate
15/160/195 mm, below: steel plate 15/100/100 mm
9 Sleeve foundation, DN150
10 Steel frame/wood screwed joint: M 8 x 100, countersunk flush with surface, spacers
made from round washers, hot-dip galvanized DB 702, d = 3 cm. Height above: 20 mm.
Height below: 30 mm, drill hole, d = 1.5 cm

SEATING CABINET IN OSCHATZ, GERMANY

Weidinger Landschaftsarchitekten, Berlin
Completion: 2006

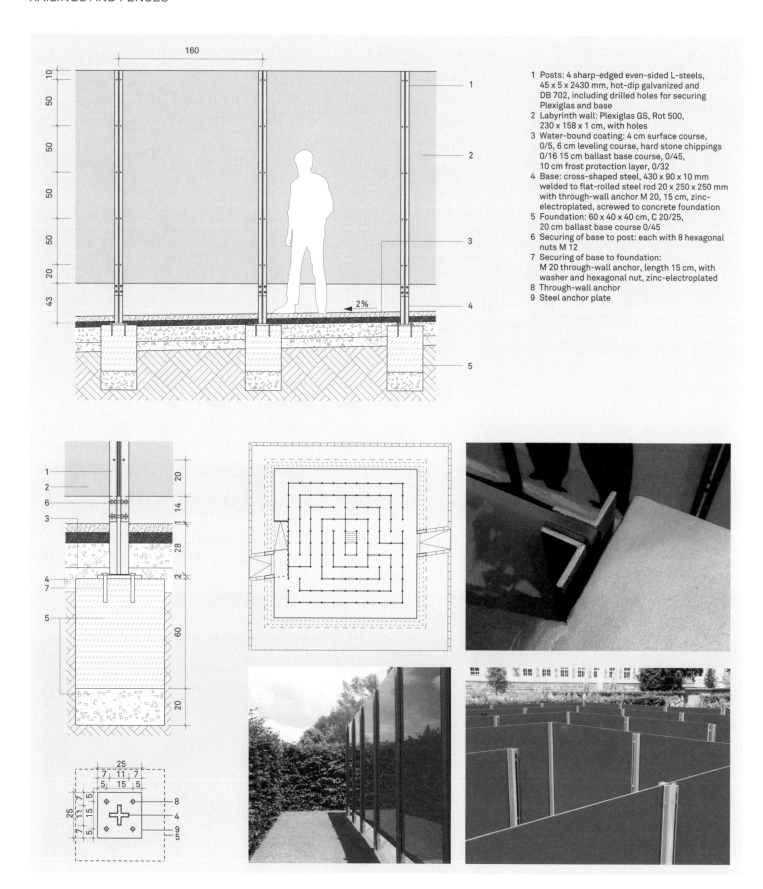

1 Posts: 4 sharp-edged even-sided L-steels,
   45 x 5 x 2430 mm, hot-dip galvanized and
   DB 702, including drilled holes for securing
   Plexiglas and base
2 Labyrinth wall: Plexiglas GS, Rot 500,
   230 x 158 x 1 cm, with holes
3 Water-bound coating: 4 cm surface course,
   0/5, 6 cm leveling course, hard stone chippings
   0/16 15 cm ballast base course, 0/45,
   10 cm frost protection layer, 0/32
4 Base: cross-shaped steel, 430 x 90 x 10 mm
   welded to flat-rolled steel rod 20 x 250 x 250 mm
   with through-wall anchor M 20, 15 cm, zinc-
   electroplated, screwed to concrete foundation
5 Foundation: 60 x 40 x 40 cm, C 20/25,
   20 cm ballast base course 0/45
6 Securing of base to post: each with 8 hexagonal
   nuts M 12
7 Securing of base to foundation:
   M 20 through-wall anchor, length 15 cm, with
   washer and hexagonal nut, zinc-electroplated
8 Through-wall anchor
9 Steel anchor plate

LABYRINTH, OSCHATZ, GERMANY

Weidinger Landschaftsarchitekten, Berlin
Completion: 2006

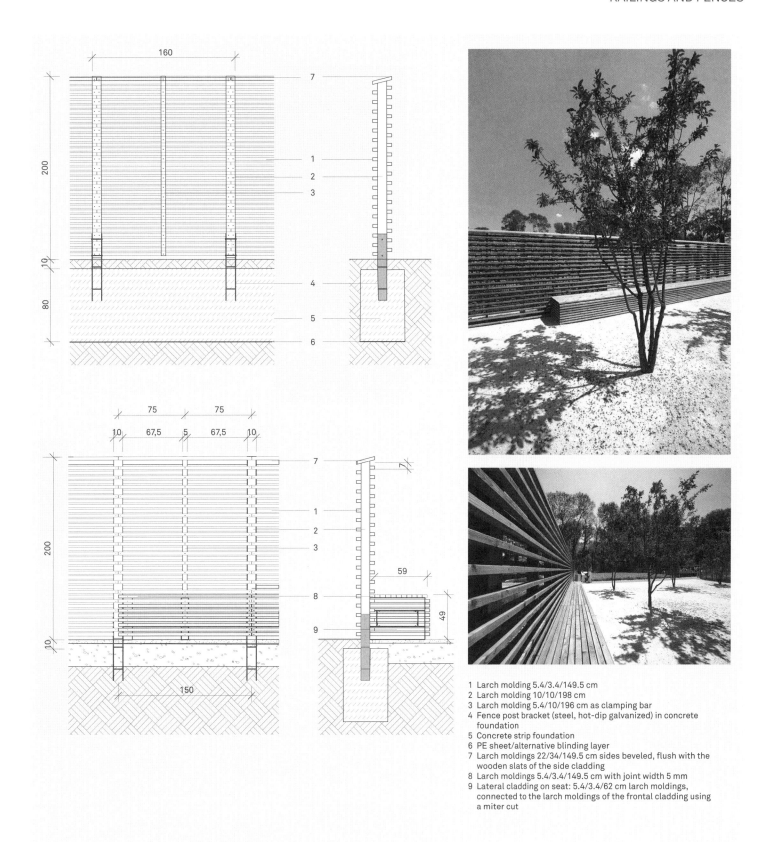

1 Larch molding 5.4/3.4/149.5 cm
2 Larch molding 10/10/198 cm
3 Larch molding 5.4/10/196 cm as clamping bar
4 Fence post bracket (steel, hot-dip galvanized) in concrete
   foundation
5 Concrete strip foundation
6 PE sheet/alternative blinding layer
7 Larch moldings 22/34/149.5 cm sides beveled, flush with the
   wooden slats of the side cladding
8 Larch moldings 5.4/3.4/149.5 cm with joint width 5 mm
9 Lateral cladding on seat: 5.4/3.4/62 cm larch moldings,
   connected to the larch moldings of the frontal cladding using
   a miter cut

SLATTED WOOD FENCE, TULLN, AUSTRIA

hutterreimann + cejka landschaftsarchitekten, Berlin
Completed: 2008

3.5 WALLS

PRINCIPLES

FREESTANDING WALLS

RETAINING WALLS
· Gravity walls
· Angle support walls
· Drainage of retaining walls
· Special retaining wall types

NONSTABLE CONSTRUCTION METHODS
· Drystone walls made from natural stone
· Soil and stone gabions

STABLE CONSTRUCTION METHODS
· One-shelled walls
· Two-shelled walls
· Joints
· Wall coverings

SPECIMEN PROJECTS

Maik Böhmer

3.5 WALLS

Fig. 3.5.2: Freestanding concrete wall, Geschichtspark Ehemaliges Zellengefängnis, Berlin-Moabit

Due to the high number of possible construction methods and materials, walls used for outdoor structures can have very varied functions. The distinction between the two types of wall in German *(Mauern and Wände)* presumably originated with the materials used. A wall in the classical sense consists of masonry *(Mauerwerk)*—i.e. it is a construction element made from natural or artificial stone. The other kind of wall *(Wand)* would originally be a clay-daubed supportive weave. They could be considered wall panels in the sense that they re upright panels. This type of wall has a space-defining, dividing and demarcating function. The timber framework construction evolved from the woven construction. However, this kind of wall can also be constructed from masonry. In modern usage, the two "walls" are synonymous.

As well as the numerous standards, recommendations, specifications and requirements, the importance of outdoor wall elements in design terms should not be forgotten. Walls give a space an unmistakable character and significantly influence the atmosphere of any space.

PRINCIPLES

Depending on the materials used, walls can be classified as solid-construction walls made from masonry or steel-reinforced concrete, wood or clay, and special forms such as glass construction block walls. They can be further classified by function. A distinction is made between freestanding walls and support walls with a loadbearing function. > Fig. 3.5.1 In Germany, masonry construction is standardized and primarily governed by DIN 1053—Masonry. Alongside classic construction methods using solid construction materials such as stone and concrete, lightweight construction materials such as steel and wood extend the field of possible designs. Techniques taken from high-rise construction, such as curtain facades, can also be used, opening up a vast spectrum of material usage and surface design.

FREESTANDING WALLS

Freestanding walls are built without reinforcement from transverse walls or bracing. The are usually constructed using the solid method. As a rule they can absorb only their own weight and horizontal loads such as wind loads. > Chapter 2.1

Construction methods are restricted by the permitted wall height, which is related to wall width. According to German standards, for a cement mortar-bonded masonry construction method with width less than 8.00 m, assuming a stone density of 2.0 t/m³, height and width are calculated using the following formula:

Required wall height d $[m] = \sqrt{h\,[m]\,/\,22}$
or:
Permitted wall height h [m] = 22 × d² [m]

The calculation result provides a reference value and must be calculated precisely by computer in concrete individual cases. Deviations can occur as a result of the wind and traffic loads to be applied and to meet higher or lower safety margins. The formula can also be applied as an approximate value for concrete walls as well (normal concrete on average 2.4 t/ m³).

1 applied soil
2 slope removal
3 existing soil

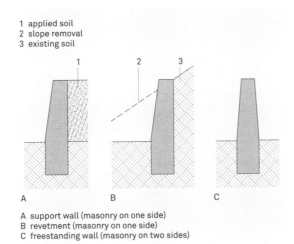

A support wall (masonry on one side)
B revetment (masonry on one side)
C freestanding wall (masonry on two sides)

Fig. 3.5.1: Outdoor wall functions

Wall width d (cm)	17,5	24,0	30,0	36,5
Calculation weight (t/m³)	Wall height (cm) (h=22 d²)			
2.4 (h=+20%)	80	152	238	352
2.0 (Formula relation h = 100%)	67	127	198	293
1.8 (h= -10%)	60	114	178	264
1.4 (h = -30%)	47	89	139	205
Basis for calculating : masonry joint/foundation = OK terrain				

Tab. 3.5.1: Permissible wall widths and heights for freestanding, unstiffened brick walls

The formula value is to be reduced by approx. 5% per reduced kN stone weight. For total wall heights above 8 m the values are to be reduced by 25%.

Definitions of terms
Stone density = dry density = calculation weight: kN/m³; kg/dm³)
Stone compressive strength = stone strength N/mm²

The density of natural stone is usually somewhere in the range 2.4–2.9 t/m³. Natural stone masonry is accordingly more stable than the value assumed for these principles of measurement.
The heights given above can be greater or the wall thicknesses less if the wall is stiffened using piers and rigid edge beams (made, for instance, from steel-reinforced concrete finished parts). In these cases, DIN 1053 gives the permitted wall surface area size, pillar spacing and masonry reinforcement, according to the strength class of the stone used. > Fig. 3.5.3, and tabs. 3.5.2 and 3.5.6
According to DIN, construction without an upper edge beam is irregular. However, if walls need only lateral stiffening, the masonry should be additionally reinforced with steel rods. In this case, the reinforcement rods are installed in the horizontal joints so that where the maximum interval between rods is 25 cm, there are at least 4 rods per meter of wall height. The horizontal joints involved should not be thicker than 2.0 cm, but must ensure a minimum covering for the reinforcement of 5 mm. > Fig. 3.5.4 The reinforcement must be anchored in the pillars. The statics for the pillars must be verified. Freestanding walls can also be stabilized using stiffening wall section arrangements (giving the wall an L, T or U-shaped ground plan, for instance) or by giving the wall a circular or curved ground plan. Freestanding walls can of course also be constructed using concrete. > Chapter Stable construction methods Steel or wood frame constructions—with special fills or cladding if required—can also be used, depending on the designer's intentions. In this case, manufacture is mainly based on steel and wood construction requirements.

RETAINING WALLS
Retaining walls are one of the classic retaining structures used to regulate changes in terrain height where slopes are undesirable in design terms or cannot be permitted due to building constraints. Important examples of support structures are gravity walls and angle retaining walls. There are other modern retaining construction methods, including gabions and crib walls, as well as systems based on the reinforced earth principle, and cushion walls (made from geotextile). > Chapter 3.1 What all these construction methods have in common is that construction begins at the bottom, assuming sufficient working space is available.

Gravity walls
This wall-reinforcing principle, which existed before the invention of steel-reinforced concrete and can be seen, for instance, in many fortified castles, involves opposing the lateral and oblique-acting forces of the bulk of the

Wall thickness [cm]	Wall surface area size [m²]		
	ε = 1.0	1.0 < ε < 2.0	ε ≥ 2.0
11.5	16 (24*)		10.6 (16*)
17.5	20 (40*)	to be interpolated	14 (28*)
24.0	36 (72*)		25 (50*)

Aspect ratio ε = h/l, if h ≥ l or ε = l/h l ≥ h
* Aspect ratio ε = h/l ≥ 2,0 and compressive strength ≥ 20 (e.g. natural stone)

Tab. 3.5.2: Permitted wall surface area size, depending on wall height. Aspect ratio ε = l/h

Wall thickness [cm]	Wall height [m]	Spacing of pillars [m]	Pillars made from	
			Steel molding S235JR, hot-dip galvanized	Steel concrete * b/d [cm]
11.5	0–2.00	5.00	IPE 140	12/24
	2.00–3.00	4.00		
17.5	0.70–2.00	6.00	IPE 200	24/18
	2.00–3.00	5.00		
24.0	1.30–2.00	8.00	IPE 260	24/24
	2.00–3.00	6.00		

* according to statics calculations

Tab. 3.5.3: Standard values for pillar spacing for stiffened walls

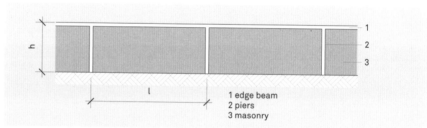

1 edge beam
2 piers
3 masonry

Fig. 3.5.3: Stiffened wall with pillars and edge beams

Wall thickness d [cm]	Pillar spacing * [m]
11.5	3.00
17.5	5.00
24.0	6.00

* Reinforcement with concrete steel rods 4 m long, Bst III/Ø 6 mm

Tab. 3.5.4: Standard values for pillar spacing for reinforced, freestanding walls

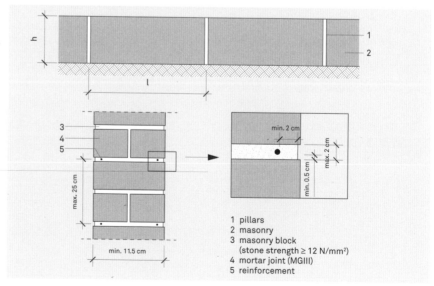

1 pillars
2 masonry
3 masonry block (stone strength ≥ 12 N/mm²)
4 mortar joint (MGIII)
5 reinforcement

Fig. 3.5.4: Reinforced masonry, placement of reinforcement rods

Fig. 3.5.5: Gravity walls of
Hohenzollern Castle, Hechingen

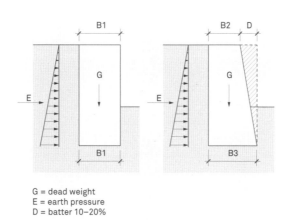

Fig. 3.5.6: Functioning principle of gravity walls

G = dead weight
E = earth pressure
D = batter 10–20%

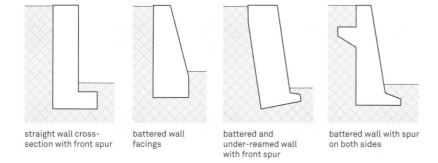

straight wall cross-
section with front spur

battered wall
facings

battered and
under-reamed wall
with front spur

battered wall with spur
on both sides

Fig. 3.5.7: Differently shaped types of gravity walls

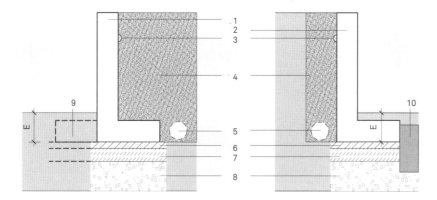

1 angle with outer visible side and T-element
   (backfilling, nonbonding)
2 angle with inner visible side
   (backfilling, nonbonding)
3 transport lugs, height dependent on height
   of element, sleeve dowel optional)
4 backfill with drainable, compacted material
5 drainage
6 5 cm screed mixture
7 10 cm concrete C16/20
8 30 cm frost-safe material, e.g. ballast
9 lateral spread as T-element possible
10 abutment should be constructed in situ

E = key depth = min. height of sole thickness

Fig. 3.5.9: Installation of angle supports

Fig. 3.5.8: Angle support wall—made from pre-cast
concrete components

soil, to the dead weight of the wall. > Fig. 3.5.5 Today, gravity walls are usually constructed from concrete or steel-
reinforced concrete using stable construction methods.
A rectangular wall cross section can be used for low wall
heights. As the wall height increases, the side exposed to
the air should have a 10–20% batter, adapting the wall
cross section to the stresses acting on it, which are heavi-
est at the base. With regard to the optical effect, battering a wall above eye level may be advisable, in order to
minimize its solid appearance. In addition, the earth side
of the wall can be under-reamed or given a toe wall to reduce the attacking soil pressure. > Figs. 3.5.6 and 3.5.7

Angle support walls

For an angle support wall, the additional load of the earth
on the horizontal arm is added to the dead weight of the
gravity wall. > Figs. 3.5.8 and 3.5.9 It therefore requires
less material than the gravity wall. However, the space
required for construction is broader, and the extra arm
makes the earth-moving involved more extensive, meaning that angle support walls are mainly used in backfilling
situations. To reduce the size of the needed cut into the
earth somewhat, the need for toe walls can be fulfilled on
the air-side as well. An additional air-side spur is optional
and is determined on the basis of statics and function and
calculated separately (incision reduction). > Chapter 1.7
Due to the surface area they occupy, angle support walls
can be built on ground with a lower loadbearing capacity.
Angle supports are usually made and installed as concrete finished parts. > DIN 1045 Surfaces are usually
smooth exposed concrete, but their appearance can be
adapted to the situation using surface design techniques
for concrete. Angle support walls can also be manufactured using in-situ concrete, although this usually requires a greater wall thickness than for finished parts.
For heights of up to 2.0 m, a large number of predimen-
sioned finished parts for the appropriate heights, base
and construction lengths and a variety of wall thicknesses are available, all designed for the standard loading condition of p= 5.0 kN/m². > Fig. 3.5.10 and tab. 3.5.5
Construction heights of over 2.0 m require a special
statics certificate for the specific instance. However,
walls of lesser heights can certainly pose a danger as

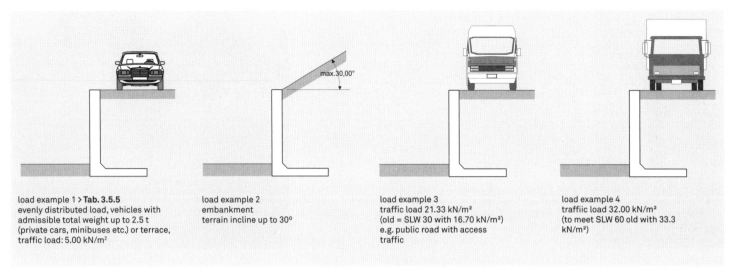

load example 1 > **Tab. 3.5.5**
evenly distributed load, vehicles with
admissible total weight up to 2.5 t
(private cars, minibuses etc.) or terrace,
traffic load: 5.00 kN/m²

load example 2
embankment
terrain incline up to 30°

load example 3
traffic load 21.33 kN/m²
(old = SLW 30 with 16.70 kN/m²)
e.g. public road with access
traffic

load example 4
traffiic load 32.00 kN/m²
(to meet SLW 60 old with 33.3
kN/m²)

Fig. 3.5.10: Loading conditions

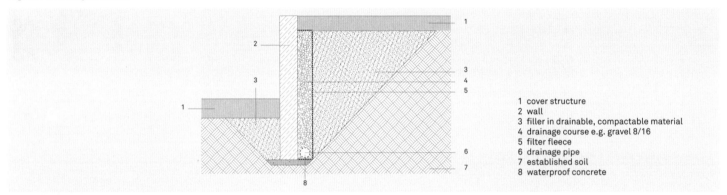

1 cover structure
2 wall
3 filler in drainable, compactable material
4 drainage course e.g. gravel 8/16
5 filter fleece
6 drainage pipe
7 established soil
8 waterproof concrete

Fig. 3.5.11: Retaining wall drain-age principle

well if fundamental statics principles are not applied.
Angle support walls should be installed on building
ground with a sufficient loadbearing capacity, preferably on a frost-safe, level concrete foundation on a ballast or gravel base course, in order to avoid any settling
or misalignment of the elements.

For construction heights of more than approx 5.0 m,
the components should be rear-anchored in backfilling
material, to prevent deformation as well as to actually
enable construction in the first place.

Drainage of retaining walls

The drainage of retaining walls is very important, as a
buildup of seepage water can endanger the stability of
the whole wall by changing the soil structure around
the wall's base, or by creating higher compressive
loads against the wall's face. To prevent this, the soil
behind the wall must be drained. This involves sealing
the excavation base with waterproofing concrete. On
top, a drainage conduit jacketed with a 30–80 cm filter
layer (depending on soil and backfill material) is laid. To
safeguard the filter's performance in the long term, a
filter fleece should be laid over the filter layer to prevent
penetration of fine soil elements into the filter element.
For the rear side of the wall, a reliably draining material
that ensures rapid dissipation of seepage water, thereby
preventing water buildup, should be applied up beneath

H	F	B	D	kg
Construction length 50				
Loading condition 1				
40	25	50	10	72
50	30	50	10	90
60	35	50	10	110
70	50	50	10	138
80	50	50	10	150
90	50	50	10	162

H	F	B	D	kg
Construction length 100				
Loading condition 1				
40	25	100	10	144
50	30	100	10	180
60	35	100	10	216
70	50	100	10	276
80	50	100	10	300
90	50	100	10	324
100	60	100	10	372

Tab. 3.5.5: Standard dimensioning of corner supports as
finished parts

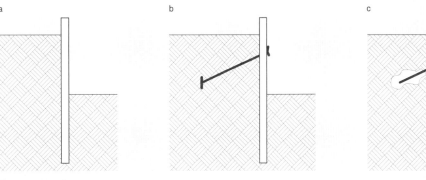

a) sheet pile wall
b) rear-anchoring using earth anchor
c) rear-anchoring using concrete anchoring

Fig. 3.5.12: Functioning principle and rear anchoring of sheet pile walls

Fig. 3.5.13 a–c): Construction of a sheet pile wall with concrete cladding

the covering on the top of the wall. All the accumulated drainage water has to drain away. > Fig. 3.5.11

Special retaining wall types

In contrast to gravity walls, angle retaining walls and console walls, palisades and sheet pile walls are protected against toppling by anchoring in the building ground rather than by their own mass.

Sheet pile walls

Sheet pile walls consist of individual moldings rammed, shaken (vibrated) or pressed in to create a secure and watertight formation. The installation method depends on both the conditions on the building ground and the permitted vibration and noise emissions. The embedment depth for a sheet pile wall increases as the required support height increases. Moldings are usually made out of steel, with varying profiles. In some cases, they may also be made of wood, steel-reinforced concrete or plastic. For greater support heights, the upper part of sheet pile walls should be rear-anchored into the ground. > Fig. 3.5.12 This reduces bending stress, allowing the embedment depth to be reduced. The top of the sheet pile wall can be additionally stiffened using a concrete beam or an appropriate steel molding.

Palisades

Palisades are usually dug in, and are available in a variety of measurements and materials such as wood, concrete and plastic. Wood palisades in particular have only

Material	Dimensions in cm				
	height above ground level to about	key depth	overall length	diameter	cross-sections
Round timber and timber thresholds	50	50	100	8	–
	105	75	180	8	–
	160	100	260	–	16/26
	180	120	300	12	–
	210	140	350	15	–
Concrete crust slabs	40	20	60	12–17	12/12
	70	30	100	20	12/12
	100	50	150	20	14/18
	130	70	200	20	14/18
Natural stone pallisade	30	20	50	–	12/12
	50	25	75	–	12/12
	70	30	100	–	12/12, 7/20
	100	50	150	–	12/12, 7/20
	170	80	250	–	10/25
Natural stone	120–200	80	~200–300		thickness: ~7–20 width: ~80–100

Tab. 3.5.6: Dimensions for pallisades and concrete crust slabs for retaining walls, standard measures

Sources include: Informationsdienst Holz, Fa. CreaBeton, Fa. Kann, Fa. Jonastone, Fa. Hubert Killing

limited suitability as support constructions. They should only be installed in permeable, compacted material, in order to reduce water buildup and rotting. Setting in a concrete foundation is not appropriate to wood's material properties.

The dimensions in the tables can be used as standard values for the installation of palisades. > Tab. 3.5.6

NONSTABLE CONSTRUCTION METHODS

As well as their basic properties as freestanding elements or supportive components, walls can be divided into stable and nonstable structures.

The essential property of a nonstable construction method is its restriction to an undemanding, simple

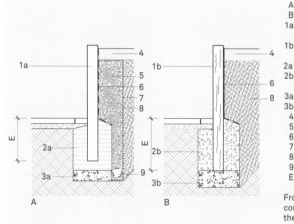

A Concrete palisade
B Wood palisade
1a Concrete or natural stone palisade
1b Wood palisade or wood threshold
2a Concrete foundation
2b Foundation, permitting drainage e.g. Aggregate 0/32
3a Clean layer
3b Drainage layer
4 Surfacing construction
5 Drainage, e. g. gravel
6 Sealing sheet
7 Filter fleece
8 Filler soil, permeable
9 Drainage pipe
E Binding depth approx. 1/3 Total length
Frostproof foundation beyond construction height above 100 cm of the ground's upper edge

Fig. 3.5.14: Installation principle for retaining wall palisades

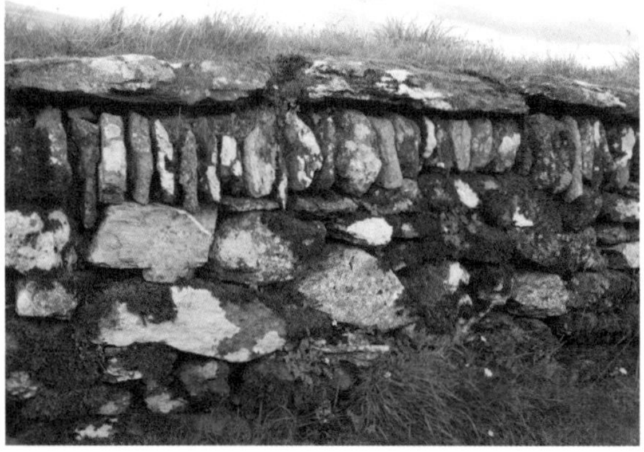

Fig. 3.5.15: Drystone wall made from layered stone slabs

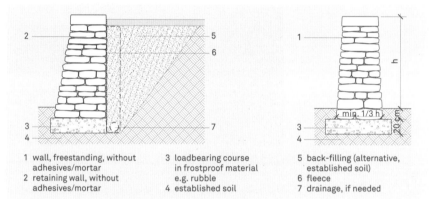

1 wall, freestanding, without adhesives/mortar
2 retaining wall, without adhesives/mortar
3 loadbearing course in frostproof material e.g. rubble
4 established soil
5 back-filling (alternative, established soil)
6 fleece
7 drainage, if needed

Fig. 3.5.16: Nonstable construction principle

Fig. 3.5.17: Soil gabions at the BUGA Gera und Ronneburg

Fig. 3.5.18: Stone gabions at the BUGA Gera und Ronneburg

Fig. 3.5.19: Detail showing steel basket with stone filling

Fig. 3.5.20: Stone gabion wall

foundation with no static function and a general lack of bonding agents. Foundations are usually low-strength gravel or ballast base courses (10–20 cm depending on grain distribution, or up to 40 cm for drystone walls) and are only able to keep out rising groundwater (frost-free foundation). The building ground must be capable of taking up the compressive forces. For this reason, nonstable construction methods are only possible on vegetated soils. On a small scale, a nonstable construction is more elastic than a stable one, allowing it to adjust to settling of the soil after installation without losing its constructive properties. As well as drystone walls, angle support walls made from finished parts below a certain height and palisades, as described in the "Retaining walls" section, are examples of this construction method. Additionally, there are special hanging systems such as crib walls made from planting dishes and finished part tubs on the market. Filled support elements such as soil or stone gabions can be constructed in a stable or nonstable fashion, depending on the desired height.

Drystone walls made from natural stone

Natural stone drystone walls may be made from simply dressed quarrystones or found stones, or from elaborately dressed stones, as described in the "Stable construction methods" section.

The major differences in individual stone wall design result from the locally available stone and its properties. > Chapter 1.5 Cavities between the stones must be as small as possible. Precisely fitting chocks wedge the stones together, replacing the bonding effect of mortar. Drystone walls can only be constructed as freestanding walls or simple gravity walls. Adding soil to the joints enables greening using rockery herbaceous plants. Construction using irregular stones put together without mortar is not covered under DIN 1053—Masonry. However, this kind of traditional drystone wall construction method is still used, relying on traditional rules and experience, although it cannot be calculated in engineering terms because standardized stones, which are the basis for such calculations, are not involved. > Figs. 3.5.15 and 3.5.16

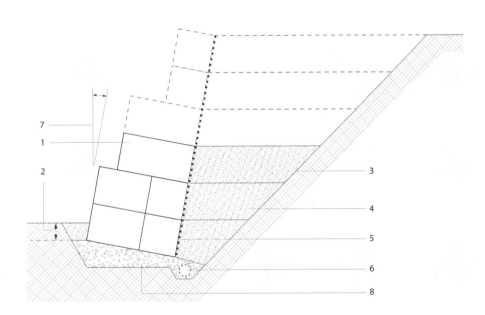

1 framework, wire baskets with soil, stone or special filler
2 keyed into the soil
3 excavated embankment
4 backfill, sealed, drainable
5 where necessary, fleece to separate from non filter-stable soil/filler materials
6 drainpipe
7 slope, achieved by tilting and/or by staggered installation (up to 6° ≡ 10.5%)
8 foundations frostproof, concrete foundation where necessary

Fig. 3.5.21: Installation principle for "box" gabions

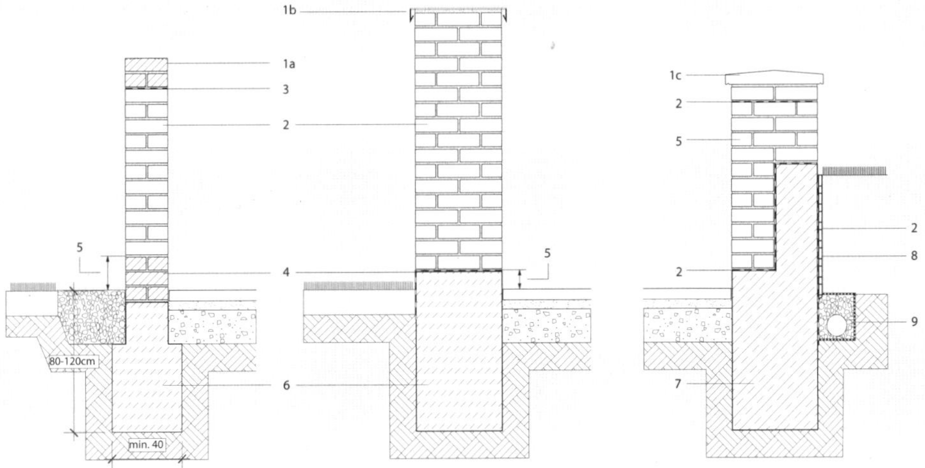

1 wall topping, a): brick blocks or chippings with slope or joints-mortar in the slope, b): sheet metal covering, c): concrete or natural stone slab with drip channel
2 Freestanding brick masonry (non-reinforced and mortared with M II or M IIa (e. g. M 2.5 or M 5 as defined by EN 998-2) and reinforced with M III (e. g. M 10 as defined by EN 998-2)
3 Barrier course/seal (e. g. bituminous sealing coat)
4 Barrier mortar in capping/ wall foundation areas
5 Splash zone protected by barrier mortar or by constructing a concrete foundation; at least 10 cm above upper edge of ground
6 concrete foundations, frostproof (C12/15–C20/25)
7 concrete foundations, frostfree, reinforced
8 drainage mat/drainage gravel
9 drainage, fleece-clad

Fig. 3.5.22: Stable construction method principle

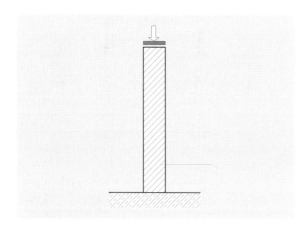

Fig. 3.5.23: Principle for one-shelled walls

Soil and stone gabions

Gabions are a type of filled support element. They function like gravity walls. Here, however, filling materials like stones, soil and broken glass are packed into a casing to create the necessary weight. To prevent the casing, which usually consists of wire netting, being deformed by the pressure of the filling material, struts must be built in between the casing walls. Due to the higher dead weight, stone filling reduces the necessary volume of the support element in relation to soil filling. For soil gabions, the material is kept within the casing by a geotextile, and can be greened. > Fig. 3.5.17 Gabions are usually manufactured in blocks. Prefabricated grid boxes are filled and stacked on top of each other. > Figs. 3.5.18–3.5.20 Alternatively, two initial walls can be built and then connected together. Finally, the filling material is added. Like retaining walls, gabions should be protected by appropriate drainage. A batter and in some cases angling the wall by tipping it over slightly (up to 10°) is also advisable for walls above a certain height. With the block construction method, a batter can easily be created through stepped arrangement of the individual elements. A gabion wall is generally founded on a frost-free layer. > Fig. 3.5.21 On building ground with a low loadbearing capacity, a stable concrete foundation is required.

STABLE CONSTRUCTION METHODS

Stable construction methods have frost-safe foundations and are held together by hardened bonding agents (mortar). > Fig. 3.5.27 and chapter 2.3 Foundations This rigid construction is required to prevent movement caused by frost or settling of the building ground, as this could cause cracks in the construction. Vital minimum requirements for a stable construction method are the use of a frost-safe bonding agent, appropriate expansion joints along the course of the wall and a covering for the wall crown as protection from rainwater penetration, as well as a concrete foundation at least 80 cm deep (up to the soil's vegetation layer if necessary). Apart from concrete, the most commonly used materials are brick and natural stone. However, older construction materials such as clay or wood, or modern ones such as steel, glass or plastics can also be used.

One-shelled walls

For one-shelled walls, the whole cross section is involved in load transfer. Where the wall's core and the

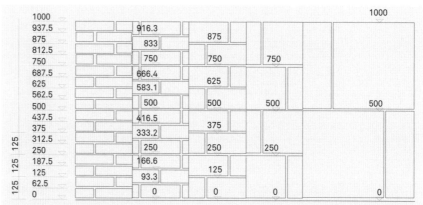

	NM	NM	NM	DM	NM	DM	DM
Stone height (mm)	52	71	113	123	238	248	499
Horizontal joint thickness (mm)	10.5	12.3	12	1–3	12	1–3	1–3
Layer height (mm)	62.5	83.3	125	125	250	250	500
Specimen forms	DF	NF	1.5 NF	2 DF	4 DF	planned element	

NM = normal mortar, DM = thin bed mortar

Fig. 3.5.24: Stone and layer heights

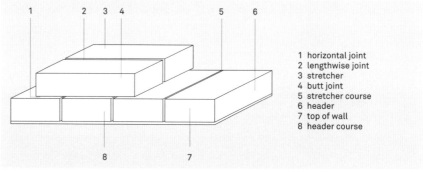

1 horizontal joint
2 lengthwise joint
3 stretcher
4 butt joint
5 stretcher course
6 header
7 top of wall
8 header course

Fig. 3.5.25: Terms in masonry construction

exposed surfaces are made of different materials, these form a structure. > Fig. 3.5.23

Full masonry

With full masonry, which can be made from brick, sand-lime brick or natural stone, the external facing stones are laid in a regular bond with the core wall stones, using mortar.

The thickness of freestanding walls can be calculated as described in the "Freestanding walls" section.
The wall thicknesses can further be calculated by the standardized wall stone formats. For this, the preferred dimensions are normal format (NF) at 240 x 115 x 71 and thin format (DF) at 240 x 115 x 52 mm. Further intermediate formats can be derived from these, allowing a variety of wall cross sections to be composed. > Fig. 3.5.24 and chapter 1.6 Brick and clinker

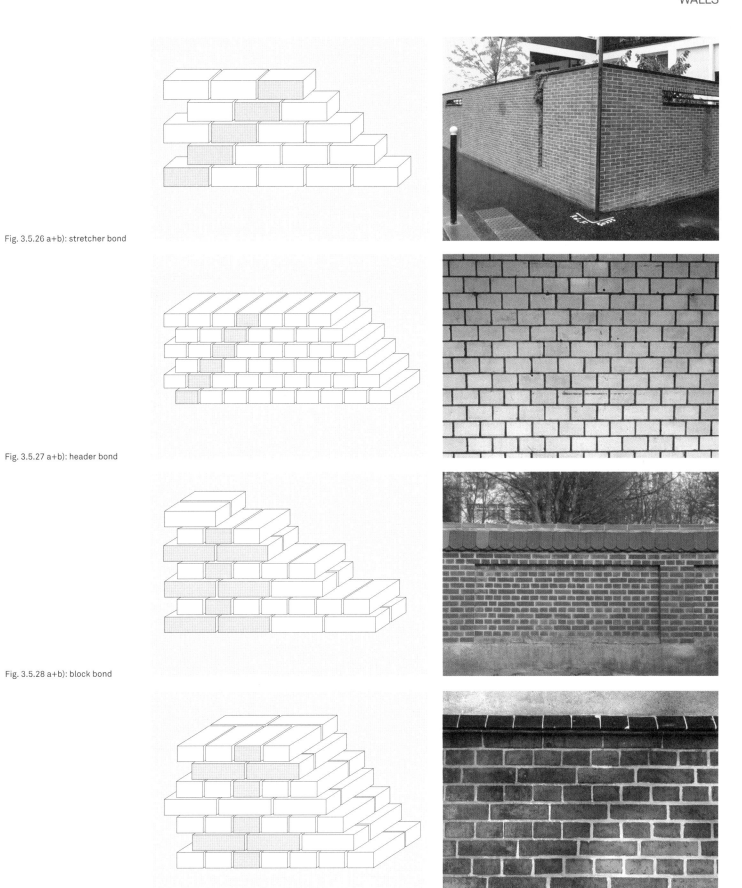

Fig. 3.5.26 a+b): stretcher bond

Fig. 3.5.27 a+b): header bond

Fig. 3.5.28 a+b): block bond

Fig. 3.5.29 a+b): cross bond

10 mm is usually added to these stone formats to allow for the horizontal joints, and 12 mm for the vertical butt joints (depending on the absorption capacity of the stones and the mortar used). This makes two stone breadths and a butt joint equal to a stone's length. > Fig. 3.5.25 This standardizing of the format allows different precisely fitting masonry bonds to be created. The formats are also based on a brick height of 1.00 m.

If walls are not plastered, their minimum width should be 30 cm, to enable the construction to resist driving rain. The wall should be constructed to keep out damp, as this can endanger the stability of the whole wall. As well as taking measures against seepage water in the surrounding soil, a barrier layer should be installed 15–20 cm above covering height to exclude rising damp. Otherwise, the result will be undesired lime efflorescence in the cement mortar, and growth of mold and algae. > Chapter 2.3 Foundations

Brick masonry bonds

Bonds are necessary to uniformly distribute and transfer load. For one-shelled brick walls, it is essential to ensure that the facing bricks and any backing-up bricks within the wall have the same water absorption ratio, the same capillary conduction capacity and the same strength. In general, the following courses are distinguished for a wall, from which a variety of bonds can be created: stretcher course = the long side is exposed; header course = the narrow side is exposed; upright course = narrow side, on-edge is exposed side. There are also special courses such as diagonal courses (with bricks laid face down or on their side), for which the bricks are placed together at an angle.

When bonds are laid, the stones must be installed on top of continuous horizontal joints and in alignment. To ensure stability, butt joints in different courses must be offset in relation to each other. This is usually done by laying half a stone across. The offset must be at least 0.4 times the stone height (at least 4.5 cm). All joints must be closed completely using suitable mortar from the appropriate mortar group, so that stones are laid with total surface contact and irregularities can be evened out.

Four basic bonds and further decorative bonds can be derived from these courses. > Figs. 3.5.26–3.5.29 The use of decorative bonds for facing including colored stones is another area where considerable regional differences exist.

Well-known decorative bonds include Gothic bond, flying or monk bond, Flemish, and Tannenburg bond. > Figs. 3.5.30–3.5.34 Decorative bonds generally have no loadbearing function and are either integrated into the masonry behind by individual headers or constructed as two-shelled masonry. Other masonry bonds widespread on the regional level often do not strictly meet standards, but can still be carried out by individual specialists drawing on traditional experience. These constructions often show a striking play of forms, colors and materials, sometimes possible only by ignoring normative

Fig. 3.5.30: Gothic bond   Fig. 3.5.31: Dutch bond

Figs. 3.5.32–3.5.34: Various decorative bonds

Fig. 3.5.35 a+b): Rubblestone masonry, cemetery in Chur, Switzerland

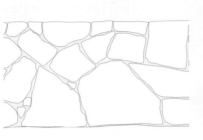

Fig. 3.5.36 a+b): Cyclopean masonry

Fig. 3.5.37 a+b): Coursed rubble masonry

constraints. However, these construction methods usually involve traditional minimum requirements and rules that the master builders observe.

Natural stone masonry bonds

As well as the nonstable drystone wall construction method, there are also stable mortared masonry structures made from natural stone, which heighten the formal variety of natural stone walls via more irregular joint patterns and a wider range of stone formats. The following types of natural stone masonry bonds exist:

Rubblestone masonry: A variety of different forms and sizes of minimally dressed, usually regional quarrystones gives the masonry a heterogeneous appearance. Due to this heterogeneity, only low compressive stresses are permitted. The total thickness of the masonry must be balanced perpendicular to the direction of force, with vertical intervals of 1.50 m maximum. Stone

sizes from 200 x 100 x 50 mm to 900 x 450 x 450 mm are used. The joint breadth is 10–15 mm. Wall thicknesses begin at 450 mm and increase in increments of 250 mm.

Cyclopean masonry: This is a variant of rubblestone masonry. The joints are made diagonal by the mainly rounded or polygonal stones.

Coursed rubble masonry: This has a more regular appearance than the masonry bonds mentioned above, due to the worked horizontal and butt joints in the visible surfaces, which must have a depth of at least 12 cm. The course thickness can change in between courses, and within a course. The same stone sizes, wall and joint thicknesses as for rubblestone masonry are used. A balance in the direction of force is also advisable here.

Fig. 3.5.38 a+b): Irregular-coursed rubble masonry

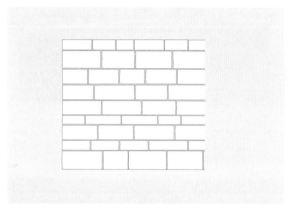

Fig. 3.5.39 a+b): Regular-coursed rubble masonry

Fig. 3.5.40 a+b): Ashlar masonry

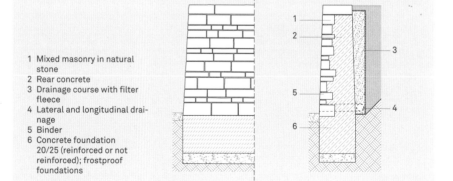

1 Mixed masonry in natural
  stone
2 Rear concrete
3 Drainage course with filter
  fleece
4 Lateral and longitudinal drainage
5 Binder
6 Concrete foundation
  20/25 (reinforced or not
  reinforced); frostproof
  foundations

Fig. 3.5.41: Combined masonry   Fig. 3.5.42: Principle of concrete-backed wall

Irregular-coursed rubble masonry: Horizontal and butt joints must be exactly vertical in relation to each other and to the surface. The worked butt and horizontal joint depth here is 15 cm, with a maximum joint width for the visible surface of 3 cm. The courses and course heights are still allowed to change.

Regular-coursed rubble masonry: Specifications the same as for irregular coursed rubble masonry. However, a change in stone height within a course is no longer permitted. The stones must be worked to the horizontal joint throughout the wall's thickness. Wall thicknesses are 240 mm and upwards, derived from the standard formats for wall stones. The joint breadth is 8–22 mm for butt joints and 10–15 mm for horizontal joints.

Ashlar masonry: The natural stone must be worked precisely to the measurements derived from the wall thicknesses. This affects all butt and horizontal joints along their whole length. All the stones in a course must be of the same height. Wall thicknesses are derived from the standard formats.

Combined masonry

In order to reduce costs, expensive natural stone or clinker is often only used for the outer, facing layer. It can be integrated with the core to form a loadbearing cross section. This is described as nonleading facing masonry. To achieve static unity, the facing stones must be laid in a bond with the stones behind them. The facing layer must also contain at least 30% header

Fig. 3.5.44: In-situ concrete wall, kindergarten Griechische Allee, Berlin-Treptow

stones. The headers must be at least 24 cm long and be embedded at least 10 cm deep in the masonry lying behind. Headers lying above or below must be at least 115 cm long, and the length must be equal to at least 1/3 of their exposed height. Where natural stones are integrated into the wall's core, every third course must be a header course.

Combined masonry walls usually have concrete backing, i.e. are constructed with a concrete core. > Fig. 3.5.42

In-situ and exposed concrete walls

In-situ and exposed concrete walls are erected using in-situ concrete or as finished concrete parts on a frost-safe foundation, constructed onsite. The various technical requirements for the construction of concrete structures depending on installation site, function, dimensions and the desired surface appearance should

Fig. 3.5.43: In-situ concrete wall, park on ULAP grounds, Berlin-Mitte

Fig. 3.5.45: Slender concrete steles (628 x 70 x 12 cm), combined heat and power plant, Darmstadt

Fig. 3.5.46: Material detail on rammed clay wall

Fig. 3.5.47: Rammed clay wall, Bundesgartenschau Schwerin

Fig. 3.5.48: Rammed clay wall with horizontal brick bands, Gärten der Welt, Berlin-Marzahn

Fig. 3.5.49: Rammed concrete wall, Erzbischöfliches Diözesanmuseum, Cologne

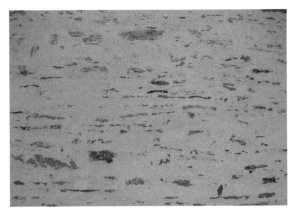

Fig. 3.5.50: Material detail: whitewashed masonry

Fig. 3.5.52: Whitewashed masonry, Sammlung Bastian, Berlin-Mitte

Fig. 3.5.51: Colorfully stuccoed wall, Bundesgartenschau Munich

be taken into account. > Chapter 1.7 Concrete As well as the precise concrete formula, the type of reinforcement and the construction of the joints are significant for construction. The fundamental difference between the design quality of concrete construction parts in architecture and, for instance, in structural engineering, where a different set of technical regulations applies. Apart from the static precepts, minimum wall thicknesses derive primarily from the covering required for reinforcement and the intervals between the reinforcement elements, as well as—particularly in high-rise construction—minimum fire protection standards. The usual wall thickness is therefore around 15–20 cm. > Figs. 3.5.43–3.5.45, and chapter 1.7 Concrete

Rammed earth walls

Rammed clay walls are one of the oldest known wall construction methods, although in many areas they have been forgotten. More recently, the clay construction method, which in our part of the world was traditionally used in timber-frame construction, has enjoyed a minor renaissance. Among other factors, this is unquestionably due to the properties of clay as a flexible construction material with a high loadbearing capacity. If certain rules are observed, clay can also be durable when used outdoors. Its major design properties are the natural feel of the material, the clay color tones and the surface texture. Dryness and moisture cause clay to shrink and swell. By adding mineral or plant aggregates, dryness shrinkage and crack formation can be minimized, the tensile, compressive and abrasive resistance strength increased, and the water sensitivity

reduced. Monolithic rammed clay walls must always be founded on a solid pedestal and foundation, preferably made of concrete and frost-free. To protect from spray water, the pedestal should be at least 50 cm high, as continual dampness will destroy the clay. Rising damp must also be prevented in construction by using a barrier layer. On the solid pedestal and using formwork, as with concrete construction, special layers of high-strength rammed clay is installed damp, in layer thicknesses of 10–15 cm and well compacted. The layers remain visible. It is important to ensure that the clay does not become wet during installation. The structure must therefore be protected from water until it dries out, and indeed in the long term. A cover on top of the wall is therefore essential.

With modifications, a similar effect can be created using rammed concrete. > Figs. 3.5.46–3.5.49

Stuccoed and whitewashed masonry

Walls are usually stuccoed for design reasons (e.g. color), but stucco may also be important in construction terms (e.g. repel water and dirt). A distinction is made between stucco with mineral and organic bonding agents. Stucco is applied in one or several layers, and only takes on its final form after hardening on the construction. Stucco usually consists of special mortars. Before application, the ground must be prepared by spraying, roughened and wet until it reaches the required level of dryness, so that the stucco can bond durably with the structure. The stucco layer thickness, including primer, is usually about 20 mm. If masonry is to be provided with a barrier layer to prevent rising damp, then reinforced under- and

Fig. 3.5.54: Stainless steel walls as a structural element

Fig. 3.5.53: Soundproofing wall made from freestanding, edged steel sheets, Berlin-Spandau

Fig. 3.5.55: Material detail wickerwork

Fig. 3.5.56: Blackthorn-brushwood walls, Landesgartenschau Wolfsburg

Fig. 3.5.57: Wickerwork as a structural element, Castle La Roche-Jagu, Ploëzal

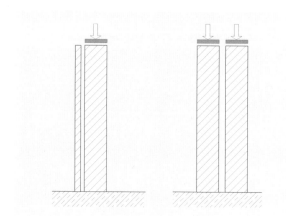

1 support plane
2 anchor rail
3 bracket anchor
4 facing/cladding masonry

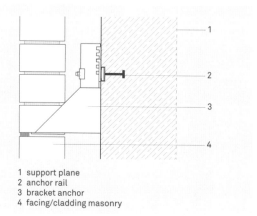

Fig. 3.5.58: Two-shelled wall principle

Fig. 3.5.60: Anchoring of facing masonry

Fig. 3.5.59: Facing, basalt natural stone masonry

over-rendering should be added and continued beyond the barrier layer. The rendering reinforcement is bonded tightly with the masonry. Stucco can be grouped according to the type of surface treatment involved. A distinction is made between smoothed stucco (worked with a smoothing trowel), textured stucco (rubbed down using various tools), trowel-thrown stucco (thrown at the wall), troweled stucco (spread in fan and fishscale shapes), gunned stucco (applied using stucco guns), scraped stucco (patterned by scraping with a nailboard) and washed stucco (bonding slurry is washed away before hardening). > Figs. 3.5.50–3.5.52

A historical type of stucco involves applying hydraulic lime, which differs from the average modern-day cement mortar due to its bonding agents (Portland cement was first discovered and brought into circulation in the early to mid-19th century.) Lime was often used for its disinfecting properties, or for physical construction reasons (e.g. its tendency to heat up less due to the white surface that reflect the sunlight), especially in southern countries. This kind of stucco has recently been rediscovered. Here also, the ground must be wet well beforehand. The hydraulic lime can then be applied using small or large brushes or a spatula, or sprayed on.

Simple steel walls

For design purposes, metal sheets can also be used to enclose smaller changes in terrain height. These must be worked to have the correct profile and stiffened on the rear side to prevent bowing. An angle that allows the additional load on the horizontal arm to be harnessed statically is favorable. With metals, corrosion behavior should be taken into account, as this factor limits durability. This can be counteracted by using corrosion-resistant metal types or sufficient material thickness, or by giving the rear side a corrosion-resistant coating. > Chapter 1.8 On the whole, however, metals are rather unsuitable for installing in direct contact with the soil. They are more suited to two-shelled construction with an air gap. > Figs. 3.5.53 and 3.5.54

Wickerwork

In British and French gardens in particular, supports made from wickerwork, traditionally used to enclose high beds, were once and are now once again becoming widespread. Taking into account their limited durability, impressive low-height surrounds and elements for controlling changes in height can be created. > Figs. 3.5.55–3.5.57 This involves creating a horizontal weave similar to a basket in between vertical wood rods. > Fig. 3.1.9c In order to increase durability and retain the soil, a geotextile should be installed on the soil side.

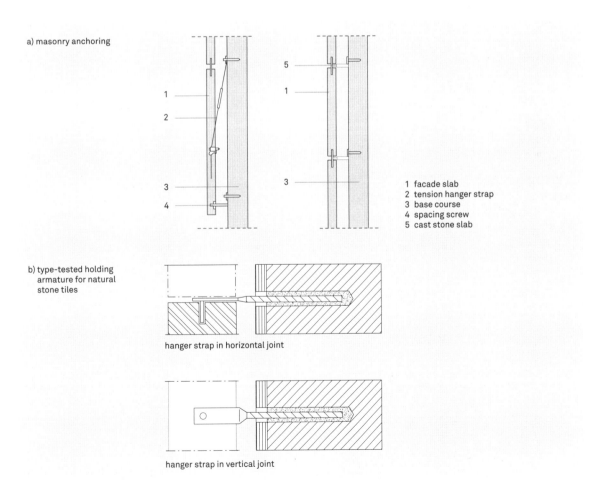

a) masonry anchoring

1
2
3
4

5
1
3

1 facade slab
2 tension hanger strap
3 base course
4 spacing screw
5 cast stone slab

b) type-tested holding armature for natural stone tiles

hanger strap in horizontal joint

hanger strap in vertical joint

Fig. 3.5.61: Specimen anchoring methods

Fig. 3.5.62: Detailed view of anchor with natural stone tile

Fig. 3.5.63: Loadbearing steel subconstruction

Fig. 3.5.64: Mounting the natural stone plates in layers using anchors

Fig. 3.5.65: Natural stone clad steel construction, Berlin-Mitte

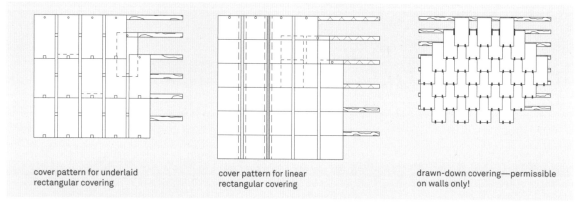

cover pattern for underlaid rectangular covering

cover pattern for linear rectangular covering

drawn-down covering—permissible on walls only!

Fig. 3.5.66: Facade cladding using slate covering

Two-shelled walls

Unlike the one-shelled wall, the two-shelled wall has a second facing layer with no static function. This permits a still greater freedom of surface design, as no static bond is required between the two shells. However, it does make an appropriately safe and durable anchoring necessary. > Fig. 3.5.58

Facing masonry for facing shell

The term faced brickwork is used if the veneer is → 90 mm. If the veneer is thinner, the terms mortar and masonry (55-90mm) exterior wall cladding are used. The cladding can be applied to the wall in the form of very thin sheets (e.g. tiles) using thick or thin plaster or mortar beds. Veneers of 90-115 mm thickness may protrude above the support to a max. height of 15 mm.

Classical masonry made from bricks or other masonry stones or natural stones > Fig. 3.5.59 can usually be used more economically to construct facings separate from the loadbearing construction. The loadbearing wall core is usually made from steel-reinforced concrete. On one side or both, a recess is provided in the loadbearing construction as a console to accommodate the facing. The facing may be rear ventilated or have solid mortar filling without cavities. It is a good idea to connect the facing masonry with the wall's core using anchors made from corrosion-resistant material (e.g. stainless steel). The anchors can be directly installed in the concrete core beforehand (e.g. anchor bars) or subsequently

hammered into the wall's surface. Alternatively, a wire anchor can be used. The number of anchors per surface unit and their thickness is determined according to the distance between the masonry shells and the height of the wall. The anchors contribute to a certain degree of load distribution in the construction. They are not visible on the outside after completion. > Fig. 3.5.60

Curtain facades

Other materials such as natural stone or concrete tiles, steel plates or steel weave, glass panes and wood or plastic slabs can be hung in front of loadbearing subconstructions using the curtain facade principle. The loadbearing construction is usually made from concrete or constructed from steel or wood frames. The construction requires precise planning, so that the anchors' grid pattern, which corresponds to the tile dimensions and joint widths, can subsequently be kept entirely consistent. For a freehanging construction method, wind loads must be borne in mind during construction. > Figs. 3.5.61–3.5.65

Sheet materials such as metal weaves or plastic membranes are usually stretched and secured on frame constructions made for the individual project. Other materials such as wood shingles or slate tiles can be secured to the wood subconstruction, in a manner similar to roof tiling. > Fig. 3.5.66

Fig. 3.5.67: Essential spatial joints as a design element in an exposed concrete wall, Bundesgartenschau Potsdam

Fig. 3.5.68: Stucco joints as decorative and structural elements, Schloss Köpenick, Berlin

Fig. 3.5.69: Ribbed joints, Friedrichswerdersche Kirche, Berlin

Fig. 3.5.70: Masonry and stucco covering, Sollbrüggenpark Krefeld

Fig. 3.5.73: Inclined upright clinker course as covering

Fig. 3.5.74: Roofing brick as covering

Joints

Due to shrinkage (reduction in mortar and concrete volume in the course of drying out) and temperature differences (from summer to winter), support walls change in length. To prevent these changes in length from causing uncontrolled crack formation, expansion joints should be included at intervals of approx. 6–8 m. They should be constructed to compensate for changes in length of approx. 2–8 mm. To absorb variations in soil pressure stresses, expansion joints can be constructed with interlocking teeth to prevent differences in incline.

As well as the necessary expansion, construction and spatial joints, visible concrete surfaces can be given dummy joints as a surface decoration element. This can be done via the formwork. For concrete elements, joints do not always have to be vertical and uniform. > Figs. 3.5.67 and 3.5.68 By means of intelligent joint design and arrangement, effective decoration can be created in this way. The minimum construction requirements for concrete joints, however, should be borne in mind. > Chapter 2.3 Connections For curtain facades, the joints between individual plates can be left open or closed using a permanently elastic filler material (e.g. silicone).

IIn masonry construction in particular, joints are a significant way of structuring the surface. As well as the mortaring of masonry joints necessary for construction, a number of possibilities exist for individual joints. > Fig. 3.5.69 There are a range of preserved historical joint construction methods, varying according to region and the masonry bonds used. The construction of unfilled vanity lines is also very significant.

Wall coverings

The wall's top must also be effectively protected against rainwater penetration. Like rising damp, it would do lasting damage to the structure. The surface should therefore have a lateral slope of at least 0.5% to allow the water to run off immediately. Only cross-joints are permitted in the covering. This minimizes the number of potential penetration points. To prevent the water from running over the visible surface, the covering should ideally protrude at least 3 cm, giving it a drip lip. A suitable inclined finished concrete part can be laid to form the covering. Alternatively, a metal covering can be mounted. For natural stone walls, covering tiles can be made of the same material; for brick masonry, inclined upright courses of thick clinker bricks can be used. Painstaking, cavity-free mortaring using trass-lime mortar is essential for a satisfactory result. > Figs. 3.5.70–3.5.73

Fig. 3.5.71: Metal cap covering

Fig. 3.5.72: Natural stone blocks of the same material as the wall as covering, Isola Bella, Italy

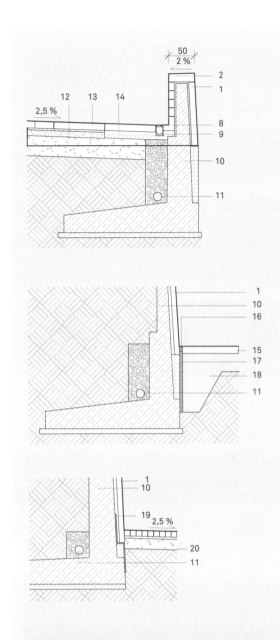

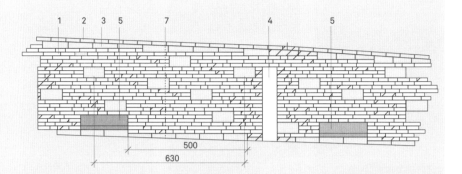

1 Wall facing: split limestone (thickness 10 cm, height 14.4 cm), in 3 different lengths 30–90 cm; sandstone ground 44.4 x 89.4 x 10 cm, natural-cleft sandstone compensating stones for stretcher rows; joints 6 mm, 5% batter, bars and T-head tie rods installed in shell of construction
2 Top of wall, sandstone 60 x 50 x 15 cm, joints 6 mm
3 Intermediate stones: sandstone, ground 10 cm thick, stone height above: 29–14 cm below: 45–50 cm.
4 Wall drainage construction, b = 60 cm, top fits precisely to horizontal joints
5 Wall bench made from sandstone (199 x 53.6 x 15–12 cm) with integrated backrest (199 x 50.3 x 10 cm) made from sandstone, ground, seat height 34–40 cm with 1% gradient
6 Expansion joint in concrete core
7 Toothed expansion joints in wall facing in area of expansion joint construction shell: horizontal joints 6 mm, butt joints 2 cm, securing of facing stones in area of expansion joints: At least 70% of the stone lengths are secured to one of the two construction shell L-stones, the remainder freely overlapping the expansion joint. Joint filling with permanently elastic material in the standard joint color.
8 L-stone special element: slope towards channel
9 Drainage channel
10 Concrete core with 5% batter
11 Drainage DN 150 in gravel packing 16/32 40 cm wide in geotextile
12 Asphalt surface (construction road) layer thickness: 10 cm
13 Magnum tiles 90+45/60/12 cm on 4 cm chippings 4/8, joints filled with hard stone crushed sand 0/3
14 Concrete C12/15
15 Basalt lava step, 10 cm thick
16 Permanently elastic joint filler, 10/5
17 Softboard mat
18 Connection to steps
19 Bituminous liquid film
20 Small stone 8/10 on 5 cm chippings 2/5

NATURAL STONE WALL IN BONIFATIUSPARK,
FRANKFURT AM MAIN, GERMANY

Bernard und Sattler Landschaftsarchitekten, Berlin
Completion: 2006

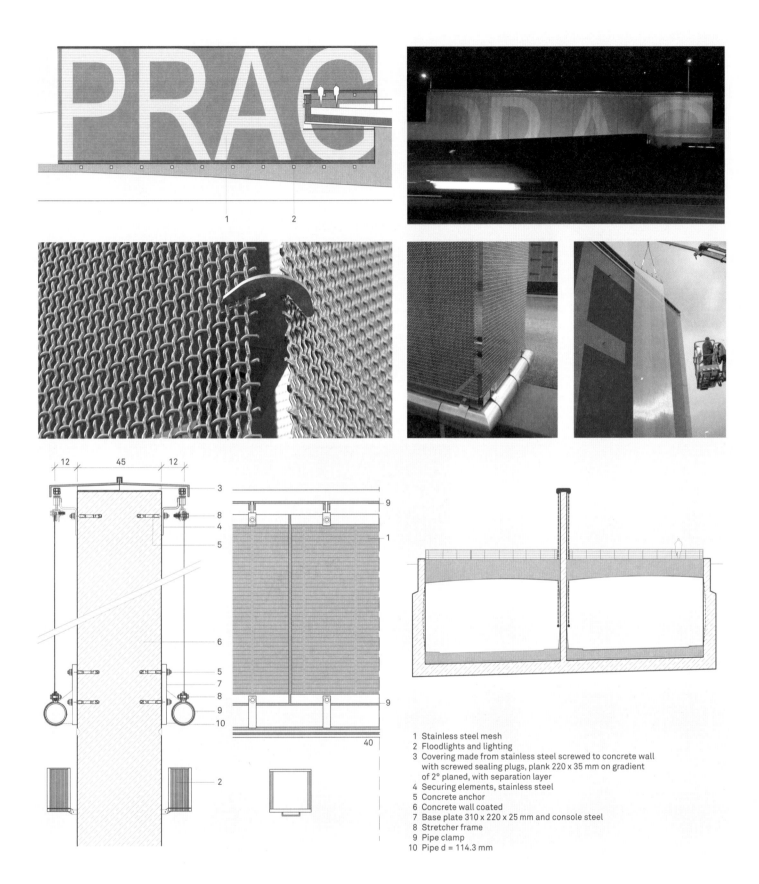

1 Stainless steel mesh
2 Floodlights and lighting
3 Covering made from stainless steel screwed to concrete wall
   with screwed sealing plugs, plank 220 x 35 mm on gradient
   of 2° planed, with separation layer
4 Securing elements, stainless steel
5 Concrete anchor
6 Concrete wall coated
7 Base plate 310 x 220 x 25 mm and console steel
8 Stretcher frame
9 Pipe clamp
10 Pipe d = 114.3 mm

IN-SITU CONCRETE WALL WITH METAL CURTAIN:
PRAGSATTEL-LÖWENTOR TUNNEL PROJECT,
STUTTGART, GERMANY

Architects: SCALA, Esefeld & Prof. Nagler, Stuttgart
Completion: 2007

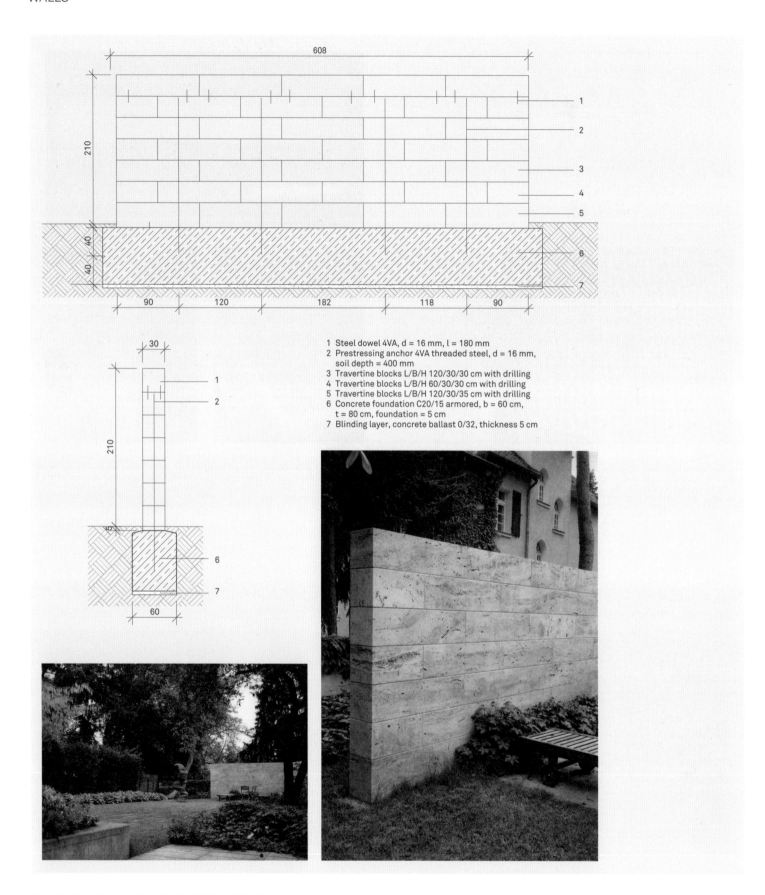

1 Steel dowel 4VA, d = 16 mm, l = 180 mm
2 Prestressing anchor 4VA threaded steel, d = 16 mm,
   soil depth = 400 mm
3 Travertine blocks L/B/H 120/30/30 cm with drilling
4 Travertine blocks L/B/H 60/30/30 cm with drilling
5 Travertine blocks L/B/H 120/30/35 cm with drilling
6 Concrete foundation C20/15 armored, b = 60 cm,
   t = 80 cm, foundation = 5 cm
7 Blinding layer, concrete ballast 0/32, thickness 5 cm

TRAVERTINE WALL, PRIVATE GARDEN, BERLIN,
GERMANY

LA.BAR Landschaftsarchitekten, Berlin
Completion: 2001

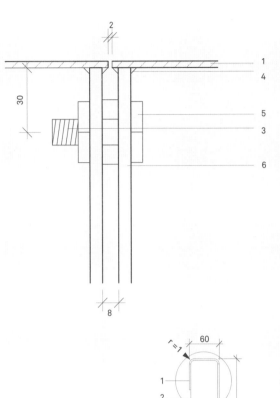

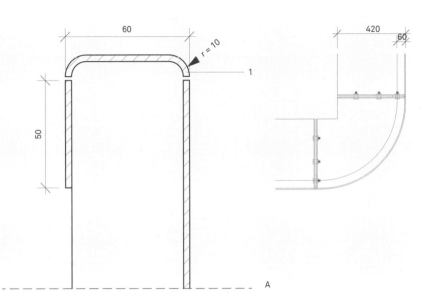

1 Steel plate 3 mm, rust-free acid-resistant steel
  AISI 316L with polished surface
2 Stiffening plate 6 mm steel PL6
3 Mounted bolts M12
4 Welding seams
5 Conical spring washer PL 8/30/30 mm
6 6 mm stringer steel plate c/c 1.5 m

STEEL SHEETING FOUNDATION CURB, PRAGS
BOULEVARD, COPENHAGEN, DENMARK

Arkitekt Kristine Jensens Tegnestue, Århus
Completion: 2005

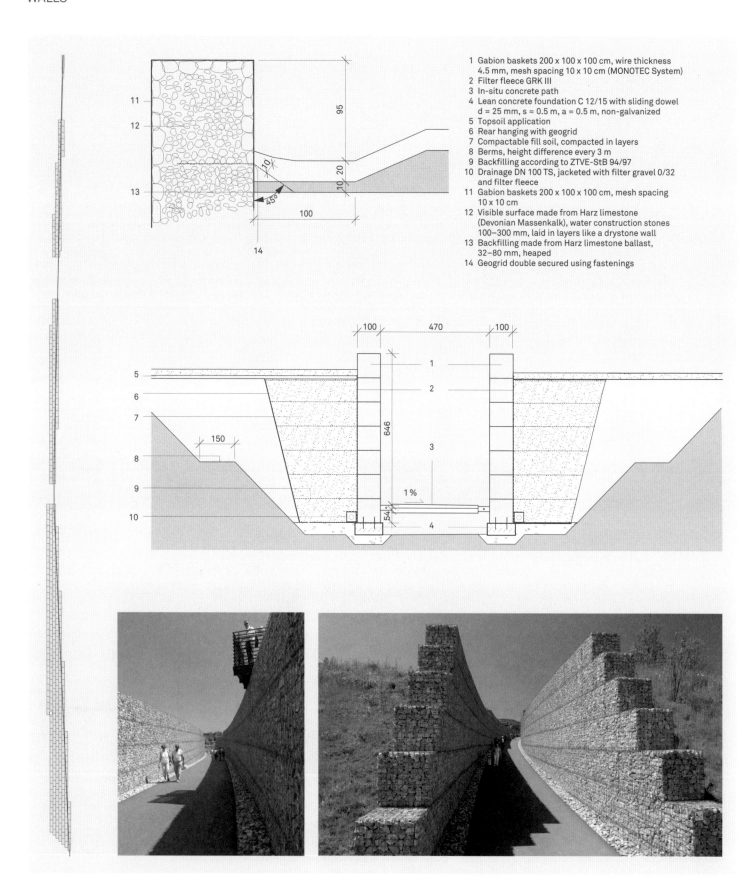

1 Gabion baskets 200 x 100 x 100 cm, wire thickness
   4.5 mm, mesh spacing 10 x 10 cm (MONOTEC System)
2 Filter fleece GRK III
3 In-situ concrete path
4 Lean concrete foundation C 12/15 with sliding dowel
   d = 25 mm, s = 0.5 m, a = 0.5 m, non-galvanized
5 Topsoil application
6 Rear hanging with geogrid
7 Compactable fill soil, compacted in layers
8 Berms, height difference every 3 m
9 Backfilling according to ZTVE-StB 94/97
10 Drainage DN 100 TS, jacketed with filter gravel 0/32
   and filter fleece
11 Gabion baskets 200 x 100 x 100 cm, mesh spacing
   10 x 10 cm
12 Visible surface made from Harz limestone
   (Devonian Massenkalk), water construction stones
   100–300 mm, laid in layers like a drystone wall
13 Backfilling made from Harz limestone ballast,
   32–80 mm, heaped
14 Geogrid double secured using fastenings

GABION WALL, WERNIGERODE, GERMANY

hutterreimann + cejka Landschaftsarchitektur,
Berlin, Vienna
Completion: 2006

1 Concrete finished part 3.0 m
x 3.0 m between high and low
tide lines on quay wall hung
using Halfen rails
2 Concrete finished part 2.0 m
x 0.60 m cover stone for quay
wall between high and low tide
lines on quay wall

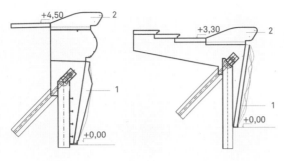

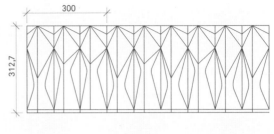

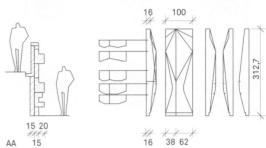

Facade clinker according to DIN 105 blank thick clinker,
especially suitable for water construction, DF 240 x 115 x 52 mm,
laid on concrete finished part
1 Alt berlin fo—anthracite-silver blue, structured
2 Speyer fo—sand colored-red nuances, structured
3 Heide fo—red moiré, structured

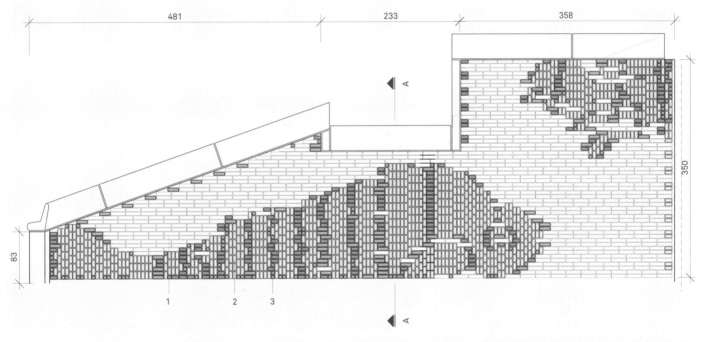

1   2   3

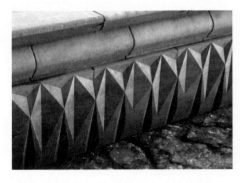

MARCO POLO SQUARE, HAFENCITY HAMBURG, GERMANY

Architects: Benedetta Tagliabue, Miralles Tagliabue
EMBT Miralles
Project leader: Karl Unglaub
Project architects: Stefan Geenen, Elena Nedelcu
Completion: 2007

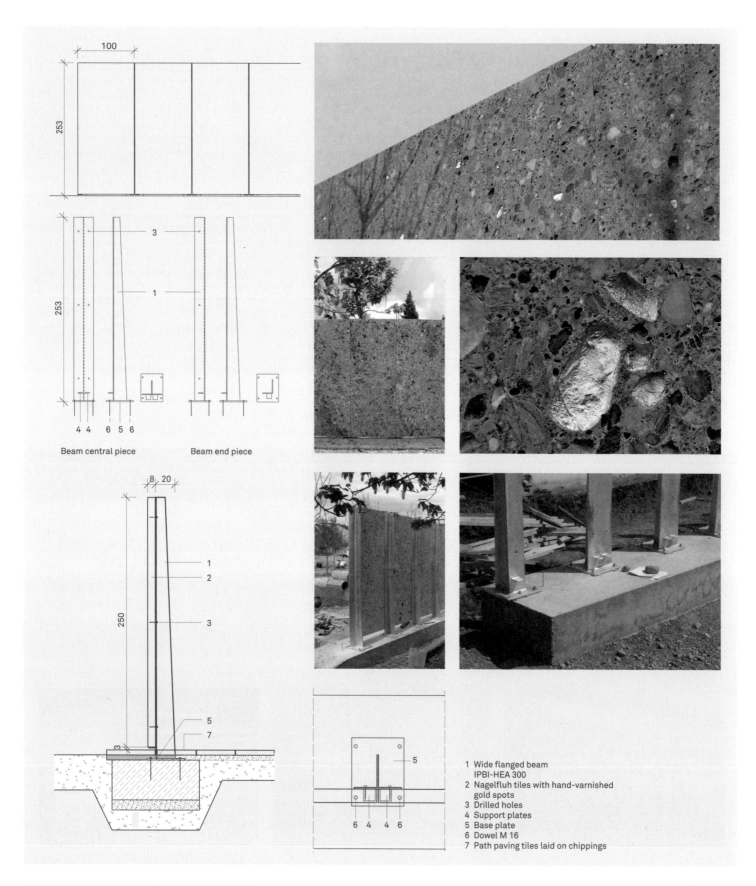

Beam central piece   Beam end piece

1 Wide flanged beam
  IPBI-HEA 300
2 Nagelfluh tiles with hand-varnished
  gold spots
3 Drilled holes
4 Support plates
5 Base plate
6 Dowel M 16
7 Path paving tiles laid on chippings

WALL WITH GOLD INCLUSIONS, STONE WALL
IN STADTPARK BURGHAUSEN, GERMANY

Rehwaldt Landschaftsarchitekten, Dresden
Completion: 2004

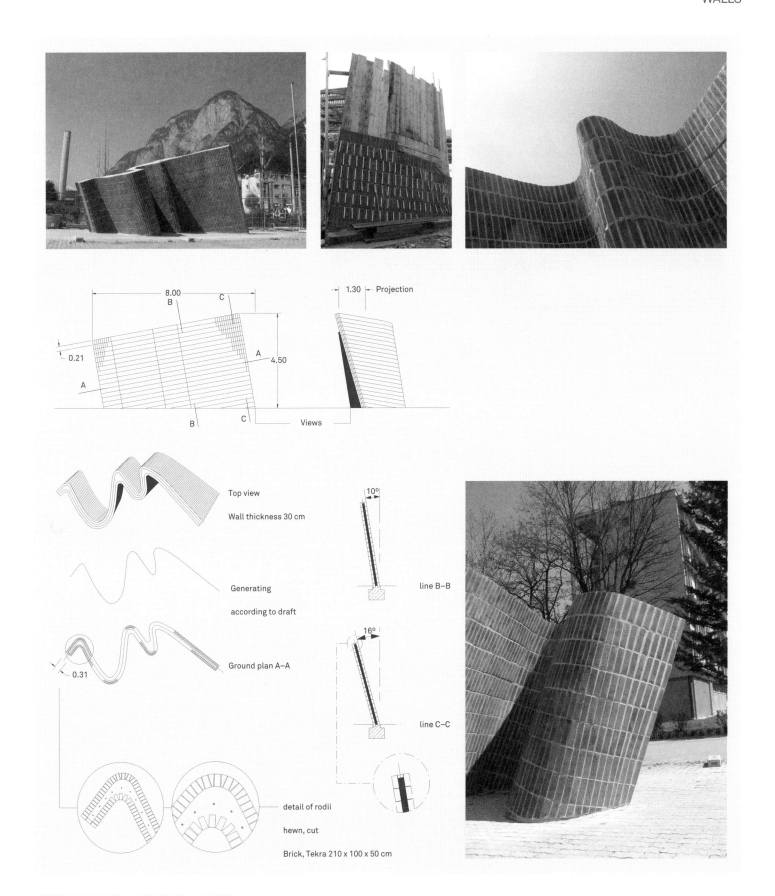

8.00

B
C

0.21

A
A

4.50

B
C

Views

1.30 — Projection

Top view

Wall thickness 30 cm

Generating

according to draft

Ground plan A–A

0.31

detail of rodii

hewn, cut

Brick, Tekra 210 x 100 x 50 cm

10°

line B–B

16°

line C–C

BRICK SCULPTURE, INNSBRUCK, AUSTRIA

Studio 3—Students of the University of Innsbruck
under Prof. Volker Gienke and Assistant Prof. Walter Prenner
Completion: 2006

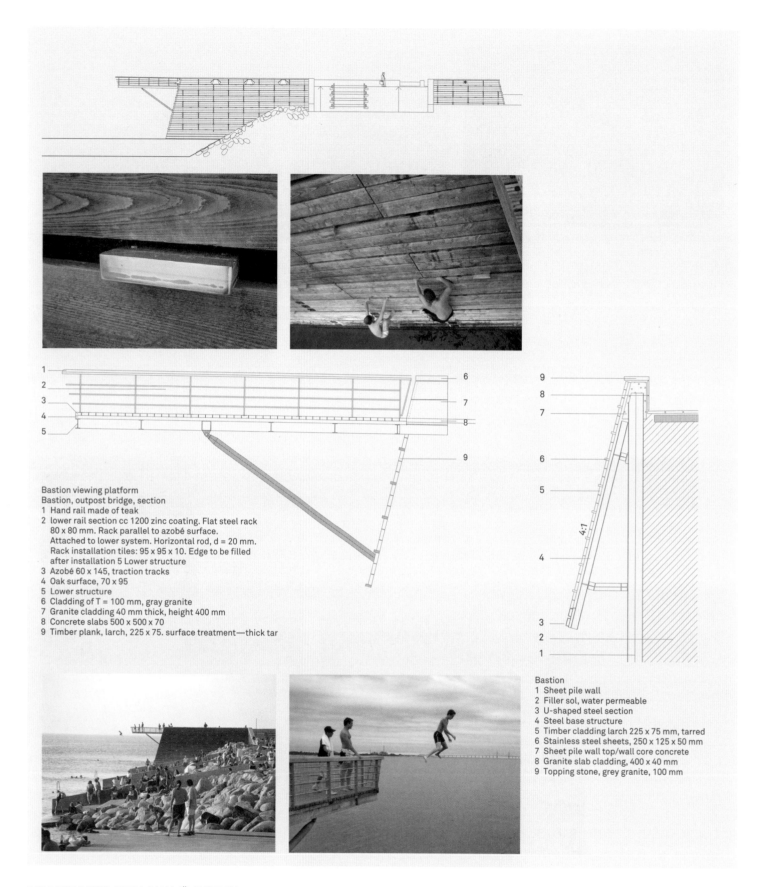

Bastion viewing platform
Bastion, outpost bridge, section
1 Hand rail made of teak
2 lower rail section cc 1200 zinc coating. Flat steel rack
   80 x 80 mm. Rack parallel to azobé surface.
   Attached to lower system. Horizontal rod, d = 20 mm.
   Rack installation tiles: 95 x 95 x 10. Edge to be filled
   after installation 5 Lower structure
3 Azobé 60 x 145, traction tracks
4 Oak surface, 70 x 95
5 Lower structure
6 Cladding of T = 100 mm, gray granite
7 Granite cladding 40 mm thick, height 400 mm
8 Concrete slabs 500 x 500 x 70
9 Timber plank, larch, 225 x 75. surface treatment—thick tar

Bastion
1 Sheet pile wall
2 Filler sol, water permeable
3 U-shaped steel section
4 Steel base structure
5 Timber cladding larch 225 x 75 mm, tarred
6 Stainless steel sheets, 250 x 125 x 50 mm
7 Sheet pile wall top/wall core concrete
8 Granite slab cladding, 400 x 40 mm
9 Topping stone, grey granite, 100 mm

WALLS IN DANIA-PARK, MALMÖ, SWEDEN

Landscape architects: SLA A/S, Copenhagen,
Stig L. Andersson
Completion: 2002

Small bastion with wooden
shingles
1 Teak covering, in front steel
slab to shade
surrounding lighting
2 Galvanzed steel girders with
teak handrail
3 Internal cladding, wooden
planks 38 x 25
4 Walking surface in 50 x 50
planks laid on loadbearing
45 x 70 plank
5 Shingles in untreated
timber
6 Loadbearing timber sub-
structure
in 45 x 120 planks
in post sockets
in concrete foundations

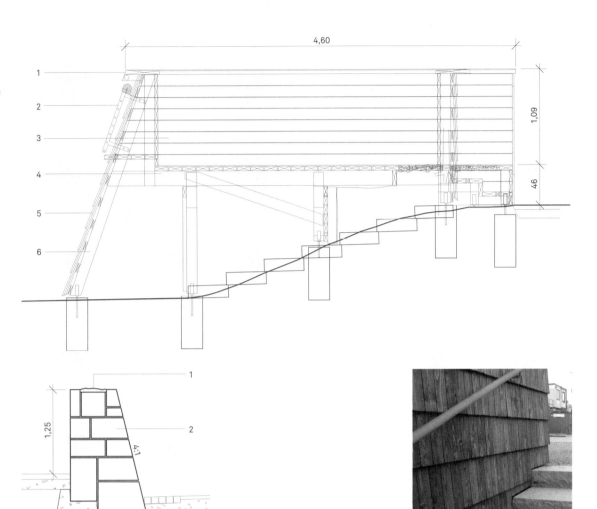

Drystone wall
1 Sedum
2 Granite block
3 Compressed material packed
   to frost-free depth

3.6 SMALL STRUCTURES AND PERGOLAS

CONSTRUCTION AND USE OF MATERIALS FOR SMALL STRUCTURES

· General construction
· Body
· Roof

CONSTRUCTION AND USE OF MATERIALS FOR PERGOLAS

· General construction
· Vertical components
· Horizontal components

SPECIMEN PROJECTS

Caroline Rolka

3.6 SMALL STRUCTURES AND PERGOLAS

Small structures and pergolas are small buildings that relate to their surroundings very directly. They generally have a unique character, being tailored to a particular location.

Their design involves defining an interior and an exterior. This is what anyone making use of them perceives as space. In this way, the fundamental human need for protection is fulfilled in their construction by wall structures and, in the case of pavilions, also by a roof.

As Figs. 3.6.1 and 3.6.2 demonstrate, "small" is a subjective perception that is difficult to pin down to a precisely definable size. > Figs. 3.6.1 and 3.6.2

CONSTRUCTION AND USE OF MATERIALS FOR SMALL STRUCTURES

The basic typological characteristics are a roofed-over single-room construction, usually with a symmetrical pattern; and minimal or absent integrated technology, such as thermal insulation, noise protection or electricity, as these objects are generally used only in favorable weather.

Simple housings and roofing, e.g. for bicycle parks or refuse huts, are not different from small structures in construction terms, and accordingly the following construction methods apply to them too. > Fig. 3.6.13

General construction

The basis for any pavilion is the body of the building with its closed or open wall systems and a roof.

The floor plan of small structures usually has a simple geometrical form. However, many kinds of cubage are possible. Beyond these construction characteristics, a small structure is further characterized by a variety of details such as roof superstructures or forward extensions, decorative facade elements, window and door design, floor coverings, and furnishing. > Fig. 3.6.3

Fig. 3.6.1: Greenhouse-like small structure, a space-filling construction between two residential buildings: "Glasbubbla" in Malmö by Monika Gora

Fig. 3.6.2: Glass pavilion with "sky roof," Louisiana Museum of Modern Art, Denmark

Fig. 3.6.3: Pavilion consisting of a body with only one closed side and a curved tent roof

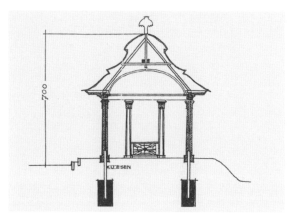

Fig. 3.6.4: Sectional view of a pavilion, historical drawing from 1916

Fig. 3.6.5: Elevated point foundation for a reinterpreted pavilion in Eubabrunn/Vogtland

This can be seen in in the example of a historical architectural drawing for a garden pavilion from 1916. The object is conceived as an eight-sided structure, crowned with a pagoda-like central roof, very much in the tradition of the outgoing 19th century. The wall construction consists of eight columns closed with spanning walls. The sectional drawing shows the pavilion's columns, grounded on point foundations. Iron U-moldings act as anchors between the foundation and the columns.
> Fig. 3.6.4

The roof framework is constructed as a collar beam roof. Echoing the basic form of the body, the collar beams are intercrossed and then each connected with a rafter. The connection method is not described. Traditionally, however, the rafter structure would be interleaved or

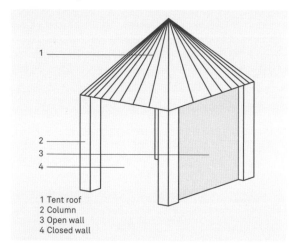

1 Tent roof
2 Column
3 Open wall
4 Closed wall

Fig. 3.6.6: Basic structure of a pavilion

Fig. 3.6.7: Open pavilion with system of reinforced concrete supports

Fig. 3.6.8: Wooden garden pavilion with historical skeleton design in Dresden Blasewitz

Fig. 3.6.9: Wooden garden pavilion with closed design in Krusenstiernska Gården in Kalmar, Sweden

mortised. > Chapter 2.3 Connections, Timber connections The inner ceiling of the depicted pavilion is designed as a flat dome. As for decoration, a roof crown and several decorative capitals are represented.

Foundation

In small structures, simple fills, point or strip foundations or—for solid designs—raft foundations are used. > Fig. 3.6.5 and chapter 2.3 A concrete foundation is not an essential condition for construction (historically, constructions are known where the foundations were created solely from stamped earth) but is normal in modern-day construction standards.

Body

The body of a small structure consists of at least three corner pillars, but usually four. This is described as an open construction, consisting only of loadbearing components, the corner pillars. On the other hand, a construction with again at least three corner pillars as loadbearing components turned into a closed space by infill (stiffening components), facings or wall cladding (non-loadbearing components) is described as a closed construction. > Fig. 3.6.6

Closed stone wall systems: Small stone structures are given their primary character by the individual features of different rock types. Artificial stone, such as brick or concrete, or natural stone such as sandstone, slate or boulders, creates an optical impact that emphasizes the mood and atmosphere of the location, most significantly through the materials used.

Closed small structures executed as masonry often make a very compact impression, even appearing habitable. > Fig. 3.6.9 However, stone is rarely used as a solid construction material for open pillar constructions due to its visual heaviness. Construction materials that can be used monolithically such as concrete allow the pavilion's typological characteristic of openness to be realized due to their specific properties. > Fig. 3.6.7 and specimen project Carport in Egg For this reason they are preferred for open building methods in the loadbearing system area.

Loadbearing wooden wall systems: A skeleton construction consisting of individual supports, also described as a frame construction, has become particularly well established for small wood structures. > Figs. 3.6.8 and 3.6.15 The structure's components are primarily loadbearing. They generally have no spatially enclosing function. Other construction methods, e.g. block design, are only exceptionally used, as the defined ease of construction no longer applies here.

Loadbearing metal wall systems: Metal working materials, especially steel and iron, have a very high compressive and bending strength, even where their sections are very thin. Skeleton metal constructions allow an optimal combination of aesthetic appeal and functionality in a small structure. Due to the slender

Fig. 3.6.10: Metal pavilion in newly interpreted kitchen garden, Laklö Slott, Sweden. The round pavilion at the end of a pergola (point de vue) is covered by an open bell roof. The individual steel box moldings are welded together.

Fig. 3.6.11: Pavilion with steel supports and a timber wall system

support system, a metal-constructed pavilion comes closest to a pavilion's original definition as a light tent structure. > Figs. 3.6.10 and 3.6.11

Infill and wall cladding: The loadbearing construction, made from wood, metal, stone or other materials, can be closed in by cladding or infill. The wall cladding has a decorative function, and may also protect the wall. The infill (also described as the support spanning, > Fig. 3.6.13), on the other hand, is not solely a decorative element. It fills the empty spaces between the individual support pillars of the frame construction at the level of the pillars, thereby having a static stiffening effect. > Fig. 3.6.5

The range of variation in pavilion design today is nearly inexhaustible. As well as the classical construction materials—wood, rock, steel, brick, or brick clay—concrete, glass, plastics and even withies and asphalt can be used. Cables, metal sheeting or thin rock tiles can also be used as infill. > Figs. 3.6.12 and 3.6.14, and specimen projects Asphalt Chapel and Carport in Egg

Roof

The design of the roof—its form and the materials used for tiling—has a significant influence on the overall appearance of small structures. At the same time, the roof encloses the structure from above, which is characteristic for the typology of the described objects.

Simply constructed cubatures, resulting from the generally quadratic, rectangular or round floor plan of the central space, are commonly used for small structures.

Fig. 3.6.12: Zinc sheets joined by standing seams, wall cladding for a pavilion in Christianshavn, Copenhagen

Fig. 3.6.13: Wall cladding made up of irregularly perforated metal plates; pavilion-like dustbin shelter in Copenhagen.

Fig. 3.6.14: Pavilion made from living withies, which form a green wall over time. The fixed roof skin consists of weather-safe, layered polyester weave.

a | b

Fig. 3.6.15: Wall cladding a) with bamboo canes, b) with wooden laths in a frame structure

Fig. 3.6.16: Pavilion in Miami, Florida, with curved flat roof

Fig. 3.6.17: Tent roof on a wooden pavilion

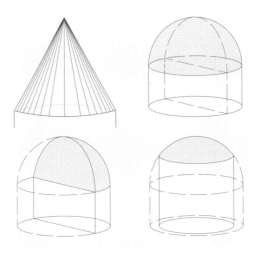

Fig. 3.6.18: Schematic structure of a conical roof,
flat dome and half dome

Fig. 3.6.19: The domed roof of a monopteros in Leipzig

Fig. 3.6.20: Simplest pavilion building method in the Parc du 26ème Centenaire, Marseille: an open structure with roofing that still creates a usable space.

As well as the classic tent roof, bell roofs, > Fig. 3.6.10 onion-domed or capped roofs, and folded roofs are known in mock-historical pavilions. Due to their clear, simple forms, the use of tent roof, domed and conical roof, flat roof and lean-to roof design forms has increased in modern landscape architecture.

The tent roof is erected over a quadratic or rectangular building. It is defined by several—at least three—roof surfaces, which incline toward each other and converge to form the tip, or crown. > Fig. 3.6.17

Domed or conical roofs are used for small structures with a round floor plan. If the dome curve is only a dome section, or calotte, it is described as a flat dome. The half dome is erected over a semicircular floor plan (exedra). > Figs. 3.6.18 and 3.6.19

Special forms like the roof of a pavilion in Miami dating from the 1930s experiment with the idea of lightness typical of this building style. > Fig. 3.6.16

The flat roof, on the other hand, is distinguished by the fact that it barely appears as a design component. Roof tiling with pantiles does not occur with flat roofs. Instead, the roof surface is rainproofed with roof sheets or metal sheeting. Flat roofs are usually constructed as cold roofs. > Chapter 3.14 Here the roofing membrane is usually laid directly on the loadbearing structure. The construction must have an incline of at least 3% for drainage purposes, so that rainwater can flow away via a roof gully or gutter. > Fig. 3.6.21

A single sloping roof surface with a greater incline than a flat roof is described as a lean-to roof. It has a half-rafter roof framework. > Fig. 3.6.22

To create the required 3% roof incline, a layer of sloping concrete (sloping screed) or sloping roof insulation panels are applied. For wood and metal sheeting roof

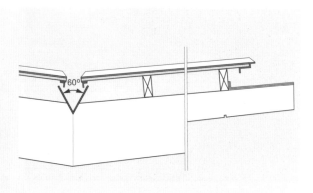

a | b

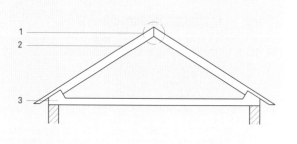

Fig. 3.6.21 a+b): Pavilion in Kaivopuisto, Helsinki: flat roof with internal drainage gutter

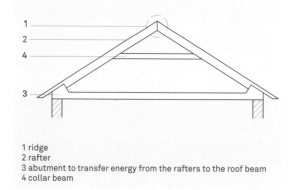

1 ridge
2 rafter
3 abutment to transfer energy from the rafters to the roof beam

Fig. 3.6.22: Schematic rafter roof construction

constructions, the incline can be achieved by sloping the substructure as wished.

In order to prevent water entering the loadbearing construction, junctions in the roof skin must be absolutely tight. As well as this, all flat roofs must have at least two outlets so that water can drain away. A gravel layer with a thickness of 5–10 cm, green roofs, slate chippings or ceramic grit will protect from direct sunlight, wind drag and mechanical damage.

Roof framework for small structures: The wood or metal loadbearing framework of the roof, which absorbs all forces acting on the roof and transmits them to the building's walls, is described as the roof framework. Due to the generally open form of the inner ceiling construction in small structures, the rafters and purlins are visible, as well as the roof sheathing. This should be borne in mind during the design process.

The roof truss must support itself in addition to the roof sheathing and the roof skin. In addition, a roof truss must be able to take the load of snow and wind. In order to absorb the forces acting on the roof framework, the roof truss is anchored directly to the body of the building. Additionally, the rafters are connected to the joists and purlins. The two most important roof truss types for small structures are rafter roofs and collar beam roofs. This kind of construction generally requires a structural analysis with regard to ultimate load.

The rafter roof consists of a series of independently secured rafter connectors (the rafter system). At the roof ridge, the rafters are solidly connected. Together with the ceiling below or a beam they form a nondeformable triangle. This allows the rafters to conduct wind and

1 ridge
2 rafter
3 abutment to transfer energy from the rafters to the roof beam
4 collar beam

Fig. 3.6.23: Schematic collar beam roof construction

superimposed load forces downward. These are then taken up by an abutment, the knee wall (or jamb wall). The great advantage of a rafter roof is that there are no beams to optically disrupt the roof space. > Fig. 3.6.22

The collar beam roof is a further development of the rafter roof. In this roof framework construction, the paired rafters are supported not only at the ridge, but also on the collar beams. The collar beams shorten the rafters' span, thereby avoiding folding and bending stress. Smaller rafter cross sections are possible, as well as larger spans. The collar beams, which are visible in the pavilion's roof space, should be integrated into the design. > Fig. 3.6.23

The roof covering (roof skin) is one of the most important aesthetic characteristics. It sets the tone for a unified structural body and the overall appearance of the location.

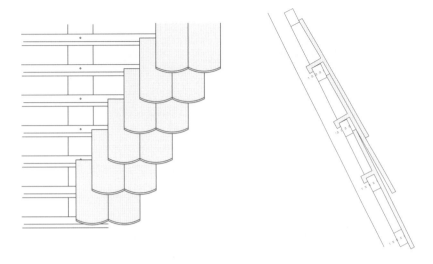

Fig. 3.6.24: Transparent roof covering on a steel girder loadbearing structure

Fig. 3.6.25: One way of laying roof tiles

The roof skin, laid on the roof framework, is the building's upper, rain-safe seal. It generally consists of level or profiled tile or tabular-shaped covering material, overlapping in scale fashion. As well as the common roof slab and roof tile covering, aluminum, zinc, stainless steel, and copper roofs are manufactured for small structures. Other common materials include corrugated tiles made from fiber-reinforced concrete, acrylic cellular tiles, and polycarbonate cellular tiles. > Fig. 3.6.25 For flat and lean-to roofs, bitumen is particularly suitable. More rarely, slate or organic construction materials—thatch or bulrushes—are used. The choice of materials essentially depends on roof incline, the function and situation of the building, and its intended appearance.

Roof tiles are laid using laths, on which they are hung by means of a handle on their undersides. > Fig. 3.6.24 Metal and corrugated tiles are nailed to the roof framework. The metal tiles are connected to each other by seams at their edges. The meeting edges of individual plastic tiles can be sealed to each other using specific adhesives. Stone shingle roof coverings (e.g. slate tiles) are generally nailed directly to the roof sheathing.

The way the shingle covering is laid is important for the roof's appearance. A distinction is made between a straight laying direction and one that is crosswise to the roof edge. > Fig. 3.6.27

Fig. 3.6.26: Artistically formed hip tiles on a Chinese-style corner pavilion in Radebeul

Fig. 3.6.27: Crosswise laying direction for slate shingles on a garden pavilion in Hartenstein

CONSTRUCTION AND USE OF MATERIALS FOR PERGOLAS

General construction

In contrast to a pavilion, a pergola is a space-defining alley of columns or pillars, either freestanding or adjoining one or several walls. Typically, it is constructed so as to be half open to the sky. > Fig. 3.6.28
A pergola usually serves as a protection from the sun or wind, as a tendril support structure for climbing plants, or simply as decoration.
A distinction is made between slatted and frame pergolas; the latter are sometimes known as a frame-and-panel pergola.

Vertical components

The loadbearing components of a pergola are the supports or posts. These are grounded in the pergola's base so as to be torsionally rigid, generally using point foundations. This is subject to dispersal of load at points into the onsite soil. Masonry constructed from artificial or natural stone, wood supports, or steel molding constructions may serve as material for the posts. However, plastic and glass are also used for the vertical construction elements of pergolas. If the post construction consists of a single elongated stone, the term used is "monolith pergola."

Horizontal components

Horizontal pergola components are divided between loadbearing and nonloadbearing components. For lamella pergolas, the loadbearing components are the purlins. For cassette pergolas this role is taken by the frame constructions. The purlins are the load-bearing elements in the slatted pergola, for the frame pergola, the frame takes the load. The elements at the top, which are non-loadbearing in statical terms, are called topping, top timbers or ceiling structure in the slatted pergola, and in the frame pergola the filler panels in the frame structure perform this function. For cassette and frame pergolas, in contrast to lamella pergolas, the loadbearing and nonloadbearing structural elements are on the same level.
> Figs. 3.6.27 and 3.6.31
The lamella pergola, whose name derives from the Late Latin word "lamella" meaning "thin slice," is a construction with long, thin slices, slivers or blades as supports. The lamellae and false rafters are usually arranged with their side edges parallel. > Fig. 3.6.29 and specimen projects on p. 337 and p. 340

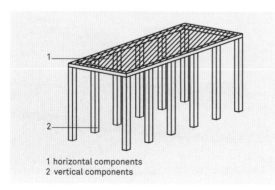

1 horizontal components
2 vertical components

Fig. 3.6.28: Schematic pergola structure

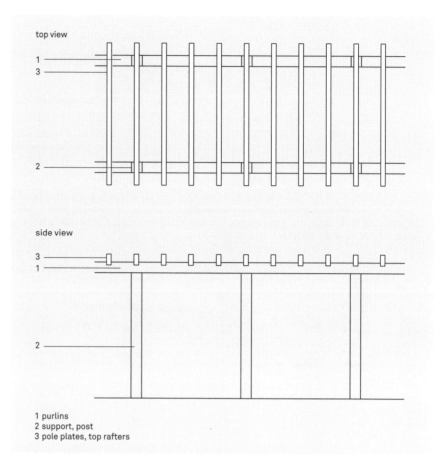

top view

side view

1 purlins
2 support, post
3 pole plates, top rafters

Fig. 3.6.29: Schematic lamella pergola structure

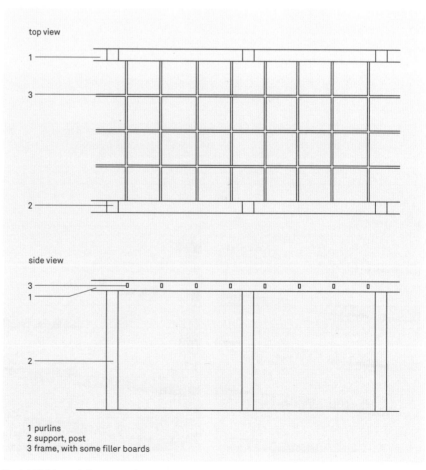

top view

side view

1 purlins
2 support, post
3 frame, with some filler boards

Fig. 3.6.30 Schematic frame pergola structure

For frame or cassette pergolas, the frame construction is integrated solidly with the loadbearing vertical components via a groove, so that a generally quadratic area, a "little box" is created. > Figs. 3.6.30–3.6.32

If the box is paneled, the pergola is described as a cassette pergola. This upper enclosure gives a definite roof-like impression, which has a decisive impact on the look of the object.

The pergola can be additionally stabilized by connecting it with a structurally stable edifice (a building or wall). Executing corner connections as a "rigid triangle" can also increase stability. Alternatively, the fields between two supports or props can be stiffened by guying, cross rods or infills—usually at the beginning and end of a construction. > Fig. 3.6.33

The possibilities of expanded material use and the changed spectrum of functions for small structures and pergolas are increasingly leading to a relaxation of stringent construction assemblages for both types of structure. All aspects of the rigid forms are softened, leading to a blending of vertical and horizontal forms into a single construction element and away from standardized descriptive models. > Figs. 3.6.34–3.6.36

a | b

Fig. 3.6.31:
a) Frame pergola in the newly interpreted kitchen garden of Laklö Slott, Sweden
b) Detail: bent laminated wood with a mortised joint

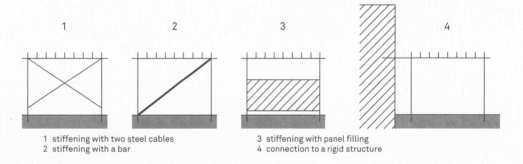

Fig. 3.6.32: Pergola in town park of Exjö, Sweden. Pairs of posts are statically and securely connected together by an overlaid purlin. In this system the lamellae rest freely on top. By means of cross-lathing, the ends of the lamellae are bound together to form a frame construction and connected to the corner posts so that a combination of lamella construction and frame construction is created.

1 stiffening with two steel cables
2 stiffening with a bar
3 stiffening with panel filling
4 connection to a rigid structure

Fig. 3.6.33: Various possibilities for stiffening pergolas in order to stabilize their structure

Fig. 3.6.34: Pergola-like construction as a "climbing structure" made up of welded steel profiles.

Fig. 3.6.35: Wooden pergola with corrugated laminated wood

Fig. 3.6.36: Small structure made from crash barriers, Künstlergruppe Observatorium

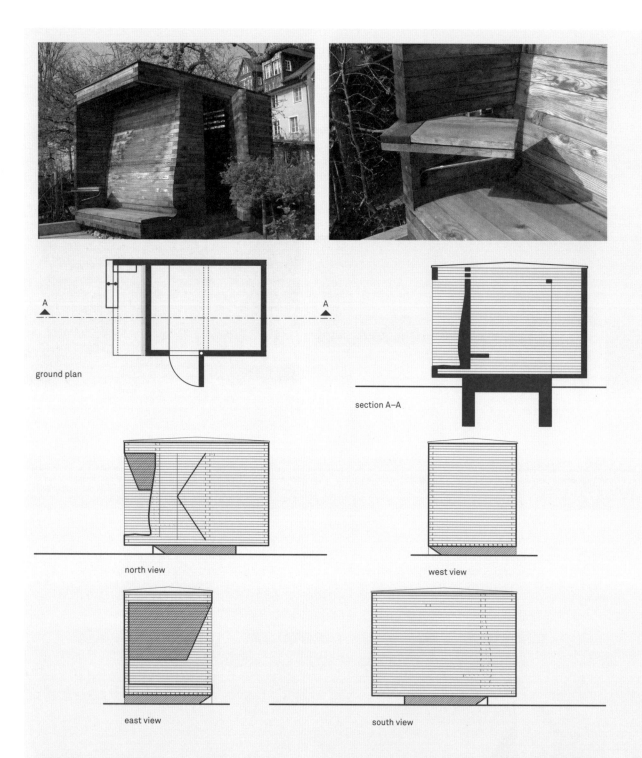

ground plan

section A–A

north view

west view

east view

south view

This bathing house, a summerhouse and changing cabin combined, also provides a place to sit with a view of the sea.
This wooden construction sits on a single "tide-safe" concrete foundation, laid to resist undermining.
The horizontal arrangement of the wood sections allows the structure to overhang the small foundation. At the same time, the horizontal timber grid (6 x 12 cm) provides the dimensions for the rest of the construction. The larchwood planks are screwed and glue laminated.
The door bolt and plate are made of oak timber, making them more resistant to mechanical loads and weathering. The door hinge has a flat washer placed beneath it at every timber plank position, to reduce the turning area.
The roof consists of 3 mm thick steel sheets, welded, galvanized, and painted. They are then watertight.

BATHING HOUSE, LINDAU ISLAND, GERMANY

Architect: Philip Lutz, Lochau (A)
Completion: 2000

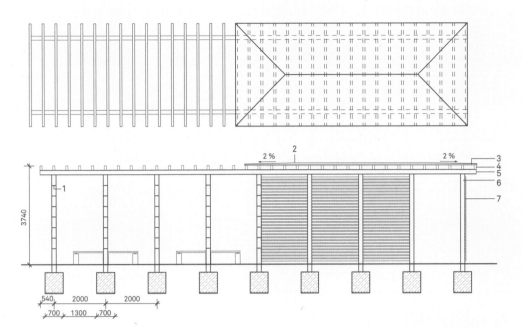

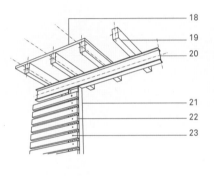

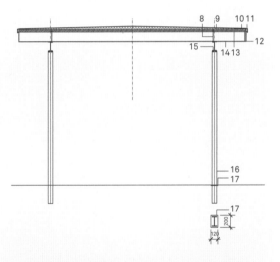

1 Tendril support: steel web 10/10 mm soldered
   with IPE molding
2 Roof incline to the edge with hip
3 Roof: 2-ply gripping plate, untreated
4 Purlins: two-by-four, untreated larch 8/16 cm
5 IPE 160 varnished DB 703
6 IPE 160 varnished DB 703
7 Wall lamellae and cladding 40/80 mm untreated
   larch with 3.5 cm joint
8 Rafters secured only in inner field
9 Inclined wedge
10 Glued bitumen sheet, with 15 cm overlap
11 Fascia board, titanium sheeting with water drip
12 Purlin cap tile larch 2 cm
13 Watertight laminated wood tiles, d = 2 x 2 cm
14 Purlins: two-by-four, untreated larch 8/16 cm
15 Props on cap plates with 4 screws
16 IPE 160 varnished DB 703
17 Base plate 120/200/10 mm
18 Roof
19 Purlins: two-by-four, untreated larch 8/16 cm
20 Steel prop IPE 160 varnished DB 703
21 Steel support IPE 160 varnished DB 703
22 Wall lamellae
23 Countersunk bolts

PERGOLA, GROSSENHAIN (SAXONY), GERMANY

Architect: SAUERZAPFE ARCHITECTS, Berlin
Landscape architects: Weidinger Landschafts-
architekten, Berlin
Completion: 2002

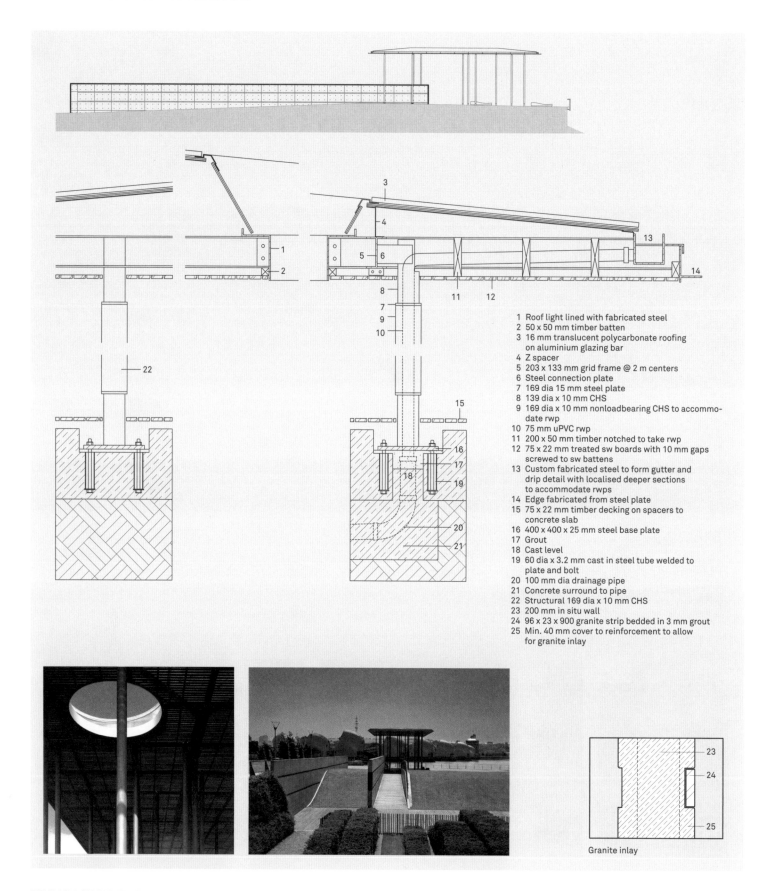

1 Roof light lined with fabricated steel
2 50 x 50 mm timber batten
3 16 mm translucent polycarbonate roofing on aluminium glazing bar
4 Z spacer
5 203 x 133 mm grid frame @ 2 m centers
6 Steel connection plate
7 169 dia 15 mm steel plate
8 139 dia x 10 mm CHS
9 169 dia x 10 mm nonloadbearing CHS to accommodate rwp
10 75 mm uPVC rwp
11 200 x 50 mm timber notched to take rwp
12 75 x 22 mm treated sw boards with 10 mm gaps screwed to sw battens
13 Custom fabricated steel to form gutter and drip detail with localised deeper sections to accommodate rwps
14 Edge fabricated from steel plate
15 75 x 22 mm timber decking on spacers to concrete slab
16 400 x 400 x 25 mm steel base plate
17 Grout
18 Cast level
19 60 dia x 3.2 mm cast in steel tube welded to plate and bolt
20 100 mm dia drainage pipe
21 Concrete surround to pipe
22 Structural 169 dia x 10 mm CHS
23 200 mm in situ wall
24 96 x 23 x 900 granite strip bedded in 3 mm grout
25 Min. 40 mm cover to reinforcement to allow for granite inlay

Granite inlay

PAVILION OF REMEMBRANCE, THAMES BARRIER
PARK, LONDON, UNITED KINGDOM

Designers: Groupe Signes and Patel Taylor
Engineering: Arup
Completion: 2000

1 Roofing plate, 3100/3100/15 mm
   untreated steel
2 L-steel 100/12 mm, l = 2900 mm
3 Grid construction of oak 10/10/350 cm
   two-by-four, with V2A steel screws
   screwed in from above
4 Hot-galvanized 100/100/6.3 mm square
   steel pipe, l = 4160 mm, filled with
   C12/15 concrete
5 Concrete foundation, constructed
   frost-free, 60/60/110 cm

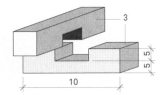

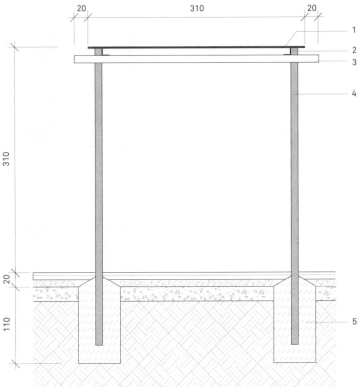

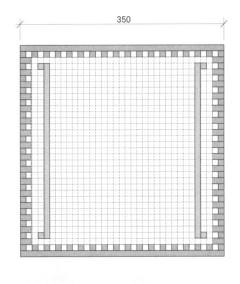

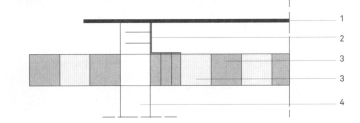

RIVERSIDE PROMENADE STRALAU PENINSULA,
BERLIN, GERMANY

Landscape architects: hutterreimann + cejka, Berlin/
Vienna
With Ingenieurbüro Wittig, Berlin
Completion: 2005

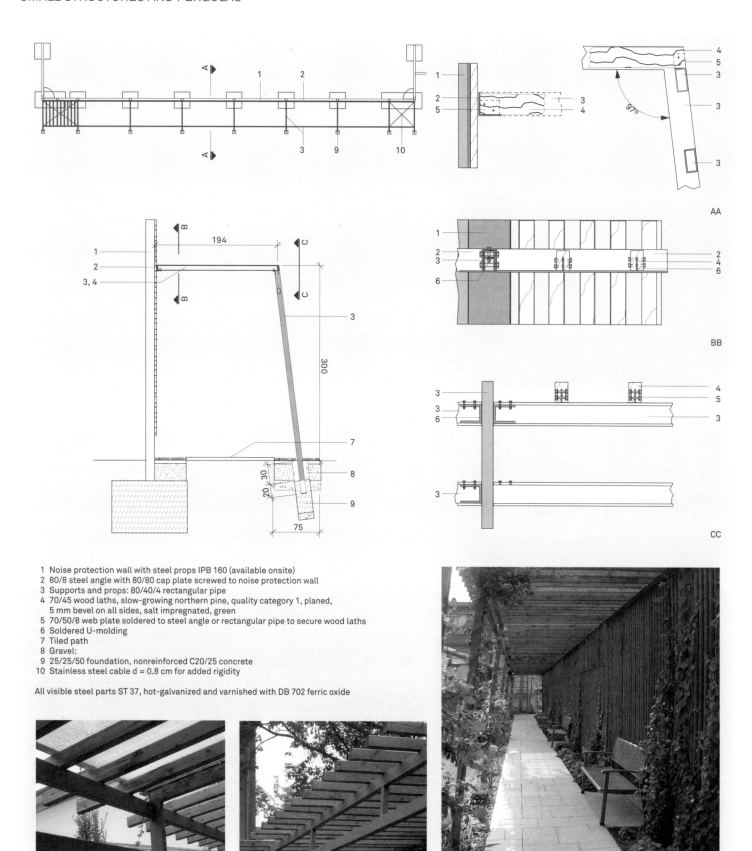

1 Noise protection wall with steel props IPB 160 (available onsite)
2 80/8 steel angle with 80/80 cap plate screwed to noise protection wall
3 Supports and props: 80/40/4 rectangular pipe
4 70/45 wood laths, slow-growing northern pine, quality category 1, planed,
   5 mm bevel on all sides, salt impregnated, green
5 70/50/8 web plate soldered to steel angle or rectangular pipe to secure wood laths
6 Soldered U-molding
7 Tiled path
8 Gravel:
9 25/25/50 foundation, nonreinforced C20/25 concrete
10 Stainless steel cable d = 0.8 cm for added rigidity

All visible steel parts ST 37, hot-galvanized and varnished with DB 702 ferric oxide

PERGOLA, GARDEN OF THE EVANGELISCHER
LUTHERSTIFT STEGLITZ, BERLIN, GERMANY

Landscape architects: LA.BAR, Berlin
Completion: 2006

1 Steel tapping screw M16
2 Reinforcing bars, d = 10 mm
3 Rubber bearing, approx. 5 mm

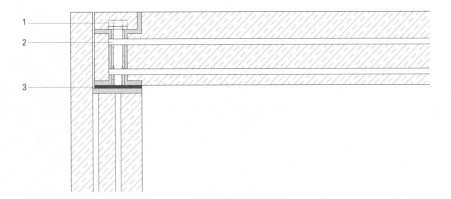

CARPORT IN EGG, AUSTRIA

Architect: Georg Bechter, Stuttgart
Track system planning: Eric Leitner, Schröcken (A)
Completion: 2006

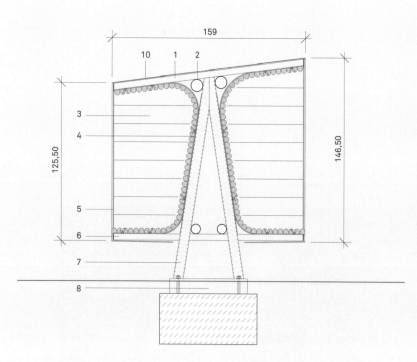

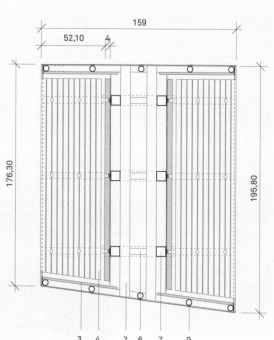

1 Steel molding 50 x 50 x 5
2 Round steel 101.6 x 6.3 mm
3 Oak boards, planed on all sides, 145 x 18 mm
4 Oak timber 40 x 40 mm
5 Flat steel 70 x 5

6 Round steel 50 x 50 x 5
7 Round steel 80 x 80 x 5
8 Concrete foundation finished part
9 Round steel 51 x 4 mm
10 Copper plate

SHELTER IN SNEFJORD, FINNMARK, NORWAY

Architects: Pushak, Oslo
Completion: 2005

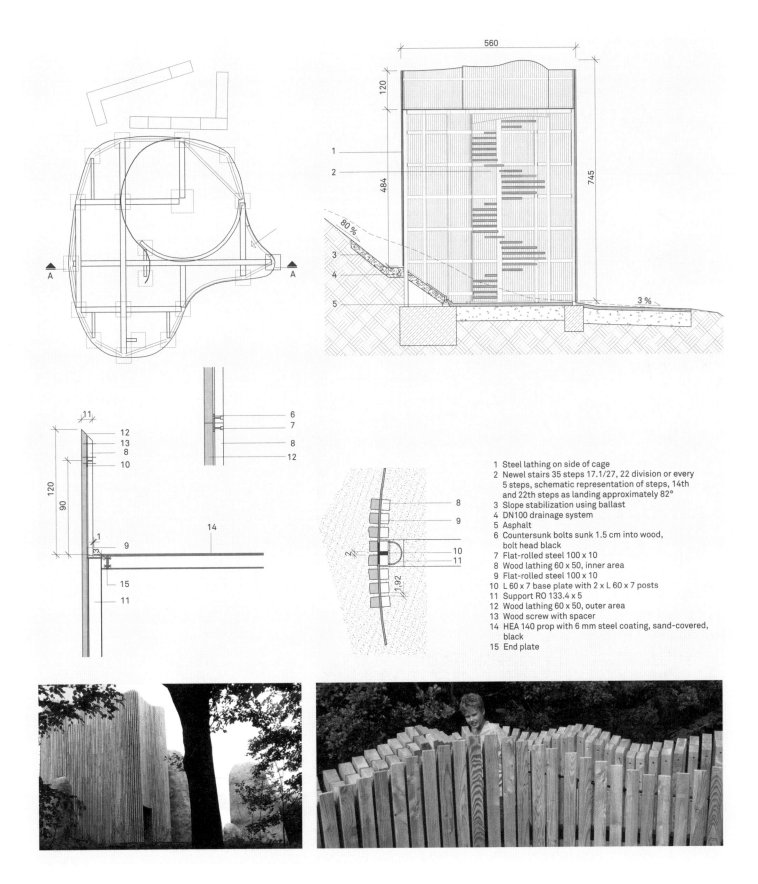

1 Steel lathing on side of cage
2 Newel stairs 35 steps 17.1/27, 22 division or every
   5 steps, schematic representation of steps, 14th
   and 22th steps as landing approximately 82°
3 Slope stabilization using ballast
4 DN100 drainage system
5 Asphalt
6 Countersunk bolts sunk 1.5 cm into wood,
   bolt head black
7 Flat-rolled steel 100 x 10
8 Wood lathing 60 x 50, inner area
9 Flat-rolled steel 100 x 10
10 L 60 x 7 base plate with 2 x L 60 x 7 posts
11 Support RO 133.4 x 5
12 Wood lathing 60 x 50, outer area
13 Wood screw with spacer
14 HEA 140 prop with 6 mm steel coating, sand-covered,
   black
15 End plate

BAOBAB VIEWING TOWER IN ZOO, WUPPERTAL, GERMANY

Landscape architects: Rehwaldt Landschaftsarchitekten,
Dresden
Completion: 2007

ASPHALT CHAPEL, ETSDORF NEAR AMBERG,
GERMANY

Planning: Wilhelm Koch
Static planning: Thomas Beck, a.k.a. engineers, Munich
Completion: 2001 in Altötting, transferred 2002

This construction/artwork, which can be entered, was planned and realized in Altötting by the communications designer Wilhelm Koch on the occasion of the Oberbayerische Kulturtage.
The 10 cm thick components were poured into a formwork with steel reinforcement inside. The "finished parts" were joined together in situ after formwork removal and connected using steel moldings.

3.7 SMALL BRIDGES

GENERAL STRUCTURE OF A BRIDGE

BRIDGE SUPPORT STRUCTURES

SPECIMEN PROJECTS

Astrid Zimmermann, Bernd Funke

3.7 SMALL BRIDGES

Bridges do not simply allow ditches or other obstacles to be crossed quickly and easily. They can also be particularly eye-catching elements or the setting for a scenic crossing, and they can enhance the element of playfulness in a play area. Bridges built for pedestrians and cyclists in or around an open public space significantly influence its appearance. Whether they fit in to the surrounding grounds spatially, act as a contrast or are designed as special locations in their own right is in the hands of the planner. These decisions cannot be separated from the structure's material and construction, which are usually decided in collaboration with a support structure planner. > Fig. 3.7.1

The text below is a brief introduction to this theme. Walkway constructions, a special case in beam bridge construction, are described in more detail in Chapter 3.8.

Fig. 3.7.1: Arch bridge in Wörlitz Park: a visual feature and a scenic crossing

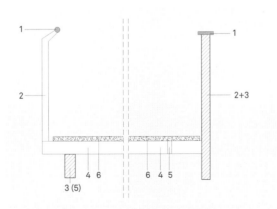

1 rail
2 banister (rails)
3 support structure
4 transverse support
5 longitudinal support
6 bridge deck/covering

Fig. 3.7.2: Schematic cross section through a bridge

GENERAL STRUCTURE OF A BRIDGE

Bridges generally show the following schematized structure in cross section: the support structure consists of longitudinal supports with transverse supports stretched in between, with the bridge deck or floor covering lying on top. If the floor covering is to be arranged crosswise, additional longitudinal supports may be required, depending on the span of the bridge. Rails should be provided as fall protection along the sides. > Fig. 3.7.2 Parts of the construction can also be unified. For instance, laterally arranged support beams can also function as rails, or the substructure of longitudinal and transverse supports can form a beam grid.

BRIDGE SUPPORT STRUCTURES

Three basic forms of support structure exist for bridge constructions: beam, arch, and suspension bridges. By varying and combining these basic forms, a variety of construction methods can be created. > Fig. 3.7.3 The simple beam—laid across a ditch—can be regarded as the original bridge form. This is the simplest variation of the beam bridge, for which the load is transferred to the abutments at either end of the bridge by one or more beams. > Fig. 3.7.4 Both tensile and compressive forces act on the beam. There are also construction types with two or more beams as longitudinal supports, with the shorter beams resting on them as cross supports and with the bridge deck resting on these in turn. The supports can be placed under the bridge deck or laterally to it. For bridges with only one beam, the cross supports or a plate must project laterally from the beam (a cantilever). In this respect, beams are subjected in the longitudinal direction to torsion stress (bending caused by asymmetrical load) as well as bending stress. This construction method is often used for small steel-concrete bridges in the form of T-beam cross sections or for steel bridges with torsionally rigid box girder longitudinal supports. > Fig. 3.7.5

Beam bridges are easy to manufacture, but have a relatively high materials requirement.

One approach to this problem is to extensively distribute the beam's cross section (the highest possible construction height), for instance by using a framework or a lower or upper span. > Fig. 3.7.6

A series of several beams and pedestals allows larger expanses to be bridged. In this case, the materials required can be reduced by constructing one continuous support over several props/pedestals. Walkway construction is also based on this principle. > Chapter 3.8

If only one pedestal can be used, the bridge structure must be constructed using a cantilever (a cantilever bridge).

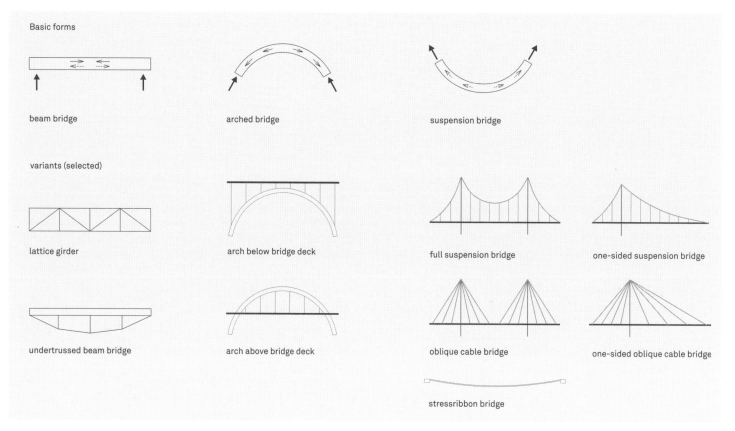

Fig. 3.7.3: Basic forms of support structure with some variants

Fig. 3.7.4: Basic "beam bridge" principle

Fig. 3.7.5 a+b): pedestrian bridge on BUGA grounds in Potsdam:
the lateral bridge supports have a box construction. Together with
the bridge deck, they create a U-shaped support structure.

a | b

Fig. 3.7.6: Wooden beam bridge

Fig. 3.7.7: "Raised" beam bridge

Fig. 3.7.8: Frame bridge in
Amsterdam: the framework is
made from T-moldings welded
to form framework stays.

Arch bridges permit the use of construction materials lacking tensile strength (e.g. masonry) as well as a significant reduction in the necessary cross section (larger spans with the same consumption of material), as the arch form converts all the active forces into compressive forces acting on the foundations. Traditionally, arch bridges are mainly built out of natural stone, but wood constructions are quite common for bridges in parks and gardens. > Fig. 3.7.1 Modified forms of arch bridge, often involving concrete and steel, can be constructed with the bridge deck above, below or in the middle of the arch. In these cases, the load is transferred to the arches via props (usually vertical) or tension rods, which are usually placed vertically. > Fig. 3.7.9

The principle of the suspension bridge is similar to that of the arch bridge, with tensile forces absorbing the loads instead of compressive forces. The bridge deck hangs from suspension cables that connect with the main cables, forming the shape of an "inverted" arch (the cable line). The main cables usually connect to pylons or masts and are anchored to the ends of the bridge. Alternatively, the cables can be anchored directly in the abutment. For small bridges in particular, chains or even cables made from natural fibers can be used instead of steel cables. Types of suspension bridge are often used in play areas or in high rope courses. > Fig. 3.7.11

For cable-stayed bridges, the load is conducted directly to the pylons via the cables.

The stress ribbon bridge is a special form of suspension bridge. It is only used for small loads and is therefore particularly suitable for pedestrian bridges. Here, the bridge covering is laid directly on the cables, which are anchored at the ends of the bridge. > Fig. 3.7.12

Fig. 3.7.9: Arch bridge with centrally placed bridge deck over the gondola pond in Grossenhain, Saxony

a | b

Fig. 3.7.10: New Traversina footbridge across the Viamala gorge:
a) abutment to anchor cable forces
b) cable suspension bridge with stepped walking surface

a | b

Fig. 3.7.11:
a) Cable suspension bridge
   as part of a play complex
b) Chain suspension bridge

a | b

Fig. 3.7.12 a+b): Stress ribbon bridge across the Viamala gorge: Stone tiles made from Andeer gneiss lie on a tensile ribbon of non-rusting flat-rolled steel.

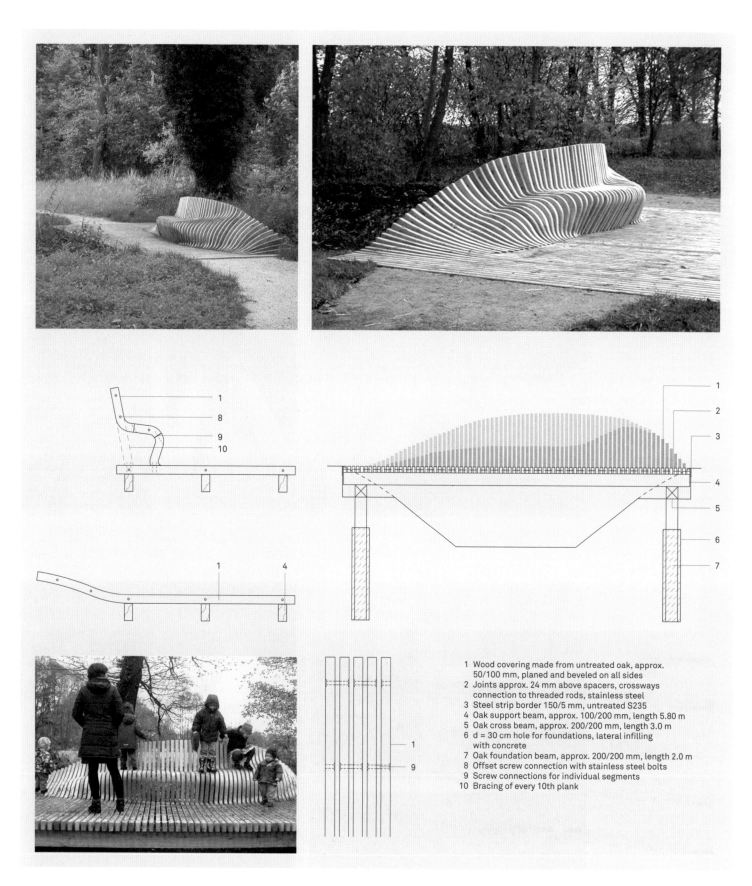

1 Wood covering made from untreated oak, approx.
  50/100 mm, planed and beveled on all sides
2 Joints approx. 24 mm above spacers, crossways
  connection to threaded rods, stainless steel
3 Steel strip border 150/5 mm, untreated S235
4 Oak support beam, approx. 100/200 mm, length 5.80 m
5 Oak cross beam, approx. 200/200 mm, length 3.0 m
6 d = 30 cm hole for foundations, lateral infilling
  with concrete
7 Oak foundation beam, approx. 200/200 mm, length 2.0 m
8 Offset screw connection with stainless steel bolts
9 Screw connections for individual segments
10 Bracing of every 10th plank

BEAM BRIDGE IN LENNÉPARK, BARUTH/MARK, GERMANY

Architects: Britta Aumüller and Tobias Hamm, Stuttgart
Timber construction firm, statics: kernholz GmbH,
Ulrich Link, Berlin
Completion: 2004

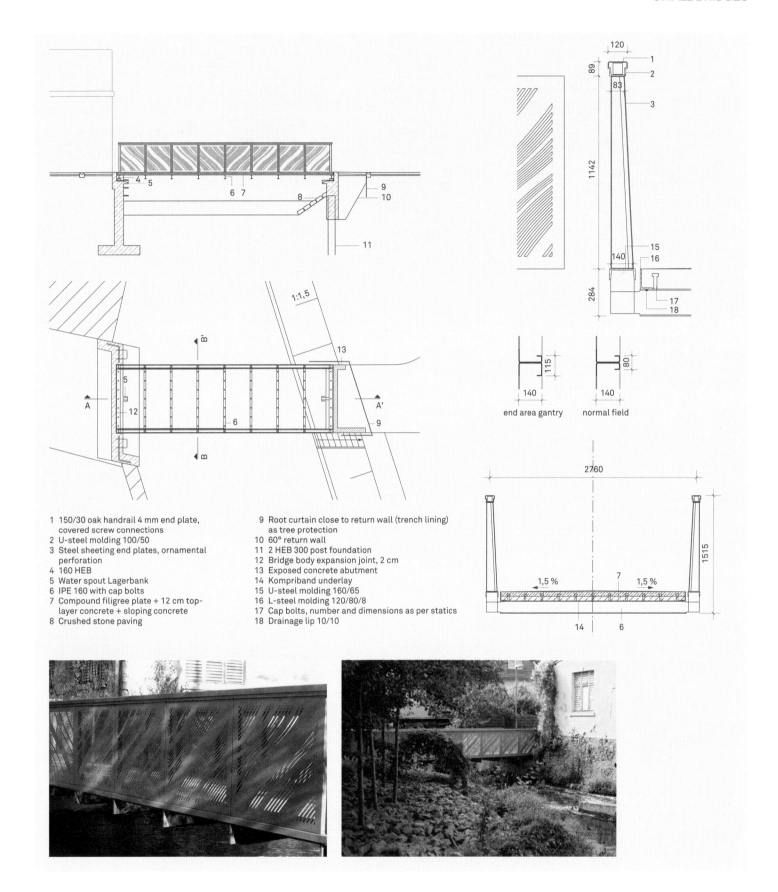

1 150/30 oak handrail 4 mm end plate,
   covered screw connections
2 U-steel molding 100/50
3 Steel sheeting end plates, ornamental
   perforation
4 160 HEB
5 Water spout Lagerbank
6 IPE 160 with cap bolts
7 Compound filigree plate + 12 cm top-
   layer concrete + sloping concrete
8 Crushed stone paving

9 Root curtain close to return wall (trench lining)
   as tree protection
10 60° return wall
11 2 HEB 300 post foundation
12 Bridge body expansion joint, 2 cm
13 Exposed concrete abutment
14 Kompriband underlay
15 U-steel molding 160/65
16 L-steel molding 120/80/8
17 Cap bolts, number and dimensions as per statics
18 Drainage lip 10/10

KATHARINENBRÜCKE, GROSSENHAIN (SAXONY), GERMANY

Architect: Sauerzapfe Architekten, Martin Sauerzapfe, Berlin
Landscape architect: Weidinger Landschaftsarchitekten, Berlin
Support structure planning: ifb frohloff staffa kühl ecker, Berlin
Completion: 2001

The bordered sheet metal panels of this beam bridge are screwed to truss
girders, forming the loadbearing system and effectively serving as railings.
The vertical edges look like upright bars and the laser-cut ornamentation
like tension diagonals, becoming wider towards the edge, which makes
statical sense. Even though the sheets are only 4 mm thick, the structure
achieves a loadbearing strength of at least 5 tons.

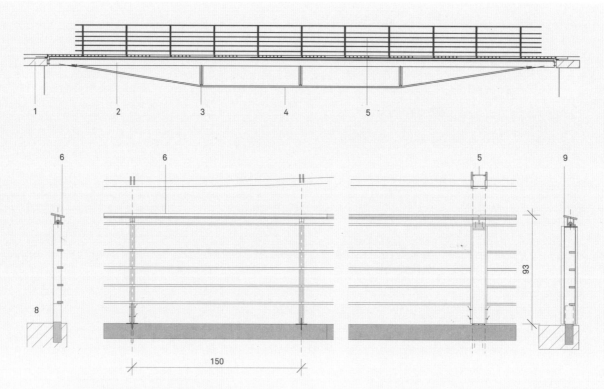

1 Support beams, concrete finished parts
2 HEB 220 steel stays, covered on both sides with 15 x 240 steel
3 Substructure: HEA 100 steel support and 70/5.6 steel pipe
4 Tension rod d = 30 mm, soldered to flat iron bar
5 Land-side railing module of bridge consisting of 10/70 flat-rolled steel posts, 20/70 flat-rolled steel handrail, 4 15/50 flat-rolled steel cross struts and a d = 20 mm round steel bar as the lowest crossbar

6 Land-side railing module of bridge, same as 5 but with applied stainless steel bezel for continuous strip lighting with light-emitting diodes
7 60/115 wood beam with anti-slip profile on steel substructure
8 Top of quay wall, reinforced concrete
9 Broader posts, approx. every 9 m with ELT-lead for strip lighting

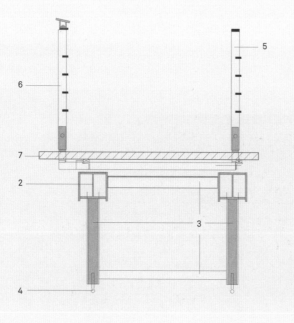

BRIDGE WITH LOWER SPAN, DANUBE QUAY, NEUBURG AN
DER DONAU, GERMANY

Architects: Herle & Herrle, Neuburg
Landscape architects: keller landschaftsarchitekten Munich
Completion: 2001

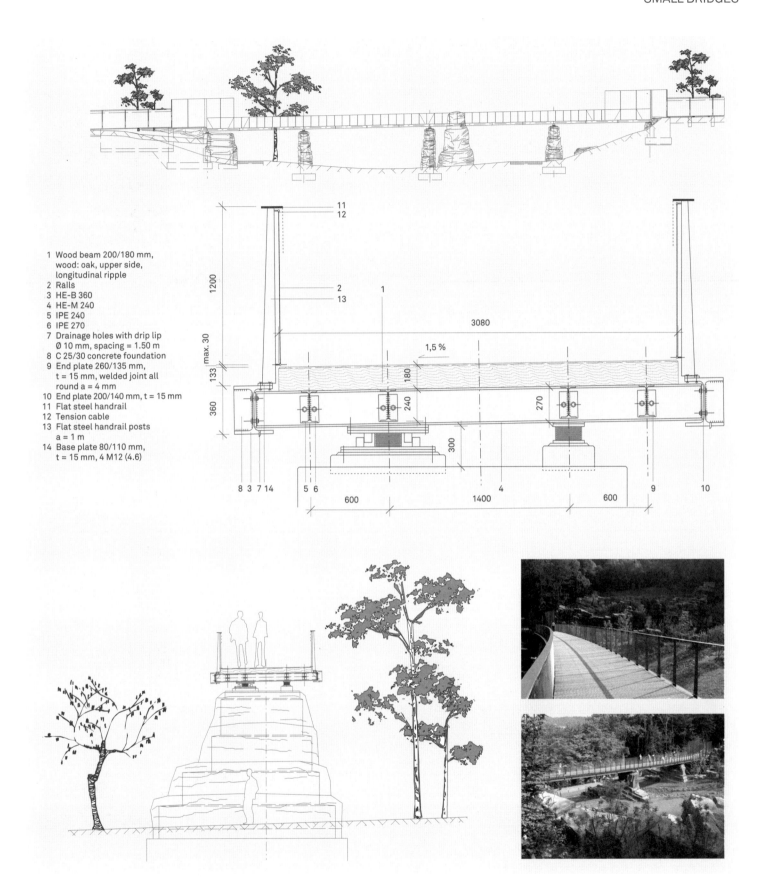

1 Wood beam 200/180 mm,
 wood: oak, upper side,
 longitudinal ripple
2 Ralls
3 HE-B 360
4 HE-M 240
5 IPE 240
6 IPE 270
7 Drainage holes with drip lip
 Ø 10 mm, spacing = 1.50 m
8 C 25/30 concrete foundation
9 End plate 260/135 mm,
 t = 15 mm, welded joint all
 round a = 4 mm
10 End plate 200/140 mm, t = 15 mm
11 Flat steel handrail
12 Tension cable
13 Flat steel handrail posts
 a = 1 m
14 Base plate 80/110 mm,
 t = 15 mm, 4 M12 (4.6)

PEDESTRIAN AND CYCLING BRIDGE IN ZOO, WUPPERTAL, GERMANY

Landscape architects: Rehwaldt Landschaftsarchitekten
Engineering firm: Kling Consult, Krumbach
Completion: 2007

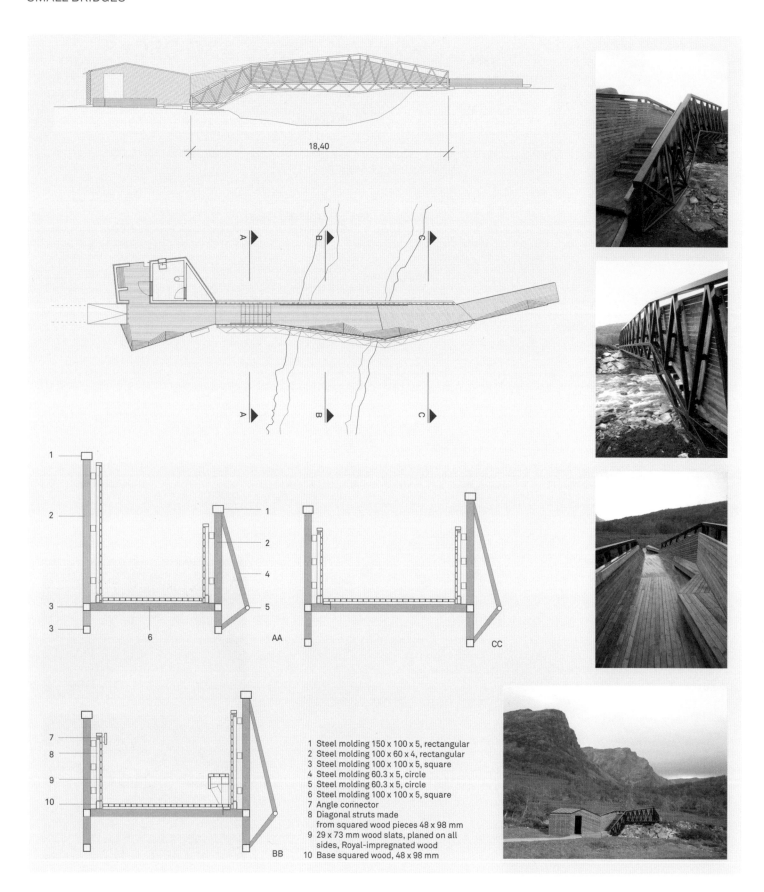

18,40

A   B   C

A   B   C

1

2

3

3   6   AA

1

2

4

5

CC

7

8

9

10

BB

1 Steel molding 150 x 100 x 5, rectangular
2 Steel molding 100 x 60 x 4, rectangular
3 Steel molding 100 x 100 x 5, square
4 Steel molding 60.3 x 5, circle
5 Steel molding 60.3 x 5, circle
6 Steel molding 100 x 100 x 5, square
7 Angle connector
8 Diagonal struts made
   from squared wood pieces 48 x 98 mm
9 29 x 73 mm wood slats, planed on all
   sides, Royal-impregnated wood
10 Base squared wood, 48 x 98 mm

BRIDGE IN LILLEFJORD, NORWAY

Architect: Pushak, Oslo
Completion: 2006

3.8 WALKWAYS AND DECKS

GENERAL ESSENTIALS

FOUNDATION

SUBSTRUCTURE/SUPPORT CONSTRUCTION

COVERING

SPECIMEN PROJECTS

Marianne Mommsen

3.8 WALKWAYS AND DECKS

Walkways and decks are traditional design elements in private and public open spaces. Jetty walkways connect land with sea. In swamp or dune landscapes, walkways open up impassable terrain. In public parks, they present themselves as inviting sun decks. They are associated with private houses as terraces. **> Figs. 3.8.1–3.8.3**
Walkways and decks are usually raised in relation to the surrounding terrain, offering design-accentuated paths and places to linger. Using them is extremely attractive, as there is always a playful, adventurous aspect to leaving solid ground behind. Traversing walkway and deck constructions is a varied haptic experience. Often, the heightened perspective reveals new views of the surroundings.

The walkways and decks described in this chapter are constructions that rise above land or water, with small spans. The forces acting on the superstructure are dispersed by broad foundations or by a grid of strip or point foundations. Walkways and decks generally consist of stakes or posts, horizontal loadbearing components, stiffening struts, and a surface covering. Walkways have a linear, connective orientation, and act as paths. Decks, on the other hand, are expansive and primarily create resting places.

GENERAL ESSENTIALS

Whether the planned walkway or deck is a structure requiring planning permission according to the local regulations, and whether legislators demand a stability check (statics) for any support construction elements involved, can be clarified by the local planning authority if necessary. Building inspections place significantly higher requirements on loadbearing and/or stiffening construction components. In general, the more complex a walkway or deck construction plan is, the more disturbance to the environment and potential risk to

Fig. 3.8.2: Wooden walkway, Palais de Tokyo, Paris

Fig. 3.8.1: Jetty, Krienicke Park in Spandau, Berlin

Fig. 3.8.3: Wooden deck, Köpenick

people and property and the more need for an accompanying building inspection.

The main issue is achieving an appropriate construction. For instance, there should be no broad lengthwise joints in the direction of travel if bicycle traffic and wheelchairs can be expected, and no gratings if high heels are common footwear in the area of use.

For open-air public facilities, accessibility must be ensured. If walkways and decks are planned for a playground environment, the general safety requirements for playground apparatus should be observed. In particular, there should be no places where body parts or clothing could become trapped.

If the difference in level with the ground surface on either side is more than 1 m, a breastwork should be included, as specified by the building regulations. > Chapter 3.4

In choosing suitable coverings with the necessary roughness or profile, it should be ensured that walkways and decks are non-slip even during wet weather or frost. The laying direction of the covering elements and the resulting joint pattern also affects skidproofing. A wooden plank covering laid across the direction of travel, for instance, is favorable.

Regular walkway and deck maintenance is necessary to retain traffic safety. Potential risks due to chippings, sharp-edged ridges, projecting nails and screws, warped planking, and faulty components should be removed.

Out of doors, walkways and decks are exposed to weathering and contact with water surfaces or soil. Leaves, dirt, and soil can be expected to collect, preventing the construction from easily drying out. For this reason, when choosing materials, durability under usage conditions should be factored in. For wood constructions, wood types with sufficient natural durability (e.g. robinia, oak, and sometimes larch and Douglas fir) or timbers protected with preventative chemicals, usually boiler pressure-impregnated native woods, are used. > Chapter 1.4

For constructions and connectors made of steel, adequate corrosion resistance should be ensured, either by using nonrusting steels or by protecting steel parts using a suitable zinc coating. Stainless steel is generally used for the connectors to avoid rust stains dirtying the construction, despite the higher cost. This also rules out corrosive influences from the tannic acid exuded by some wood species (e.g. oak), or by chemical wood protection agents. If different metals are used, contact corrosion should be avoided as far as possible. > Chapter 1.8

As well as a suitable choice of materials, the correct construction of details is important for the longevity of walkways and decks. In principle, whole constructions can be protected from direct weathering by the form and construction of a roof. Individual components can be protected by an impermeable covering. Standing water should also be avoided by creating appropriate slopes and possibilities for drainage. Prompt and controlled drainage of moisture as well as good air circulation for all components should be the aim: this ensures quick drying. Deposits of dirt, which store moisture in particularly high amounts, should be minimized through appropriate construction, and removed as part of regular maintenance.

FOUNDATION

The type of foundation used for walkways and decks depends on the loads involved, the support construction and the loadbearing capacity of the building ground. > Chapter 2.3

Ramming in stakes or posts is particularly appropriate where concrete foundations are more difficult, e.g. for jetties. The embedment depth depends on the building ground's composition. Otherwise, concrete isolated footings are usual for raised walkways and decks —those for which the loads are transmitted to the foundation level by uprights. For wood constructions, the concrete foundation and the uprights are connected by steel fittings. If the loadbearing capacity of isolated footings is insufficient, strip or raft foundations are constructed. If walkways or decks are laid level to the ground and no uprights are needed, it is possible to lay the horizontal loadbearing components on strip foundations or wide-surface foundations. Wide-area foundations can be created as rigid concrete raft foundations or nonrigid gravel or ballast base courses. > Fig. 3.8.4

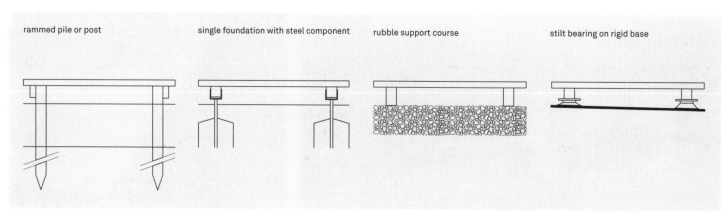

Fig. 3.8.4: Different foundation types for walkways and decks

SUBSTRUCTURE/SUPPORT CONSTRUCTION

The support structure or substructure absorbs the forces acting on the covering and transmits them to the foundation. Its design should therefore be decided in connection with the choice of materials. It is tailored to the static demands.

Good weathering protection should be assured for the support construction, as its maintenance is usually made difficult by its being out of sight and requiring significant effort to replace. Walkways and decks that "float" above the surface of the ground are safer from weathering than structures at terrain height, in direct contact with soil or water. The contact faces between the upper components and the support construction should be as narrow as possible, as a minimal contact face ensures rapid drying. For an ideally constructed wood deck or walkway, a hard rubber strip or narrow oak fillet, for instance, is laid between the board layer and the loadbearing timbers. In addition, protective coverings on the upper side of the loadbearing timbers increase the life expectancy of the wood construction. Places where connectors penetrate these coverings should be sealed to be as watertight as possible, using continuous strips of neoprene, for instance. > Fig. 3.8.5

Steel substructures are more durable and also enable longer spans, if protected from corrosion. > Fig. 3.8.6

COVERING

The covering is the uppermost part of walkways and decks, and is therefore decisive for functional comfort and optical appearance. In practice, wooden plank or board coverings and metal gratings have become established for normal usage conditions. Walkways and decks made from sheet-metal moldings, steel plates, concrete, plastic, or armored glass are rarer. > Figs. 3.8.7 and 3.8.8

The covering elements generally lie crosswise to the walking/driving direction. The laying direction and joint formation can however also be modified for design purposes. For larger surfaces, there are two basic possibilities: to stagger the joints at regular intervals or to align them in a row, so that closed fields are created. > Fig. 3.8.9

Wooden planks can be connected directly with the substructure as separate elements or prefabricated as wood grids. Wood grid coverings have the advantage of being easy to remove and replace. Attaching the wood grids to the substructure should be done in such a way that horizontal loads are redirected and rattling is avoided. Wood grids are commercially available as a standard element. If they have been produced individually, the dimensions should be restricted to allow easy handling by two people (< 2.5 m^2).

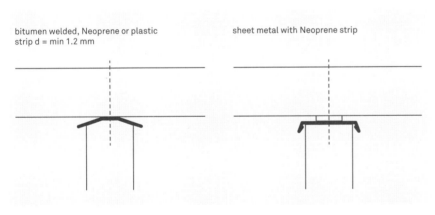

bitumen welded, Neoprene or plastic strip d = min 1.2 mm

sheet metal with Neoprene strip

Fig. 3.8.5: Covering loadbearing timbers

Fig. 3.8.6: Steel walkway with wood covering, I-supports as beams, circular hollow moldings as supports

Fig. 3.8.7: Ground-level deck made of glass, Oberbaum City in Berlin

Fig. 3.8.8: Overhanging steel walkway

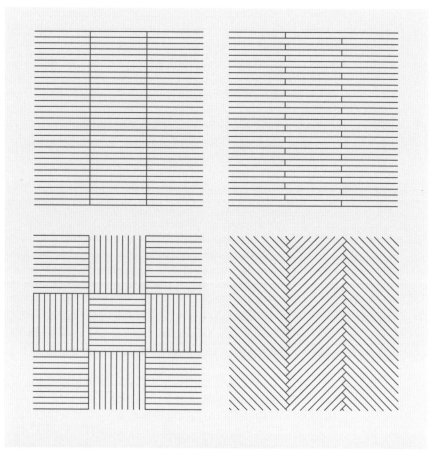

Fig. 3.8.9: Effect of joints and end-meetings, seen in a wood deck

The planks' cross sections are determined by static stresses. A correct distance between the loadbearing timbers (50–80 cm), or, for larger plank support spans, the mounting of non-loadbearing wooden spacers on planks' undersides, is important to prevent warping. The wooden planks are secured with two special nails or wood screws to each mounting. However, screws are preferred as they make removal of damaged planks easier. Joint gaps of 6–8 mm are a proven method for open plank coverings. However, as planks are often laid with a wood moisture content of > 20%, it makes sense to install with narrower joint gaps (approx. 3 mm), as the joint gap will increase due to wood shrinkage.

Gratings consist of vertical support bars arranged in parallel, crossed by filler bars. For standard pressure-locked gratings, filler bars are pressed into slots in the support bars at high pressure. Gratings in which the support bars and the filler bars are at the same height are described as full gratings. The bar construction is enclosed by iron bars or U-moldings at the edges. Gratings are produced with quadratic or rectangular spacing and with a variety of dimensions. They are manufactured from steel, stainless steel or aluminum.
> Fig. 3.8.10

The grating's lateral contact face with the substructure should be at least 30 mm. Grids should be secured to the substructure using connective elements. They may also be installed in a frame construction (angle frame) to prevent slippage.

Fig. 3.8.10: Different pressure gratings: pressure-locked grating with steel bar border, pressure-locked grating with U-molding border and full grating

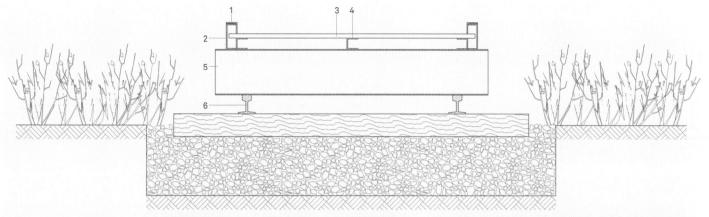

1 Angle frame, nonalloy,
  80 x 80 x 7 mm
2 U molding, nonalloy, 180 mm
3 Galvanized grating,
  MW 31/9 mm, 1000 x 1800 mm
4 U-steel, nonalloy, 80 mm
5 Steel pipe, nonalloy,
  323.9 x 6.3 mm, length 200 cm
6 Existing rails

NATURE PARK SCHÖNEBERGER SÜDGELÄNDE,
BERLIN, GERMANY

Artist: Gruppe Odious: Klaus Duschat, Klaus H.
Hartmann, David Lee Thompson
Completion: 1998

The sensitive biotope in the grounds of the former Tempelhof marshalling yard is made
accessible to the public nondestructively by means of a 600 m steel walkway floating
50 cm above the ground.
Steel pipes welded to steel supports on their upper sides lie along the remaining rails.
Gratings enclosed laterally by spur posts made of steel grille moldings are secured to this
substructure.

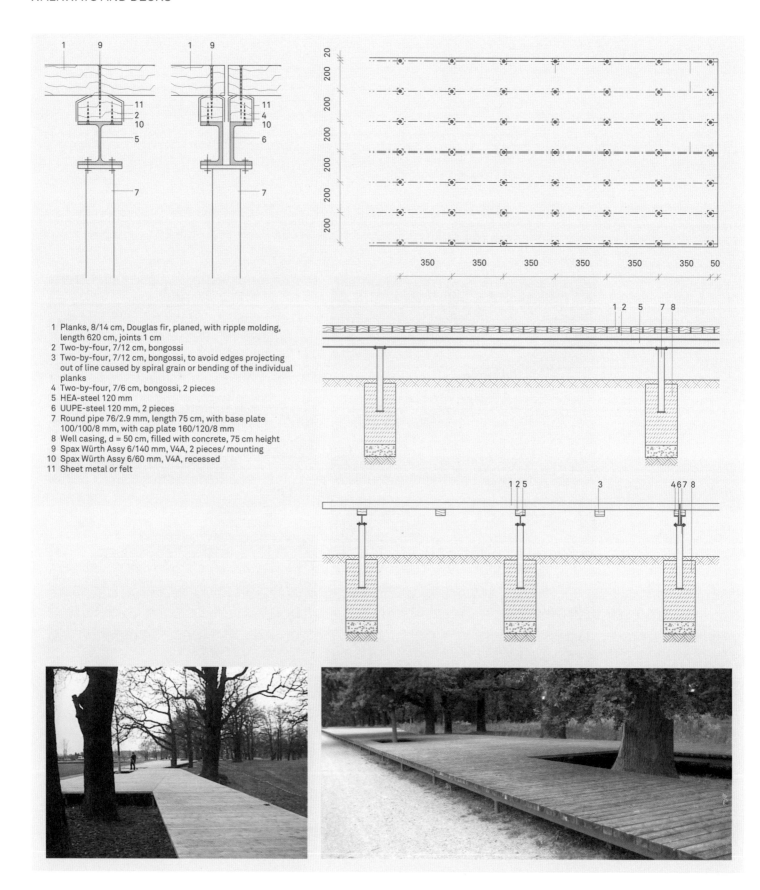

1 Planks, 8/14 cm, Douglas fir, planed, with ripple molding,
  length 620 cm, joints 1 cm
2 Two-by-four, 7/12 cm, bongossi
3 Two-by-four, 7/12 cm, bongossi, to avoid edges projecting
  out of line caused by spiral grain or bending of the individual
  planks
4 Two-by-four, 7/6 cm, bongossi, 2 pieces
5 HEA-steel 120 mm
6 UUPE-steel 120 mm, 2 pieces
7 Round pipe 76/2.9 mm, length 75 cm, with base plate
  100/100/8 mm, with cap plate 160/120/8 mm
8 Well casing, d = 50 cm, filled with concrete, 75 cm height
9 Spax Würth Assy 6/140 mm, V4A, 2 pieces/ mounting
10 Spax Würth Assy 6/60 mm, V4A, recessed
11 Sheet metal or felt

WOODEN PLATFORM, VIERECKREMISE, POTSDAM, GERMANY

Planungsgemeinschaft Remisenpark Potsdam:
AG Freiraum Jochen Dittus and Andreas Böhringer
Pit Müller Freier Landschaftsarchitekt
Construction directed by: Stötzer und Neher GmbH

Structural engineer: Harald Albrecht
Completion: 2001
The loadbearing substructure consists of steel tubes and moldings. The steel supports
allow a further grid to be realized, to restrict the trees' root space as little as possible.
To secure the covering timbers on the steel substructure, squared bongossi timbers are
placed in between. Where the covering planks meet, the steel molding is divided, so that
any water seeping in can escape downwards.

1 Boards, 3.5/14.5 cm, larch,
   planed
2 Boards, 3.5/14.5 cm, larch,
   planed, with sloped face
3 Boards, 3.5/14.5 cm, larch,
   planed, with ripple molding
4 Boards, 3.5/12.5 cm, larch,
   planed
5 Two-by-fours, 9/9 cm, larch
   as a substructure, with folded
   sheets
6 Two-by-fours, 9/9 cm, larch
7 Bolts with washers
8 Drainage mat
9 Sandpit
10 Height and slope adjustable
   stilt bearing
11 Asphalt cover (existing)

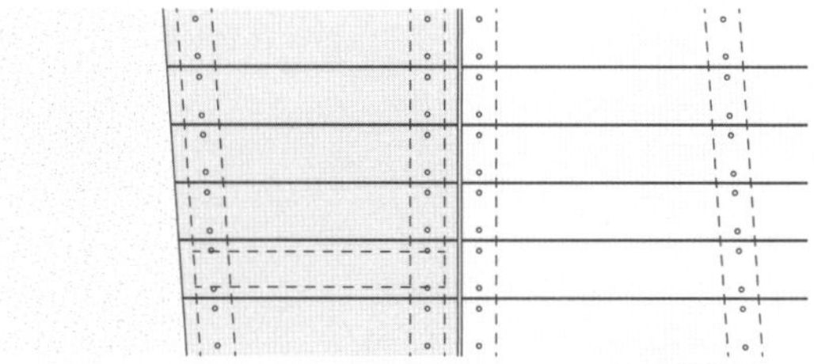

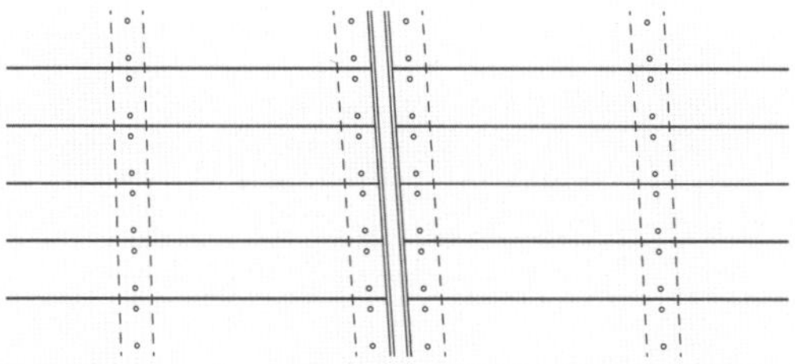

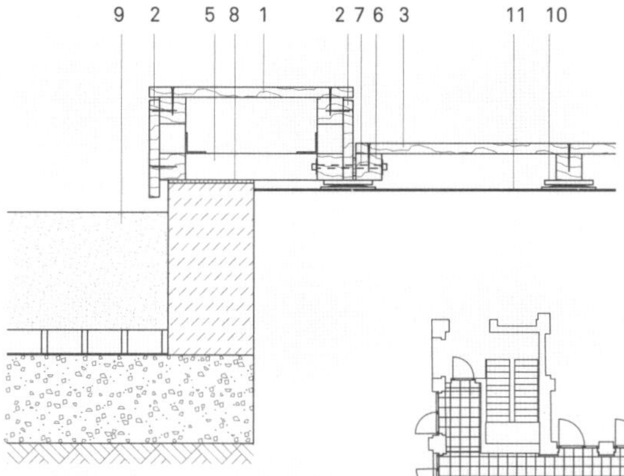

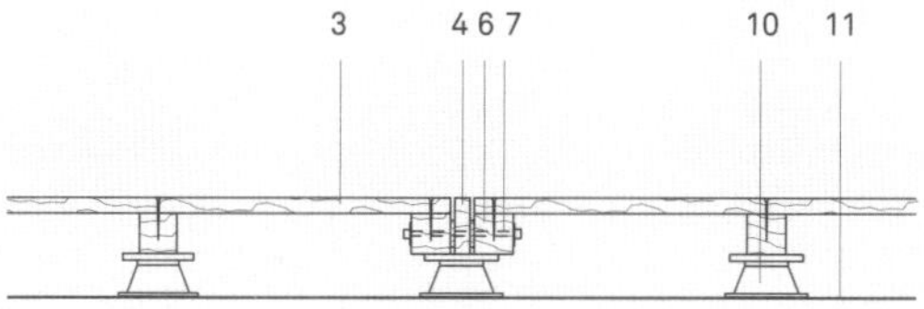

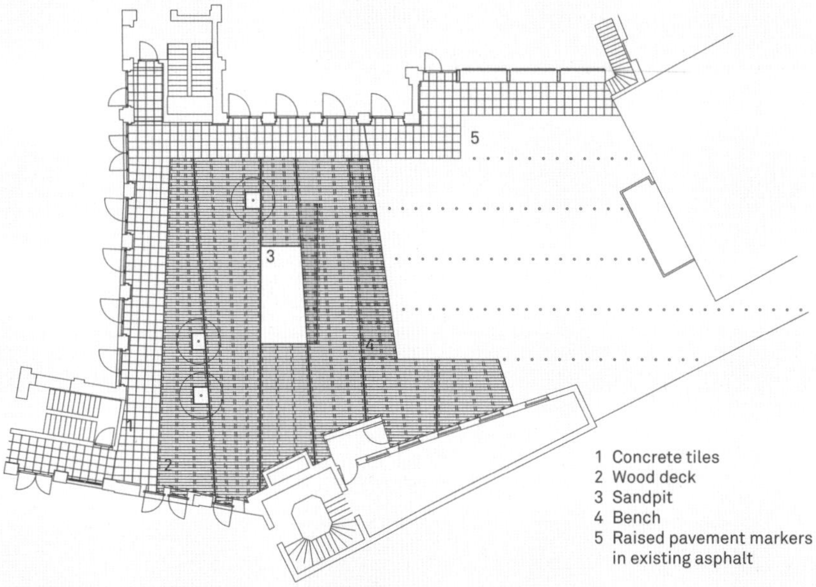

1 Concrete tiles
2 Wood deck
3 Sandpit
4 Bench
5 Raised pavement markers
   in existing asphalt

WOOD DECK IN INNER COURTYARD OF ALTE
DRUCKEREI, HANOVER, GERMANY

relais Landschaftsarchitekten
Completion: 2005

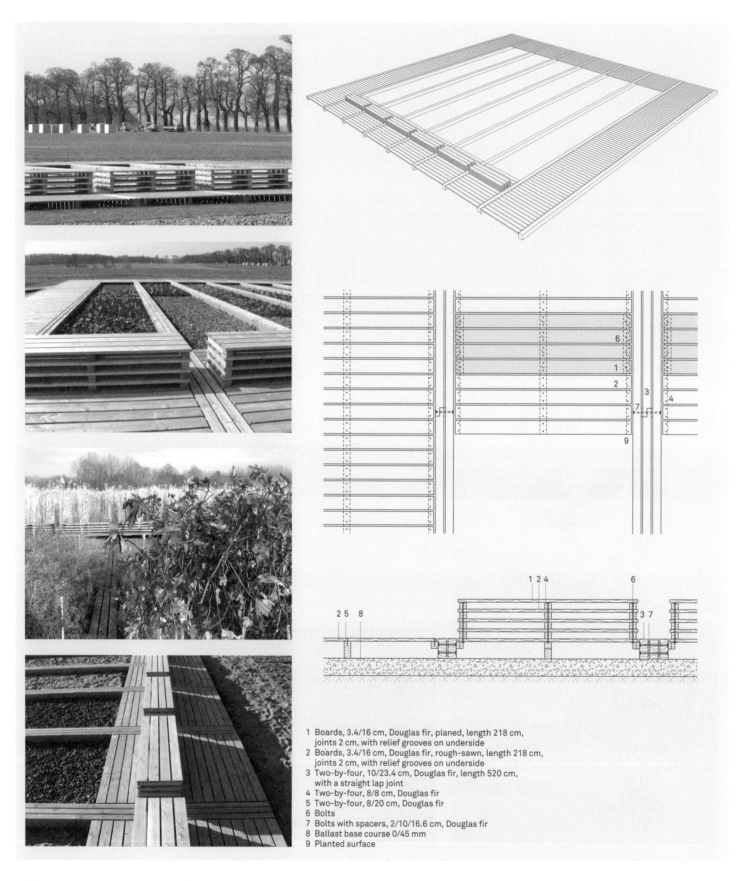

1 Boards, 3.4/16 cm, Douglas fir, planed, length 218 cm, joints 2 cm, with relief grooves on underside
2 Boards, 3.4/16 cm, Douglas fir, rough-sawn, length 218 cm, joints 2 cm, with relief grooves on underside
3 Two-by-four, 10/23.4 cm, Douglas fir, length 520 cm, with a straight lap joint
4 Two-by-four, 8/8 cm, Douglas fir
5 Two-by-four, 8/20 cm, Douglas fir
6 Bolts
7 Bolts with spacers, 2/10/16.6 cm, Douglas fir
8 Ballast base course 0/45 mm
9 Planted surface

WOODEN CARGO DECK, ZENTRUM FÜR GARTENKUNST
SCHLOSS DYCK, GERMANY

relais Landschaftsarchitekten
Completion: 2002

This themed garden at a regional garden show is designed to last for five years. Nine wood ribs, each made of two to three parallel two-by-fours bolted together with a gap in between, structure the garden. They support a continuous belt of wood boards. The boards are laid with wide gaps at the joints, in order to evoke associations with industrially produced wood pallets. The continuous wood frame is laid on a ballast base course. In the planting area, the wood ribs have rammed-in robinia wood pillars as foundations.

1 Supporting wall, exposed concrete finished parts
2 Bolts 4.5/14.5 cm, larch, rough-sawn, length 249.5 cm,
   joints 1 cm
3 Two-by-four, 9/9 cm, larch
4 Roofing felt
5 Concrete tile 25/25/4 cm
6 Ballast base course, 0/45 mm
7 Shortened sheet pile wall, irregular course (existing)
8 HEB 120 spacer with under-hook protection TB 60
9 U-steel 280 mm skirting protection
10 Water

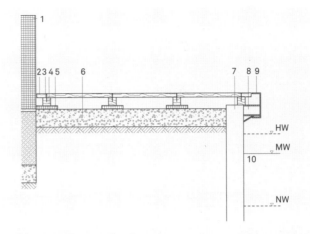

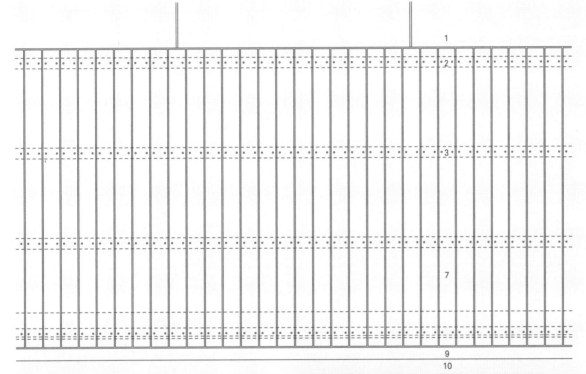

HARBOR WALKWAY, MASELAKEPARK, SPANDAU,
BERLIN, GERMANY

relais Landschaftsarchitekten
Completion: 2007

The change in levels between the wood walkway and the elevated continuous promenade part is eliminated by a combined support and seating wall made from exposed concrete finished parts. On the seaward side, a skirting protection made of steel U-moldings encloses the wood walkway. The existing sheet pile walls were shortened by 1 m. The irregular sheet piling line is balanced optically by the protruding wood walkway, forming a straight edge.

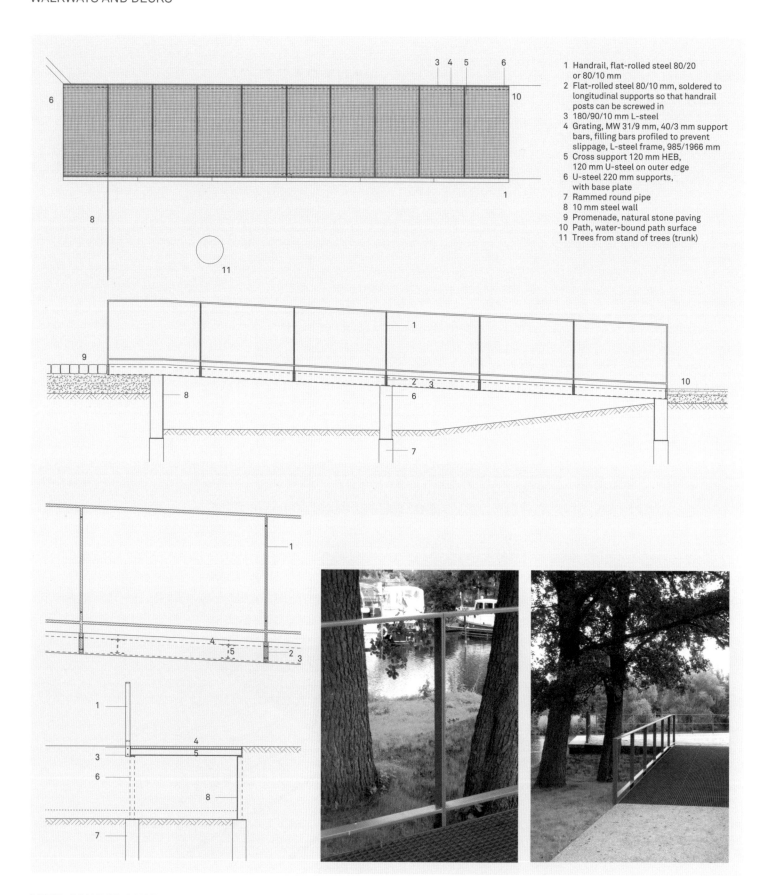

1 Handrail, flat-rolled steel 80/20
   or 80/10 mm
2 Flat-rolled steel 80/10 mm, soldered to
   longitudinal supports so that handrail
   posts can be screwed in
3 180/90/10 mm L-steel
4 Grating, MW 31/9 mm, 40/3 mm support
   bars, filling bars profiled to prevent
   slippage, L-steel frame, 985/1966 mm
5 Cross support 120 mm HEB,
   120 mm U-steel on outer edge
6 U-steel 220 mm supports,
   with base plate
7 Rammed round pipe
8 10 mm steel wall
9 Promenade, natural stone paving
10 Path, water-bound path surface
11 Trees from stand of trees (trunk)

METAL WALKWAY, MASELAKEPARK BERLIN-SPANDAU,
GERMANY

relais Landschaftsarchitekten
Completed: 2007

To connect the raised harbor area with a continuing lower-
lying foot and cycle path, a steel walkway standing on supports was constructed. This walkway avoided further filling
of the terrain, protecting a distinctive stand of alders.

3.9 PLANTING TECHNIQUE AND CARE OF VEGETATION SURFACES

BASICS OF PLANT GROWTH
· Fundamental site conditions
· Development phases and maintenance
· Plant protection

PLANTING WOODY PLANTS
· Planting woody plants in existing soil
· Road-lining tree planting in sealed areas
· Maintenance

PLANTING AND MAINTENANCE OF HERBACEOUS PLANTS
· Planting
· Maintenance

PLANTING AND MAINTENANCE OF GEOPHYTES

SEASONAL ORNAMENTAL PLANTS

SPECIMEN PROJECTS

Ute Rieper

3.9 PLANTING TECHNIQUE AND CARE OF VEGETATION SURFACES

BASICS OF PLANT GROWTH

Fundamental site conditions

Plant health is affected by various different factors. The most significant of these are the availability of nutrients, soil conditions, climatic conditions, and competition pressures arising between different plant species.

Soil serves plants for root anchorage and as a nutrient and water reservoir. Good soil aeration, maintained by an adequate percentage of air-conducting coarse pores, good water drainage, no waterlogging, and a normal soil layer thickness are required for root growth. Loamy / clayey soils have a relatively high capacity for nutrient and water storage, but tend towards compaction and poor aeration. For this reason, mixed soil types such as loamy sands or sandy loams are the most favorable.

The most important nutrient elements are N (nitrogen, for leaf mass), P (phosphorus, for flower formation) and K (potassium, for firm, frost-resistant tissues). These are commonly stored by humus particles or clay minerals in the soil. Adding nutrients to the soil via fertilizers or compost is mainly necessary for extremely sandy soils, in case of continual nutrient removal (e.g. where hedges are clipped), or for high nutrient-intake cultures such as bedding roses. Where possible, leaves or cut herbaceous plant material should be left on the area to preserve the nutrient cycle. Trees are able to tap nutrients at great depths due to their deep penetrating roots.

The growth of plants is also strongly influenced by climate. It is above all the severity and duration of frosts that limits the choice of suitable plants. The atlas shown in **Fig. 3.9.1.** gives a rough overview of winter hardiness zones in Europe.

Corresponding indications of the frost resistance of species and varieties can be found in reference books and tree nursery catalogues. Regional climate and microclimate determine the actual effect frost will have. Heavy, wet soils,

Organism	Fertilizing during planting (or finalizing maintenance)	Fertilizing during upkeep maintenance
Isolated woody plant, in virgin soil	controlled-release complete fertilizer if soil is extremely sandy	compost or leafmold humus, targeted doses of single nutrient fertilizer if deficiencies appear
Road-lining tree in planting trench	-	possibly K-rich controlled release fertilizer
Hedge	controlled-release complete fertilizer if soil is extremely sandy	compost or low dose of complete fertilizer
Bed roses or climbing roses	complete fertilizer at beginning of growing period	low-chloride complete fertilizer, 2x per year
Ornamental and bedding herbaceous plants	minimal to moderate dose of complete fertilizer in the first spring	compost and/or complete fertilizer annually
Large herbaceous plant on rich site	as for bedding herbaceous plants	annual cut material mulch, compost, possibly complete fertilizer
Planting in dry, meager sites	-	-
Woodland herbaceous plants	possibly as for herbaceous bedding plants	leafmold mulch or compost for good humus provision annually
Geophytes, winter hardy	-	for tulip and narcissus hybrids, complete fertilizer doses when leaves shoot
Geophytes, frost-sensitive	compost or controlled release complete fertilizer during planting as needed	supplementary fertilizing if deficiencies appear
Spring and summer bedding flowers	controlled release complete fertilizer during planting	additional P-rich fertilizers if necessary. Occasionally the nutrient content should be checked through soil analysis, to optimize the dosage and avoid eutrophication
Tub plants	controlled release complete fertilizer, compost, manure	possibly additional complete fertilizer

Tab. 3.9.1: Fertilizer requirements of different organisms

Winter hardiness zones and their temperature spreads, average annual minimum temperatures ($t_{min J}$)		
Zone	°F	°C
1	< -50	< -45.5
2	-50 to -40	-45.5 to -40.1
3	-40 to -30	-40.0 to -34.5
4	-30 to -20	-34.4 to -28.9
5	-20 to -10	-28.8 to -23.4
6	-10 to 0	-23.2 to -17.8
7	0 to 10	-17.7 to -12.3
8	10 to 20	-12.2 to -6.7
9	20 to 30	-6.6 to -1.2
10	30 to 40	-1.1 to 4.4
11	> 40	> 4.4

Fig. 3.9.1: Winter hardiness zones
in Europe (taken from: Heinze and
Schreiber 1984)

sun exposure and wind aggravate frost damage: frost directly damages the cells, which freeze and burst if their water content is high. Evergreens in particular are vulnerable to frost drought. If the sun shines on their leaves during a frost and water evaporates, it cannot be replenished by the frozen soil, causing the affected plants to dry out and eventually die. Effective protection measures include mulching of the root area (for insulation) and low-N, high-K fertilizer to make cells frost-resistant, as well as shading for evergreen woody plants.

The way that geography shapes the climate is also significant. Areas near the sea have a maritime climate, with less difference between summer and winter temperatures, high precipitation levels, cool summers and mild, rainy winters. As distance from the sea increases, the landmass creates a continental climate, with lower precipitation and a greater summer-winter temperature difference. Summers are hotter, while winters bring severe frost with low precipitation (black frost). As plants are adapted to the climate of their original location, moving them to a location with a dissimilar climate often creates problems. Species that prefer a continental climate tend to develop increased fungal diseases and winter root rot when exposed to a maritime climate, while maritime species resettled in a continental climate tend to develop frost damage and suffer from the dryness and low humidity in summer.

Competition exists between plants—between plants of the same species (for instance in a birch grove) and between different organisms (for instance, between the trees and the plants in the herb layer in a mixed deciduous wood), for the resources of light, water, root space and placement, as well as nutrients. Species with similar requirements are in direct competition with each other. This usually leads to a single species becoming dominant. It is therefore better to combine species whose requirements tend to complement each other.

Development phases and maintenance
Succession—the establishment and development of plant communities—can take place anywhere on open soil. In a temperate, mid-European climate, the end result is usually a mixed, deciduous forest. > Fig. 3.9.3

Fig. 3.9.2: Shading after transplanting

Garden plantings are also subject to this dynamic, which causes changes in overall plant composition. Long-term maintenance measures are therefore necessary, in order to preserve a planting.

The term maintenance describes the sum of all measures and interventions that preserve and promote the desired function and form of a planting in the long term. In plant sociology terms, maintenance means halting or delaying the natural succession. It influences and to some extent prevents the processes of competition.

Separate maintenance stages are recognized, depending on a planting's developmental state.
Finalizing maintenance follows the first planting. It is intended to ensure the growth of plants, concluding with them reaching an acceptable state. It includes watering, weeding and possibly fertilizing, with plant protection measures if necessary. This kind of maintenance usually lasts for a full growing period after completion.
Development maintenance describes the phase ending with the desired function and form being achieved, e.g. achieving an even shrub layer in woody plant groups or reaching the desired crown height in road-lining trees. This phase is very labor-intensive, so that efforts are often made to keep it short via planning strategy and choice of materials.

An even vegetation layer can be created onsite as early as the first or second year, by seeding a herb layer in

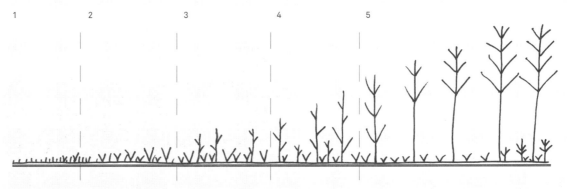

1) pioneer stage, 2) grass-shrub stage, 3) transitional stage, 4) bush stage, 5) forest stage. Soil development and maturation occur from 1) to 5), the species become increasingly more long-lived, competitive and more tolerant of shade.

Fig. 3.9.3: Schematized succession process

woody plant groups or by using fast-developing pioneer species in herbaceous plantings. Where older specimens are used, partial training involving clipping may take place in the tree nursery. This may be the best option if expert maintenance cannot be expected. Open soil can also be covered with mulch. Organic or mineral materials may be used for this. Mulching improves moisture conservation and, when organic material is used, improves humus and nutrient content. Mulch containing wood initially binds nitrogen, and should therefore be used in combination with a complementary fertilizing process. As the mulch layer is reduced over time by dispersal and decomposition, it should be renewed every 2–4 years as needed. > Tab. 3.9.2

Development maintenance involves weeding, watering and fertilizing as needed, training clipping of woody plants and possible plant protection measures. It can be expected to last 2–3 years for herbaceous plantings, 5–8 years for woody plant groups, and 10–15 years for road-lining trees.

Upkeep maintenance preserves and improves the achieved shape and function. This includes rejuvenating and filling gaps in herbaceous plantings, and regular clipping of hedges.

Plant protection

Damage and diseases are usually caused by insects, rodents, viruses, bacteria, and fungi. It is mainly weakened plants that are infested; regular mass infestations thus usually indicate a problem with the location. Applications of synthetic sprays are usually only effective in the short term. The concept of "integrated plant protection" is represents a more sensible and sustainable strategy. In terms of planning, this involves a precise description of the site and taking care to choose plants appropriate to it. Another possibility is using especially robust, disease-tolerant or resistant species or varieties.

In terms of long-term upkeep maintenance, this means ensuring optimal species-specific provisions. Some species may need to be kept particularly dry with a low nutrient intake. In the longer term this also means adapting and replacing older plant stock, for instance if tree growth overshadows formerly sunny sites.

The introduction of pests, in connection with global commodities transport, is a particular problem. As their new host plants are unable to develop defensive mechanisms or resistance, the pests can cause extremely severe damage. For this reason, a health certificate or prescribed quarantine is required for plant imports from non-European countries.

PLANTING WOODY PLANTS

Planting woody plants in existing soil

Preparing the site

Unfavorable soil types should be improved. Sandy soils can be made more cohesive and water-retentive in the root zone by admixtures of supplements such as bentonite (clay minerals). Soils that are too heavy and loamy

Material	Use	Notes
Chippings, diverse (hard) mineral types	herbaceous plants: sunny sites/open space, road-lining trees	N-neutral, decoration for planting with gaps
Lava tuff	herbaceous plants: sunny sites, road-lining trees	N-neutral, decoration for planting with gaps
Brick chippings	herbaceous plants: open space, rockeries, occasionally road-lining trees	N-neutral, color tone often difficult to combine with plants
Bark mulch	herbaceous plants: woodland herbaceous plants, open space, bedding herbaceous plants, woody plants	N-binding, complementary fertilizer to be renewed after 2–3 years
Wood fiber	herbaceous plants: sunny to shady, not for rockeries/steppe or similar	N-binding (see above)
Chopped wood	woody plants, herbaceous plants except for locations/rockeries or similar	N-binding (see above) woody plants: risk of introducing disease factors if origin of chopped wood unknown. Chopped cut material (from maintenance clipping) harmless. Do not apply too much. It may be a good idea to take the existing herb layer into account
Cocoa bean husks	as an N-providing admixture	if applied unmixed, this often causes salt damage to herbaceous plants as well as groundwater contamination via high-nutrient seepage water, due to high N, P and K content.

The layer thickness should be about 5–7 cm for herbaceous plants and 7–10 cm for woody plants.

Tab. 3.9.2: Mulching materials

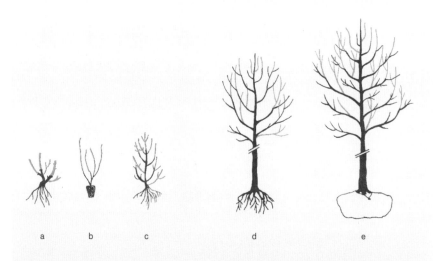

a) Take bare-rooted roses down to 3–5 eyes (buds), b) reduce climbers such as *Clematis* to approx. 30 cm, c+d Bare-rooted stock: Competing roots and damaged, inward-growing or crossing branches are removed. Heavy trimming of the crown promotes growth in some species, including Robinia and Salix (willow). e) Usually, container stock plants are merely thinned out and modified with regard to growth pattern.

Fig. 3.9.4: Plant clipping

Fig. 3.9.5: Plant clipping on a horizontal standard tree

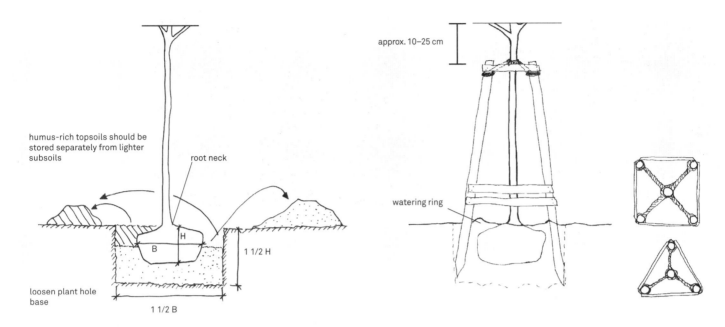

Fig. 3.9.6: Tree planting and anchoring

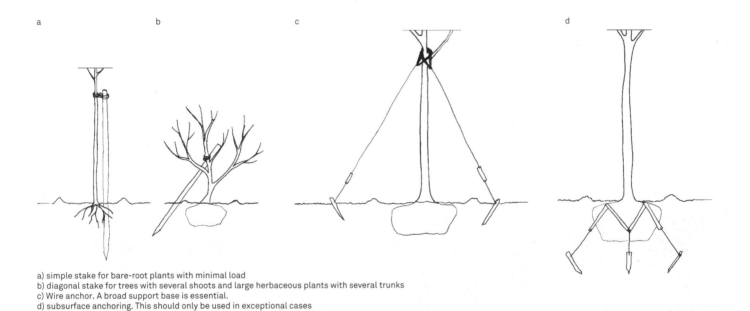

a) simple stake for bare-root plants with minimal load
b) diagonal stake for trees with several shoots and large herbaceous plants with several trunks
c) Wire anchor. A broad support base is essential.
d) subsurface anchoring. This should only be used in exceptional cases
 A relatively large and firm rootball is a requirement. The rootball is often squashed or folded during placement.

Fig. 3.9.7: Light anchoring techniques and subsurface anchoring

should be loosened, for instance by adding sand or tuff. If necessary, the topsoil should be additionally improved by adding humus. If planting holes are dug out in very cohesive soil and filled with substrate offering seepage, there is a danger that water will accumulate there. As most woody plants die when waterlogged, the planting should be abandoned if drainage cannot be provided.

Plant clipping

Plant clipping is intended to restore the balance between root volume and shoot mass, thereby enabling vigorous shoot formation as well as good rooting. This is generally carried out before planting. Bare-rooted stock plants are cut back about 1/3 in autumn, and about 1/2 to 1/3 in spring (a and b). Rootball plants are generally modified on site (c). > Fig. 3.9.4

The woody plant is aligned in the planting hole. The roots should be submerged as deeply as they were in the tree nursery. When filling in, the soil is compacted carefully, to avoid significant settling. Finally, the soil is thoroughly watered, to improve the roots' contact with the earth, and a watering ring about the same size as the rootball is laid.

Anchoring woody plants

Secure tying is intended to allow undisturbed growth of fine feeder roots. Anchoring should last for three growing periods and can then be removed. For road-lining trees, a three- or four-legged jack stand is needed. For

Fig. 3.9.8: Coconut rope binding

Fig. 3.9.9: A young standard trunk strangled by over-tight synthetic binding

lesser loads and lower quality, lighter anchoring systems can be used. > Fig. 3.9.7

The binding must have a broad contact area and must not rub or constrict. Coconut rope is a tried and tested material. There are also a variety of synthetic materials, which may only be suitable under certain circumstances (> Schneidewind 2003). As vigorous young trees can increase considerably in girth, the binding must be checked regularly (annually) and loosened if necessary, as the binding may be overgrown by wood or even strangle the trunk. > Figs. 3.9.8 and 3.9.9

It is primarily young standard trunks, without an impervious outer bark, that need to be additionally protected against sun burning by means of trunk protection. Mats made from reeds or bamboo canes are particularly effective. > Fig. 3.9.10a

Road-lining tree planting in sealed areas

If the existing soil is not suitable as a tree planting site, a tree trench can be arranged. It should be at least 12 m³ in size and at least 1.5 m deep. For areas without pressure caused by use, simple tree substrate can be used. For moderate functional pressure areas, a self-supporting tree grate can be built in above. Grilles or tiles intercept the active forces and prevent the substrate from being compacted. > Fig. 3.9.11

Where higher loads are present, due, for instance, to pedestrians, cyclists and light traffic, loadbearing substrate capable of acting as subsoil can be used. It is compacted sufficiently to support a load, after which it still possesses enough air and water capacity for healthy root growth. In confined sites, root space can be additionally expanded using construction measures such as

Fig. 3.9.10:
a) Three-legged jack stand for road-lining tree with a belt binding and reed matting trunk protection
b) Diagonal stake with synthetic binding for a young red oak in a park
c) Three-legged jack stand with belt binding and protection against animal browsing

a | b | c

Fig. 3.9.11: Self-supporting
overbuilt tree grates:
a) compound tree grille
   with durable trunk protection
b) tree grilles with relatively
   small openings may have to be
   removed or replaced before
   the base of the trunk becomes
   too big

a | b

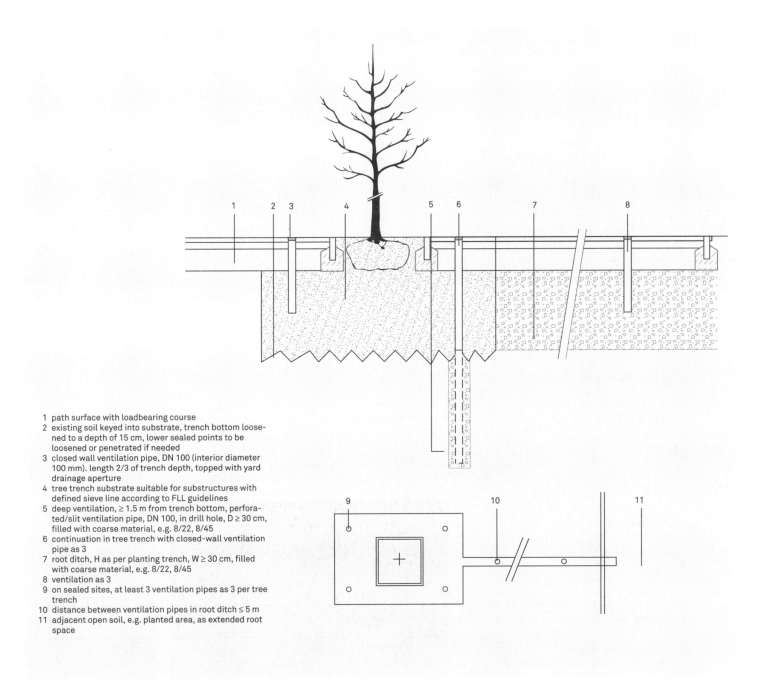

1 path surface with loadbearing course
2 existing soil keyed into substrate, trench bottom loosened to a depth of 15 cm, lower sealed points to be
   loosened or penetrated if needed
3 closed wall ventilation pipe, DN 100 (interior diameter
   100 mm). length 2/3 of trench depth, topped with yard
   drainage aperture
4 tree trench substrate suitable for substructures with
   defined sieve line according to FLL guidelines
5 deep ventilation, ≥ 1.5 m from trench bottom, perfora-
   ted/slit ventilation pipe, DN 100, in drill hole, D ≥ 30 cm,
   filled with coarse material, e.g. 8/22, 8/45
6 continuation in tree trench with closed-wall ventilation
   pipe as 3
7 root ditch, H as per planting trench, W ≥ 30 cm, filled
   with coarse material, e.g. 8/22, 8/45
8 ventilation as 3
9 on sealed sites, at least 3 ventilation pipes as 3 per tree
   trench
10 distance between ventilation pipes in root ditch ≤ 5 m
11 adjacent open soil, e.g. planted area, as extended root
   space

Fig. 3.9.12: Tree trench with loadbearing substrate, standard and deep
aeration and root ditches

deep aeration or a root ditch, in which roots can be directed towards neighboring unsealed areas.

Maintenance

Finalizing maintenance involved is described under
> Chapter Basics of plant growth, Development phases and maintenance
The constructive clip and training clip are carried out during the development stage. > Figs 3.9.13 and 3.9.14. They are important as the basis for the tree's shape, static crown form, and how it will age over the next few decades, especially for road-lining trees.

A new approach to planning low-maintenance woody plant groups is based on the different species-specific competing strengths of the plants used. This concept aims to create woody plant groups with good tree cover that age well and largely regulate themselves during the development stage. To achieve this, woody plants that are durable for the foreseeable future and are actually intended to fulfill the function of the woody plant group (dazzle and wind protection, space creation, habitat, etc.) are combined with weakly competitive, short-lived filler woody plants. These subordinate woody plants are intended to create even cover and reserve the growth

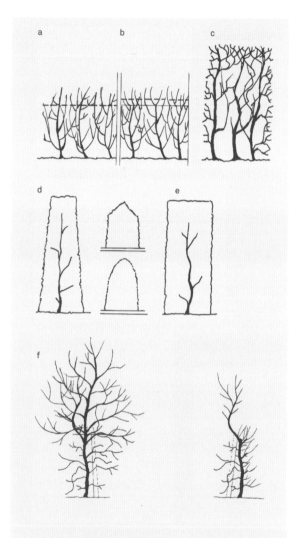

a) clip height approx. 60 cm at planting
b) new shoots and clipping back in the first vegetation period
c) 1.5 m final height achieved after approx. 5 years; frequent clipping ensures dense branches
d) normal hedge outline: the hedge tapers towards the top, so that the lower parts are exposed to sufficient light and do not become bald
e) only shade-loving varieties such as yew or beech are suitable for vertical hedge cross-sections
f) untended hedges can be tapered if the plant species is capable of wide growth. These included species such as yew, hornbeam or common maple. The first stage is to reduce the height on one side. The clipping line lies about 15 cm below the intended height. As soon as strong new growth has been achieved, the second side can be cut back. It is important to maintain a good supply of water and nutrients to promote new growth.

Fig. 3.9.13: Training clip and rejuvenation clip for hedges

No.	Woody plant planting type	Finalizing maintenance	Development maintenance	Upkeep maintenance
1	isolated woody plant, bush or tree	water, weed, check binding	check tree binding (risk of strangulation), water during summer for approximately 2–3 years, possibly shape or modify crown, possibly use frost protection until plant becomes established	remove dead wood. thin out bushes (continual rejuvenation) water during shoot production in dry locations
2	road-lining tree	as for 1	as for 1, lop according to clearing pattern	regular checking of trees, removal of dead wood, treat calluses, possibly fertilize if deficiencies are manifested
3	clipped hedges	water, weed, clip hedge	1–2 clippings annually. Water if soil is sandy. Fertilize if necessary	clip hedge 1 to 2x annually, remove weeds and woody plant seedlings, add compost or fertilizer if soil is poor. Plant protection if necessary
4	form-clipped woody plants	as for 1	as for hedges. Create unusual forms using wires	1–3 clippings annually, otherwise as for hedges. Shelter during winter in exposed situations
5	large trees	as for 1	water, fertilize if necessary, plant protection, check long-term anchoring	due to slow development, long-lasting development care is often required. Otherwise, see 1
6	woody plant groups	as for 1	depending on plan, thin out, weed, mulch as necessary	thin out at intervals to rejuvenate, remove tree seedlings
7	creepers and climbing plants	water, weed	water, shape if required or train to trellis, e.g. Wisteria	cut back annually or every 3 years, depending on species. Keep vulnerable parts of buildings or neighboring plants clear
8	roses (bedding roses and climbers)	as for 7. Fertilize	train climbing roses to trellis if necessary. create support framework, fertilize, cut	fertilize 2x annually, cut back in spring, deadhead, plant protection, cut back in autumn
9	conifer woody plants	as for 1	shelter sensitive species in young phase during winter. Mulch root area	water additionally in unsuitable locations. Complementary fertilizing if necessary, frost protection for only partially frost-hardy species, measures against snow breakage if necessary (park trees)

Tab. 3.9.3: Comparing maintenance of different woody plant types

Fig. 3.9.14: a) Free-form hedge (*Prunus laurocerasus*),
b) *P. laurocerasus* stump shoot after rejuvenation clip

a | b

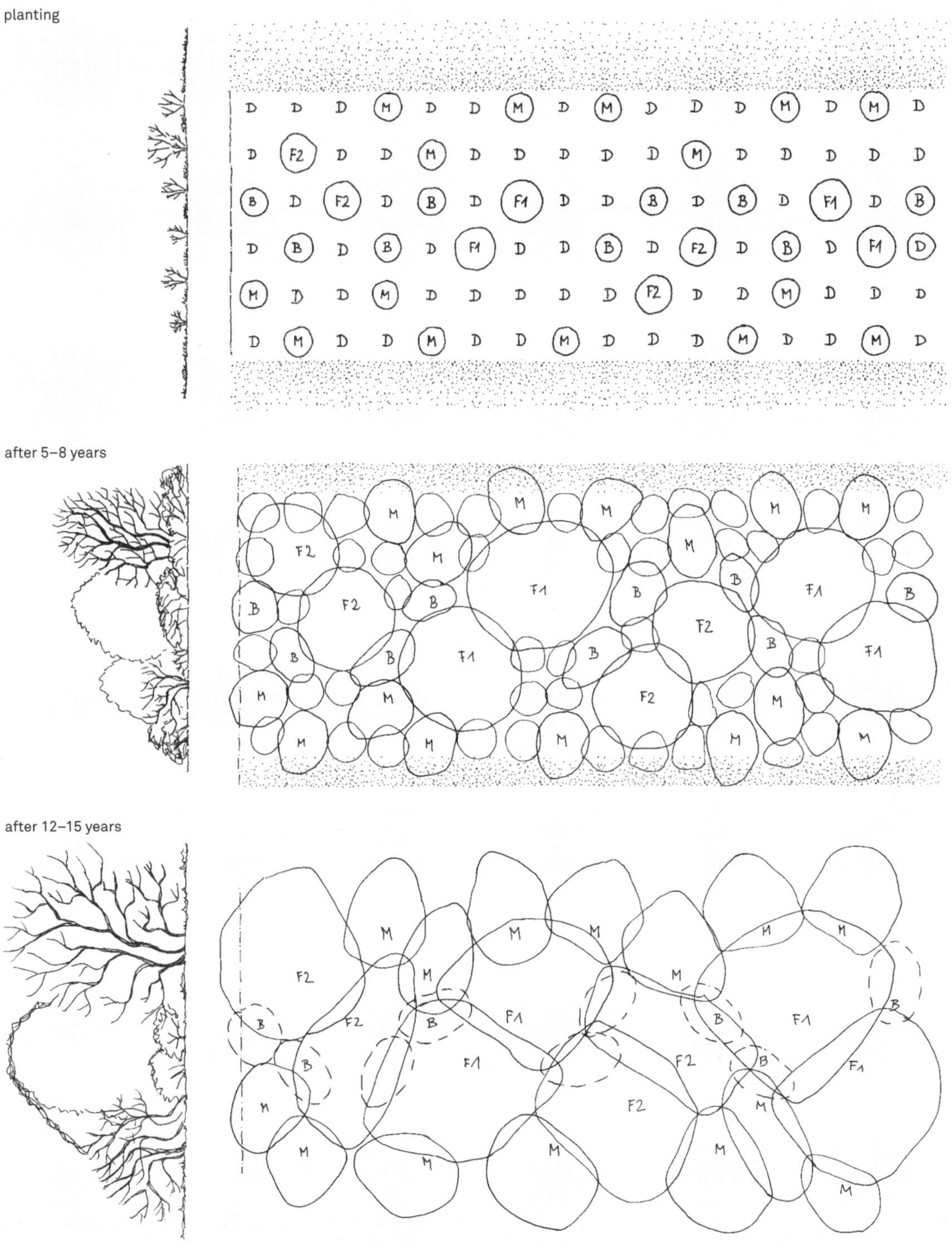

planting

after 5–8 years

after 12–15 years

Symbol	Description	Percentage of total plant stock
F1, F2	main woody plants (F1 larger than F2). Functional part of planting. Tall-growing, long-lived, strong competitors, shade-tolerant	approx. 8%
M	cover woody plants: similar to F1 and F2 lower-growing. Used for edge areas	approx. 15%
B	companion woody plants: for undergrowth. Very shade-tolerant. Rather low-growing	approx. 8%
D	temporary filler plants, restricted to development phase: Light-loving, low growth size, short-lived, weak competitors. Alternatively, a herb layer (sown/planted herbaceous plants) can serve to keep the space open	approx. 70%

Fig. 3.9.15: Development schema for a woody plant group (taken from Brahe 2000)

space for the long-term trees for approximately 15 years, by which time they should have grown out. Development maintenance is restricted to weeding and above all the removal of tree seedlings. In addition, it is essential to replace any long-term woody plants that are lost. The regular thinning required by traditional plantings is not necessary, as the long-term woody plants will generally simply grow over the filler woody plants. Knee-high to grove-like plantings can be designed using this concept. An FLL guide provides detailed information.

PLANTING AND MAINTENANCE OF HERBACEOUS PLANTS

Planting

The planting times for herbaceous plants are in spring (from around March to May) and autumn (September–November), provided there is no frost. Autumn planting is generally more favorable to growth. If soil is heavy with a waterlogging problem and frosts are severe, spring should be chosen.

In preparation, the whole surface area is loosened, and any previous growth must be entirely removed, including rhizomes able to shoot. Unfavorable soils should be improved. > Planting woody plants in existing soil Dry potted root balls should be immersed to saturation before the herbaceous plants are arranged, removed from pots and planted. If sun and wind are strong, the plants must not be allowed to dry out. Finally, the planting is watered and the surface is loosened and mulched if necessary. Plant density depends closely on the type and function of the planting.

Maintenance

Finalizing maintenance generally consists of watering and weeding. Bought topsoil is often very rich in nutrients, offering favorable conditions for weed seeds as well as ruderal plants (rubble plants) and segetal plants (wild plants found on cultivated land). It is essential to weed these out before germination. The subsequent development maintenance should be kept as short as possible by using mulch or pioneer species.

Development maintenance primarily consists of weeding until an even vegetation layer becomes established and watering. Fast-growing pioneer varieties should be removed for the sake of slow-growing late developers if necessary.

Upkeep maintenance (of herbaceous plants)

Long-term maintenance is required for a planting to develop the full potential envisaged in its planning. Inexpert maintenance, on the other hand, can utterly destroy the planner's intentions. Maintenance work can be significantly reduced without any decrease in aesthetic quality if long-term care is geared to the growth behavior of plant types.

Plants/m²	Situation
8	average, e.g. mixed planting
5	tall-growing species in long-lived plantings
10–15	smaller species
15–25	garden shows, short-term only

Tab. 3.9.4: Plant density for different herbaceous plantings

Level 1	**Minimum maintenance** (regular) only combating weeds
Level 2	**Basic maintenance** (1 or 2x per year) includes winter clipping/ post-flowering cutting back
Level 3	**Complete maintenance** (not regular) includes mulching, fertilizing, winter protection, plant protection, transplanting, removal of seedlings
Level 4	**Optimum maintenance** (depending on need/requirement) includes cosmetic measures (deadheading, untying etc.)
Level 5	**Constituting maintenance** rare. Renewal of planting

increasing
design quality

Tab. 3.9.5: Maintenance levels for herbaceous plantings in public green spaces (taken from Schmidt 2005)

Fig. 3.9.16: Example species:
a) c-strategist *Eupatorium fistulosum*
b) s-strategist *Rosmarinus officinalis*
c) r-strategist *Digitalis purpurea*

a | b | c

C-strategists	R-strategists	S-strategists
Eupatorium fistulosum	Aquilegia spec.	Asarum europaeum
Leucanthemella serotinum	Digitalis purpurea	Avenella flexuosa
Lythrum salicaria	Iris barbata hybrids	Rosmarinus officinalis
Sylphium laciniatum	Rudbeckia hirta	Sempervivum spp.
Symphyotrichum novae-angliae (syn. Aster novae-angliae)	Verbascum spp.	Thymus spp.

Tab. 3.9.6: Species that exemplify the different competition types

R-maintenance plan for disturbance-tolerant plant types	C-maintenance plan for strongly competitive plant types	S-maintenance plan for stress-tolerant plant types
Typical for: · temporary flowering areas, exacting herbaceous bed borders, annual meadows, and new complexes during the initial phase	Typical for: · edge woodland, open spaces, tall herbaceous meadows, tall grass prairie, meadow-like plantings, North American herbaceous beds in cool to damp locations	Typical for: · Heath and steppe, expansive heath, stone steppe, rockeries, short grass prairie plantings, woodland areas, marsh areas, water bodies
Characteristics: · fast-growing, but short-lived plants in different life areas (pioneers, ruderal types, annuals, perennials), · good site conditions without deficiency (no stress, no growth restrictions)	Characteristics: · long-lived, high-growth species, some with suckers, some slow developers for ± undisturbed locations, · dense, medium to tall growing growth types from strong competitor species with high biomass production, · ± good site conditions without deficiency (low restriction on growth)	Characteristics: · long-lived low-growing species found in undisturbed locations with growth restrictions, · low-growing or mat-like growth types with low biomass production, · adapted to locations' disadvantages, specialists, often weak competitors
Maintenance: · open expanses or open soil required (competition-free locations), · development is promoted by disturbances (e.g. tilling or hoeing)	Maintenance: · avoid open soil, disturb minimally (mulch, encourage ground-covering growth), · recycle nutrients via a closed circulation (leave fine cut material on the area), · never hoe!	Maintenance: · extreme location conditions should be preserved and promoted by maintenance (e.g. keep soil poor by removing cut material, use mineral substrates or mulches, exploit lack of light and root pressure beneath woody plants, etc.)
Maintenance work: · continually quite high (depending on the percentage of short-lived species), · more favorable for sown annual surfaces)	Maintenance work: · moderate to low	Maintenance work: · low to very low on a favorable site (high to very high on an unfavorable site!)

Tab. 3.9.7: Maintenance plan correlated with plant type, taken from Schmidt 2005

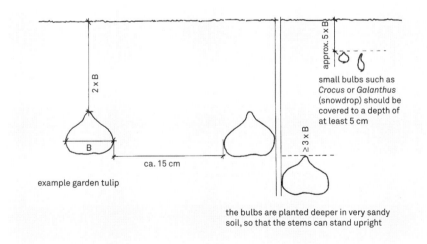

Fig. 3.9.17: Planting depth for geophytes

Meticulous planning can reduce the effort involved in maintenance. The more formal a design is, the more formidable its upkeep, as one is continually working against vegetation dynamics. Natural designs, in which this dynamic is integrated into the planning, therefore require significantly less maintenance. Herbaceous plantings should be optimized for their location. In addition, the location may have to be improved with reference to their requirements and growth behavior. > **Tab. 3.9.4**
A model taken from Grime's Plant Sociology distinguishes between three main types: Competition strategists (c-strategists), ruderal strategists (r-strategists), and stress-tolerant strategists (s-strategists). C-strategists have high competitive abilities and are able to exploit available light, space, nutrients, and water equally. They are relatively long-lived and are not adapted to scarcity situations or disturbances. R-strategists are fast-growing species that last for one year to a few years. They reproduce in large numbers via seeds, but are weak as competitors. They can tolerate disturbances and quickly settle newly created habitats (pioneer plants). S-strategists are generally long-lived, low-growth species that occur in unfavorable (dry, low-nutrient, lacking in light, low pH, etc.) locations. On well-supplied soil, they are crowded out. > **Tab. 3.9.7** With sufficient knowledge of plant species, the Grime model can be used to plan plantings adapted to the location and optimize maintenance work.

PLANTING AND MAINTENANCE OF GEOPHYTES

Spring-flowering geophytes can be planted from roughly after the middle of August to the middle of November. The earlier they are planted, the more time the bulbs have to develop. Later planting times usually mean delayed flowering the following spring. Planting depth depends on species. The rule of thumb is to plant a bulb three times as deep as it is thick. > **Fig. 3.9.17**
Bulb distribution should be harmonized with the planting's style. In formal gardens and for non-permanent floral bedding out, regular intervals are usual. In natural-styled plantings, they should be loosely scattered, with varied intervals and different sized groups. Where geophytes are companion plants in herbaceous plantings, a suggested ratio is 15–25 plants/m². For very small bulbs such as Crocus, a plan should include 50–100 plants per m².

SEASONAL ORNAMENTAL PLANTS

For a new layout, soil preparation is the same as for herbaceous plants. When the flowering stock is changed, the soil is usually loosened after being cleared (tilling, turning) and sometimes mixed with a slow-release fertilizer. Plants are laid out and planted according to the pattern. For formal patterns, the plants should be planted in a regular grid. Spring flowers can be planted in October/November. Where geophytes are included, first the plants and then the bulbs are planted. Summer flowers are planted from the beginning to the middle of May after the frost, depending on the weather.
Maintenance largely consists of watering, weeding and deadheading. For high-profile plantings, weekly maintenance tours should be planned for the summer.

A grove of European aspen (*Populus tremula* 'Erecta') with ivy as undertree planting is planted in the inner courtyard, atop building structure (an intensive green roof). These species are used to avoid a space problem in the long term. The trees' development, enabled by the strong soil composition and high nutrient storage capacity of the natural slightly loamy soil used, is very good. Maintenance is undertaken by an appointed master gardener, who is able to react knowledgeably and immediately to problems like pest infestation or drought.

Substrate composition: 3 cm mulch layer, 0/8 lava tuff, 30 cm topsoil, 70 cm noncohesive subsoil, 10 cm drainage layer (lava)
Planting of 5000 *Hedera helix* (ivy) (10 plants/m²) and 62 *Populus tremula* 'Erecta', solitaire, 3 x planted, balled, H 3.0–3.50 m

Maintenance work: mainly consists of regularly checking the health of and availability of resources for the woody plants, fertilizing (8 g N, 2 g P, 8 g K, 1 g Mg /a/m²) and watering in summer as needed (150 l/ trees)

a	b
c	d

a) New planting 1997
b) 1999, 2 years after completion
c) 1999, view from building
d) 2002, autumn coloration

PAPPELHOF, ENBW ZENTRALE, KARLSRUHE, GERMANY

Landscape architects: Klahn + Singer + Partner, Karlsruhe
Completion 1997, 2005 maintenance plan assignment

a) View of Parco Nord from the north, approx. 10 years after completion
b) The central circle of trees and the surrounding expanse of woody plants approx. 15 years after planting
c) A ring of trees, formed from a double row of *Carpinus betulus* 'Fastigiata' and *Quercus robur*, crossed by an avenue of *Tilia platiphyllos* approx. 15 years after completion
d) The avenue of *Carpinus betulus* 'Fastigiata' at the tree ring, approx. 15 years after planting
e) Meadows and woodland areas on re-cultivated steel slag heaps

a	b
c	d

e

Construction begun in 1987, 400 ha completed in 2005, still under construction
Location: approximately 1050 ml annual precipitation, with drought in summer, gravelly-sandy soil with a low storage capacity. Some of the land was previously used for agriculture.
Planting: approx. 250,000 woody plants, bare-rooted, year-old managed forest stock for area planting, young trees, H 1.8–2.0 m and H 3.5–4.0 m, with rootballs, for avenues
Common species: *Acer platanoides, Alnus incana, Gleditsia triacanthos, Populus alba, Quercus robur, Tilia cordata, Tilia platiphyllos, Ulmus carpinifolia*

A former industrial area was gradually converted to a green area. As well as natural woodland-like areas, there are clearly structured, intensively maintained park areas. The avenue trees were trained and cut for 2 years. For the first few years, they were watered using underground drip irrigation. Wide-area woody plantings were watered by sprinkling the sloping terrain. Upkeep maintenance mainly consists of mowing the sown meadow surfaces and checking the woody plants.

PARCO NORD, MILAN, ITALY

Planning: Architect Francesco Borella, Milan, with landscape architect Andreas Kipar, KLA kipar landscape architects milano_duisburg www.kiparland.com
Total area: 600 ha

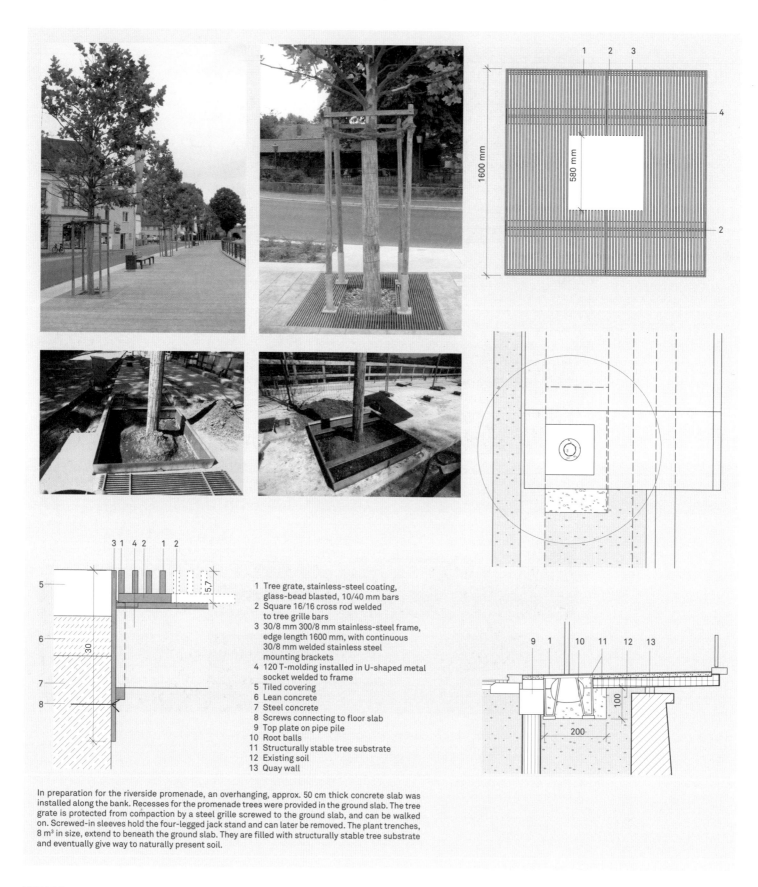

1 Tree grate, stainless-steel coating,
   glass-bead blasted, 10/40 mm bars
2 Square 16/16 cross rod welded
   to tree grille bars
3 30/8 mm 300/8 mm stainless-steel frame,
   edge length 1600 mm, with continuous
   30/8 mm welded stainless steel
   mounting brackets
4 120 T-molding installed in U-shaped metal
   socket welded to frame
5 Tiled covering
6 Lean concrete
7 Steel concrete
8 Screws connecting to floor slab
9 Top plate on pipe pile
10 Root balls
11 Structurally stable tree substrate
12 Existing soil
13 Quay wall

In preparation for the riverside promenade, an overhanging, approx. 50 cm thick concrete slab was
installed along the bank. Recesses for the promenade trees were provided in the ground slab. The tree
grate is protected from compaction by a steel grille screwed to the ground slab, and can be walked
on. Screwed-in sleeves hold the four-legged jack stand and can later be removed. The plant trenches,
8 m³ in size, extend to beneath the ground slab. They are filled with structurally stable tree substrate
and eventually give way to naturally present soil.

TREE GRATE, OVERBUILT, SELF-SUPPORTING,
NEUBURG AN DER DONAU, GERMANY

Landscape architects: keller landschaftsarchitekten, Munich
Architects: Herle & Herrle, Neuburg an der Donau
Completion: 2001

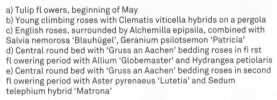

a) Tulip fl owers, beginning of May
b) Young climbing roses with Clematis viticella hybrids on a pergola
c) English roses, surrounded by Alchemilla epipsila, combined with
Salvia nemorosa 'Blauhügel', Geranium psilotsemon 'Patricia'
d) Central round bed with 'Gruss an Aachen' bedding roses in fi rst
fl owering period with Allium 'Globemaster' and Hydrangea petiolaris
e) Central round bed with 'Gruss an Aachen' bedding roses in second
fl owering period with Aster pyrenaeus 'Lutetia' and Sedum
telephium hybrid 'Matrona'

The rose garden was laid out in 1909, and redeveloped and made smaller in 1974. Due to increasing problems with soil fatigue and disease, the planting became unattractive. In 2004 it was decided to renew it, with a plan requiring lower maintenance. About 1000 roses of about 80 varieties (modern and historical bedding roses, English and Old Garden roses, and climbing roses) were planted. Resistance to disease was an important factor in selecting varieties. About 5000 herbaceous plants, grasses and *Clematis viticella* as well as about 17,000 geophytes were also planted, in order to present appealing combinations out of rose flowering season. This gave the flowering a series of different faces from late winter to autumn. Due to the soil fatigue that often occurs with *Rosaceae* (plants of the rose family) the soil was replaced to a depth of 70 cm before commencement of the new planting. Maintenance consists of spring and autumn clipping, repeated weeding and deadheading during the flowering season and plant protection methods as needed.

RECREATION OF ROSE GARDEN IN TIERGARTEN,
BERLIN, GERMANY

Landscape architect: Christian Meyer, Berlin
Completion: 2006
Size: 1400 m²

a) *Salvia nemorosa* 'Tänzerin' and Allium 'Globemaster' in early summer
b) Massed flowers of *Achillea filipendulina* hybrid. 'Coronation Gold'
c) Red-leaved *Foeniculum vulgare* 'Atropurpureum' contrasted
   with the compact cushion plants
d) *Salvia* in second blossoming period and *Agastache* forming
   the August scene
e) Asters, *Stipa gigantea* and *Sedum telephium* influence the autumn
   color scene

This area located on a traffic island was to be redeveloped following construction work. In cooperation with the ministry for green spaces, Marc Köppler initiated herbaceous planting. The criteria for selection were competitive strength, drought-tolerance and unaided reproduction via seeding or runners. Additionally, a good appearance from a distance, with abundance of flowering and strong colors, was important.
Location: slightly loamy, disturbed urban soil, approx. 650 ml annual precipitation with pronounced dryness in summer
Soil application: After removal of topsoil, application of approx. 15 cm sandy-mineral soil mixture, with about 15 cm basalt chippings.
Planting: 1800 herbaceous plants and semi-bushes in groups as well as approx. 3400 crocuses, ornamental allium plants and botanical tulips

A specimen selection of species: *Artemisia pontica, Buddleia 'Nanho Blue', Echinacea pallida, Euphorbia cyparissias, Foeniculum vulgare, Gaura lindheimeri, Perovskia abrotanoides, Salvia sklarea var. turkestanica, Stipa gigantea*
Seasonal scenes: Bulbs provide the first flowers in the spring. The main blossoming period is in spring and summer. In autumn, the grasses and some late blossoms set the tone. In winter, the year-round seed stock of herbaceous plants and grasses remains.
Maintenance: The planting is not watered. Appropriate care consists of an annual clearing cut in late winter, regular weeding out of the few weeds, collecting of waste and dog excrement, and selective removal of individual plants to refine the overall picture.

DESERT HERBACEOUS PLANTING AT BERSARINPLATZ,
BERLIN FRIEDRICHSHAIN, GERMANY

Landscape architects: Marc-Rajan Köppler,
Christian Meyer, Berlin
Completion: 2006
Size: approx. 500 m²

a	b
c	d
e	

a) Narcissus flowers in April
b) Tulip hybrids, *Brunnera macrophylla* and *Primula elatior* in May
c) Bartiris, *Geranium sanguineum* 'Album' as well as *Allium* 'Globemaster' and *A.* 'Mt. Everest' at the beginning of June
d) *Alchemilla mollis, Salvia nemorosa* 'Rügen' and *Delphinium elatior* hybrids at the end of June
e) High summer flowers such as *Achillea filipendulina, Rudbeckia fulgida* and *R. nitida, Phlox paniculata, Veronicastrum virginicum* and the grass *Pennisetum alopecuroides*

Planting: approx. 3500 herbaceous plants and grasses, additional geophytes
The ornamental border at Savignyplatz in Charlottenburg, Berlin dates from the end of the 19th century, was redesigned by Erwin Barth in 1926, and was restored in the 1980s. By 2004, it was in need of renewal, as the planting had become patchy and unsightly. A classical decorative herbaceous planting with bedding herbaceous plants was laid out. Imposing herbaceous plants such as *Delphinium* and *Phlox paniculata* hybrids form the main flowering aspect. Through the use of geophytes, early summer flowers and grasses, additional flowering scenes for the spring and late autumn are created. The year-round grass stems create an additional winter scene. Maintenance, which is carried out about once a month, consists of cutting back in autumn and early spring, fertilizing, weeding, watering, untying, and cutting back to promote a second flowering. The planting's appearance can be improved if the planner gives instructions to the gardener in charge of maintenance.

NEW PLANTING OF HISTORICAL ORNAMENTAL
BORDER AT SAVIGNYPLATZ, BERLIN, GERMANY

Landscape architect: Christian Meyer, Berlin
Completion: 2005
Planted surface: approx. 720 m²

3.10 LAWNS AND MEADOWS: LAYING OUT AND CARE

LAWNS
- Site requirements
- Seeding lawns
- Prefabricated lawns
- Lawn maintenance

MEADOWS
- Laying out
- Meadow maintenance

SEEDING ORNAMENTAL ANNUALS

SPECIMEN PROJECTS

Ute Rieper, Alexander von Birgelen

3.10 LAWNS AND MEADOWS: LAYING OUT AND CARE

LAWNS

Site requirements

Sunny sites with loamy-sandy soil and pH of 5.5–6.5 as well as good water drainage are best suited to lawn surfaces. Unfavorable soil conditions should be improved to conform to this. Waterlogging can be corrected by deep soil loosening. This is particularly necesssary when the area will be in heavy demand for play, as in the case of sports fields, for example. > Fig 3.10.1

To prepare the soil, the topsoil is loosened to a depth of about 10–15 cm and leveled out. The leveled ground for the seed bed should be uniform and without depressions or holes, in which moisture might otherwise collect. If the terrain is modeled, the soil should be stored separately and relaid over the top afterwards. The gradient should be at least 1%, allowing the surface to dry out more quickly. With increased incline, overall maintenance becomes more time-consuming. Virtually unrestricted use of machines is possible on any slope of less than 15%. > Fig. 3.10.1 and 3.10.12

Large stones, refuse and weed roots should be collected up. The seed bed is then rolled or trodden down, to prevent settling, and finely leveled to finish. For sports field or golf course turf, a special base course is usually used due to the high playability requirements.

Seeding lawns

Autumn is a good time for sowing, as long as the soil is still warm (from September to October). In spring, the

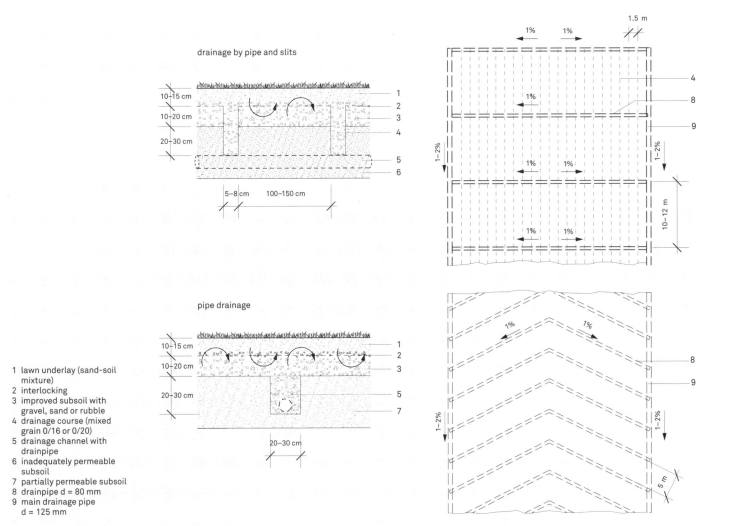

1 lawn underlay (sand-soil mixture)
2 interlocking
3 improved subsoil with gravel, sand or rubble
4 drainage course (mixed grain 0/16 or 0/20)
5 drainage channel with drainpipe
6 inadequately permeable subsoil
7 partially permeable subsoil
8 drainpipe d = 80 mm
9 main drainage pipe d = 125 mm

Fig. 3.10.1: Draining sports fields with insufficient natural drainage.

Fig. 3.10.2: Mowing stripes caused by too steep a slope

soil will be warm enough from April onwards, although the need for watering will be greater due to rising temperatures. The minimum temperature for germination is 5 °C. The optimum temperature lies between 16–21 °C. Depending on the seed mixture, about 12–20 g/m² is applied. Sowing too densely increases vulnerability to fungal diseases and is disadvantageous to slow-germinating fine grass types. The seed is worked into the surface only, and is finally rolled or pressed in.

Until proper roots have developed, the seed must be kept moist. The upper 3–4 cm of the soil is moistened every 1–5 days, depending on the weather. The lawn is cut for the first time when it has grown to a height of 6–8 cm. For slow-growing mixtures such as ornamental lawn mixtures without *Lolium* a preceding clearance cut may be necessary to remove the faster-growing seed-spread weeds. Cutting height depends on lawn type and is usually about 1.5–4 cm. Cutting encourages grasses to

form a dense layer. After the first cut, a starter fertilizer can be administered (4–6 g N/m²). A seeded lawn is usable after about 3–4 months.

Prefabricated lawns

Soil preparation is the same as for a seeded lawn. Rolled sod can be processed almost all year round, except in periods of frost and intense heat. The grass sod is laid on the supportive finely leveled ground manually or by machine. The separate parts are arranged in a staggered pattern. Overlapping, cross-shaped junctions and wide joints should be avoided. To finish, the surface is rolled. > Fig. 3.10.2 and 3.10.1

The prefabricated lawn must be kept moist for 2–3 weeks, until new roots have formed. In extreme heat, this may involve watering several times a day. A phosphorus-rich fertilizer will encourage root growth. The first cut takes place after about 6–10 days, and the first fertilizing takes place after 4–6 weeks. Rolled sod is functional after 3–5 weeks.

Lawn maintenance

Lawns require regular maintenance. The type and extent of this is primarily determined by lawn function and intensity of usage. The higher the functional or aesthetic requirements, the more intensive the maintenance. Football pitches, golf greens or ornamental lawns require more intensive maintenance measures than natural lawns, for instance. If cutting frequency and amounts of water and fertilizer are reduced, then a lawn with a more varied species makeup is created. Due to the lower percentage of grass, these produce less clippings and have a higher percentage of flowering plants.

Fig. 3.10.3: Mechanical turg laying
a) machine for laying large rolls;
b) mechanical laying of jumbo rolls

Description	Formats	Installation
Rolled sod	0.40 x 2.50 m (1 m²)	laid by hand, approx. 20 kg/m²
Large sod rolls	0.6 m x 15–20 m, approx. 1.5 cm thick	mechanically installed
Large sod rolls, thick sod	0.6–2.20 m x 15–20 m, 2.5–3 cm thick	installed using laying apparatus, approx. 40 kg/m², instantly usable (e.g. refurbishing a goal area)

Tab. 3.10.1:
Common sod formats

Fig. 3.10.4: Level path and lawn edges make mowing easier

Fig. 3.10.5: Aerifier

Fig. 3.10.6: Sanding a sports field

Mowing

Cutting encourages grasses to form a dense layer, keeps high-growing wild plants in check and retains the lawn's ability to be walked on. To create a thick fine grass mat, the cut should remove about 1/3 of growth. If half of the growth is cut, regeneration takes longer and the lawn mat becomes somewhat rougher. The lawn is first cut around March, after grass growth has begun, and the last cut is carried out at the end of October to the beginning of November, after grass growth has finished, as long grass is more vulnerable to winter fungal infections.

Watering

To develop deeper roots, a lawn should be watered less often but more thoroughly, at about 20–25 l/m². At the first signs of wilting (footprints remain visible, as the blades do not spring up) the lawn should be watered. The early morning is a good time for this, as the lawn dries quickly over the course of the day (fungal disease avoidance). When temperatures are high, lawns should not be watered during the day, as this causes very high evaporation loss.

Fertilizing

Lawns are usually serviced with N-rich complete fertilizer, primarily in order to promote leaf blade growth. This allows even heavy-duty lawns to grow well enough to regenerate. In addition, wild plants are not competitive enough to become established in a well-supplied, frequently mown lawn. To create an even fertilizer profile, fast and slow-release nutrients are usually combined. Fertilizers should be applied in several small doses, to prevent contamination of groundwater with an excess of easily washed-out nitrate. K-rich fertilizer is generally used in the winter, to increase disease and frost resistance.

Scarifying

Scarifying is intended to provide air to the grass mat and encourage grasses to grow more thickly. Special blades or rakes slit the grass mat, thereby removing moss and matted dead grass. Low-growing wild herbs such as *Bellis perennis* or *Prunella vulgaris* are decreased or removed.

Aeration

Aeration involves loosening and ventilating the upper soil level to a depth of about 10 cm. The faster drainage and higher percentage of air in the soil this creates is intended to promote grass root and shoot growth. This involves removing plugs of soil using hollow prongs (about 250–400 per m²) and then filling the holes with sand. > Fig. 3.10.5

Sanding

Applying 0/2 sand levels out small humps and depressions and improves water permeability, especially in combination with aeration. > Fig. 3.10.6

Weed elimination and plant protection

It is primarily in heavy-duty turf that persistent, low-growing wild herbaceous plants and some of the "weed grasses" have to be combated to retain the functionality and playing quality of the turf. Various herbicides, effective for different species, exist for this purpose. There is no need to remove wild herbaceous plants on a normal hard-wearing lawn. Lawns with an herb element often have higher drought tolerance and present attractive flowering scenes. > Figs. 3.10.7 and 3.10.8

Pests occasionally appear in large numbers. For instance, gnat larvae can eat the grass roots. In this situation, it may make sense to combat the pests, beginning

Fig. 3.10.7: *Primula vulgaris* in a low-nutrient lawn, which is partially shaded in summer

Fig. 3.10.8: Extensively maintained functional lawn with *Bellis perennis* and *Ranunculus repens* in April

at the first signs of infestation. Pesticides are usually necessary. Most lawn diseases are caused by fungi. Excessively moist, over-fertilized and young lawns are especially vulnerable. Mild winters and particularly warm summers also encourage fungal infectious agents to multiply. Using special fungicides may be a good idea, but this must go hand in hand with a plan to optimize the critical site factors. Heavy-duty turf and golf courses are the types most affected by this. Infectious agents are also spread by the international trade in materials and by golf tourism.

MEADOWS

Laying out

In populous areas, meadow seeding using commercial seed is the most common method. Seed mixtures can also contain exotic species if they are intended solely for decorative purposes. Meadows on the edge of populous areas or within the natural landscape should be created using local native plant seed, especially when they are created for nature conservation purposes. Ideally, the soil should be low in nutrients—on rich soils, meadows with few species dominated by grasses develop. This can be achieved by removing the humus topsoil (Ah horizon) so that seeding takes place on the mineral subsoil (B-horizon).

About 2–5 g/m² of seed is applied to a fine-crumbed soil seeding bed. Spring (February–May) and autumn (end of August–November) are good times for this. Unfavorable site factors such as waterlogging, compaction or significant lack of nutrients create specialized meadows, and do not necessarily need to be corrected. As meadow herbs or wild herbaceous plants develop relatively slowly, a clearance cut to remove seed-spread weeds may be necessary. Many wild herbaceous plants flower in their second year at the earliest.

If local, native seed has to be used, there are a number of methods for obtaining seed in a rural environment. Hay transfer involves mowing a donor area when the desired type of seed is mature and immediately transferring the mown hay to the seeding surface. The ratio of donor to seeding surface is approximately 1:2. For threshed hay seed, the hay is machine-threshed. Additional drying gives the seeding material a (limited) storage life. The seeding amount is 50–1000 g/m². Hay flower seed describes seeds and hay residue from a hayloft. In this case, species composition and germination power are unknown. The amount of seed used is 100–2000 g/m². Another possibility is the conversion of existing frequently cut meadows. Mowing frequency is reduced to 2–3 cuts per year and the cuttings are removed in order to make the soil less rich. Depending on the original conditions, it will take longer than 10 years before the

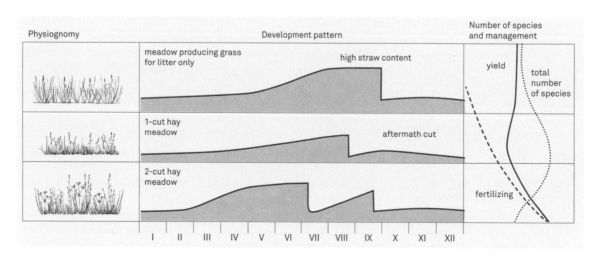

Fig. 3.10.9: Influence of mowing on species composition (taken from Ellenberg 1996)

Maintenance measures	Decorative lawns	Heavy-duty turf (football)	Hard-wearing lawns	Natural lawns	One-cut meadow	2–3 cut meadow
Cut frequency/year	30–60	25–45	6–15	0–3	1	2–3
Growth height	2–3 cm	6–9 cm	5–10	6–20	approx. 80–120	approx. 60–100
Cut height	1.5–3	3–5	4–6	approx. 8	approx. 10–15	approx. 10–15
Watering (frequency)	every 3–7 days	every 3–7 days	as needed (0.5–1x/ week)	-	-	-
Amount of fertilizer N-P-K g/m²/a	N 15–20 P 0–8 K 0–16	N 15–25 P 0–8 K 0–16	N 6–10 P 0–8 K 0–16	-	manure, liquid manure in case of hay production	manure, liquid manure in case of hay production
Thatching/year	min. 1x	1–3	0–1	-	-	-
Aeration	-	1–3	if necessary for restoration	-	-	-
Sanding	-	1–5	-	-		-
Plant protection	as needed	as needed	-	-	-	-
Combating weeds	routine, chemical and manual	routine, chemical	manual if necessary, localized	-	localized in case of hay production (poisonous plants)	localized in case of hay production (poisonous plants)

Tab. 3.10.2: Overview of upkeep maintenance

site becomes so low in nutrients that meadow herbs can compete against grasses and become established.

Meadow maintenance (mowing)

Meadows must be mown at least once a year, as otherwise they become overgrown with bushes. Depending on the meadow's function, the time for cutting is determined by, for instance, seed ripeness, species protection issues, or value as animal fodder. One-cut hay meadows have the highest number of species, and 2- and 3-cut meadows remain relatively species-rich. After 4 or more cuts per year, the number of species decreases incrementally. > Figs. 3.10.9 and 3.10.10, Tab. 3.10.2

SEEDING ORNAMENTAL ANNUALS

Annuals are best suited to temporary greening. Species mixtures can be created even for dry, sparse, grit-like soils, although they may look unattractive after a dry summer. Repeated seeding is like cultivating field crops, as the soil has to be dug over and prepared every year. As most species require high germination temperatures, the seeding bed must be free of weeds, as it will otherwise be overgrown by cold-germinating, strongly competitive field weeds. This can be achieved by working with machines or by using total herbicides containing glyphosphates. Sowing usually takes place at the beginning through to the middle of May. Only a few species can be sown on open land earlier, from March or April. Depending on the species mixture and location, 1–5 g/m² is sown and worked into the surface only. During germination, dryness, late frost and slugs can cause

Fig. 3.10.10: Meadow contrasted with a functional lawn in a public green space

losses. Flowering usually begins from July onwards. For certain combinations of species, it can last until the beginning of the frost. Maintenance mainly consists of watering and fertilizing if necessary. To uproot the weeds would be very time-consuming and probably too demanding for the maintenance gardener's plant recognition, and treading on it usually causes damage to the thick-growing meadow-like cover.

The "landform" was conceived as a sculpture that could be walked on and would continually offer viewers new vistas due to its variety of curved forms. Due to safety constraints for public green spaces, the sculpture as a whole was made less steep and more solid (slope bases secured using steel and concrete instead of elm boards).

In the period from Easter to the end of September, intensive upkeep maintenance is carried out. From March to September, mowing is carried out about once a week. On the slopes, strimmers and hover-mowers are used. The banks are watered daily, as they dry out quickly. Level surfaces are fertilized in spring and autumn using kelp granulate fertilizer (50 g/m2), and the slopes are fertilized with liquid kelp fertilizer every 2 months. The north faces of the sculpture are treated once a year with moss killer. Weeds are treated locally with herbicide as needed.

Location: approx. 670 ml annual precipitation
Soil composition: mainly compacted oil-shale slag, 5 cm loamy subsoil and 5 cm topsoil
Seed: hard-wearing, heavy-duty lawn mixture

$$\frac{a}{\frac{b}{c}}$$

a) View of the "landform" from the museum
b) Stepped seating near the museum
c) View towards the museum

UEDA LANDFORM, NATIONAL GALLERY, EDINBURGH, UNITED KINGDOM

Planning: Charles Jencks, London, with Terry Farrell & Partners and Ian White Associates
Completion: 2002
Surface: approx. 3000 m²

Location:
The soil in the central area is rough-soil-type gravel. Up to 40 cm topsoil was applied to edge areas. In accordance with a land use plan incorporating green space planning, the area was to be permanently developed as dry meadow serving as a habitat for special-ized sparse turf fauna, as part of a system of connected habitats.

Seed:
Mown harvest of about 9 sparse meadow sites with added acceptance species from local native plants

Maintenance:
Single mow in September, approx. 20% of the surface is left standing over the winter as winter shelter for fauna.

a	b
c	d

a) Growth is still sparse in the first year after sowing. Particularly appealing varieties such as *Papaver rhoeas* (corn poppy) and *Anthemis tinctoria* (golden marguerite) are starting to flower, summer 2000
b) Blossom apects including *Rhinanthus alectorolophus* (greater yellow rattle), *Anthemis tinctoria* and the occasional *Linum perenne* (perennial flax), summer 2004
c) Blossom aspects including the pale yellow *Rhinanthus alectorolophus* in their mature state, summer 2007
d) Pale pink flowers of *Securigera varia* (crownvetch), summer 2008

DRY MEADOW IN RIEMER PARK, MUNICH, GERMANY

Haase & Söhmisch Büro für Landschaftsarchitektur und Planung, Freising
Completion: 1999
Surface: approx. 1.3 ha

a	
b	c
d	e

a) *Papaver rhoeas* (corn poppy) as appealing varieties in the first year since planting
b) Blue-yellow aspect with *Echium vulgare* (viper's bugloss) and *Anthemis tinctoria* (golden marguerite))
c) *Dianthus carthusianorum* (Carthusian pink) and *Lotus corniculatus* (bird's-foot trefoil) from the 2nd year
d) *Leucanthemum vulgare* (ox-eye daisy) and *Salvia pratensis* (meadow clary) from the 2nd year
e) *Onobrychis viciifolia* (sanfoin), *Galium mallugo* (hedge bedstraw) and *Rhinanthus minor* (yellow rattle) from the 2nd year

SAGE AND TALL OATGRASS MEADOW IN RIEMER PARK, MUNICH, GERMANY

Landscape architect: Heiner Luz, Munich
Seed years 2001–2004
Surface: approx. 70 ha

Location: Soil predominantly newly modeled, with specially created vegetation base layer on Ecotype seed, 2.5 g/m², with additional "acceptance species" (flowering in first year) mixed in.
Maintenance: Alternate single and double mowing. Parts of the surface are left for animals over the winter.

3.11   SURFACE DRAINAGE

CREATING SLOPES
· Determining slope
· Slope types

CONSTRUCTION METHODS FOR DRAINAGE SYSTEMS
· Drainage facilities
· Conduits and inspection shafts
· Rainwater seepage systems

BASIC CALCULATIONS AND PARAMETERS
· Establishing degree of rainfall
· Dimensions of drainage facilities

SPECIMEN PROJECTS

Astrid Zimmermann

3.11 SURFACE DRAINAGE

In order to ensure safe and largely nonweather-dependant usage, precipitation must be directed away from hard surfaces (paths, areas, steps) by creating a slope. In principle, the same applies to lawn surfaces, especially when they are intended for intensive use, e.g. as sports or play areas. For hard areas, drainage also prevents damage to the pavement through invasive or standing water—due to frost, for instance. Water is redirected, either via drains or by lateral drainage into neighboring planted areas. For permeable ground coverings, this is combined with direct seepage into the soil. > Fig. 3.11.1

To take pressure off sewers, to avoid floods due to freak heavy rain, and to return the precipitation into the local water cycle, on-site seepage is preferable to directing water into receiving water courses (natural or artificial streams) or purification facilities. Seepage takes place above ground via surface and trench seepage, and below ground via through trenches. On-site seepage is now a legal requirement in many municipalities.

Precipitation water from roof surfaces should also be included in these considerations. A green roof can reduce the amount of water to be redirected. > Chapter 3.14

As early as the planning phase, drainage options that incorporate design and functional solutions for the necessary on-site seepage should be looked into and developed, taking connection heights and standing heights into account.

The essential elements of drainage outside of buildings are regulated by the multipart EN 752. It also refers readers to further information sources for specific regions.

CREATING SLOPES

Determining slope

Water is directed away by a surface's incline.
The composition of the surface also affects the speed of the flowing water. Different minimum and maximum values for slope formation should be factored in depending on site use. > Tab. 3.11.1

Fig. 3.11.1: Possibilities
for redirecting water:
a) linear drainage
b) point drainage
c) drainage via seepage joints
and neighboring planted areas

Surface construction	Recommended slope	Limitations due to special usage requirements
Concrete and asphalt cover	≥ 1.5–2.0%	public roads (transverse gradient) ≥ 2.5 sports areas * with stamped earth/artificial turf covering 0.8%, plastic coating ≤ 1%, on tennis courts ≤ 0.5% seating areas, especially those with tables (e.g. on terraces) 1–2%, Transverse inclines on steps and ramps in exceptional cases only > **Chapter 3.3**
Concrete and natural stone tiles	≥ 2.0%	
Concrete and clinker paving	≥ 2.5%	
Natural stone paving	≥ 2.5–3.0%	
Water-bound and other non-bonded path surfaces	3.0–6.0%	
Turf	≥ 1.0–2.0%	sports areas ≥ 0.5% and ≤ 1.0%
* indications given in current guidelines and regulations apply		

Tab. 3.11.1: Slope formation depending on ground covering and usage requirements

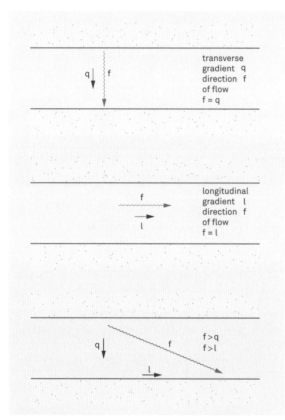

Fig. 3.11.2: Direction of flow depending on lengthwise gradient and transverse gradient

Fig. 3.11.4: Channel below an individual step

Fig. 3.11.5: Arrangement with open channels on both sides

Fig. 3.11.6: Open transverse channel

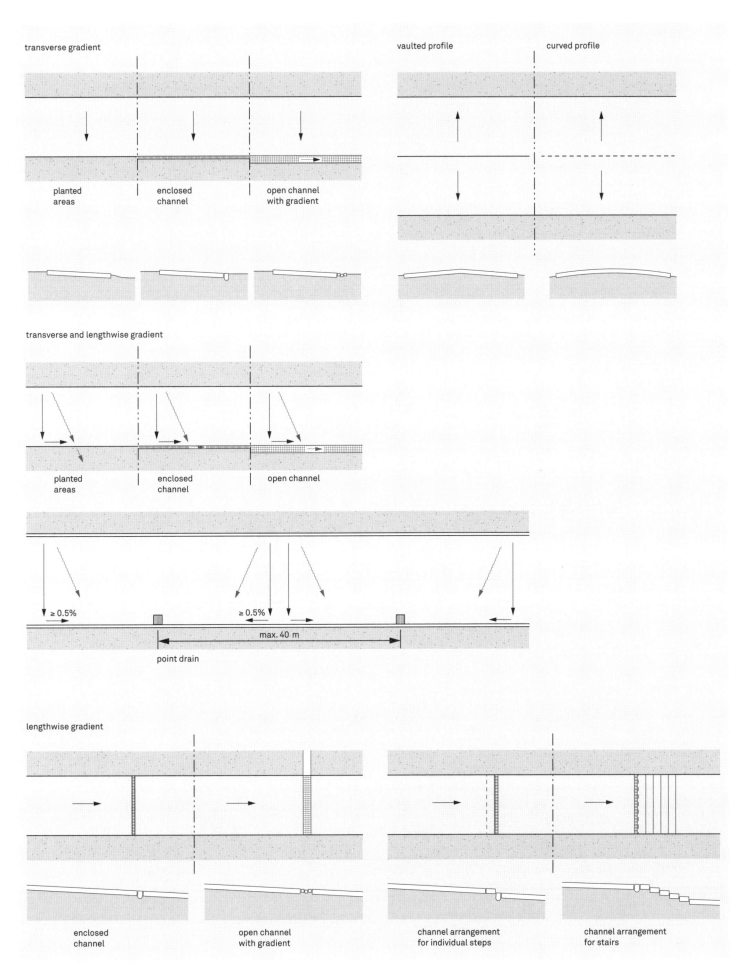

transverse gradient

planted
areas

enclosed
channel

open channel
with gradient

vaulted profile

curved profile

transverse and lengthwise gradient

planted
areas

enclosed
channel

open channel

≥ 0.5%

≥ 0.5%

max. 40 m

point drain

lengthwise gradient

enclosed
channel

open channel
with gradient

channel arrangement
for individual steps

channel arrangement
for stairs

Fig. 3.11.3: Specimen linear surface drainage

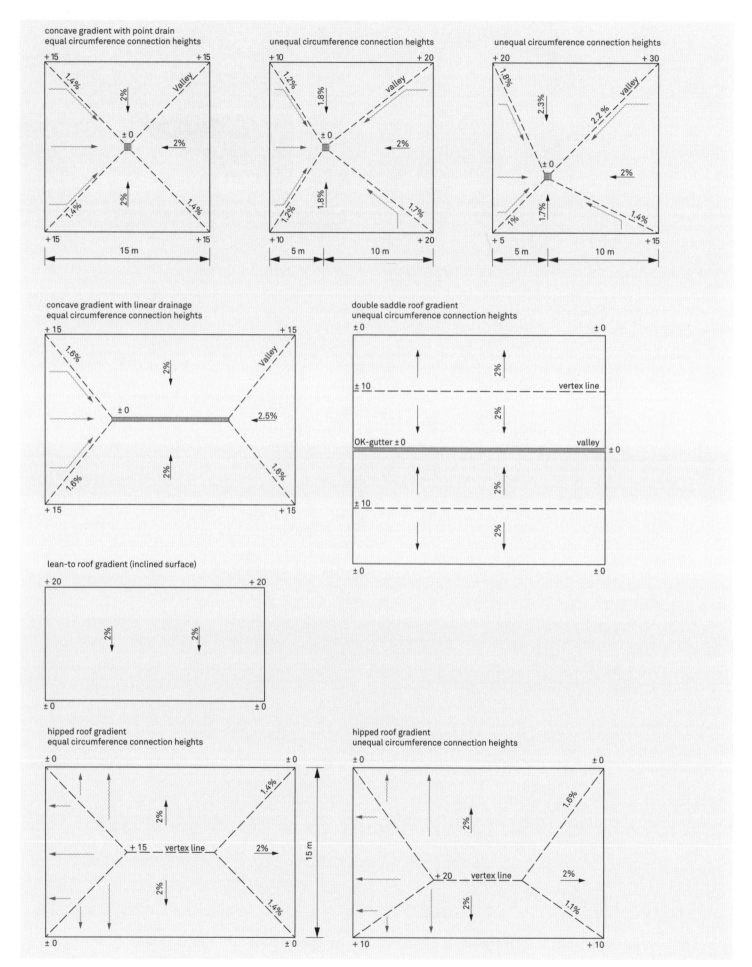

Fig. 3.11.7: Specimen drainage of area surfaces

Fig. 3.11.8: Asphalt covering with concave gradient

Slope types

For roads and paths, a distinction is made between lengthwise gradient (s), which follows the path direction, and transverse gradient (q), which runs crosswise over the path. A diagonal incline—a combination of the lengthwise and transverse gradients—forms the greatest gradient on the plot, and therefore determines the water's actual flow direction (f). The diagonal incline can be calculated using the formula $f = \sqrt{q^2 + L^2}$. > Fig. 3.11.2

Paths are usually drained via a transverse slope into the planted areas at either side, or via a channel. If the water is directed away from both sides, this is described as a vaulted profile or curved profile.

The combination of lengthwise and transverse gradient is also used for roads, which are kept free of water by a point drain at the edge of the road. In this case, a high curb is generally used to direct water toward the drain. A lengthwise gradient is primarily found on hillside paths, as well as on ramps and steps, as these may only have a transverse gradient in exceptional cases. For lengthwise gradient, channels are installed crossways to the path direction. > Figs. 3.11.3–3.11.6

In area surface drainage, a distinction is made between concave and convex gradients. > Fig. 3.11.7 With a concave gradient, the water is directed to a low-lying point in the surface where a point drain or channel is placed. The connection heights with the outer edges may be equal or unequal. To create sufficient incline, the low point will not lie in the center if the exterior heights are unequal. For smaller, more angular ground plans and steeper gradients, the concave form often creates a fold line in the covering. This "valley," in which the redirected water collects, is difficult to construct using tiles and large-format paved covering, especially where these are in elongated formats. Small formats and quadratic formats are more suitable, as are asphalt and concrete coverings. > Figs. 3.11.8 and 3.11.9

A convex gradient is generally more optically appealing. The water is directed away from an elevated ridge (the vertex line) towards nearby plants or a drainage element—usually a channel. A distinction is made between saddle, lean-to, and hipped roof gradients.

For lean-to and saddle roof gradients, the connection heights around the outside are never all at the same height. The surrounding terrain must therefore be formed accordingly or intercepted by raised edging. The hipped roof gradient is particularly suited to areas with continuous equal connection heights and where drainage within the surface is undesirable or not possible, as with sports areas. For smaller sports areas, the lean-to roof gradient may be used, while for areas over 40 m wide, only the saddle or hipped roof gradient can be used. More precise gradient specifications can be found in the relevant regulations and guidelines for sports areas.

Paths for pedestrians and wheelchair users may have a lengthwise gradient of more than 6% only in exceptional cases, but on area surfaces, greater inclines in a single direction are possible. Under normal circumstances, the maximum lengthwise incline for traffic surfaces is 10%, excluding hilly stretches and special cases. The drainage of a surface is admittedly made more difficult by a steep gradient and the corresponding increase in flow speed. In this case, the channels should be appropriately wide channels (nominal values of 150–300 mm), and meshed or spanning bar grilles should be used as drain covers.

The transverse incline should be 2.5% for footpaths, 4% for cycle paths, and no greater than 6–8% for roads.

Tab. 3.11.2: Load classes for drainage systems and their application areas (according to EN 1433 and EN 124)

Class	Areas of use
A 15	areas used exclusively by pedestrians and cyclists
B 125	footpaths and pedestrian areas, parking surfaces for passenger cars
C 250	non-traffic-used road shoulders and gutters
D 400	road lanes, pedestrian roads used by cars, shoulders and parking surfaces for all road vehicle types
E 600	surfaces with high wheel loads, e.g. in harbor areas
F 900	surfaces with especially high wheel loads, e.g. air traffic surfaces

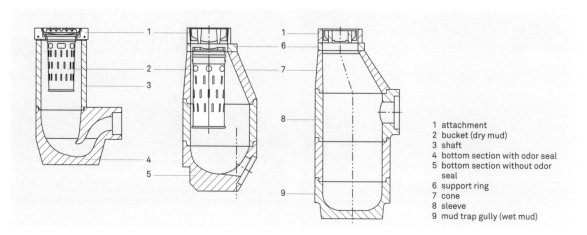

1 attachment
2 bucket (dry mud)
3 shaft
4 bottom section with odor seal
5 bottom section without odor seal
6 support ring
7 cone
8 sleeve
9 mud trap gully (wet mud)

Fig. 3.11.10: Cutaway view of drains

CONSTRUCTION METHODS FOR DRAINAGE SYSTEMS

Drainage facilities

Yard and road drains are point drainage facilities. Yard drains have lower water uptake capacities than road drains and are designed for smaller traffic volumes. > Tab. 3.11.2 Drains consist of an attachment, a shaft and the base. For larger drains, the shaft is replaced by a connecting part and a shaft cone.

If the outlet is in the base, coarse impurities in the water are captured in a bucket (dry mud collection). Larger drains have a mud trapping gully instead. This can collect greater amounts of mud in the lower area of the drain (wet mud collection). In this case, the water drain is located higher up, on the "sleeve." > Fig. 3.11.10 In mixed water systems, an odor trap must be installed in drains that are less than 2 m from the living space of nearby buildings. > Fig. 3.11.10b In special areas, separators are also used—e.g. light liquid separators to deal with oil or gasoline residues.

Enclosed and open channels are a form of linear drainage facility. Open channels direct the water over the surface to a drainage point. The channel itself must therefore be set sufficiently deep into the surface and have a gradient. > Figs. 3.11.11 and 3.11.12, and chapter 3.2 Enclosed channels conduct the rainwater to be diverted beneath the surface to an outlet instead. They consist of the channel body (made, for instance, from concrete, polymer concrete, plastic or steel) and a cover grille. The slot gutter is a special construction method. > Fig. 3.11.13 The nominal widths (NW) are 100 mm, 150 mm, 200 mm or greater, up to 1000 mm. Channels have either a base slope or step slope, or no intrinsic slope at all. In this case, the water flow is regulated by the water level, or by installing the channel at a gradient. Construction elements with and without an intrinsic slope can also be combined—in order to minimize installation depth, for instance. To conduct the water away, a trash box or a connection to a pipe in the channel's bottom should be included at the end of the channel (and for longer channels additionally along the channel length). > Fig. 3.11.14

Drainage channels and drains are installed on concrete foundations. > Figs. 3.11.15 and 3.11.16

On roof surfaces, balconies and terraces with superstructures that permit seepage, special forms are used which are installed directly on the surface. > Chapter 3.14 Park and side paths are also drained by means of transverse abatements (simple channels made using wood). > Fig. 3.11.17

The choice of cover is determined by the location (roads, pedestrian areas) and design requirements.

In theory, gutter covers offer maximum loadbearing capacity. Gratings or grilles made from spanning or crossbars have the maximum inlet cross sections. Perforated grilles tend to have smaller inlet cross section and only a low loadbearing capacity. Special elements can be made from concrete or natural worked stone. > Figs. 3.11.18 and 3.11.19

The anticipated load is a key criterion when choosing drainage systems; it is given by the load class. > Tab. 3.11.2

While the actual inlet cross section capacity of standardized covers can often handle more than this in reality, the drainage area should be about 400 m² for road drains and 200 m² for yard drains.

The following standard value can be used to roughly calculate capacity: 1 cm² inlet cross section to roughly 1 m² of surface to be drained.

The dimensions of drainage channels are usually determined by channel cross section and the size of the pipe's exit where it meets the channel. However, a greater inlet cross section can be necessary for quick removal of rainwater, particularly on traffic surfaces.

Conduits and inspection shafts

From drainage facilities, water is directed into sewer conduits or into any seepage systems. Plastic pipes are generally used for draining plots of ground. They are also described as basic sewer pipes (KG). Pipes made from PVC are often used. Other materials include HDPE and stoneware.

For buried conduits, nominal widths from 100 mm upwards are used. The necessary diameter is determined by the amount of accumulated water, the pipe's gradient and the possibilities of connecting to channels and drains. Branches (max. 45°) for connecting two pipes and saddle fittings and connector nozzles (including

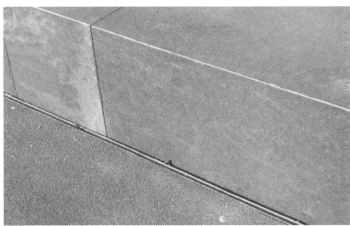

Fig. 3.11.13: Closed channels:
a) channel with drain cover
b) slot gutter

Fig. 3.11.11: Natural stone channel with drain

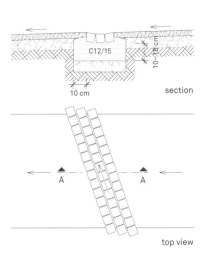

Fig. 3.11.12: Specimen paved channel design

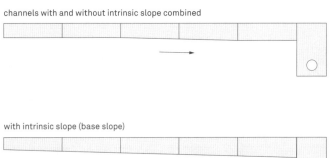

without intrinsic slope, with water level slope

without intrinsic slope, with terrain slope

with step slope

channels with and without intrinsic slope combined

with intrinsic slope (base slope)

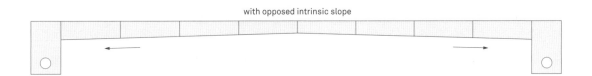

with opposed intrinsic slope

Fig. 3.11.14: Different channel gradients showing position of trash box

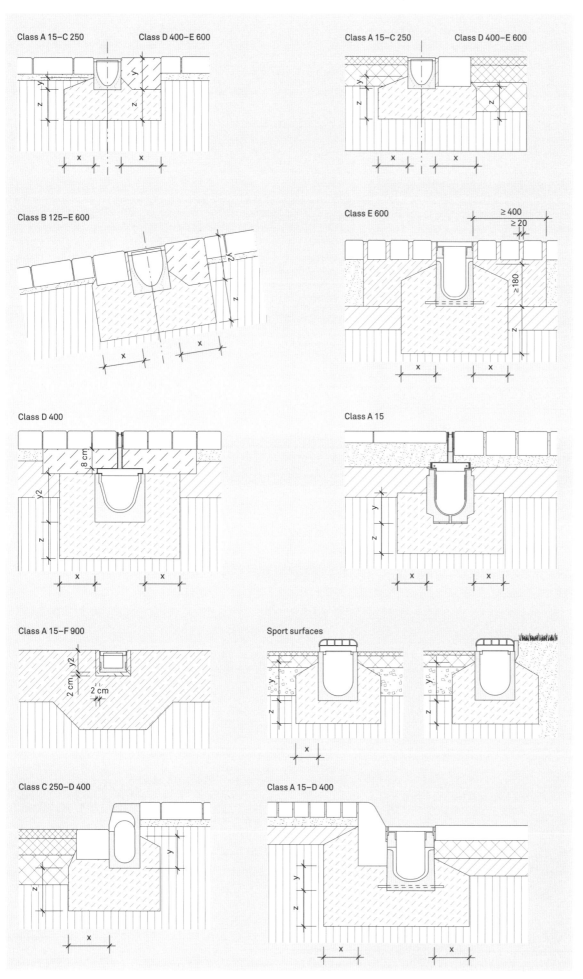

Fig. 3.11.15: Specimen representation of listed installation classes. The type and thickness of the path construction may vary, depending on the situation.
> Chapter 3.2 Paths and Squares

Fig. 3.11.16: Specimen drain installations

Class A 15–B 125

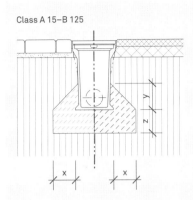

Class E 600–F 900

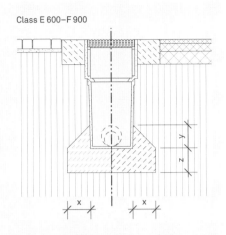

dimensions of foundations:
yard drains x/y/z = 10 cm,
road drains x/y/z = 20 cm,
for higher load classes raise
y to the bedding level

Average foundation dimensions			Concrete quality	
			frost risk	no frost risk
x	≥ 10–20 cm	depending on nominal width, load class, channel height and installation [1]	C 25/30 [2]	C 20/25 [2]
y	≥ 10–25 cm			
y[2]	= height of channel			
z	≥ 15–20 (25) cm			
[1] The manufacturer's installation instructions must be followed!			[2] C12/15 may also be included for class A15 only, and only where loadbearing capacity requirements are very low.	

a | b

Fig. 3.11.17 a+b): Transverse finish

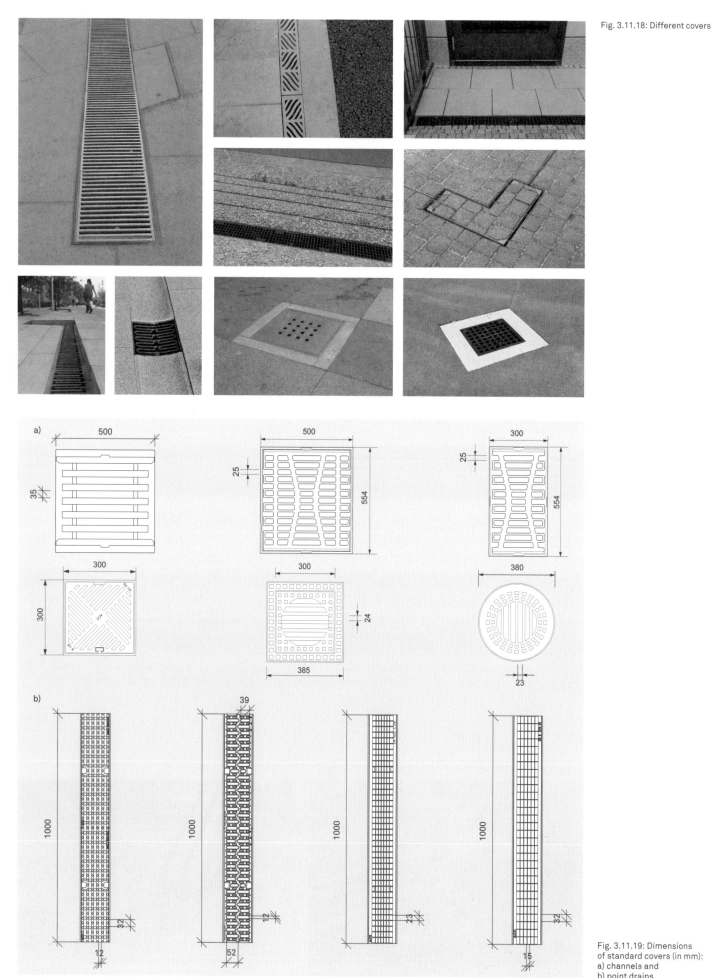

Fig. 3.11.18: Different covers

Fig. 3.11.19: Dimensions
of standard covers (in mm):
a) channels and
b) point drains

types for stoneware or concrete pipes) for creating other kinds of junctions are available. Adaptors or reducers enable transitions to the next biggest or next smallest pipe diameter. Changes in direction are created using bends (15°, 30° and 45°).

Conduits must always be dug with a gradient in order to ensure quick drainage and prevent buildup of sediment. The necessary slope depends on the amount of outflow and the pipe's diameter. > **Dimensions of drainage facilities** Water pipes in open spaces must be laid so as to be free of frost.

Pipe trenches may have scarped or vertical walls. Scarped walls take up more space and may put more load on the pipes due to greater amounts of fill soil. Where the walls are vertical, a distinction is made between trench depths of up to 1.25 m, up to 1.75 m and over 1.75 m. > **Chapter 3.1**

The bottom of the trench must be level and stable. If the soil is not loose or fine-grained enough, a bedding (e.g. sand) of ≥ 10 cm in thickness should be provided. If the soil is rocky and firm, the bedding should be ≥ 15 cm (> EN 1610).

Inspection shafts (inspection openings) must be provided to allow checking and cleaning of conduit systems. They are sited where two or more conduits meet or where flow direction or gradient changes. Access shafts must also be provided at regular intervals (> EN 476). The inner diameter for these is ≥ 1000 mm (round cross section) or ≥ 750 x 1200 mm (rectangular cross section). Steps should be provided in the shaft's inner wall. > **Fig. 3.11.20** Shafts are often made from concrete finished parts, (partially) from brickwork, or from plastic. These last are suitable for areas than are inaccessible to heavy construction machinery due to their low weight. Shaft covers are usually made from cast iron. In order to fit into the surrounding road covering, they are also available with grooves so that they can be paved or with a concrete surface. > **Fig. 3.11.21**

Rainwater seepage systems

If above- or below-ground seepage systems are planned, the subsoil must permit sufficient seepage. The seepage space beneath the planned seepage system (e.g. a vegetated swale or through trench) should be at least 1 m at average highest groundwater level (MHGW). If rainwater discharges with a low level of substance contamination are being handled through above-ground seepage, then this minimum distance may be decreased in exceptional cases. Water containing pollutants (e.g. from heavily used roads) must absolutely not be passed through below-ground seepage systems.

For rainwater with low contamination (e.g. from lightly used roads and parking areas), below-ground seepage may be possible in exceptional cases. In this case, the seepage space should be as large as possible in order to make sufficient use of the soil's filtration effect. A legal permit should always be obtained for below-ground seepage systems and for systems near water-protection zones.

One, or a combination, of the seepage types below should be chosen, depending on the locality's features.

In surface seepage, rainwater passes directly into the water-permeable soil layers and seeps through. If only small areas are involved, the surface water can seep into a neighboring planted bed or lawn surface. If there is insufficient space, trenches with horizontal bases can be laid out, providing interim storage for the water on the surface. To prevent the surface from becoming compacted or covered with mud, as well as damage to the vegetation, the accumulation period should be limited. This results in a maximum permitted accumulation height of 30 cm and a required soil permeability of at least $k_f = 5 \times 10^{-6}$ m/s. The inflow should be distributed across the whole surface as uniformly as possible. Often the surface is laid out as a vegetated swale. Planting with ground-cover plants and tall herbaceous plants is possible. > **Figs. 3.11.22–24, and tab. 3.11.1c+d** Using water-permeable path coverings

Fig. 3.11.20: Road manhole

Fig. 3.11.21: Shaft covers: cast-iron

allows a percentage of the rainwater to seep directly through the hard surface. > Chapter 3.2

Filled drainage trenches, piped and filled drainage trenches

Drainage trench elements are below-ground drainage ditches filled with a cavity-rich material (e.g. gravel). The result is delayed seepage of water via this below-ground storage space into the subsoil.

Rainwater is delivered to a drainage trench above ground, usually via a seepage trough located above.

In a French drain, the water-uptake capacity is increased by embedding a seepage pipe. French drains are used where a large enough surface is not available or unreachable due to situation (e.g. altitude). Water is delivered to the French drain via a conduit system or an inflow shaft in the seepage pipe. Water is dispersed into the drainage trench and thereby into the surrounding soil through perforations in the seepage pipe. A cavity-rich material (e.g. 16/32 gravel) should be used as filling material. The average pipe size is about DN 300. The sides of the drainage trench should be protected from finer soil particles forming mud using fleece. > Fig. 3.11.25 Alternatively, cavity-rich plastic elements can be used (a packing drainage trench). These are distinguished by their low weight and a particularly high storage capacity. > Fig. 3.11.26 Drainage trenches are installed without a gradient. An overflow should be provided to prevent heavy rain events causing backing up.

Surface (trough) and underground filled drainage trenches

For a trough-trench element, the above ground seepage is combined with subsurface seepage. > Fig. 3.11.27 The trough can also be provided with an overflow that directs water into the through trench via an overflow pipe or a gravel packing off to the side in case of a peak in precipitation. > Fig. 3.11.28 The overflow can also regulate the water level, keeping it to the maximum permitted height of 30 cm. Through-trough trench elements can be used if the permeability of the soil onsite is below $k_f \geq 10^{-6}$ m/s. If the permeability of the soil is $k_f < 10^{-6}$ m/s, an outlet control is required, as the seepage rate can no longer be leveled out by the interim storage of runoff. This is also described as a trough-trench system. This allows both seepage and the conduction of water unable to take the seepage route into a pipe system or a ditch. > Fig. 3.11.29 Seepage shafts represent an alternative for when there is not enough space even for subsurface drainage trenches or the upper soil levels are not permeable enough. They are made from concrete or plastic. The nominal width should be 1000 mm. > Fig. 3.11.30

Seepage basins or ponds are central reservoirs with a construction similar to seepage troughs. However, due to the greater inflow, a soil permeability of $k_f \geq 10^{-5}$ m/s is required. To prevent deposits (colmation) on the basin's bottom, the water should pass through sedimentation basins (and in the case of areas near roads, light liquid separators if necessary) first.

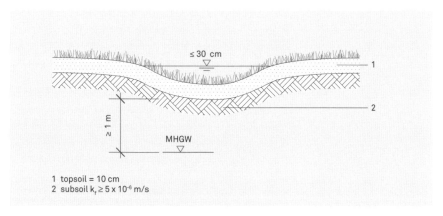

1 topsoil = 10 cm
2 subsoil $k_f \geq 5 \times 10^{-6}$ m/s

Fig. 3.11.22: Seepage trench, construction method

Fig. 3.11.23: Seepage trench with delivery pipe leading from the road

Fig. 3.11.24: Seepage trench. Steel plates divide the trench into individual horizontal reservoirs. Overflow height = 30 cm

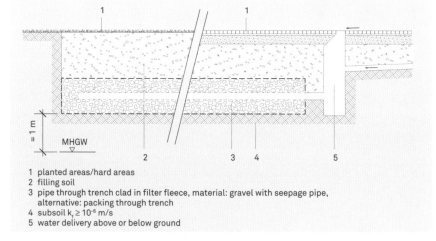

1 planted areas/hard areas
2 filling soil
3 pipe through trench clad in filter fleece, material: gravel with seepage pipe, alternative: packing through trench
4 subsoil $k_f \geq 10^{-6}$ m/s
5 water delivery above or below ground

Fig. 3.11.25: Longitudinal section of pipe through trench

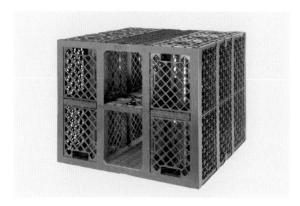

Fig. 3.11.26: Packing through trench made using plastic

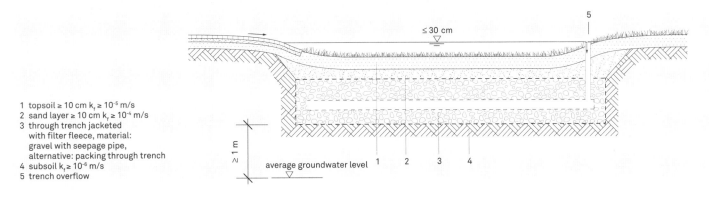

1 topsoil ≥ 10 cm
  k_f ≥ 10^{-5} m/s
2 sand layer ≥ 10 cm
  k_f ≥ 10^{-4} m/s
3 through trench (e.g. gravel)
  jacketed with filter fleece
4 subsoil k_f ≥ 10^{-6} m/s

Fig. 3.11.27: Trench-through trench without seepage pipe

BASIC CALCULATIONS AND PARAMETERS

Establishing degree of rainfall

Depending on frequency and duration of rainfall, different amounts of water will occur. Different "calculated rainfall levels" may be used. The average values for a particular site can be learned from local authorities or the weather service.

As some of the rainwater seeps directly into the surface it falls on, the actual incoming amount is reduced by an amount equal to the runoff coefficient on the "runoff-producing surface" (A_u). > Tab. 3.11.3

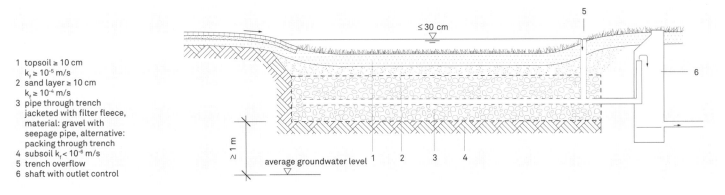

1 topsoil ≥ 10 cm k_f ≥ 10^{-5} m/s
2 sand layer ≥ 10 cm k_f ≥ 10^{-4} m/s
3 through trench jacketed
  with filter fleece, material:
  gravel with seepage pipe,
  alternative: packing through trench
4 subsoil k_f ≥ 10^{-6} m/s
5 trench overflow

Fig. 3.11.28: Trench-through trench element with seepage pipe

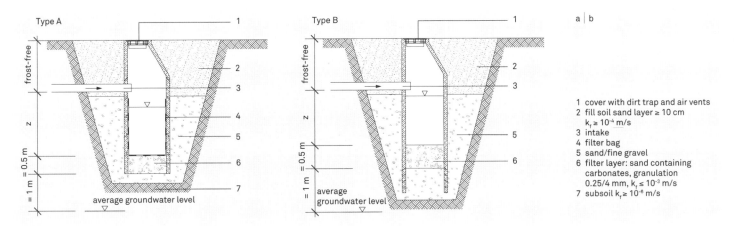

1 topsoil ≥ 10 cm
  k_f ≥ 10^{-5} m/s
2 sand layer ≥ 10 cm
  k_f ≥ 10^{-4} m/s
3 pipe through trench
  jacketed with filter fleece,
  material: gravel with
  seepage pipe, alternative:
  packing through trench
4 subsoil k_f < 10^{-6} m/s
5 trench overflow
6 shaft with outlet control

Fig. 3.11.29: Trench-through trench system with outlet control

1 cover with dirt trap and air vents
2 fill soil sand layer ≥ 10 cm
  k_f ≥ 10^{-4} m/s
3 intake
4 filter bag
5 sand/fine gravel
6 filter layer: sand containing
  carbonates, granulation
  0.25/4 mm, k_f ≤ 10^{-3} m/s
7 subsoil k_f ≥ 10^{-6} m/s

Fig. 3.11.30: Variant seepage shafts (according to DWA-A 138): a) type A, b) type B

The following formula gives the rainwater runoff in general terms:

$$Q_r = r_{(D,T)} \cdot \psi \cdot A$$

Q_r = rainwater runoff [l/s]
A = runoff-producing surface (horizontal projection) [m²]
ψ = runoff coefficient > **Tab. 3.11.3**
$r_{(D,T)}$ = calculated rainfall level [l/(s · ha)], where D is duration and T is frequency

Dimensions of drainage facilities

Conduits

In calculating the dimensions for conduits on a plot of ground, a rainfall of 5 min. duration and a frequency of 2 years (or 5 years in town centers > EN 752-4) is generally assumed. This is used a the basis for calculating rainwater runoff according to the formula below:

$$Q_r = r_{(5,2)} \cdot \psi \cdot A / 10.000 \, [l/s]$$

Q_r = rainwater runoff [l/s]
$r_{(5,2)}$ = calculated rainfall level [l/(s·ha)]
ψ = runoff coefficient > **Tab. 3.11.3**
A = runoff-producing surface [m²]

Buried conduits must not be smaller than DN 100. The gradient must be at least 1:DN. $h/d_i = 0.7$ should be taken as the maximum degree of filling. Together with the calculated rainwater runoff Q_r, this gives a pipe diameter as listed in Table 3.11.4.

Seepage systems

The basic calculations below apply to systems with a maximum drainage area of 200 ha and DWA-A 138—Planning, Construction and Operation of Facilities for the Percolation of Precipitation Water. More detailed construction specifications and additional calculation formulae can be found in the DWA-A 138 spreadsheet.

Surface seepage

$$A_S = \frac{A_u}{\left(k_f \cdot 10^{-7} / 2 \cdot r_{D(0.2)}\right) - 1}$$

A_S = seepage surface (horizontal projection)
A_u = surface to be drained $(A_E) \cdot \psi$, ψ > **Tab. 3.11.3**
k_f = permeability coefficient (> **Tab. 1.1.3**) $\geq 2 \cdot r_{D(0.2)} \cdot 10^7$
$r_{D(0.2)}$ = rainfall frequency where T = 5a
D = 10–15 min.

Trough seepage (calculating volume required)

$$V_M = \left[(A_u + \text{erf. } A_S) \, 10^{-7} \cdot r_{D(0.2)} - \text{erf. } A_S \cdot \frac{k_f}{2} \right] \cdot D \cdot 60 \cdot f_z$$

V_M = volume of trough in m³
erf. $A_S = 0.1 \cdot A_u$ (soil type MSa, FSa),
$0.2 \cdot A_u$ (soil type siSa, saSi, Si)
$r_{D(0.2)}$ = rainfall frequency where T = 5a
D = variable*
k_f = permeability coefficient > **Tab. 1.1.3**
f_z = safety factor (generally 1.2)

> proof of emptying time (tE)< 24 h must be provided with the result for V:

$$t_E = 2 \cdot (V / A_S) / k_f = t_E \,(\text{in seconds}), \, t_E/3600 = t_E \, h$$

> calculating accumulation height $z_M = V / A_S$
French drain seepage
(Calculation of necessary length of trench for thin-walled plastic pipes)

$$S_{RR} = \frac{S_R}{b_R \cdot h} \left[b_R \cdot h + \frac{\pi \cdot d^2}{4} \left(\frac{1}{S_R - 1} \right) \right]$$

S_R = storage coefficient of filler material > percentage of pores in filler material (e.g. 8/32 gravel > $S_R = 0.35$)
d = pipe diameter (where thin-walled pipes are used)

Path covering	Runoff coefficient ψ according to DIN 1986-100	
	according to DWA-A 117	
Hard areas		
· asphalt and concrete surfaces	1.0	(0.9 *)
· paving with joint grouting	1.0	
· paved or tiled covering on sand/chippings bedding	0.7	(0.75 *)
· paved coverings with > 15% joints	0.6	(0.5 *)
· artificial surfaces/turf	0.6	
· stamped earth surfaces on sports areas	0.4	
· water-bound surfaces	0.3	
· lawn grid paving stones	0.0 [on smaller surfaces. e.g. single car parking areas and their access ways]	(0.15 *)
· garden paths made from water-bound covering	0.0	
Roof surfaces		
· roof surfaces	1.0	(0.9–1.0 *)
· gravel roofs	0.5	(0.7 *)
· extensive green roofs < 10 cm structure thickness	0.5	(0.5 *)
· extensive green roofs ≥ 10 cm structure thickness	0.3	(0.3 *)
· intensive green roof surfaces	0.3	(0.3 *)
Non-hard areas		
· turf surfaces (sports surfaces)	0.30	
· lawns and planted areas in gardens and parks	0.0	(0.0–0.3 *) [depending on slope]
· rolled gravel surfaces and ballast floors	0.0	(0.3 *)

Tab. 3.11.3: Runoff coefficients

$$L_R = \frac{A_u \cdot 10^{-7} \cdot r_{D(0.2)}}{\dfrac{b_R \cdot h \cdot S_{RR}}{D \cdot 60 \cdot f_z} + \left(b_R + \dfrac{h}{2}\right) \cdot \dfrac{k_f}{2}}$$

$$z = \frac{A_u \cdot 10^{-7} \cdot r_{D0.2)} - \left(\dfrac{\pi \cdot d_a^2}{4^a} \cdot \dfrac{k_f}{2}\right)}{\dfrac{d_i^2 \cdot \pi}{4 \cdot D \cdot 60 \cdot f_z} + \dfrac{d_a \cdot \pi \cdot k_f}{4}}$$

$r_{D(n)}$ = rainfall frequency where n = 0.2
b_R = drainage trench width, h = drainage trench height
D = variable*
S_{RR} = total storage coefficient > for drainage trenches A S_R, for French drains > formula for S_{RR}

z = accumulation height in shaft
$r_{D(0.2)}$ = rainfall frequency where T = 5a
d_a = outer diameter of shaft
d_i = inner diameter of shaft

Trough-drainage trench seepage (length of trough-
drainage trench element)

* calculation of maximum value through varying of rain duration D
(> change in runoff speed with increased rainfall duration)

$$L = \frac{(A_u + A_{s,M}) \cdot 10^{-7} \cdot r_{D(0.2)} - \dfrac{Q_{dr} - V_M}{D \cdot 60 \cdot f_z}}{\dfrac{b_R \cdot h \cdot S_{RR}}{D \cdot 60 \cdot f_z} + \left(b_R + \dfrac{h}{2}\right) \cdot \dfrac{k_f}{2}}$$

$A_{s,M}$ = seepage surface of trough (estimated) = 0.1 $\cdot$ A_u
r_{DT} = rainfall frequency where T ≤ 5a
Q_{dr} = outlet control in m³/s (for drainage trenches = 0)
V_M = trough volumes, to calculate see above
> the result for L must correspond to the following
equation:

existing $A_{s,M} = L \cdot b_R < A_{s,M} (0.1 \cdot A_u)$

shaft seepage (calculating the required accumulation
height z > Fig. 3.11.27)

Slope	Runoff capacity in l/s for nominal width						
% (cm/m)	DN 100 d_i = 96 mm	DN 125 d_i = 113 mm	DN 150 d_i = 146 mm	DN 200 d_i = 184 mm	DN 225 d_i = 207 mm	DN 250 d_i = 230 mm	DN 300 d_i = 290 mm
5.0	9.4	14.6	28.8	-	-	-	-
4.5	8.9	13.8	27.3	50.5	-	-	-
4.0	8.4	13.0	25.8	47.6	-	-	-
3.5	7.9	12.2	24.1	44.5	60.9	-	-
3.0	7.3	11.3	22.3	41.2	56.3	74.4	-
2.5	6.7	10.3	20.3	37.6	51.4	67.9	125.4
2.0	5.9	9.2	18.2	33.6	45.9	60.7	112.1
1.5	5.1	7.9	15.7	29.1	39.7	52.5	97.0
1.4	5.0	7.7	15.2	28.1	38.4	50.8	93.7
1.3	4.8	7.4	14.6	27.1	37.0	48.9	90.3
1.2	4.6	7.1	14.1	26.0	35.5	47.0	86.7
1.1	4.4	6.8	13.5	24.9	34.0	45.0	83.0
1.0	4.2	6.5	12.8	23.7	32.4	42.8	79.1
0.9	slope ≤ 1:DN	6.1	12.2	22.5	30.7	40.6	75.0
0.8		5.8	11.5	21.2	29.0	38.3	70.7
0.7			10.7	19.8	27.1	35.8	66.1
0.6				18.3	25.0	33.1	61.2
0.5				16.7	22.8	30.2	55.8
0.4				20.4	27.0	49.9	

Tab. 3.11.4: Drainage capacity of drainage pipe systems not in buildings where the amount of filler h/d_i = 0.7 (according to EN 752-2 and DIN 1986-100)

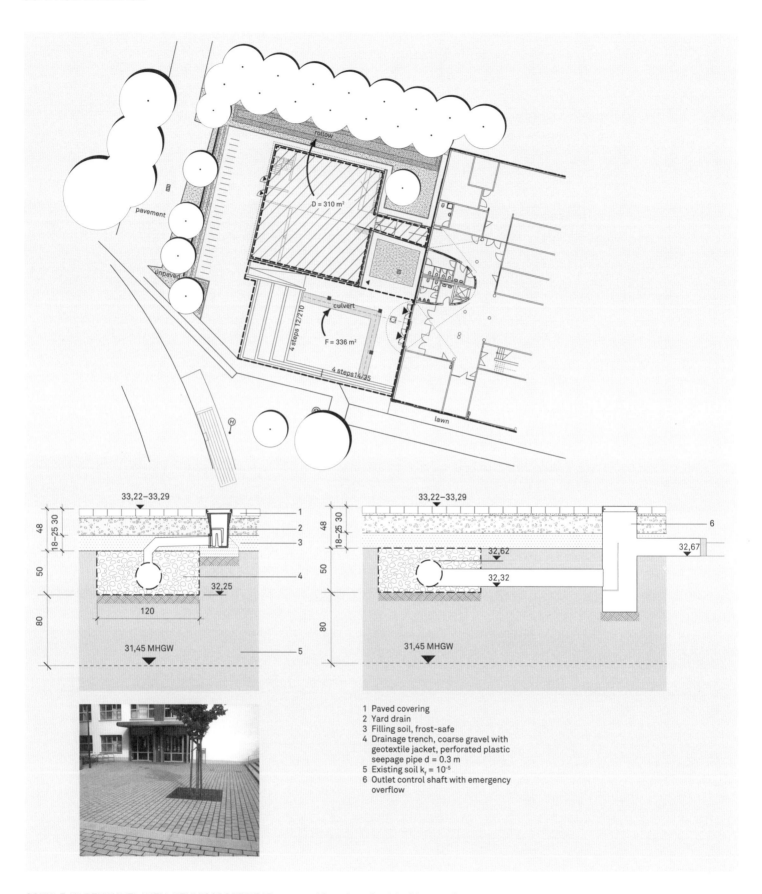

1 Paved covering
2 Yard drain
3 Filling soil, frost-safe
4 Drainage trench, coarse gravel with
geotextile jacket, perforated plastic
seepage pipe d = 0.3 m
5 Existing soil $k_f = 10^{-5}$
6 Outlet control shaft with emergency
overflow

SCHULE AN DEN HAVELAUEN, HENNIGSDORF NEAR
BERLIN, GERMANY

Architects: Fromme und Linsenhoff with Norbert
Müggenburg, landscape architect, Berlin
Completion: 2003

After the school had been refurbished and extended the precipitation must have seeped away on site. As an example, calculations are presented for the new building roof areas (pit seepage near the building) and for the paved areas of the forecourt (pipe-drainage ditch). As the forecourt is lower than the adjacent terrain, it was not possible to drain into adjacent vegetation areas.

Initial data:

Groundwater level 31.45 m (DHHN 92)

Soil type in area around seepage system according to survey: fine sand, $k_f = 10^{-5}$

Localized rainfall for a rain event with a frequency of 5 years (n = 0.2), duration variable. Calculations based on the KOSTRA values (levels of heavy rain in Germany), issued by Deutscher Wetterdienst, 1997:

Duration (D)	$r_{D(0.2)}$ l/(s·ha)
5 min	363.2
10	231.5
15	177.6
20	147.7
30	114.8
45	87.5
60	72.8
90	52.9
120	42.4
180	31
240	24.6
360	17.8

Calculation of amounts discharged

Description of area/ upper surface	Area in m²	Runoff coefficient acc. DWA-A 138	A_u	Drainage type	Rainwater runoff = plan-ned discharge amount in l/s[1]
F paved covering	336	0.75	= 252	French drain	4.9 l/s
D flat roof with gravel covering	310	0.7	= 217	trough	4.2 l/s

[1] Rain level where D = 15 min., T = 2 plus 10% tolerance = 195 l/(s·ha)

Specimen calculation Surface D for trough seepage

$$V_M = \left[(A_u + erf.A_S) \cdot 10^{-7} \cdot r_{D(0.2)} - erf.A_S \cdot \frac{k}{2} \right] \cdot D \cdot 60 \cdot f_z$$

with: $A_u = 217$ m², $A_S = 33$ m², $f_Z = 1.2$
gives:

$$V_M = \left[(217 + 33) \cdot 10^{-7} \cdot r_{D(0.2)} - 33 \cdot \frac{5 \cdot 10^{-5}}{2} \right] \cdot D \cdot 60 \cdot 1.2$$

$$V_M = \left[0.000025 \cdot r_{D(0.2)} - 0.000825 \right] \cdot D \cdot 72$$

Calculating the maximum value using the values under D and $r_{D(0.2)}$:

Duration (D)	$r_{D(0.2)}$	V in m³
15	177.6	3.9
20	147.7	4.1
30	114.8	4.42
45	87.5	4.41
60	72.8	4.3
90	52.9	3.2
120	42.4	2.0

The maximum required storage volume is $V - 4.42$ m³.
$z_M = 4.42$ m³ / 33 m² = 0.14 m
Accumulation height where size is 33 m² = 0.14 m.
Length x width of planned trough = 29 m · 1.20 m.

The base of the trough is at a height of 33.55 m DHHN 92. Given the groundwater level, this gives a seepage space of 2.10 m.

Specimen calculation Surface F for French drain seepage

$$S_{RR} = \frac{S_R}{b_R \cdot h} \left[b_R \cdot h + \frac{\pi \cdot d^2}{4} \left(\frac{1}{S_R - 1} \right) \right]$$

$$L_R = \frac{A_u \cdot 10^{-7} \cdot r_{D(0.2)}}{\frac{b_R \cdot h \cdot S_{RR}}{D \cdot 60 \cdot f_z} + \left(b_R + \frac{h}{2} \right) \cdot \frac{k_f}{2}}$$

Estimate of width and height of drainage trenches:
b_R = 1.2 m, h = 0.5 m
Use of plastic pipes with d = 0.3 m
S_R = storage coefficient of drainage trench filler materials
= 0.35
k_f = 10^{-5}
f_z = additional factor = 1.2
A_u = 217 m²

If the following is true for S_{RR}:

$$S_{RR} = \frac{0.35}{1.2 \cdot 0.5} \cdot \left[1.2 \cdot 0.5 + \frac{3.1416 \cdot 0.3^2}{4} \left(\frac{1}{35} - 1 \right) \right]$$

$$S_{RR} = 0.583 \cdot [0.6 + 0.071 \quad 1.857] = 0.726$$

and for L:

$$L_R = \frac{252 \cdot 10^{-7} \cdot r_{D(0.2)}}{\frac{1.2 \cdot 0.5 \cdot 0.726}{D \cdot 60 \cdot 1.2} + \left(1.2 + \frac{0.5}{2} \right) \cdot \frac{0.00001}{2}}$$

$$L_R = \frac{0.0000252 \cdot r_{D(0.2)}}{\frac{0.436}{D \cdot 72} + 0.00000725}$$

Calculating the maximum necessary French drain length where b = 1.2 m and h = 0.5 m using the values under D and $r_{D(0.2)}$:

Duration (D)	$r_{D(0.2)}$	L in m
15	177.6	10.9
20	147.7	12
30	114.8	13.8
45	87.5	15.8
60	72.8	17
90	52.9	17.8
120	42.4	18.5
180	31	19.2
240	24.6	19.1
360	17.8	18.7

The maximum required length of the planned drainage trench is 19.2, rounded up to 20.

The bottom of the trench is at a height of 32.25 m DHHN 92, allowing 0.8 m space above the groundwater. Nonobservation of the required 1 m distance was authorized by a legal permit. To prevent flooding of the entrance, an emergency overflow was set up to ensure the discharge of excess water if necessary.

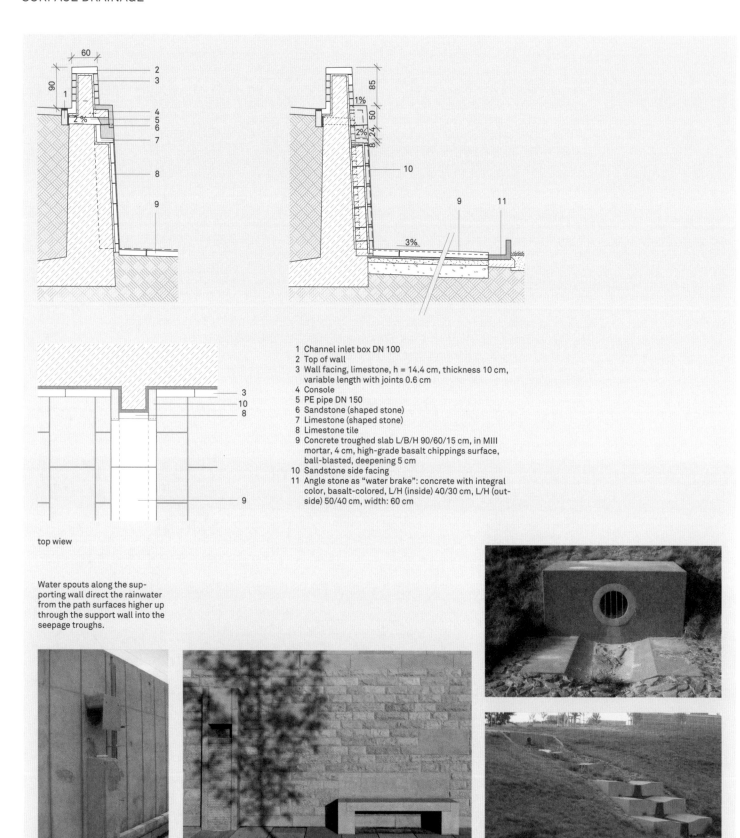

1 Channel inlet box DN 100
2 Top of wall
3 Wall facing, limestone, h = 14.4 cm, thickness 10 cm, variable length with joints 0.6 cm
4 Console
5 PE pipe DN 150
6 Sandstone (shaped stone)
7 Limestone (shaped stone)
8 Limestone tile
9 Concrete troughed slab L/B/H 90/60/15 cm, in MIII mortar, 4 cm, high-grade basalt chippings surface, ball-blasted, deepening 5 cm
10 Sandstone side facing
11 Angle stone as "water brake": concrete with integral color, basalt-colored, L/H (inside) 40/30 cm, L/H (outside) 50/40 cm, width: 60 cm

top wiew

Water spouts along the supporting wall direct the rainwater from the path surfaces higher up through the support wall into the seepage troughs.

DRAINAGE FACILITIES IN BONIFATIUSPARK,
FRANKFURT AM MAIN, GERMANY

Landscape architects: Bernhard und Sattler with Norbert
Müggenburg, Berlin
Completion: 2006

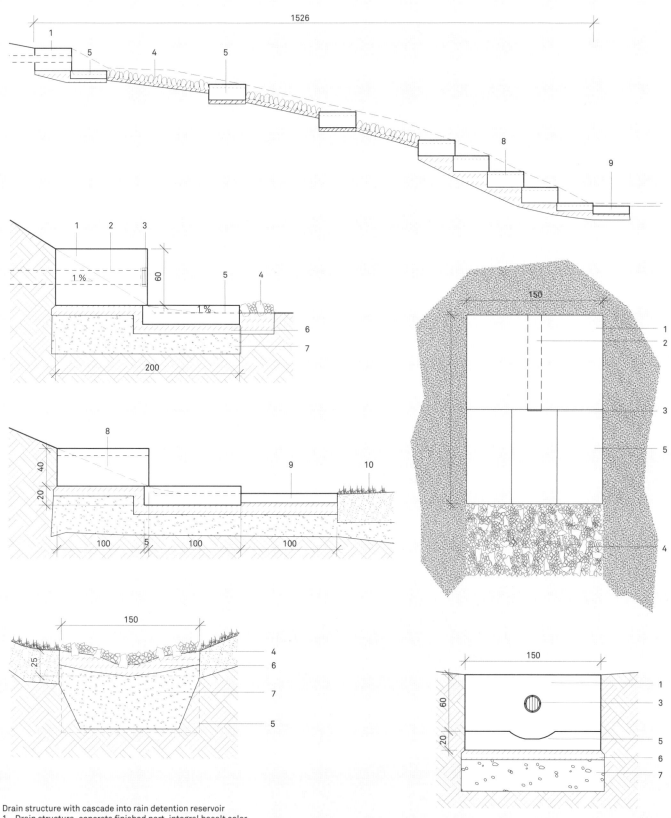

Drain structure with cascade into rain detention reservoir
1   Drain structure, concrete finished part, integral basalt color,
    with mini-bevel, sand-blasted
2   PE rain pipe DIN 150
3   Stainless steel cover grate, vertical, spacing width 6–8 cm
4   Water bricks as size 10.15 rubble stones, on concrete C25/30
5   Troughed slab, concrete finished part with 8 cm downwarping
6   Concrete foundation C25/30, 15 cm
7   Frost-protection layer 0/32, 65 cm
8   Cascade step, concrete finished part with 8 cm downwarping
9   Final concrete slab (without trough) level with bottom of rain
    detention reservoir, gradient 0%
10 Bottom of rain detention reservoir

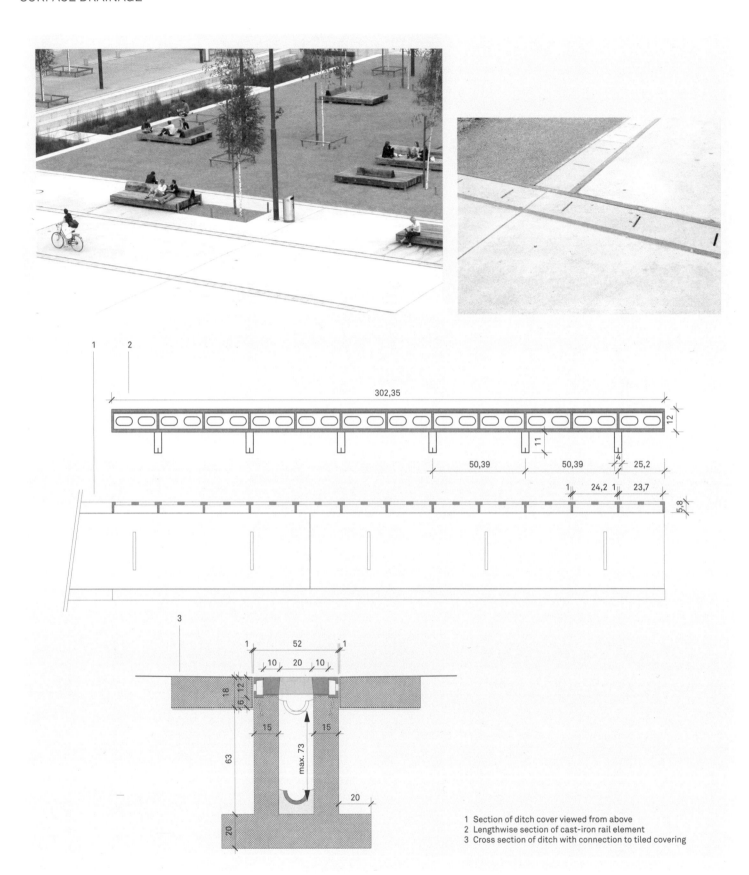

1 Section of ditch cover viewed from above
2 Lengthwise section of cast-iron rail element
3 Cross section of ditch with connection to tiled covering

TURBINENPLATZ, ZURICH, SWITZERLAND

Architects: ADR Sarl, Julien Descombes and
Marco Rampini, Geneva
In collaboration with Tobias Eugster, Zurich
Completion: 2002

Large areas of water-bound paving and shot-peened in-situ concrete are intended to emphasize the size of the turbine area. A gutter systems captures rainwater, drains it into an open seepage pool and thus structures the public space with steel framing at the same time.

3.12   WATER INSTALLATIONS

GENERAL BUILDING METHODS AND CHOICE OF LOCATION

CONSTRUCTION METHODS
·   Profiling
·   Ponds
·   Architectural pools
·   Water connections and penetration
·   Technical plant

PLANTING POOLS AND PONDS
·   Aquatic plants
·   Substrates and plant areas

SPECIMEN PROJECTS

Astrid Zimmermann

3.12 WATER INSTALLATIONS

Water as an element does not merely enhance open spaces with its reflections and light effects on the surface of the water. It also offers other visual, acoustic and tactile attractions as a habitat for aquatic plants and in the form of moving water. Water affects the microclimate positively as well.

The desired effect or use make different demands in terms of building methods, the depth of the water and the profiling of the water feature. Possibilities extend from natural-looking ponds with sloping banks to formal architectural designs with vertical pool borders. > Fig. 3.12.1

GENERAL BUILDING METHODS AND CHOICE OF LOCATION

Water installations can be built as rigid or nonrigid structures. The nonrigid method uses soil with lining, which is particularly suitable for pools with natural-looking profiling. Sheeting and clay are the commonest lining materials. The rigid method involves a solid structure in reinforced concrete, fiberglass reinforced plastic, natural stone, and masonry.

Designs for natural-looking pools should relate to the shape and position of the natural location. Round or organic forms are usually derived from the existing topography. Positioning at a low point on the terrain comes closest to a natural site. This clearly suggests itself if a pond that makes a natural impression is required.

On the other hand, architectural pools using the architectural construction method can be positioned as wished. Protrusions and raised borders are possible with appropriate dimensions. Their situation is more likely to derive from formal necessities. Geometrical shapes and lucidly formulated bank areas or framing features are typical. It is possible to combine rigid and nonrigid construction methods. So, for example, an architectural pool can be framed by a wall, but have a nonrigid liner.

It is essential to ensure stability of the subsoil; this also applies to laterally adjacent bodies of soil for nonrigid structures lined with sheeting.

Locations with alternating shade and sun over the course of a day offer the best possible conditions for biological equilibrium in a pond. It should be exposed to direct sunlight for 5–7 hours, ideally distributed over the morning and afternoon. Partial shade can also be achieved by using plants with floating leaves. Organic matter should not be introduced in undue quantities, and equally deciduous trees and shrubs should not be planted in the immediate vicinity because of falling leaves, and particularly not in the line of the prevailing wind.

The larger the pond and the deeper the water, the more likely it is that stable biological equilibrium will be achieved. This also means that the pond will require less care and attention.

a
—
b

Fig. 3.12.1: a) Natural-looking pond, b) architectural pool

Pools without plants should also be protected against the introduction of organic substances. As it is not possible to achieve biological equilibrium and contamination soon becomes a problem, regular maintenance is required. The water quality in installations with regularly changing water or circulating water (e.g. in water features and fountains) is better than in stagnant water.

In order to avoid frost damage, water should be drained from pools with mainly vertical sides in the winter months in frost-prone areas. In ponds, the formation of a shallow water zone usually offers sufficient protection against ice damage. It can make sense to lower the water level by 10–20 cm in winter in order to protect the sensitive border of the pool.

All ponds and pools must have a water supply nearby so that they can be filled and then topped up. If possible, soft water with low nutrient levels should be used. An outlet at the bottom of the pool makes it easier to empty it completely. An overflow allows water to escape if required, and regulates the water level. Permission is needed to create large water installations in Germany. Local building regulations should be consulted to establish whether this is necessary, and from what size upwards.

CONSTRUCTION METHODS

Profiling

Profiling the cross section of the pond or pool depends on the nature of the installation, the amount of space needed and the possible introduction of plants. If the installation is to be planted, then water zones have to be planned in that are appropriate to the habitats of the particular plants. > Planting pools and ponds In natural-looking installations, this is usually done by creating shallow slopes in the pool, possibly combined with terracing, to establish different water zones. Slopes in ponds should not exceed a ratio of 1:2. Shallower inclines are better, as this prevents soil slipping down deeper in the water. Substrates and pebbles can be prevented from slipping by stone ramparts, little walls, or by installing pond bags (geotextile sacks filled with gravel).

Even if the circumstances are somewhat restricted there must still be a shallow peripheral area and sufficient depth: terracing can link a shallow zone by the bank to the deep water zone via a steeper slope, or one side could be a bank with a steep edge. > Fig. 3.12.2
For architectural pools, the depth of the water or the height of the structure are dictated mainly by design requirements. If plants are needed, the depth of the pool should be appropriate for the habitat of the desired plants. > Fig. 3.12.3

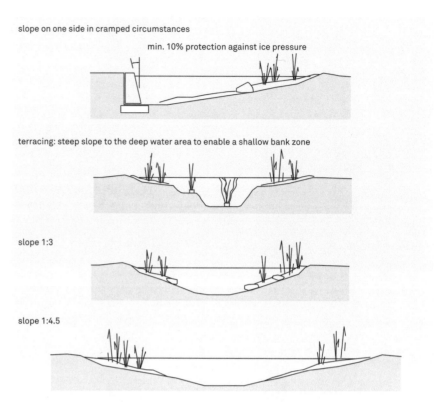

slope on one side in cramped circumstances

min. 10% protection against ice pressure

terracing: steep slope to the deep water area to enable a shallow bank zone

slope 1:3

slope 1:4.5

Fig. 2.12.2: Profiling ponds

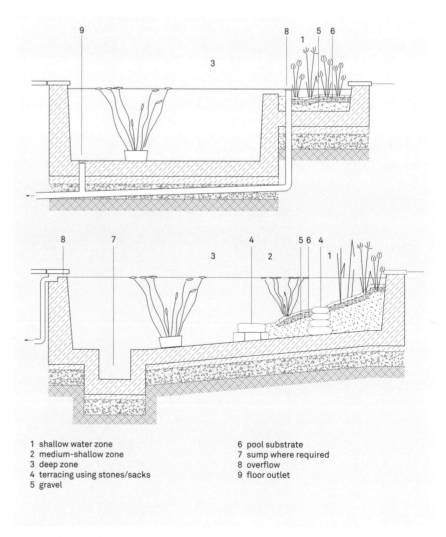

1 shallow water zone	6 pool substrate
2 medium-shallow zone	7 sump where required
3 deep zone	8 overflow
4 terracing using stones/sacks	9 floor outlet
5 gravel	

Fig. 3.12.3: Profiling planted architectural pools

Ponds

The surface water in ponds should cover at least 30 m², so that ecological equilibrium can be established. Smaller ponds can be created if little space is available (but at least 10 m²).

Water over 1 m deep prevents overheating in summer and permits adequate circulation in the water. If the water is deeper than the frost penetration depth this will also create survival space for water organisms in the winter months.

Ponds are sealed off from the surrounding soil with plastic sheeting or with mineral sealant (clay-based liner) in the nonrigid construction method. The material should be protected from damage by the ground beneath it. If the subsoil is stony, a fleece can additionally be installed on top of a leveling course of sand. Lining in the form of clay tiles can be laid directly on the subsoil. If additional loads such as gravel are placed on the pond liner there should be protective layers above the liner as well. For greater loads (large stones of foundations for structural components) building protection mats are used. On the peripheries, gravel, sand or other substrates should be provided, offering protection against UV radiation or damage from other sources. This is not needed for plastic liner sheets in deeper water, but if groundwater levels are high, weighting with loose material can stop the sheeting from floating upwards. > Fig. 3.12.4

Plastic sheet liners are very flexible and can be used in ponds of almost any shape. Sheeting for ponds is made of PVC, EPDM, flexible polyolefins (FPO), or polythene (PE). Their properties and their environment-friendliness in manufacture and recyclability can differ greatly in some cases, and should be considered when choosing materials. > Tab. 3.12.1 In general, sheet thicknesses of 1.2–1.5 mm are suitable for ponds with normal loading. Manufacturers' recommendations should be followed.

Creases should be avoided when laying the liner sheet, but undulating folds are permissible and also unavoidable when adapting to an organic pond shape on site. However, tailor-made sheets manufactured to planning requirements provide a lining that will fit exactly. EPDM sheets are tailor-made as a matter of course. Edges should always be taken 5 cm above the planned water level. It is good for plastic liners to finish vertical at the

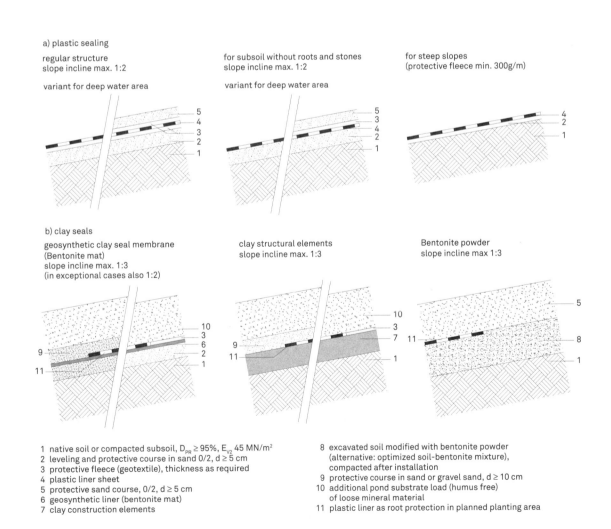

a) plastic sealing

regular structure
slope incline max. 1:2

variant for deep water area

for subsoil without roots and stones
slope incline max. 1:2

variant for deep water area

for steep slopes
(protective fleece min. 300g/m)

b) clay seals

geosynthetic clay seal membrane
(Bentonite mat)
slope incline max. 1:3
(in exceptional cases also 1:2)

clay structural elements
slope incline max. 1:3

Bentonite powder
slope incline max 1:3

1 native soil or compacted subsoil, $D_{PR} \geq 95\%$, E_{V2} 45 MN/m²
2 leveling and protective course in sand 0/2, d ≥ 5 cm
3 protective fleece (geotextile), thickness as required
4 plastic liner sheet
5 protective sand course, 0/2, d ≥ 5 cm
6 geosynthetic liner (bentonite mat)
7 clay construction elements

8 excavated soil modified with bentonite powder
   (alternative: optimized soil-bentonite mixture),
   compacted after installation
9 protective course in sand or gravel sand, d ≥ 10 cm
10 additional pond substrate load (humus free)
   of loose mineral material
11 plastic liner as root protection in planned planting area

Fig. 3.12.4: Accumulating layers using the non-rigid construction method: a) plastic liners, b) clay liners

Material	Flexibility and malleability	Durability, weathering properties	Jointing techniques, tightness	Environmental friendliness (manufacture and recycling *)	Color spectrum	Additional points
Plastic liners						
PVC-P	very flexible, brittle under pressure	not quite as resistant to cold as EPDM (also dependent on color), not UV resistant in the long term (> plasticizers)	thermal welding and solvent bonding, glued joints for penetration	questionable in terms of health because of plasticizers in the manufacturing process, recyclable	dyes well, available in turquoise or beige, for example, as well as black or olive green	comparatively cheap and easy to work
EPDM	very elastic, stretches even with subsequent settling	highly flexible when cold, workable even at low temperatures, not to be installed in damp conditions, UV- and weather-resistant, and very dimensionally stable	installed only tailor-made, penetration possible with glued joints on site	environmentally friendly in production reused as recycling granulate	only in black	
FPO	harder	very durable	thermal welding	more environmentally friendly than PVC in production	can be dyed in many colors	expensive to work
PE-LD	very flexible and adaptable	workable only when dry and at minimum temperature	not available tailor-made	recyclable	black	
Clay-based liners						
Clay structural elements	no steep slopes, max. 1:3, better 1:5, larger areas good to model	highly resistant to aging, needs protection against drying out	100% tightness not guaranteed	ecologically safe	natural color shade from necessary covering layer, but not defining	economical to work, especially for larger installations
Bentonite powder (mixed-in-place)		needs protection against drying out				
Bentonite powder (mixed-in-plant)						
Bentonite mat	comparable with plastic sheeting	no moisture action during storage and installation	laid overlapping very tight, but tightness test possible only after covering layers have even installed	base material in geoplastics		more economical than the other clay-based linings

* Recycling possible only when the material is known, so it is essential to possess the necessary knowledge about the material at the time of disposal; this is best guaranteed by information provided on the material.

Tab. 3.12.1: Survey of currently available linings and their properties for the non-rigid construction method

edges, so that water does not diffuse into adjacent areas. This also makes it less easy for the sheets to be uncovered. > Figs. 3.12.5 and 3.12.6

To guarantee that the liner is rootproof (and thus sealing correctly), only certified liners should be used for sealing.

Lining with clay makes it possible to create a "natural" pond. In addition, subsequent disposal and any residue left in the soil will not create environmental problems. If the existing soil is sufficiently cohesive, it can be sealed directly, but other processes are generally used to ensure even and secure sealing.

Working with clay construction materials, e.g. clay tiles, is comparatively more elaborate. As the material is so heavy, high transport costs for delivering the material have to be taken into account as well if the installed thickness is 10–30 cm.

Bentonite is an alternative material, a clay mineral that can swell considerably, which closes the pores in the grain structure and thus increases the waterproof qualities of the soil. The material can be worked into the existing soil on site in powder form (mixed-in-place process) or ready-mixed with soil in fixed proportions at the factory (mixed-in-plant process). The mixed-in-place process in cheaper, but the mixed-in-plant process produces the best possible mixture.

Geosynthetic clay liners (bentonite mats) are geotextile liners made of mechanically bonded layers of fleece material with a bentonite filling. They are laid on site

Fig. 3.12.5: Incompletely covered plastic sheet, supported by gravel at the sides

edging for plastic sheets

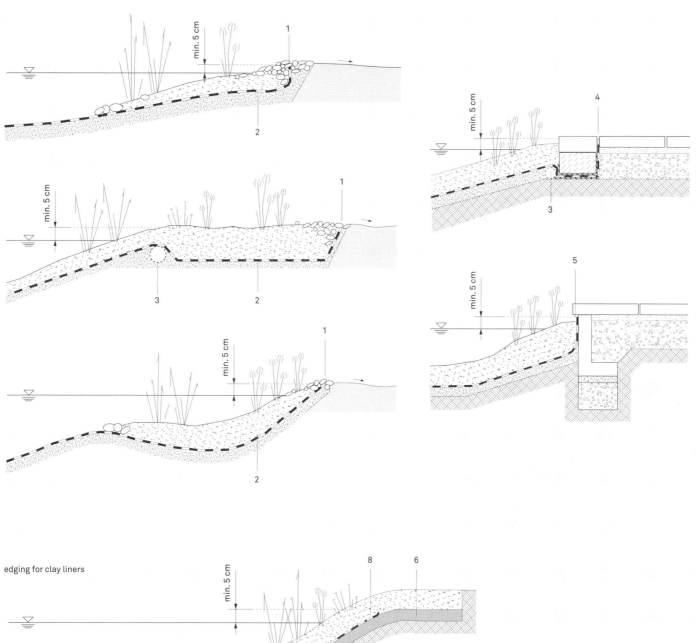

edging for clay liners

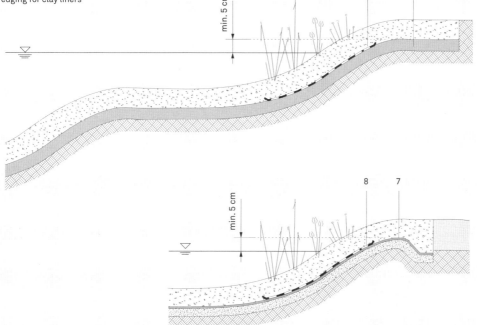

1 capillary break created by raised liner/laying in coarse gravel
2 plastic liner with protective fleece > Fig. 3.12.4
3 stabilizing the plastic sheet, e.g. with drainage pipe
4 liner taken behind the surround, foundation clad in protective fleece
5 plastic liner raised at edge, where necessary provide wall fixing > Fig. 3.12.9
6 clay liner
7 bentonite mat
8 root protection

Fig. 3.12.6: Pond peripheries

and covered with a protective layer of gravel sand mixture 0/32 and an additional layer of pond substrate where necessary. Laying bentonite mats is a comparatively practicable and reasonably priced variant when using clay liners (low transport costs, simple to install, almost independently of the weather). > Fig. 3.12.4

To prevent clay linings from drying out, loose material able to break the capillary effect should be installed on the peripheries. Courses no less than 20 cm thick should be provided. > Fig. 3.12.6

Ponds can also be constructed using waterproof concrete or asphalt. But these materials make sense only for large installations and are comparatively expensive; fine modeling is not possible.

Ready-made ponds are available in fiberglass reinforced plastics, though only in small sizes. They can also be supplied locally in any shape by specialist firms. Manufacturing such ponds or pools is significantly more expensive, but they are very durable, and fold-free.

Architectural pools

A very wide variety of materials can be considered for architectural pools and water features. > Fig. 3.12.7 The tightness of the structure is also crucially important here. A common construction method uses waterproof concrete, > Chapter 1.7 Concrete which can also serve as a substructure for a surface clad in steel, natural stone, or tiles. > Fig. 3.12.8 Working and movement joints must be watertight. > Chapter 2.3 Connections, Concrete connections If the pool is not constructed in waterproof concrete, a plastic linier must be laid on the concrete surface. The same applies if the structure is in masonry. Liners must be protected against damage and raised above the maximum water level when connecting to raised edges and buildings, and where necessary additionally secured with parallel clamps or compound metal sheeting sections. > Fig. 3.12.9 As a rule, a concrete pool is places on a clean layer (C 12/15) and a support course where necessary.

To arrive at the required minimum wall thickness both the horizontal pressure from the pool water and also—in the case of inset pools—the horizontal pressure of the oil on the outside wall of the pool should be taken into account.

Fountains and small pools can also be made monolithically from a single natural stone.

Fig. 3.12.7: Architectural pools and fountains

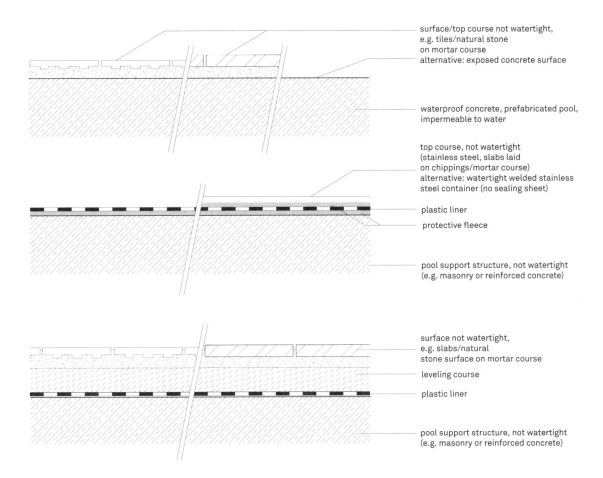

surface/top course not watertight,
e.g. tiles/natural stone
on mortar course
alternative: exposed concrete surface

waterproof concrete, prefabricated pool,
impermeable to water

top course, not watertight
(stainless steel, slabs laid
on chippings/mortar course)
alternative: watertight welded stainless
steel container (no sealing sheet)

plastic liner

protective fleece

pool support structure, not watertight
(e.g. masonry or reinforced concrete)

surface not watertight,
e.g. slabs/natural
stone surface on mortar course

leveling course

plastic liner

pool support structure, not watertight
(e.g. masonry or reinforced concrete)

Fig. 3.12.8: Course structure
for architectural pools

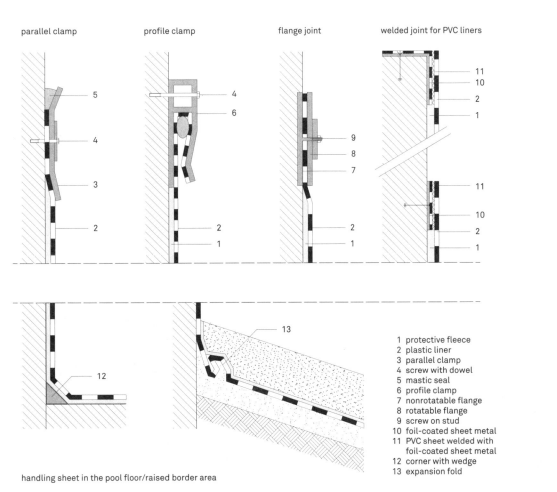

parallel clamp   profile clamp   flange joint   welded joint for PVC liners

handling sheet in the pool floor/raised border area

1 protective fleece
2 plastic liner
3 parallel clamp
4 screw with dowel
5 mastic seal
6 profile clamp
7 nonrotatable flange
8 rotatable flange
9 screw on stud
10 foil-coated sheet metal
11 PVC sheet welded with
   foil-coated sheet metal
12 corner with wedge
13 expansion fold

Fig. 3.12.9: Connecting buildings
to plastic liners

Water connections and penetration

Penetration of the waterproof wall of a pond or pool is always a potential weakness. It is possible to arrange inlets on the surface, but this does not always work for overflows, and not at all for outlets.

If a nonrigid construction method is being used, then the required pipework should be stabilized outside the pool, with concrete foundations, for example. Suitable clamp or sleeve joints are available for watertight pipe penetration. Incompatibilities must be borne in mind, especially between plastics, and appropriate jointing parts used. When sealing clay, the material is applied directly to the penetrating object, and the area around the pipe is fixed with bentonite powder. > Fig. 3.12.10

Casing pipes or tap holes with seal insert or flanged pipes with seal flange are used for pipes running through waterproof concrete. The pipe penetration must always be executed at right angles to the wall or the floor slab.

Technical plant

Natural-looking ponds do not usually need any pool technology if their size means biological equilibrium can be anticipated. For smaller ponds in particular, it can make sense to use fountains, waterfalls or aeration systems to raise the oxygen content.

It is essential to change the water for cleaning purposes in architectural pools. This can be done with a mobile water pump, or as for water features with a permanent flow of water provided by a pumping system. Technical equipment is usually installed in cooperation with a specialist fountain and pump technology planner, or in consultation with the manufacturers of appropriate plant.

For emptying the pool, a pump sump or a pump chamber should be installed on the floor of the pool, so that water can accumulate there and then be pumped out. Appropriate shaft systems have to be installed if needed for the installation of other hydraulic technical equipment, especially for circulating pumps.

PLANTING POOLS AND PONDS

Aquatic plants

Aquatic plant habitats are characterized by different depths: a distinction is drawn between the marshy area in the intermittently wet bank area, the shallow water zone, with a depth of about 0 to 30 cm, the medium-shallow zone from 30–50 cm, and the subsequent deep water area. > Figs. 3.12.11–3.12.13

Aspects other than the depth of the water are significant for the choice of water plants. Oxygenating plants are particularly interesting, as they make a significant contribution to improving water quality. These include the bulrush (*Schoenoplectus*), for example, manna grass (*Glyceria*), and submerged aquatic plants such as hornwort (*Ceratophyllum demersum*).

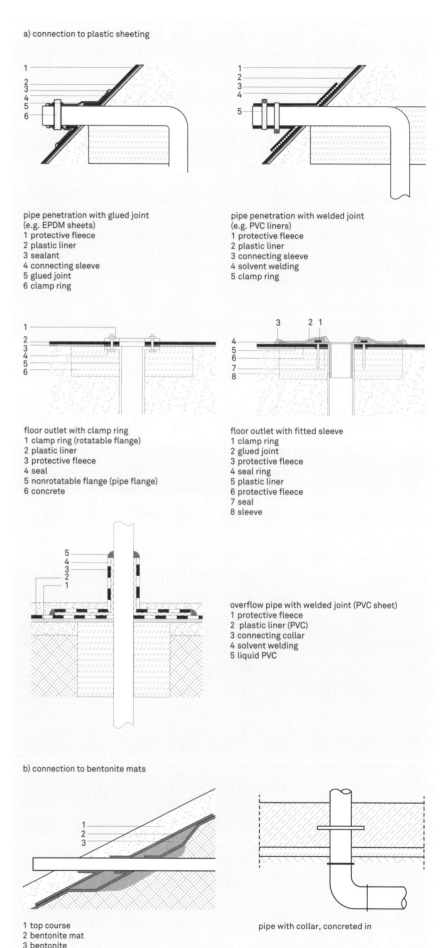

a) connection to plastic sheeting

pipe penetration with glued joint
(e.g. EPDM sheets)
1 protective fleece
2 plastic liner
3 sealant
4 connecting sleeve
5 glued joint
6 clamp ring

pipe penetration with welded joint
(e.g. PVC liners)
1 protective fleece
2 plastic liner
3 connecting sleeve
4 solvent welding
5 clamp ring

floor outlet with clamp ring
1 clamp ring (rotatable flange)
2 plastic liner
3 protective fleece
4 seal
5 nonrotatable flange (pipe flange)
6 concrete

floor outlet with fitted sleeve
1 clamp ring
2 glued joint
3 protective fleece
4 seal ring
5 plastic liner
6 protective fleece
7 seal
8 sleeve

overflow pipe with welded joint (PVC sheet)
1 protective fleece
2 plastic liner (PVC)
3 connecting collar
4 solvent welding
5 liquid PVC

b) connection to bentonite mats

1 top course
2 bentonite mat
3 bentonite

pipe with collar, concreted in

Fig. 3.12.10: Pipe penetrations

Plants with floating leaves also help to regulate biological equilibrium. Their leaves shade the water, so that it does not heat up unduly, thus restricting the growth of algae. Care should also be taken that no plants with aggressive root growth or a tendency to spread invasively are used. These include reeds (*Phragmites*), in particular, which are often found as the main plant in botanical sewage disposal systems.

Complementing the above-mentioned aspects, aesthetics plays a particular part in plant use. In natural-looking ponds the selection should feature a wide variety of species, while a reduced number of plant species produces a more succinct effect in architectural pools.

Substrates and plant areas

Undue nutrient input should be avoided in all water installations, which is why nonorganic soils should be used. The preferred pool substrates are thus nutrient-poor clayey sands, and 5–10 cm courses of these are perfectly adequate. The substrate should be covered with gravel, to prevent it from floating off. To prevent aquatic plants from proliferating unduly or to control spreading, the plants can be set in contained areas or in special aquatic plant baskets. These plant baskets in plastic mesh are also suitable for plants that have to be taken out of the pool, e.g. in the winter months or for cleaning purposes. > Fig. 3.12.14

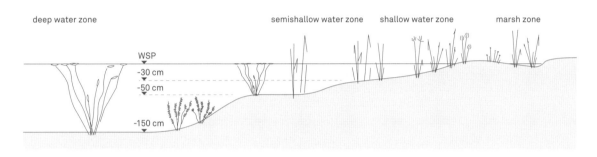

Fig. 3.12.11: Aquatic plant habitats

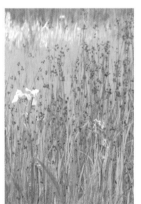

a | b | c

Fig. 3.12.12: Aquatic plants:
a) flowering rush: *Butomus umbellatus* (shallow water)
b yellow flag: *Iris pseudacorus* and *Scirpus* (shallow water)
c) white water lily: *Nymphaea alba* (deep water)

a | b

Fig. 3.12.13:
a) Planting in a sunken pool area
b) Water lilies in plant baskets for a temporary installation

Genus, species, English name

Group	Species
Underwater plants	*Elodea Canadensis,* Canadian waterweed
	Ranunculus aquatilis, common water crowfoot
	Hottonia palustris, water violet
	Callitriche palustris, vernal water starwort
Plants with floating leaves	*Nuphar lutea,* yellow water lily
	Nymphaea alba, white water lily
	Potamogeton natans, broad-leaved pondweed
	Nymphaea hybrids and varieties
	Nymphoides peltata, fringed water lily
	Polygonum amphibium, water smartweed
Floating plants	*Stratiotes aloides,* water soldier
	Hydrocharis morsus-ranae, frogbit
	Trapa natans, water chestnut
	Ceratophyllum demersum, hornwort
Marsh and river-bank plants	*Schoenoplectus (Scirpus) lacustris,* Te common clubrush
	Phragmites australis, common reed
	Typha angustifolia, lesser bulrush
	Hippuris vulgaris, mare's tail
	Sagittaria sagittifolia, arrowhead

Location, depth of water in cm (■ = suitable range)

Depth	Zone	Elodea	Ranunculus	Hottonia	Callitriche	Nuphar	Nymphaea alba	Potamogeton	Nymphaea hyb.	Nymphoides	Polygonum	Stratiotes	Hydrocharis	Trapa	Ceratophyllum	Schoenoplectus	Phragmites	Typha	Hippuris	Sagittaria
humid river-banks																				
0–10	shallow water									■	■					■	■	■		
10–20	shallow water				■					■	■					■	■	■	■	■
20–30	shallow water	■		■	■					■	■		■		■	■	■	■	■	■
30–40	semi-deep water	■	■	■	■			■		■	■		■		■	■	■	■	■	■
40–50	semi-deep water	■	■	■	■			■		■	■	■	■		■	■	■		■	■
50–60	deep water	■	■	■		■	■	■	■	■	■	■	■	■	■					
60–70	deep water	■	■	■		■	■	■	■	■	■	■	■	■	■					
70–80	deep water	■	■			■	■	■	■	■	■	■	■	■	■					
80–90	deep water	■	■			■	■	■	■	■	■	■	■		■					
90–100	deep water	■	■			■	■	■	■	■	■	■	■		■					
100–110	deep water	■	■			■	■					■	■		■					
110–120	deep water	■	■			■						■	■		■					
120–130	deep water	■				■						■			■					
130–140	deep water	■				■						■								
140–150	deep water	■				■						■								

Growth height in cm (above water level)

Elodea	Ranunculus	Hottonia	Callitriche	Nuphar	Nymphaea alba	Potamogeton	Nymphaea hyb.	Nymphoides	Polygonum	Stratiotes	Hydrocharis	Trapa	Ceratophyllum	Schoenoplectus	Phragmites	Typha	Hippuris	Sagittaria
–	10–20	30		–		inflorescence: 5–10	–	–	–	inflorescence: 20	inflorescence: 5	–	–	200	60–250	200	20–30	40–70

Light requirements

Elodea	Ranunculus	Hottonia	Callitriche	Nuphar	Nymphaea alba	Potamogeton	Nymphaea hyb.	Nymphoides	Polygonum	Stratiotes	Hydrocharis	Trapa	Ceratophyllum	Schoenoplectus	Phragmites	Typha	Hippuris	Sagittaria
○–◐	○	○–◐	○–◐	○–◐	○	○–◐	○	○–◐	○–◐	○–◐	○–◐	○	○–◐	○–◐	○–◐	○	○–◐	○–◐

Flowering

Elodea	Ranunculus	Hottonia	Callitriche	Nuphar	Nymphaea alba	Potamogeton	Nymphaea hyb.	Nymphoides	Polygonum	Stratiotes	Hydrocharis	Trapa	Ceratophyllum	Schoenoplectus	Phragmites	Typha	Hippuris	Sagittaria
V–VIII	VI–VIII	V–VI	VI–VII	VI–VIII	VI–IX	VII–VIII	VI–IX	VII–VIII	VI–VIII	V–VIII	VII–VIII	VI–VIII	VI–IX	VI–VIII	VII–XI	VI–VIII	V–VIII	VI–VIII

Purification effect

Elodea	Ranunculus	Hottonia	Callitriche	Nuphar	Nymphaea alba	Potamogeton	Nymphaea hyb.	Nymphoides	Polygonum	Stratiotes	Hydrocharis	Trapa	Ceratophyllum	Schoenoplectus	Phragmites	Typha	Hippuris	Sagittaria
	x			x	x	x		x	x	x			x	x	x	x		x

Oxygenation

Elodea	Ranunculus	Hottonia	Callitriche	Nuphar	Nymphaea alba	Potamogeton	Nymphaea hyb.	Nymphoides	Polygonum	Stratiotes	Hydrocharis	Trapa	Ceratophyllum	Schoenoplectus	Phragmites	Typha	Hippuris	Sagittaria
x	x	x								x	x		x					

Hints

Species	Hint
Elodea Canadensis	green in winter, very vigorous growth
Hottonia palustris	on long stems, floating under water
Nuphar lutea	creeping rhizome, 'Minima' variety grows at a depth of 30–50 cm
Potamogeton natans	inclined to proliferate, and then forms large carpets under the surface of the water, good for shade, but not in small ponds
Nymphaea hybrids	creeping rhizome, flower color and location vary considerably by variety
Nymphoides peltata	spreads considerably in favorable locations, creeping stems
Polygonum amphibium	proliferates considerably
Stratiotes aloides	above surface only when in flower, otherwise belowt
Hydrocharis morsus-ranae	bud winters on bottom
Trapa natans	roots in mud
Ceratophyllum demersum	flourishes when floating freely
Schoenoplectus lacustris	seeds heavily
Phragmites australis	proliferates considerably, inclines to "monoculture", only for very large ponds or separated areas, can damage the pool membrane
Typha angustifolia	forms runners
Hippuris vulgaris	rhizome creeps and proliferates

Tab. 3.12.2: Aquatic plants and their use (selected)

Marsh and river-bank plants

Plant	Height/depth (cm)	Light	Flowering	x	Notes
Typha latifolia, bulrush	100–200	○	VI–VIII	x	only for large ponds and marshes, spreads considerably
Pontederia cordata, pickerel weed	50	○	VI–VIII	x	creeping rhizome, not guaranteed hardy in winter, so winter frost-free (min. 50 cm deep)
Butomus umbellatus, flowering rush	80–100	○–◐	VI–VIII		
Sparganium erectum, branched bur-reed	30–60	◐	VII–VIII	x	grows vigorously, forms runners
Acorus calamus, common sweet flag	60–100	○–◐	VI–VII	x	forms rhizome and creeps
Alisma plantago-aquatica, common water plantain	30–80	○–◐	VII–IX		tuberous rhizomes, self-seeding, also suitable for small pools
Ranunculus lingua, water spearwort	60–100	○	VI–VIII		grows vigorously, forms runners
Typha minima, dwarf reed mace	60	○	V–VII	x	suitable for small ponds (does not proliferate like other Thypha varieties), delicate, forms runners
Veronica beccabunga, brooklime	20–30	○–◐	V–VIII		
Iris laevigata, Japanese water iris	70	◐	VII–VIII	x	
Caltha palustris, kingcup	30	○–◐	IV–V	x	forms rhizome, creeps
Calla palustris, bog arum	20–30	○–◐	VI–VIII	x	creeping rhizomes
Iris pseudacorus, yellow flag	50–90	○–◐	V–VII	x	
Eriophorum angustifolium, common cottongrass	15–30	○	VI–VII		moorland plant
Glycera maxima 'Variegata', variegated manna grass	60	○	VII–VIII	x	proliferates less than the species
Iris versicolor, harlequin blueflag	60	○–◐	VI–VII		
Juncus effuses, corkscrew rush	70–80	○–◐	VII–VIII	x	inclined to proliferate
Juncus ensifolius, swordleaf rush	30	○	VI–VIII		grows thickly
Lysimachia nummularia, creeping jenny	5–10	○–◐	VI–VII	x	ground cover, shoots root above ground, well suited for pond edges
Lysimachia vulgaris, yellow loosestrife	60–120	○	VII–VIII	x	runners below ground, also suitable for dry banks
Lythrum salicaria, purple loosestrife	60–100	○–◐	VII–IX	x	
Myosotis palustris, common forget-me-not	20–40	○–◐	V–VIII	x	seeds easily in favorable locations

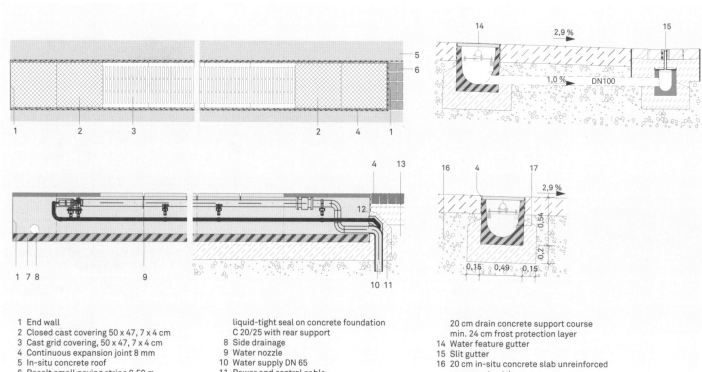

1 End wall
2 Closed cast covering 50 x 47, 7 x 4 cm
3 Cast grid covering, 50 x 47, 7 x 4 cm
4 Continuous expansion joint 8 mm
5 In-situ concrete roof
6 Basalt small paving strips 0.50 m
   with expansion joint on one side
7 Gutter undersection without own
   incline sealant in safety joint between
   gutter section and end wall creating

liquid-tight seal on concrete foundation
C 20/25 with rear support
8 Side drainage
9 Water nozzle
10 Water supply DN 65
11 Power and control cable
12 End wall, drilled through
13 Basalt small paving, 8 x 8 x 12 cm
   (5 mm higher than top gutter covering)
   3 cm mortar bed

20 cm drain concrete support course
min. 24 cm frost protection layer
14 Water feature gutter
15 Slit gutter
16 20 cm in-situ concrete slab unreinforced
   as concrete strip
   min. 35 cm frost protection layer
17 Power and control cable in empty pipes

WATER FEATURE, HAUPTTORPLATZ LEUNA, GERMANY

Landscape architects: Weidinger Landschaftsarchitekten,
Berlin
Completion: 2005

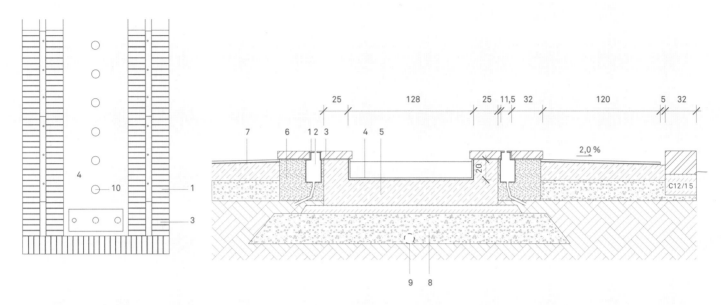

1 Bronze cover plate, drilled with neoprene coating
2 Nozzle case
3 Sandstone covering as chippings course with mortar joint, Polish "Hockenau" sandstone
4 Water-repellent Moroccan tiles, joined with 2-component epoxy resin joint mortar
5 Pool support structure in waterproof concrete on clean course C 12/15

6 Like-grained concrete
7 Moroccan tiles on reinforced concrete slab
8 Recycled support course 0/32
9 Drainage pipe DN 160
10 UV lamp

LONG POOL IN THE ORIENTAL "GARDEN OF THE FOUR RIVERS" ERHOLUNGSPARK MARZAHN, BERLIN, GERMANY

Landscape architect: Kamel Louafi, Berlin
Company implementing project: Andalous Design, Morocco
Hydraulics: Joachim Kudlek
Completion: 2005

water table, top view

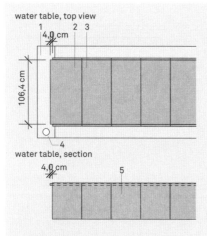

water table, section

1 Catch basin
2 Covering in Oberdorla muschelkalk,
   106.5 x 54 x 3 cm
3 Covering in Oberdorla muschelkalk,
   106.5 x 50 x 3 cm
4 Outlet DN 100
5 Sidewall covering Oberdorla muschelkalk,
   50 x 60 x 3 cm

water table, top view

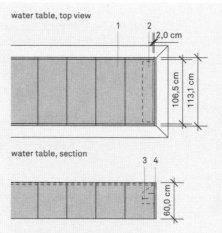

water table, section

1 Covering Oberdorla muschelkalk,
   106.5 x 50 x 3 cm
2 Water inlet box
3 Baffle plates
4 End wall behind, Oberdorla muschelkalk
   suspended in front, 113.1 x 60 x 3 cm

water inlet box

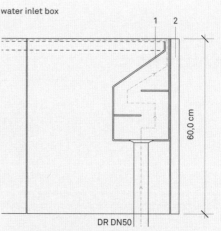

1 Water inlet box with baffle plates, pressure tube
   connection DN50
2 End wall behind, Oberdorla muschelkalk suspended in front, 113.1 x 60 x 3 cm

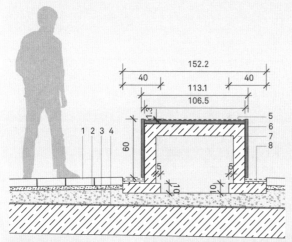

section A–A'

1 Cast stone, thickness 8 cm
2 Sand bed 4 cm
3 Gravel support course
4 Drainage mat on top edge
   of multistory car park
5 Water level 0.5 cm
6 Natural stone cover 3 cm,
   Oberdorla muschelkalk,
   fixed with epoxy resin
   mortar for underwater area
7 Reinforced concrete
   support structure C25
8 Stainless steel gutter
   23 cm on mortar bed,
   water level 2 cm

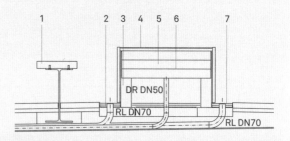

cross-section A–A'

1 Bench
2 Water return channel, V4A stainless steel, 200 x 200 mm,
   with inlaid natural stone slab
3 Water table with natural stone covering 3 cm, on reinforced
   concrete support structure C25
4 Water table water level 0.5 cm
5 Water inlet box in V4A stainless steel, 1000 x 300 x 200 mm
6 Baffle plates
7 Water return channel, water level 2 cm

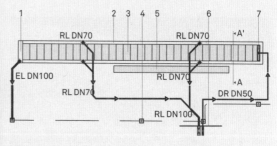

1 Catch basin, 1500 x 300 x 150 mm
2 Water return channel, 200 x 200 mm
3 Water table
4 Rainwater connection, 300 x 300 mm
5 Bench
6 Connection pump room, domestic services
7 Water inlet box, 1000 x 300 x 200 mm

WATER TABLE, INNER COURTYARD
AT 17 SCHUMANNSTRASSE, BERLIN, GERMANY

K1 Landschaftsarchitekten, Berlin
Completion: 2003

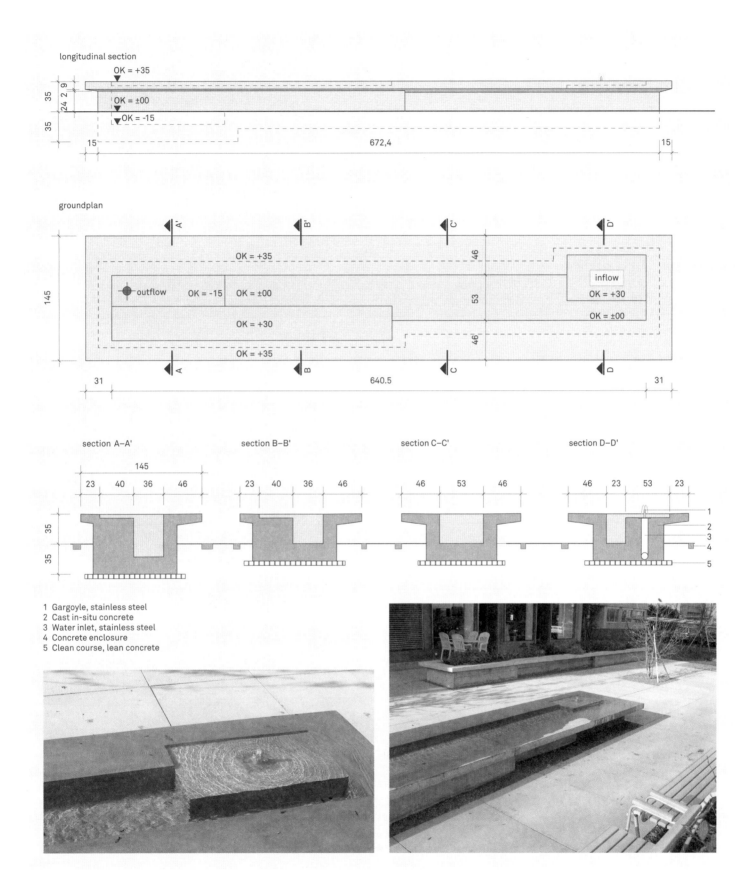

longitudinal section

OK = +35
OK = ±00
OK = -15

35
24 2 9
35

15
672,4
15

groundplan

A'
B'
C'
D'

OK = +35
46

outflow   OK = -15   OK = ±00
inflow
OK = +30

145
53

OK = +30
OK = ±00

OK = +35
46

A
B
C
D

31
640.5
31

section A–A'   section B–B'   section C–C'   section D–D'

145
23 40 36 46   23 40 36 46   46 53 46   46 23 53 23

35
35

1 Gargoyle, stainless steel
2 Cast in-situ concrete
3 Water inlet, stainless steel
4 Concrete enclosure
5 Clean course, lean concrete

1
2
3
4
5

POOL, BACHWIESEN CARE CENTRE, ZURICH,
SWITZERLAND

Kuhn Truninger Landschaftsarchitekten, Zurich
Completion: 2004

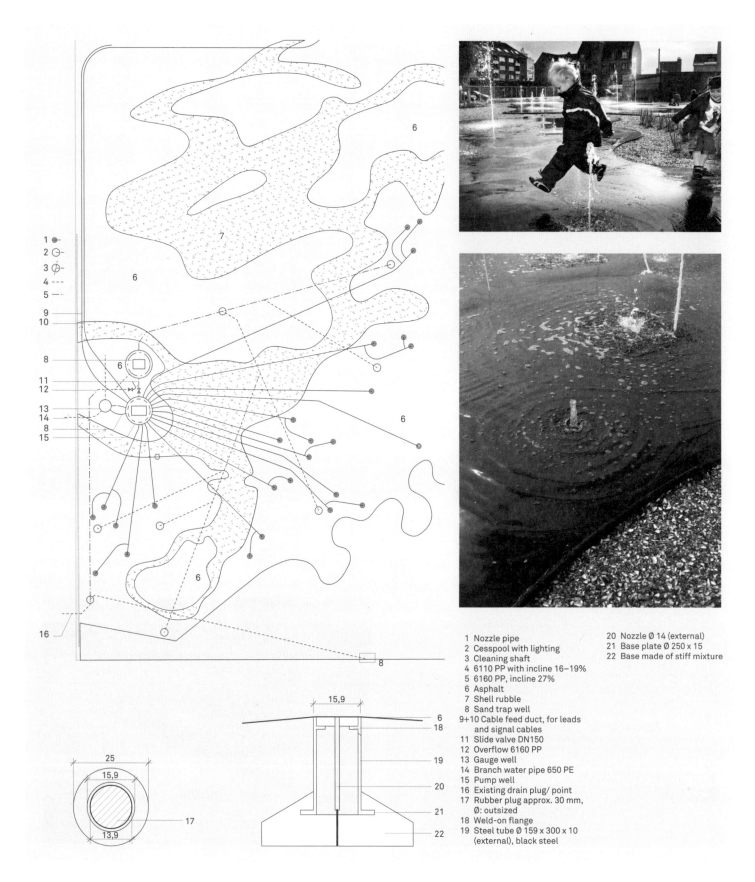

1 Nozzle pipe
2 Cesspool with lighting
3 Cleaning shaft
4 6110 PP with incline 16–19%
5 6160 PP, incline 27%
6 Asphalt
7 Shell rubble
8 Sand trap well
9+10 Cable feed duct, for leads
    and signal cables
11 Slide valve DN150
12 Overflow 6160 PP
13 Gauge well
14 Branch water pipe 650 PE
15 Pump well
16 Existing drain plug/ point
17 Rubber plug approx. 30 mm,
    Ø: outsized
18 Weld-on flange
19 Steel tube Ø 159 x 300 x 10
    (external), black steel

20 Nozzle Ø 14 (external)
21 Base plate Ø 250 x 15
22 Base made of stiff mixture

WATER FEATURE IN THE "URBAN GARDEN",
NØRRESUNDBY, DENMARK

Landscape architects: SLA A/S, Copenhagen
Completion: 2005

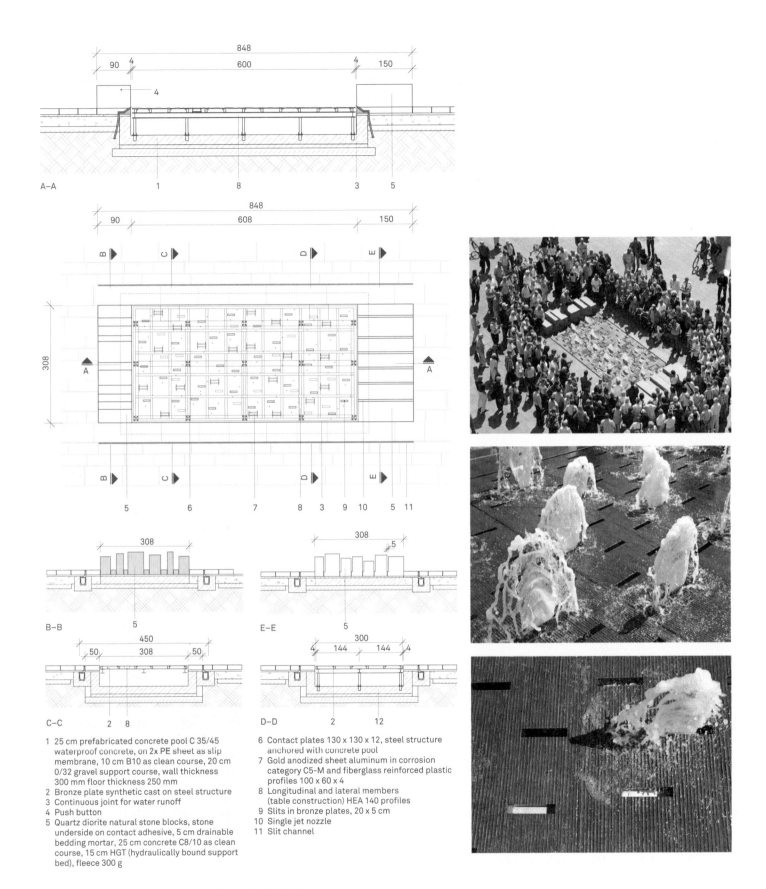

848
90 4 600 4 150
A–A 1 8 3 5

848
90 608 150
308

B C D E
A   A
B C D E
5 6 7 8 3 9 10 5 11

308
B–B 5

308 5
E–E 5

450
50 308 50
C–C 2 8

300
4 144 144 4
D–D 2 12

1 25 cm prefabricated concrete pool C 35/45 waterproof concrete, on 2x PE sheet as slip membrane, 10 cm B10 as clean course, 20 cm 0/32 gravel support course, wall thickness 300 mm floor thickness 250 mm
2 Bronze plate synthetic cast on steel structure
3 Continuous joint for water runoff
4 Push button
5 Quartz diorite natural stone blocks, stone underside on contact adhesive, 5 cm drainable bedding mortar, 25 cm concrete C8/10 as clean course, 15 cm HGT (hydraulically bound support bed), fleece 300 g

6 Contact plates 130 x 130 x 12, steel structure anchored with concrete pool
7 Gold anodized sheet aluminum in corrosion category C5-M and fiberglass reinforced plastic profiles 100 x 60 x 4
8 Longitudinal and lateral members (table construction) HEA 140 profiles
9 Slits in bronze plates, 20 x 5 cm
10 Single jet nozzle
11 Slit channel

"GOLDSOLE" WATER FEATURE, MARKTPLATZ IN HALLE
AN DER SAALE, GERMANY

Rehwaldt Landschaftsarchitekten, Dresden
Completion: 2006

1 Granite slab 20 to 50 cm on 3 cm mortar compensation course, 20 cm reinforced concrete base slab, 100 cm reinforced concrete strip foundations, 30 cm subsoil improvement
2 Water outlet stainless steel slit and jets
3 Installation shaft for hydraulic technology
4 Overflow with pump
5 Water-course block, water bricks category LMB 10/60, natural stone "Maui black"
6 20–30 cm mineral mixture 0/45
7 Intermediate planting reed sods 3 per m²
8 Water outlet, bronze flap "Aqua G", water outlet slit 50 x 2 cm, stainless steel, thickness 2 mm
9 Water steps, 3 cm mortar compensation course, 20 cm reinforced concrete base plate
10 Glass, translucent, color gold-yellow, underside reflective, glued with silicone adhesive
11 "Maui black" with circular gaps

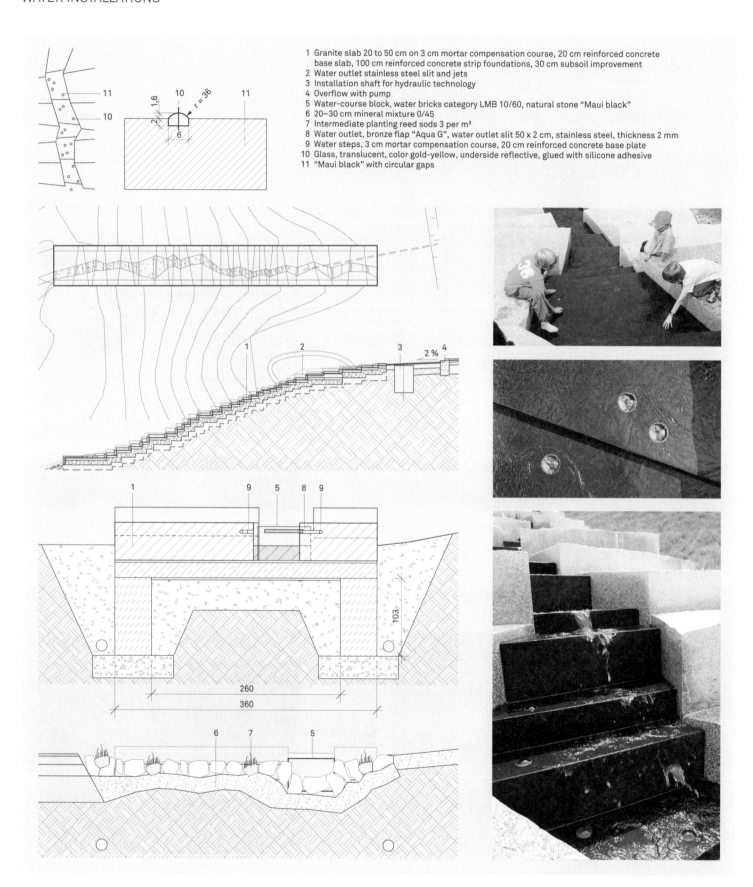

WATER STEPS, STADTPARK WALDKIRCHEN, GERMANY

Rehwaldt Landschaftsarchitekten, Dresden
Completion: 2007

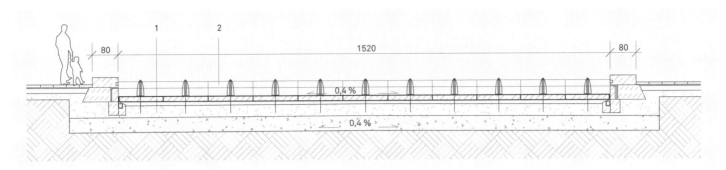

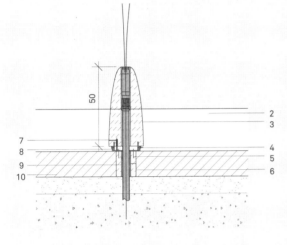

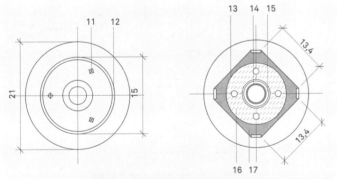

1 Pool floor, reinforced concrete slab faced with polished terrazzo, thick watertight jointing, 10 cm compensation course chippings 0/8, 35 cm mineral mixture 0/32, min. 35 cm mineral mixture 0/54
2 Water level
3 Concrete hump, Ø max. 21 cm, color coating with glitter chips, color as chosen by company
4 Adjustable blocking with internal hexagonal screw DIN 912-A2
5 4 anchor bolts M10 x 50
6 Grouting mortar
7 Threaded bush M5 x 40, internal hexagonal screw M5 x 65
8 Flat steel ring A2, 50 x 5 mm, cast in at factory
9 Continuous joint seal 8 mm
10 Sheet stainless steel base plate A2, 134 x 134 mm with 4 link plates welded on 20 x 20 x 5 mm with thread M5 and bore 50 mm

Concrete hump
11 3 threaded bushes M5 x 40,
12 Flat steel ring A2, Ø = 15 cm, 50 x 5 mm, cast in factory

Fixing
13 Drilling in concrete base slab, Ø = 12 cm
14 Intruder detection lead DN40
15 Joint seal
16 Grouting mortar
17 Flat steel base plate A2, 134 x 134 x 5 mm with 4 link plates welded on 20 x 20 x 5 mm with thread M5, 4 drill holes 12 mm and 1 drill hole 50 mm

"AQUASONUM" WATER FEATURE, WALDKIRCHEN, GERMANY

Rehwaldt Landschaftsarchitekten, Dresden
Completion: 2007

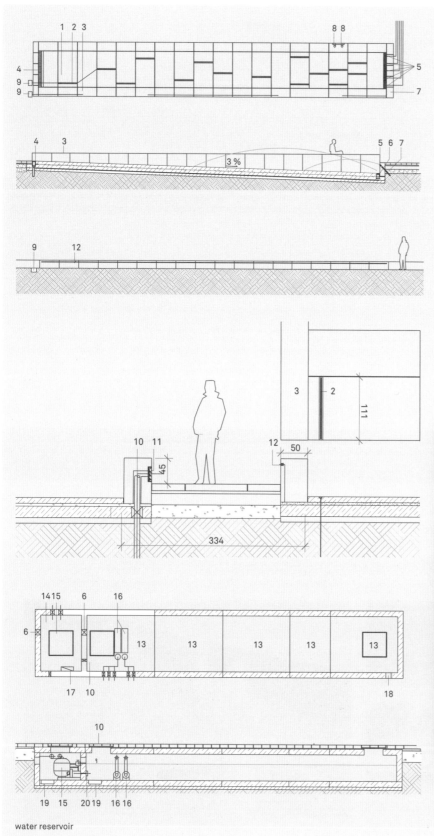

1 Slabs (prefabricated) 1.12 x 2.02 x 0.15 m, all joints watertight, mastic 3 cm, with gap for light band/decorative sheet metal copper, substructure: drainage mortar 20 cm C25/30; PE sheet 0.5 mm; 10 cm clean layer; lean concrete C8/10
2 "Decorative sheet" copper, sheet copper with light slit (LED lamp)
3 Border: squared granite, B/ T 1.12 x 0.5 m, H = 0.6–1.22 m, border 0.45 m above top border G, installed on sloping concrete slab, subsoil as 1
4 Drainage gutter DN 150, grille cover, bar grate on frame, sloped to correspond with top edge of pool fl oor, stainless steel with outlet, return 2, constantly open, connection DN 150
5 Individual jets shooting to different heights, feed pipes in drill holes, 45° through granite block, jets 0.41 m apart, 10 cm under top edge of end stone
6 Return, channel DN 150 with grille cover
7 End stones HBT 0.75 x 0.60 x 0.30 m; 5 in all
8 Inward and outward ventilation pipework services room 2 x 200 mm, each stone clad at end and from below aperture in stone, fl ush, cladding stainless steel grille, bar grate dimensions approx, 0.7 x 0.25 m
9 Transformer
10 Inward and outward ventilation well house KG 100, aperture DN 200
11 Ventilation grille, coated stainless steel DB 703, approx. 25 x 70 mm
12 Gap for light band LED lamp HBT 2.5 x 2.5 x 2.5 cm cable duct in empty pipe drill hole in natural stone
13 Prefabricated concrete part LBH 2.5 or 1.5/2/0.9 m, clear space
14 Well house
15 Sand fi lter plant
16 Pump
17 Controls
18 Emergency overfl ow DN 100
19 Mobile pump sump to empty water reservoir and well house
20 Connection to RW network suction fi lter basket

water reservoir

"STEINSCHWÄRZE" WATER FEATURE, MARKTPLATZ
EBERSWALDE, GERMANY

Rehwaldt Landschaftsarchitekten, Dresden
Completion: 2007

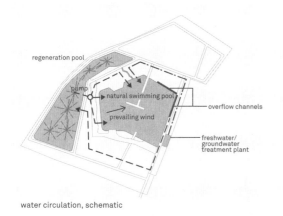

water circulation, schematic

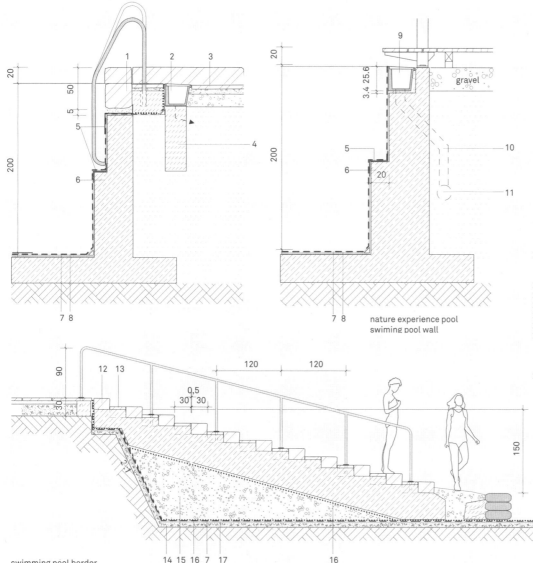

nature experience pool
swiming pool wall

swimming pool border

1 Solid step approx. 30 x 30
2 Overflow channel
3 Polygonal slabs
4 Strip foundation
5 Sheet metal with foil
6 Rest step
7 Pool liner 1.5 mm
8 Underlay fleece 200 g/m²
9 Overflow channel on mortar bed
10 Pipe DN 100
11 Pipe DN 150
12 Solid steps, 30 x 20 cm
13 Concrete slabs, 20 x 20 x 5 cm
14 Clean course, Sand 0/2
15 Gravel 16/32 lime content 62%
16 Protective layer
17 Underlay fleece 300 g/m²
18 Concrete slabs 40 x 40 x 8(5) cm, on
   3 cm mortar bed and 20 cm macadam
   course
19 Angle stone, 55 cm high, set on 5 cm
   mortar and 20 cm capillary-breaking
   course
20 Regeneration pool border area: 8 cm
   gravel 16/32, color gray/white, 15 cm
   pool substrate, fleece, 170 g/m²
21 Zeolite
22 Drainpipe DN100
23 PVC pressure feed DN63
24 Distributor shaft 60 x 120 cm
25 Topsoil
26 Continuous gravel strip without plantingwidth approx. 80 cm gravel cover
   course in this area consisting of gravel
   16/32 and 32/64
27 Drainpipe

NATURE EXPERIENCE POOL IN GROSSENHAIN
(SAXONY), GERMANY

Weidinger Landschaftsarchitekten, Berlin
Springer Architekten, Berlin
R. Grafinger, Bionova Badeteiche, Bergkirchen
Completion: 2001

The basic principle of the public nature pool complex is based on a dual chamber system in which the swimming and the regeneration pool are arranged separately. The swimming pool water is pumped directly into the regeneration pool floor filter for purification by a water circulation system. The purified water is taken from the surface of the regeneration pool and fed back to the swimming pool.

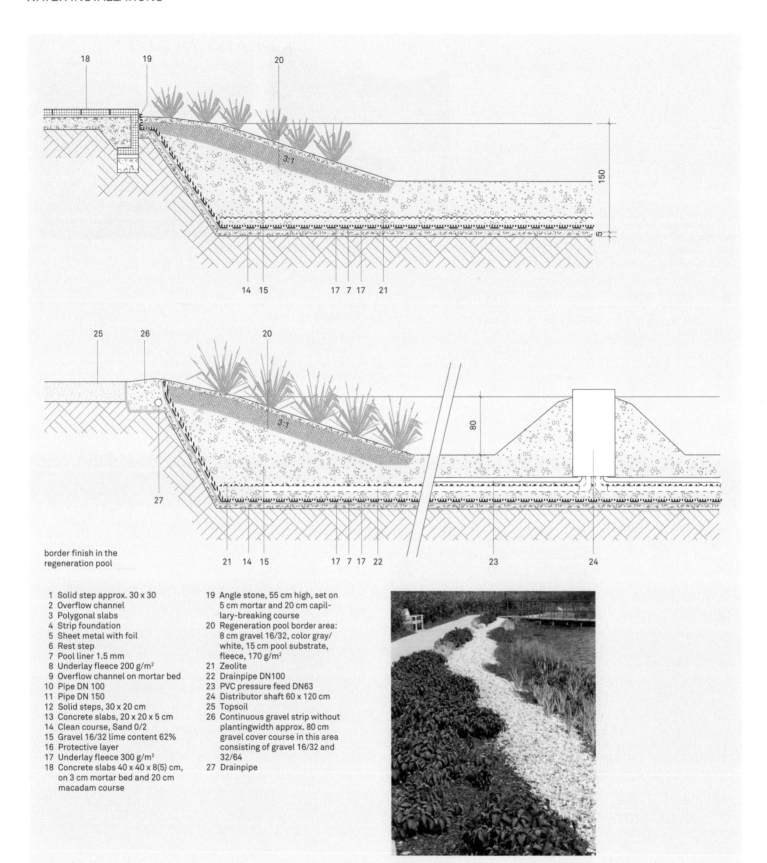

border finish in the
regeneration pool

1 Solid step approx. 30 x 30
2 Overflow channel
3 Polygonal slabs
4 Strip foundation
5 Sheet metal with foil
6 Rest step
7 Pool liner 1.5 mm
8 Underlay fleece 200 g/m²
9 Overflow channel on mortar bed
10 Pipe DN 100
11 Pipe DN 150
12 Solid steps, 30 x 20 cm
13 Concrete slabs, 20 x 20 x 5 cm
14 Clean course, Sand 0/2
15 Gravel 16/32 lime content 62%
16 Protective layer
17 Underlay fleece 300 g/m²
18 Concrete slabs 40 x 40 x 8(5) cm,
   on 3 cm mortar bed and 20 cm
   macadam course

19 Angle stone, 55 cm high, set on
   5 cm mortar and 20 cm capillary-breaking course
20 Regeneration pool border area:
   8 cm gravel 16/32, color gray/
   white, 15 cm pool substrate,
   fleece, 170 g/m²
21 Zeolite
22 Drainpipe DN100
23 PVC pressure feed DN63
24 Distributor shaft 60 x 120 cm
25 Topsoil
26 Continuous gravel strip without
   plantingwidth approx. 80 cm
   gravel cover course in this area
   consisting of gravel 16/32 and
   32/64
27 Drainpipe

3.13   VERTICAL PLANTING

CREATIVE AIMS
- Typical appearance
- Self-supporting climbers
- Spreading climbers
- Creepers
- Free-standing plants for vertical planting

**STRUCTURES AND ATTACHMENT MODES
FOR TRELLIS CLIMBERS**

CONSTRUCTION REQUIREMENTS

LOADS

PROBLEMS WITH CLIMBING PLANTS

MAINTENANCE AND CHECKING

SPECIMEN PROJECTS

Cordula Loidl-Reisch

3.13 VERTICAL PLANTING

Vertical planting means growing climbing plants on more or less vertical sections of buildings or in the spaces between them. This includes planting on traditional arbors and pergolas, and on walls, industrial halls, multistory car parks, and sound insulation screens.

Climbing plants grow upwards towards the light. Rapid growth in terms of length not matched by equivalent thickness serves them well as a "tactic," which they have evolved from adapting to dark forest locations as their original habitat. The disadvantage here is that they continue to depend on a support.

Although upward growth predominates at first, some perennial climbing plants grow strikingly in thickness as well (increased diameter).

A distinction can be made between two typical climbing strategies: that adopted by tendril climber—plants with tendrils or other parts used for attaching themselves that still require support if they are to be planted on a wall—and "autonomous," self-supporting climbers. > Fig. 3.13.2

One alternative here is another facade planting type, protected by copyright, developed a few years ago by botanist Patrick Blanc: "Le Mur Végétal". He chooses not to use climbing plants here, and the plants used are not in the usual soil. Instead, special light plastic elements mounted in frames on the facade take over the mechanical aspect of soil function. In this way an opaque "green wall" is created, automatically soaked

climbing plant growth height 1–4 m (used on the base/ground floor zone, for single-story houses, for penthouses, in plant troughs, etc.)

- Clematis alpina
- Actinidia kolomikta
- Clematis tanguitica
- Jasminum nudiflorum
- Lonicera brownii
- Clematis viticella
- Clematis Hybriden
- Rambler roses
- Lonicera heckrotti
- Lonicera henryi
- Lonicera caprifolium
- Lonicera periclymenum

climbing plant growth height 4 m (used for tall buildings)

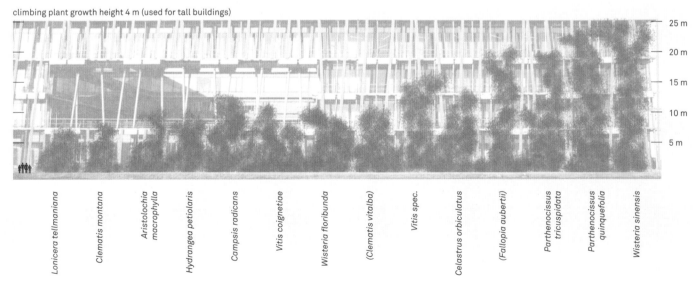

Lonicera tellmaniana · Clematis montana · Aristolochia macrophylla · Hydrangea petiolaris · Campsis radicans · Vitis coignetiae · Wisteria floribunda · (Clematis vitalba) · Vitis spec. · Celastrus orbiculatus · (Fallopia aubertii) · Parthenocissus tricuspidata · Parthenocissus quinquefolia · Wisteria sinensis

25 m / 20 m / 15 m / 10 m / 5 m

Fig. 3.13.1: Growth heights for climbing plants

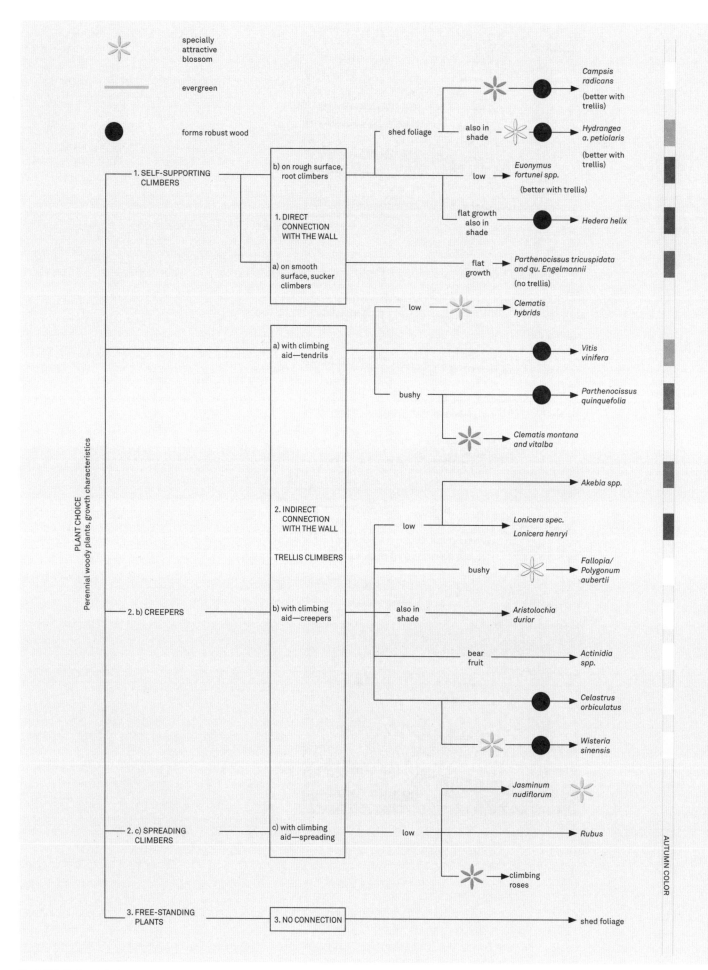

Fig. 3.13.2: Choice of plants

Fig. 3.13.3: Facade planting with cable-net structures covering the whole area

Fig. 3.13.4: Stainless steel wire cable "stoppers," Nordspangenpark, Graz

Fig. 3.13.5: *Mur Végétal*

First-class industrial products for fixing tendril elements combined with the "ideal" qualities of these "conquerors of clear space" make perennial climbing plants more attractive than ever for use in the urban environment. Consequently vertical planting, with roof planting, offer excellent ways of compensating for the lack of greenery in densely built-up areas. This is particularly true in megalopolises, where the underground car parks in the towering buildings and the general scarcity of land mean that open spaces are increasingly sited in artificial locations.

CREATIVE AIMS

Planted facades change the surroundings and outward appearance of buildings. This raises questions about the creative aims, which are particularly strongly associated with specific plant qualities in the case of vertical planting. Should the growth be spread evenly? Is it about filigree "green lines"? Should a three-dimensional, apparently solid structure be created? Is the idea "airy light green" or "compact dark green"? Should the full height of the building be planted, or just part of it (e.g. just the ground floor)? Is the situation sunny or shady? Considerations of this kind affect the choice of plants. > Fig. 3.13.1

Growth across a whole area is best achieved with autonomous climbing plants. Both dark, evergreen ivy (*Hedera*) and also the fresh green Boston Ivy (*Parthenocissus tricuspidata* "Veitchii") are able to "cover" entire buildings on their own.

But if full growth over a wall is to be achieved with trellis climbers alone, the whole facade area should be fitted with trellis or cable-net structures. > Fig. 3.13.3

Linear planting can be achieved with a few single cables, rods or narrow grids running in parallel. Here the structures must no always run vertically, diagonal "spillikin-style" cables within a space create an interesting effect. But plants are less inclined to climb at angles under 45°. Particularly suitable for linear planting are creepers (*Actinidia*, *Akebia*, *Aristolochia*, *Celastrus*, *Wisteria*), and trailing plants such as *Parthenocissus quinquefolia*. If the cable is fitted with "stoppers" the plants are less likely to slip off. > Fig. 3.13.4

The architectural plasticity of a building can be enhanced by emphasizing projections on the building with planted steel elements or grids; recesses can be "deepened" with dark ivy.

To create combined planting, linear and more expansive elements are brought together or used in parallel for structuring. A wide range of possible combinations is available here: constructions made up of cables, steel cable-nets, carbon steel mats, perforated sheet metal, or expanded meta or stable grids (NB: plants that grow to large diameters need sufficiently large apertures) can be developed, in combination with linear, vertical or diagonal steel rods, or with weatherproof fiberglass rods. Where there are distances between individual supporting elements to be bridged, it should be remembered that climbing plants cannot cope with unduly wide gaps, so the sections of the structure should not be more than 30–50 cm apart.

with water and fertilizer, and planted over its full area with a variety of low plants adapted to steep locations. (2002, sensio, Paco p. 257) > Fig. 3.13.5

A lot of arguments can be cited in favor of vertical planting: aesthetic and micro-climatic reasons, protecting facades against heavy rain, the desire for shade and the beneficial effect of planted, green facades on the psyche.

Fig. 3.13.6: Green scenic effect in an inner courtyard

Fig. 3.13.7: Claret leaves in Virginia creeper

Fig. 3.13.8: Ivy

Low-climbing plants can also be used for partially greening tall facades if adequately large, water plant containers are attached on the higher levels.

Sculptural vertical planting based on stainless steel wire cables can make a scenic effect between buildings or posts. The "volume", almost invisible at the beginning, initially materializes as a result of the plant growth. > Fig. 3.13.6

One important design motif can be the color of climbing plants, showing up in different green foliage shades, the color of the blossom and to an extent in very marked autumn coloring (claret, fox-red, yellow). > Fig. 3.13.7

Typical appearance

The plant's characteristic climbing strategy and habit in combination with the wall or the trellis structure created typical vertical planting images. They can generally be trimmed to the desired shape.

Self-supporting climbers

Ivy (*Hedera helix*) is a particularly robust, shade-loving root climber, with dark green foliage. It can create dense, enormously high evergreen walls (up to 30 m) if it is allowed to develop freely. Its ample multiple fruits are attractive, though these do no appear until the plant is a few years old, and they make the plant more vulnerable to storms. > Fig. 3.13.8

Care is needed however: ivy is top of the "rankings" for plants that cause damage (cf. Althaus). Walls that are already slightly damaged make ideal victims.

The trumpet vine (*Campsis radicans*) also climbs with anchoring roots and tends to develop into a kind of extended tree crown. The plant produces striking orange trumpet flowers on the sunny upper side. Its roots can penetrate cracks and joints in the wall and cause damage. A light structural support should be provided to prevent storms from tearing parts of the plant off the wall.

The climbing hydrangea (*Hydrangea petiolaris*) attaches itself to rough walls, cracks and joints with its anchoring roots. It is shade-loving and slow-growing, develops a full and pendulous appearance with attractive, protruding corymbose cymes, which makes the plant vulnerable to being torn off in storms and under snow, which is why structural protection should be afforded.

Boston Ivy is striking because of its precisely defined appearance: no other climbing plant grows so flat, in a way that is reminiscent of a roof shingle run. > Fig. 3.13.9 Tiny anchor discs enable this climbing plant to cover entire walls with its trilobate foliage even without a trellis. Boston Ivy has no trouble in climbing to heights of 15–20 m. Shade spurs it on to grow even more quickly, and it rapidly develops real trunks. The branches in the darker areas then lose their leaves, and the wall or support structure then catch people's eyes. > Fig. 3.13.10

Spreading climbers

Spreading climbers, such as sun-loving climbing roses, jasmine and blackberries are appealing because of their abundant, pretty blossom. As they grow to only about 5 m high, they can be used practically speaking only for partial planting for something like the height of

Fig. 3.13.9: *Parthenocissus tricuspidata* 'Veitchii'

Fig. 3.13.10: Protective grid for *Parthenocissus tricuspidata* 'Veitchii'

Fig. 3.13.11: Climbing rose on horizontal wooden trellis

a single floor. Because individual branches spread over the trelliswork they always tend to look a little messy and unkempt. A climbing construction made up of horizontal slats, cables, rods or a large-mesh grid structure is needed to prevent the thorns or protruding side shoots from slipping off. > Fig. 3.13.11
Winter jasmine (*Jasminum nudiflorum*, fam. Oleaceae) tends to be overhanging, with its shoots hanging down in curves up to 2 m long.

Creepers

If left to their own devices, creepers tend to look bushy, but they can be confined to a more disciplined shape by trimming. But the plants must be accessible for trimming purposes, which can be a limiting factor in terms of height. The shade-tolerant pipevine (*Aristolochia macrophylla*, fam. Artistolochiaceae) radiates the refined elegance of classical plants in arbors, and at the same time creates a jungly-tropical image with its very large, light green leaves. > Fig. 3.13.12

The climbing oriental bittersweet (*Celastrus orbiculatus*, Celastraceae) is a green summer creeper with an alarming name in German—*Baumwürger*, tree strangler. Care is needed if actually planting oriental bittersweet by trees, as the plant quickly takes over the crown, and soon only the bittersweet leaves can be seen. This "false crown" looks pretty when it turns yellow in the autumn, but the host tree quickly suffers from the lack of light. Young trees can be literally choked by the plant in their trunk area, so the experience can be bittersweet indeed.
Celastrus (also known as *Campsis* or *Wisteria*) is a good choice, however, when the design intention is to create little "false trees" on an interesting substructure. > Fig. 3.13.13
Horticultural species of clematis hybrids (Fam. Ranunculaceae) attract attention with their large flowers, but they grow slowly and thus remain small.
The much more vigorous *Clematis Montana* carries an abundance of smaller flowers and "crochets" itself gracefully around the trellis structures.
Traveler's Joy or Old Man's Beard (*Clematis vitalba*) forms a green ball over a wild entanglement of branches, with new shoots constantly appearing above older twigs on its side facing the sun, so that the plant increasingly trails. It is also striking in winter when it has no leaves and the whitish blossom glows in the sunlight. This wild variety grows higher, winding itself around every little branch or projecting object.

Fig. 3.13.12: Aristolochia macrophylla

Fig. 3.13.13: Wisteria as a false "small tree" on a substructure

The same applies—despite a different climbing technique—to the silver or lemon lace vine *Fallopia aubertii* (fam. Polygonaceae).

Particular care is needed with this plant that tries to cling on by twining as it tend to grow into gutters, drainpipes, etc., as it grows considerably faster than the rest. > **Fig. 3.13.14** Lemon lace vine "reaches out" for every little thing that could offer purchase, and grows fuller from year to year: unusual "topiaries" grow up, presenting the opposite to architectural form, which can be entirely desirable. Otherwise, regular trimming is necessary. Their white panicles are very decorative.

If some protection against being overlooked is needed in winter as well in densely urban situations, then evergreen honeysuckle (*Lonicera henryii*, fam. Caprifoliaceae) is the best choice. The significance of this plant, which grows to only a few meters high but is well suited for partial planting in semi-shady locations will increase correspondingly in the next few years. Its bushy growth can be controlled by trimming. Here, the correct partners are grids, stretched wires or trellises.

The "five-fingered" Virginia creeper *Parthenocissus quinquefolia* (fam. Vitaceae) is the perfect "tightrope walker" and one of the most vigorous of the climbers that grows here, reaching heights of up to 25 m. It uses its tendrils to climb up vertical, diagonal and horizontal cables. In the case of cables, Virginia creeper likes to let individual twigs with foliage on them hang down like plaits, and these can develop into "curtains" hanging down to a length of several meters. > **Fig. 3.13.15**

Vitis, the vine (fam. Vitaceae) is the commonest deciduous plant in wine-growing areas. > **Fig. 3.13.16**

If the common grape vine (*Vitis vinifera*) is grown for its grapes, it has to be pruned back each year to ensure that fruit will be produced. After pruning, the eye is then drawn for months to structures and walls. Unpruned, this climbing plant can grow to a height of 10–12 m using its winding tendrils, developing a romantic, bushy appearance.

Much the same applies to other vines—the riverbank or frost grape (*Vitis riparia*), the fox grape (*V. labrusca*), and the crimson glory vine (*V. coignetiae*). Remember that the wood of all vines grows to the thickness of small tree trunks in time.

Wisteria (fam. Leguminosae) is one of the most beautiful climbing flowering woody plants for warm and sunny locations because of its magnificent white or blue racemes. The light green of its pinnules makes a pleasant impression in the surrounding area. It wraps itself around its support structure, which has to be particularly robust as Wisteria can grow to over 15 m high.

Fig. 3.13.14: *Fallopia aubertii* on wire mesh

Fig. 3.13.15: Virginia creeper hanging down in plaits

Fig. 3.13.16: Common grape vine

Free-standing plants for vertical planting

Walls can also be planted with woody espalier stock (fruit trees, e.g. apple, pear) and other woody plants that can be pruned, such as *Acer campestre* (field maple), *Carpinus betulus* (hornbeam), *Pyracantha* (firethorn), *Taxus* (yew), *Tilia* (lime), etc. If they are constantly pruned they can be kept as narrow as the wall; wires can be used for additional shaping, but the plants are self-supporting. This kind of facade planting is very labor-intensive. It was very common until the early years of the 20th century, but has now become a rarity.

STRUCTURES AND ATTACHMENT MODES FOR TRELLIS CLIMBERS

Thanks to the enormous development of solid structural elements, vertical planting has been able to emancipate itself in recent decades as an independent outdoor type, generating considerable interest. The best example of this is the large-scale urban garden arbor in Zurich's MFO Park (p. 664, *DETAIL* 6/2004).

As they are exposed to the weather all the time, only robust materials that function over a long period can be used. This means, first and foremost, stainless steel constructions that direct climbing plants to the kind of exposed location they would not reach otherwise. Regular checks on trellis or scaffold structures and care for the climbing plants themselves must also be ensured at great heights and in exposed locations.

There are various possible means of attaching trellis structures. These include bracing, hanging, screwing to the wall, and post-and-beam structures placed in front of the facade. This applies to all the elements listed below: thin (∅ of a few centimeters) steel rods, hollow steel sections, and also compound materials such as weatherproof fiberglass bars (GFK) and high-quality timber rods. These last should, however, only be used for planting at base story level or in penthouse areas that are easier to manage.

All wall fastenings—e.g. with anchor bolts, tree rods, sleeves, or anchors—must comply with DIN 18515-1 by being attached to loadbearing walls, and should also be compatible with its structure (e.g. thermal insulation facade, curtain facade, etc.).

Cold-drawn, high-strength steel cables in stainless, acid-resistant steel wire (material complying with EN 10264-4) with steel reinforcement and diameters of 4–8 mm, in combination with various terminal fittings are extremely important for linear and also cross bracing.

Weatherproof grids are suitable for wide construction areas. They can be made of construction steel, expanded metal or also rack screens. Perforated sheet metal with large apertures, or grids made up of cross-clamped cables are also suitable, as they can offer wide spacing between the individual cables for climbing plants whose trunks grow to a considerable width.

"Modern mesh"—robust stainless steel nets—make it possible to plant large areas of facade over several stories, using bracing.

A wide range of elegant connecting elements in stainless, acid-resistant steel is available: binding heads and fork crowns, angle joints, eyes, ring bolts, loops, shackles, spacer or supporting cable holders, stirrups, brackets, cross clamps, cable retainers, etc.

CONSTRUCTION REQUIREMENTS

Construction requirements arise from the plants' specific climbing strategies. *Campsis*, *Celastrus*, *Hedera*, *Hydrangea*, *Parthenocissus*, *Vitis* and *Wisteria* must be kept sufficiently far from the wall (approx. 20 cm) because their trunks thicken. The root areas should be screened off by a protective grid.

Grid-style constructions (steel mats, cable structures) have proved their worth for climbing plants with tendrils. Vines (*Vitis*), which have shoot tendrils, need to be some distance apart (15–20 cm), while plants such as clematis that have leafstalk tendrils are better with smaller gaps (10 x 10 to max. 15 x 15 m). The recommended diameter for tendril aids is approx. 1.1–1.9 cm for shoot tendrils (for Virginia creeper max. 1.3 cm), and 0.4–1.2 cm for plants with leafstalk tendrils.

Vertical frame structures with circular cross sections (cables, tubes, rods are advantageous for creepers, to avoid squashing. They should be 0.6–5 cm in diameter. Unduly week tubular structures can be crushed by high-diameter wood growth. The tendency to self-strangulation on species that twine quite powerfully can be reduced by attaching only one main shoot to the bracing wire. > Fig. 3.13.17

Distances between vertical elements should be approx. 30–80 cm for creepers, or up to 150 cm for plants whose stems thicken considerably (e.g. Wisteria). Anti-slip devices should be 0.5–2 m apart.

Fig. 3.13.17: Tendency to self-strangulation in a wisteria that is twining too tightly

Horizontal strips or rods up to 40 cm apart or grids with widths up to 30–50 cm (strips, rods, cable constructions) set about 5 cm from the wall are very suitable for spreading climbers.

LOADS

The structure to be planted must be able to absorb the additional loads. Climbing aids must be stable and able to bear loads.

Vertical loads include the weight of all parts of the planting for the building: the weight of the plants (1–50 kg/m^2; weight of wood plus foliage), of the climbing aids plus rain sleet and snow on the structure and the plants; here the total weight can be double or threefold for evergreen plants in winter.

Forces resulting from wind pressure and wind suction occur as horizontal loads and can be greater than the winter weight of plants.

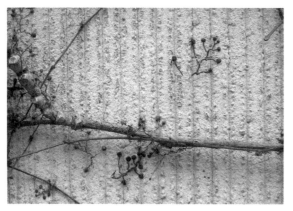

Fig. 3.13.18: Remains of adhesive discs on rendered facade

PROBLEMS WITH CLIMBING PLANTS

Negative phototropic growth—plant growth on the side of the plant facing away from the light, typical of root tips, but also of the shoots of climbing plants such as *Aristolochia* or *Fallopia*—can trigger problems if the wrong plants are chosen and cause damage if they grow into open joints in ventilated facades, for example.

Damage to walls by root climbers exacerbated by existing structural faults can scarcely be avoided in the long term. But it is possible to prevent or remove parts of root climbers that have been torn off in storms from hanging down by using wire bracing, or by trimming them.

If a plant like Boston Ivy with disc attachment tendrils has to be removed from the facade, remains of lignified adhesive discs will still be attached to the wall. This is particularly problematic if the wall has to be repainted regularly. > **Fig. 13.3.18**

If the spaces between the trellis elements and the wall are too small, plants that form thick trunks can force structures apart or the plant itself can be crushed. > **Fig. 13.3.19**

Climbing plants placed fewer than 50 cm from the building in a rain shadow can be damaged by drought. This also applies to climbing plants in tubs if the containers are too small and watering has not been arranged.

MAINTENANCE AND CHECKING

Essential maintenance work for vertical planting involves guaranteeing sufficient water and nutrient supplies, checking anchorage and structures and regular trimming. Thinning out, cutting back to the required shape, prevented undue growth and growing into blinds, gutters, downpipes and roofing tiles, as well as the removal of dead wood and dried plant parts are included in this. > **Fig. 3.13.20**

Fig. 13.3.19: *Wisteria* crushed by an unduly tight grid

Fig. 3.13.20: Tangled *Fallopia aubertii* branches

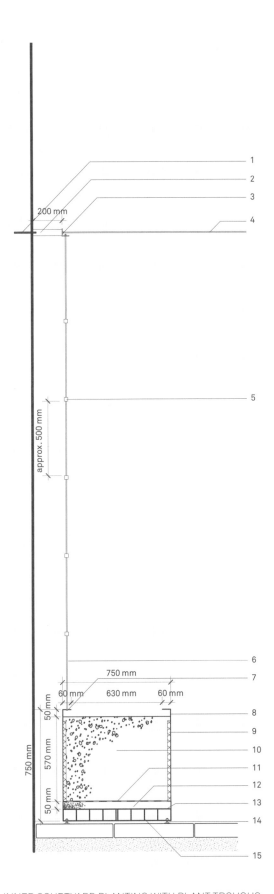

200 mm

approx. 500 mm

750 mm

60 mm · 630 mm · 60 mm

50 mm

50 mm

570 mm

50 mm

1 Wall anchoring conforming with static requirements
2 Spacer
3 Stainless steel angle-iron 50/50/5 in conformity with EN 10056-1: 1998, with drill holes
4 Stainless steel cable, 6 mm
5 Stopper
6 Stainless steel cable in conformity with EN 10088-32005, 6 mm, pressed with binding head
7 Drill hole d = 6 mm (5 per trough)
8 Stainless steel sheet in conformity with EN 10088-2:2005 (anti-slip plate) approx. 3 mm, tilted approx. 60 mm top and bottom
9 Weatherproof insulation plate, d = 2 cm
10 Body of vegetation approx 0.3 m³ (garden substrate with storage capacity)
11 Filter fleece
12 Expanded clay, layer 5 cm thick
13 Tilted stainless steel perforated sheet, 2 items
14 Adjustable feet e.g. stainless hexagonal screws with nuts and washers
15 Flat steel, welded on edge to trough, 10 x 80/740/3

INNER COURTYARD PLANTING WITH PLANT TROUGHS
AND INTEGRATED CABLE BRACING, VIENNA, AUSTRIA

Landscape architect: C. Loidl-Reisch

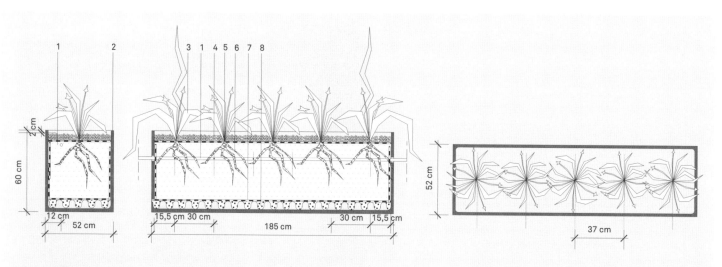

1 Drip watering
2 Fibrous concrete
3 Plant species from planting concept
4 8/11 chippings covering, 5 cm
5 Non-woven divider fabric
6 Vegetation support layer 1/8 according to FLL approx 4.5 cm
7 Non-woven system filter 100 g
8 Polythene drainage elements 60 x 1000 x 2000 filled
  with bulk mineral material

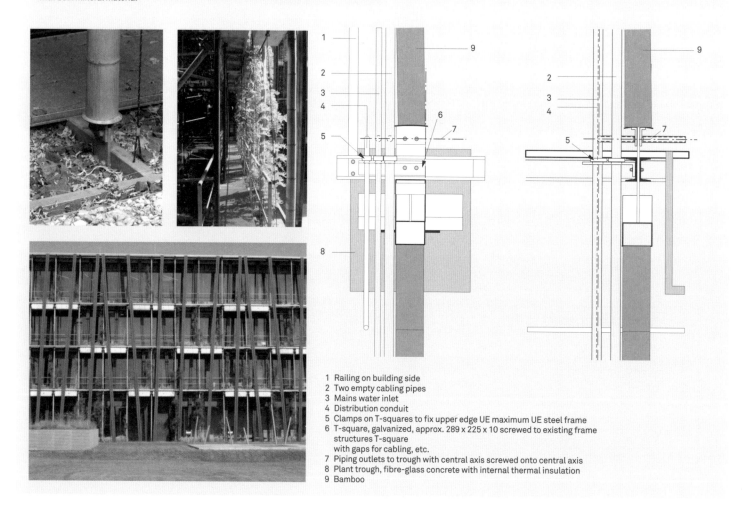

1 Railing on building side
2 Two empty cabling pipes
3 Mains water inlet
4 Distribution conduit
5 Clamps on T-squares to fix upper edge UE maximum UE steel frame
6 T-square, galvanized, approx. 289 x 225 x 10 screwed to existing frame
  structures T-square
  with gaps for cabling, etc.
7 Piping outlets to trough with central axis screwed onto central axis
8 Plant trough, fibre-glass concrete with internal thermal insulation
9 Bamboo

BERLIN MODEL URBAN ECOLOGY PROCESS, EXTERIOR
AREAS AND FACADE PLANTING
DEPARTMENT OF PHYSICS, HUMBOLDT-UNIVERSITÄT
ZU BERLIN, GERMANY

Architects: Augustin und Frank Architekten, Berlin

Landscape architect: S. Tischer with Joerg Th. Coqui
Project direction phases 1–3: Ippolita Nicotera
Specialist advice on rainwater management and monitoring
ecological construction process: Marco Schmidt, TU Berlin
Completed: 2003

3.14 GREEN ROOFS

FORMS OF GREEN ROOF

**CONSTRUCTION REQUIREMENTS
AND CONSTRUCTIVE ELEMENTS**
· Roof types and loadbearing capacity
· Roof incline and pitch
· Watering and drainage systems
· Edge formation, fire prevention and wind action

DESIGNS AND LAYERS IN GREEN ROOFS

GREENING METHODS
· Types of greening
· Forms of vegetation

IMPLEMENTING A GREEN ROOF

SPECIMEN PROJECTS

Eike Richter

3.14 GREEN ROOFS

The field of green structure incorporates green roofs and facade greening. Their historical predecessors are Scandinavia's earth and turf lawns, and the green roofs of the Middle East, such as the Hanging Gardens of Babylon. Green roofs have become more widespread with the development of roof seals and root barriers and the emergence of the ecology movement that followed the 1960s. > Fig. 3.14.1

Green roofs compensate for interventions in the landscape and provide plants and animals with new habitats in an urban environment. They are an important aspect of sustainable building planning. Compared with conventional roof constructions, they improve roof protection and building insulation. > Fig. 3.14.2

Developing areas above other structures, such as terraces, inner courtyards and roofs, creates usable open space. The retentive properties of green roofs also allow water to be better managed. Rainwater runoff is slowed down and reduced, leveling out spikes in precipitation and taking the pressure off channeling systems. 40–60% annual mean water retention is created by extensive green roofs, 60–90% for intensive green roofs. Consequently the microclimate also improves, as the increase in water vapor balances extremes of temperature and the vegetative surface filters fine dust and heavy metals out of the air.

FORMS OF GREEN ROOF

Technical requirements (roof incline, roof load), climatic conditions in context (amount of precipitation, exposure, wind direction, etc.) as well as intended function and desired appearance determine the type of green roof. A distinction is made between extensive green roofs, simple intensive green roofs, intensive green roofs and hard surfaces. > Figs. 3.14.3–3.14.5

An extensive green roof is indicated when a roof will only tolerate minimal superstructure and loads, and the roof is not intended to be walked on. Creating and

Fig. 3.14.1: Extensive sloping green roof: in the tradition of grass roofs

Fig. 3.14.2: Construction intervention in a sensitive landscape compensated for by green roofs

Fig. 3.14.5: Intensive roof greening in an inner courtyard

Fig. 3.14.3: Extensive greening with minimal structure ("light roof")

Fig. 3.14.4: Small-scale simple intensive greening of a carport with water surfaces

maintaining these is comparatively inexpensive. Except during the growing phase, maintenance is extensive. The superstructure layers are 5 to approximately 15 cm thick. An extensive green roof imposes functional loads on the roof construction of from 60 kg/m² to approximately 240 kg/m². Due to the minimal structure and the extensive maintenance, only very robust and drought-resistant plants are used. Shrubs, grasses, lichens and mosses or, more rarely, ground-covering woody plants are used. Many of these plants originate in high alpine locations. > **Figs. 3.14.6 and 3.14.7**

Simple intensive green roofs are the intermediate form of extensive and intensive green roofs. They can be used where a high roof load is possible (180–300 kg/m²) and a varied range of plants is desired. As well as plants used in the extensive green roof, low woody plants and more demanding shrubs can be used. Simple intensive green roofs involve superstructures of about 15–25 cm. When designing a simple intensive green roof, its more labor-intensive care, especially with regard to watering and fertilizing, must be taken into account. > **Fig. 3.14.8**

With an intensive green roof, there are practically no limits as regards functionality or use of plants. A load-bearing roof is required, with a capacity of over 300 kg/m². Depending on construction, this can be increased to 1500 kg/m². As well as the plants already mentioned, bushes, small trees and lawn areas can be included. Adequate watering, usually involving water accumulation or irrigation systems, is invariably necessary. Height of superstructures varies from about 25 cm to 150 cm in some cases. > **Fig. 3.14.9** For lawns "a layer thickness of 15–20 cm is adequate in exceptional cases, if one is prepared to put up with a higher degree of maintenance" (Kolb and Schwarz 1999, p. 52).

Hard surfaces and terraces are often created in combination with intensive green roofs. **Fig. 3.14.10**. Roof load permitting, asphalt, paved or tiled paths, wooden decking or enclosing walls are possible. These surfaces and components usually have the same substructure as the intensive green roof.

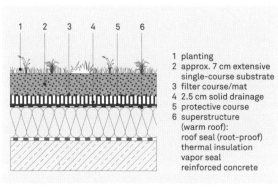

1 planting
2 approx. 7 cm extensive single-course substrate
3 filter course/mat
4 2.5 cm solid drainage
5 protective course
6 superstructure (warm roof):
  roof seal (root-proof)
  thermal insulation
  vapor seal
  reinforced concrete

Fig. 3.14.6: Standard extensive green roof structure

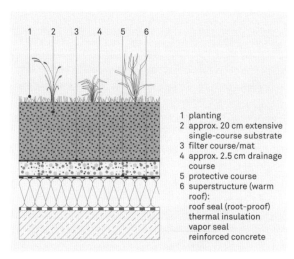

1 planting
2 approx. 20 cm extensive single-course substrate
3 filter course/mat
4 approx. 2.5 cm drainage course
5 protective course
6 superstructure (warm roof):
  roof seal (root-proof)
  thermal insulation
  vapor seal
  reinforced concrete

Fig. 3.14.8: Standard simple intensive green roof structure

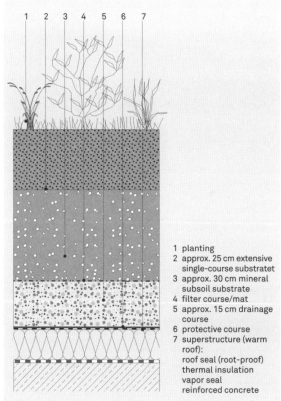

1 planting
2 approx. 25 cm extensive single-course substratet
3 approx. 30 cm mineral subsoil substrate
4 filter course/mat
5 approx. 15 cm drainage course
6 protective course
7 superstructure (warm roof):
  roof seal (root-proof)
  thermal insulation
  vapor seal
  reinforced concrete

Fig. 3.14.7: Extensive green roof containing many species in an ecological housing development

Fig. 3.14.9: Standard intensive green roof structure

Fig. 3.14.10: A variety of green roof types on different levels of a building

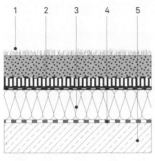

1 roof planting structure
(extensive):
planting
vegetation support
course
filter course/mat
drainage course
protective course
superstructure:
2 roof sealing (root-proof)
3 thermal insulation
4 vapor seal
5 reinforced concrete roof

Fig. 3.14.11: Standard warm roof construction

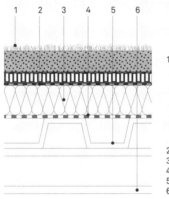

1 roof planting structure
(extensive):
planting
vegetation support
course
filter course/mat
drainage course
protective course
superstructure:
2 roof sealing (root-proof)
3 thermal insulation
4 vapor seal
5 trapezoidal sheet metal
6 steel section

Fig. 3.14.12: Standard warm roof construction (light shell)

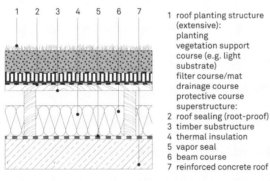

1 roof planting structure
(extensive):
planting
vegetation support
course (e.g. light
substrate)
filter course/mat
drainage course
protective course
superstructure:
2 roof sealing (root-proof)
3 timber substructure
4 thermal insulation
5 vapor seal
6 beam course
7 reinforced concrete roof

Fig. 3.14.13: Standard cold roof construction

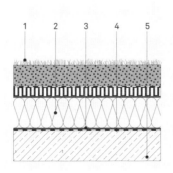

1 roof planting structure
(extensive):
planting
vegetation support
course
filter course/mat
drainage course
trickle protection/
separation fleece
structure open
to diffusion
superstructure:
2 thermal insulation
3 protective course
4 roof sealing (root-proof)
5 reinforced concrete roof

Fig. 3.14.14: Standard inverted roof construction

1 roof planting structu
(extensive):
planting vegetation
support course, filter
course/mat drainage
course, trickle protec-
tion/separation fleece
structure open to diffu-
sion
superstructure:
2 thermal insulation
3 roof sealing (root-
proof—only in areas
with penetration)
4 waterproof concrete
("White Tub")

Fig. 3.14.15: Standard watertight concrete roof construction

CONSTRUCTION REQUIREMENTS AND CONSTRUCTIVE ELEMENTS

Roof types and loadbearing capacity

When planning a green roof, the first thing to do is to check the construction and loadbearing capacity of the roof. For new structures, the intended form of green roof should be determined at an early stage, so that the roof can be designed accordingly. It should be ensured that the required roof seals are designed to be impenetrable to roots.

For a warm roof, the roof seal is above the thermal insulation, which in turn lies atop the loadbearing construction. This form of roof is widespread and is generally suitable for green roofs without special requirements. The thermal insulation must be able to tolerate the pressure. A vapor barrier should be installed above the roof skin, covering the above-ground construction, as otherwise condensation water may get into the building. > Fig. 3.14.11

A single-shell roof with no thermal insulation is different from a warm roof in that insulation and vapor barrier are absent. This roof form is used, for instance, in underground garages and unheated outbuildings. Given sufficient loadbearing capacity, this creates no problems for a green roof. As the roof may freeze through, cold-sensitive plants should not be included. > Fig. 3.14.12

For a cold roof (also known as a multishell roof), condensation is prevented from forming during roof construction by ventilation slits above the insulation. As an additional layer beneath the roof seal, usually a light wood construction, is involved, this often means that only an extensive green roof is possible. > Fig. 3.14.13

The inverted roof is a special case. Here, thermal insulation is above the roof seal. This means that the water-carrying layer is beneath the insulation, which in turn means that all materials used for the green roof must allow diffusion. If this is borne in mind, all forms of green roof are possible. > Fig. 3.14.14

With watertight concrete roofs, as with inverted roofs, the insulation is on top of the roof skin, or is absent. Watertight concrete gives the optimum protection from condensation and root damage. This makes whole-surface roof seals, vapor barriers and root barriers unnecessary. The watertight cement roof is generally suitable for all forms of green roof. Any openings and joints in the roof should be protected by a locally applied rootproof seal. > Fig. 3.14.15

a | b

Fig. 3.14.16: Flat roof renovation:
a) condition before renovation,
b) following green roof
implementation

Fig. 3.14.17: Sloping green roof

Fig. 3.14.20: Intensive sloping green roof with turf and integrated guttering

Fig. 3.14.21: Installing a claw mat to prevent slippage

Roof incline and pitch

Roof incline is an important technical consideration in choosing a green roof. Roofs with 0–2% roof incline are particularly suited to intensive green roofs with water-accumulation irrigation. Tolerances in building construction do not preclude puddles forming at the drainage layer. For this reason, the roof seal should be laid to measure especially and a drainage level should always be provided (the same applies to extensive green roofs!). Roofs with 2–5% incline are generally optimal for green roofs and are also favorable for water retention. Where water accumulation irrigation is in place, water accumulation thresholds may have to be provided. The roof pitch means that excess water quickly flows out of the drainage system. Where construction tolerances permit a siphon effect or insufficient downward water movement, these must be eliminated.

Depending on steepness, measures relating to water retention and delivery as well as slippage prevention should be put in place for sloping roofs with a 5–58% incline. These begin with shear barriers at drainage level and extend to the upper vegetation layer, with erosion resistant weaves or similar measures. For more demanding vegetation types and intensive utilization, rooftop irrigation should be put in place. In principle, a variety of green roof forms are possible given careful planning. > **Figs. 3.14.17–3.14.21**

Watering and drainage systems

The number and placement of drainage installations such as roof drains, roof guttering, water spouts, and emergency overflows is a function of the structure's pitch and the green roof's construction. Roof drains on the roof skin should be designed to be visible via

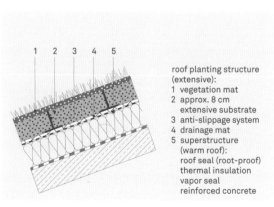

roof planting structure
(extensive):
1 vegetation mat
2 approx. 8 cm
 extensive substrate
3 anti-slippage system
4 drainage mat
5 superstructure
 (warm roof):
 roof seal (root-proof)
 thermal insulation
 vapor seal
 reinforced concrete

Fig. 3.14.18: Standard extensive sloping roof construction

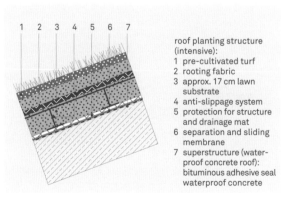

roof planting structure
(intensive):
1 pre-cultivated turf
2 rooting fabric
3 approx. 17 cm lawn
 substrate
4 anti-slippage system
5 protection for structure
 and drainage mat
6 separation and sliding
 membrane
7 superstructure (water-
 proof concrete roof):
 bituminous adhesive seal
 waterproof concrete

Fig. 3.14.19: Standard sloping roof lawn construction

a | b

Fig. 3.14.22: water draining
from a sloping roof into an outer
gutter:
a) construction phase with shear
barriers,
b) finished green roof

Fig. 3.14.23: Water channel molding

Fig. 3.14.24: Drainage and inspection shaft

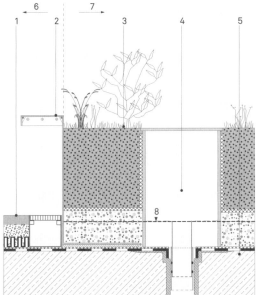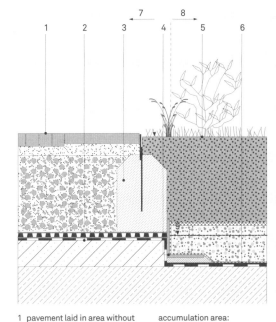

1 slab surface structure:
  concrete slab
  (60 x 30 x 3.5 cm)
  natural stone chippings
  solid drainage
  drainage gutter
  building protection mat
2 plant bed framed with
  steel wall,
  waterproof screw
  attachment to mortar
  strip foundation
3 intensive planting by
  accumulated water
  filter mat (plastic fiber)
  drainage course
  solid drainage

  building protection mat
4 inspection shaft (30/30)
  with accumulated water
5 superstructure (water-
  proof concrete):
  roof seal (root-proof)
  reinforced concrete
6 area without water accumulation
7 area with water accumu-
  lation
8 top edge of accumulated
  water 5 cm under bottom
  edge of intensive sub-
  strate

Fig. 3.14.25: Water accumulation on roof with 0% incline

1 pavement laid in area without
  water accumulation:
  approx. 3 cm chippings 2/5
  crushed stone 2/32
  building protection and drainage mat (car type)
2 superstructure (waterproof
  concrete):
  roof seal (root-proof), screed
  (outside water accumulation),
  reinforced concrete
3 steel band in point foundation
  (C12/15)
4 fiber concrete angle (15/15)
  on mortar bed (C12/15), root
  protection strip glued to angle
5 intensive planting in water

  accumulation area:
  plant bed approx. 37–41 cm,
  intensive substrate, filter
  mat (plastic fiber), approx.
  15 cm drainage course, building protection mat/protec-
  tion mat
6 superstructure (waterproof
  concrete):
  roof seal (root-proof), reinforced concrete
7 area without water accumulation
8 area with water accumulation
9 top edge of accumulated
  water 5 cm under bottom

Fig. 3.14.26: Water accumulation with above-ground drip lip

Fig. 3.14.27: Irrigation machine in shaft

Fig. 3.14.28: Inspection shaft for a simple water accumulation irrigation device

inspection shafts in the surface. Gravel traps or similar measures should be used to ensure that the roof drains do not become clogged. For sloping roofs, both inner and outer gutters are possibilities. In case of curves in the pitch of the roof, special drainage layers should be provided. > Figs. 3.14.22–3.14.26

Irrigation systems must also be suitable for the type of green roof and for the structure. Accumulation barriers are used, some already integrated into the structure of the roof construction, but installations for automatic water accumulation, recessed sprinklers, or drip irrigation can also be added. Ducts should be provided within the roof and inside the building for water delivery and control leads. For extensive green roofs, at least one water outlet is required for manual watering. > Figs. 3.14.27 and 3.14.28

Edge formation, fire prevention and wind action

In edge formation for green roofs, a distinction must be made between junctions and terminations. Junctions are found around rising components and those that penetrate the roof, e.g. chimneys. Roof seals and root barriers of at least 10 cm—or, for roofs with less of an incline, as much as 15 cm—above the upper edge of the top layer or the green roof should be introduced in these areas. In order to avoid excessive swelling caused by water release, the water-carrying layer can be lowered by means of gratings. > Fig. 3.14.29

The terminations are at the lateral roof edges (attic story). Roof seals and root barriers—5 or 10 cm above the water-carrying layer, depending on the roof's incline—should be introduced in these areas,

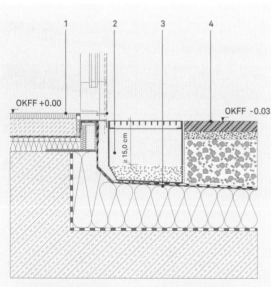

1 interior with threshold
2 steel gutter with gravel trap and packing: water-bearing course 15 cm lower
3 superstructure (warm roof) roof seal (root-proof) slanting thermal insulation (foam glass sheets) vapor barrier

4 natural stone slab surface crushed sand 0/5 crushed stone 2/32 drainage mat protective course

Fig. 3.14.29: Junction with terrace door with low threshold

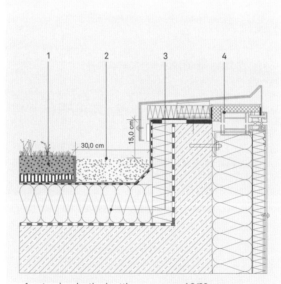

1 extensive planting in attic area: planting approx. 7 cm extensive single-course substrate filter course/mat 2.5 cm solid drainage protective course
2 edging strip on attic floor: gravel strip (80 x 5)

gravel 8/32 protective layer
3 superstructure (warm roof): roof seal (root-proof) thermal insulation vapor barrier reinforced concrete
4 sheet metal covered attic storey with seal to a height of 15 cm

Fig. 3.14.30: Junction with attic

Fig. 3.14.33: Attic story edging strip with lawn paving on gravel to resist wind drag

Fig. 3.14.31: Edge strip of gravel and kick plates bordering a rising structural component

Fig. 3.14.32: Damage caused by wind drag

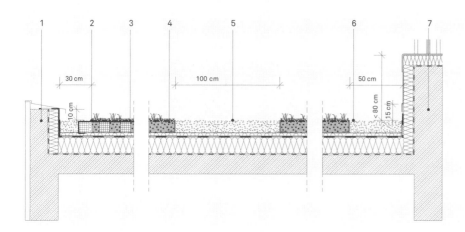

Fig. 3.14.34: Extensive green roof: fire prevention, wind drag protection, junctions with attics and rising components

1 superstructure:
  sheet metal covered attic storey with seal to a height of 30 cm
2 edging strip on attic storey:
  gravel (8/32)
  filter course/mat
  drainage element (unfilled)
  protective course
3 edging strip to resist wind suction
  erosion protection fabric
  lawn grid 40 x 60 x 11:
4 extensive roof planting:
  planting with shallow balls approx. 10 cm extensive substrate
  filter course/mat

drainage element (unfilled)
protective course
5 fire protection strip (where fire cells necessary)
6 edging strip on facade (W = 50 cm)
  gravel 8/32
  gravel strip
  filter course/mat
  drainage element (unfilled)
  protective course
7 facade with seal 15 cm high and parapet/window (< 80 cm)

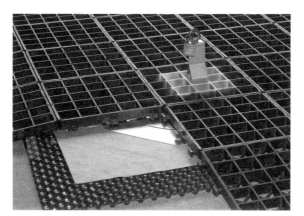

Fig. 3.14.35: Rope anchor safety system anchored to solid drainage system

Fig. 3.14.36: Personnel protection involving rope anchorage systems

and vegetation-free strips—generally > 30 cm wide—should be included. > Fig. 3.14.30

Intensive green roofs are considered hard roofing due to their irrigation, and therefore require no special fire precautions. Extensive green roofs have shorter maintenance intervals and more minimal construction. They are therefore at greater risk from airborne burning matter. For this reason, the junctions must be provided with vegetation-free protective strips of gravel or tiles 50–100 cm wide. > Fig. 3.14.31

For loosely laid roof layers, particularly in inverted roofs, precautions should be taken to ensure that the whole roof construction is safe from wind drag. Roofs above 20 m eaves height as well as the corners and edges of the green roof should be protected against wind drift by laying vegetation-free strips (e.g. heavy tiles), or by using filled-in lawn paving or vegetation mats. In exposed areas, the need to increase the weight of superstructures (as protection against wind load) may have to be balanced with the static roof load that can be tolerated. > Figs. 3.14.32–3.14.34

Fall protection should be provided for all green roofs. This may comprise either secure rails or special systems of holds for maintenance work, such as rope sockets and rope anchors. > Figs. 3.14.35 and 3.14.36

DESIGNS AND LAYERS IN GREEN ROOFS

A fundamental distinction is made between single-layer and multilayer designs. One-layer designs consist of a vegetation base layer, which performs both drainage and filtration functions, and sometimes supplementary protective and filtering fleeces.

Depending on the construction chosen, the following elements are found in a multilayered construction method: Protective plies protect the roof seal from mechanical damage, especially during the construction phase.

These are usually made of plastic or screed. If the roof seal is not rootproof, root barrier sheets are also included in the protective plies. > Figs. 3.14.37

The function of the drainage layer is to conduct precipitation water away evenly so that no waterlogging occurs. The aim is controlled storage of water for use while expanding the area for roots. The drainage layer may be formed of natural mineral substances such as sands, gravels or lava, or synthetic mineral substances such as expanded clay, expanded slate, or recycled substances. Drainage layers made from artificial substances, such as hard plastic tiles or foam drainage tiles are also in common use. It is possible to combine these materials—for instance, by filling in plastic storage elements with mineral bulk materials. > Figs. 3.14.38 and 3.14.41

Fig. 3.14.37: Protection and storage fleece

Fig. 3.14.38: Drainage mats for use on inclined roofs

Fig. 3.14.39: Solid drainage system for extensive green roof, 2.5 cm thick with protective and filtration fleeces

Fig. 3.14.40: Solid drainage system for transport routes (1.2 cm) with mounted filtration fleece

Fig. 3.14.41: Expanded slate 8/16 for drainage layers

Fig. 3.14.42: Predominantly mineral substrate for one-layer extensive green roof

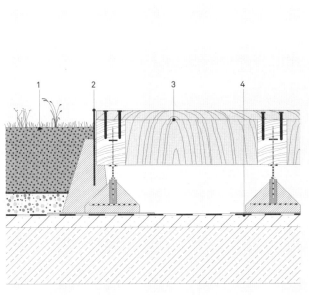

1 roof planting structure (intensive):
approx 20 cm intensive substrate
filter course/mat
approx. 6 cm drainage course
2 steel band in point foundation (C12/15)
3 wooden terrace structure:
wooden planks fastened with V2/A torx screws
beam course
stiffening plank
point foundation with post supports,
support base (galvanized with fin)
protective layer under point foundation
4 superstructure (waterproof concrete roof):
roof seal (root-proof)
sloping screed
reinforced concrete

Fig. 3.14.44: Wood covering at junction with lawn

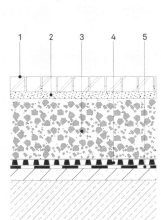

1 paving
2 approx. 3 cm chippings 2/5
3 approx. 20 cm crushed stone 2/32
4 building protection and drainage mat (car type)
5 superstructure (waterproof concrete)
roof seal (root-proof)
sloping screed
reinforced concrete

Fig. 3.14.43: Paved surface, able to take weight

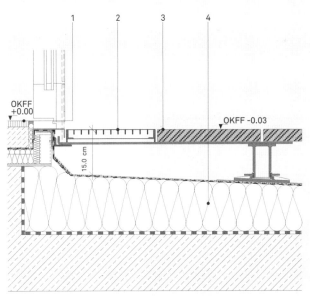

1 interior with threshold
2 steel grating as facade gutter
3 terrace structure:
natural stone slabs
metal angle as support for cantilever arm
cantilever arm in galvanized steel,
material approx. 2 mm thick
stilt course, adjustable height with joint dividers
protective course in stilt course area
building protection mat
4 superstructure (warm roof)
roof seal (root-proof)
sloping thermal insulation
(foam glass sheets)
vapor seal
reinforced concrete

Fig. 3.14.45: Terrace covering on stilt bearing, door junction

In multi-layer superstructures, the filtration layer filters out sediments, e.g. humus substances, in order to safeguard drainage layer function in the long term. Geotextiles are commonly used. > Figs. 3.14.41 and 3.14.42
The vegetation base layer is where the plants are actually located. It must be structurally stable—i.e. it must not be allowed to sag. Its plant substrate therefore has significantly lower levels of humus. For one-layer extensive green roofs, the FLL guidelines stipulate no more than 4% organic substances. This value can reach 6–12% for multi-layer designs, depending on design and gross density. As for grain size distribution, the allowed percentage of fine-grained sand and clay components is greater for intensive green roofs (max. 20%) than for extensive green roofs (max. 7%). The goal is good permeability together with optimum water retention. Topsoil mixtures with grain size distribution and humus content that meet the above requirements, e.g. which contain a high proportion of sandy soil, can be used for the vegetation base layer. The use of mineral bulk materials such as lava, pumice and expanded slate or recycled substances such as crushed brick with added organic substances and clay is widespread. > Figs. 3.14.43–3.14.45
Hard surfaces and timber decking are often constructed in combination with the plant surfaces, especially in intensive green roofs. This means that the protective layer, and usually the drainage and filtration layers as well, are always continued beneath the hard surface to permit unobstructed water flow. For water accumulation irrigation, however, the drainage layer is interrupted at the accumulation threshold.
Paved and tiled surfaces can be laid in chippings directly on protective fleeces or filtration layers. Alternatively, adjustable-height stilt bearings are possible. This allows weight to be reduced, but reduces the loadbearing capacity of the surface. This may have to be balanced out by laying a thicker tiled surface.

GREENING METHODS

Types of greening

Various possibilities exist for applying the actual vegetation. Dry-seeding is largely used to create meadow-like grass and herb stands or dry grasslands. These are extensive or semi-intensive green roofs with low requirements as regards wind loads and erosion. In hydro-seeding, the seed is applied to the vegetation base layer mixed with adhesive components. In particular, this method is used for wide-area extensive green roofs. It guarantees a uniform distribution of the seed and an instant protection against wind and rain erosion. In the course of a year, dry and hydro-seeding create 60–80% cover.

Sprout-seeding, in particular seeding with sedum sprouts, can be used alone or in combination with both the above methods. > Figs. 3.14.47 and 3.14.48

A vegetation mat green roof is suitable where increased erosion protection requirements exist and a higher immediate degree of cover is required. Precultivated vegetation mats with a variety of compositions are available, with grass, herbaceous plants, or sedum. Both biodegradable and permanent support materials are available. > Fig. 3.14.49

Lawn areas for intensive green roofs should generally be created using turf. Where pitch is especially problematic, reinforcement of the support material or additional fastening with wooden nails (be aware of the construction's height!) are recommended. Shrubs are added either as tub plants or as shallow root ball shrubs. They are most often available as precultivated multipot tiles. > Fig. 3.14.46 and 3.14.51

Woody plants for intensive green roofs are generally planted as root ball or container plants. Solitaire woody plants and trees should be anchored on the roof so that they are stable. > Fig. 3.14.50. This can be done using trunk guys or root ball anchors. The anchoring must not damage the roof skin. For this reason, it should be laid flat on the drainage system so as to distribute the weight or secured by means of piers, eyelets, etc.

Forms of vegetation

While a well-nigh endless variety of plants and designs exists for intensive green roofs, for simple intensive green roofs a distinction is made between the following categories of vegetation (according to FLL guidelines for green roofs):

· grass and herbaceous green roofs > Fig. 3.14.54
· wild shrub-woody plant green roofs > Fig. 3.14.53
· woody plant-shrub green roofs > Fig. 3.14.52
· woody plant green roofs.

The following vegetation categories are suitable for extensive green roofs:
· moss-sedum green roofs
· sedum-moss-herbaceous green roofs > Fig. 3.14.55
· sedum-herbaceous-grass green roofs > Fig. 3.14.56
· grass-herbaceous green roofs Fig. 3.14.57

A specimen plant selection for a green roof in transition from an extensive green roof to a semi-intensive green roof can be found in the planting plan reproduced here. > Figs. 3.14.59 - 3.14.61.

Fig. 3.14.46: Planting of shallow root ball shrubs

Fig. 3.14.47: Application of sedum sprouts

Fig. 3.14.48: Spray greening

Fig. 3.14.49: Laying sedum mats

Fig. 3.14.51: Intensive green roof: woody plant roof on underground garage

Fig. 3.14.50: Shallow root ball shrubs (sedum)

Fig. 3.14.52: Simple intensive green roof: woody plant-bush green roof

Fig. 3.14.53: Wild shrub-woody plant green roof

Fig. 3.14.54: Grass-herbaceous green roof

Fig. 3.14.55: Extensive green roofs: sedum-moss-herbaceous green roof

Fig. 3.14.56: Sedum-herbaceous-grass green roof

Fig. 3.14.57: Grass-herbaceous green roof (Steinrosenflor)

Fig. 3.14.58: Sedum roof

Fig. 3.14.59: Example of an extensive green roof: Bundesministerium für Verkehr, Bau und Stadtentwicklung, Berlin

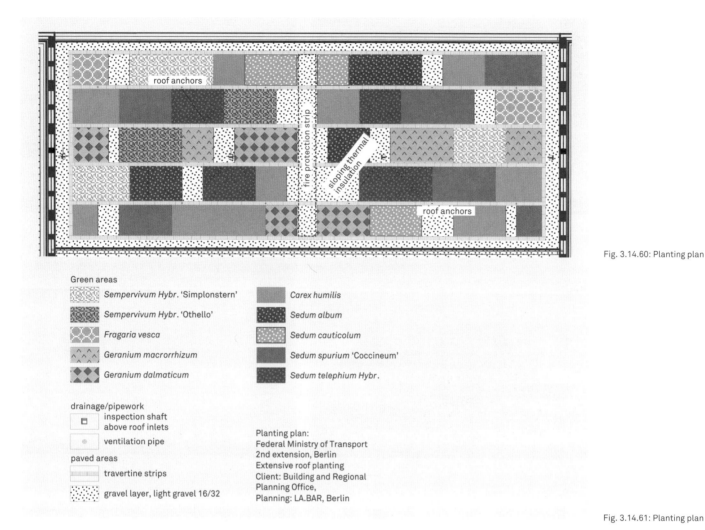

Fig. 3.14.60: Planting plan

Green areas

Sempervivum Hybr. 'Simplonstern'   Carex humilis

Sempervivum Hybr. 'Othello'   Sedum album

Fragaria vesca   Sedum cauticolum

Geranium macrorrhizum   Sedum spurium 'Coccineum'

Geranium dalmaticum   Sedum telephium Hybr.

drainage/pipework

inspection shaft
above roof inlets

ventilation pipe

paved areas

travertine strips

gravel layer, light gravel 16/32

Planting plan:
Federal Ministry of Transport
2nd extension, Berlin
Extensive roof planting
Client: Building and Regional
Planning Office,
Planning: LA.BAR, Berlin

Fig. 3.14.61: Planting plan key

IMPLEMENTING A GREEN ROOF

Immediately before beginning construction, a test of the roof's impermeability should be performed, e.g. by flooding with water. If unusual demands with regard to roof protection are involved, a building protection mat should be used on above-ground areas. In all cases, it must be ensured that both roof construction and green roof can function independently.

Whether the bulk materials can be transported onto the roof using a Big Bag and a crane, or whether this will be done with the aid of pneumatic technology, using suitable vehicles and via tubes, should also be ascertained. > Fig. 3.14.62

Figs. 3.14.63–3.14.65 show the progress of various green roof constructions in pictures.

It is generally possible to assemble the layer construction at any time of the year, provided the weather is not frosty. However, seals and ventilation sheets require a certain minimum temperature. The actual greening (planting, dry, and hydro-seeding) can only be carried out in the months from April to June and from September to November. Woody plants can be introduced as container plants at any time. Turf lawns and vegetation mats should ideally be laid in late spring to early

autumn. Planting shrubs in autumn in inner-city areas risks harming birds in their search for food.

Removal of seeding surfaces takes place when 12–15 months have elapsed, when the required 60% cover has been attained. Complementary maintenance should be carried out until then. This is different for intensive and extensive green roofs. For extensive green roofs, this mainly involves removing alien plants, keeping edges and any incorporated structures clear, reseeding if necessary and applying fertilizer and water during the growing phase. For intensive green roofs, the maintenance effort required for a traditional green space effectively has to be performed together with the specific requirements of a rooftop situation. Particular attention must be paid to controlling the irrigation and drainage systems. Lawns should be mown regularly in order to ensure that the roots penetrate the substrate thoroughly. > Figs. 3.14.67 and 3.14.69

For intensive and extensive green roofs, removal is followed by developmental and management maintenance. > Chapter 3.9 The intensity and measures involved in this maintenance depend on the type of green roof, and equate to complementary maintenance. For intensive green roofs in particular, it should first be ensured that this is an extreme location barely tenable without maintenance, or one that might actually be a hazard for the building without maintenance. > Figs. 3.14.66 and 3.14.68

Fig. 3.14.62: Pneumatic transport of bulk materials onto a roof

Fig. 3.14.63: Green roofs for flat
and sloping roofs:
a) above-ground roof seal
b) fleece installation, shear
   protection water channel
   moldings
c) applying substrate
d) appearance of roof after
   vegetation has been applied

a	b
c	d

Fig. 3.14.64: Sloping green roof:
a) after roof seal, drainage mats
   and shear protection system
   have been added
b) substrate transport with Big
   Bag
c) distribution of substrate
d) applying vegetation mats

a	b
c	d

Fig. 3.14.65: Extensive green roof for a summerhouse:
a) installation of fleeces and gravel strips,
b) application of substrate and protective fleeces,
c) planting shallow root ball shrubs,
d) finished green roof

Fig. 3.14.66: Overgrowth of woody plants due to a lack of maintenance

Fig. 3.14.68: > 90% coverage on an extensive roof: target vegetation after developmental maintenance

Fig. 3.14.67: Overgrown edge strip

	Planting			
Completion tending	12–15 months	Minimum acceptability requirements		
		· seeding:	60% surface cover	
			60% of the species sown ascertainable	
		· shoots:	75% of the shoots mature and	
			60% surface cover	
		· turf:	95% surface cover	
		· vegetation mats:	80% surface cover	
		-> acceptable condition		
Development tending	usually 2 years	1–2 inspections per year measures: · providing nutrients · trimming and keeping safety strips clear · removing unwanted vegetation · replanting and watering if necessary **target vegetation achieved: 90% ground cover**		
Maintenance		continuing care maintenance of target vegetation measures as above		

Fig. 3.14.69: Acceptance and maintenance scheme (in accordance with FLL 2002)

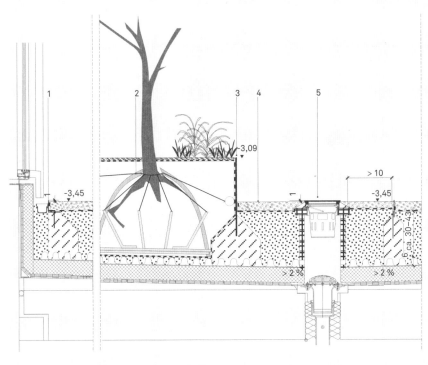

1 safety gutter 10 x 7.5 cm on mineral bulk solids 4/16
   every 1 m on mortar sacks
2 root ball attachment
   premounted ground plate
   retaining cable with black rubber sleeve
   root ball anchorage
   eyelets for tree anchoring
3 Corten steel wall
4 bulk gravel structure
   bulk solids 32/56 e.g. crushed brown glass
   liner fleece 100% polypropylene, 68 g/sq m
   mineral bulk solids 4/16
   drainage element, polypropyene 60 x 1000 x 2000
   filled with mineral bulk solids
   system filter 100 g
5 Outlet combination of
   top in plastic reinforced mortar, class A
   support ring
   bulk solds adapted briefly to thermal insulation and
   gutter inflow
   galvanized bucket
   min. 10 cm bulk solids around outlets

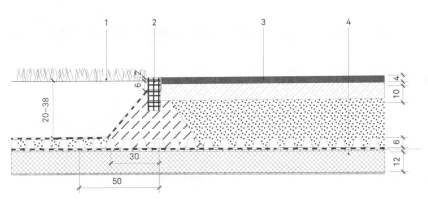

1 green area structure
   lawn
   vegetation layer 1/8 acc. to FLL
   system filter fleece 100 g
   drain element, polythene 60 x 1000 x 2000 cm filled with mineral bulk material 4/16 acc.to FLL
   dividing and liner fleece, polypropylene 80 g/m2
2 deep concrete kerbstone, 8 x 20 x 100 cm:
   strip foundation, 20–50 cm
   bituminous grouted joint 1 cm to asphalt floor
3 path structure
   poured asphalt 4 cm, reinforcement 500/550 Q 131, expansion joint every 5 m
   concrete loadbearing course approx. 10 cm
   drainage element, polythene 60 x 1000 x 2000 cm filled with mineral bulk material acc.
   to FLL 0–34 cm, in middle 17 cm
   dividing and liner fleece, polypropylene 80 g/m2
4 structure of inverted roof on building side

SÄCHSISCHE LANDES-, UNIVERSITÄTS- UND
STAATSBIBLIOTHEK (SLUB), DRESDEN, GERMANY

Stefan Tischer and Joerg Th. Coqui, Berlin
Construction directed by: Krüger Landschafts-
architekten, Dresden; Architecture: Ortner + Ortner,
Berlin, Vienna; Completion: 2004

About 10,000 m² in size, the library roof blends seamlessly with the campus. It is divided into areas with different designs that are all constructed as a green roof atop an inverted roof. The roof substrate is a special mixture enriched with zeolite. The paths made from poured asphalt on a concrete foundation are of particular interest. The precipitation seeps down to the plot of ground into the drainage layer into a retention trough and finally into rainwater through trenches.

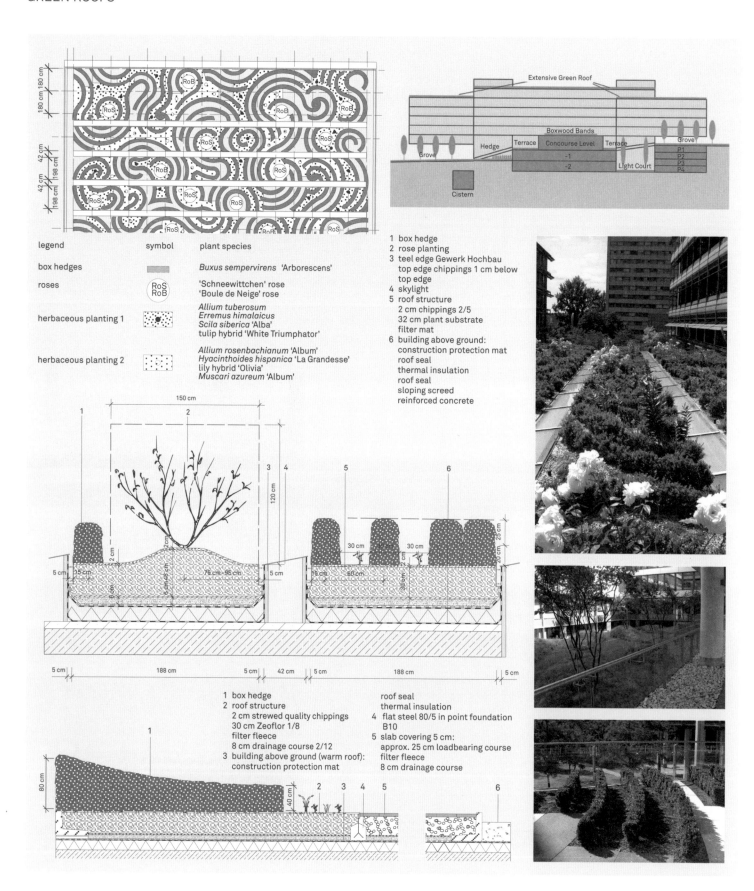

legend

legend	symbol	plant species
box hedges		*Buxus sempervirens* 'Arborescens'
roses	RoS RoB	'Schneewittchen' rose 'Boule de Neige' rose
herbaceous planting 1		*Allium tuberosum* *Erremus himalaicus* *Scila siberica* 'Alba' tulip hybrid 'White Triumphator'
herbaceous planting 2		*Allium rosenbachianum* 'Album' *Hyacinthoides hispanica* 'La Grandesse' lily hybrid 'Olivia' *Muscari azureum* 'Album'

1 box hedge
2 rose planting
3 teel edge Gewerk Hochbau
  top edge chippings 1 cm below
  top edge
4 skylight
5 roof structure
  2 cm chippings 2/5
  32 cm plant substrate
  filter mat
6 building above ground:
  construction protection mat
  roof seal
  thermal insulation
  roof seal
  sloping screed
  reinforced concrete

1 box hedge
2 roof structure
  2 cm strewed quality chippings
  30 cm Zeoflor 1/8
  filter fleece
  8 cm drainage course 2/12
3 building above ground (warm roof):
  construction protection mat

roof seal
thermal insulation
4 flat steel 80/5 in point foundation
  B10
5 slab covering 5 cm:
  approx. 25 cm loadbearing course
  filter fleece
  8 cm drainage course

ZUSATZVERSORGUNGSKASSE DES BAUGEWERBES,
WIESBADEN, GERMANY
Landscape architects: Latz und Partner, Kranzberg
Construction directed by: Latz Riehl Partner, Kassel
Architecture: Herzog und Partner, Munich
Completion: 2003

The interaction of building and open space creates working and recreational spaces that are optimal in terms of light and energy.
In the sunken courts between the underground garage and new office development, water-sprayed stone and plant structures have been created, assisting building climate control. The large-scale greening of the high roofs has a positive effect on the urban climate.

Structure of the extensive roof planting:
    flat ball plants, 16 per m²
    vegetations substrate,
    80 l/m²
    system filter
    drainage and water storage
    element 25 mm
    moisture retaining protection
    mat
    root protection sheet
    roof seal on above-ground
    building side

1 edging strip structure:
    edging strip in granite gravel
    bulk solids 16/32, at least 0.5 m
    metal edge
    system filter
    drainage and water retention
    element 25 mm, filled with mineral bulk solids
    insulating protection mat
    brown root protection sheet
    dividing and protection mat
    roof seal on above-ground
    building side

2 structure of intensive roof
    planting:
    plants
    vegetation substrate 240 l/ m²
    height approx. 25 cm substrate,
    160 l/m², hight approx. 15 cm
    system filter
    drainage and water retention
    element 60 mm filled with mineral bulk solids
    insulating protection mat
    brown root protection sheet
    dividing and protection mat
    roof seal on above-ground
    building side

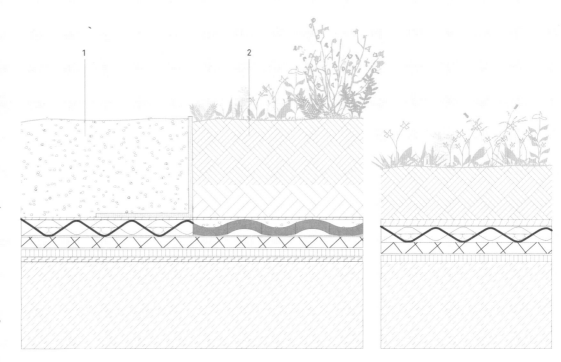

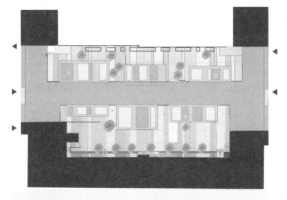

EXTENSION FOR THE LANDESAMT
FRIEDRICHSTRASSE, BERLIN-KREUZBERG, GERMANY

Exterior facilities: ST raum a, Berlin
Architecture: KSP Engel und Zimmermann Architekten
Completion 2005

The six roofs of the labor exchange extension building are on both sides of it. Strips of roof planting and gravel are separated by steel edging from a strip of gravel running all the way round. Each area is planted with a mixture of Sedum varieties and rock-garden plants. The areas area built up as follows: plant layer, plant substrate, fleece, drainage course, retention course and roof protection. Structural thickness derives from the plants used on the roofs.

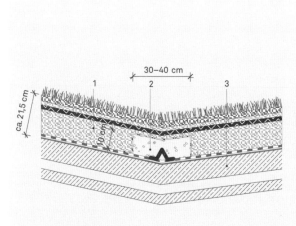

1 Roof planting structure
precultivated turf
lawn substrate, 17cm thick
building protection and drainage mat, artificial fiber
separation and liner sheet, approx. 0.2 mm thick
2 drainage channel:
water management element, h = 50 mm
drainage pack, 16/32, washed
filter fleece, approx. 3 mm thick, artificial fiber
3 above ground:
bituminous adhesive seal on waterproof concrete, rootproof
ceiling waterproof concrete

1 Roof structure:
precultivated turf
rooting fabric, 20 mm thick
lawn susbstrate, 17 cm thick
building protection and drainage mat,
plastic fiber
dividing and liner sheet, approx.
0.2 mm thick
2 anti-shear measures:
T-shaped anti-shear system, h = 8 cm,
suitable up to 45°
shear threshold
shear support
angle profile, hot-galvanized steel, 200
x 100 x 16 mm, length 200 mm, anchored with adhesive dowel

3 above-ground structure:
bituminous adhesive seal on waterproof concrete, rootproof
ceiling waterproof concrete
underground railway roof foundation
4 lawn with drainage pack:
structure lawn park, 2 layers:
15 cm topsoil (top layer) enriched
with lava and compost, 15 cm topsoil
(lower layer)
filter fleece, approx. 3 mm thick,
plastic fiber
gravel, 16/32, washed

1 Roof structure:
precultivated turf
rooting fabric, approx. 20 mm thick
lawn substrate, 17 cm thick, less in channel area
building protection and drainage mat, artificial fiber
separation and liner sheet, approx. 0.2 mm thick
water management element, h = 50 mm
drainage pack, 16/32, washed
2 triangle inspection shaft as roof outlet for above-ground
structure:
3 steel outflow pipe DN 100
4 roof outflow recess
5 bituminous adhesive seal on waterproof concrete, rootproof
—ceiling waterproof concrete
6 aluminium wall connection element
7 section of inspection shaft in front of water management
element
8 section of inspection shaft through water management
element

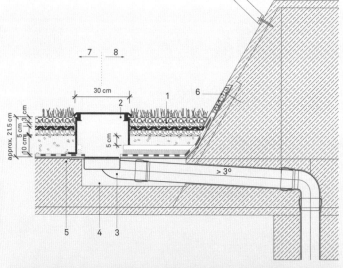

ZENTRALE MITTE HOCHSCHULCAMPUS GARCHING,
GERMANY

LA.BAR Landschaftsarchitekten, Berlin; Construction directed by: Mutter Landschaftsarchitekten, Schrobenhausen;
Architect/General planner: Léon Wohlhage Wernik Architekten, Berlin; Static framework for subway roofs: WTM
ENGINEERS, Munich; Completion: 2007

The new campus park above the Garching-Forschungszentrum subway station is laid
out as an urban green space. Three subway entrances are integrated into the tectonic
rhythm of the folded lawn surfaces and connected to its path system. The folded,
passable subway roofs, made from exposed concrete, are intensive green roofs, incorporating lawns, and have a continuous steel concrete parapet with rails. To protect
against slippage turf with a specified amount of grass seed incorporated, rooting
weaves, substrate with a stable structure and a shear protection system were used.

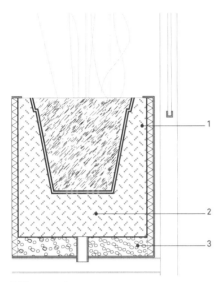

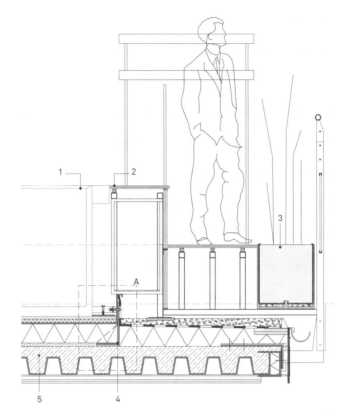

1 Plant trough
  stainless steel 1.4404, 2 mm, grain 250 polished
  insulation 2 cm XPS
  fleece
  double plant trough (tree nursery container)
  substrate from tree nursery
2 roof garden intensive substrate (for perennials
  between the containers)
3 drainage/outlet
  Leca (expanded clay for drainage)
  static tube DN 30 mm welded as seal
  static tube protrusion for drip

1 Pool:
  stainless steel with bench, 260 x 600 x 100 cm
  internal dimensions, 5 m³ water content,
  approx. 15 t weight incl. equipment, load transferred via 16 regulating screws
  trough:
  2.5 cm Sylomer (PUR elastomer)
  4 cm XPS
  2 mm steel tub
  16 cm foam glass cast in bitumen
  reinforced concrete ceiling
2 terrace paving:
  2.5 cm planks in Thermobuche
  4 cm laths in larch (ventilated by corrugated
  shaping)
  compression-molded stainless steel structure
  1.4301
3 plant trough:
  stainless steel with static tube 40 mm, 2 piece
  per linear metre

insulation with 2 cm XPS
  Leca to upper edge of static tube
  fleece
4 angle element for pool anchoring acc. T 12
  Stylomer statics for thermal separation
5 roof structure: warm roof
  trapezoidal metal sheets between steel
  girders
  approx. 16 cm concreted thermal insulation
  triple moisture insulation
  building protection mat
  chippings 8/16 mm

ROOF GARDEN IN VIENNA, AUSTRIA

stalzer lutz | gartenarchitektur, Weidling
Completion: 2006

This Vienna roof garden consists of a stainless steel pool
with surrounding wooden terraces made from roasted
beech and plants in steel troughs. A pool on a roof must satisfy numerous requirements: functional moisture fastness, exclusion of acoustic conduction through the
roof and particular static requirements concerning laterally acting forces. The planting
combines winter-hardy shrubs and woody plants with exotic plants. The non-winter-
hardy plants are planted in double tree nursery pots that can be moved into greenhouses in the autumn. The troughs drain directly into the gravel bed on the flat roof or
into the guttering via tubes.

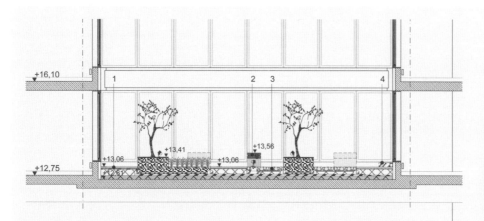

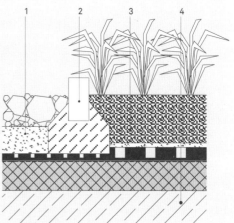

1 path structure:
  4 cm travertine slabs
  4 cm chippings bed 2/5
  3 cm drainage course filled with chippings 2/5
  protection and insulation mat
  13 cm insulation with rootproof seal
  roof shell
2 seating element ST 37
3 rubble area structure:
  15 cm crushed tarvertine rubble 5/15 cm
  10 cm extruded hard foam with topped with filter fleece
  6 cm drainage course filled with mineral substance
  13 cm insulation with roofproof seal
4 travertine plinth 15 cm

1 rubble area structure:
  15 cm travertine rubb;e
  13 cm expanded clay, crushed
  3 cm drainage element with filter fleece
2 concrete prefabricated element B/H: 10/20 cm, top edge
  8 cm above substrate level.concrete foundation C12/15
3 planting structure
  Corex variegata
  23 cm light substrate
  2 cm expanded clay, crushed
  filter fleece
  6 cm drainage element filled with mineral substance
  separation fleece
4 above-ground structure:
  14 cm insulation
  roof shell waterproof concrete

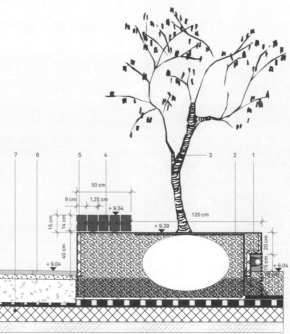

1 fluorescent tube
2 plant trough structure:
  drip irrigation
  light substrate
  lower substrate mineral
  2 cm expanded con-
  crete, crushed
  drainage element, 6 cm
  filled with mineral substance + filter fleece
  separation fleece
3 Malus sargentii
4 seating element:
  thermo-timber screwed
  with threaded rods and
  steel sections
5 plant trough setting:
  plant trough, steel galvanized, lacquered St37
  3 cm extruded hard
  foam
6 natural stone area
  structure:
  4 cm travertine stone
  slabs
  4 cm chippings bed 2/5
  filter fleece
  20 cm expanded clay,
  crushed
  3 cm drainage element
  separation fleece
7 above-ground structure:
  heat insulation
  roof seal in joint area,
  apertures
  shell ceiling waterproof
  concrete

ATRIUM COURTYARD, COMERCIAL BUILDING
TAUENTZIENSTRASSE, BERLIN, GERMANY

LA.BAR Landschaftsarchitekten, Berlin
Architect: Weinmiller Architekten, Berlin
Completion: 2006

This atrium court is on the third floor. Its travertine tiles (laid with fixed width and variable length) pick up on the materials of the surrounding facades. The beds are planted mainly with carex and festuca, and are formally structured using strips of travertine bulk materials and Carrara concrete elements. The steel planting troughs are planted with decorative apple trees (*Malus toringo sargentii*) cut into an umbrella form. The planted surfaces are maintained by an automatic irrigation system.

3.15   SPECIAL ELEMENTS

LIGHTING ELEMENTS
· Technical principles
· Lamps

PLAY AND SPORTS ELEMENTS
· Technical requirements
· Materials
· Fall protection
· Artificial climbing apparatus
· Skating facilities

SPECIMEN PROJECTS

SEATING ELEMENTS

SPECIMEN PROJECTS

Katja Heimanns

3.15 SPECIAL ELEMENTS

Outdoor furnishing may be installed as standard elements or designed individually by the planner. The main technical principles for planning lighting elements as well as requirements for play apparatus, sports facilities, and seating elements are described briefly below.

LIGHTING ELEMENTS

Light changes the impression spaces make. The outdoor use of artificial light is therefore important not only for safety, but also for the perception of architecture and landscape. Light can illuminate a space atmospherically, dramatically, and with rich contrast, emphasizing materials and objects, enhancing or muting colors, and blurring or redrawing spatial boundaries through combinations of light and darkness.

Technical principles

Our perception of color and lightness is based on electromagnetic waves, the frequency of which lie within the visible area of the spectrum. The spectrum of visible light ranges from approximately 370 nm (short waves, violet) to 750 nm (long waves, red). Sunlight, which falls evenly across this spectrum, therefore creates optimum color rendering.

For colors to appear the same under artificial light as we are accustomed to seeing them in sunlight, the spectrum of any light source should be similar to that of sunlight. In choosing an illuminant, color rendering (R_a) and color temperature (K), as well as technical and economic factors such as light yield (lm/W) and lifespan (hrs), therefore play important roles. > **Tab. 3.15.1**

Lamps

Thermal radiators (incandescent lamps, halogen incandescent lamps) create light via an incandescent metal coil. In a halogen incandescent lamp, halogens (usually iodine) are added to the filler gases. This causes the tungsten given off by the coil to combine and form a metal halogenide inside the relatively cool bulb. A very bright, white light is created. Thermal radiators give off up to 95% of their energy as heat. This gives them a short lifespan and makes outdoor use problematic due to the amount of heat generated. > **Tab. 3.15.2**

Lamps in which gases or metal vapors are caused to glow by electrical discharges between electrodes are called discharge lamps. To operate these lamps, a suitable electrical ballast is required. To initiate the discharge, a starter must be present. The starter is usually integrated into the lamp holder. The electrical ballast is usually external due to its size. There are two types of discharge lamps: high pressure discharge lamps (sodium vapor, mercury, and halogen metal vapor lamps) and low pressure discharge lamps.

As well as sodium vapor lamps, the low pressure discharge lamps include fluorescent lamps. In this case, a layer of

Term	Unit	Description
Luminous flux	lm (lumen)	The total light power emitted by a lamp, taking into account the eye's varying sensitivity to different areas of the spectrum. A radiant flux of 1 W at the maximum point of the spectrum (555 nm) creates a luminous flux of 683 lm.
Luminous intensity	cd (candela)	The luminous flux (lm) radiated in a particular direction, in relation to the solid angle (steradian).
Luminance	cd/m^2	Measurement of lightness. Luminance is obtained from the relationship of luminous intensity to surface area. The human eye perceives differences in luminance as differences in lightness.
Illuminance	lx (lux)	Measurement of luminous flux falling on a surface. If a luminous flux of 1 lm impacts uniformly on a 1 m^2 surface, the illuminance is 1 lx.
Light yield (efficiency)	lm/W (lumen/watt)	The light yield or level of efficiency is a measurement of the conversion of electrical energy (W) into visible light (luminous flux in lm). Light yield measures how economically a lamp functions. The higher this value, the better it functions.
Light color		Light color is the color of the light emitted by a light source, and is given by the x and y coordinates on the CIE standardized color table.
Color temperature	K (Kelvin)	Color temperature classifies the temperature a black body must reach before its light creates the same color impression as that of the actual light source. At 800 K, the body begins to glow (deep red light color). Further heating can make it appear yellow, white or even blue. (Planck Radiation Formula). White light colors are divided into three categories: warm white (ww) < 3300 K, neutral white (nw) 3300–5300 K and daylight white (tw) > 5300 K.
Color rendering	color rendering index R_a	The color rendering index R_a describes how well a lamp can render the total color spectrum of sunlight (R_a = 100). The quality of color rendition in an irradiated object results from the spectral composition of the light source. Example: some objects lose their color in the yellow light of a sodium lamp, as these lamps radiate very little green and red light.

Tab 3.15.1: Physical units in lighting engineering

	Lamps	Light intensity (W) all values according to manufacturer's data	Light yield lm/W	Additional operation device	Color temperature K	Color rendering index R_a (max. 100)	Lifespan hrs	Outdoor application	Special properties
Thermal radiators	incandescent lamp	25–150	< 15	no	approx. 2800	> 90	1000	sometimes still used in recessed lights, but increasingly replaced by other lamps	only approx. 5% light yield, 95% warmth, economical cost
	low voltage halogen incandescent lamp	20–100	20–28	yes	3000	> 90	4000	special effect lighting	very small lamp, expensive to install
	high voltage halogen incandescent lamp	40–500	20	no	3200	> 90	2000	now rarely used	especially bright light
Low pressure discharge lamps	fluorescent lamp	8–70	< 100	yes	3000–4000	60–69	18,000	e.g. linear lighting of bridges, railings etc. Floodlighting	long-life, relatively economical in terms of energy use. Not especially popular.
	compact fluorescent lamp (energy-saving lamp)	5–55	60–70	yes	2300–7000	80–89 (at 2700 K)	15,000	Orientation lights, headlights, bollard lights, garden lights	a smaller development of the fluorescent lamp
	sodium vapor low pressure lamp (LST)	18–185	100–200	yes	< 2500	25	16,000	used in street lighting to mark pedestrian bridges, tunnels and danger spots	yellow light, with poor color rendering, suitable for illuminating surfaces only in exceptional cases (e.g. soiling sandstone), causes fewer insect problems
High pressure discharge lamps	sodium vapor high pressure lamp (HSE, HST)	50–250	70–150	yes	< 2500	25–40	25,000	standard street lighting and industrial lighting. Also used in plant cultivation.	light color between pink and light orange
	mercury vapor lamp (HME)	50–400	60	yes	4000	40–59	10,000	e.g. street lighting	cold, neutral-white light color. The illuminant's high UV level attracts insects. Poor efficiency.
	halogen metal vapor lamp (HIT, HIE, HIR)	20–400	60–100	yes	> 3000	70	12,000	e.g. sports venues	increasingly used to light outdoor facilities. Due to their light color, they are replacing the less economical mercury vapor lap. Higher costs.
	xenon	35	30–50 (bis 150)	yes	4000–5000	no data	< 6000	mainly used for car headlights	very bright light
Electroluminescence	light-emitting diodes (LED) (white)	0,1–5	40–90	yes	3000–5500	80	> 50,000	decorative accentuation, orientation lights, not suitable for larger-scale illumination. Signaling facilities	low size, robust, dynamic color changes (RGB)

Tab. 3.15.2: Lamps and their outdoor applications

fluorescent pigment is applied to the inner side of the glass bulb. With the help of photoluminescence, this converts the discharge into visible radiation (light). As well as linear tubes, fluorescent lamps are also manufactured as compact fluorescent lamps (energy-saving lamps). However, as they contain mercury, lead and strontium, they must be disposed of as hazardous waste. > Tab. 3.15.2

LEDs (Light Emitting Diodes) are a type of electroluminescent radiator. They are based on semiconductor connections that convert electric current directly into light. LEDs exist in a variety of colors, forms, and sizes. The different colors are created by different semiconductor crystals. Ropelights and luminous foils consist of electroluminescent cells. Their diameter is approximately 3 mm. The lamp is flexible and bendable, allowing it to form curves. > Tab. 3.15.2

Fiber-optics are flexible cables using transparent, translucent fibers made from glass, plastic or other materials that transport light or infrared radiation. Light rays that are fed into one end of the fibers (by LEDs or focused incandescent lamps, for instance) are reflected in the boundary layer between the core and mantle glass. Fiber-optic lamps do not emit heat, and use little electricity. They are particularly suited to decorative lighting or the manufacture of translucent concrete. > Tab. 3.15.2 and chapter 1.7 Concrete

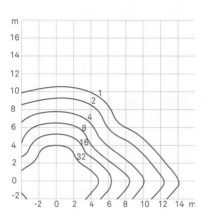

Fig. 3.15.1: Isolux line

low radiating

wide radiating

obliquely radiating

free radiating

high radiating

low/high radiating

Fig. 3.15.2: Polar representation of luminous intensity distribution

Fig. 3.15.3: Path illumination: mast lights

a | b   Fig. 3.15.5: Orientation lights: paving stones with LED lights

Fig. 3.15.4: Railing handrail with fluorescent lamp, light arc: Donaukai, Neuburg

Fig. 3.15.6: Directional floor flood

Isolux diagrams and light intensity distribution curves provided by lighting manufacturers give information on the intensity and direction of a light. Isolux diagrams show illuminance distribution on a plane. Isolux lines connect points with the same illuminance. For lighting where the light-emitting point is fixed for construction reasons, such as street lights with a prescribed mast height, the possible intervals between lights while maintaining the required illuminance can be directly calculated from this.
> Fig. 3.15.1

Luminous intensity distribution curves show the direction and intensity with which a lamp emits light.
> Fig. 3.15.2

Fig. 3.15.7: Orientation lights as a design element

PLAY AND SPORTS ELEMENTS

Alongside the use of mass-produced elements, individual design is becoming ever more significant. This ranges from simple play apparatus to complex play landscapes and skating facilities. A variety of technical standards and safety regulations must be observed during planning. Depending on the national legislation, these must be proven by a final examination and certified (in Germany, for instance, this is the GS certification mark awarded by the TÜV).

Technical requirements

Play and sports apparatus is subject to Europe-wide standards and the valid legal regulations of individual countries. EN 1176 and EN 1177 regulate technical safety requirements for installation, ground composition, and safety distances for all public play area equipment. Apparatus and facilities used as play area apparatus despite not having been manufactured for this purpose are also subject to these standards. Adventure play areas (fenced-in, protected play areas, often equipped with apparatus constructed by the owner) and some other categories are exempt from standard EN 1176. Play apparatus made and erected before EN 1176 came into force in 1998 comes under provisions to safeguard existing standards, if it does not represent a serious accident risk.

Materials

The stability and longevity, and also the design and use possibilities of play apparatus are significantly influenced by the choice of materials.

As a natural construction material, wood is more susceptible to weathering than other materials and tends to crack. This endangers its stability. On the other hand, wood is a suitable material for making play apparatus precisely because of its natural properties: pliability, workability, distinctive growth, relative lightness, and "warmth".

As the most durable type of European wood, robinia is particularly suited for play apparatus construction. Even when in contact with the ground, non-impregnated robinia can remain in place for 20 years and more. However, due to its growth pattern, robinia is only available in a limited range of measurements. Often only peeled trunks left in their natural, irregular form are used. Their characteristic form makes them striking. > Fig. 3.15.8

To avoid cracks, sliced squared timbers and watertight glue are often used for play apparatus. > Fig. 3.15.9
In order to keep the play apparatus stable and durable in the long term, constructive wood protection at soil level should always be observed. > Fig. 3.15.10

Fig. 3.15.8: Play apparatus made from robinia wood

Fig. 3.15.10: Climbing apparatus in the form of a "humpbacked bridge": the bottoms of the round timbers are anchored in long steel sleeves, providing optimal water protection.

Fig. 3.15.9: Sundry elements made from solid wood and composite lumber, Allerpark Wolfsburg

Fig. 3.15.13: Metal play tower, bark mulch as fall protection

Fig. 3.15.11: Play apparatus with flexible plastic elements

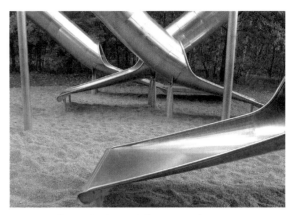

Fig. 3.15.12: Slide with tubes made from non-rusting steel

Fig. 3.15.14: Swings, bark mulch as fall protection

Fig. 3.15.15: Climbing wall made from red sprayed concrete: a) under construction, b) following completion.

a | b

Plastics are of interest for use in play apparatus due to their high durability, high tear and breakage strength, and lack of splinters. Elastomers > **Chapter 1.9** are used where elastic properties are required. > **Fig. 3.15.11**

Steel has the best durability and vandalism resistance. Where steel play apparatus is in contact with the ground, there is no risk of rotting, as long as appropriate corrosion protection is in place. > **Chapter 1.8**

Direct sunlight can cause the surface to heat up substantially. This is a disadvantage, particularly for slides. However, steel slides work better than the plastic equivalent, so they are often chosen for older children and adolescents. > **Fig. 3.15.12**

Sprayed concrete allows varied modeling of play figures and climbing walls. These free forms are often created from steel matting, sprayed concrete, and sprayed mortar, applied in several layers using dry shotcreting. > **Fig. 3.15.15**

Fall protection

In order to prevent injuries caused by falling, the fall space and the impact surface must be free of obstacles and also shock-absorbing. For fall heights of up to 1.50 m, the fall space—i.e. the space around the play apparatus—should always be at least 1.50 m. The free fall height should not be more than 3.00 m. The space required (minimum space) for the impact surface depends on the free fall height.

As a general rule, the fall space should be made larger as the height of the play apparatus increases. For free fall heights of over 1.50 m the length of the impact surface should be calculated using the formula below:

Length of impact surface (m) = [(2/3 of free fall height) + 0.5] m.

With the exception of impact surfaces for turning or swinging apparatus, impact surfaces can overlap.

In principle, all flooring in child play areas is subject to certain requirements. For play area apparatus with a free fall height of up to 60 cm, the flooring should have shock-absorbing properties. However, an assessment of the critical fall height is not required. For play area apparatus with a free fall height of more than 60 cm, however, play area flooring must have particular shock-absorbing properties across its whole impact area. The choice of play area flooring depends on the free fall height. > **Figs. 3.15.13 and 3.15.14, and tab. 3.15.3**

Artificial climbing apparatus

A climbing wall consists of either individual elements (size approx. 1 x 1 m) made of wood, GRP or other materials, or boulder-like elements, often made from sprayed concrete. To increase friction, surfaces may be given a coating containing sand. The individual handgrips are

Flooring material	Subsoil requirements	Minimum layer thickness cm	Max. fall height cm
Concrete/stone	-		≤ 60
Bitumen-bound floorings			
Water-bound coverings	-		≤ 100
Topsoil			
Turf	-		≤ 150
Chipped wood [1]	machine-chipped wood (no derived timber products without bark or leaves. Grain size 5–30 mm	20	
Bark mulch [1]	chipped conifer bark. Grain size 20–80 mm	20	≤ 300
Sand [1]	no silty or clayey components, washed. Grain size 0.2–2 mm	20	
Gravel [1]	grain size 2–8 mm	20	
Synthetic fall protection	assessment according to EN 1177		

[1] Loose material should be applied with a 20 cm higher layer thickness due to its tendency to become displaced.
[2] Bark mulch and chipped wood should be applied to a subsoil that does not allow water to collect.

Tab. 3.15.3: Subsoil in fall area of play area apparatus according to EN 1177

secured to the wall at intervals of approx. 20–30 cm using screws.

On a climbing wall, people either climb freely (bouldering) or on a rope. Climbing walls with free fall heights of over 2 m are a distinct category. > **Fig. 3.15.15**

Skating facilities

Besides skateboards, skating facilities are mainly used for BMX bicycles and inline skates.

The composition of the skating surfaces and safety areas must be in line with national standards (for Germany, DIN 33943). They must be separate in spatial and construction terms from play areas, sports areas, leisure parks, and similar facilities. For fall heights greater than 100 cm, suitable falling protection must be put in place. A distinction is made between individual elements, facilities built out of individual skate elements and skate parks.

In contrast to the setting up of individual elements, skate parks are modeled to fit into the terrain. > **Fig. 3.15.16**

These elements are usually manufactured from reinforced concrete with a plastic or synthetic coating. Concrete has the advantage of a long lifespan and therefore low maintenance costs, as well as optimum skating properties and muting of wheel noise.

Preferably, joints are hard (preferably using a synthetic resin-sand mixture) and are therefore easier to maintain than soft silicone joints, which can be loosened by wheel pressures. The edges of the skating surfaces should be protected with hard rubber, stainless steel or hot-dip galvanized moldings. For copings (skating elements made from metal pipes) with a diameter of approx. 5–7 cm, the materials should be either low-maintenance and long-lived stainless steel or galvanized steel. For "grinds" (slides), the sliding properties of galvanized steel are significantly better. One disadvantage is the occasional appearance of spots of rust. As with edges and copings, non-screwed installation is advisable, in order to avoid injuries caused by projecting screws, etc. > **Fig. 3.15.17**

a
b

Fig. 3.15.16: Skating facilities:
a) skate park in Oschatz modeled to fit into the landscape
b) individual elements on the BUGA in Munich

a | b

Fig. 3.15.17: Copings and edge protection

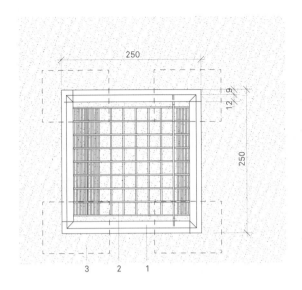

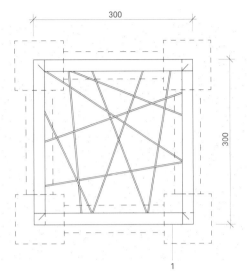

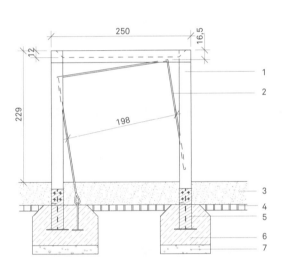

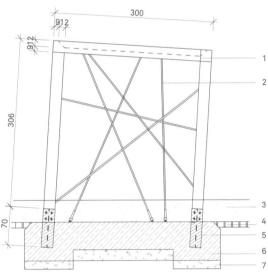

1 Frame made from oak beams 21/21 cm, upper face beveled 45° joint with stainless steel sheet 10 mm, screwed
2 Climbing rope made from polyamide-jacketed 6-stranded steel cables, d = 19 mm, color: hemp. Crossing points formed by stainless steel S-clamps, d = 8 mm, securing to wooden frame; stainless steel press sockets, fitted to ropes, adjustable, anchoring in foundation; steel anchor, ropes with turnbuckles and U-clamps, adapted to ropes
3 Play sand, 40 cm
4 Lawn grid paving
5 Post in stainless steel beam bracket, Profile HE-B 220, l = 70 cm, with welded-on base plate, 4-fold bolting
6 Foundations C25/30, reinforced, according to static requirements, post foundations approx. 90/90/70 cm, continuous strip foundations approx. 50/50 cm
7 Ballast 0/45.15 cm
8 Anchoring in foundation

CLIMBING DEVICE, MASELAKEPARK, BERLIN, GERMANY

Landscape architect: relais Landschaftsarchitekten, Berlin
Completion: 2007

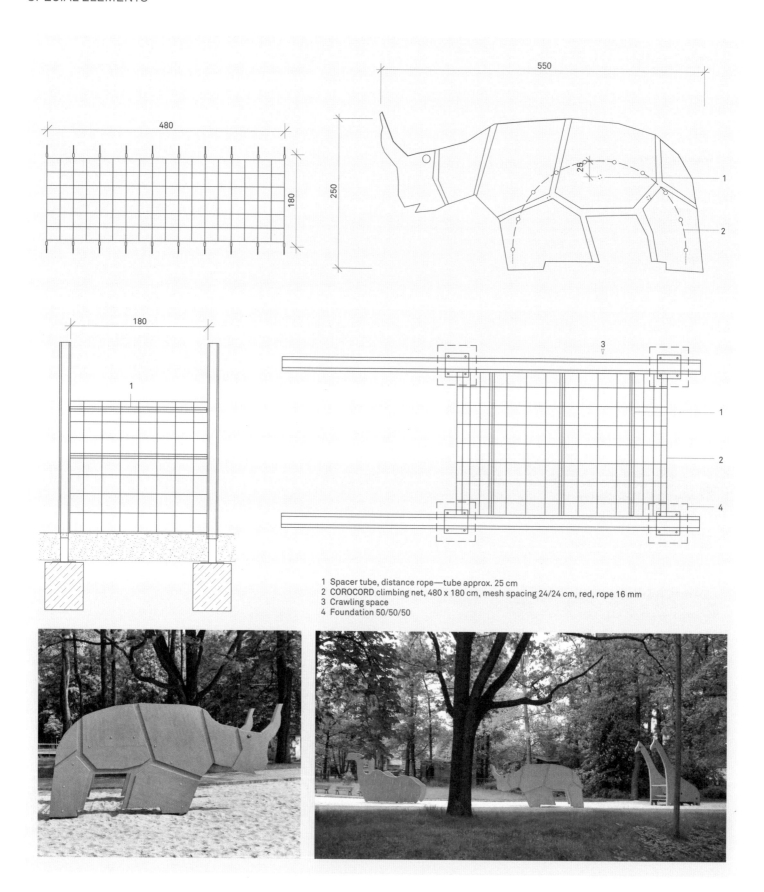

1 Spacer tube, distance rope—tube approx. 25 cm
2 COROCORD climbing net, 480 x 180 cm, mesh spacing 24/24 cm, red, rope 16 mm
3 Crawling space
4 Foundation 50/50/50

PLAY ANIMALS "ARCHE NOAH" PLAY AREA
PELZMÜHLE, CHEMNITZ, GERMANY

Landscape architect: Rehwaldt Landschaftsarchitekten,
Dresden
Completion: 2004

1 15 mm EPDM-plastic granulate as surface layer
2 Steel mat reinforcement, two-ply. After manufacture, apply first
   layer of sprayed concrete to relief
3 Spring boss 3 mm PCC cosmetic mortar
4 12 mm fine layer C25/30, XF1
5 14 cm sprayed concrete C25/30, XC4, XF1b reinforced, multiply
6 70 cm subsoil stabilization sand 04 with 3% of weight cement
7 Drainage DN80, jacketed with coconut fiber
8 KG PVC 100
9 20 cm topsoil-sand mixture (on a slope of < 1:2), grass seed
10 Drainage layer with 5% slope relative to the terrain, 20 cm
   drainage layer, filter chippings 4/ 8 on filtration fleece
11 Seat, swiveling
12 Sleeve with console for 4 screws, sleeves welded to posts,
   galvanized and powder-coated
13 Pole, diameter 100 mm, l = 3500 mm with hot-dip galvanized
   base plate, powder-coated
14 Speaking tube
15 Sleeve flush with foundation, secured to foundation by means
   of 6 heavy-load anchors M12
16 Arches 45°, KG PVC pipe DN100
17 Foundation, concrete C25/35, XF1
18 KG PVC pipe DN100
19 Sheeting diameter 100.5 mm, d = 4 mm, 1 per perch, tightly welded
   in to form the top
20 Pole, steel pipe diameter 108 x 3.6 mm, hot-dip galvanized, three
   different heights: 3 m, 4 m and 5 m above upper-edge fall protection
21 Seat cushion, artificial resin, glass-fiber-reinforced, screwed to
   console from beneath
22 Sleeve with console, consisting of a steel pipe 114.3 x 3.2.l = 110 mm,
   ring internal diameter 110 mm, external diameter 190 mm,
   thickness 10 mm, 4 drill holes 12 mm, 1 for each perch
23 Climbing aid
24 Ring internal diameter 110 mm, external diameter 190 mm,
   1 per perch

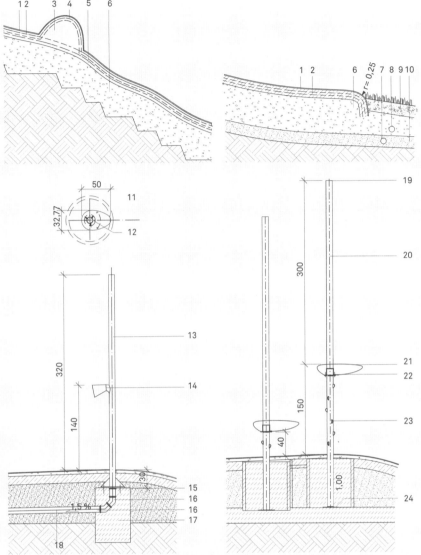

"HANGRUTSCHE", STADTPARK WALDKIRCHEN,
GERMANY

Landscape architect: Rehwaldt Landschaftsarchitekten,
Dresden
Completion: 2007

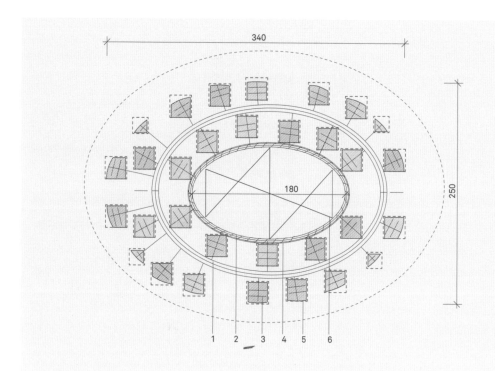

1 Outer ring stainless steel pipe 76.1 x 3.6 mm, S235
2 Inner ring stainless steel pipe 40 x 4 mm, S235
3 Bracing steel sheet t = 10 mm, S355, welded to rings, bolted to squared timbers
4 Continuous stainless steel net as fall protection with mesh spacing 7 x 7 cm, wire thickness 2 mm, circumference approx. 4.8 m, heights 0.5 m; 3.5 m and 2.75 m
5 Squared timber 220 x 238 mm to 10.5 m long
6 Rope ladder, Corocord System, reinforcement according to manufacturer's data
7 Grating screwed to flat-rolled steel fishplate with M12 x 45 flat-rolled steel 110 x 50 x 10 mm, stainless steel, welded to steel pipe
8 Flat-rolled steel 40 x 3 mm, stainless steel, bent, soldered to struts of grating
9 Stainless steel pipe S 235 80 x 4 mm as pedestal for grating
10 Sheet S 235, t = 10 mm with 9 bar dowels Ø16
11 Glue wood strip to cover sheet
12 Grating stainless steel, V2A, pickled, mesh spacing 5 x 5 cm, base height 4 cm, with no sharp edges, in accordance with play apparatus regulations
13 Steel pipe subconstruction, powder-coated, 80 x 40 x 4 mm
14 Flat-rolled steel 40 x 3 mm, bent, welded to grating
15 Support sheet t = 10 mm, 5, welded to moldings, a = 5 mm

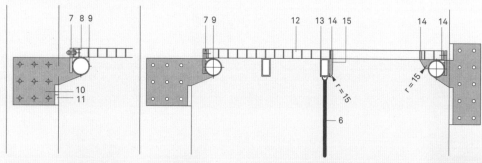

"TRAXINGTANNE" CLIMBING TOWER, STADTPARK
WALDKIRCHEN, GERMANY

Landscape architect: Rehwaldt Landschaftsarchitekten, Dresden
Statics: Büchting und Streit, Waldkirchen
Completion: 2007

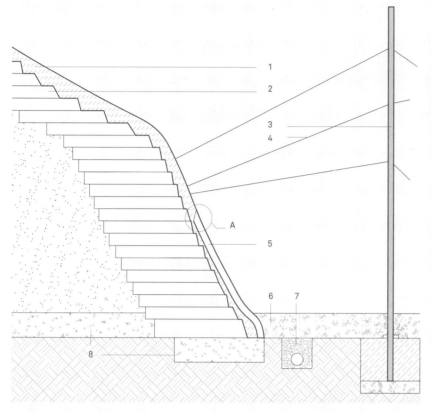

1 Poured concrete with fine layer
2 RC concrete tiles with pores
3 Climbing pole, height 5 m
4 Climbing ropes secured to lifting eye nuts
5 Fall protection coating (EPDM plastic) 11 cm with 10 mm plastic granulate as surface layer
6 Fall protection gravel 2/5
7 Through trench 50 x 50
8 Frost-protection gravel 0/45
9 12 mm sprayed concrete fine layer C25/30

10 10 cm sprayed concrete C25/30 multiply
11 4–5 cm sprayed concrete C8/10 as blinding layer
12 10 mm EPDM-plastic granulate as surface layer
13 11 cm EPDM fall protection coating
14 Wood strut with post bracket (for wood platform)
15 Threaded rod M16 with locking nut
16 Foundation 50 x 50 x 80 cm

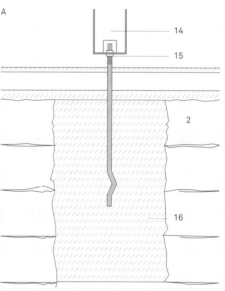

PLAY HILLS, STADTPARK BURGHAUSEN, GERMANY

Landscape architect: Rehwaldt Landschaftsarchitekten, Dresden
Completion: 2004

SEATING ELEMENTS

Seating elements are made from very diverse materials or combinations of materials. As well as design aspects, weathering and vandalism resistance are important when choosing materials and designs. Plastic covering is often used instead of wood, as plastic is more durable. For the seat, comfort is especially important. Seat surfaces made from wood offer the most comfortable surface.

In general, care should be taken that slats are not too narrow, to guarantee sitting comfortably. > Fig. 3.15.21 Benches are also often made from concrete finished parts or in-situ concrete, due to their high stability and the variety of designs. > Fig. 3.15.20

Two things should be borne in mind for all seating elements: prevention of water collecting on the seat surface, and stability and firm anchoring. The surfaces should also be easy to clean. Joint widths should be designed either so that no refuse becomes lodged in them or so that it can easily be removed. Given the opportunity, skaters often misuse bench edges as grinds (slides). In this case, edges should be reinforced using steel moldings. Alternatively, the whole bench should be made of metal. Benches made from metal are very durable, and easy to maintain even when much used. They are however of-ten considered uncomfortable.

Fig. 3.15.18: Wooden seating elements

Fig. 3.15.19: Metal benches and table with wood covering

Fig. 3.15.20: Seating ensemble made from finished concrete parts

Fig. 3.15.21: Concrete seating elements using plastic planks, wood covering, and EPDM covering

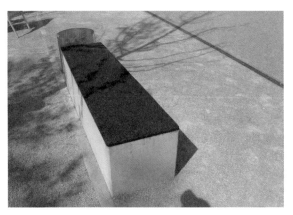

a | b | c

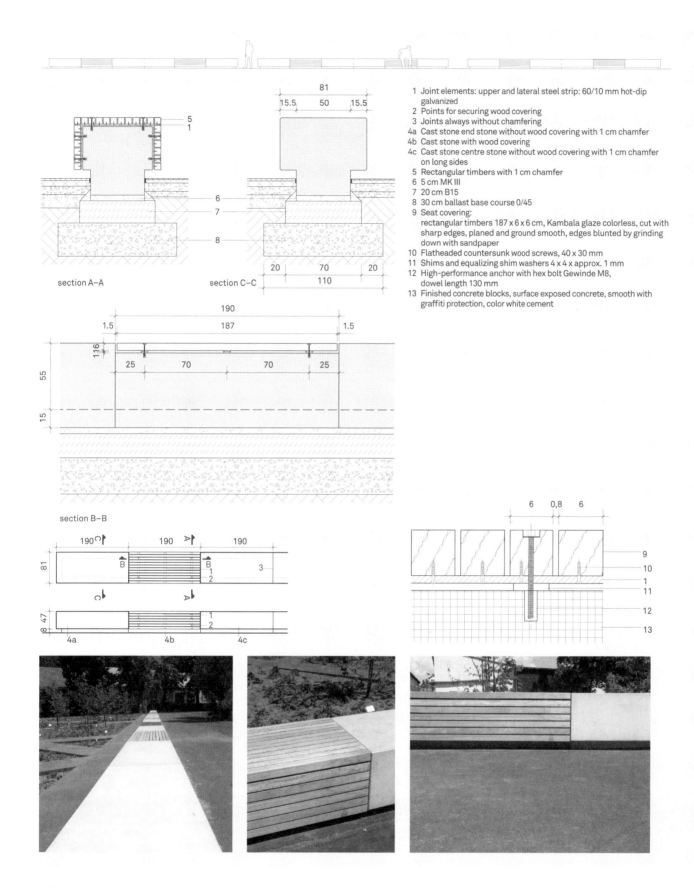

1 Joint elements: upper and lateral steel strip: 60/10 mm hot-dip galvanized
2 Points for securing wood covering
3 Joints always without chamfering
4a Cast stone end stone without wood covering with 1 cm chamfer
4b Cast stone with wood covering
4c Cast stone centre stone without wood covering with 1 cm chamfer on long sides
5 Rectangular timbers with 1 cm chamfer
6 5 cm MK III
7 20 cm B15
8 30 cm ballast base course 0/45
9 Seat covering:
  rectangular timbers 187 x 6 x 6 cm, Kambala glaze colorless, cut with sharp edges, planed and ground smooth, edges blunted by grinding down with sandpaper
10 Flatheaded countersunk wood screws, 40 x 30 mm
11 Shims and equalizing shim washers 4 x 4 x approx. 1 mm
12 High-performance anchor with hex bolt Gewinde M8, dowel length 130 mm
13 Finished concrete blocks, surface exposed concrete, smooth with graffiti protection, color white cement

section A–A

section C–C

section B–B

CONCRETE BENCH WITH WOOD COVERING, OSCHATZ, GERMANY

Landscape architect: Weidinger Landschaftsarchitekten
Completion: 2006

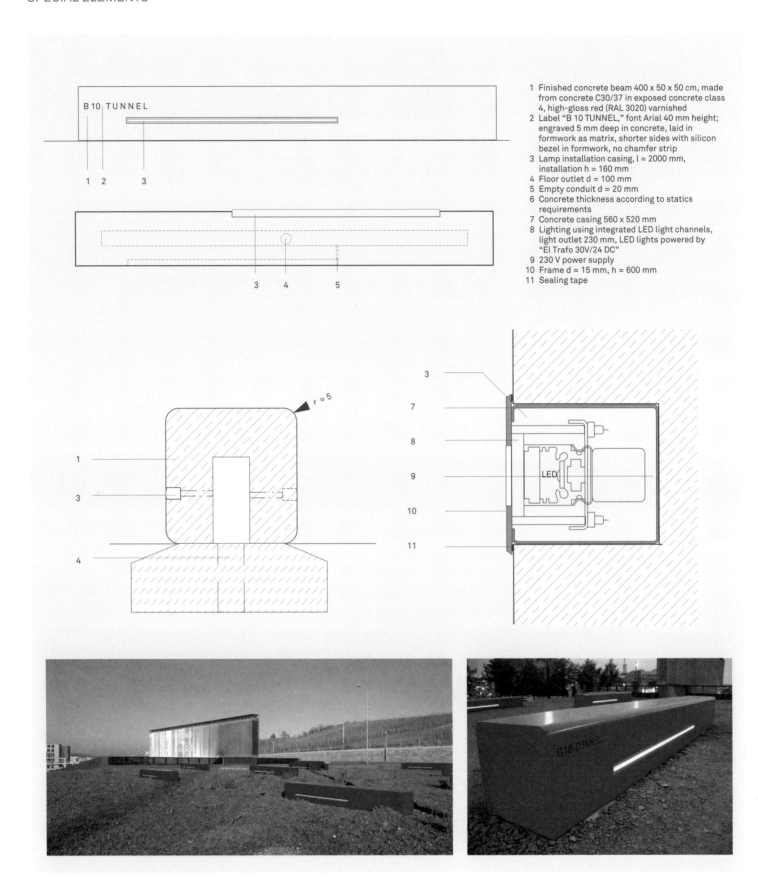

1 Finished concrete beam 400 x 50 x 50 cm, made from concrete C30/37 in exposed concrete class 4, high-gloss red (RAL 3020) varnished
2 Label "B 10 TUNNEL," font Arial 40 mm height; engraved 5 mm deep in concrete, laid in formwork as matrix, shorter sides with silicon bezel in formwork, no chamfer strip
3 Lamp installation casing, l = 2000 mm, installation h = 160 mm
4 Floor outlet d = 100 mm
5 Empty conduit d = 20 mm
6 Concrete thickness according to statics requirements
7 Concrete casing 560 x 520 mm
8 Lighting using integrated LED light channels, light outlet 230 mm, LED lights powered by "El Trafo 30V/24 DC"
9 230 V power supply
10 Frame d = 15 mm, h = 600 mm
11 Sealing tape

"ROTER BALKEN": PRAGSATTEL-LÖWENTOR TUNNEL
PROJECT, STUTTGART, GERMANY

Architects: SCALA, Esefeld & Prof. Nagler, Stuttgart
Completion: 2000

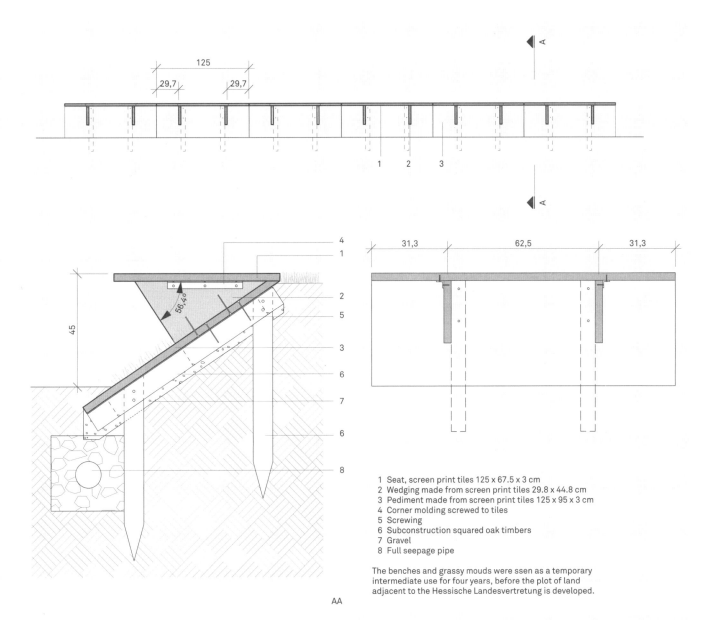

1 Seat, screen print tiles 125 x 67.5 x 3 cm
2 Wedging made from screen print tiles 29.8 x 44.8 cm
3 Pediment made from screen print tiles 125 x 95 x 3 cm
4 Corner molding screwed to tiles
5 Screwing
6 Subconstruction squared oak timbers
7 Gravel
8 Full seepage pipe

The benches and grassy mouds were ssen as a temporary
intermediate use for four years, before the plot of land
adjacent to the Hessische Landesvertretung is developed.

AA

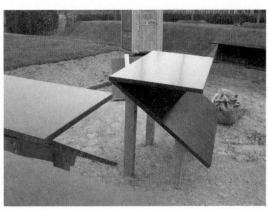

BENCH SET IN EARTH MOUND: HESSISCHE
LANDESVERTRETUNG, BERLIN, GERMANY

Landscape architect: Bernard und Sattler
Completion: 2007

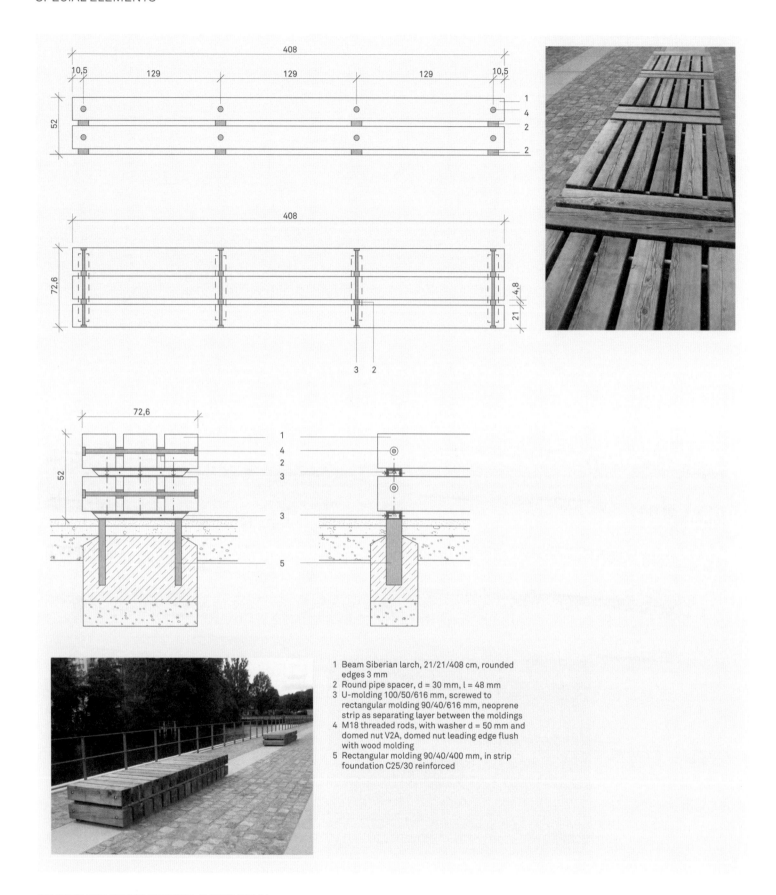

1 Beam Siberian larch, 21/21/408 cm, rounded
   edges 3 mm
2 Round pipe spacer, d = 30 mm, l = 48 mm
3 U-molding 100/50/616 mm, screwed to
   rectangular molding 90/40/616 mm, neoprene
   strip as separating layer between the moldings
4 M18 threaded rods, with washer d = 50 mm and
   domed nut V2A, domed nut leading edge flush
   with wood molding
5 Rectangular molding 90/40/400 mm, in strip
   foundation C25/30 reinforced

BENCH IN THE UFERPARK MASELAKE ZENTRUM,
BERLIN, GERMANY

Landscape architect: relais Landschaftsarchitekten,
Berlin
Completion: 2006

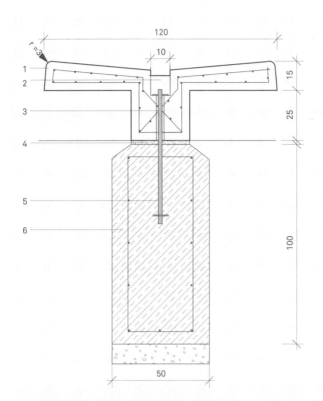

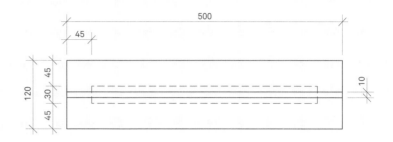

1   Concrete finished part, polished
2   Tile 80/80/5
3   Corrugated sheath, grouted with epoxy resin
4   Mortar MGIII 2 cm
5   Threaded rod M20
6   Concrete C20/25 on gravel 0/32

BENCH AT AXEL-SPRINGER-HAUS, BERLIN, GERMANY

Landscape architect: Birgit Hammer Landschaftsarchitektur, Berlin
Completion: 2000

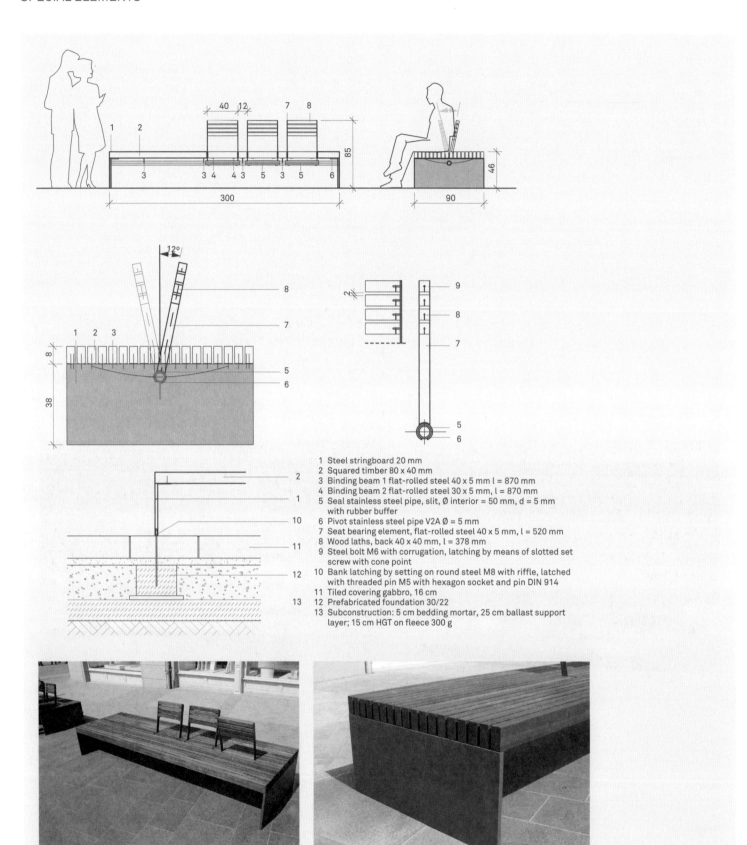

1 Steel stringboard 20 mm
2 Squared timber 80 x 40 mm
3 Binding beam 1 flat-rolled steel 40 x 5 mm l = 870 mm
4 Binding beam 2 flat-rolled steel 30 x 5 mm, l = 870 mm
5 Seal stainless steel pipe, slit, Ø interior = 50 mm, d = 5 mm with rubber buffer
6 Pivot stainless steel pipe V2A Ø = 5 mm
7 Seat bearing element, flat-rolled steel 40 x 5 mm, l = 520 mm
8 Wood laths, back 40 x 40 mm, l = 378 mm
9 Steel bolt M6 with corrugation, latching by means of slotted set screw with cone point
10 Bank latching by setting on round steel M8 with riffle, latched with threaded pin M5 with hexagon socket and pin DIN 914
11 Tiled covering gabbro, 16 cm
12 Prefabricated foundation 30/22
13 Subconstruction: 5 cm bedding mortar, 25 cm ballast support layer; 15 cm HGT on fleece 300 g

FOLDING BENCH, MARKTPLATZ HALLE / SAALE,
GERMANY

Landscape architect: Rehwaldt Landschaftsarchitekten,
Dresden
Completion: 2006

1 Exposed concrete without facing, black—anthracite
2 Light exposed concrete

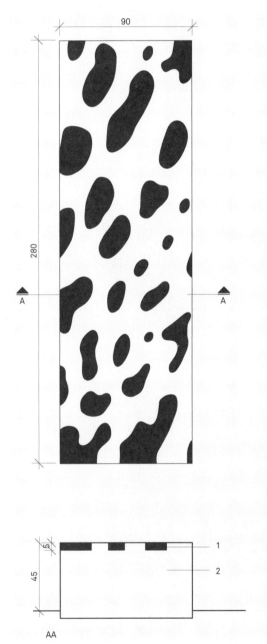

BENCHES IN FRONT OF ZOO IN WUPPERTAL,
GERMANY

Landscape architect: Rehwaldt Landschaftsarchitekten,
Dresden
Completion: 2007

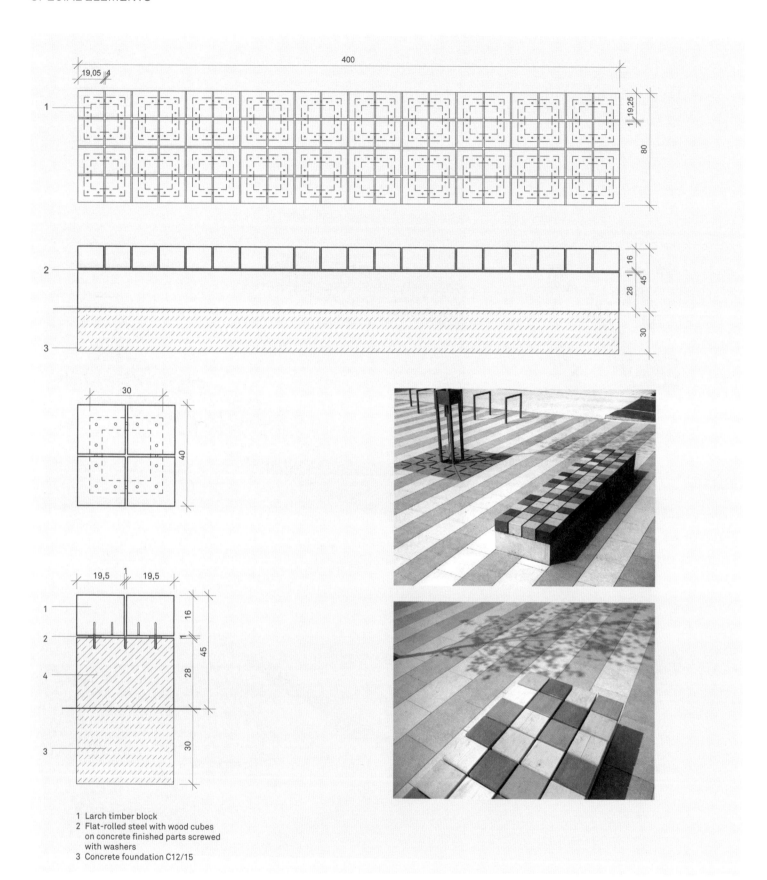

1 Larch timber block
2 Flat-rolled steel with wood cubes
  on concrete finished parts screwed
  with washers
3 Concrete foundation C12/15

BENCHES AT MEDICAL-THEORETICAL CENTER,
TU DRESDEN, GERMANY

Landscape architect: Rehwaldt Landschaftsarchitekten,
Dresden
Completion: 2006

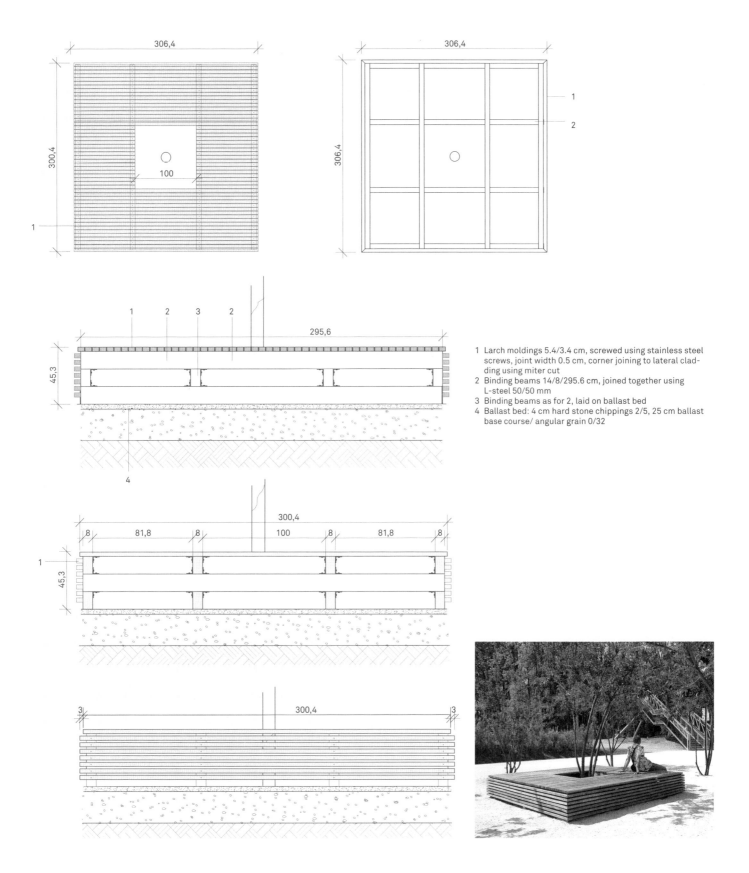

1 Larch moldings 5.4/3.4 cm, screwed using stainless steel screws, joint width 0.5 cm, corner joining to lateral cladding using miter cut
2 Binding beams 14/8/295.6 cm, joined together using L-steel 50/50 mm
3 Binding beams as for 2, laid on ballast bed
4 Ballast bed: 4 cm hard stone chippings 2/5, 25 cm ballast base course/ angular grain 0/32

GARDEN PLOTS AT THE GARTENSCHAU IN TULLN, AUSTRIA

Landscape architect: hutterreimann + cejka, Berlin
Completion: 2008

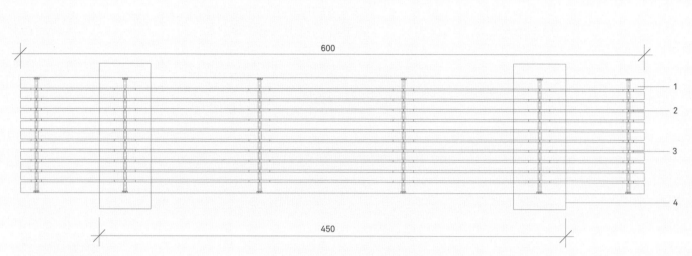

1 Larch timber 600 x 10 cm
2 Threaded rod, galvanized steel
3 Spacer
4 Granite stone 100 x 50 cm

BENCH IN DANIA-PARK, MALMÖ, SWEDEN

Landscape architects: Thorbjörn Andersson, SWECO
FFNS Architects, Stockholm
Completion: 2002

APPENDIX

LITERATURE, STANDARDS AND DIRECTIVES,
ADDITIONAL INFORMATION

PICTURE CREDITS

INDEX

LITERATURE, STANDARDS AND DIRECTIVES, ADDITIONAL INFORMATION

European standards (EN) and international standards adopted in Europe (EN ISO) are listed without identifying the countries concerned. The current national published version applies.

ESSAY

Baur, Eva Gesine: *Was kommt, was bleibt. Prognosen für das nächste Jahrtausend.* dtv, Munich 1999

Bertaux, Pierre: *La mutation humaine.* Payot, Paris 1964

Friedell, Egon: *A Cultural History of the Modern Age.* Knopf, New York 1930

Hegger, Manfred; Drexler, Hans; Zeumer, Martin: *Basics Materials.* Birkhäuser Verlag, Basel 2007

Poethig, Kurt; Schneider, Camillo: *Hausgartentechnik. Das Handwerk der Anlage, Pflanzung und Pflege.* Bücher der Gartenschönheit, vol. 12, Berlin 1929

Virilio, Paul: *The Aesthetics of Disappearance.* Semiotext(e), New York 1991

Wagner, Karlheinz: Fragil bauen. In: *Zuschnitt,* issue no. 19, September 2005 (pp. 8–9). Published by: proHolz Austria—Arbeitsgemeinschaft der österreichischen Holzwirtschaft

1 MATERIALS AND WORKING WITH BUILDING MATERIALS, GENERAL

Beier, Harm-Eckart; Niesel, Alfred; Petzold, Heiner: *Lehr-Taschenbuch für den Garten- Landschafts- und Sportplatzbau.* Ulmer Verlag, Stuttgart 2003

Bell, Victoria Ballard: *Materials for Architectural Design.* King, London 2006

Beylerian, George M.; Dent, Andrew; Moryadas, Anita: *Material Connexion. Innovative Materialien fur Architekten, Künstler und Designer.* Prestel, Munich 2005

Brownell, Blaine: *Transmaterial: A Catalog of Materials that Redefine our Physical Environment.* Princeton Architectural Press, New York 2006

Hegger, Manfred; Auch-Schwelk, Volker; Fuchs, Matthias; Rosenkranz, Thorsten: *Construction Materials Manual.* Birkhäuser Verlag, Basel 2006

Jørgensen, Kim Tang; Holgersen, Søren; Stausholm, Anne Fischer; Meyle, Eva: *Danske Anlægsgartnere: Normer og Vejledning i anlægsgartnerarbejde.* 2006

Lefteri, Chris: *Best of Materials for Inspirational Design.* RotoVision, Hove 2007

Niesel, Alfred (ed.): *Bauen mit Grün—Die Bau- und Vegetationstechnik des Landschafts- und Sportplatzbaus.* Ulmer Verlag, Stuttgart 2003

Schäffler, Hermann; Bruy, Erhard; Schelling, Günther: *Baustoffkunde.* Vogel, Würzburg 2005

Wendehorst, Reinhard: *Baustoffkunde.* Vincentz, Hanover 2004

SIA 318 Garten- und Landschaftsbau

Bundesvereinigung Recycling-Baustoffe e.V.—www.recycling-baustoffe.de

1.1 SOIL

Duchaufour, Philippe : *Abrégé de pédologie. Sol, vegetation, environnement.* Masson, Paris 1997

Ellenberg, Heinz und Lehrstuhl für Geobotanik der Universität Göttingen: *Zeigerwerte der Pflanzen in Mitteleuropa (Indicator values of plants in Central Europe).* Goltze, Göttingen 2001

Hill, M. O., Mountford, J. O., Roy, D. B.; Bunce, R. G. H.: *Ellenberg's Indicator Values for British Plants.* Series: Ecofact Research Report Series 2b. Technical Annex to Ecofact Volume 2. Institute of Terrestrial Ecology 1999

Plaste, Edward: *Soil Science & Management.* Thomson Delmar Learning, New York 2002

Rosenheinrich, Günther; Pietzsch, Wolfgang: *Erdbau.* 3rd revised edition, Werner, Düsseldorf 1998

EN ISO 14688-1 Geotechnical investigation and testing . Identification and classification of soil. Part 1: Identification and description, 2002

EN ISO 14688-2 Geotechnical investigation and testing. Identification and classification of soil. Part 2: Principles for a classification, 2004

EN 12620 Aggregates for concrete

EN 13043 Aggregates for bituminous mixtures and surface treatments for roads, airfields and other trafficked areas

EN 13042 Aggregates for unbound and hydraulically bound materials for use in civil engineering work and road construction

EN 13055-1 Lightweight aggregates. Part 1: Lightweight aggregates for concrete, mortar and grout

EN 13139 Aggregates for mortar

EN 13285 Unbound mixtures—Specifications

EN 13383-1 Armourstone—Specification

DIN 18196 Erd- und Grundbau—Bodenklassifikation für bautechnische Zwecke

DIN 18300 VOB Vergabe- und Vertragsordnung für Bauleistungen—Teil C: Allgemeine Technische Vertragsbedingungen für Bauleistungen (ATV)—Erdarbeiten

DIN 18915 Vegetationstechnik im Landschaftsbau—Bodenarbeiten

DS 404 Nomenklatur for sand-, grus- og stenmaterialer

ÖNORM L 1050 Boden als Pflanzenstandort—Begriffsbestimmung, Untersuchungsverfahren

ÖNORM L 1061 Physikalische Bodenuntersuchungen; Bestimmung der Korngrössenverteilung des mineralischen Feinbodens

ÖNORM B 4400 Erd- und Grundbau; Bodenklassifikation für bautechnische Zwecke und Methoden zum Erkennen von Bodengruppen

ÖNORM B 4412 Erd- und Grundbau : Untersuchung von Bodenproben; Korngrössenverteilung

SN 640 581: Erdbau, Boden, Grundlagen

Forschungsgesellschaft für Strassen- und Verkehrswesen (FGSV) (publ.):
- *Technische Lieferbedingungen für Gesteinskörnungen im Strassenbau (TL Gestein-StB 04).* FGSV-Verlag, Cologne 2007

Federal Office for the Environment FOEN (www.bafu.admin.ch):
- Directive pour la valorisation, le traitement et le stockage des matériaux d'excavation et déblais/ Direttiva per il riciclaggio, il trattamento e il deposito di materiale di scavo. Bern 1999
- Construire en préservant les sols/ Costruire proteggendo il suolo. LFU Nr. 10, Bern 2001
- Directive pour la valorisation des déchets de chantier minéraux/ Direttiva per il riciclaggio dei rifiuti edili minerali. Bern 2006

Gütegemeinschaft Substrate für Pflanzenbau e.V. (Quality Assurance Association Growing Media for Plant Cultivation)— www.substrate-ev.org
Dachverband Lehm e.V.—www.dachverband-lehm.de
Bund/Länder-Arbeitsgemeinschaft Abfall (LAGA)— www.laga-online.de
Bundesgütegemeinschaft Recycling-Baustoffe e.V.— www.recycling-bau.de
EU-Recycling—the portal for waste, water, soil, air— www.recyclingportal.eu
Umweltportal Deutschland—www.portalu.de

1.2 PLANTS

Alanko, Pentti; Kahila, Pirkko: Köynnöskasvit. Tammi, 2003
Armitage, Allan M.: Armitage's garden annuals. Timber Press, Portland 2004
Balder, H.; Flechner, H.-P., Klein, W. und Krüger, G.: Unter der Lupe: angelieferte Pflanzware. In: LA—Landschaftsarchitektur 1995, 05, 1
Bayer, E.; Buttler, Kp. ; Finkelzeller, X. ; Grau, J.: Guide de la flore méditerranéenne : caractéristiques, habitat, distribution et particularités de 536 espèces. Delachaux et Niestlé, Paris 2005
Berg, Johann; Heft, Lothar: Rhododendron und immergrüne Laubgehölze. Ulmer Verlag, Stuttgart 1991
Hansen, Richard; Stahl, Friedrich: Die Stauden und ihre Lebensbereiche in Gärten und Grünanlagen. Ulmer Verlag, Stuttgart 1997
Hämet-Ahti, Leena e.a. (ed.): Suomen puu- ja pensaskasvio. 2., uudistettu painos. Dendrologian Seura—Dendrologiska Sällskapet r.y. Helsinki 1992 (Publications of the Finnish Dendrological Society 6, pp. 373)
Hvass, Niels: Plantning af træer. European Tree Planting Guide 2005
Jelitto, Leo; Schacht, Wilhelm; Simon, Hans: Die Freiland-Schmuckstauden. Ulmer Verlag, Stuttgart 2002
Kawollek, Wolfgang: Kübelpflanzen, Südländische Gehölze für die Kultur in Töpfen und Kübeln. Ulmer Verlag, Stuttgart 1997
Krüssmann, Gerd: Handbuch der Nadelgehölze. Parey, Berlin/ Hamburg 1983
Krüssmann, Gerd: Handbuch der Laubgehölze. Blackwell, Berlin 1999
Mathew, Brian; Swindells, Philip: Blomsterløg og knolde. Politikkens Forlag og Det Danske Haveselskab 1994
McClaren, Bill: Encyclopedia of Dahlias. Timber Press, Portland/ Cambridge 2004
Olsen, Ib Asger: Planter i Miljøet. Grønt miljø 1998
Phillips, Roger; Rix, Martyn: Bulbs. Macmillan Publishers, London 1989
Phillips, Roger; Rix, Martyn: Perennials. Vol. 1 Early Perennials. Macmillan Publishers, London 1994
Phillips, Roger; Rix, Martyn: Perennials. Vol. 2 Late Perennials. Macmillan Publishers, London 1996

Phillips, Roger; Rix, Martyn: Annuals and Biennials. Macmillan Publishers, London 1999
Polese, Jean-Marie: Arbres et arbustes de Méditerranée. Edisud, Aix-en-Provence 2007
Räty, Ella (ed.): Viheralueiden puut ja pensaat. Taimistoviljelijät ry. 4. uudistettu painos. 2007
Schul, Jane: Hvilken Plante hvor. Politikken i samarbejde med Det Danske Haveselskab 1999
Seitz, Birgit; Kowarik, Ingo; Starfinger, Uwe (eds.): Perspektiven für die Verwendung gebietseigener Gehölze. NEOBIOTA 2, 2003, pp. 3–26
Sirviö, Jenni (ed.): Viheralueiden kasvualustat. Viherympäristöliitto ry, VYL julkaisu 31. 2004
Toomey, Mary; Leeds, Everett: An illustrated Encyclopedia of Clematis. Timber Press, Portland 2001
Tossavainen, Anne; Räty, Ella (eds.): Viherammattilaisen perennakirja. Viherympäristöliitto ry.
Vollrath, Birgit: Autochthonie im Praxistest. AFZ—Der Wald. 2006/8, 435–437. Deutscher Landwirtschaftsverlag, Hanover and Munich 2006
Warda, Hans-Dieter: Das grosse Buch der Garten- und Landschaftsgehölze. Bruns Pflanzen Export GmbH im Eigenverlag, Bad Zwischenahn 2001

European Technical and Quality Standards for Hardy Nursery stock, including Roses, Fruit Trees, Herbaceous Perennials. (Nov. 1996), E.N.A. (European Nurserystock Association)

DIN 18916 Vegetationstechnik im Landschaftsbau—Pflanzen und Pflanzarbeiten
ÖNORM L 1110 Pflanzen—Vegetationstechnische Arbeiten— Pflanzengüteanforderungen, Sortierungsbestimmungen

Qualitätsbestimmungen des Verbands Schweizer Baumschulen (VSB) vom 24.02.2005
Forschungsgesellschaft Landschaftsentwicklung Landschaftsbau e. V. (FLL) (publ.):
- Gütebestimmungen für Baumschulpflanzen. Eigenverlag, Bonn 2004
- Gütebestimmungen für Stauden. Eigenverlag, Bonn 2004
Danske Anlægsgartnere og Dansk Planteskoleforening: Kvalitetssikring af Planteleverancer, 1996
Danske Anlægsgartnere: Pleje af grønne områder, 2003

ISU internationale Stauden-Union—www.isu-perennials.org
Gemeinschaftliches Sortenamt der EU—www.cpvo.europa.eu
European Bamboo Society (EBS)—www.bamboo-society.org.uk
World Federation of Rose Societies—www.worldrose.org
Zentralverband deutscher Gartenbau—www.g-net.de
Grünflächenamtsleiterkonferenz—www.galk.de
Bund Deutscher Baumschulen—www.bund-deutscher-baumschulen.de
Allgemeine Deutsche Rosenneuheitenprüfung (ADR)— www.adr-rose.de
Bund deutscher Staudengärtner (BdS)—www.stauden.de
Polish Nurserymen Association—www.polskierosliny.pl; www.zielentozycie.pl
Royal Horticultural Society (RHS)—www.rhs.org.uk
British Bedding & Potplant Association—www.thebbpa.org.uk
International Flower Bulb Centre—www.bulbsonline.org
Gesellschaft Schweizer Staudenfreunde—www.staudenfreunde.ch

Unternehmerverband Gärtner Schweiz—www.jardinsuisse.ch
Die Vereinigung Schweizerischer Stadtgärtnereien und Garten-
bauämter—www.vssg.ch
Österreichische Gartenbaugesellschaft—www.garten.or.at
Bundesverband Österreichischer Gärtner—www.gartenbau.or.at
Plantedirektotatet—www.plantedir.dk

1.3 LAWNS AND OTHER SEEDED AREAS

Ellenberg, Heinz: *Vegetation Mitteleuropas mit den Alpen.* Ulmer
Verlag, Stuttgart 1996
Gandert, Klaus-Dietrich: *Rasen im Garten.* BfG. VEB Deutscher
Landwirtschaftsverlag, Berlin 1982
Hentinen, Hanna: *Kotipihan nurmikko-opas: Perusta nurmikko
helposti.* Viherympäristöliiton julkaisuja no 5. Viherympäristöli-
itto ry. Helsinki 1997
Hope, Frank: *Rasen. Anlage und Pflege von Zier-, Gebrauchs-,
Sport- und Landschaftsrasen.* Ulmer Verlag, Stuttgart 1983
Klapp, Ernst; Opitz von Boberfeld, Wilhelm: *Taschenbuch der
Gräser.* 12th revised edition, Paul Parey Verlag, Berlin and Ham-
burg 1990
Mertz, Peter: *Pflanzenwelt Mitteleuropas und der Alpen. Hand-
buch und Atlas der Pflanzengesellschaften.* Nikol Verlagsgesell-
schaft, Hamburg 2002
Rasen/Turf/Gazon mit Greenkeepers Journal, Fachzeitschrift.
Köllen Druck + Verlag GmbH
Rothmaler, Werner; Jäger, Eckhart: *Exkursionsflora von
Deutschland.* Vol. 4., 10th edition, Spektrum Akademischer
Verlag, Munich 2005

Council Decision 93/626/EEC of 25 October 1993 concerning the
conclusion of the Convention on Biological Diversity
66/401/EEC Directive of 14 June 1966 on the marketing of fodder plant seed

DIN 18035-4 Sportplätze—Teil 4: Rasenflächen
DIN 18917 Vegetationstechnik im Landschaftsbau—Rasen und
Saatarbeiten (RSM verankert)
DIN 18918 Vegetationstechnik im Landschaftsbau—Ingeni-
eurbiologische Sicherungsbauweisen—Sicherungen durch
Ansaaten, Bepflanzungen, Bauweisen mit lebenden und nicht
lebenden Stoffen und Bauteilen, kombinierte Bauweisen (RSM
verankert)
ÖNORM B 2606-1 Sportplatzbeläge—Rasenbeläge

Forschungsgesellschaft Landschaftsentwicklung und Land-
schaftsbau e.V.(FLL):
- *Empfehlungen für Bau und Pflege von Flächen aus Schotterra-
sen,* Eigenverlag der FLL, Bonn 1999
- *RSM 2006. Regel-Saatgut- Mischungen Rasen.* Eigenverlag der
FLL, Bonn 2005

Deutsche Rasengesellschaft e.V.—www.rasengesellschaft.de
Deutsche Saatveredlung AG—www.dsv-saaten.de und www.
rasen.de
Bundessortenamt—www.bundessortenamt.de (biennially publishers *Beschreibende Sortenliste Rasengräser*)

1.4 WOOD

Detail. Zeitschrift für Architektur + Baudetail: *Timber Construction.* Ausgabe 10/2006. Institut für internationale Architektur-
Dokumentation GmbH & Co. KG, Munich

Geza Ambrozy, Heinz; Giertlová, Zuzana: *Planungshandbuch.
Holzwerkstoffe. Technologie—Konstruktion—Anwendung.*
Springer Verlag, Vienna 2005
Hallmann, Heinz W.; Rohn, Heinz W.; Lingnau, Günter: *Bauen mit
Holz in Park und Garten. Anregungen zur Gestaltung und Konst-
ruktion.* Callwey Verlag, Munich 1984
Herzog, Thomas et al.: *Timber Construction Manual.* Birkhäuser
Verlag, Basel 2003
Lefteri, Chris: *Wood.* RotoVision, Hove 2005
Mombächer, Rudolf (ed.): *Holz-Lexikon. Nachschlagewerk für
die Holz- und Forstwirtschaft.* 3rd newly revised edition, DRW
Verlag, Leinfelden-Echterdingen 1988
Petersen, Dorte klarskov: *Miljøvenlig brug af træ.* Have og
Landskabsrådet 2001
Sell, Jürgen: *Eigenschaften und Kenngrößen von Holzarten.* 3rd
slighly revised edition, Baufachverlag AG, Zurich 1989
Wagenführ, Rudi: *Holzatlas.* 5th updated and extended edition,
Fachbuchverlag Leipzig im Carl Hanser Verlag, Munich 2000
Winterbottom, Daniel M.: *Wood in the Landscape. A Practical
Guide to Specification and Design.* John Wiley, New York 2000

EN 335-1 Durability of wood and wood-based products—Definition of use classes—Part 1: General; Trilingual version
EN 335-2 Durability of wood and wood-based products—Definition of use classes—Part 2: Application to solid wood; Trilingual version
EN 350-1 Durability of wood and wood-based products—Natural
durability of solid wood—Part 1: Guide to the principles of testing
and classifikation of the natural durability of wood; Trilingual
version
EN 350-2 Durability of wood and wood-based products—Natural durability of solid wood—Part 2: Guide to the natural durability and treatability of selected wood species of importance in
Europe; Trilingual version
EN 351-1 Durability of wood and wood-based products Preser-
vatives-treated solid wood—Part 1: Classification of preservative penetration and retention; Trilingual version
EN 460 Durability of wood and wood-based products—Natural
durability of solid wood—Guide to the durability requirements
for wood to be used in hazard classes; Trilingual version
EN 599-1 Durability of wood and wood-based products—
Performances of wood preservative as determined by biological
tests—Part 1: Specification according to hazard class
EN 599-2 Durability of wood and wood-based products—
Performance of preventive wood preservatives as determined
by biological tests—Part 2: Classification and labelling
DIN 1052 Entwurf, Berechnung und Bemessung von Holzbau-
werken—Allgemeine Bemessungsregeln und Bemessungsre-
geln für den Hochbau
DIN 4074-1 Sortierung von Holz nach der Tragfähigkeit,
Teil 1: Nadelschnittholz
DIN 4074-5 Sortierung von Holz nach der Tragfähigkeit—
Teil 5: Laubschnittholz
DIN 68800-2 Holzschutz—Teil 2: Vorbeugende bauliche Mass-
nahmen im Hochbau
DIN 68800-3 Holzschutz—Teil 3: Vorbeugender chemischer
Holzschutz
NTR Dokument nr. 1 Nordisk træbeskyttelse
RT 21-10823 *Lämpökäsitelty puu*
RT 21-10880 *Kyllästetty puutavara*
RT 29-10567 *Maalaustarvikkeet. Maalit ja pinnoitteet*
RT 89-10241 *Kestopuiset pihalaatat*

Puurakenteet 1: *Puu materiaalina*. Rakentajain kust. Helsinki 1981

Puurakenteet 3: Liitokset. Rakentajain kust. Helsinki 1982

Informationsdienst Holz—www.informationsdienst-holz.de

LIGNUM—Holzwirtschaft Schweiz—www.lignum.ch

LIGNUM—Office Romand—www.cedotec.ch

proHolz Austria—Arbeitsgemeinschaft der österreichischen Holzwirtschaft—www.proholz.at

Træbranchens Oplysningsråd—www.top.dk

1.5 STONE

Baetzner, Alfred: *Natursteinarbeiten*. Ulmer Verlag, Stuttgart 1991

Bradley, Frederick; Studio Marmo: *Natural Stone. A Guide to Selection*. Norton, New York 1998

Detail. Zeitschrift für Architektur und Baudetail. *Building with Stone*. Issue 6/1999. Institut für internationale Architektur-Dokumentation GmbH, Munich

Deutscher Naturwerksteinverband (DNV) (publ.): *Bautechnische Informationen Naturwerkstein*. Würzburg 1996

Deutscher Naturwerksteinverband (DNV) (publ.): *Pflasterdecken und Plattenbeläge aus Naturstein für Verkehrsflächen*. Würzburg 2000

Germann, Albrecht (ed.): *Naturstein-Lexikon: Gesteinskunde and Handelsnamen; Naturstein im Innen- und Aussenbereich; Kunstgeschichte und Architektur*. Callwey, Munich 2003

Grimm, Wolf-Dieter: *Bildatlas wichtiger Denkmalgesteine der Bundesrepublik Deutschland*. Arbeitsheft 50 des Bayerischen Landesamtes für Denkmalpflege, Karl M. Lipp Verlag, Munich 1990

Holzman, Malcolm: *Stone Work*. Images Publishing Group, Mulgrave, Victoria 2001

Hugues, Theodor; Steiger, Ludwig; Weber, Johann: *Dressed Stone: Types of Stone, Details, Examples* (Detail Practice). Birkhäuser, Basel 2005

Mackler, Christoph: *Werkstoff Naturstein. Material, Konstruktion, Zeitgenössische Architektur*. Birkhäuser Verlag, Basel 2004

Mehling, Günther: *Natursteinlexikon*. Munich 1981

Mehling, Günther (ed.): *Natursteinlexikon*. 5th completed revised and updated new edition, Callwey Verlag, Munich 2003

Mesimäki, Pekka: *Luonnonkivikäsikirja*. Kiviteollisuusliitto ry. Helsinki 1997

Topos. European Landscape Magazine. Vol. 43: *Gestalten mit Stein*. Callwey Verlag, Munich 2003

Wanetschek, Margret and Horst (ed.): *Naturstein und Architektur. Fassaden, Innenräume, Aussenanlagen, Steintechnik*. Callwey, Munich 2000

Weber, Johann: Oberflächenbearbeitung von Naturstein. In: *Detail—Zeitschrift für Architektur und Baudetail. Bauen mit Naturstein*. 11/2003, p. 1304ff

EN 771-6 Specification for masonry units—Natural stone masonry units

EN 1341 Slabs of natural stone for external paving—Requirements and test methods

EN 1342 Setts of natural stone for external paving—Requirements and test methods

EN 1343 Kerbs of natural stone for external paving—Requirements and test methods

EN 933-4: Tests for geometrical properties of aggregates—Part 4: Determination of particle shape—Shape index

EN 1467 Natural stone—Rough blocks—Requirements

EN 1468 Natural stone test methods—Rough slabs—Requirements

EN 1469 Natural stone products—Slabs for cladding—Requirements

EN 1925 Natural stone test methods—Determination of water absorption coefficient by capillarity

EN 1926 Natural stone test methods—Determination of uniaxial compressive strength

EN 1936 Natural stone test methods—Determination of real density and apparent density, and of total and open porosity

EN 12059 Natural stone products—Dimensional stone work—Requirements

EN 12326 Slate and stone products for discontinuous roofing and cladding

EN 12370 Natural stone test methods—Determination of resistance to salt crystallization

EN 12371 Natural stone test methods—Determination of frost resistance

EN 12372 Natural stone test methods—Determination of flexural strength under concentrated load

EN 12407 Natural stone test methods—Petrographic examination

EN 12440 Natural stone—Denomination criteria

EN 12670 Natural stone—Terminology

EN 13161 Natural stone test methods—Determination of flexural strength under constant moment

EN 13364 Natural stone test methods—Determination of the breaking load at dowel hole

EN 13373 Natural stone test methods—Determination of geometric characteristics on units

EN 13755 Natural stone—Test methods—Determination of water absorption at atmospheric pressure

EN 14066 Natural stone test methods—Determination of resistance to ageing by thermal shock

EN 14146 Natural stone test methods—Determination of the dynamic elastic modulus of elasticity (by measuring the fundamental resonance frequency)

EN 14147 Natural stone test methods—Determination of resistance to ageing by salt mist

EN 14157 Natural stones—Determination of abrasion resistance

EN 14158 Natural stone test methods—Determination of rupture energy

EN 14205 Natural stone test methods—Determination of Knoop hardness

EN 14580 Natural stone test methods—Determination of static elastic modulus

EN 14581 Natural stone test methods—Determination of linear thermal expansion coefficient

DIN 52100-2 Naturstein—Gesteinskundliche Untersuchungen—Allgemeines und Übersicht

DIN 52104-2 Prüfung von Naturstein; Frost-Tau-Wechsel-Versuch; Verfahren Z

DS 404 Nomenklatur for sand-, grus- og stenmaterialer

OENORM B 3120-1 Natürliche Gesteine; Probenahme; allgemeine Grundlagen und gesteinskundliche Beschreibung

OENORM B 3120-2 Natürliche Gesteine; Probenahme; Festgesteine

RT 30–10314 *Luonnonkivet, suomalaiset rakennuskivet*

SN 640 560b Randabschlüsse aus Naturstein und Kunststeinen

SN 567 246 Natursteinarbeiten—Beläge, Bekleidungen und Werkstücke

Fédération Belge des Associations de Maîtres Tailleurs des Pierres—www.pierresetmarbres.be

Deutsches Naturstein-Archiv—www.deutsches-naturstein-archiv.de

TU München—Fakultät für Architektur—Lehrstuhl für Baukonstruktion und Baustoffkunde—Baustoffsammlung, EBB—www.ebb.ar.tum.de

Deutscher Naturwerkstein Verband e.V.—www.natursteinverband.de

Bayerischer Industrieverband Steine und Erden e.V.—www.steine-erden-by.de

Bundesinnungsverband des Deutschen Steinmetz-, Stein- und Holzbildhauerhandwerks—www.biv-steinmetz.de

Bundesverband Mineralische Rohstoffe (MIRO)—www.bv-naturstein.org

Bundesanstalt für Materialprüfung—www.bam.de

Finstone - Suomalainen kivi (The Finnish Natural Stone Association)—www.finstone.com

Institut Supérieure de recherche et de formation aux métiers de la Pierre—www.institut-de-la-pierre.com

British Stone—www.bpindex.com

National Association of Memorial Masons (Namm)—www.namm.org.uk

Stone Federation Great Britain—www.stone-federationgb.org.uk

Mc Keon Stone federation—www.mckeonstone.ie

Associazione Italiana Marmomacchine—www.assomarmomacchine.com

Norsk Byggtjeneste A/S (Norwegian Building Centre)—www.nobb.no

Stenindustriens Landssammenslutning—www.stenindustrien.no

Vereinigung Österreichischer Natursteinwerke (VÖN)—www.pronaturstein.at

ASSIMAGRA (Associação Portuguesa dos Indústriais de Mármores, Granitos e Ramos Afins)—www.assimagra.com

Association Romande des Métiers de la Pierre (ARMP)—www.armp.ch

F.D.P. Federacion Española de la Piedra Natural—www.fdp.es

Verband Dänischer Steinmetze—www.stenhuggerlauget.dk

1.6 BRICK AND CLINKER

Altaha, Nasser: *Säure und Wasser? Vorsicht! Ursachen und Vermeidung von Ausblühungen.* In: Bautenschutz + Bausanierung. Zeitschrift für Bauinstandsetzung und Denkmalpflege, issue 6, pp. 14–18. Rudolf Müller Verlag, Cologne 1998

Auer, Gerhard et al. (eds.): *DAIDALOS—Triumpfe des Backsteins / Triumphs of Brick.* Issue 43, Bertelsmann Fachzeitschriften, Gütersloh 1992

Bender, Willi: *Lexikon der Ziegel.* Bauverlag, Wiesbaden/Berlin 1995

Bender, Willi; Händle, Frank (eds.): *Handbuch für die Ziegelindustrie: Verfahren und Betriebspraxis in der Grobkeramik.* Bauverlag, Wiesbaden and Berlin 1995

Bender, Willi: *Vom Ziegelgott zum Industrieelektroniker. Geschichte der Ziegelherstellung von den Anfängen bis heute.* Bundesverband der Deutschen Ziegelindustrie, Bonn 2004

Brunskill, Ronald W.: *Brick Building in Britain.* Victor Gollancz with Peter Crawley, London 1997

Distel, Walter: *Modern Bauen mit Backstein.* Schweizerische Zieglerorganisation, Zurich 1934

Fester, Mark; Kraft, Sabine; Kuhnert, Nikolaus; Uhlig, Günther (eds.): *Zeitschrift für Architektur und Städtebau—Arch+ Mit Fug und Stein.* Issue 84, ARCH+ Verlag, Aachen 1986

Gurcke, Karl: *Bricks and brickmaking: A Handbook for Historical Archaeology.* The University of Idaho Press, Moscow 1987

Lefteri, Chris: *Keramik.* Material—Herstellung—Produkte. Av edition GmbH, 2005

Lynch, Gerard: *Brickwork: History, technology and practice.* Vol. 1, 2. Donhead, London 1994

Murerfagets Oplyaninaråd på: *Tegl—Fuger i murværk.* Forgalet Tegl, Copenhagen 1999

Peirs, Giovanni: *Construire en brique en Europe.* Editions Lannoo sa, Tielt 1994

Peirs, Giovanni: *La Terre cuite. L'Architecture en terre cuite après.* Pierre Mardaga Editeur, Liège 1982

Schrader, Milla: *Mauerziegel als historisches Baumaterial.* Edition: anderweit Verlag, Suderburg-Hösseringen 1997

Schumacher, Fritz: *Das Wesen des neuzeitlichen Backsteinbaus.* Callwey Verlag, Munich, Reprint 1985 (1920)

Sovinski, Rob W.: *Brick in the Landscape.* John Wiley & Sons Inc., New York 1999

Zadel-Sodtke, Petra: *Wahrnehmungsorientiertes Gestalten von Ziegelsichtmauerwerk im Aussenraum.* Dissertation, Berlin 2006

Zimmerschied, Gerd: *Ziegel als gestaltendes Element.* Verlag Interbuch, Berlin 1961

EN 771-1 Specification for masonry units—Part 1: Clay masonry units

EN 772-1 Methods of test for masonry units—Part 1: Determination of compressive strength

EN 772-3 Methods of test for masonry units—Part 3: Determination of net volume and percentage of voids of clay masonry units by hydrostatic weighing

EN 772-5 Methods of test for masonry units—Part 5: Determination of the active soluble salts content of clay masonry units

EN 772-7 Methods of test for masonry units—Part 7: Determination of water absorption of clay masonry damp proof course units by boiling water

EN 772-13 Methods of test for masonry units—Part 13: Determination of net and gross dry density of masonry units (except for natural stone)

EN 772-16 Methods of test for masonry units—Part 16: Determination of dimensions

EN 993-1 to 18 Methods of test for dense shaped refractory products

EN 1344 Clay pavers—Requirements and test methods

EN ISO 10545-1 to 16 Ceramic tiles

BS 8221-1 and 2 Code of practice for cleaning and surface repair of buildings—Cleaning of natural stones, brick, terracotta and concrete

DIN V 105-100 Mauerziegel—Teil 100: Mauerziegel mit besonderen Eigenschaften (preliminary standards)

DIN 18158 Bodenklinkerplatten

DIN 18503 Pflasterklinker—Anforderungen und Prüfverfahren

OENORM B 3200 Mauerziegel—Anforderungen und Prüfungen—Klassifizierung und Kennzeichnung—Ergänzende Bestimmungen zu OENORM EN 771-1

RT 34-10761 *Keraamiset laatat*

RT 34-10763 *Keraamiset laatat, laatoitukset*

RT 35-10500 Poltetut tiilet. Muuraustarvikkeet

Fédération Européenne des Fabricants de Tuiles et de Briques (TBE)—www.cerameunie.net

Fédération Belge de la Brique—www.brique.be

Kalk-og Teglvaerksforeningen af 1893—www.byg-i-tegl.dk, www.mur-tag.dk

Bundesverband der Deutschen Ziegelindustrie e.V.—
www.ziegel.de
Arbeitsgemeinschaft Pflasterklinker e.V.—www.pflaster-
klinker.de
Arbeitsgemeinschaft Ziegelelementbau im Bundesverband der
Deutschen Ziegelindustrie e.V.—www.Ziegelelementbau.de
Forschungsstelle der Deutschen Ziegelindustrie e.V.—
www.ziegel-forschung.de
Institut für Ziegelforschung e.V.—www.izf.de
Deutsche Gesellschaft für Mauerwerksbau e. V.—
www.dgfm.de
Bauhaus-Universität Weimar, Fakultät Bauingenieurwesen,
Fachgebiet Aufbereitung von Baustoffen und Wiederverwen-
dung—www.uni-weimar.de/Bauing/aufber/
Fédération Française des Tuiles et de Briques—www.fftb.org
Association of Greek Heavy Clay Industries—www.sevk.gr
The Brick Development Association Ltd. BDA—www.brick.org.uk
Associazione Nazionale degli Industriali die Laterizi, ANDIL-
Assolaterizi—www.laterizio.it
Koninklijk Verbond van Nederlandse Baksteenfabrikanten—
www.knb-baksteen.nl
Verband Österreichischer Ziegelwerke—www.ziegel.at
Zwiazek Pracownikow Ceramiki Budowlanej i Silikatow—
www.zwiazek.org.pl
APICER—Portuguese Association of Ceramic Industry—
www.apicer.pt
CC Höganäs Byggkeramik AB—www.cchoganas.se
Verband Schweizerische Ziegelindustrie. VSZ—www.domo-
terra.ch
HISPALYT Asociación Española de Fabricantes de Ladrillos y
Tejas de Arcilla Cocida—www.hispalyt.es
Ceramic & reractory Manufacturers´ Associacion—www.turkish-
ceramics.com
Cihlarsky svaz Cech a Mravy—www.cscm.cz
Magyar Téglás Szövetség—www.teglapont.hu

1.7 CONCRETE

Baus, Ursula: *Sichtbeton—Architektur, Konstruktion, Detail.*
Dt. Verlags-Anstalt, Munich 2007
Collectif. Presses Polytechniques et Universitaires Romandes:
Construire avec les bétons. Le Moniteur, Lausanne 2000.
Kind-Barkauskas, Friedbert (ed.): *Beton und Farbe—Farbsys-
teme, Ausführung, Instandsetzung.* DVA, 2003
Kind-Barkauskas, Friedbert; Kauhsen, Bruno; Polonyi, Stefan:
Concrete Construction Manual. Birkhäuser, Basel 2002
Peck, Martin: *Technik des Sichtbetons—Praktische Hinweise zur
Planung und Ausführung glatter Sichtbetonflächen.* Verlag Bau +
Technik, Düsseldorf 2007

EN 196 Methods of testing cement
EN 197 1-2 Cement
EN 206 1-3 Concrete
EN 450 Fly ash concrete
EN 12878 Pigments for the colouring of building materials
based on cement and/or lime
DIN 51043 Trass
DIN 1164 Zement mit besonderen Eigenschaften
DIN 1100 Hartstoffe für zementgebundene Hartstoffestriche
DS 400 Betonvarer
DS 423 Betonprøvning, 45 delstandarder fra forskellige år
DS 481 Beton materialer
RT 31-10066 Mosaiikkibetoni, yleiset laatuvaatimukset

ÖNORM B 3310 Zement für Bauzwecke
ÖNORM B 4200-10 Beton—Teil 10: Herstellung, Verwendung
und Gütenachweis
ÖNORM B 4710-1 Beton—Teil 1: Festlegung, Herstellung, Verwendung und Konformitätsnachweis

Deutscher Ausschuss für Stahlbeton:
- *Richtlinie selbstverdichtender Beton*
- *Richtlinie Beton mit verlängerter Verarbeitungszeit*

Deutscher Beton Verein:
- *Merkblatt Sichtbeton*
- *Merkblatt Betondeckung und Bewehrung*
- *Merkblatt Trennmittel für Beton*
- *Merkblatt Stahlfaserbeton*
- *Merkblatt Glasfaserbeton für Fertigteile*

Österreichischer Betonverein:
- *Richtlinie Wasserundurchlässige Betonbauwerke—Weisse
Wannen,* March issue 1999
- *Richtlinie Beton—Herstellung, Transport, Einbau, Gütenach-
weis,* February issue 1999
- *Richtlinie Innenschalenbeton,* March issue 1995

ÖVBB Richtlinie: *Geschalte Betonflächen (Sichtbeton)*

Belægningsgruppen Dansk Beton—
www.belaegningsfraktionen.dk
Deutscher Ausschuss für Stahlbeton (DAfStb)—www.dafstb.de
Deutscher Beton Verein—www.betonverein.de
Pihakivi—www.pihakivi.com
Suomen Betonitieto Oy—www.betoni.com
Österreichische Vereinigung für Beton- und Bautechnik—
www.concrete-austria.com
Bundesverbände der Deutschen Zement-, Transportbeton- und
Betonfertigteilindustrie—www.beton.org
Verein Deutscher Zementwerke e.V.—www.vdz-online.de

1.8 METALS

Collectif: *Construire avec les aciers.* Le Moniteur, Paris 2002
Friedrich, Wilhelm: *Tabellenbuch Bau und Holztechnik.* Dümm-
lers Verlag, Bonn 1974/1983
Grimm, Friederich: *Stahlbau im Detail.* Weka Baufachverlag,
Augsburg 1994
Euro Inox (ed.): *Guide to Stainless Steel Finishes.* Brussels 2005
Kindmann, Rolf (ed.): *Stahlbau kompakt: Bemessungshilfen,
Profiltabellen.* Stahleisen, Düsseldorf 2006
LeCuyer, Annette: *Stahl & Co. Neue Strategien für Metalle in der
Architektur,* Birkhäuser Verlag, Basel 2003
Lefteri, Chris: *Metals. Materials for Inspirational Design.* RotoVi-
sion, Hove 2004
Reichel, Alexander et al.: *Building with Steel.* Institut für inter-
nationale Architektur-Dokumentation, Munich 2006
Schneider, Ulrich; Bruckner, Heinrich; Bölcskey, Elmar: *Alumi-
nium / Glas—Baustoffe und ihre Anwendung.* Vol. 1. Springer,
Vienna 2002
Schneider-Bürger, Martha: *Stahlbau-Profile.* Stahleisen, Düs-
seldorf 2004
Schulitz, Helmut C.; Sobek, Werner; Habermann, Karl J.: *Steel
Construction Manual.* Institut für internationale Architektur-
Dokumentation und Deutscher Stahlbau-Verband (publ.).
Birkhäuser Verlag, Basel, 2000 (in French: *Construire en acier.*
Presses Polytechniques et Universitaires Romandes, 2003)

EN ISO 1461 Hot dip galvanized coatings on fabricated iron and steel articles—Specifications and test methods
EN ISO 3506 Mechanical properties of corrosion-resistant stainless steel fasteners—Part 2: Nuts
EN ISO 12944-1 Paints and varnishes—Corrosion protection of steel structures by protective paint systems—Part 1: General introduction
EN ISO 12944-2 Paints and varnishes—Corrosion protection of steel structures by protective paint systems—Part 2: Classification of environments
EN ISO 12944-5 Paints and varnishes—Corrosion protection of steel structures by protective paint systems—Part 5: Protective paint systems
EN 10020 Definition and classification of grades of steel, 2000
EN 1172 Copper and copper alloys—Sheet and strip for building purposes
EN 1179 Zinc and zinc alloys—Primary zinc
EN 1560 Founding—Designation system for cast iron—Material symbols and material numbers
EN 1561 Founding—Grey cast irons
EN 1562 Founding—Malleable cast irons
EN 1563 Founding—Spheroidal graphite cast irons
EN 10017 Steel rod for drawing and/or cold rolling—Dimensions and tolerances
EN 10025-1 Hot rolled products of structural steels—Part 1: General technical delivery conditions
EN 10025-2 Hot rolled products of structural steels—Part 2: Technical delivery conditions for non-alloy structural steels
EN 10025-3 Hot rolled products of structural steels. Part 3: Technical delivery conditions for normalized/normalized rolled weldable fine grain structural steels
EN 10025-4 Hot rolled products of structural steels—Part 4: Technical delivery conditions for thermomechanical rolled weldable fine grain structural steels
EN 10025-5 Hot rolled products of structural steels—Part 5: Technical delivery conditions for structural steels with improved atmospheric corrosion resistance
EN 10027-1 Designation systems for steels—Part 1: Steel names
EN 10027-2 Designation systems for steel; numerical system
EN 10056-1 Structural steel equal and unequal leg angles—Part 1: Dimensions
EN 10079 Definition of steel products
EN 10080 Steel for the reinforcement of concrete—Weldable reinforcing steel—General
EN 10088-1 Stainless steels—Part 1: List of stainless steels
EN 10088-2 Stainless steels—Part 2: Technical delivery conditions for sheet/plate and strip of corrosion resisting steels for general purposes
EN 10088-3 Stainless steels—Part 3: Technical delivery conditions for semi-finished products, bars, rods, wire, sections and bright products of corrosion resisting steels for general purposes
EN 10088-4 Stainless steels—Part 4: Technical delivery conditions for sheet/plate and strip of corrosion resisting steels for construction purposes
EN 10264-4 Steel wire and wire products—Steel wire for ropes—Part 4: Stainless steel wire
EN 10340 Steel castings for structural uses
RT 39-10260 Sinkitys teräksen suojana
RT 39-10367 Kuparimetallit
RT 39-10451 Alumiini

Stahl-Informations-Zentrum:
- *Merkblatt 434—Wetterfester Baustahl.* Düsseldorf 2004
- *Merkblatt 329—Korrosionsschutz durch Feuerverzinken (Stückverzinken).* Düsseldorf 2001

Institut Feuerverzinken GmbH: *Korrosionsschutz durch Duplex-Systeme (Feuerverzinken + Beschichten).* Düsseldorf o.J.

Wirtschaftsvereinigung Metall—www.wvmetalle.de
Metallic colour system—www.mcscolour.com
Natural Color Systems—www.ncscolour.com
RAL Deutsches Institut für Gütesicherung und Kennzeichnung e. V.—www.ral.de
EAA—European Aluminium Association—www.eaa.net
OECAM—Organisation of European Copper Alloy Ingot Makers—www.oecam.org
Gesamtverband der Aluminiumindustrie e.V.—www.aluinfo.de
www.copperinfo.com
www.kupfer-institut.de
www.oecam.org
www.kupfer-institut.de
Access Steel—www.access-steel.com
Acier construction—www.acierconstruction.com
Associazione fra i Costruttori in Acciaio Italiani—www.acaiacs.it
Bauen mit Stahl e.V.—www.bauen-mit-stahl.de
Bouwen met Staal—www.bouwenmetstaal.nl
Centre Technique Industriel de la Construction Métallique—www.cticm.eu
Deutscher Ausschuss für Stahlbau. DASt—www.deutscher-stahlbau.de
European Convention for Constructional Steelwork—www.steelconstruct.com
Euro Inox—The European Stainless Steel Development Association—www.euro-inox.org
Informationsstelle Edelstahl Rostfrei—www.edelstahl-rostfrei.de
Informationsstelle für nichtrostende Stähle SWISS INOX—www.swissinox.ch
Stahlbau Zentrum Schweiz / Centre suisse de la construction métallique / Centrale svizzera per le costruzioni in acciaio—www.szs.ch
Stahl-Informations-Zentrum—www.stahl-info.de
Institut Feuerverzinken—www.feuerverzinken.com
European General Galvanizers Association (EGGA)—www.egga.com

International Zinc Association (IZA)—www.zincforlife.org/
Initiative Zink—www.initiative-zink.de

1.9 OTHER BUILDING MATERIALS
Plastics

Elias, Hans-Georg: *An Introduction to Plastics.* Wiley-VCH 2003
Lefteri, Chris: *The Plastic Handbook.* RotoVision, Hove 2008
Schwarz, Otto; Ebeling, Friedrich-Wolfhard: *Kunststoffkunde.* Vogel, Würzburg 2007
Ashby, Mike; Johnson, Kara: *Materials and Design.* 3rd edition, Butterworth-Heinemann, Oxford 2004
Braun, Dietrich: *Kunststofftechnik für Einsteiger.* Carl Hanser Verlag, Munich, Vienna 2003
Domininghaus, Hans: *Die Kunststoffe und ihre Eigenschaften.* VDI-Verlag, 5th edition, Düsseldorf 1999
Ehrenstein, Gottfried W.: *Mit Kunststoffen konstruieren.* 2nd edition, Carl Hanser Verlag, Munich, Vienna 2001

Erhard, Gunter: *Konstruieren mit Kunststoffen*. Carl Hanser Verlag, Munich, Vienna 1993

Flemming, M.; Ziegmann, G.; Roth, S.: *Faserverbundbauweisen—Fertigungsverfahren mit duroplastischer Matrix*. Springer Verlag, Berlin and Heidelberg 1999

Franck, Adolf: *Kunststoff-Kompendium*. 5th edition, Vogel Fachbuchverlag, Würzburg 2000

Lefteri, Chris: *The Plastic Handbook*. RotoVision, Hove 2008

Lörcks, Jürgen: *Biologisch abbaubare Kunststoffe*. Fachagentur Nachwachsende Rohstoffe e.V., 2003

Saechtling, Hansjürgen; Oberbach, Karl: *Kunststoff Taschenbuch*. 28th edition, Carl Hanser Verlag, Munich and Vienna 2001

Schwarz, Otto: *Kunststoffkunde*. 6th edition, Vogel Verlag, Würzburg 2002

Wintermantel, Erich; Ha, Suk-Woo: *Biokompatible Werkstoffe und Bauweisen*. Springer Verlag, Leipzig 1998

Bitumen and asphalt

Beratungsstelle für Gussasphalt e.V. (publ.): *Informationen über Gussasphalt*. Bonn 1998

Zardini, Mirko: *Asfalto: il carattere della città*. Mondadori Electa, Milan 2003

Glass

Achilles, Andreas et al.: *Glasklar—Produkte und Technologien zum Einsatz von Glas in der Architektur*. Deutsche Verlags-Anstalt, Munich 2003

Flachglas AG (publ.): *Das Glashandbuch*. 1982

Klindt, Ludwig B. and Klein, Wolfgang: *Glas als Baustoff*. Verlagsgesellschaft R. Müller, Cologne 1977

Lefteri, Chris: *Glass*. RotoVision, Hove 2002

Schittich, Christian et al.: *Glass Construction Manual*. 2nd revised and extended edition, Birkhäuser Verlag, Basel 2006

Schneider, Ulrich; Bruckner, Heinrich; Bölcskey, Elmar: *Aluminium / Glas—Baustoffe und ihre Anwendung*. Volume 1. Springer, Vienna 2002

Bitumen and asphalt

EN 12591 Bitumen and bituminous binders—Specifications for paving grade bitumens

EN 13108-1 bis 8 Bituminous mixtures—Material specifications

Glas

EN 572-1 Glass in building—Basic soda lime silicate glass products—Part 1: Definitions and general physical and mechanical properties

EN 572-2 Glass in building—Basic soda lime silicate glass products—Part 2: Float glass

RT 38-10316 Lasilevyt, paksuuden mitoitus

RT 38-10901 Rakennuslasit, tasolasit

Plastics

Arbeitsgemeinschaft PVC und Umwelt e.V.—www.agpu.de

Arbeitsgemeinschaft Verstärkte Kunststoffe e.V.—www.avk-tv.de

Deutsche Kautschuk-Gesellschaft e.V.—www.rubber-dkg.de

DVS—Deutscher Verband für Schweissen und verwandte Verfahren e.V.—www.die-verbindungs-spezialisten.de

Fachverband Schaumkunststoffe e. V.—www.fsk-vsv.de

Gesamtverband kunststoffverarbeitende Industrie e.V.—www.gkv.de

Kunststoff-Portal der Schweiz—www.kunststoff-schweiz.ch

Bitumen and asphalt

Eurobitume, The European Bitumen Association—www.eurobitume.org

Arbeitsgemeinschaft der Bitumenindustrie—www.arbit.de

Aspahltberatung—www.asphaltberatung.de

vdd Industrieverband Bitumen-Dach- und Dichtungsbahnen e.V.—www.derdichtebau.de; www.vdd-technische-regeln.de

Verband der Belgischen Bitumenindustrie—www.beneluxbitume.org

Associatione Italiana Bitume Asfalto Strade—www.siteb.it

Glass

Bundesverband Flachglas (BF)—www.bundesverband-flachglas.de

PART 2 THE PRINCIPLES OF LOADBEARING STRUCTURES

Dierks, Klaus; Schneider, Klaus-Jürgen: *Baukonstruktion*. 2nd edition, Werner Verlag, Düsseldorf 1990

Engel, Heino: *Tragsysteme/Structure Systems*. Hatje Cantz Verlag, Ostfildern-Ruit 1999

Frohmann, Martin: *Tabellenbuch Landschaftsbau*. Eugen Ulmer, Stuttgart 2003

Goris, Alfons; Schneider, Klaus-Jürgen: *Bautabellen für Architekten mit Entwurfshinweisen und Beispielen*. 17th edition, Werner-Verlag, Cologne 2006

Hegger, Manfred; Auch-Schwelk, Volker; Fuchs, Matthias; Rosenkranz, Thorsten: *Construction Materials Manual*. Birkhäuser Verlag, Basel 2006

Meistermann, Alfred: *Tragsysteme*. Birkhäuser Verlag, Basel 2007

Neumann, Dietrich; Hestermann, Ulf; Rongen, Ludwig; Weinbrenner, Ulrich: *Frick/Knöll Baukonstruktionslehre 1*. 34th edition, Vieweg+Teubner 2006

Neumann, Dietrich; Hestermann, Ulf; Rongen, Ludwig; Weinbrenner, Ulrich: *Frick/Knöll Baukonstruktionslehre 2*. 33rd edition, Vieweg+Teubner 2008

Schneider, Klaus-Jürgen; Volz, Heinz: *Entwurfshilfen für Architekten und Bauingenieure*. Bauwerk Verlag GmbH, Berlin 2004

Simmer, Konrad: *Grundbau 1, Bodenmechanik, Erdstatische Berechnungen*. 19th edition , B. G. Teubner, Stuttgart 1994

Simmer, Konrad: *Grundbau 2, Baugruben und Gründungen*. 18th edition , B. G. Teubner, Stuttgart 1999

Smoltczyk, Ulrich: *Grundbau-Taschenbuch, Teil 1–3*. 6th edition, Ernst & Sohn, Berlin 2001

Wetzell, Otto W.: *Wendehorst Bautechnische Zahlentafeln*. 32nd edition , B. G. Teubner, Wiesbaden 2007

Zilch, Konrad; Diederichs, Claus Jürgen; Katzenbach, Rolf: *Handbuch für Bauingenieure*. Springer Verlag, Berlin Heidelberg 2002

EN ISO 898-1 Mechanical properties of fasteners made of carbon steel and alloy steel—Part 1: Bolts, screws and studs

EN ISO 4034 Hexagon nuts—Product grade C

EN ISO 22475-1 Geotechnical investigation and testing—Sampling methods and groundwater measurements—Part 1: Technical principles for execution

EN ISO 22476-1 Geotechnical investigation and testing—Field testing—Part 1: Electrical cone and piezocone penetration tests

EN ISO 22476-2 Geotechnical investigation and testing—Field testing—Part 2: Dynamic probing

EN ISO 22476-3 Geotechnical investigation and testing—Field testing—Part 3: Standard penetration test
EN ISO 4762 Hexagon socket head cap screws
EN 287 Qualification test of welders—Fusion welding
EN 1991 Actions on structures
EN 1992 (EC 2) Design of concrete structures
EN 1993 (EC3) Design of steel structures
EN 1995 (EC 5) Design of timber structures
EN 1996 (EC 6) Design of masonry structures
EN 1997 (EC 7) Geotechnical design
EN 14399-4 High-strength structural bolting assemblies for preloading—Part 4: System HV—Hexagon bolt and nut assemblies
EN 14399-6 High-strength structural bolting assemblies for preloading—Part 6: Plain chamfered washers

DIN 1045-1 bis 3 Tragwerke aus Beton, Stahlbeton und Spannbeton
DIN 1052 Entwurf, Berechnung und Bemessung von Holzbauwerken—Allgemeine Bemessungsregeln und Bemessungsregeln für den Hochbau
DIN 1054 Baugrund—Sicherheitsnachweise im Erd- und Grundbau
DIN 1055 Einwirkungen auf Tragwerke
DIN 4021 Baugrund; Aufschluss durch Schürfe und Bohrungen sowie Entnahme von Proben
DIN 18127 Baugrund—Untersuchung von Bodenproben—Proctorversuch
DIN 18134 Baugrund; Versuche und Versuchsgeräte—Plattendruckversuch
DIN 18800 Stahlbauten
ÖNORM B 4418—Erd- und Grundbau: Untersuchung von Bodenproben; Proctorversuch

Forschungsgesellschaft für Strassen- und Verkehrswesen (FGSV) (publ.):
- RStO 01, Richtlinien für die Standardisierung des Oberbaues von Verkehrsflächen. FGSV Verlag, Cologne 2001
- ZTV E-StB 97, Zusätzliche Technische Vertragsbedingungen und Richtlinien für Erdarbeiten im Strassenbau. FGSV Verlag, Cologne 1997

PART 3 CONSTRUCTIONS, GENERALLY

Armbuster, Georg et al. (eds.): Regelgerechte Bauausführung im Garten-, Landschafts- und Sportplatzbau. WEKA Baufachverlag, Augsburg from 1999
Asensio Cerver, Francisco: Landscape Architecture: Urban Space Details. Whitney Library of Design, New York 1998
Basal, Prof. Dr. Metin; Özdemir, Dr. Aydin: Sustainable Site Design Approaches. (Turkish title: SURDURULEBILIR PEYZAJ TASARIM YAKLASIMLARI), Ankara University Publishing 2008
Beier, Harm-Eckart; Niesel, Alfred; Petzold, Heiner: Lehr-Taschenbuch für den Garten-, Landschafts- und Sportplatzbau. Ulmer Verlag, Stuttgart 2003
Blake, James: Introduction to Landscape Design and Construction. Gower Publishing, Brookfield 1999
Boyer, Annie; Rojat-Lefebvre, Elisabeth: Aménager les espaces publics. Le Moniteur, Paris 1994.
Ching, Francis D.K.: Bildlexikon der Architektur. Campus Verlag, Frankfurt and New York 1996
Frick, Otto; Knöll, Karl; Neumann, Dietrich: Baukonstruktionslehre—Teil 2. Teubner, Stuttgart 2003

Frohmann, Martin (ed.): Tabellenbuch Landschaftsbau. Ulmer Verlag, Stuttgart 2003
Harris, Charles W.; Dines, Nicholas T.: Time-Saver Standards for Landscape Architecture: Design and Construction Data. Second Edition, McGraw-Hill Publishing Company, New York 1998
Hopper, Leonard J.: Landscape Architectural Graphic Standards. Hoboken, John Wiley & Sons 2007
Jørgensen, Kim Tang; Holgersen, Søren; Stausholm, Anne Fischer; Meyle, Eva: Danske Anlægsgartnere: Normer og Vejledning i anlægsgartnerarbejde. 2006
Mc Leod, Virginia: Detail in Contemporary Landscape Architecture. Laurence King Publishing Ltd., London 2008
Mahabadi, Mehdi: Konstruktionsdetails im Garten- und Landschaftsbau. Vieweg Verlagsgesellschaft, Wiesbaden and Berlin 1996
Niesel, Alfred (ed.): Bauen mit Grün—Die Bau- und Vegetationstechnik des Landschafts- und Sportplatzbaus. Ulmer Verlag, Stuttgart 2003
Sauter, David: Landscape Construction. Delmar Learning, New York 2005
Thompson, Ian H.; Dam, Torben; Nielsen, Jens Balsby (eds.): European Landscape Architecture—Best Practice in Detailing. Taylor & Francis, London 2007

ÖNORM L 1111 Gartengestaltung und Landschaftsbau—Technische Ausführung
SIA 318 Garten- und Landschaftsbau

Bundesverband Garten-, Landschafts- und Sportplatzbau e. V. (BGL)—www.galabau.de
The Landscape Research, Development & Construction Society (Forschungsgesellschaft Landschaftsentwicklung und Landschaftsbau e.V. - FLL)—www.f-l-l.de/english.html

3.1 GROUND MODELING AND EARTHWORKS

Dachroth, Wolfgang R.: Handbuch der Baugeologie und Geotechnik. Springer, 2002
Eymer, Wilfrid: Grundlagen der Erdbewegung. Kirschbaum, 2nd edition, Bonn 2006
Florineth, Florin: Pflanzen statt Beton. Patzer Verlag, Berlin 2004
Floss, Rudolf: ZTVE—StB 94, Kommentar mit Kompendium Erd- und Felsbau. Kirschbaum Verlag, Bonn 1997
Müller-Rochholz, Jochen: Geokunststoffe im Erd- und Verkehrswegebau. 2nd edition, Werner, Neuwied 2008
Müller-Rochholz, Jochen: Geokunststoffe im Erd- und Strassenbau. Werner, Düsseldorf 2005
Deutsche Gesellschaft für Geotechnik (DGGT): Empfehlungen für Bewehrungen aus Geokunststoffen (EBGEO). Wiley-VCH Verlag, Weinheim GmbH 1997
Petschek, Peter: Grading for Landscape Architects and Architects. Birkhäuser Verlag, Basel 2008
Schmidt, Hans-Henning: Grundlagen der Geotechnik. 3rd edition, Teubner B.G. GmbH, 2006
DIN 4124 Baugruben und Gräben. Böschungen, Verbau, Arbeitsraumbreiten
DIN 18300 Erdarbeiten
DIN 18918 DIN 18918 Vegetationstechnik im Landschaftsbau—Ingenieurbiologische Sicherungsbauweisen—Sicherungen durch Ansaaten, Bepflanzungen, Bauweisen mit lebenden und nicht lebenden Stoffen und Bauteilen, kombinierte Bauweisen
ÖNORM B 2205 Erdarbeiten—Werkvertragsnorm

RT 81-10590 Routasuojausrakenteet
SN 640 581 Erdbau, Boden; Grundlagen
SIA 318 Garten- und Landschaftsbau

Saxon Textile Research Institute—www.geokunststoffe.com/en

3.2 PATHS AND SQUARES

Deutscher Asphaltverband (DAV) (publ.): *Ausschreiben von As-phaltarbeiten.* Bonn 2003
Eifert, Helmut: *Strassenbau heute—Tragschichten.* Verlag Bau+Technik, Düsseldorf 2006
Eifert, Vollpracht, Hersel: *Strassenbau heute—Betondecken.* Verlag Bau+Technik, Düsseldorf 2004
Holgersen, Søren; Dam, Torben: *Befæstelser.* Forlaget Grønt Miljø 2006
Littlewood, Michael: *Landscape Detailing Vol. 2: Surfaces.* 3rd edition, Architectural Press, 1993
Richter, Dirk: *Monolithische Betonböden.* Vol S 13, Landschafts-entwicklung und Umweltforschung, Schriftenreihe der Fakultät Architektur Umwelt Gesellschaft, TU Verlag, Berlin 2003
Stolze Møller, C. J.: *Brolæggerfaget.* Erhvervsskolernes Forlag 1984
Thagesen, Bent: *Veje og Stier.* Polyteknisk Forlag 1998

EN 1338 Concrete paving blocks—Requirements and test methods
EN 1339 Concrete paving flags—Requirements and test methods
EN 1340 Concrete kerb units; Requirements and test methods
EN 1341 Slabs of natural stone for external paving—Require-ments and test methods
EN 1342 Setts of natural stone for external paving—Require-ments and test methods
EN 1343 Kerbs of natural stone for external paving—Require-ments and test methods
EN 1344 Clay pavers—Requirements and test methods
EN 13285 Unbound mixtures—Specifications
EN 13877 Concrete pavements
EN 14877 Synthetic surfaces for outdoor sports areas—Specification
DIN 18035–5 Sportplätze, Tennenflächen
DIN 18300 Erdarbeiten
DIN 18315 Verkehrswegebauarbeiten, Oberbauschichten ohne Bindemittel
DIN 18316 Verkehrswegebauarbeiten, Oberbauschichten mit hydraulischen Bindemitteln
DIN 18317 Verkehrswegebauarbeiten, Oberbauschichten aus Asphalt
DIN 18318 Verkehrswegebauarbeiten, Pflasterdecken, Platten-beläge, Einfassungen
ÖNORM B 2214 Pflasterarbeiten—Werkvertragsnorm
ÖNORM B 2606-2 Sportplatzbeläge—Teil 2: Tennenbeläge
Forschungsgesellschaft für Straßen- und Verkehrswesen (FGSV) (publ.):
- *RStO 01, Richtlinien für die Standardisierung des Oberbaues von Verkehrsflächen.* FGSV Verlag, Cologne 2001
- *RuA-StB, Richtlinien für die umweltverträgliche Anwendung von industriellen Nebenprodukten und Recycling-Baustoffen im Strassenbau.* FGSV Verlag, Cologne 2001
- *TL Gestein StB 04, Technische Lieferbedingungen für Gesteins-körnungen im Strassenbau.* FGSV Verlag, Cologne 2004
- *TL Min-StB 2000, Technische Lieferbedingungen für Mineral-stoffe im Strassenbau (Gesteinskörnungen und Werksteine im Strassenbau).* FGSV Verlag, Cologne 2000
- *ZTV Asphalt-StB 01, Zusätzliche Technische Vertragsbedin-gungen und Richtlinien für den Bau von Fahrbahndecken aus Asphalt.* FGSV Verlag, Cologne 2001
- *ZTV Beton-StB 01, Zusätzliche Technische Vertragsbedingun-gen und Richtlinien für den Bau von Fahrbahndecken aus Beton.* FGSV Verlag, Cologne 2001
- *ZTV Pflaster-StB 06, Zusätzliche Technische Vertragsbedin-gungen und Richtlinien zur Herstellung von Pflasterdecken, Plat-tenbelägen und Einfassungen.* FGSV Verlag, Cologne 2006
- *ZTV T-StB 2002, Zusätzliche Technische Vertragsbedingungen und Richtlinien für Tragschichten im Strassenbau.* FGSV Verlag, Cologne 2002

Deutscher Asphaltverband (DAV) (publ.): *Gestalten mit Asphalt und Technik im Asphaltbau.* Bonn 2005

Deutscher Naturwerkstein Verband (DNV) (publ.):
- *Bautechnische Information Naturwerkstein Bodenbeläge, aussen.* Würzburg 2008
- *Bautechnische Information Naturwerkstein Mörtel für Aussen-arbeiten.* Würzburg 1996
- *Merkblatt Pflasterdecken und Plattenbeläge aus Naturstein für Verkehrswegeflächen.* Würzburg 2002

3.3 STEPS

Baus, Ursula; Siegele, Klaus: *Stahltreppen. Konstruktion, Gestalt, Beispiel.* Deutsche Verlags-Anstalt, Stuttgart 1999
Blondel, François: *Cours d'architecture.* Paris 1683
Daidalos. *Extreme der Topografie, vol. 63.* Bertelsmann Fach-zeitschriften GmbH, Gütersloh 1997
Detail—Zeitschrift für Architektur + Baudetail. *Stairs.* Ausgabe 4/2002. Institut für internationale Architektur-Dokumentation GmbH & Co. KG
Ehrmann, Walter; Nutsch, Wolfgang: *Der Holztreppenbau.* Verlag Europa Lehrmittel, Haan-Gruiten 2004
Hartisch, Karl: *Treppen in Stahl, Beton und Holz.* Karl Krämer, Stuttgart and Zurich 1993
Mader, Günter: *Kleine Mathematik des Treppenbaus.* In: Der Gar-tenbau, issue 35/2002
Mielke, Friedrich: *Handbuch der Treppenkunde.* Th. Schäfer, Hanover 1993.
Pech, Anton; Kolbitsch, Andreas: *Treppen / Stiegen. Baukonst-ruktionen vol. 10.* Springer, Vienna 2005
Gut, D.: Gedankengänge. In: Deplazes, Andrea: *Architektur kon-struieren.* Birkhäuser Verlag, Basel 2005
Informationsstelle Edelstahl Rostfrei: *Geländer und Treppen aus Edelstahl.* Rostfrei, Dokumentation 871, Düsseldorf 1998

EN 14076 Timber stairs. Terminology
DIN 18065-1 Treppen in Gebäuden
DS 105-E. Udearealer for alle. Anvisning for planlægning og indretning med henblik på handicappedes færden.
ÖNORM B 1600 Barrierefreies Bauen—Planungsgrundsätze
ÖNORM B 5371 Gebäudetreppen—Abmessungen

Stahl-Informations-Zentrum:
- *Merkblatt 255—Aussentreppen aus Stahl*
- *Merkblatt 355—Entwurfshilfen für Stahltreppen*

3.4 RAILINGS AND FENCES

Baus, Ursula; Siegele, Klaus: *Stahltreppen.* Dt. Verl.-Anst., Stuttgart 1999

Boeminghaus, Dieter: *Zäune aus Holz: klassische Lösungen und neue Beispiele.* Callwey Verlag, Munich 1986

Gladischefski, Hans; Halmburger, Klaus: *Treppen in Stahl.* Bauverlag, Wiesbaden 1974

Goldelius, Hans-Walter: *Balkon- und Treppengeländer.* Verlagsgesellschaft Rudolf Müller GmbH & Co. KG, Cologne 2008

Littlewood, Michael: *Landscape Detailing Vol. 1: Enclosures.* 3rd edition, Elsevier Ltd., Oxford 1993

Mader, Günter; Zimmermann, Elke: *Zäune und Tore aus Holz und Metall.* DVA, Munich 2006

Warnes, Jon: *Living Willow Sculpture.* Search Press, 2000

DIN 18024-1 Barrierefreies Bauen—Teil 1: Strassen, Plätze, Wege, öffentliche Verkehrs- und Grünanlagen sowie Spielplätze (will be replaced by DIN 18030)

DIN 18024-2 Barrierefreies Bauen—Teil 2: Öffentlich zugängige Gebäude und Arbeitsstätten, Planungsgrundlagen (will be replaced by DIN 18030)

SIA 358 Geländer und Brüstungen

Documentation SIA D 0158 *Geländer und Brüstungen—Aspekte zur Anwendung der Norm SIA 358*

Bundesverband Metall: *Technische Richtlinie des Metallhandwerks—Geländer und Umwehrungen aus Metall.* Charles Colemann Verlag GmbH & Co KG, Lübeck; new edition planned for 2008

Schweizerische Beratungsstelle für Unfallverhütung (BFU): *Dokumentation "Geländer und Brüstungen"* (www.bfu.ch)

Stahl-Informations-Zentrum:

- *Merkblatt 255—Aussentreppen aus Stahl*
- *Merkblatt 355—Entwurfshilfen für Stahltreppen*

3.5 WALLS

Baetzner, Alfred: *Natursteinarbeiten.* Ulmer Verlag, Stuttgart 1991

Dachverband Lehm e.V. (publ.): *Lehmbau Regeln.* 2nd edition, Vieweg, Braunschweig/Wiesbaden 2002

Friederich, Volker: *Mauern aus Natursteinen.* Ulmer Verlag, Stuttgart 2001

Garner, Lawrence: *Dry Stone Walls.* Shire Publications Ltd., Buckinghamshire 2005

Kapfinger, Otto: *Martin Rauch—rammed earth. Lehm und Architektur.* Birkhäuser Verlag, Basel 2001

Littlewood, Michael: *Landscape Detailing Vol. 1: Enclosures.* 3rd edition, Elsevier Ltd., Oxford 1993

Mader, Günter; Zimmermann, Elke: *Mauern—Elemente der Garten- und Landschaftsarchitektur.* DVA Architektur, Munich 2008

Pfeifer, Günther et al.: *Mauerwerk Atlas.* 6th edition, Birkhäuser Verlag, Basel 2001

Radford, Andy: *A Guide to Dry Stone Walling.* Crowood Press Ltd., 2005

Reichel, Alexander; Hochberg, Anette; Köpke, Christine: *Plaster, Render, Paint and Coatings: Details, Products, Case Studies (Detail Practice Series).* Birkhauser Verlag, Basel 2005

Stiftung Umwelt Einsatz Schweiz SUS (ed.): *Trockenmauern im Berggebiet*—8. Internationaler Trockenmauerkongresses 29–31 August 2002, Visp, Schweiz (conference publication)

Tufnell, Richard; Rumpe, Frank; Ducommun, Alain; Hassenstein, Marianne: *Trockenmauern—Anleitung für den Bau und die Reparatur.* Hauptverlag, Bern 1996

EN 338 Structural timber—Strength classes

EN 998-2 Specification for mortar for masonry—Part 2: Masonry mortar

EN 1993- 5 (EC 3) Design of steel structures—Part 5: Piling

EN 1995-1-1 (EC5) Design of timber structures—
Part 1-1: General—Common rules and rules for buildings

EN 1996-1-1 (EC 6) Design of masonry structures—
Part 1-1: General rules for reinforced and unreinforced masonry structures

EN 14487-1 Sprayed concrete—Part 1: Definitions, specifications and conformity

EN 14487-2 Sprayed concrete—Part 2: Execution

DIN 1045 Tragwerke aus Beton und Stahlbeton—Teil 1: Bemessung und Konstruktion—Kommentierte Kurzfassung

DIN 1053-1 Mauerwerk—Teil 1: Rezeptmauerwerk; Berechnung und Ausführung

DIN 1053-2 Mauerwerk—Teil 2: Mauerwerk nach Eignungsprüfung; Berechnung und Ausführung

DIN 18330 Mauerarbeiten

DIN 18332 Naturwerksteinarbeiten

DIN 18515-1 Aussenwandbekleidungen—Teil 1: Angemörtelte Fliesen oder Platten; Grundsätze für Planung und Ausführung

DIN 18515-2 Aussenwandbekleidungen; Anmauerung auf Aufstandsflächen; Grundsätze für Planung und Ausführung

DIN 18516 Ausbruchlast am Ankerdornloch

DS 415 Norm for fundering

SIA 178 Natursteinmauerwerk

SIA 225 Mauerwerk aus künstlichen Steinen, Leistung und Lieferung

SIA 226 Natursteinmauerwerk, Leistung und Lieferung

SN 567 246 Natursteinarbeiten—Beläge, Bekleidungen und Werkstücke

SN 640 383 Mauertypen

SN 640 385 Fundamente

SN 640 386 Maueransichten

SN 640 387 Fugen

SN 640 388 Mauerkronen

SN 640 389 Entwässerung und Hinterfüllung

Bundesverband der Deutschen Ziegelindustrie (publ.): *Merkblatt 1-3.11 Freistehende Mauern—Einfriedungen, Sichtblenden, Schutzmauern.* Bonn 1994

Deutscher Natursteinverband:

- *Bautechnische Information Naturwerkstein: 1.1 Massiv- und Verblendmauerwerke.* 1996
- *Bautechnische Information Naturwerkstein: 1.6 Mörtel für Aussenarbeiten.* 1996
- *Bautechnische Information Naturwerkstein: 1.7 Bauchemische und bauphysikalische Einflüsse Aussenarbeiten.* 1995
- *Bautechnische Information Naturwerkstein: 4.1 Wissenswertes über Naturwerkstein.* 1996

Schweizer Ziegelindustrie (publ.): *Backstein Mauerwerk—Planung, Eigenschaften, Ausführung.* Schweizer Ziegelindustrie Informationsstelle, Zurich 1977

Dry Stone Walling Association of Great Britain (DSWA)—Handouts:

- *Notes on Building a Cairn*
- *Specification for simple Retaining Walls*
- *Butts for Shelter, Shooting or Watching*
- *Craftsman Certification Scheme*
- *Possible Grant Sources for Dry Stone Walling & Dyking*
- *Bee Boles*
- *Walls need Friends*
- *Working for the Professional Waller or Dyker*
- *Dry Stone Walls and Wildlife*

Dry Stone Walling Association of Great Britain—
www.dswa.org.uk
Bundesverband der Deutschen Ziegelindustrie—www.ziegel.de
Dachverband Lehm e.V.—www.dachverband-lehm.de
BetonMarketing Deutschland GmbH—www.beton.org
Verein Deutscher Zementwerke e.V.—www.vdz-online.de
Deutscher Beton- und Bautechnik-Verein e.V.—
www.betonverein.de
Fachverband Baustoffe und Bauteile für vorgehängte hinter-
lüftete Fassaden—www.fvhf.de
Gesamtverband Deutscher Holzhandel e.V.—
www.holzhandel.de
Stahl-Informations-Zentrum—www.stahl-info.de
Verband des Zimmerer- und Holzbaugewerbes Baden-
Württemberg—www.holzbau-online.de

3.6 SMALL STRUCTURES AND PERGOLAS

Engelmann, Fritz: *Kleine Holzbauwerke. Balkone, Pergolen,
Zäune, Wartehäuschen, konstruktiver Holzschutz.* Bruder,
Karlsruhe 1995
Jesberg, Paulgerd: *Lust zum Gartenhaus.* Coppenrath Verlag,
Münster 1995
Littlewood, Michael: *Landscape Detailing Vol. 3: Structures.*
3rd edition, Architectural Press, 1997
Niederstrasser, Michael; Spalink-Sievers, Johanna; Weddige, Rü-
diger: *Gartenhaus, Laube, Pergola.* Callwey Verlag, Munich 1986
Zentralverband des Deutschen Dachdeckerhandwerks—Fach-
verband Dach-, Wand- und Abdichtungstechnik e.V.: *Deutsches
Dachdeckerhandwerk—Regeln für Dachdeckungen.* Rudolf Mül-
ler Verlag, Cologne 2007

3.7 SMALL BRIDGES AND
3.8 WALKWAYS AND DECKS

Baus, Ursula: *Fussgängerbrücken: Konstruktion—Gestalt—
Geschichte.* Birkhäuser Verlag, Basel 2008
Euro Inox (ed.): *Pedestrian Bridges in Stainless Steel.* Brussels
2004
Hallman, Heinz W.; Rohn, Heinz W.; Lingnau, Günter: *Bauen mit
Holz in Park und Garten—Anregungen zur Gestaltung und Konst-
ruktion.* Callwey, Munich 1984.
Oster, Hans J. (ed.): *Fussgängerbrücken—Jörg Schlaich und
Rudolf Bergermann.* Catalogue for an exhibition at ETH Zürich,
Zurich 1992
Ruske, Wolfgang (ed.): *Aussenanlagen im Detail.* WEKA-Verlag,
Kissing 1987
Ruske, Wolfgang (ed.): *Bauten in der Landschaft.* WEKA-
Verlag, Kissing 1987
Stahl-Informations-Zentrum: *Fussgängerbrücken aus Stahl.
Dokumentation 577.* Düsseldorf 2004

3.9 PLANTING TECHNIQUES AND CARE
OF VEGETATION SURFACES

Ball, Liz; Anderson, Jim: *Composting.* Workman Publishing 1998
Frey, Wolfgang; Lösch, Rainer: *Lehrbuch der Geobotanik.* Fischer
Verlag, Stuttgart 1998
Greenwood, Pippa; Halstead, Andrew: *Dumont's Grosses
Gartenhandbuch Schädlinge & Krankheiten.* Dumont Verlag,
Cologne 1998
Greenwood, Pippa; Halstead, Andrew and The Royal Horticultu-
ral Society, *Pest & Diseases.* Dorling Kindersley, London, 1997
Kaiser, Klaus (1998): Pflanzen. Zur Rose die Staude. In: *Garten +
Landschaft,* 9/1998, pp. 23–24
Krüssmann, Gerd: *Taschenbuch der Gehölzverwendung: ein
Leitfaden für die richtige Verwendung der in den Baumschulen
erhältlichen Gehölze.* Parey Verlag, Berlin 1970
Lacher, Jean-Luc; Gelgon, Thierry: *Aménagement et maintenance
des surfaces végétales.* Tech.& Doc./Lavoisier, 2000
Lapouge-Déjean, Brigitte; Klecka, Virginie : *Jardin sans eau ! Re-
portages, idées, portraits de plantes.* Edisud, Aix-en-Provence,
2007
Le Bret, Jean: *Les Plantes vivaces de lumière.* Paris, 1989
Niesel, Alfred (ed.): *Grünflächenmanagement. Dynamische Pfle-
ge von Grün.* Ulmer Verlag, Stuttgart 2006
Roloff, Andreas; Thiel, Andreas; Weiß, Henrik (Hrsg.): *Urbane
Gehölzverwendung im Klimawandel und aktuelle Fragen der
Baumpflege.* Selbstverlag der Fachrichtung Forstwissenschaft
der TU Dresden, Tharandt 2007
Ruyten, Frits: Der integrale Bepflanzungsplan. In: *Garten +
Landschaft,* 8/1997, pp. 29–31
Sachweh, Ulrich: *Grundlagen des Gartenbaues.* Ulmer Verlag,
Stuttgart 1985
Scheffer, Fritz; Schachtschabel, Paul: *Lehrbuch der Bodenkunde.*
Spektrum Akademischer Verlag, Heidelberg 2002
Schmidt, Cassian: Neue Pflegekonzepte für nachhaltige Stau-
denpflanzungen. *Stadt + Grün,* 3/2005, pp. 30–35
Schneidewind, Axel: *Vergleichsuntersuchung von Verankerungs-
methoden und Baumbindematerialien für Jungbäume.* In: Duje-
siefken, Dirk; Kockerbeck, Petra (ed.): *Jahrbuch der Baumpflege.*
Thalacker Verlag, Braunschweig, 2003, pp. 86–106

DIN 18916 Vegetationstechnik im Landschaftsbau—Pflanzen
und Pflanzarbeiten
DIN 18919 Vegetationstechnik im Landschaftsbau—Entwick-
lungs- und Unterhaltungspflege von Grünflächen
DIN 18920 Schutz von Bäumen, Pflanzenbeständen und Vege-
tationsflächen bei Baumassnahmen
ÖNORM B 2241 Gartengestaltung und Landschaftsbau
ÖNORM L 1040—Pflanzen-Vegetationstechnische Arbeiten
SN 640 577 a Schutz von Bäumen—Protection des arbres
SN 640 677 Alleebäume, Grundlagen
SN 640 678 Alleebäume, Baumartenwahl
FLL—Forschungsgesellschaft Landschaftsentwicklung und
Landschaftsbau e. V. (publ.): *Additional Technical Contractual
Terms and Guidelines for Tree Care,* 2004

ELCA European landscape contractors association—
www.elca.info/en
ISA International society of arboriculture—www.isa-arbor.com

Deutsche Dendrologische Gesellschaft e.V. DDG—
www.ddg-web.de

Perenne e. V. Verein für Staudenzüchtung und Sortimentsent-
wicklung—www.perenne.de
Staudensichtung des Bundes deutscher Staudengärtner—
www.staudensichtung.de
British association of landscape industries BALI—
www.bali.co.uk
Landscape Institute—www.landscapeinstitute.org
Österreichische Gartenbaugesellschaft—www.garten.or.at
Landwirtschaftskammer Österreich—www.landwirtschafts-
kammer.at
Bodenkundliche Gesellschaft der Schweiz—www.soil.ch/BGS
Bund Schweizer Baumpflege—www.baumpflege-schweiz.ch
Schweizerische Stiftung für die kulturhistorische und geneti-
sche Vielfalt von Pflanzen und Tieren—www.prospecierara.ch
Schweizer Dendrologische Gesellschaft—www.dendrolo-
gie.ch

3.10 LAWNS AND MEADOWS: LAYING OUT AND CARE

Beard, James B.: *Beards Turfgrass Encyclopedia: For Golf Cour-
ses, Grounds, Lawns, Sports Fields.* State University Press,
Michigan 2005
Brochard, Danierl: *Pelouses et gazons: les conseils d'un spécia-
liste pour choisir, installer et entretenir votre tapis vert.*
Hachette, Paris 1994
Ellenberg, Heinz: *Vegetation Mitteleuropas mit den Alpen.* Ulmer
Verlag, Stuttgart 1996
Gandert, Klaus; Bures, Frantisek: *Handbuch Rasen. Grund-
lagen—Anlage—Pflege.* Deutscher Landwirtschaftsverlag, 1992
Gandert, Klaus-Dietrich; Bures, Frantisek: *Handbuch Rasen.*
Deutscher Landwirtschaftsverlag, Hanover 1991
Hoppe, Frank: Rasen. *Anlage und Pflege von Zier- Gebrauchs-,
Sport- und Landschaftsrasen.* Ulmer Verlag, Stuttgart 1983
Jencks, Charles: *The Garden of Cosmic Speculation.* Frances
Lincoln Limited, London 2003—www.charlesjencks.com
Kauter, Dirk: *Entwicklung der Rasenkultur in Mitteleuropa—
Ein Überblick vom Mittelalter bis ins angehende 19. Jahrhun-
dert.* Köllen Druck und Verlag, Bonn 2002
Loyd, Christopher; Hunningher, Erica (eds.): *Meadows.* Timber
Press, Portland 2004
Orell, Christine: Skurriler Sommerflor. In: *Gartenpraxis* Nr.
5/2004, pp. 14–17

DIN 18035-2 Sportplätze Teil 2—Bewasserung von Rasen- und
Tennenflächen
DIN 18035-3 Sportplätze Teil 3—Entwässerung
DIN 18035-4 Sportplätze Teil 4—Rasenflächen
DIN 18917 Vegetationstechnik im Landschaftsbau—Rasen-
und Saatarbeiten
DIN 18918 Vegetationstechnik im Landschaftsbau—Ingeni-
eurbiologische Sicherungsbauweisen—Sicherungen durch
Ansaaten, Bepflanzungen, Bauweisen mit lebenden und nicht
lebenden Stoffen und Bauteilen, kombinierte Bauweisen
ÖNORM B 2605 Sportplätze—Planungsrichtlinien und Ausfüh-
rungshinweise
ÖNORM B 2606-1 Sportplatzbeläge—Rasenbeläge

FLL—Forschungsgesellschaft Landschaftsentwicklung und
Landschaftsbau e. V. (publ.):
- *Richtlinie für den Bau von Golfplätzen.* 2000
- *Empfehlung für Bau und Pflege von Flächen aus Schotterrasen.*
2000

ÖAG (Österr. Arbeitsgemeinschaft für Grünland u. Futterbau und
BAL Bundesamt für Alpenländische Landwirtschaft Gumpen-
stein) (publ.): Richtlinie für standortgerechte Begrünungen. 2000

Deutsche Rasengesellschaft (DRG)—www.rasengesell-
schaft.de
Société des Gazons Française—www.gazonsfg.org
EIGCA European Institute of Golf Course Architects—
www.eigca.org
The Sports Turf Research Institute—www.stri.co.uk

3.11 SURFACE DRAINAGE

Geiger, Wolfgang F.; Dreiseitl, Herbert: *Neue Wege für das
Regenwasser—Handbuch zum Rückhalt und zur Versickerung
von Regenwasser in Baugebieten.* Verlag R. Oldenbourg, Munich
2001.
Mahabadi, Mehdi: *Regenwasserversickerung. Planungsgrund-
sätze und Bauweisen.* Thalacker Medien, Braunschweig 2001
Heinrichs, Franz-Josef; Rickmann, Bernhard; Sondergeld,
Klaus-Dieter: *Gebäude- und Grundstücksentwässerung.
Planung und Ausführung. DIN 1986-100 und DIN EN 12056-4.*
Deutsches Institut für Normung e.V., Berlin, 2008
Sieker, Friedhelm; Kaiser, Mathias; Sieker, Heiko: *Dezentrale
Regenwasserbewirtschaftung im privaten, gewerblichen und
kommunalen Bereich. Grundlagen und Ausführungsbeispiele.*
Fraunhofer IRB Verlag, Stuttgart 2006

EN 124 Gully tops and manhole tops for vehicular and pedest-
rian areas
EN 752-1 Drain and sewer systems outside buildings—
Part 1: Generalities and definitions
EN 752-2 Drain and sewer systems outside buildings—
Part 2: Performance requirements
EN 752-3 Drain and sewer systems outside buildings—
Part 3: Planning
EN 1433 Drainage channels for vehicular and pedestrian areas.
Classification, design and testing requirements, marking and
evaluation of conformity
EN 1610 Construction and testing of drains and sewers
DIN 1986-100 Entwässerungsanlagen für Gebäude und Grund-
stücke—Teil 100: Zusätzliche Entwässerungsanlagen für Ge-
bäude und Grundstücke

Deutsche Vereinigung für Wasserwirtschaft, Abwasser und
Abfall e.V.:
- Arbeitsblatt DWA-A 117: *Bemessung von Regenrückhalteräu-
men.* 2006
- Arbeitsblatt DWA-A 138: *Planung, Bau und Betrieb von Anla-
gen zur Versickerung von Niederschlagswasser.* 2005
- Arbeitsblatt ATV-DVWK-A 156: *Regeln für den Kanalbetrieb—
Regenbecken und -entlastungen.* 2000
- Arbeitsblatt ATV-DVWK-A 157: *Bauwerke der Kanalisation.*
2000
- Arbeitsblatt ATV-A 166: *Bauwerke der zentralen Regenwas-
serbehandlung und -rückhaltung—Konstruktive Gestaltung und
Ausrüstung.* 1999

FLL—Forschungsgesellschaft Landschaftsentwicklung und
Landschaftsbau e. V. (publ.):
- *Empfehlung zur Versickerung und Wasserrückhaltung.* 2005
- *Richtlinie für die Planung, Ausführung und Unterhaltung von
begrünbaren Flächenbefestigungen.* 2008

3.12 WATER INSTALLATIONS

Bahamón, Alejandro: *Water Features.* Loft Publications, Barcelona 2007

Dreiseitl, Herbert; Grau, Dieter (eds.): *Waterscapes—Planning, Building and Designing with Water.* Birkhäuser Verlag, Basel, Berlin, Boston 2001

Dreiseitl, Herbert; Grau, Dieter; Ludwig, Karl H.C.: *New Waterscapes—Planning, Building and Designing with Water.* Birkhäuser Verlag, Basel, Berlin, Boston 2005

Junker, Lars: *Vand i haven.* Politiken forlag i samarbejde med Det Danske Haveselskab, 2007

Littlewood, Michael: *Landscape Detailing Vol. 4: Water.* 3rd edition, Elsevier Ltd., Oxford 2001

Lohmann, Michael: *Den frodige vandhave.* Skarv/Høst og Søn, 1993

Stadelmann, Peter: *Kommas bog om vand i haven.* Komma, 1989

Wachter, Karl; Bollerhey, Herbert; Germann, Theo: *Der Wassergarten.* Ulmer Verlag, Stuttgart 2005

Weixler, Richard; Hauer, Wolfgang: *Garten- u. Schwimmteiche— Bau, Bepflanzung, Pflege.* Leopold Stocker Verlag, Graz 1998

DIN 18195-1 to 10 Bauwerksabdichtungen, Teile 1–6

FLL—Forschungsgesellschaft Landschaftsentwicklung und Landschaftsbau e.V. (publ.):
- *Recommendations for the Planning, Construction, Servicing and Operation of Public Swimming and Bathing Pond Facilities, 2003*
- *Recommendations for the planning, construction, maintenance of private swimming and natural pools, 2006*

Internationale Gesellschaft für naturnahe Badegewässer— www.igb.cc

Schweizerischer Verband für naturnahe Badegewässer und Pflanzenkläranlagen—www.svbp.org

3.13 VERTICAL PLANTING

Alanko, Pentti; Kahila, Pirkko: *Köynnöskasvit.* Tammi, 2003

Althaus, Christoph: *Fassadenbegrünung. Ein Beitrag zu Risiken, Schäden und präventiver Schadensverhütung.* Patzer Verlag, Berlin, Hanover 1987

Baumann, Rudi: *Begrünte Architektur. Bauen und Gestalten mit Kletterpflanzen.* Callwey Verlag, Munich 1983

Blanc, Patrick: The Vertical Garden. In: *Nature and the City.* New York 2008. See also www.verticalgardenpatrickblanc.com/ 2008-07-14

Bundesverband Metall, Vereinigung Deutscher Metallhandwerke (publ.): *Fassadenbegrünung—Gestaltung, Bemessung, Ausführung.* Charles Coleman Verlag, Cologne 2000

Detail. Zeitschrift für Architektur + Baudetail: *Urban Planning Details.* Ausgabe 6/2004. Institut für internationale Architektur-Dokumentation GmbH & Co. KG, Munich

Dunnett, Nigel; Kingsbury, Noel: *Planting Green Roofs and Living Walls.* Portland, Oregon 2008

Gunkel, Rita: *Fassadenbegrünung. Kletterpflanzen und Klettergerüste.* Stuttgart 2004

Hoyland, John: Keep climbers in check. In: *Gardens Illustrated,* issue no. 127, July 2007, pp. 78–81

International Design: The Vertical Gardens of Patrick Blanc. In: *Gardens Illustrated,* issue no. 128, August 2007, pp. 86/87

Köhler, Manfred: *Fassaden- und Dachbegrünung.* Ulmer Verlag, Stuttgart 1993

Lambertini, Anna; Ciampi, Mario: *Vertical Gardens: Bringing the City to Life.* Thames & Hudson, London 2007

Minke, Gernot: *Häuser mit grünem Pelz—ein Handbuch zur Hausbegrünung.* Fricke, Frankfurt 1982

EN 13119 Curtain walling—Terminology; Trilingual version
EN 20273 Fasteners; clearance holes for bolts and screws.
EN 20898-2 Mechanical properties of fasteners; part 2: nuts with specified proof load values; coarse thread (ISO 898-2:1992)
EN 28839 Mechanical properties of fasteners; nonferrous metal bolts, screws, studs and nuts (ISO 8839:1986)
DIN 18515-1 Aussenwandbekleidungen—Teil 1: Angemörtelte Fliesen oder Platten; Grundsätze für Planung und Ausführung
DIN 18515-2 Aussenwandbekleidungen; Anmauerung auf Aufstandsflächen; Grundsätze für Planung und Ausführung
DS 410 Norm for belastning på konstruktioner
ÖNORM B 2241 Gartengestaltung und Landschaftsbau— Werkvertragsnorm
ÖNORM L 1110 Pflanzen—Güteanforderungen, Sortierungsbestimmungen
ÖNORM L 1111 Gartengestaltung und Landschaftsbau— Technische Ausführung

FLL (Forschungsgesellschaft Landschaftsentwicklung und Landschaftsbau e.V.):
- *Richtlinie für die Planung, Ausführung und Pflege von Fassadenbegrünungen mit Kletterpflanzen.* Bonn 2000

EFB-Europäische Föderation Bauwerksbegrünung— www.efb-bauwerksbegruenung.com
Associazione Italiana verde pensile (AIVEP)—www.aivep.org
Fachverband Bauwerksbegrünung e. V. (FBB)—www.fbb.de
Stadsingeniorens direktorat Kobenhavn—Grønne mure— www.vejpark2.kk.dk/publikationer/pdf/005_groenne_mure.pdf
Schweizerische Fachvereinigung Gebäudebegrünung (SFG)— www.sfg-gruen.ch
VBB Vereniging van Bouwwerk Begroeners—www.bouwwerk-begroeners.nl
VFB Verband für Bauwerksbegrünung—www.gruendach.at
ZEOSZ Zöldtetöepitök Országos Szövetsége—www.zeosz.hu

3.14 GREEN ROOFS

Ahrendt, Jana: *Historische Gründächer, Ihr Entwicklungsgang bis zur Erfindung des Eisenbetons.* Dissertation, TU Berlin, 2007

BGL (publ.): *Jahrbuch Dachbegrünung.* Thalacker Medien, Braunschweig 2002

Detail, Zeitschrift für Architektur + Baudetail, *Roof Construction,* Ausgabe 7–8/2002, Verlag Institut für internationale Architekturdokumentation, Munich

Dubbeling, M.; Bleuze, P.: *Begroeide daken,* Stuurgroep Experimenten Volkshuisvesting, Rotterdam 1999

Dunett Nigel; Kingsbury Noel: *Planting Green Roofs and Living Walls,* Timber Press, Portland OR, 2008

Ernst, Wolfgang: *Dachabdichtung Dachbegrünung, Fehler— Ursachen, Auswirkungen und Vermeidung,* Fraunhofer IRB Verlag, Stuttgart 2002

Garten + Landschaft, Themenheft Dachgrün, Ausgabe 10/2003, Callwey Verlag, Munich

Garten + Landschaft, Themenheft Eco Value, Ausgabe 1/2008, Callwey Verlag, Munich

Grützmacher, Bernd: *Grasdach und Dachbegrünung.* Callwey Verlag, Munich 1993

Hopper, Leonard J.: *Landscape Architectural Graphic Standards.* Hoboken, N.J., John Wiley & Sons (Chapter: Living Green Roofs and Landscapes over Structure pp. 713–23), 2007

Köhler, Manfred: *Fassaden- und Dachbegrünung.* Ulmer Verlag, Stuttgart 1993

Köhler, Manfred: *Gründächer international.* In: Stadt + Grün, 10/2006, pp. 54–56

Kolb, Walter; Schwarz, Tassilo: *Dachbegrünung, intensiv und extensiv.* Verlag Eugen Ulmer, Stuttgart 1999

Krupka, Bernd: *Dachbegrünung, Pflanzen- und Vegetationsanwendung an Bauwerken.* Verlag Eugen Ulmer, Stuttgart 1992

Møller, Angela Beck: *Det grønne tag.* Grønt miljøs småbøger 2003

Liesecke, H.-J.: *Extensive Dachbegrünung, Teil 1: Von den ersten Entwicklungsansätzen bis zur praktischen Umsetzung.* In: Stadt + Grün, 10/2006, p. 47 ff.; *Teil 2: Die Vermittlung von Forschungsergebnissen.* In: Stadt + Grün, 11/2006, p. 52 ff.

Liesecke/Krupka/Lösken/Brüggemann (publ.: FLL): *Grundlagen der Dachbegrünung.* Patzer Verlag, Hanover 1989

Loon, A. van: *Ruimte voor de stadsboom.* Blauwdruk, Wageningen 2003

Ngan, Goya: *Soka-Bau Green Roof Case Study,* Canada Mortgage and Housing Corporation (publ.) "Innovative Buildings" series, self-published/internet (www.cmhc.ca), Ottawa 2004

Osmundsen, Theodore: *Roof Gardens: History, Design, and Construction.* W.W. Norton & Company, New York, 1999

Peck, Steven; Kuhn Monica: *Design Guidelines for Green Roofs,* Canada Mortgage and Housing Corporation (publ.), self-published/internet (www.cmhc.ca), Ottawa n. y.

Snodgrass Edmund; Snodgrass Lucie: *Green Roof Plants, A Resource and Planting Guide.* Timber Press, Portland OR, 2006

Stifter, Roland: *Dachgärten, Grüne Inseln in der Stadt.* Verlag Eugen Ulmer, Stuttgart 1988

Teeuw, P.G.; Ravesloot, C.M.: *Begroeide daken in Nederland.* Delft University Press, Delft 1998

Werthmann, Christian: *Green Roof: A Case Study: Michael Van Valkenburgh Associates' Design for the Headquarters of the American Society of Landscape Architects.* Princeton Architectural Press, New York, 2007

DIN 18338 Dachdeckungs- und Dachabdichtungsarbeiten

DIN 18531 Dachabdichtungen; Begriffe, Anforderungen, Planungsgrundsätze (für Extensivbegrünungen)

DIN 18195 Bauwerksabdichtungen (für Intensivbegrünungen)

DIN 18531 Dachabdichtungen; Begriffe, Anforderungen, Planungsgrundsätze (für Extensivbegrünungen)

ÖNORM B 2209-1—Abdichtungsarbeiten für Bauwerke, Werkvertragsnorm

ÖNORM B 2209-2—Abdichtungsarbeiten für genutzte Dächer, Werkvertragsnorm

ONR 12 11 31 Qualitätssicherung im Grünraum—Gründach-Richtlinien für die Planung, Ausführung und Erhaltung, Vienna 2002

UNI 11235 Istruzioni per la progettazione, l'esecuzione, il controllo e la manutenzione di coperture a verde, Rome 2007

Bundesinnung der Dachdecker und Pflasterer Österreichs: *Richtlinien für die Ausführung von Flachdächern*

Internationale Förderation des Dachdeckerhandwerkes (IFD): *Richtlinien für die Planung und Ausführung von Dächern mit Abdichtungen (Flachdachrichtlinien)*

Forschungsgesellschaft Landschaftsentwicklung und Landschaftsbau (FLL): *Guideline for the Planning, Execution and Upkeep of Green-Roof Sites, 2002*

Schweizerische Fachvereinigung Gebäudebegrünung (SFG):
- *Gründachrichtlinie für Extensivbegrünung:* Teil 1: "Wasserhaushalt und Vegetation"
- *Gründachrichtlinie für Extensivbegrünung:* Teil 2: "Labelvergabe und Ökobilanz"
- *Empfehlung zur Pflege und zum Unterhalt von extensiven Dachbegrünungen*

Schweizerischer Ingenieur- und Architektenverein (SIA):
- *Empfehlung Nr. 493: Deklaration ökologischer Merkmale von Bauprodukten*
- *Empfehlung Nr. 271/2: Flachdächer zur Begrünung*

ASLA (American Society of Landscape Architects), "Green Roof Project"—www.asla.org/land/050205/greenroofcentral.html

Associazione Italiana Verde Pensile (AIVEP)—www.aivep.org

Deutscher Dachgärtner Verband e.V.—www.dachgaertnerverband.de

European Federation of Green Roof Associations (EFB)—www.efb-greenroof.eu

Fachvereinigung Bauwerksbegrünung (FBB)—www.fbb.de

Green Roofs for Healthy Cities North America—www.green-roofs.org

International Green Roof Association—www.igra-world.com

Livingroofs.org Ltd.—www.livingroofs.org

Österreichischer Verband für Bauwerksbegrünung—www.gruendach.at

Schweizerische Fachvereinigung Gebäudebegrünung (SFG)—www.sfg-gruen.ch

SGRA/SGRI—Scandinavian Green Roof Association/Institute—www.greenroof.se

Plattform zur Dachbegrünung—www.gruendaecher.de

Vereniging Bouwwerk Begroeners (V.B.B.)—www.bouwwerkbegroeners.nl

Zentralverband des Deutschen Dachdeckerhandwerks (ZVDH)—www.dachdecker.de

ZEOSZ Zöldtetöepitök Országos Szövetsége—www.zeosz.hu

3.15 SPECIAL ELEMENTS

Lighting elements

ASL Landscape Design Institute et al.: *Landscape Lighting Design Book.* Callwey Verlag, Munich 1998

Bean, Robert: *Lighting: Interior and Exterior.* Architectural Press, Oxford 2004

Egan, M. David; Olgyay, Victor W.: *Architectural Lighting.* McGraw-Hill, New York 2002

Flagge, Ingeborg: *Licht und Architektur 2000, Jahrbuch.* Rudolf Müller Verlag, Cologne 2002

Lange, Horst: *Handbuch der Beleuchtung.* ecomed Verlag, Landsberg 2002

Narboni, Roger; Jousse, François: *La Lumière urbaine: éclairer les espaces publics.* Le Moniteur, Paris 1995

Narboni, Roger: *La Lumière et le paysage: Créer des paysages nocturnes.* Le Moniteur, Paris 2003

Osborne, Michèle: *Lighting Gardens*. Mitchell Beazley, London 2005
Schricker, Rudolf: *Licht-Raum, Raum-Licht*. Deutsche Verlags-Anstalt (DVA), Stuttgart 1994

EN 12193 Light and lighting—Sports lighting
EN 13201-2 Road lighting—Part 2: Performance requirements
EN 13201-3 Road lighting—Part 3: Calculation of performance
EN 13201-4 Road lighting—Part 4: Methods of measuring lighting performance
EN 15193 Energy performance of buildings—Energy requirements for lighting
EN 1838 Lighting applications—Emergency lighting
SEV 4006 Leitsätze für die Beleuchtung von Tennisplätzen und -hallen (1962)
SEV 8902 Leitsätze für die Beleuchtung von Leichtathletik-, Spiel- und Turnanlagen (1970)
SEV 8903 Leitsätze für die Beleuchtung von Fussballplätzen und Stadien für Fussball und Leichtathletik (1971)
SEV 8907 Leitsätze für öffentliche Beleuchtung: 1. Teil—Strassen und Plätze, 2. Teil—Strassentunnel und Unterführungen

Leuchtdioden Rechercheportal—www.led-info.de
International Commission on Illumination (CIE)—www.cie.co.at
DIAL—Deutsches Institut für Angewandte Lichttechnik GmbH—www.dial.de

Play and sports elements
EN 1176-1 Playground equipment and surfacing—Part 1: General safety requirements and test methods
EN 1176-2 Playground equipment and surfacing—Part 2: Additional specific safety requirements and test methods for swings
EN 1176-3 Playground equipment and surfacing—Part 3: Additional specific safety requirements and test methods for slides
EN 1176-4 Playground equipment and surfacing—Part 4: Additional specific safety requirements and test methods for cableways
EN 1176-5 Playground equipment and surfacing—Part 5: Additional specific safety requirements and test methods for carousels
EN 1176-6 Playground equipment and surfacing—Part 6: Additional specific safety requirements and test methods for rocking equipment
EN 1176-7 Playground equipment and surfacing—Part 7: Guidance on installation, inspection, maintenance and operation
EN 1176-10 Playground equipment and surfacing—Part 10: Additional specific safety requirements and test methods for fully enclosed play equipment
EN 1176-11 Playground equipment and surfacing—Part 11: Additional specific safety requirements and test methods for spatial network
EN 1177 Impact attenuating playground surfacing—Determination of critical fall height
EN 12572-1 Artificial climbing structures—Part 1: Safety requirements and test methods for ACS with protection point
DIN 18035-1 Sportplätze; Freianlagen für Spiele und Leichtathletik; Planung und Masse
DIN 18035-2 Sportplätze; Bewässerung
DIN 18035-2 Sportplätze; Entwässerung
DIN 33942 Barrierefreie Spielplatzgeräte—Sicherheitstechnische Anforderungen und Prüfverfahren

PICTURE CREDITS

Some of the drawings are based on the script "Technisch-konst-ruktive Grundlagen I", prepared at the TU Berlin by Prof. Heinz W. Hallmann, working with Sandra Rösler and Friederike Flötotto. The drawings for the sample projects were revised graphically on the basis of original drawings from the planning practices. It is essential when using the DIN standards to consult the version of most recent date, available from Beuth Verlag GmbH, Burggrafen-strasse 6, 10787 Berlin.

1.1 SOIL
Figs. 1.1.1a, b + 1.1.2: Fine Aufmkolk
Figs. 1.1.3 to 1.1.6a–d: Astrid Zimmermann
Fig. 1.1.7: © LBEG Hanover, Landesamt für Bergbau, Energie und Geologie

1.2 PLANTS
All figures Ute Rieper, except:
Figs. 1.2.3 and 1.2.4 a–d: H. Lorberg Baumschulerzeugnisse GmbH & Co. KG (www.lorberg.com)
Fig. 1.2.7: Marc-Rajan Köppler
Fig. 1.2.8 c: Wolfgang Stenglin, Lemwerder-Altenesch
Fig. 1.2.11: Alexander von Birgelen

1.3 LAWNS AND OTHR SEEDED AREAS
Fig. 1.3.1: Astrid Zimmermann
Fig. 1.3.2: Astrid Zimmermann; b-d: Alexander von Birgelen
Fig. 1.3.3: Ivette Grafe
Fig. 1.3.4: Simon Colwill
Figs. 1.3.5 and 1.3.6: Alexander von Birgelen, after Heinz Ellen-berg, 1996, p. 787
Figs. 1.3.7 and 1.3.8: Norbert Kühn
Fig. 1.3.9: Alexander von Birgelen
Fig. 1.3.10: Cassian Schmidt

1.4 WOOD
Fig. 1.4.1: Binderholz GmbH / FeuerWerk—HolzErlebnisWelt/Fügen (www.binder-feuerwerk.com)
Fig. 1.4.2: FSC Arbeitsgruppe Deutschland e.V., PEFC Deusch-land e.V.
Fig. 1.4.3: Michael Volz
Fig. 1.4.4: Holzforschung Munich, Fotografie und Multimedia
Fig. 1.4.5: after Mägdefrau, 1951
Figs. 1.4.6 to 1.4.17: Gero Heck
Fig. 1.4.18: Mehling & Wiesmann GmbH
Figs. 1.4.19 to 1.4.21: Gero Heck

1.5 STONE
Fig. 1.5.1: Astrid Zimmermann
Fig. 1.5.5: Rüdiger Amend
Fig. 1.5.6: Burkhard Paetow
Fig. 1.5.7: Astrid Zimmermann
Fig. 1.5.8: Raderschall Landschaftsarchitekten AG, Zurich, Switzerland
Fig. 1.5.9: Hartmut Holl
Fig. 1.5.10: Burkhard Paetow
Fig. 1.5.12: Astrid Zimmermann
Fig. 1.5.13: Birgit Schmidt
Fig. 1.5.16: Astrid Zimmermann

Fig. 1.5.17: Hanna Bornholdt after Müller 2001, p. 216f. and Detail Praxis Natursteinwerk 2002
Fig. 1.5.18a–i: Theodor Hugues, Ludwig Steiger, Johann Weber
Tab. 1.5.2: Hanna Bornholdt after Müller 2001
Tab. 1.5.3: Hanna Bornholdt after Müller 2001, p. 230ff. and Detail Praxis – Natursteinwerk 2002, p. 58ff.

1.6 BRICK AND CLINKER
All figures Petra Zadel-Sodtke, except:
Fig. 1.6.2a–d: Astrid Zimmermann after Willi Bender: Handbuch für die Ziegelindustrie, 1995
Fig. 1.6.3a: Petersen Tegl, b: Randers Tegl
Fig. 1.6.5a–f: Petra Zadel-Sodtke/Astrid Zimmermann
Fig. 1.6.6: Randers Tegl
Fig. 1.6.7a–o: Petra Zadel-Sodtke/Astrid Zimmermann
Fig. 1.6.8: A•K•A Ziegelgruppe GmbH, Peine
Fig. 1.6.9: Astrid Zimmermann (original: Bernhard Ziegelwerke)
Fig. 1.6.10: Astrid Zimmermann (originals: 2nd from left: Arbeits-gemeinschaft Pflasterklinker, 3rd and 4th from left: Vereinigte Ziegelwerke)
Fig. 1.6.11 A•K•A Ziegelgruppe GmbH
Fig. 1.6.12 a, b: belTerra®, Bauhaus-Universität Weimar, Professur Aufbereitung von Baustoffen und Wiederverwertung
Fig. 1.6.20a, b, d, g, h, i, n, o: Petersen Tegl; c, t: Wienerberger; e, j, m, p: Randers Tegl; f, l, v, y, z: Wittmunder Kinker; k: Gima, Girn-ghuber GmbH; q, r, x: Astrid Zimmermann; s, w: Simon Colwill; u: A•K•A Ziegelgruppe GmbH

1.7 CONCRETE
Figs. 1.7.1: Thomas Brunsch
Fig. 1.7.2: Thomas Brunsch; design: Matthias Lanzendorf, execution: Thomas Queck/Matthias Lanzendorf
Fig. 1.7.3 and Fig. 1.7.4: Thomas Brunsch
Fig. 1.7.5: Sandra Brunsch
Fig. 1.7.6: Thomas Brunsch
Fig. 1.7.7: Sandra Brunsch
Fig. 1.7.8: Sandra Rösler
Fig. 1.7.9: Sandra Brunsch
Fig. 1.7.10a: Thomas Brunsch; b: Astrid Zimmermann (Guhl garden chair in Eternit); c: Urban Design by Concrete® Sportanlagen GmbH
Fig. 1.7.11: Astrid Zimmermann
Fig. 1.7.12: Sandra Brunsch
Fig. 1.7.13: Astrid Zimmermann
Figs. 1.7.14a–d to 1.7.16: Sandra Brunsch
Fig. 1.7.17a, b: Thomas Brunsch; c: Astrid Zimmermann
Fig. 1.7.18: Astrid Zimmermann
Fig. 1.7.19: Sandra Brunsch
Figs. 1.7.20 to 1.7.23: Thomas Brunsch

1.8 METALS
All figures Astrid Zimmermann, except:
Fig. 1.8.1: Joachim Zimmermann
Fig. 1.8.3: Martin Linz
Fig. 1.8.4: Sandra Rösler
Fig. 1.8.5: Astrid Zimmermann after Stahlbauprofile, Verlag Stahleisen GmbH, 2004

Fig. 1.8.6: after BAUEN MIT STAHL e.V./Stahlbau Arbeitshilfe—1.1 Korrosionsschutzgerechte Gestaltung
Figs. 1.8.9a–g to 1.8.11: Jörn Mikoleit
Fig. 1.8.12: Informationsstelle Edelstahl-Rostfrei, Düsseldorf
Fig. 1.8.13: Jörn Mikoleit
Fig. 1.8.15b: Stefan Wolf
Fig. 1.8.16a: Ingeburg Zimmermann; b: Jörn Mikoleit
Fig. 1.8.18: KME/Christian Richters (design: modulorbeat—ambitious urbanists & planners, Marc Günnewig, Jan Kampshoff)

1.9 OTHER BUILDING MATERIALS

All figures Astrid Zimmermann, except:
Fig. 1.9.1: Stefan Müller-Naumann; b: Martin Wegner /Jennefer Richter
Fig. 1.9.2: Stefan Wolf; f: Ulrike Kirstein
Fig. 1.9.3a, b: Stefan J. Cichosz; c: Doreen Kittner
Fig. 1.9.4a: Stefan Müller-Naumann (BUGA Munich, design: Rainer Schmidt); b, c, d: Swissfiber AG, Zurich
Fig. 1.9.6: Jörn Mikoleit
Fig. 1.9.7: Stefan J. Cichosz
Fig. 1.9.8b: Asphalt + Bitumen Beratung GmbH
Fig. 1.9.9: Asphalt + Bitumen Beratung GmbH
Fig. 1.9.10a, b: Thilo Folkerts
Fig. 1.9.11a, b: Asphalt + Bitumen Beratung GmbH
Fig. 1.9.13b: Jörn Mikoleit
Fig. 1.9.19d: Carolin Russler

2.1 LOADBEARING STRUCTURES AND THEIR DIMENSIONS

All figures Bernd Funke, except:
Fig. 2.1.1: Gabriele Zimmermann-Rall
Figs. 2.1.2 to 2.1.9a–c: Bernd Funke
Fig. 2.1.10: Tim Krüger
Fig. 2.1.11a–d: Bernd Funke based on Heino Engel, 1997
Fig. 2.1.13a–c and 2.1.15a–d: Bernd Funke based on Heino Engel, 1997
Fig. 2.1.16: Astrid Zimmermann
Fig. 2.1.17a–d: Bernd Funke based on Heino Engel, 1997
Fig. 2.1.18: Anonymous
Fig. 2.1.19: Stefan Müller for Thomanek Duquesnoy Boemans Landschaftsarchitektur
Fig. 2.1.21: Bernd Funke after Wilhelm Scholz: Baustoffkenntnis, 1995
Fig. 2.1.23: Stefan Müller for Thomanek Duquesnoy Boemans Landschaftsarchitektur
Fig. 2.1.24: Bernd Funke after Heinz Buchenau/Albrecht Thiele: Stahlhochbau, 1986
Fig. 2.1.27: Astrid Zimmermann
Fig. 2.1.30a–d: Bernd Funke based on Otto W. Wetzel, 2007
Fig. 2.1.32: Thomanek Duquesnoy Boemans Landschaftsarchitektur
Figs. 2.1.35a–d and 2.1.36a, b: Bernd Funke based on Klaus-Jürgen Schneider/Heinz Volz, 2004

2.2 FOUNDATIONS

All figures Bernd Funke, except:
Fig. 2.2.2: Bernd Funke based on Konrad Simmer, 1994
Fig. 2.2.3: Bernd Funke based on Achim Hettler: Gründung von Hochbauten, 2000
Fig. 2.2.4: Bernd Funke after Konrad Simmer, 1987
Fig. 2.2.6: Bernd Funke based on Klaus-Jürgen Schneider: Bautabellen mit Berechnungshinweisen und Beispielen, 9th edition, 1990

Fig. 2.2.7: Bernd Funke based on Frick/Knöll/Neumann/Weinbrenner: Baukonstruktionslehre Teil 1, 29th edition, 1987
Fig. 2.2.8: Bernd Funke based on Konrad Simmer, 1994
Fig. 2.2.9: Bernd Funke based on Konrad Simmer, 1994
Fig. 2.2.10a: Bernd Funke based on Otto W. Wetzel, 2007; b: Bernd Funke based on Konrad Simmer, 1994
Fig. 2.2.11: Bernd Funke based on Konrad Simmer, 1994
Fig. 2.2.12a, b: Bernd Funke based on Ulrich Smoltczyk, 1992
Fig. 2.2.13: Bernd Funke based on Konrad Simmer, 1994
Fig. 2.2.15: Bernd Funke based on Frick/Knöll/Neumann/Weinbrenner: Baukonstruktionslehre Teil 1, 33rd edition, 2002
Fig. 2.2.18: Bernd Funke based on Ulrich Smoltczyk, 1992
Fig. 2.2.19a–c: Bernd Funke after Achim Hettler: Gründung von Hochbauten, 2000

2.3 CONNECTIONS

All figures Bernd Funke, except:
Fig. 2.3.1: Bernd Funke based on Informationsdienst Holz, Mechanische Verbindungen
Figs. 2.3.4a–u, 2.3.5a–d and 2.3.6a–j: Bernd Funke after Manfred Gerner: Handwerkliche Holzverbindungen der Zimmerer, 1992
Fig. 2.3.10a–e: Bernd Funke based on Informationsdienst Holz, Mechanische Verbindungen
Fig. 2.3.11: Bernd Funke after Dierks/Schneider: Baukonstruktion, 1990
Fig. 2.3.13a, b: Bernd Funke based on Dierks/Schneider: Baukonstruktion, 1990
Fig. 2.3.15a–c: Bernd Funke after Gerhard Werner: Holzbau, part 1, Grundlagen, 4th edition, 1991
Fig. 2.3.16a, b: Bernd Funke after Frick/Knöll/Neumann/Weinbrenner: Baukonstruktionslehre, part 2, 1988
Fig. 2.3.18a, b: Bernd Funke after Frick/Knöll/Neumann/Weinbrenner: Baukonstruktionslehre, part 2, 1988
Fig. 2.3.19: Bernd Funke after Dierks/Schneider: Baukonstruktion, 1990
Fig. 2.3.20: Bernd Funke based on Dierks/Schneider: Baukonstruktion, 1990
Fig. 2.3.21: Bernd Funke based on Gerhard Werner: Holzbau, part 1, Grundlagen, 4th edition,1991
Fig. 2.3.22a, b: Bernd Funke based on Informationsdienst Holz, Mechanische Verbindungen
Fig. 2.3.23a, b: Bernd Funke after Otto W. Wetzel: Wendehorst Bautechnische Zahlentafeln, 32nd edition, 2007
Fig. 2.3.24a, b: Bernd Funke after Eduard Kahlmeyer: Stahlbau after DIN 18 800 (11.90), Bemessung und Konstruktion, Träger — Stützen — Verbindungen, 1993
Fig. 2.3.25a: Bernd Funke based on Kindmann/Krahwinkel: Stahl- und Verbundkonstruktionen, 1999; b+c: Bernd Funke after Frick/Knöll: Baukonstruktionslehre, part 1, 2002; d: Bernd Funke
Fig. 2.3.26: Bernd Funke after Buchenau/Thiele: Stahlhochbau 1, 1986
Fig. 2.3.27a, b: Bernd Funke after Wolfram Lohse: Stahlbau 2, 20th edition, 2005; c+d: Bernd Funke after Kindmann/Krahwinkel: Stahl- und Verbundkonstruktionen, 1999; e: Bernd Funke after Wolfram Lohse: Stahlbau 2, 20th edition, 2005
Fig. 2.3.28a, b: Bernd Funke after Lohmeyer/Bergmann/Ebeling: Stahlbetonbau, 7th edition, 2006
Fig. 2.3.29a, b: Bernd Funke after: Produktunterlage Fa. Peca Verbundtechnik GmbH; c: Bernd Funke
Fig. 2.3.30a1: Bernd Funke after: Produktunterlage Fa. Halfen GmbH & Co.KG, a2+a3: Bernd Funke, b, c: Bernd Funke

Fig. 2.3.31a–d: Bernd Funke after Lohmeyer/Bergmann/
Ebeling: Stahlbetonbau, 7th edition, 2006
Fig. 2.3.32a, b: Bernd Funke based on Lohmeyer/Bergmann/
Ebeling: Stahlbetonbau, 7th edition, 2006
Fig. 2.3.33a–c: Bernd Funke based on Lohmeyer/Bergmann/Ebe-
ling: Stahlbetonbau, 7th edition, 2006
Fig. 2.3.34a: Bernd Funke after Frick/Knöll/Weinbrenner/
Hestermann/Rongen: Baukonstruktionslehre, part 1, 2002;
b: Bernd Funke after Konrad Bergmeister: Betonkalender 2005,
part 2
Fig. 2.3.35: Bernd Funke after Zilch/Diederichs/Katzenbach:
Handbuch für Bauingenieure, 2002
Fig. 2.3.36a, b: Bernd Funke after Frick/Knöll/Weinbrenner/
Hestermann/Rongen: Baukonstruktionslehre, part 2, 2003
Fig. 2.3.41a: Bernd Funke based on Frick/Knöll/Weinbrenner/Hes-
termann/Rongen: Baukonstruktionslehre, part 1, 2002;
b: Bernd Funke based on Kindmann/Krahwinkel: Stahl- und Ver
bundkonstruktionen, 1999
Fig. 2.3.42a: Bernd Funke after Dierks/Schneider: Baukonstruktion, 2nd edition, 1990, b1+b2: Bernd Funke based on Kind-
mann/Krahwinkel: Stahl- und Verbundkonstruktionen, 1999;
c: Bernd Funke based on Dierks/Schneider: Baukonstruktion, 2nd
edition, 1990
Fig. 2.3.43a: Bernd Funke after Buchenau/Thiele: Stahlhochbau 1,
21st edition, 1986; b: Bernd Funke based on Kindmann/Krahwin-
kel: Stahl- und Verbundkonstruktionen, 1999
Fig. 2.3.44a, b: Bernd Funke after Zilch/Diederich/Katzenbach:
Handbuch für Bauingenieure, 2002
Figs. 2.3.45a, b and 2.3.46a, b: Bernd Funke after Steinle/Hahn:
Bauen mit Betonfertigteilen im Hochbau, 1991
Fig. 2.3.49a–c: Bernd Funke based on Frick/Knöll: Baukon-
struktionslehre, part 2, 2003
Fig. 2.3.50: Bernd Funke based on Dierks/Schneider: Baukon-
struktion, 2nd edition, 1990
Fig. 2.3.51a: Bernd Funke, b: Bernd Funke based on Frick/Knöll/
Weinbrenner/Hestermann/Rongen: Baukonstruktionslehre, part
2, 2003
Fig. 2.3.52a–d: Bernd Funke after Frick/Knöll/Weinbrenner/Hester-
mann/Rongen: Baukonstruktionslehre 1, 33rd edition, 2002

3.1 GROUND MODELING AND EARTHWORKS
All figures Astrid Zimmermann except:
Fig. 3.1.2: Astrid Zimmermann after Martin Frohmann: Bautechnik
1, p. 156, Stuttgart 1986 and Floss, p. 233, 1997
Fig. 3.1.3: Astrid Zimmermann after Martin Frohmann: Bautechnik
1, p. 89, Stuttgart 1986 and Holger Seipel: Fachkunde für Garten-
und Landschaftsbau, p. 80, Hamburg 2007
Fig. 3.1.7: Astrid Zimmermann after Beier/Niesel/Petzold: Lehr-
Taschenbuch für den Garten- Landschafts- und Sportplatzbau,
Stuttgart 2003 und Werner Knaupe: Erdbau, Berlin 1975, altered
Fig. 3.1.9: Astrid Zimmermann after Produktinformation Tensar
International GmbH (www.tensar.de), altered
Fig. 3.1.10a–c: Astrid Zimmermann after Florin Florineth, 2004 and
Ingenieurbiologische Bauweisen, Studienbericht Nr. 4, BWG, 2004
(www.bbl.admin.ch/bundespublikationen), altered
Fig. 3.1.11: Astrid Zimmermann after Dywidag Systems Internatio-
nal (www.dywidag-systems.com)
Fig. 3.1.13: Astrid Zimmermann after Produktinformation TenCate
(www.tencate.com), Tensar International GmbH
(www.tensar.de), REHAU AG+Co (www.rehau.de), altered
Fig. 3.1.14: Astrid Zimmermann after Tensar International GmbH
(www.tensar.de), altered
Fig. 3.1.16: Zimmermann after Florineth, altered and with additions; photograph: Jörn Mikoleit
Tab. 3.1.2: Astrid Zimmermann after Floss, altered and with additions
Tab. 3.1.3: Astrid Zimmermann after Martin Frohmann: Bautechnik
1, p. 89, 1986

Steep slope by the Kurmittelhaus: drawings + photographs: Land-
schaftsarchitekturbüro Birgit Hammer
Ronnenburg—south terrace: drawings + photographs: Land-
schaftsarchitekturbüro Fagus GmbH
Stone embankments—Mobile Life Campus: drawings: Land-
schaftsarchitekturbüro Topotek 1; photographs: Hanns Joosten
Sloping lawn, Munich Airport: drawings: Rainer Schmidt Landschaftsarchitekten; photographs: Stefan Müller-Naumann

3.2 PATHS AND SQUARES
All figures Axel Klapka:
Fig. 3.2.5: Axel Klapka after RStO
Fig. 3.2.11a–c and f–h: Deutscher Asphaltverband (DAV)
Fig. 3.2.16 Keller Landschaftsarchitekten
Fig. 3.2.21a–h: dispo GmbH
Barcelona Botanic Garden: drawings: Ferrater/Canosa/Figueras;
photographs: Axel Klapka
Urban renewal, Schmalkalden: drawings: Terra Nova; photograph
left-hand page: Terra Nova, photographs right-hand page: Reich—
Stadt Schmalkalden (left), Boris Storz (right)
Morelondon, London: Townshend Landscape Architects/Foster
Architects; photographs: Foster Architects
Stadtlounge, St. Gallen: drawings + photographs: Carlos Martinez
Architekten AG
Beatline, Munich: drawings + photographs: Keller Landschaftsar-
chitekten
Asphalt lake: photographs: Wilhelm Koch

3.3 STEPS
All figures Astrid Zimmermann, except:
Fig. 3.3.1: Friederike Flötotto
Figs. 3.3.2 and 3.3.3: Astrid Zimmermann after Skript FG Land-
schaftsbau/Objektbau TU Berlin
Fig. 3.3.7a: Simon Colwill, c: Thilo Folkerts
Fig. 3.3.8: Astrid Zimmermann after Skript FG Landschaftsbau/
Objektbau TU Berlin
Fig. 3.3.10: Astrid Zimmermann after Pech/Kolbitsch 2005, altered
with additions
Figs. 3.3.23/3.3.26a/3.3.28: Astrid Zimmermann after Skript FG
Landschaftsbau/Objektbau TU Berlin
Fig. 3.3.31b: Stefan J. Cichosz
Fig. 3.3.32: Astrid Zimmermann after Hans Gladischefski: Treppen
in Stahl, 1974 altered with additions
Fig. 3.3.35a–c: Astrid Zimmermann after Ehrmann/Nutsch 2004,
altered with additions
Fig. 3.3.36: Yvonne Schwerk
Fig. 3.3.37a: Friederike Flötotto
Steel stairs by the Schloss: drawings: Weidinger Landschaftsar-
chitekten; photographs: Astrid Zimmermann
Clinker steps in Charlottenlund, Denmark: drawings: Alexander
Damsbo; photographs: Timme Hovind
Lesserstiege in Nordhausen: drawings: Atelier Worschech and
Julian Reisenberger (bottom left); photographs: Dr. Horst Schro-
eder (center and right) Julian Reisenberger (left)
Steps with timber covering, Markkleeberger See: drawings and
photographs: Rehwaldt Landschaftsarchitekten
Staris, Festhalle Weissach: drawings: relais Landschaftsarchitek-
ten; photographs: Stefan Müller
Steps with rubber covering: drawings + photographs: SLA

3.4 RAILINGS AND FENCES
All figures Astrid Zimmermann, except:
Fig. 3.4.1: Astrid Zimmermann after Godelius 2008, altered with
additions
Fig. 3.4.3: Carolin Russler
Fig. 3.4.4/3.4.6: Astrid Zimmermann after Godelius 2008,
altered with additions
Fig. 3.4.7: Simon Colwill

Fig. 3.4.10: Sandra Rösler
Fig. 3.4.12: Keller Landschaftsarchitekten
Fig. 3.4.23: © Sue Jackson, reproduced courtesy of CABE
Fig. 3.4.37: Astrid Zimmermann after Godelius 2008
Fig. 3.4.41: Astrid Zimmermann after Pech/Kolbitsch 2005,
altered with additions
Fig. 3.4.43: Astrid Zimmermann after Lomer/Koppen 2001
Tab. 3.4.1: Astrid Zimmermann after Niesel, 2002 and Boeming-
haus, 1986, with additions
Railings on the Textima site: drawings + photographs: Weidinger
Landschaftsarchitekten
Railings in the Maselakepark: drawings + photographs (center
and right): relais Landschaftsarchitekten; photograph left:
Astrid Zimmermann
Railings with handrail, Wernigerode: drawings: hutterreimann
+ cejka Landschaftsarchitektur; photographs: Lichtschwärmer
(center) and Astrid Zimmermann
Wooden fence, Motalavej: drawings + photographs: SLA
Wooden fence with gate: drawings + photographs: Kuhn Trunin-
ger Landschaftsarchitekten
Steel fence and gate at the Lutherstift: drawings + photo-
graphs: LA.BAR Landschaftsarchitekten
Playing field, Prags Boulevard: drawings: Arkitekt Kristine Jen-
sens Tegnestue; photographs: Simon Høgsberg
Fence, Prags Boulevard: drawings: Arkitekt Kristine Jensens
Tegnestue; photographs: Christina Capetillo
Sitting room in Oschatz: drawings: Weidinger Landschaftsarchitekten; photographs: Weidinger Landschaftsarchitekten
(right) and Astrid Zimmermann
Maze, Oschatz: drawings: Weidinger Landschaftsarchitekten;
photographs: Astrid Zimmermann
Slatted timber fence, Tulln: drawings: hutterreimann + cejka
landschaftsarchitektur; photographs: Lichtschwärmer (Franziska Poreski and Christo Libuda)

3.5 WALLS
All figures Maik Böhmer, except:
Fig. 3.5.1: Maik Böhmer after Skript FG Landschaftsbau/
Objektbau TU Berlin
Fig. 3.5.2: Simon Colwill
Fig. 3.5.3a, b: Maik Böhmer/Astrid Zimmermann after Niesel,
2006; Heiko Müller
Fig. 3.5.4: Maik Böhmer/Astrid Zimmermann after Niesel, 2006
Fig. 3.5.5: Maik Böhmer
Figs. 3.5.6 and 3.5.7a: Maik Böhmer/Bernd Funke
Fig. 3.5.7b: Michael Lahmann
Fig. 3.5.8: Rekers Betonwerk GmbH & Co. KG
Fig. 3.5.9: Maik Böhmer, after Herstellerangaben Westerwelle
Figs. 3.5.15 to 3.5.18: Simon Colwill
Figs. 3.5.19 and 3.5.20: Astrid Zimmermann
Fig. 3.5.26b: Heiko Müller
Fig. 3.5.27b: Heiko Müller
Fig. 3.5.28b: Astrid Zimmermann
Fig. 3.5.29b: Heiko Müller
Fig. 3.5.31: Simon Colwill
Figs. 3.5.32 to 3.5.34: Heiko Müller
Fig. 3.5.35a: Maik Böhmer after Niesel, 1995; b: Astrid
Zimmermann
Fig. 3.5.36a: Maik Böhmer Niesel, 1995; b: Astrid Zimmermann
Fig. 3.5.37a: Maik Böhmer Niesel, 1995; b: Michael Lahmann
Fig. 3.5.38a: Maik Böhmer Niesel, 1995 ; b: Astrid Zimmermann
Fig. 3.5.39 b: Gabriele Zimmermann-Rall
Fig. 3.5.40 Astrid Zimmermann
Fig. 3.5.41: Thilo Folkerts

Fig. 3.5.43: Simon Colwill
Fig. 3.5.45: Heiko Müller
Figs. 3.5.46 to 3.5.48: Simon Colwill
Fig. 3.5.50: Heiko Müller
Fig. 3.5.51: Simon Colwill
Fig. 3.5.52: Heiko Müller
Fig. 3.5.53: Häfner/Jimenez
Fig. 3.5.54: Astrid Zimmermann
Figs. 3.5.55 and 3.5.56: Maik Böhmer
Fig. 3.5.57: Ulrike Zimmermann
Figs. 3.5.58 and 3.5.59: Maik Böhmer
Fig. 3.5.60: Maik Böhmer
Fig. 3.5.61a: after Befestigungstechnik vorgefertigter Betonfassa-
den, Merkblatt der Fachvereinigung Deutscher Betonfertigteil-
bau e.V. (06/2006); b: Bautechnische Information Naturwerkstein
1.1 Massiv- und Verblendmauerwerk
Figs. 3.5.62 to 3.5.65: Maik Böhmer
Fig. 3.5.66: Astrid Zimmermann
Fig. 3.5.67: Maik Böhmer
Fig. 3.5.68: Maik Böhmer
Fig. 3.5.69: Astrid Zimmermann
Fig. 3.5.70: Maik Böhmer
Fig. 3.5.71: Astrid Zimmermann
Figs. 3.5.72: Maik Böhmer
Figs. 3.5.73 to 3.5.75: Astrid Zimmermann
Tab. 3.5.1: Maik Böhmer
Tabs. 3.5.3 and 3.5.4: after Ziegelbauberatung, Merkblatt 1.3.11
Freistehende Mauern
Tab. 3.5.5: after Herstellerangaben Westerwelle
Natural stone wall in the Bonifatiuspark: drawings + photo-
graphs: Bernard:Sattler Landschaftsarchitekten
In-situ concrete wall with metal curtain, Pragsattel-Löwentor:
drawings + photographs: SCALA Architekten
Travertine wall: drawings + photographs: LA.BAR Landschafts-
architekten
Sheet steel edging, Prags Boulevard: drawings: Arkitekt Kristine
Jensens Tegnestue; photographs: Simon Høgsberg
Gabion wall: drawings: hutterreimann + cejka Landschafts-
architektur; photographs: Lichtschwärmer (Franziska Poreski
and Christo Libuda)
Marco Polo Square: drawings and photographs: Miralles
Tagliabue EMBT
Wall with gold inserts, Burghausen: drawings and photographs:
Rehwaldt Landschaftsarchitekten
Brick sculpture: drawings and photographs: Studio 3 — Univer-
sität Innsbruck
Walls in the Dania-Park: drawings: SWECO FFNS Architects; pho-
tographs: Jens Lindhe, Åke E:son Lindman, Steffen Meyhöfer

3.6 SMALL STRUCTURES AND PERGOLAS
All figures Caroline Rolka, except:
Fig. 3.6.1: Åke E:son Lindman
Fig. 3.6.7: Astrid Zimmermann
Fig. 3.6.11: Tanja Gallenmüller
Fig. 3.6.13 Simon Colwell
Fig. 3.6.14: Weidenprinz
Fig. 3.6.15a: Astrid Zimmermann
Fig. 3.6.16-3.6.20: Simon Colwell
Fig. 3.6.21a: Roy Mänttäri Architekten; b: Astrid Zimmermann/
Roy Mänttäri Architekten
Fig. 3.6.24: Astrid Zimmermann
Fig. 3.6.33: Caroline Rolka after Hallman/ Rohn/Lingnau, 1984, p. 16
Figs. 3.6.34 to 3.6.36: Astrid Zimmermann
Bath-house, Insel Lindau: drawings + photographs: Philip Lutz

Pergola: drawings: SAUERZAPFE ARCHITEKTEN; photographs: SAUERZAPFE ARCHITEKTEN (center) and Astrid Zimmermann

Pavilion of Remembrance, Thames Barrier Park, London: drawings + photographs: Groupe Signes and Patel Taylor

Shore promenade, Stralau peninsula: drawings: hutterreimann + cejka Landschaftsarchitektur; photographs: Lichtschwärmer (Christo Libuda and Franziska Poreski) and Astrid Zimmermann (bottom)

Pergola Lutherstifts: drawings and photographs: LA.BAR Landschaftsarchitekten

Carport in Egg: drawing: Eric Leitner; photographs: Georg Bechter

Protective hut in Snefjord: drawings and photographs: Pushak Architekten

Zoo tower—Baobab: drawings and photographs: Rehwaldt Landschaftsarchitekten

Asphalt chapel: photographs: Wilhelm Koch

3.7 SMALL BRIDGES

All figures Astrid Zimmermann, except:

Fig. 3.7.4: Doreen Kittner

Fig. 3.7.8: Ulrike Böhm

Fig. 3.7.9: Martin Sauerzapfe

Fig. 3.7.11a: Doreen Kittner

Beam bridge in the Lennépark: drawings + photographs: Britta Aumüller and Tobias Hamm

Katharinenbrücke: drawings + photograph left: SAUERZAPFE ARCHITEKTEN; photographs right: Astrid Zimmermann

Undertrussed bridge, Donaukai: drawings: Herle & Herrle Architekten; photograph: Claudia Wenz

Pedestrian and cycle bridge in the zoo: drawings: Kling Consult; photographs: Rehwaldt Landschaftsarchitekten

Bridge in Lillefjord: drawings + photographs: Pushak Architekten

3.8 WALKWAYS AND DECKS

Fig. 3.8.1: Julia Jiménez Ramos (Krienicke Park, Wasserstadt Berlin-Spandau, HÄFNER/JIMENEZ Büro für Landschaftsarchitektur)

Fig. 3.8.2: atelier le balto (Le jardin sauvage, Palais de Tokyo, atelier le balto)

Fig. 3.8.3: atelier le balto (Licht-Garten, Kunst+Architektur in Alt Köpenick-Berlin, atelier le balto)

Figs. 3.8.4 and 3.8.5: Marianne Mommsen

Fig. 3.8.6: Astrid Zimmermann

Fig. 3.8.7: Marianne Mommsen (courtyards in Rother Strasse, Berlin, Prof. Gustav Lange)

Figs. 3.8.8 and 3.8.9: Marianne Mommsen

Fig. 3.8.10: E-Stahl Ltd.

p. 293: drawing: Odious/Marianne Mommsen; photographs: Marianne Mommsen

p. 294: drawings: Planungsgemeinschaft Remisenpark Potsdam/Marianne Mommsen; photographs: Planungsgemeinschaft Remisenpark (left), Marianne Mommsen (right)

p. 295: drawings: relais Landschaftsarchitekten; photographs: Stefan Müller

pp. 296 to 298: drawings + photographs: relais Landschaftsarchitekten

3.9 PLANTING TECHNIQUE AND CARE OF VEGETATION SURFACES

All figures Ute Rieper, except:

Fig. 3.9.1: Astrid Zimmermann after Heinze/Schreiber 1984

Fig. 3.9.3: Ute Rieper after Wolfgang Frey & Rainer Lösch 1998

Figs. 3.9.6 and 3.9.7: Ute Rieper after FLL: Empfehlungen für Baumpflanzungen, Teil 1: Standortvorbereitungen für Neupflanzungen 2005; and also Teil 2: Planung, Pflanzarbeiten, Pflege 2004

Fig. 3.9.12 Ute Rieper after FLL: Empfehlungen für Baumpflanzungen, Teil 1: Standortvorbereitungen für Neupflanzungen 2005; and also Teil 2: Planung, Pflanzarbeiten, Pflege 2004

Fig. 3.9.15 Ute Rieper after Peter Brahe 2000

Tab. 3.9.2: Ute Rieper after Bernd Hertle et al. 1996

Tab. 3.9.5: Ute Rieper after Cassian Schmidt 2005

Tab. 3.9.6: Ute Rieper after Grimes

Pappelhof, EnBW Zentrale: photographs: Klahn + Singer + Partner

Parco Nord, Milan: photographs: Andreas Kipar

Tree section, Neuburg an der Donau: drawings + photographs: keller landschaftsarchitekten

Rose garden: photographs: Christian Meyer

Dry shrub planting in Bersarinplatz: photographs: Marc-Rajan Köppler

Savignyplatz: photographs: Christian Meyer

3.10 LAWNS AND MEADOWS: LAYING OUT AND CARE

All figures Ute Rieper, except:

Fig. 3.10.1: Ute Rieper after Florineth 2004

Fig. 3.10.3a+b: Otto Hauenstein Samen, Rafz

Figs. 3.10.5 and 3.10.6: Otto Hauenstein Samen, Rafz

Fig. 3.10.9: Astrid Zimmermann after Ellenberg, Heinz: Vegetation Mitteleuropas mit den Alpen, Stuttgart, 1996

Fig. 3.10.10: Ute Rieper

Ueda Landform: photographs: Charles Jencks

Dry lawn in the Riemer Park: photographs: Haase & Söhmisch

Sage and false oat grass meadow in the Riemer Park: photographs: Heiner Luz

3.11 SURFACE DRAINAGE

All figures Astrid Zimmermann, except:

Fig. 3.11.1b: Simon Colwill

Fig. 3.11.2: Astrid Zimmermann based on Niesel, 2002, p. 354

Fig. 3.11.4: Friederike Flötotto

Fig. 3.11.5: Carolin Russler

Fig. 3.11.12 Astrid Zimmermann after Skript FG Landschaftsbau/Objektbau, TU Berlin

Figs. 3.11.15 and 3.11.16: Astrid Zimmermann after Produktvorlagen der Hersteller Aco, Hauraton and Anrin

Fig. 3.11.18b, h: Simon Colwill; c: Yvonne Schwerk; f, g: Steffen Meyhöfer

Fig. 3.11.19: Symbolbibliothek Programm Vektorworks

Fig. 3.11.21: Petra Zadel

Fig. 3.11.22: Astrid Zimmermann based on DWA-A 138

Fig. 3.11.23: Astrid Zimmermann

Fig. 3.11.24: relais Landschaftsarchitekten

Fig. 3.11.25: Astrid Zimmermann based on DWA-A 138

Fig. 3.11.26: Fränkische Rohrwerke, Gebr. Kirchner GmbH & Co. KG (Rigofill inspect)

Figs. 3.11.27 to 3.11.29a+b: Astrid Zimmermann based on DWA-A 138

Trough and ditch drainage: drawings: Astrid Zimmermann; photograph: Ulrike Zimmermann

Bonifatiuspark: drawings: BERNARD:SATTLER with Norbert Müggenburg; photographs: BERNARD:SATTLER

Turbinenplatz: drawings + photographs: ADR Sarl, Julien Descombes and Marco Rampini

3.12 WATER INSTALLATIONS

All figures Astrid Zimmermann, except:

Fig. 3.12.1a: Simon Colwill

Fig. 3.12.2: Astrid Zimmermann after Thomas Brunsch/Skript FG Landschaftsbau/Objektbau TU Berlin

Fig. 3.12.5: Gisela Mourão

Fig. 3.12.8: Astrid Zimmermann after Skript FG Landschaftsbau/Objektbau TU Berlin

Fig. 3.12.9: Astrid Zimmermann based on FLL-Empfehlungen für Planung, Bau und Instandhaltung von Abdichtungssystemen für Gewässer im Garten-, Landschafts- und Sportplatzbau, edtion 2005, Mahabadi 1996

Fig. 3.12.10: Astrid Zimmermann, parts based on Firestone Building Products (www.firestonebpe.com) and Herbst Handel + Transportgesellschaft mbH/www.bentonit.de

"Wasserfisch"/Leuna: drawings and photographs right: Weidinger Landschaftsarchitekten; photograph left: Bernd Hiepe

Pool/"Garten der vier Ströme": drawings: Kamel Louafi; photographs: Kamel Louafi (left) and Astrid Zimmermann (right)

Water table/Schumannstrasse: drawings: K1 Landschaftsarchitekten; photographs: Mathias Schrumpf (right) and K1 Landschaftsarchitekten

Pool/Pflegezentrum Bachwiesen: drawings + photographs: Kuhn-Truninger Landschaftsarchitekten

Water feature/"Urban Garden", Nørresundby: site plan: Rambøll; Detail-drawings + photographs: SLA

Water feature "Goldsole": drawings + photographs: Rehwaldt Landschaftsarchitekten

Cascade/Waldkirchen: drawings + photographs: Rehwaldt Landschaftsarchitekten

Water feature "Aquasonum": drawings + photographs: Rehwaldt Landschaftsarchitekten

Water feature "Steinschwärze": drawings + photographs: Rehwaldt Landschaftsarchitekten

Nature experience pool in Großenhain: drawings: Weidinger Landschaftsarchitekten; photographs: Astrid Zimmermann

---

3.13 VERTICAL PLANTING

All figures Cordula Loidl-Reisch, except:

Fig. 3.13.4: Fink + Jocher, Munich

Courtyard planting in Vienna: drawings + photograph: Cordula Loidl-Reisch

Facade planting Institut für Physik: drawings + photographs: Joerg Th. Coqui; photograph left: Astrid Zimmermann

---

3.14 GREEN ROOFS

All figures Eike Richter/ LA.BAR, except:

Fig. 3.14.1c: Zinco
Fig. 3.14.2: Dachgrün, Vienna
Figs. 3.14.3 and 3.14.4: Optigrün
Fig. 3.14.5: Dachgrün, Vienna
Fig. 3.14.7: Zinco
Fig. 3.14.10: John Wilhelm
Fig. 3.14.16a+b: Wankner+Fischer, Optigrün
Figs. 3.14.17 and 3.14.20: Zinco
Fig. 3.14.21: Dachgrün, Vienna
Fig. 3.14.22a: Optigrün; b: Zinco
Figs. 3.14.23 + 3.14.24: Optigrün
Fig. 3.14.27: Optigrün
Figs. 3.14.28 and 3.14.31: John Wilhelm
Figs. 3.14.32 and 3.14.33: Martin Küster
Fig. 3.14.35: Zinco
Figs. 3.14.36 to 3.14.39: Optigrün
Fig. 3.14.40: Martin Küster
Figs. 3.14.41 and 3.14.42: Optigrün
Figs. 3.14.46 and 3.14.47: Optigrün
Fig. 3.14.48: Zinco
Fig. 3.14.49: Dachgrün
Figs. 3.14.50 to 3.14.56: Optigrün
Fig. 3.14.57: Zinco
Fig. 3.14.58: Dachgrün, Vienna
Fig. 3.14.62: Martin Küster
Fig. 3.14.63a–d: Optigrün
Fig. 3.14.64a–d: Martin Küster
Fig. 3.14.65a–d: Dachgrün, Vienna
Figs. 3.14.66 and 3.14.67: Optigrün

Fig. 3.14.68: John Wilhelm

Sächsische Landes-, Universitäts- und Staatsbibliothek: drawings: Stefan Tischer/Joerg Th. Coqui; photographs: Joerg Th. Coqui

Zusatzversorgungskasse des Baugewerbes: drawings + photographs: Latz und Partner

Extension to the Landesarbeitsamt Friedrichstraße: drawings + photographs: ST raum a

Depot Mitte Hochschulcampus Garching: drawings: LA.BAR Landschaftsarchitekten; photographs: Thomas Mutter (left bottom) and LA.BAR Landschaftsarchitekten (center left and bottom right)

Roof garden in Vienna: drawings: stalzer lutz gärten; photographs: Clemens Lutz

Atrium courtyard, Tauentzienstraße: drawings + photographs: LA.BAR Landschaftsarchitekten

---

3.15 SPECIAL ELEMENTS

All figures Katja Heimanns, except:

Fig. 3.15.3a: Simon Høgsberg; b: Astrid Zimmermann
Fig. 3.15.4: Claudia Wenz.
Figs. 3.15.5 to 3.15.7: Astrid Zimmermann
Figs. 3.15.8, 3.15.10 and 3.15.11: Doreen Kittner
Fig. 3.15.12: Astrid Zimmermann
Fig. 3.15.15a+b: LA.BAR Landschaftsarchitekten
Fig. 3.15.16a: Astrid Zimmermann. (Design for Oschatz skate park: Concrete Sportanlagen and Weidinger Landschaftsarchitekten), b: Astrid Zimmermann
Fig. 3.15.17a+b: Concrete Sportanlagen
Fig. 3.15.19: Carolin Russler
Fig. 3.15.21: b: Astrid Zimmermann
Fig. 3.15.22: Astrid Zimmermann

Climbing frame/Maselakepark: drawings + photographs: relais Landschaftsarchitekten

Play animals/Noah's Arche /"Hanging slide"/climbing tower "Traxingtanne"/play hills: drawings + photographs: Rehwaldt Landschaftsarchitekten

Concrete bench with wooden overlay: drawings: Weidinger Landschaftsarchitekten; photographs: Astrid Zimmermann

Red beam—Pragsattel-Löwentor: drawings + photographs: SCALA Architekten

Bench on grassy mount—Hessische Landesvertretung: drawings + photographs: Bernard : Sattler Büro für Landschaftsarchitektur

Bench/Maselakepark: drawings + photographs: relais Landschaftsarchitekten

Bench by the Axel-Springer-Haus: drawings + photographs: Birgit Hammer Landschaftsarchitektur

Folding bench/seating benches at zoo in Wuppertal/benches at the Med.-Theoret. Zentrum: drawings + photographs: Rehwaldt Landschaftsarchitekten

Garden seating/Tulln: drawings: hutterreimann + cejka landschaftsarchitekten; photograph: Lichtschwärmer

Bench/Dania-Park: drawings: SWECO FFNS Architects; photograph: Åke E:son Lindman

INDEX

A

abrasion resistance — 55, 71, 106, 124
accelerants — 96
accessibility — 358
access shafts — 404
accumulated moisture — 47, 75
accumulation — 409, 412–413, 458, 460–462, 465
additives — 87, 95–96, 222
adsorption water — 16
aeration — 44, 98, 369, 375–376, 391, 428
aggregates — 13, 20–24, 75, 79, 87–88, 95, 99–100, 126, 129, 149, 202, 221, 309
air entrainers — 96
allowable bearing pressures — 166
allowable load on the subsoil — 166
alloy elements — 106, 109, 112
alloys — 105–107, 112, 114, 118
aluminum — 103, 105, 107, 112, 117–118, 131, 133, 332, 360, 437
anatomic structure — 53
anchor holes — 100, 278
anchoring roots — 448
anchoring woody plants — 373
anchor plate — 279–280, 290
anchors — 178, 191–195, 258, 268, 277, 279, 312, 328, 451, 464, 466, 487, 491
anchor screws — 192
anchor spacings — 194
angle of elevation — 201
angle steps — 252
angle support wall — 296
anisotropy — 55
annuals — 39, 48, 379, 387, 393
anti-slip precautions — 244
apical growth — 30
aquatic plant — 429
area loads — 143
ashlar masonry — 307
asphalt concrete — 130, 222–224
asphalt surface courses — 221
asphalt surfaces — 129–130, 221–222
austenitic chromium-nickel steels — 114

B

balanced form — 145
balance of forces — 138–139
ballast — 20, 72, 84, 167, 216–217, 219–220, 224, 226, 229–231, 239, 277, 282, 290, 297, 300, 316, 318, 343, 358, 364, 412, 479, 491, 496, 499
bar-active loadbearing systems — 146
bare-root goods — 29
bark humus — 24
bark mulch — 23
barrier-free construction — 257, 268
barrier layer — 112, 302, 309
basalt — 67–69, 71, 73, 235, 310, 384, 416–417

base course — 102, 129, 213, 215–217, 219–222, 224–231, 234–235, 238–239, 290, 297, 311, 364–365, 389, 491, 499
base slab — 248–249, 252–253, 438–439
basic sewer pipes — 404
battering — 296
beams on two supports — 138
bearing forces — 138–139
bedding roses — 34, 369, 376, 383
benches — 106, 126, 490
bending efficiency — 148
bending strength — 71, 142, 147, 154, 329
bent-back starter bars — 187
bentonite — 23, 372, 423, 425–426, 428
bentonite mat — 423, 425, 428
bentonite powder — 423, 428
berm — 199
binding — 124, 202, 372, 374, 376, 451, 453
binding agents — 124, 202
biological equilibrium — 421–422, 428–429
bitumen — 112, 114, 124, 128–129, 215, 221–224, 227, 239, 332, 337
blast furnace slag — 23
blinding layer — 169, 291, 489
bolted joints — 274
bolts and threaded rods — 176
bolt strength grades — 181
bonds, decorative — 304
bond, flying or monk — 304
bonded anchors — 192, 195
bonded expansion anchors — 192
borders — 141, 219, 231, 379, 421
brass — 118
brick — 41, 46, 79–87, 89–90, 226, 252–253, 302, 304, 308, 313, 329–330, 465
brick formats — 81–82
brick gravel — 84
brick paving stones — 90
brick proportions — 81
brick steps — 252
bricks, peat-fired — 89
bricks, semi-dry pressed— 79
bricks, vitrified — 89
bronze — 118, 133, 437–438
building ground — 215–217, 219, 221, 224, 226, 229–232, 297–302, 358
building protection mats — 126, 128, 423
bulbs of pressure — 168
bulk density — 55–56, 71
bulk material — 216–217
butt joints — 183–184, 302, 304–305, 307, 314

C

cables — 106, 123–124, 145–146, 248–249, 271, 274–276, 335, 349, 436, 447–451, 480, 485
caissons — 169
calcareous tuff — 67, 69, 71, 73
calcium carbonate — 68, 149
calcium hydroxide — 149
cantilever staircase — 249

capillary water — 16
captured water — 15
carbonatization — 149–150
carbon dioxide welding — 183
carpentry joints — 62, 173–174
casing pipes — 426
cassette pergolas — 334–335
cast-in channels — 191–192, 194
cast-in plates — 192
cast steel — 107
cement — 75, 95–101, 112, 131, 149–150, 169, 184, 191, 204, 215–216, 219–220, 227, 295, 302, 311, 460, 487, 491
cement mortar — 112, 131, 204, 227, 295, 302, 311
cement paste — 95, 149
channels — 75, 111, 126, 130, 191–192, 194, 400, 403–405, 408, 492
chippings — 20–24, 68, 72, 90, 129, 211, 217, 222–225, 229–230, 237, 261, 277–278, 290, 314, 320, 331, 358, 372, 384, 412, 416, 433, 439, 454, 465, 487, 499
circulating pumps — 428
clamp — 280, 315, 427–428
clay — 16–20, 23, 29, 67–68, 79, 87, 89, 96, 160, 163, 166, 169, 201, 216, 219, 229, 260, 295, 302, 308–309, 330, 369, 372, 421, 423–426, 428, 453, 464–465
clay-based liner — 423
clay-humus complex — 20
clay structural elements — 424
clay tiles — 23, 423–424
cleaning methods — 75
climbing apparatus — 477, 483
climbing roses — 34, 369, 376, 383, 448
clinker — 77, 79, 81–82, 84, 86–87, 89, 96, 215, 224, 226, 252–253, 269, 302, 307, 313, 319, 400
close-tolerance bolts — 176, 180, 183, 195
coal-fired bricks — 89
coating process — 118
cohesion — 18, 161, 163, 165
cold plastic — 129–130
color — 30–31, 35, 45, 53, 55, 62, 67, 69, 71–72, 87–89, 96, 99–100, 106, 111–115, 118, 123–124, 128–130, 133, 219, 226, 229, 258–259, 309, 314, 335, 372, 384, 416–417, 424, 438–439, 441–442, 448, 479–480, 485, 491
colorants — 99, 129–130
color pigments — 96, 99
color rendering — 479–480
color systems — 111
color temperature — 479
column footing — 277, 289
columns — 33, 71–72, 108, 161, 167, 187, 192, 194–195, 328, 334
compactability — 16, 160, 202, 215, 219
compact compression members — 151
compaction — 98, 100, 160, 162, 166, 169, 200, 222, 225, 227, 229–230, 369, 382, 392
competition — 369, 371, 379
component cross section — 141
compost — 24, 230, 369, 376
compression and tension zone — 153
concrete backing — 307
concrete connections — 221
concrete cover — 98, 150, 215, 282
concrete formulas — 100
concrete, finished — 95, 100, 221, 297, 307, 313, 490
concrete, gunned, see also concrete, sprayed — 204, 206, 208
concrete, in-situ — 95, 98, 100, 102, 252
concrete paints — 100
concrete paving — 98, 216, 224–225, 230
concrete, exposed — 96, 99–100, 105, 297, 307, 313, 365, 474, 491–492, 497
concrete, photo — 100

concrete, polished — 93, 100
concrete slab foundations — 245
concrete-steel connections — 191
concrete steel mats — 97, 204
concrete steel rods — 97, 296
concrete surfaces — 98, 100, 130, 219–221, 277, 313, 412
concrete-timber connections — 194
condensation — 15, 110, 194, 459
conduits — 106, 125, 404, 409, 412
cone penetration test — 160
conical roof — 331
conifers — 32–34, 147
connections between different materials — 189
connections with cast-in items — 191
connections with drilled anchors — 192
connections with pockets — 193
connectors — 62, 173–174, 176–179, 189, 192, 194, 274, 279, 332, 358–359
consistency — 16, 20, 29, 86, 96, 100, 160, 221
constant loads — 143
construction joints — 98, 168, 174–175, 184, 187–189
construction of details — 358
construction steel — 97–98, 107, 110, 112, 283, 451
contact corrosion — 109–110, 112, 114, 116, 358
containers — 29–30, 33–34, 36, 128, 448, 452
contamination — 20, 24, 372, 391, 409, 422
continental climate — 371
contraction joints — 150, 189
copings — 484
copper — 100, 105, 107, 112, 118–119, 332, 440
coring or perforation types — 79
corner brackets — 99
corrosion — 59, 62, 97–98, 105–106, 109–114, 116–118, 149, 178, 184, 191–192, 194, 204, 269, 279, 281, 311–312, 358–359, 437, 483
corrosion resistance — 114, 116, 191–192, 358
corrosion-resistant coating — 311
corrugated bituminous boards — 189
counter-lever arm — 268
coursed rubble masonry — 305–307
cover grille — 404
coverings — 59, 75, 84, 109, 111, 118, 124, 215–216, 226–227, 229–230, 293, 313, 327, 331, 333, 358–360, 399, 403, 410, 412, 484
crack-control reinforcement — 189
crack-inducing joints — 189
creepers — 34, 38, 376, 447, 449, 451
crib walls — 296, 300
critical buckling load — 152
crossbars — 270–271, 273–274, 276, 404
cross beams — 249, 251–252, 255, 258
cross-beam staircases — 247
cross-beam structures — 249
cross section — 81, 148–149, 153, 187, 189, 221, 271, 274, 296–297, 302, 307, 347, 349, 404, 409, 422
crushed sand — 20–22, 90, 215–216, 224–226, 230, 261, 314
crushed stone — 20, 46–47, 68, 95, 99–100
crushed stone aggregate — 100
c-strategists — 379
curbstones — 99
curtain facades — 295, 313
cut bricks — 83
cyclopean masonry — 305

D
----

deep foundations — 167, 169
deep roots — 202
deformation — 106, 143, 147, 149, 160–161, 163, 166, 169, 173, 177, 183, 189, 216, 222, 298
deformation values — 143

degree of compaction — 159–160
degree of compression — 159
degree of rainfall — 397, 411
de-icing agents — 97
developmental and management maintenance — 468
diabas/dolerite — 68
diorite — 67–68, 71, 437
discharge lamps — 479–480
diseases — 371–372, 390, 392
dolomite — 67, 69, 71, 73
double and multiple shear — 176–177
dowels — 173–174, 176–177, 180, 189, 191, 488
drainage — 17, 19–20, 22–24, 75, 84, 106, 114, 118, 123–124, 126,
129, 197, 200, 202, 207, 211, 215–216, 218, 222, 227, 230–231, 237,
245, 256, 277, 297–298, 301, 314, 331–332, 338, 343, 358, 369, 373,
380, 389, 391, 397, 399, 401–404, 409–410, 412–413, 415, 425, 432,
440, 454–455, 460, 462–466, 468–469, 471, 487
drainage clinker — 84
drainage facilities — 118, 397, 404, 409, 412
drainage layer — 380, 460, 464–465, 471, 487
drainage trench — 410, 413, 415
drilled piles — 169
drilling — 62, 72, 81, 109, 111, 116, 133, 176, 194, 316, 439
drip lip — 282, 313, 353, 461
drive-over tests — 160
drop height — 267
dry density — 159–160
drying — 24, 38, 51, 55, 59, 61, 79, 96, 102, 126, 161, 245, 313,
358–359, 392, 424, 426
dry masonry — 150
dry mud collection — 404
dry pressed bricks — 79
dry-seeding — 466
drystone wall — 301, 305, 318
dummy joints — 187, 313
duplex system — 109–119
duroplast — 123, 128
dynamic course — 229
dynamic loads — 143, 166
dynamic penetration test — 160

E
----
earth surcharge — 163
edge beams — 295–296
edge distances — 176, 194–195
edge formation — 462
edge protection — 484
elastically bedded plates — 169
elasticity — 55, 123–124, 147, 149, 215
elasticity module — 147
elastic strength — 147
elastomers — 123–124, 126, 128
electroluminescent radiator — 480
embankment — 84, 161, 163, 218, 245–246
embedment depth — 162–163, 166–167, 188, 194, 268, 299, 358
end bearing — 169
end grain — 179–180, 194
engineering biology techniques — 204
engineering clinker — 79
engineering timber construction — 62
EPDM — 124, 126–127, 231, 239, 287, 423–424, 428, 487, 489–490
equilibrium moisture content — 55
erosion protection mats — 202
exceptional loads — 143, 231
expanded metal — 187–188, 451
expanding waterstops — 189
expansion force — 194
expansion joints — 102, 150, 187, 189, 302, 313–314

expansion sleeve — 194
expansion-type waterstops — 189
exposure classes — 149
extensive green roof — 457–459, 464, 466–467
external cut — 139
extruded grids — 254
extruded profiles — 117
extruder bricks — 79

F
----
facing bricks — 79, 81, 89, 304
facing concrete — 99
facing masonry — 75, 307, 310, 312
facings — 297, 312, 329
facing shell — 312
facing stones — 302, 307, 314
facing tiles — 79
fall protection — 126, 230, 347, 483–484, 487, 489
fertilizing — 48, 369, 371–372, 376, 378, 380, 385, 390, 392–393,
458
fiber and particle composite plastics — 126
fiber-reinforced plastics — 128, 131
fibers — 55, 97–98, 128, 131, 147, 149, 151, 349, 480
fiber saturation — 55–56
field-fired bricks — 89
filler bars — 360
filler elements — 271
fillet welds — 183–184
filter fleece — 207, 211, 298, 318, 410–411
filtration layer — 465
finalizing maintenance — 369
fine grinding — 72
finger joints — 59, 180
finger tests — 24
fires — 131, 229, 309, 455, 462–463
firing method — 86
fitness for purpose — 148
flanged pipes with seal flange — 428
flat dome — 329, 331
flat roof — 331–332, 415, 475
flights — 243–245, 249, 254
floatglass — 130
floods — 399
floor tiles — 79
fluidity — 149, 227
force — 62, 111, 114, 126, 137–139, 141–144, 151, 153–155, 161–162,
164, 166, 168, 177, 182, 191, 194, 204, 229, 305, 452, 482
force exerted by weight — 137
forking trunks — 30
form-active loadbearing systems — 144, 146
form cracks — 221
formwork — 75, 95, 98–102, 124, 130, 165, 168–169, 184, 187–189,
191–192, 206, 221, 231, 248, 309, 313, 344, 492
foundation base — 17, 206, 249
foundation base slabs — 249
foundation concrete — 100
foundations — 17–20, 24, 97, 143, 154, 157, 159–162,
167–169, 192, 206–207, 233, 245, 249–252, 255–256, 259, 269, 277,
280, 302, 328–329, 334, 349–350, 357–358, 364, 404, 406, 423, 428,
438, 485
fountain and pump technology — 428
fountain basins — 72
FPO — 124, 423–424
frame — 60, 258, 270–271, 273–274, 280, 282, 289, 296, 309, 312, 315,
329–330, 334–335, 338, 360–361, 364, 366, 382, 440, 451, 454, 485
french drain — 410, 412, 414–415
fresh concrete — 95, 98–100
friction-grip (GV) — 182

frost action zone — 216–217
frost and de-icing salt resistance — 95, 226
frost- and weather-resistant — 79
frost attack — 97
frost drought — 371
frost heave — 167
frost-protected — 249
frost protection course — 215–217, 219, 221, 224, 226–227, 232, 235, 256
frost resistance — 68, 70–71, 98, 369, 391
full masonry — 302
fuming — 62
funicular line — 145
fusion welding — 183

G

gabbro — 67–68, 71, 496
gabions — 204, 293, 296, 300–301
Gang-Nail — 178–179
geofleece — 215, 219
geogrids — 204, 206
geophytes — 27, 29, 35, 37, 39, 379, 383, 385
geotextiles — 204, 206–207
glass — 95, 98–101, 117, 124–126, 128–133, 147, 162, 211, 269, 295, 301–302, 312, 330, 334, 359, 382, 480, 487
glass beads — 130
glass blocks — 131
glazed bricks — 79, 88
gluing — 60, 118, 173–174
grading — 61, 86, 96, 98, 216, 222, 227
grading curve — 96, 98
graffiti — 75, 491
grain distribution — 216, 300
grain patterns — 55, 71
grain size — 16–18, 20, 22–24, 216, 222, 465, 484
granite — 67–68, 70–74, 101, 234–235, 249, 272, 322, 338, 440
grassed areas — 466
grasses — 27, 35–36, 38, 41, 43–47, 49, 202, 383–385, 390–393, 458
gratings — 274, 358–361, 404, 462
gravel — 16–24, 59, 75, 84–86, 90, 95, 98, 100, 160, 167, 169, 201, 204, 211, 216–217, 224, 226, 230, 237, 239, 249, 297, 300, 314, 318, 331, 358, 395, 410–412, 414–415, 422–426, 429, 437, 441–442, 463, 470, 475, 489, 495
gravity walls — 296–298, 301
gray cast iron — 106–107
greenable covers — 229
greening methods — 466
green roofs — 199, 331, 412, 455, 457–460, 462–468, 474
grille — 269–270, 274, 280–281, 286, 361, 375, 382, 404, 440
ground composition — 482
ground failure — 162–163
ground slabs — 161, 187, 221
groundwater — 16, 23–24, 163, 168, 189, 215, 300, 372, 391, 409, 415, 423
grout — 169, 189, 192, 194, 338
grouting mortar — 277, 439
growth forms — 29, 44
GVP — 183

H

habitats of herbaceous plants — 34
half dome — 331
hammer-head bolts — 191
hammer masonry — 305

handrail — 84, 192, 244, 254, 257, 267–271, 278–280, 283, 351–352, 366, 481
hand-struck bricks — 79, 86–87
hard surfaces — 399, 414, 457
hay flower seed — 392
hay transfer — 392
header — 253, 302–304, 307
heartwood — 53, 55–56
heat-treated timber — 59
heave failure — 162, 166
heavy-duty anchors — 277
heavy-duty paving — 225
hedge brush layers — 204
herbaceous plants — 29–30, 35–38, 202, 301, 367, 369, 372–373, 377–379, 383–385, 391–392, 409, 466
hexagon head bolts — 180–181, 290
high-grade steel — 97–98, 112
high pressure discharge lamps — 479
high-strength friction-grip bolts — 180
hinges — 162, 177, 280
historic bricks — 84
hogging — 161–162
holding-down bolts — 192–193, 195
hole clearance — 180–181, 183
horizontal loads — 143, 268, 359, 452
hot-dip galvanizing — 109, 111, 191, 194
hot plastic — 129–130
humus — 15, 18–20, 24, 29, 34, 36–37, 48, 199, 369, 372–373, 392, 423, 465
hydratation — 149
hydraulic lime — 311
hydro-seeding — 466, 468

I

ice lenses — 167
illuminant — 479–480
impregnations — 75
incision — 199, 218
incline — 197, 199, 201, 204, 206, 231, 243, 245, 263, 313, 331–332, 337, 389, 399, 403, 432, 436, 455, 457, 460–463
individual loads — 143
infill — 329–330
inflow shaft — 410
inhomogeneity — 148
injected piles — 169
injection hoses — 189
inseparable joints — 116
in-situ concrete, see also concrete — 95, 98, 100–102, 168, 171, 187, 221, 252, 272, 297, 307, 418, 432, 435, 490
in-situ construction — 184
in-situ density D — 159
inspection openings — 409
inspection shafts — 397, 404, 462
intensive green roof — 380, 412, 458, 466–467
intensive roots — 202
intermediate storage — 24
internal and external waterstops — 189
internal cut — 139
internal forces — 138–141, 143–144, 151, 153
intrinsic slope — 404
inverted roof — 459, 471
irregular-coursed rubble masonry — 305
irregular course masonry — 311
irrigation systems — 458
isolated footings — 358
isolating bearing pad to prevent rising moisture — 194
isolux lines — 358

J
----

jetty — 357
joint dowelling — 191
joint edges — 183
joint filling compounds — 228
joint formation — 359
joint gaps — 360
jointing techniques — 118
joint mortar — 227, 433
joints — 51, 59, 62–63, 75, 83–84, 90, 98, 102, 114,
116–118, 130, 150–151, 168–169, 171, 173–175, 177–178, 180,
183–184, 187–189, 191, 221, 225, 227, 229–230, 237, 252, 274, 277,
280–281, 296, 301–302, 304–305, 307, 313–314, 358–360, 362,
364–365, 390, 399, 412, 416, 424, 426, 428, 440, 448, 451–452,
460, 484
joints, glued — 180, 424
joints, horizontal — 83, 90, 296, 302, 304, 307, 314
joints, sleeve— 428
joints, welded — 151, 183–184

K
----

kerbstones — 72, 130

L
----

lamella pergola — 334
laminated limestone — 69
laminated timber — 60, 178–180, 195
laminated wood — 151, 335, 337
lap length — 187
laser technology — 72
late-flowering — 35
lateral removal — 199
lattices — 154
lava — 20, 67–69, 72–73, 230, 314, 380, 464–465
lawn — 41, 43–47, 84–85, 126, 202, 219, 229–230,
389–394, 399, 409, 412, 458, 460, 463, 465, 474
lawn areas — 458
lawn maintenance — 390
layer installation — 199
layer removal — 199
laying direction — 333, 358–359
leaching — 75, 133
LED — 178, 440, 480–481, 492
lengthwise gradient — 400, 403
leverage effect — 268
license — 180, 184
light liquid separators — 404, 410
lightweight expanded clay — 20
light yield — 479–480
lime efflorescence — 302
limestone — 67, 69–74, 149, 237, 314, 318, 416
limit of elasticity — 55, 149
linear drainage facility — 404
lining elements — 206
loadbearing — 15, 17, 20, 22, 59–62, 71, 75, 108–109,
114–115, 125, 128, 131–132, 135, 138–139, 141, 143–154, 157, 159,
166–167, 169, 176, 178, 182, 192, 194, 204, 215–216, 219, 224–227,
229–230, 247, 249, 252, 254, 258, 268–269, 274, 276, 295, 297, 301,
304, 307, 309, 312, 329–331, 334–335, 357–360, 362, 374–375,
404, 407, 451, 455, 458–459, 465
loadbearing arches — 154
loadbearing capacity — 17, 61–62, 108, 125, 132, 141, 147–148,
150–154, 169, 176, 194, 204, 215–216, 219, 224, 226–227, 229–230,
249, 268, 297, 301, 309, 358, 404, 407, 455, 459, 465
loadbearing spar — 254

loadbearing substrate — 374–375
loam — 20, 23
low pressure discharge lamps — 479

M
----

machine-struck brick — 79
magmatite — 68
maintenance — 30–31, 34, 37, 43–44, 47, 111, 116–117, 215, 219,
224, 228, 358–359, 367, 369, 371–372, 376, 378–381, 383, 385, 387,
389–390, 393–394, 422, 452, 458, 463–464, 468, 470, 484
malleable cast iron — 106
marble — 67, 69–71
maritime climate — 371
masonry — 23, 69–70, 75, 77, 81, 83–84, 90, 150, 167, 191–192,
219, 246, 252–253, 269, 272, 274, 277, 295–296, 302, 304–307,
309–310, 312–313, 329–330, 349, 421, 426
masonry bonds — 83, 302, 304–305, 313
material strength — 135, 139, 142, 147
material testing service — 71
meadow seeding — 392
meadow types — 47–48
mechanical couplers — 187
mechanical soil improvement — 202
mechanical surface treatment, artificial stone — 72
mesh laths — 75
metal arc welding — 183–184
metal expansion anchors — 194
metal sheets — 117, 311
metal steps — 252
metamorphites — 67
micropiles — 169
milling — 106, 116
mineral-fiber boards — 189
mineral glass — 100
mineral sealant — 423
mixed masonry — 307
mixed water systems — 404
modular dimensions — 225
molded parts — 106, 117, 124
moment of plane area I — 147, 152
moment of resistance — 142, 148, 152–154
mortar — 20, 22–23, 75, 84, 90, 100, 112, 126, 131, 150, 191–192,
204, 226–227, 237, 252–253, 261–262, 277, 295–296, 301–302,
304, 311–313, 416, 432–434, 437–442, 483, 487, 496
mortar group — 150, 304
mosaic — 68, 216, 227
movement joints — 227, 426
mowing — 47–48, 201–202, 381, 391–394, 396
mud trapping gully — 404
mulch — 23–24, 46, 369, 372, 376, 378–380, 483–484

N
----

nails and staples — 176
natural soil — 15, 24, 100, 204, 206
natural soil angles — 201
natural stone — 67, 71–72, 75, 95–96, 99–100, 219, 221, 224–227,
232, 234, 236, 246–248, 252, 262, 272, 278, 282, 293, 295, 301–
302, 305, 307, 310, 312–313, 329, 334, 349, 366, 400, 421, 426, 434,
437–438, 440
natural stone walls — 75, 305, 313
negative normal force — 139, 151
nomenclature — 67
nominal cracks — 150
non-ferrous metals — 105
non-rigid construction methods — 249

non-slip surfaces — 126, 263, 358
normal format NF — 81
nutrient elements — 369
nutrient supply — 20, 44, 47

O
----
oil-shale cement — 100
one-shelled walls — 302
open cross sections — 153
outlet control — 410–411, 413

P
----
pad foundations — 167–169
painting — 106, 111
palisade fence — 271
palisades — 59, 99, 165, 298–300
particle-size distribution — 159
passive corrosion protection — 194
patina — 65, 69, 72, 84, 99–100, 105, 118
paved areas — 31, 75, 84, 90, 167
paved surfaces — 219, 222, 228
pavement — 32, 70, 167, 215–217, 219, 221–222, 227, 229, 231, 256, 363, 399
paving — 22, 67–70, 72, 75, 79, 83–84, 87, 90, 98–99, 215–216, 219, 221, 224–230, 232, 234–237, 257, 262, 282, 320, 351, 366, 400, 412, 418, 432, 463, 481, 485
paving clinker — 79, 87, 215, 226
paving stones — 72, 84, 90, 99, 216, 224–225, 230, 232, 257, 412, 481
pebble paving — 226
PE-LD — 124, 424
perforated lawn clinker — 84
perforated sleeves — 192
pergolas — 325, 327, 334–335, 445
permanent connections — 191
pests — 29, 31, 372, 391
pH — 20, 48, 149, 379, 389
picket fencing — 271
pigments — 79, 96, 99–100, 129
piled foundations — 169
pillars — 296, 329–330, 334, 364
pillar spacing — 295–296
pin-type fasteners — 176–177, 180
pipe penetration — 428
plank support spans — 360
plant clipping — 372
planting depth — 379
plant protection — 371–372, 376, 378, 383, 391
plant reproduction — 29
planum drainage — 215, 227
plastic coatings — 230
plasticity — 16, 25, 123, 160, 447
plasticizers — 96, 98, 424
plastic pad — 189
plastic sheet — 424–425
plate-active loadbearing systems — 144–145
plate bearing test — 160
plywood — 61, 180, 287
pocket foundations — 192
polishing — 68, 72, 100, 118, 128–129
ponds — 18, 128–129, 410, 419, 421–423, 426, 428–429
pool substrates — 429
pool technology — 428
porous volume — 15, 17–18
positive normal force — 139, 151
post-bar construction — 271

post-cross-lath construction — 270
post-frame construction — 271
posts — 118, 192, 194, 268–269, 271–283, 286, 334–335, 343, 352, 357–358, 361, 366, 448, 487
poured asphalt — 129–131, 222–223, 471
powder coating — 106, 111, 114, 118
powdered clay — 23
precast construction — 184
precipitation water — 75, 231, 245, 464
prefabricated concrete parts — 98
prefabricated lawns — 390
preformed gasket — 189
preformed sheet steel components — 174, 176, 178, 190
preformed sheet steel shoes — 194
preparing the site — 372
pressed bricks — 79
pressure — 16, 25, 60, 68–69, 71–72, 84, 86, 95, 124, 143–147, 151–154, 160–166, 168–169, 174, 176, 180, 182–183, 187, 225, 263, 296–297, 301, 313, 358, 360, 374, 379, 399, 422, 424, 426, 434, 441–442, 452, 457, 459, 479–480
pressure line — 145
pressure-locked gratings — 360
pressure resistance — 71
pressure welding — 183
preventive chemical timber treatment — 60
primary constructions — 191
proctor density — 159
protection against corrosion — 109, 112, 114, 149, 204
protection against erosion — 48, 202
protective courses — 463
protective plies — 464
pumice — 20, 24, 68, 465
pump chamber — 428
pump sump — 428, 440
PUR-bound EPDM granulate — 126
purlins — 191, 332, 334
PVC-P — 124, 424

Q
----
quarries — 20, 72
quarry location — 67
quarrystone masonry — 305
quartz sand — 99–100, 130–131, 192

R
----
rafters — 191, 195, 332, 334
raft foundations — 167, 169, 329, 358
rain, freak heavy — 399
rammed clay — 23, 308–309
rammed clay walls — 309
rammed piles — 169
ramming in stakes or posts — 358
ramp — 257, 268, 284
ready-made ponds — 426
receiving water courses — 399
recycled bricks — 84
recycling — 23, 106, 118, 123–124, 126, 424
refuse incineration slag — 23
regular-coursed rubble masonry — 307
reinforced concrete — 93, 96–98, 106, 132, 149, 168–169, 184, 204, 206, 249, 262, 295–296, 299, 312, 332, 352, 421, 433, 438–439, 484
reinforced earth — 204, 206, 296
reinforced masonry — 150

reinforcement — 84, 97–98, 102, 131, 149–151, 169, 184, 187–189, 199, 202, 204, 206–208, 229–230, 252, 262, 296, 307, 309, 338, 344, 451, 466, 487–488
reinforcement corrosion — 97
reinforcement, minimum— 150
reinforcement rods — 296
reinforcing steel — 98, 149, 208
releasing agents — 100
required foundation area — 168
resistance — 17, 34, 43, 45–46, 51, 55–56, 58–59, 68, 70–71, 95, 98, 105–106, 114, 116–118, 123–124, 126, 128–129, 131, 141–143, 148–149, 151–154, 160–161, 163–167, 183, 191–192, 225–227, 309, 358, 369, 372, 391, 483, 490
resistance to corrosion — 105, 117–118
resistance welding — 117, 183
rest of bodies — 138
restraint stresses — 189
retaining walls — 163, 165, 204, 293, 296, 298, 301
retarders — 96–97, 100, 102
rhizome — 30
rhyolite (porphyry) — 68, 71
rigid — 20, 55, 61, 144–145, 166, 173–174, 180, 191, 195, 215–216, 219, 227, 249, 251–252, 295, 302, 334–335, 347, 358, 421, 423–424
riveting — 117–118
road drains — 404, 406
road paving asphalt — 221
rock flour — 22, 96
rock grain — 20
roof — 23, 47, 59, 68, 75, 79, 118, 127, 144, 154–155, 187, 191, 312, 327–333, 335–336, 358, 362, 380, 399, 403–404, 412, 414–415, 432, 447–448, 455, 457–464, 466–471, 475
roof, cold— 459
roof, collar beam — 328, 332
roof covering — 332
roof eaves — 331
roof framework — 328, 331–333
roof incline — 331–332, 457, 460
roof, lean-to — 331, 403
roof, rafter — 331–332
roof ridge — 331–332
roof seal — 459–460, 464, 469
roof skin — 330–332, 459, 462, 466
roof tiles — 79
roof, warm — 459
rootball goods — 29
root climber — 448
root growth — 369, 376, 390, 429
root penetrability — 20
root system — 30, 32, 37
rough blocks — 72
roughness or profile — 358
rough stone — 68
r-strategists — 379
rubble materials — 20
rubble stone — 72
rubblestone masonry — 305
runoff coefficient — 411–412
run thickness — 184

S
----
safety coefficients — 142
safety distances — 482
safety edges — 254
safety grids — 254
sagging — 133, 161–162
salt deposits — 75
samples — 32, 72, 160

sand — 16–23, 25, 74, 79–80, 86–88, 90, 95–96, 99–100, 102, 123, 130–132, 147, 160, 163, 169, 189, 192, 200–201, 215–217, 224–226, 229–230, 237, 239, 249, 256, 261, 302, 314, 319, 343, 373, 391, 409, 411–412, 415, 417, 423, 426, 465, 483–485, 487
sand, granulated— 96
sand-lime brick — 302
sand-struck bricks — 79, 86
sapwood — 53
sawing — 60–62, 116
sawn planting — 392
sawn timbers — 60
scarifying — 391
scoria — 68
screw anchor joints — 277, 280
screwing — 117–118, 176, 278–279, 451
screw joints — 180
sealants — 96, 124, 133
seal insert — 428
seating elements — 99, 479, 490
seawater — 58, 97, 118
secondary constructions — 191
sedimentary rocks — 67, 69
seeding — 202, 371, 384, 392–393, 466, 468
seepage — 15, 22, 124–125, 202, 207, 229–230, 256, 262, 298, 302, 372–373, 397, 399, 404, 409–416, 418, 471, 493
seepage pipe — 125, 262, 410–411, 414, 493
seepage runs — 202
seepage shafts — 411
seepage space — 256, 409, 415
seepage water — 298, 302, 372
semi-precast construction — 184
sensitivity to frost — 19, 24
separators — 404, 410
settling — 17, 199, 379
shade-tolerance — 44
shallow foundations — 162, 167, 169
shallow slopes — 422
shear/bearing (SL) — 182
shear connectors — 194
shear-plate connectors — 178
shear strength — 16, 142, 161–163, 165, 204, 216
sheet metal with grooves — 254
sheet-pile walls — 299
shingle covering — 333
shrink — 55, 309
shrinkage cracks — 96, 98
shrubs — 30, 33, 36, 53, 421, 458, 466, 468, 470, 475
silicones — 126
silt — 16–20, 23, 160, 166, 200–201, 216
simple intensive green roofs — 457, 466
single loads — 143
single-sized aggregate concrete — 75
skeleton construction — 329
skin friction — 160, 169
slab foundations — 245
slabs — 68, 70, 72, 75, 79, 84, 98, 161, 187, 221, 249, 252, 258, 263, 278–279, 300, 312, 322, 441–442
slab steps — 249, 252
slag — 15, 23, 96, 381, 394
slats — 271, 289, 291, 354, 449
sleeve foundations — 277
slender compression members — 152
slipperiness — 69, 244
slip plane angle — 161, 164
slope — 163, 166, 187, 197, 199, 201–202, 204–206, 208–210, 257, 295, 313–314, 363, 389, 394, 397, 399–400, 403–404, 409, 412–413, 422, 487
slope failure — 163
slope fascines — 204

slope, shifted material — 199
slot gutter — 404–405
small paving — 232, 432
small stone — 68, 262
small structures — 117, 325, 327, 329–332, 335
soils, cohesive — 16, 18, 20, 161–163, 166, 202
soil compacting — 169
soil conditioning measures — 216
soil exchange — 169
soil modeling — 17
soil nails — 204, 206, 208
soil pressure — 154, 168, 296, 313
soil protection — 49
soil reaction — 20, 25, 47
soil report — 24
soil sample — 25, 159–160
soil structure — 15, 20, 24, 44, 49, 167, 199, 202, 298
soil type — 13, 16, 18, 20, 23–24, 38, 49, 201, 206, 412
soil volume — 200
sole plates — 194
solid masonry — 75
solid rectangular steps — 245, 247, 249, 251–252
solid timber products — 60
sorting — 199
sown planting — 392
spacers — 59, 98, 204, 225, 227, 271, 281, 289, 338, 350, 360, 364
spatial joints — 221, 313
special connectors — 176–179
special nails — 360
special sizes — 36
spheres of life — 34
spheroidal — 106
spiral staircase — 249
split-face stones — 72
sprayed concrete — 102, 483, 487, 489
sprout-seeding — 466
s-strategists — 379
stability — 15, 17–18, 20, 30, 32, 56, 96, 132, 149, 154, 167, 201, 206, 215–216, 222, 224, 226–228, 231, 277, 280, 298, 302, 304, 335, 357, 421, 482, 490
stability check — 201, 357
stable construction methods — 295–296
stainless steels — 106, 109, 114, 117
stains — 75, 358
staircase stringers — 249
stamped clay wall — 307
standard formats — 81, 307
standard loading condition — 297
starter bars — 187–188, 282
static loads — 143, 268
steel — 59, 62, 95, 97–99, 103, 105–118, 126, 133, 142, 144, 147–151, 165, 169, 171, 173–174, 176–184, 187, 189–195, 202, 204–209, 227, 231–232, 247–249, 254–255, 258, 260–262, 265, 269, 271–272, 274–291, 295–296, 299–300, 302, 310–312, 315–317, 322, 329–330, 332, 334–340, 342–344, 347, 349–352, 358–362, 365–366, 381–382, 394, 404, 417–418, 426, 434–440, 447–448, 451, 453–454, 474–476, 482–485, 487–488, 490–491, 496, 498–500
steel cable nets — 274
steel cables — 106, 271, 274–275, 335, 349, 451, 485
steel connections — 126, 171, 177, 191–193
steel fiber concrete — 98
steel lattice elements — 206
steel mat fences — 274
steel-timber connections — 191
steels, general construction — 106, 109, 112
steles — 72
stencils — 100, 102

steps — 67, 70–72, 99, 135, 142, 180, 243–249, 251–257, 260–262, 268, 271, 273, 279, 314, 343, 399–400, 403, 438, 441–442
step with underlay — 252
stiffening — 108, 135, 154–155, 272, 296, 329–330, 335, 357
stone — 13, 15–16, 20–22, 24, 41, 46–47, 65, 67–68, 70–75, 79, 89, 95–96, 99–100, 126, 129–130, 149–150, 206–207, 210, 219, 221–227, 232, 234–236, 245–249, 252–253, 256, 261–262, 272, 277–278, 282, 287, 290, 293, 295–296, 300–302, 304–305, 307, 310–314, 319–320, 329–330, 334, 349, 351, 366, 379, 400, 404–405, 416, 421–422, 426, 434, 437–438, 440–442, 472, 484, 491, 499–500
stonemasons — 72, 226
stone matrix asphalt — 129–130, 222–223
strain limit — 149
stratification density D — 159
stretcher — 253, 302–304, 314
stringers — 68, 246, 248–249, 251, 255
stringer staircases — 247
strip footings — 166–169
strip foundations — 249, 329, 358, 438, 485
structural thickness — 213, 215, 217, 219
stucco — 309, 311, 313
sub-base — 166
sub-grasses — 43
submerged arc welding — 183–184
subsoil — 20, 154, 157, 161, 166–169, 202, 210–211, 215–219, 221, 224, 226, 229–232, 245, 249, 271, 374, 380, 392, 394, 409–411, 421, 423, 438, 440, 484, 487
substructure — 215–216, 218–219, 221, 224, 226, 229–232, 347, 352, 359–363, 426, 440, 449, 458
succession — 371
superplasticizers — 96, 221
support bars — 360, 366
support construction — 331, 355, 357–359
supporting walls — 296
supports — 34, 108, 138, 140, 145, 151, 249, 254, 297–298, 311, 328–329, 334–335, 347–348, 351, 359, 361–362, 366, 491
surface and deep drainage — 202
surface and trench seepage — 399
surface courses — 20, 213, 215–217, 219, 222, 227–229, 231
surface properties — 103, 105–106, 227
surface treatment — 51, 61, 72, 75, 77, 86–87, 93, 99, 105, 109, 118, 245, 309, 322
swells — 55
syenite — 67–68, 71, 73

T

tap holes — 428
tendril climber — 445
tensile bending strength and absorbency — 71
tensile reinforcement — 206
tensile strength — 97–98, 106, 142, 147–149, 151, 181, 189, 227, 349
tension — 108, 123–124, 139, 141–142, 144–145, 147–149, 151, 153–154, 176–178, 180, 192–195, 311, 349, 351
tension-elongation diagram — 149
tent roof — 331
tents — 145
terminal buds — 35
terraces — 84, 201, 357, 400, 404, 457–458, 475
terracotta slabs — 79
terrazzo — 100, 439
thermal expansion — 71, 105, 131
thermal radiators — 479
thin format DF — 81
threaded rod — 192, 279, 282, 289
threshed hay seed — 392
trough-wall anchors — 277

tiled coverings — 215, 226–227, 331

tilting — 161, 168

timber connectors — 274

timber grade — 61

timber planks — 255

toe wall — 296

toothed-plate connectors — 178

topiary bushes — 32

topsoil — 15, 18–20, 24, 199, 207, 209–211, 230, 237, 373, 378, 380, 384, 389, 392, 394–395, 410–411, 487

torque-controlled expansion — 192–193

torsional force — 138

transverse abatements — 404

transverse gradient — 400, 403

trass — 75, 96, 227, 313

trass cement — 75, 227

travel-controlled expansion — 192–193

travertine — 67, 69–73, 476

tree trench — 374

trenches — 197, 201, 206, 382, 399, 409–410, 413, 415, 471

tropical timbers — 53

trough-trench system — 410

trunk protection — 374–375

trussing — 154

tuff — 20, 67, 69, 71, 73, 372–373, 380

turf — 43–44, 46, 202, 230, 389, 391–393, 395, 400, 412, 457, 460, 466

two-shelled wall — 311

U

U-iron — 274

undercut anchors — 194

unglazed bricks — 87

uniformity coefficient U — 159

upkeep maintenance (of herbaceous plants) — 378

upper and lower braces — 271, 274

upright course — 304

upstand on foundation — 195

use classes — 55

V

vacuum concrete — 98

vanity lines — 313

varying loads — 143, 145

vector representation of forces — 137

vegetated swale — 409

vegetation base layer — 230, 396, 464–466

vegetation forms — 466

vegetation mat — 466

vegetation support layer — 20, 23

vertical loads — 143, 163, 224

W

walkways and decks — 357–359

wall cladding — 117–118, 127, 329–330

wall coping — 84–85

wall coverings — 313

walls, freestanding— 295–296, 301–302

washers — 112, 176, 180–181, 192, 289, 363, 453, 491, 498

water accumulation irrigation — 460, 465

water-bound path surface — 228, 366

water/cement value — 95, 97–98, 100, 150

water cycle — 399

water drainage capacity — 75

watering — 38, 234, 237, 371–373, 378, 380, 385, 390, 393, 452, 454, 458, 462

water permeability — 20, 391

water-permeable asphalt — 129, 227, 238

water-permeable base courses — 227

waterproof concrete — 169, 426, 428, 433, 437

water protection — 23, 222, 482

water pump — 428

water-struck bricks — 79, 86

watertight concrete roofs — 459

water-uptake capacity — 410

water zones — 422

wattle fences — 274

wear and tear — 35, 97, 216

weathering — 15, 51, 55, 58–61, 72, 98, 100, 109, 123–124, 126, 199, 226, 249, 336, 358–359, 424, 482, 490

weatherproof — 39, 75, 105–107, 109–114, 117, 124, 254, 447, 451

weatherproof construction steels — 110

wedge-shaped steps — 252, 255

weed elimination — 391

welded connections — 182, 184, 186

welding — 109, 116–118, 128, 183–185, 191–192, 269, 282, 424, 428

wet mud collection — 404

white cement — 100–101, 491

whitewashed masonry — 309

wickerwork — 205, 310–311

wind drag — 331, 463

wire anchor — 312, 373

wire mesh fence — 276

wire netting — 301

wood, see also timber — 24, 31–32, 51, 53–63, 87, 89, 95, 99–101, 126, 133, 142, 144, 147–149, 151, 176–177, 180, 245, 255, 269–270, 274, 276, 279, 284, 289, 291, 295–296, 299, 302, 311–312, 329–331, 334–337, 340, 343, 349, 352–354, 358–360, 362, 364–365, 371–372, 374, 376, 404, 450–452, 459, 475, 482–484, 488–491, 494, 498

wooden planks — 255, 360

wooden spacers — 360

wooden steps — 252

wood grids — 359

wood joints — 59, 62–63

wood materials — 61

wood protection treatment — 55

wood screws — 176, 360, 491

wood treatment — 62

woody espalier stock — 451

woody plants — 27, 29–30, 32, 34–35, 37–38, 202, 204, 367, 371–373, 376–381, 450–451, 458, 466, 470, 475

woven fences — 204

wrought copper alloys — 118

Y

yard — 106, 361, 404, 406, 414

THE AUTHORS

Alexander von Birgelen, Dipl.-Ing., research associate in the department of Vegetationstechnik und Pflanzenverwendung (vegetation technology and plant use) at the TU Berlin

Hanna Bornholdt, Dr.-Ing., landscape architect, Hamburg

Thomas Brunsch, Dr.-Ing., dissertation on the subject of concrete

Maik Böhmer, Dipl.-Ing. (FH), Planorama Landschaftsarchitektur, Berlin

Bernd Funke, Dipl.-Ing., executive partner of CRP Planungsgesellschaft für Ingenieurbauwerke mbH, Berlin

Gero Heck, Dipl.-Ing., relais Landschaftsarchitekten, Berlin. Scientific associate of the Institut für Landschaftsarchitektur at the Universität Hannover until 2007

Katja Heimanns, Dipl.-Ing., landscape architect, Braunschweig

Marianne Mommsen, Dipl.-Ing., relais Landschaftsarchitekten, Berlin

Axel Klapka, Dipl.-Ing., K1 Landschaftsarchitektur, Berlin

Cordula Loidl-Reisch, Prof., Dipl.-Ing., landscape architect. Director of the department for Landschaftsbau-Objektbau (landscape construction and object construction) at the TU Berlin

Eike Richter, Dipl-Ing., LA.BAR Landschaftsarchitekten, Berlin

Ute Rieper, Dipl-Ing., landscape architect in Basel. Scientific associate of the department for Vegetationstechnik und Pflanzenverwendung (vegetation technology and plant use) at the TU Berlin until 2008

Caroline Rolka, Dr.-Ing., dissertation on the subject of small-scale architecture, landscape architect and heritage garden perservation, Berlin

Petra Zadel-Sodtke, Dr.-Ing., dissertation on the subject of brick/clinker. Landscape architect at bdla, Berlin

Astrid Zimmermann, Dipl.-Ing., landscape architect, Berlin. Scientific associate of the department for Landschaftsbau-Objektbau (landscape construction and object construction) at the TU Berlin until 2008

Edited by Astrid Zimmermann
Institute of Landscape Architecture and Environmental Planning, Faculty VI, TU Berlin

Collaborators:
Mareike Knocke, Sebastian Pötter, Jennifer Zelt, Sandra Rösler, Elisabeth Gallant, Heidrun Fehr, Ulrike Kirstein,
Karsten Scheffer, Stefan J. Cichosz, Alexander Roscher, David Kaufmann, Gesa Königstein, Thorsten Wolff

Picture editor:
Astrid Zimmermann

All CAD drawings were produced and laid out using the Vectorworks program **Vectorworks.**
LANDSCHAFT

The technical recommendations contained in this book reflect the current state of technology. However, they expressly require to be checked explicitly against the currently valid laws, regulations and standards of the country in question by the specialist planning bodies responsible. The author and publishing house can under no circumstances be held liable for the design, planning or execution of faulty structures.

Translation into English: Michael Robinson and Alison Kirkland (chapters 1–2.1, 3); Gerd H. Söffker and Philip Thrift (chapters 2.2, 2.3)

English copy editing: Monica Buckland

This book is also available in a German language edition (ISBN 978-3-0346-0737-7 Hardcover;
ISBN 978-3-0346-0719-3 Softcover) and in a Spanish language edition (ISBN 978-3-0346-0694-3, Softcover)

Bibliographic information published by the German National Library
The German National Library lists this publication in the Deutsche Nationalbibliografie; detailed bibliographic data are available on the Internet at http://dnb.d-nb.de.

Second, revised and expanded edition 2011
© 2011 Birkhäuser Verlag GmbH
P.O. Box, CH-4002 Basel, Switzerland
Part of ActarBirkhäuser

Printed on acid-free paper produced from chlorine-free pulp. TCF ∞

Layout and cover design: Nadine Rinderer
Typesetting: ActarPro

Printed in Spain

ISBN 978-3-0346 0736-0 (Hardcover)
ISBN 978-3-0346-0720-9 (Softcover)

9 8 7 6 5 4 3 2 1   www.birkhauser.com

Here I would like to thank all the practices, institutions and individuals who have supported and made this publication possible by making pictorial material and exensive project documentation available free of charge.
Special thanks also go to the following for research work, expert advice and other support: Simon Colwill, Birgit Funke, Jörn Mikoleit, Peter Rieper, Ulrike Zimmermann, Meika Fields, Anne-Cecile Jaquot, Nadine Kaczmarek, Martin Küster, Christian Oberbichler, Günter Mader, Karin Kragsig Peschardt, Thomas Reschke, Wolfgang Schäfer, Saara Vilhunen and Jim Wheeler.
Warmest thanks also to Annette Gref for support on concept and content, and to Prof. Heinz W. Hallmann and Prof. Cordula Loidl-Reisch in the Department of Landscape and Commercial Construction, TU Berlin.

With its 31 production sites and over 70 sales & marketing companies, ACO is an international synonym for surface and building drainage. ACO products are found around the world in numerous public spaces, transport hubs, airports and shopping streets. Over 3800 employees in Europe, America, Australia and Asia will generate a turnover of 630 million euros in 2008.

Modern landscaping has to cope with numerous ambitious design and engineering challenges. The world market leader in line drainage successfully tackles these challenges with a precisely matched range of quality products that fully satisfy the professional standards of planners and operatives. Whatever the situation—line and facade drainage, point drainage, rainwater infiltration, or tree and amphibian protection—ACO has the best solutions and systems for the creative design of public spaces, stadiums and sports grounds, domestic applications, roof gardens, or nature conservation and environmental protection. ACO's in-depth expertise in production technologies for polymer concrete, reinforced concrete, stainless steel, cast iron and plastics benefits landscaping projects and companies with a spectrum of solutions that combine aesthetics and customised design with functionality and economic efficiency. The innovative product systems are also backed up by a free service package including hydraulic calculations, manufacturer-neutral specification clauses, precise installation plans, and personal on-site consulting.

ACO Severin Ahlmann GmbH & Co. KG
Am Ahlmannkai
D-24782 Büdelsdorf
Tel. +49 (0) 4331 354-0
Fax. + 49 (0) 4331 354-130
www.aco.com

**Deutschland
Land der Ideen**
●✿●●●●●●●
Ausgewählter Ort 2008

KiC – Kunst in der Carlshütte
Eine Initiative der ACO Gruppe und der
Städte Büdelsdorf und Rendsburg